FILM THEORY AND CRITICISM

FILM THEORY AND CRITICISM

Introductory Readings

Third Edition

Gerald Mast
Marshall Cohen

New York   Oxford
OXFORD UNIVERSITY PRESS
1985

Oxford University Press

Oxford London New York Toronto
Delhi Bombay Calcutta Madras Karachi
Kuala Lumpur Singapore Hong Kong Tokyo
Nairobi Dar es Salaam Cape Town
Melbourne Auckland

and associated companies in
Beirut Berlin Ibadan Mexico City Nicosia

Copyright © 1974, 1979, 1985 by Oxford University Press, Inc.

Published by Oxford University Press, Inc.
200 Madison Avenue, New York, New York 10016

Library of Congress Cataloging in Publication Data
Mast, Gerald, 1940–
Film theory and criticism.
Bibliography: p.
1. Moving-pictures—Addresses, essays, lectures.
I. Cohen, Marshall. II. Title.
PN1994.M364 1985 791.43'01 84-27243
ISBN 0-19-503573-9 (pbk.)

Printing (last digit): 9 8 7 6 5 4 3 2 1
Printed in the United States of America

PREFACE
TO THE THIRD EDITION

The preface to the second edition of this collection noted an emerging distinction between traditional approaches to problems of film theory and those newer approaches influenced by the terms, assumptions, and methodologies of certain disciplines in the social sciences. In the five years that have elapsed between the second and this third edition, these differences between the two types of film theory have become both more pronounced and more clear. In recognition of this clarity, film theorists themselves have divided their field into two halves: "classical film theory" as opposed to "contemporary film theory" (or even "film theory" proper). The basis of this division is partly historical: the recognition that certain problems intrigued film theorists from about 1916 (the year in which the first essay anthologized in this volume was published) until the late 1960s (the years of the Viet Nam War, the student riots in Paris, and the emergence of the new academic disciplines and sensibilities partially in response to these social phenomena). It now seems clear that "classical film theory" can itself be divided into two historical waves. Its first was, broadly, formalist; from the late silent period through the early sound period, theorists such as Hugo Munsterberg, Rudolf Arnheim, and Sergei Eisenstein labored to demonstrate that film was indeed an art—not a mere copying of nature by a mere recording machine. The coming of synchronized sound and an accompanying nostalgic preference for the achievements of silent

cinema provoked a second wave of "classical theory," the realist reaction to the formalist argument. Theorists such as Erwin
Panofsky, Siegfried Kracauer, André Bazin, and Stanley Cavell
labored to demonstrate that film was not an art in opposition
to nature but somehow, and paradoxically, an art of nature.

"Contemporary film theory" arose in the 1960s both from
conditions in the world — public reaction to certain cultural
biases and economic inequities — and from conditions in
scholarly fields contiguous to that of film theory. The study of
linguistics, from the early work of C. S. Peirce, Ferdinand de
Saussure, and Roman Jakobson, to the more recent work of
Noam Chomsky and Louis Hjelmslev, explicated the bases of
the systems upon which communication and knowledge themselves rest. The structuralist anthropology of Claude Lévi-
Strauss, the cultural observations of Roland Barthes, the demystifying historical arguments of Louis Althusser and Michel
Foucault, the psychoanalytic studies of Jacques Lacan, and the
deconstructionist philosophy of Jacques Derrida have all exerted a powerful influence on film study, as they have on every
other form of humanistic inquiry. The primary effect of these
new (generally French) theories has been an undermining of
confidence in the very terms upon which the issues of classical
film theory were based — terms like art, nature, society, culture, effect, affect, reality, illusion, self, consciousness, work,
text, author, artist. "Contemporary film theory," like contemporary literary theory, is less concerned with individual works
than with the terms and assumptions required for examining
and evaluating such works.

In response to this current division in film theory, this collection maintains its historical perspective as a broad survey
of film thinking over the past eight decades. What may seem
its quantitative bias toward "classical theory" arises from several considerations. First, there is the simple difference in the
time span of the two traditions; while "contemporary theory"
is indeed contemporary, with a body of texts stretching back
less than twenty years, "classical theory" embraces arguments
about film over the entire period that there have been films to
argue about. Second, the works of "classical film theory" have
had the time to demonstrate their usefulness in thinking about
film and films; despite the limitations of these theories, they
have provided the means to focus and define certain key issues in the consideration of film as an art and cultural medium. Many of the newer pieces of film theory have not yet
demonstrated that enduring utility, nor have the more and less
useful applications of those assumptions yet been sorted out.
In its older applications, "classical film theory" continues to

provide useful insights to a new generation of student readers; in its newer formulations, "classical film theory," usually based on the American academic traditions of empiricism or phenomenology, continues to fill the gaps and plug the leaks of earlier formulations. Despite the claims that "classical film theory" is (at most) obsolete and (at least) unfashionable, many film theorists, particularly in America, continue to ask the same questions that have dominated "classical film theory" or propose answers that fuse the "classical" and "contemporary" modes. It may well be that the most adventurous, innovative, and pioneering work in film theory today can be attributed to followers of the French schools, but the "classical" works of current film theory continue to solidify the field if not expand its borders.

The most obvious influence of "contemporary film theory" on this volume can be seen in its final section, which has once again been retitled, expanded, and extensively revised. Its new title, "Film: Society, Ideology, and Psychology," indicates that the central issue of such a line of inquiry is not film itself but film's relationship to its culture and its consumers—the way films shape or reflect cultural attitudes, reinforce or reject the dominant modes of cultural thinking, stimulate or frustrate the needs and drives of the psyche. In a very broad sense, the title of this final section might more appropriately have returned to that of the first edition, "The Film Audience," rather than of the second, "Film and Society," since "contemporary film theory" treats not just social issues but psychological, political, and economic ones and the inseparable interrelation between them. Although the most extensive collection of "contemporary" essays can be found in this seventh section, the footprints of "contemporary film theory" can be tracked throughout the volume, in response to more "classical" issues—the Freudian basis of a film genre, the relationship of a movie star to sexist ideology, or the implications of television as a medium.

The other major revision of this third edition can be seen in its fifth section, which has been retitled "Film Genres" (rather than "Kinds of Film"). The shift of title indicates that the focus of this section is narrower than it previously was, concentrating exclusively on distinctions within a single kind of film—fictional Hollywood movies (or "classical Hollywood narrative cinema," as it is now called). Other than an inescapable response to the necessity of making this collection as economical as possible, the change of the section's title and focus reflects current thinking about the categorization of films, which has almost exclusively narrowed to types within the fictional Hol-

lywood narrative tradition. We must apologize for any pedagogical inconvenience or disruption which the removal of these
essays might cause—and for the excision of any others which
may have seemed useful or interesting.

We once again wish to express our sincere thanks to those
who have helped formulate the new issues and choose the new
essays for this third edition—particularly, Curtis Church, Beverle Houston, Bruce Kawin, and Joel Snyder.

PREFACE
TO THE SECOND EDITION

The Preface to the original edition of this collection closed with the following wish: "It is our hope that this anthology will contribute to the growing interest in film theory and to the practice of a more rigorous criticism than that which prevails at the present time." It is difficult to say whether the appearance of this anthology in 1974 should be taken as a prophecy, or merely as another symptom of what has become clear five years later: that the last decade has been an extremely fertile and fervent period of theorizing about film, perhaps the richest period of film theorizing in quantity, quality, and diversity since the invention of cinema itself. This recent theory is fully conscious of the context of theoretical debate, within which each new question or solution must be placed, in a way that was not true of previous generations of film theorists.

The second edition of *Film Theory and Criticism* attempts to give the reader a sense of these developments. To do so we have devoted more space to certain issues, especially to the discussion of film *genres,* and have payed greater attention to certain theoretical trends, particularly to the semiotic and structuralist approaches to film theory and criticism. Several traditional approaches to film theory continue to be employed by the most recent theory—approaches which borrow the methodologies and terminology of such related humanistic disciplines as literary criticism, art history, and aesthetics. But the newer semiotic and structuralist approaches, often influenced by the methodologies and even the conclusions of related disciplines in the social sciences—of Marxist economic historical analysis and Freudian psychoanalysis—have become increasingly important to film theory (and a subject of controversy within it) during the last decade. Writers in this tradition have offered new perspectives on such "classical" issues of film theory as the relation of film to reality or the precise characteristics of film as a "language." The sections of the anthology devoted to these questions have, therefore, been revised to give a fuller account of these approaches.

The semiotic school, particularly in its Marxist manifestations, has also been particularly concerned with the ways that films reveal the underlying social attitudes and "ideologies" of the cultures that produce them, the ways films manipulate audience beliefs, and the ways they exploit and satisfy audience desires. Although the importance of these issues is reflected throughout the anthology, we have given them a sharper focus by reconceiving and retitling the final section "Film and Society" to reflect the concern with treating a film not as a self-contained work of art, as much "classical" film theory does, but as a social-economic product and a cultural manifestation. To accommodate these additions, we have found it necessary to eliminate the discussion of Shakespeare and Film, a topic which other anthologies, devoted exclusively to it, have treated more fully.

We would like to thank all those who sent us suggestions for additions, eliminations, and emendations: Kent R. Brown; Robert E. Golden; Bruce Kawin; Barbara Leaming; Charles J. Maland; Joan Mellen; James Monaco; and William Siska. Our final decision to eliminate an essay (certainly the most difficult decision we had to make) was based both on general opinion of its usefulness as well as our opinion of its relevance to an important theoretical issue. We can only apologize if we have eliminated some of the essays readers considered most useful and interesting. We would also like to express our special thanks to Jean Shapiro, who aided us so patiently and so diligently in assembling the final manuscript.

PREFACE
TO THE FIRST EDITION

This collection of readings gathers together under one cover the most significant theories and theorists of film. Given the youth of the film art, the variety of its possibilities, and the fact that it incorporates so many other arts, it is not surprising that the general pattern of film theory is one of disagreement and diversity. Theorists have responded in many different ways to the fact that film has been both silent and with sound, in color and black-and white, short and long, plotted and plotless, realistic and fantastic, logical and irrational, two- and three-dimensional, in wide and narrow screen, fictional and factual, live and animated, entertaining and educational.

In order to give some shape to this complexity, the book organizes its selections around seven topics which have emerged as the basic subjects of film theory. In the first section, Film and Reality, the collection examines the relationship between the motion picture and the reality which it photographs. In the second, Film Image and Film Language, the theorists examine the syntax and structure of the film itself. They ask how it generates "meaning." The third section, The Film Medium, considers the term "cinematic" and asks what qualities, if any, make the film art unique. The fourth section, Film, Theater, and Literature, continues this line of questioning and asks, in particular, how the film is related to those literary arts with which it has so much in common and from which it yet differs so greatly. The fifth section, Kinds of Film, analyzes some of the main genres of film and discusses the difficulties that arise in attempting to categorize films in these ways. The sixth section, The Film Artist, investigates the question of who, if anyone, ought to be called the artist in the collaborative endeavor of filmmaking. The seventh section, The Film Audience, asks what kind of experience film provides for its audience and what kind of experience it ought to provide.

Film theory is of importance not only for its own sake but also for the contribution it can make to film criticism. Each section therefore includes, in addition to the more theoretical articles, critical essays which show how the more general issues arise in connection with specific films and filmmakers. It is our hope that this anthology will contribute to the growing interest in film theory and to the practice of a more rigorous criticism than that which prevails at the present time.

We wish to thank Dudley Andrew, Hannah Arendt, Richard Balkin, Stanley Kauffmann, Harriet Serenkin, and John Wright for their helpful advice and comments.

CONTENTS

III

THE FILM MEDIUM
209

IV
FILM, THEATER, AND LITERATURE
327

V
FILM GENRES
405

VI
THE FILM ARTIST
521

VII
FILM: PSYCHOLOGY, SOCIETY, AND
IDEOLOGY
669

I

Film and Reality

The main tradition of Western aesthetics, deriving from Aristotle's *Poetics*, adopts the view that art "imitates" nature or, in Hamlet's phrase, holds "the mirror up to nature." Painting, from the early Renaissance to the late nineteenth century, from Giotto to Manet and the impressionists, pursued this ideal with ever-increasing success. Later the novels of Balzac and Tolstoy achieved a more accurate representation of nature and society than anything literature had previously known, and the plays of Ibsen and Chekhov seemed to carry Hamlet's ideal of the theater to its limit. All these achievements were eclipsed, however, by the invention of photography. For the camera, and especially the motion picture camera, was unique in its ability to represent nature. If the ideal of art is to create an illusion of reality, the motion picture made it possible to achieve this ideal in an unprecedented way.

But is the aim of art to imitate nature at all? And if it is, what role remains for the other arts when film achieves it so simply and perfectly? An anti-realist tradition therefore denies that the goal of art is the imitation of nature. It has argued that to create a work of art is not simply to copy the world but to add another, and very special, object to the world. This object may be valuable because it offers an interpretation or idealization of the world, or even because it creates another, wholly autonomous, world. Others in this anti-realist tradition argue that the value of such an object may be that it expresses the feelings and emotions of its creator, or that the artist manages to impose a beautiful or a significant form on the materials with which he works. The artist's feelings may be expressed abstractly, and the resulting form may be purely imaginative. The work of art may not allude to nature at all.

For example, theorists of modern painting have argued that painting should not even attempt to provide a three-dimensional representation of reality but acknowledge, instead, that it is essentially the application of pigments to a two-dimensional surface. This modernist view assumes that painting cannot and should not compete with film in attempting to mirror reality. Painting must renounce that task altogether. Others have argued, however, that film cannot reproduce reality either. And, even if it could, it ought not to try. According to this anti-realist view, film, like any other art form, must offer an interpretation of the world or, by the manipulation of the camera, create an alternative world. Just as painting must acknowledge that it is not really a mirror but pigments on canvas, cinema must acknowledge that it is simply projected images on a screen. To claim that these images ought to be images of physical reality—as opposed to any other kinds of images—is pure dogma. Why should these images not liberate the imagination from the tedium of reality, introducing us to the world of abstractions or of dreams instead?

Siegfried Kracauer, the German-born film historian and aesthetician, is a leading exponent of the realist view of cinema. In his book, *Theory of Film*, Kracauer argues that because film literally photographs reality it alone is capable of holding the mirror up to nature. Film actually reproduces the raw material of the physical world within the work of art. This makes it impossible for a film to be a "pure" expression of the artist's formative intentions or an abstract, imaginative expression of his emotions. Kracauer insists that it is the clear obligation and the special privilege of film (a descendant of still photography) to record and reveal, and thereby redeem, physical reality.

Kracauer's attitude is a response to the common complaint that the abstractions and categorizations of modern science and technology make it impossible for us to appreciate the concrete world in which we live—what John Crowe Ransom called "the world's body." The distinct function of art (especially of poetic imagery) might well be to help us possess the concrete world once more. Kracauer believes that the film art actually does this; it "literally redeems this world from its dormant state, its state of virtual nonexistence, by endeavoring to experience it through the camera." For Kracauer film delivers us from technology by technology.

In his earlier work, *From Caligari to Hitler*, a study of the German cinema from 1919 to 1933, Kracauer traces the decline of German political culture as reflected in the history of its cinema. His view is that the German film's concern for artistic design and its dedication to purely formal values actually prepared the way for Hitler's rise by subtly diverting the audience from a serious appraisal of social realities. This era of German film, usually considered one of the great periods in the history of cinema, is for Kracauer an example of all that cinema must avoid. By ignoring the claims of camera reality the German cinema achieved the damnation, not the redemption, of German life.

André Bazin, who also insists on the unique realism of cinema, does so, however, from a markedly different viewpoint. Bazin, a French critic who founded the influential journal, *Cahiers du Cinéma*, in the late 1940s and whose practicing disciples include Jean-Luc Godard, François Truffaut, and Claude Chabrol, is perhaps the most important theorist of the "second" film generation, a generation for whom the experience of the silent film was no longer decisive. Unlike Kracauer, Bazin views the film's realism as an expression of the mythic, not of the scientific, spirit and believes that its function is not to redeem physical reality but to exempt us from our physical destiny. This magical aim finds expression in the "myth of total cinema," the ideal of a complete recreation of the world in its own image. Bazin welcomes the sound film as a necessary step toward this ideal. For similar reasons, he believes that *mise-en-scène* (arranging the elements of the scene and the camera's relationship to them so as to preserve their physical reality) is a more natural technique than *montage*.

But Bazin's conception of total cinema also leads to interesting questions—particularly in view of the most recent decades of film technology and film style. Would he have welcomed the widespread use of color and the advent of holography and of three-dimensional cinema, as his principles seem to indicate? And what would his attitude have been to the self-consciousness and self-referential tendencies of the film in the last decades? Devices such as slow motion, the freeze frame, the split screen, and color tinting call attention to the screen itself, rather than treating it as a simple window on the world. Although Bazin put his trust in the mechanical representation of uninterpreted reality, many of his followers have insisted on the artifice of the cinematic image.

Rudolph Arnheim, the psychologist and film aesthetician, is a leading "first generation" exponent of the anti-realist tradition in film theory. For Arnheim, if cinema were the mere mechanical reproduction of real life it could not be an art at all. Arnheim acknowledges the existence of a primitive desire to get material objects into one's power by creating them afresh, but he believes that this primitive impulse must be distinguished from the impulse to create art. The "wax museum" ideal may satisfy our primitive impulse, but it fails to satisfy the true artistic urge—not simply to copy, but to originate, to interpret, and to mold. The very properties that keep photography from reproducing reality perfectly must be exploited by the film artist, for they alone provide the possibilities for a film art. Bazin's myth of "total" cinema is nothing more than Arnheim's fallacy of the "complete" film. The pursuit of an ever more complete realism through the use of sound, color, and stereoscopic vision is simply a prescription for undermining the achievement of film art, which must respect, even welcome, the inherent limitations of the art.

For William Earle, a contemporary philosopher in the existentialist and phenomenological tradition, film art is not anti-realist by definition, but the medium is peculiarly apt for expressing an anti-realist sensibility. By severing the connection between sensations and perceptions, by divorcing things from their scientific connotations, and by calling attention to the film image itself, the antirealist tradition expresses its attitude toward an all too "boring" reality. For anti-realists the attempt of realists to record and reveal physical reality is not only naïve; it is an inauthentic attempt to allay man's anxiety about the reality of physical existence. For Earle, the realist ideal is simply an invitation to spiritual death.

V.F. Perkins, the English film critic and theorist, attempts to incorporate the insights of both the realist and the anti-realist traditions. For him the film medium is capable of both documentation and fantasy, of copying and creation. But the central achievement of film is to be found in fictional narration, and this type of movie achieves a synthesis of films' two tendencies. Cinema obscures the distinction between authentic and staged events, making us feel like eye-witnesses at what are in fact fictional events. The credibility which photography and movement confer on films' images encourages us to place an inaccurate construction on an accurate series of images. Film thereby achieves its unique blend of photographic realism and dramatic illusion.

As V.F. Perkins suggests, the consideration of film's relationship to reality has powerfully influenced evaluations of fictional, narrative films; however, William Earle also suggests the importance of such considerations to an alternative film tradition, the one called, variously, independent, experimental, or avant garde cinema. Two of the most important American contributors to that tradition, Maya Deren and Stan Brakhage, clearly reflect the debate about film and reality in both their writings and their films. Deren, the first important woman filmmaker in America, accepted the inherent realism of the photographic image, beginning with her very first film, *Meshes of the Afternoon*, in 1943. For Deren, as for Kracauer and Bazin, "The photographic image as reality . . . is the building block for the creative use of the medium." But Deren's program for the "creative use" of this photographic reality synthesizes the opposing views of the realist theorists and Rudolf Arnheim: the filmmaker creatively alters photographic reality by distorting the anticipated and familiar spatio-temporal relationships within the sequential flow of images. Deren suggests ways to alter what Arnheim called reality's "space-time continuum" — by using slow motion, reverse motion, and the freeze frame. Consistent with the terms of William Earle's categorization, Deren depends on our recognizing and understanding the perceptual reality which the photographic image presents and represents (Deren would fit Earle's categories of the surrealist and ironic filmmaker). Her films can then creatively exploit the "various attributes of the photographic image" — its fidelity, reality, and authority — by effectively undermining what we know about these realistic spaces.

Stan Brakhage, who began making his highly personal films just after the Second World War, takes an exactly opposite position. For Brakhage, the supposed reality of the photographic image is itself a conventionalized illusion, imposed by rules of perspective, compositional logic, and "lenses grounded to achieve 19th century Western compositional perspective." If Brakhage's argument looks forward to those of the post-structuralist theorists who similarly attack the ideology of perspective and the cinema apparatus (see Section VII of this volume), it also reflects the debate suggested by William Earle. For Brakhage (whose films would fit Earle's categories of both the sensory and the ironic), the goal of cinema is the liberation of the eye itself, the creation of an act of seeing previously unimagined and undefined by conventions of representation, an eye as natural and unprejudiced as that of the cat, the bee, or the infant. While the phenomenologist Earle suggests that the sensory filmmaker wishes to undermine perception, seeing, so that the viewer might experience pure sensation, Brakhage wishes to redefine the terms "perception" and "seeing" themselves. Brakhage hopes to replace the "absolute realism" of the motion picture, merely "a contemporary mechanical myth," with a new absolute realism, "unrealized, therefore potential, magic." If there is one clear link between Deren and Brakhage, it would be that both make films which satisfy Earle's definition of the "ironic." Whatever their opposing views, the films and writings of Deren and Brakhage represent reflexive, modernist meditations on the act and art of cinema itself.

SIEGFRIED KRACAUER
FROM THEORY OF FILM

BASIC CONCEPTS

Like the embryo in the womb, photographic film developed from distinctly separate components. Its birth came about from a combination of instantaneous photography, as used by Muybridge and Marey, with the older devices of the magic lantern and the phenakistoscope. Added to this later were the contributions of other nonphotographic elements, such as editing and sound. Nevertheless photography, especially instantaneous photography, has a legitimate claim to top priority among these elements, for it undeniably is and remains the decisive factor in establishing film content. The nature of photography survives in that of film.

Originally, film was expected to bring the evolution of photography to an end—satisfying at last the age-old desire to picture things moving. This desire already accounted for major developments within the photographic medium itself. As far back as 1839, when the first daguerreotypes and talbotypes appeared, admiration mingled with disappointment about their deserted streets and blurred landscapes. And in the 'fifties, long before the innovation of the hand camera, successful attempts were made to photograph subjects in motion. The very impulses which thus led from time exposure to snapshot engendered dreams of a further extension of photography in the same direction—dreams, that is, of film. About 1860, Cook and Bonnelli, who had developed a device called a photobioscope, predicted a "complete revolution of photographic art.... We will see ... landscapes," they announced, "in which the trees bow to the whims of the wind, the leaves ripple and glitter in the rays of the sun."

Along with the familiar photographic leitmotif of the leaves, such kindred subjects as undulating waves, moving clouds, and changing facial expressions ranked high in early prophecies. All of them conveyed the longing for an instrument which would capture the slightest incidents of the world about us—scenes that often would involve crowds, whose incalculable movements resemble, some-how, those of waves or leaves. In a memorable statement published before the emergence of instantaneous photography, Sir John Herschel not only predicted the basic features of the film camera but assigned to it a task which it has never since disowned: "the vivid and lifelike reproduction and handing down to the latest pos-terity of any transaction in real life—a battle, a debate, a public solemnity, a pugilistic conflict." Ducos du Hauron and other fore-runners also looked forward to what we have come to label news-reels and documentaries—films devoted to the rendering of real-life events. This insistence on recording went hand in hand with the expectation that motion pictures could acquaint us with normally imperceptible or otherwise induplicable movements—flashlike transformations of matter, the slow growth of plants, etc. All in all, it was taken for granted that film would continue along the lines of photography. . . .

PROPERTIES OF THE MEDIUM

The properties of film can be divided into basic and technical properties.

The basic properties are identical with the properties of photog-raphy. Film, in other words, is uniquely equipped to record and reveal physical reality and, hence, gravitates toward it.

Now there are different visible worlds. Take a stage performance or a painting: they too are real and can be perceived. But the only reality we are concerned with is actually existing physical reality— the transitory world we live in. (Physical reality will also be called "material reality," or "physical existence," or "actuality," or loosely just "nature." Another fitting term might be "camera-reality.") . . . The other visible worlds reach into this world without, however, really forming a part of it. A theatrical play, for instance, suggests a universe of its own which would immediately crumble were it related to its real-life environment.

As a reproductive medium, film is of course justified in reproduc-ing memorable ballets, operas, and the like. Yet even assuming that such reproductions try to do justice to the specific requirements of the screen, they basically amount to little more than "canning," and are of no interest to us here. Preservation of performances which lie outside physical reality proper is at best a sideline of a medium so particularly suited to explore that reality. This is not to deny that reproductions, say, of stage production numbers may be put to good cinematic use in certain feature films and film genres.

Of all the technical properties of film the most general and indispensable is editing. It serves to establish a meaningful continuity of shots and is therefore unthinkable in photography. (Photomontage is a graphic art rather than a specifically photographic genre.) Among the more special cinematic techniques are some which have been taken over from photography—e.g. the close-up, soft-focus pictures, the use of negatives, double or multiple exposure, etc. Others, such as the lap-dissolve, slow and quick motion, the reversal of time, certain "special effects," and so forth, are for obvious reasons exclusively peculiar to film.

These scanty hints will suffice. It is not necessary to elaborate on technical matters which have been dealt with in most previous theoretical writings on film. Unlike these, which invariably devote a great deal of space to editing devices, modes of lighting, various effects of the close-up, etc., the present book concerns itself with cinematic techniques only to the extent to which they bear on the nature of film, as defined by its basic properties and their various implications. The interest lies not with editing in itself, regardless of the purposes it serves, but with editing as a means of implementing—or defying, which amounts to the same—such potentialities of the medium as are in accordance with its substantive characteristics. In other words, the task is not to survey all possible methods of editing for their own sake; rather, it is to determine the contributions which editing may make to cinematically significant achievements. Problems of film technique will not be neglected; however, they will be discussed only if issues going beyond technical considerations call for their investigation.

This remark on procedures implies what is fairly obvious anyway: that the basic and technical properties differ substantially from each other. As a rule the former take precedence over the latter in the sense that they are responsible for the cinematic quality of a film. Imagine a film which, in keeping with the basic properties, records interesting aspects of physical reality but does so in a technically imperfect manner; perhaps the lighting is awkward or the editing uninspired. Nevertheless such a film is more specifically a film than one which utilizes brilliantly all the cinematic devices and tricks to produce a statement disregarding camera-reality. Yet this should not lead one to underestimate the influence of the technical properties. It will be seen that in certain cases the knowing use of a variety of techniques may endow otherwise nonrealistic films with a cinematic flavor.

THE TWO MAIN TENDENCIES

If film grows out of photography, the realistic and formative tendencies must be operative in it also. Is it by sheer accident that the two tendencies manifested themselves side by side immediately after the rise of the medium? As if to encompass the whole range of cinematic endeavors at the outset, each went the limit in exhausting its own possibilities. Their prototypes were Lumière, a strict realist, and Méliès, who gave free rein to his artistic imagination. The films they made embody, so to speak, thesis and antithesis in a Hegelian sense.

Lumière and Méliès

Lumière's films contained a true innovation, as compared with the repertoire of the zootropes or Edison's peep boxes: they pictured everyday life after the manner of photographs. Some of his early pictures, such as *Baby's Breakfast (Le Déjeuner de bébé)* or *The Card Players (La Partie d'écarté)*, testify to the amateur photographers's delight in family idyls and genre scenes. And there was *Teasing the Gardener (L'Arroseur arrosé)*, which enjoyed immense popularity because it elicited from the flow of everyday life a proper story with a funny climax to boot. A gardener is watering flowers and, as he unsuspectingly proceeds, an impish boy steps on the hose, releasing it at the very moment when his perplexed victim examines the dried-up nozzle. Water squirts out and hits the gardener smack in the face. The denouement is true to style, with the gardener chasing and spanking the boy. This film, the germ cell and archetype of all film comedies to come, represented an imaginative attempt on the part of Lumière to develop photography into a means of story telling. Yet the story was just a real-life incident. And it was precisely its photographic veracity which made Maxim Gorki undergo a shock-like experience. "You think," he wrote about *Teasing the Gardener*, "the spray is going to hit you too, and instinctively shrink back."

On the whole, Lumière seems to have realized that story telling was none of his business; it involved problems with which he apparently did not care to cope. Whatever story-telling films he, or his company, made—some more comedies in the vein of his first one, tiny historical scenes, etc.—are not characteristic of his production. The bulk of his films recorded the world about us for no other purpose than to present it. This is in any case what Mesguich, one of Lumière's "ace" cameramen, felt to be their message. At a time when the talkies were already in full swing he epitomized the work of the master as follows: "As I see it, the Lumière Brothers had established the true domain of the cinema in the right manner. The novel, the theater, suffice for the study of the human heart.

The cinema is the dynamism of life, of nature and its manifesta tions, of the crowd and its eddies. All that asserts itself through movement depends on it. Its lens opens on the world."

Lumière's lens did open on the world in this sense. Take his immortal first reels *Lunch Hour at the Lumière Factory (Sortie des usines Lumière), Arrival of a Train (L'Arrivée d'un train), La Place des Cordeliers à Lyon*: their themes were public places, with throngs of people moving in diverse directions. The crowded streets captured by the stereographic photographs of the late 'fifties thus reappeared on the primitive screen. It was life at its least controllable and most unconscious moments, a jumble of transient, forever dissolving patterns accessible only to the camera. The muchimitated shot of the railway station, with its emphasis on the confusion of arrival and departure, effectively illustrated the fortuity of these patterns; and their fragmentary character was exemplified by the clouds of smoke which leisurely drifted upward. Significantly, Lumière used the motif of smoke on several occasions. And he seemed anxious to avoid any personal interference with the given data. Detached records, his shots resembled the imaginary shot of the grandmother which Proust contrasts with the memory image of her.

Contemporaries praised these films for the very qualities which the prophets and forerunners had singled out in their visions of the medium. It is inevitable that, in the comments on Lumière, "the ripple of leaves stirred by the wind" should be referred to enthusiastically. The Paris journalist Henri de Parville, who used the image of the trembling leaves, also identified Lumière's over-all theme as "nature caught in the act." Others pointed to the benefits which science would derive from Lumière's invention. In America his camera-realism defeated Edison's kinetoscope with its staged subjects.

Lumière's hold on the masses was ephemeral. In 1897, not more than two years after he had begun to make films, his popularity subsided. The sensation had worn off; the heyday was over. Lack of interest caused Lumière to reduce his production.

Georges Méliès took over where Lumière left off, renewing and intensifying the medium's waning appeal. This is not to say that he did not occasionally follow the latter's example. In his beginnings he too treated the audience to sightseeing tours; or he dramatized, in the fashion of the period, realistically staged topical events. But his main contribution to the cinema lay in substituting staged illusion for unstaged reality, and contrived plots for everyday incidents.

The two pioneers were aware of the radical differences in their approach. Lumière told Méliès that he considered film nothing more than a "scientific curiosity," thereby implying that his cinematograph could not possibly serve artistic purposes. In 1897, Méliès on his part published a prospectus which took issue with Lumière: "Messrs. Méliès and Reulos specialize mainly in fantastic or artistic scenes, reproductions of theatrical scenes, etc. . . . thus creating a special genre which differs entirely from the customary views supplied by the cinematograph—street scenes or scenes of everyday life."

Méliès's tremendous success would seem to indicate that he catered to demands left unsatisfied by Lumière's photographic realism. Lumière appealed to the sense of observation, the curiosity about "nature caught in the act"; Méliès ignored the workings of nature out of the artist's delight in sheer fantasy. The train in *Arrival of a Train* is the real thing, whereas its counterpart in Méliès's *An Impossible Voyage (Voyage à travers l'impossible)* is a toy train as unreal as the scenery through which it is moving. Instead of picturing the random movements of phenomena, Méliès freely interlinked imagined events according to the requirements of his charming fairy-tale plots. Had not media very close to film offered similar gratifications? The artist-photographers preferred what they considered aesthetically attractive compositions to searching explorations of nature. And immediately before the arrival of the motion picture camera, magic lantern performances indulged in the projection of religious themes, Walter Scott novels, and Shakespearean dramas.

Yet even though Méliès did not take advantage of the camera's ability to record and reveal the physical world, he increasingly created his illusions with the aid of techniques peculiar to the medium. Some he found by accident. When taking shots of the Paris Place de l'Opéra, he had to discontinue the shooting because the celluloid strip did not move as it should; the surprising result was a film in which, for no reason at all, a bus abruptly transformed itself into a hearse. True, Lumière also was not disinclined to have a sequence of events unfold in reverse, but Méliès was the first to exploit cinematic devices systematically. Drawing on both photography and the stage, he innovated many techniques which were to play an enormous role in the future—among them the use of masks, multiple exposure, superimposition as a means of summoning ghosts, the lap-dissolve, etc. And through his ingenuity in using these techniques he added a touch of cinema to his playful narratives and magic tricks. Stage traps ceased to be indispensable; sleights-of-hand yielded to incredible metamorphoses which film alone was able to accomplish. Illusion produced in this climate depended on another kind of craftsmanship than the magician's. It was cinematic illusion, and as such went far beyond theatrical make-believe. Méliès's *The Haunted Castle (Le Manoir du diable)* "is conceivable only in the cinema and due to the cinema," says

The Two Tendencies: Lumière's *Workers Leaving the Lumière Factory* (1895) and Méliès' *The Witch* (1900). "Lumière's lens did open on the world . . . Méliès ignored the workings of nature out of the artist's delight in sheer fantasy" (KRACAUER, pages 11, 12).

Henri Langlois, one of the best connoisseurs of the primitive era.

Notwithstanding his film sense, however, Méliès still remained the theater director he had been. He used photography in a pre-photographic spirit—for the reproduction of a papier-maché universe inspired by stage traditions. In one of his greatest films, *A Trip to the Moon (Le Voyage dans la lune)*, the moon harbors a grimacing man in the moon and the stars are bull's-eyes studded with the pretty faces of music hall girls. By the same token, his actors bowed to the audience, as if they performed on the stage. Much as his films differed from the theater on a technical plane, they failed to transcend its scope by incorporating genuinely cinematic subjects. This also explains why Méliès, for all his inventiveness, never thought of moving his camera; the stationary camera perpetuated the spectator's relation to the stage. His ideal spectator was the traditional theatergoer, child or adult. There seems to be some truth in the observation that, as people grow older, they instinctively withdraw to the positions from which they set out to struggle and conquer. In his later years Méliès more and more turned from theatrical film to filmed theater, producing *féeries* which recalled the Paris Châtelet pageants.

The Realistic Tendency

In following the realistic tendency, films go beyond photography in two respects. First, they picture movement itself, not only one or another of its phases. But what kinds of movements do they picture? In the primitive era when the camera was fixed to the ground, it was natural for film makers to concentrate on moving material phenomena; life on the screen was life only if it manifested itself through external, or "objective," motion. As cinematic techniques developed, films increasingly drew on camera mobility and editing devices to deliver their messages. Although their strength still lay in the rendering of movements inaccessible to other media, these movements were no longer necessarily objective. In the technically mature film "subjective" movements—movements, that is, which the spectator is invited to execute—constantly compete with objective ones. The spectator may have to identify himself with a tilting, panning, or traveling camera which insists on bringing motionless as well as moving objects to his attention. Or an appropriate arrangement of shots may rush the audience through vast expanses of time and/or space so as to make it witness, almost simultaneously, events in different periods and places.

Nevertheless the emphasis is now as before on objective movement; the medium seems to be partial to it. As René Clair puts it: "If there is an aesthetics of the cinema . . . it can be summarized in

one word: 'movement.' The external movement of the objects per
ceived by the eye, to which we are today adding the inner movement of the action." The fact that he assigns a dominant role to
external movement reflects, on a theoretical plane, a marked feature of his own earlier films—the ballet-like evolutions of their
characters.

Second, films may seize upon physical reality with all its mani-
fold movements by means of an intermediary procedure which
would seem to be less indispensable in photography—staging. In
order to narrate an intrigue, the film maker is often obliged to stage
not only the action but the surroundings as well. Now this recourse
to staging is most certainly legitimate if the staged world is made to
appear as a faithful reproduction of the real one. The important
thing is that studio-built settings convey the impression of actuality,
so that the spectator feels he is watching events which might have
occurred in real life and have been photographed on the spot.

Falling prey to an interesting misconception, Emile Vuillermoz
champions, for the sake of "realism," settings which represent reality as seen by a perceptive painter. To his mind they are more real
than real-life shots because they impart the essence of what such
shots are showing. Yet from the cinematic point of view these allegedly realistic settings are no less stagy than would be, say, a
cubist or abstract composition. Instead of staging the given raw
material itself, they offer, so to speak, the gist of it. In other words,
they suppress the very camera-reality which film aims at incorporating. For this reason, the sensitive moviegoer will feel disturbed
by them. (The problems posed by films of fantasy which, as such,
show little concern for physical reality will be considered later on.)

Strangely enough, it is entirely possible that a staged real-life
event evokes a stronger illusion of reality on the screen than would
the original event if it had been captured directly by the camera.
The late Ernö Metzner who devised the settings for the studio-made
mining disaster in Pabst's *Kameradschaft*—an episode with the ring
of stark authenticity—insisted that candid shots of a real mining
disaster would hardly have produced the same convincing effect.

One may ask, on the other hand, whether reality can be staged so
accurately that the camera-eye will not detect any difference between the original and the copy. Blaise Cendrars touches on this
issue in a neat hypothetical experiment. He imagines two film
scenes which are completely identical except for the fact that one
has been shot on the Mont Blanc (the highest mountain of Europe)
while the other was staged in the studio. His contention is that the
former has a quality not found in the latter. There are on the mountain, says he, certain "emanations, luminous or otherwise, which
have worked on the film and given it a soul." Presumably large
parts of our environment, natural or man-made, resist duplication.

The Formative Tendency

The film maker's formative faculties are offered opportunities far exceeding those offered the photographer. The reason is that film extends into dimensions which photography does not cover. These differ from each other according to area and composition. With respect to areas, film makers have never confined themselves to exploring only physical reality in front of the camera but, from the outset, persistently tried to penetrate the realms of history and fantasy. Remember Méliès. Even the realistic-minded Lumière yielded to the popular demand for historical scenes. As for composition, the two most general types are the story film and the non-story film. The latter can be broken down into the experimental film and the film of fact, which on its part comprises, partially or totally, such subgenres as the film on art, the newsreel, and the documentary proper.

It is easy to see that some of these dimensions are more likely than others to prompt the film maker to express his formative aspirations at the expense of the realistic tendency. As for areas, consider that of fantasy: movie directors have at all times rendered dreams or visions with the aid of settings which are anything but realistic. Thus in *Red Shoes* Moira Shearer dances, in a somnambulistic trance, through fantastic worlds avowedly intended to project her unconscious mind — agglomerates of landscape-like forms, near-abstract shapes, and luscious color schemes which have all the traits of stage imagery. Disengaged creativity thus drifts away from the basic concerns of the medium. Several dimensions of composition favor the same preferences. Most experimental films are not even designed to focus on physical existence; and practically all films following the lines of a theatrical story evolve narratives whose significance overshadows that of the raw material of nature used for their implementation. For the rest, the film maker's formative endeavors may also impinge on his realistic loyalties in dimensions which, because of their emphasis on physical reality, do not normally invite such encroachments; there are enough documentaries with real-life shots which merely serve to illustrate some self-contained oral commentary.

Clashes Between the Two Tendencies

Films which combine two or more dimensions are very frequent; for instance, many a movie featuring an everyday-life incident includes a dream sequence or a documentary passage. Some such combinations may lead to overt clashes between the realistic and formative tendencies. This happens whenever a film maker bent on creating an imaginary universe from freely staged material also feels under an obligation to draw on camera-reality. In his *Hamlet* Laurence Olivier has the cast move about in a studio-built, conspicuously stagy Elsinore, whose labyrinthine architecture seems calculated to reflect Hamlet's unfathomable being. Shut off from our real-life environment, this bizarre structure would spread over the whole of the film were it not for a small, otherwise insignificant scene in which the real ocean outside that dream orbit is shown. But no sooner does the photographed ocean appear than the spectator experiences something like a shock. He cannot help recognizing that this little scene is an outright intrusion; that it abruptly introduces an element incompatible with the rest of the imagery. How he then reacts to it depends upon his sensibilities. Those indifferent to the peculiarities of the medium, and therefore unquestioningly accepting the staged Elsinore, are likely to resent the unexpected emergence of crude nature as a letdown, while those more sensitive to the properties of film will in a flash realize the make-believe character of the castle's mythical splendor. Another case in point is Renato Castellani's *Romeo and Juliet*. This attempt to stage Shakespeare in natural surroundings obviously rests upon the belief that camera-reality and the poetic reality of Shakespeare verse can be made to fuse into each other. Yet the dialogue as well as the intrigue establish a universe so remote from the chance world of real Verona streets and ramparts that all the scenes in which the two disparate worlds are seen merging tend to affect one as an unnatural alliance between conflicting forces.

Actually collisions of this kind are by no means the rule. Rather, there is ample evidence to suggest that the two tendencies which sway the medium may be interrelated in various other ways. Since some of these relationships between realistic and formative efforts can be assumed to be aesthetically more gratifying than the rest, the next step is to try to define them.

THE CINEMATIC APPROACH

It follows from what has been said . . . that films may claim aesthetic validity if they build from their basic properties; like photographs, that is, they must record and reveal physical reality. . . . One might argue that too exclusive an emphasis on the medium's primary relation to physical reality tends to put film in a strait jacket. This objection finds support in the many existing films which are completely unconcerned about the representation of nature. There is the abstract experimental film. There is an unending succession of "photoplays" or theatrical films which do not picture real-life material for its own sake but use it to build up action after the manner of the stage. And there are the many films of fantasy which neglect the external world in freely composed dreams or visions. The old German expressionist films went far in this direction; one of their champions, the German art critic Herman G. Scheffauer, even eulogizes expressionism on the screen for its remoteness from photographic life.

Why, then, should these genres be called less "cinematic" than films concentrating on physical existence? The answer is of course that it is the latter alone which afford insight and enjoyment otherwise unattainable. True, in view of all the genres which do not cultivate outer reality and yet are here to stay, this answer sounds somewhat dogmatic. But perhaps it will be found more justifiable in the light of the following two considerations.

First, favorable response to a genre need not depend upon its adequacy to the medium from which it issues. As a matter of fact, many a genre has a hold on the audience because it caters to widespread social and cultural demands; it is and remains popular for reasons which do not involve questions of aesthetic legitimacy. Thus the photoplay has succeeded in perpetuating itself even though most responsible critics are agreed that it goes against the grain of film. Yet the public which feels attracted, for instance, by the screen version of *Death of a Salesman*, likes this version for the very virtues which made the Broadway play a hit and does not in the least care whether or not it has any specifically cinematic merits.

Second, let us for the sake of argument assume that my definition of aesthetic validity is actually one-sided; that it results from a bias for one particular, if important, type of cinematic activities and hence is unlikely to take into account, say, the possibility of hybrid genres or the influence of the medium's nonphotographic components. But this does not necessarily speak against the propriety of that definition. In a strategic interest it is often more advisable to loosen up initial one-sidedness — provided it is well founded — than to start from all too catholic premises and then try to make them specific. The latter alternative runs the risk of blurring differences between the media because it rarely leads far enough away from the generalities postulated at the outset; its danger is that it tends to entail a confusion of the arts. When Eisenstein, the theoretician, began to stress the similarities between the cinema and the traditional art media, identifying film as their ultimate fulfillment, Eisenstein, the artist, increasingly trespassed the boundaries that separate film from elaborate theatrical spectacles: think of his *Alexander Nevsky* and the operatic aspects of his *Ivan the Terrible*.

In strict analogy to the term "photographic approach" the film maker's approach is called "cinematic" if it acknowledges the basic aesthetic principle. It is evident that the cinematic approach materializes in all films which follow the realistic tendency. This implies that even films almost devoid of creative aspirations, such as newsreels, scientific or educational films, artless documentaries, etc., are tenable propositions from an aesthetic point of view—presumably more so than films which for all their artistry pay little attention to the given outer world. But as with photographic reportage, newsreels and the like meet only the minimum requirement.

What is of the essence in film no less than photography is the intervention of the film maker's formative energies in all the dimensions which the medium has come to cover. He may feature his impressions of this or that segment of physical existence in documentary fashion, transfer hallucinations and mental images to the screen, indulge in the rendering of rhythmical patterns, narrate a human-interest story, etc. All these creative efforts are in keeping with the cinematic approach as long as they benefit, in some way or other, the medium's substantive concern with our visible world. As in photography, everything depends on the "right" balance between the realistic tendency and the formative tendency; and the two tendencies are well balanced if the latter does not try to overwhelm the former but eventually follows its lead.

THE ISSUE OF ART

When calling the cinema an art medium, people usually think of films which resemble the traditional works of art in that they are free creations rather than explorations of nature. These films organize the raw material to which they resort into some self-sufficient composition instead of accepting it as an element in its own right. In other words, their underlying formative impulses are so strong that they defeat the cinematic approach with its concern for camera-reality. Among the film types customarily considered art are, for instance, the above-mentioned German expressionist films of the years after World War I; conceived in a painterly spirit, they seem to implement the formula of Hermann Warm, one of the designers of *The Cabinet of Dr. Caligari* settings, who claimed that "films must be drawings brought to life." Here also belongs many an experimental film; all in all, films of this type are not only intended as autonomous wholes but frequently ignore physical reality or exploit it for purposes alien to photographic veracity. By the same token, there is an inclination to classify as works of art feature films which combine forceful artistic composition with devotion to significant subjects and values. This would apply to a number of adaptations of great stage plays and other literary works.

Yet such a usage of the term "art" in the traditional sense is misleading. It lends support to the belief that artistic qualities must be attributed precisely to films which neglect the medium's recording obligations in an attempt to rival achievements in the fields of

the fine arts, the theater, or literature. In consequence, this usage
tends to obscure the aesthetic value of films which are really true to
the medium. If the term "art" is reserved for productions like *Hamlet* or *Death of a Salesman*, one will find it difficult indeed to appreciate properly the large amount of creativity that goes into
many a documentary capturing material phenomena for their own
sake. Take Ivens's *Rain* or Flaherty's *Nanook*, documentaries saturated with formative intentions: like any selective photographer,
their creators have all the traits of the imaginative reader and curious explorer; and their readings and discoveries result from full
absorption in the given material and significant choices. Add to this
that some of the crafts needed in the cinematic process—especially
editing—represent tasks with which the photographer is not confronted. And they too lay claim to the film maker's creative powers.

This leads straight to a terminological dilemma. Due to its fixed
meaning, the concept of art does not, and cannot, cover truly
"cinematic" films—films, that is, which incorporate aspects of
physical reality with a view to making us experience them. And yet
it is they, not the films reminiscent of traditional art works, which
are valid aesthetically. If film is an art at all, it certainly should not
be confused with the established arts. There may be some justification in loosely applying this fragile concept to such films as
Nanook, or *Paisan*, or *Potemkin* which are deeply steeped in cam-
era-life. But in defining them as art, it must always be kept in mind
that even the most creative film maker is much less independent
of nature in the raw than the painter or poet; that his creativity
manifests itself in letting nature in and penetrating it.

1960

ANDRÉ BAZIN
FROM WHAT IS CINEMA?

THE MYTH OF TOTAL CINEMA

Paradoxically enough, the impression left on the reader by Georges Sadoul's admirable book on the origins of the cinema is of a reversal, in spite of the author's Marxist views, of the relations between an economic and technical evolution and the imagination of those carrying on the search. The way things happened seems to call for a reversal of the historical order of causality, which goes from the economic infrastructure to the ideological superstructure, and for us to consider the basic technical discoveries as fortunate accidents but essentially second in importance to the preconceived ideas of the inventors. The cinema is an idealistic phenomenon. The concept men had of it existed so to speak fully armed in their minds, as if in some platonic heaven, and what strikes us most of all is the obstinate resistance of matter to ideas rather than of any help offered by techniques to the imagination of the researchers.

Furthermore, the cinema owes virtually nothing to the scientific spirit. Its begetters are in no sense savants, except for Marey, but it is significant that he was only interested in analyzing movement and not in reconstructing it. Even Edison is basically only a do-it-yourself man of genius, a giant of the *concours Lépine*. Niepce, Muybridge, Leroy, Joly, Demeny, even Louis Lumière himself, are all monomaniacs, men driven by an impulse, do-it-yourself men or at best ingenious industrialists. As for the wonderful, the sublime E. Reynaud, who can deny that his animated drawings are the result of an unremitting pursuit of an *idée fixe*? Any account of the cinema that was drawn merely from the technical inventions that made it possible would be a poor one indeed. On the contrary, an approximate and complicated visualization of an idea invariably precedes the industrial discovery which alone can open the way to its practical use. Thus if it is evident to us today that the cinema even at its most elementary stage needed a transparent, flexible, and resistant base and a dry sensitive emulsion capable of receiving an image instantly—everything else being a matter of setting in order a mechanism far less complicated than an eighteenth-century clock—it is clear that all the definitive stages of the invention of the cinema had been reached before the requisite conditions had been fulfilled. In 1877 and 1880, Muybridge, thanks to the imaginative generosity of a horse-lover, managed to construct a large complex device which enabled him to make from the image of a galloping horse the first series of cinematographic pictures. However to get this result he had to be satisfied with wet collodion on a glass plate, that is to say, with just one of the three necessary elements—namely instantaneity, dry emulsion, flexible base. After the discovery of gelatino-bromide of silver but before the appearance on the market of the first celluloid reels, Marey had made a genuine camera which used glass plates. Even after the appearance of celluloid strips Lumière tried to use paper film.

Once more let us consider here only the final and complete form of the photographic cinema. The synthesis of simple movements studied scientifically by Plateau had no need to wait upon the industrial and economic developments of the nineteenth century. As Sadoul correctly points out, nothing had stood in the way, from antiquity, of the manufacture of a phenakistoscope or a zootrope. It is true that here the labors of that genuine savant Plateau were at the origin of the many inventions that made the popular use of his discovery possible. But while, with the photographic cinema, we have cause for some astonishment that the discovery somehow precedes the technical conditions necessary to its existence, we must here explain, on the other hand, how it was that the invention took so long to emerge, since all the prerequisites had been assembled and the persistence of the image on the retina had been known for a long time. It might be of some use to point out that although the two were not necessarily connected scientifically, the efforts of Plateau are pretty well contemporary with those of Nicéphore Niepce, as if the attention of researchers had waited to concern itself with synthesizing movement until chemistry quite independently of optics had become concerned, on its part, with the automatic fixing of the image.

I emphasize the fact that this historical coincidence can apparently in no way be explained on grounds of scientific, economic, or industrial evolution. The photographic cinema could just as well have grafted itself onto a phenakistoscope foreseen as long ago as the sixteenth century. The delay in the invention of the latter is as disturbing a phenomenon as the existence of the precursors of the former.

But if we examine their work more closely, the direction of their research is manifest in the instruments themselves, and, even more undeniably, in their writings and commentaries we see that these precursors were indeed more like prophets. Hurrying past the various stopping places, the very first of which materially speaking should have halted them, it was at the very height and summit that most of them were aiming. In their imaginations they saw the cinema as a total and complete representation of reality; they saw in a trice the reconstruction of a perfect illusion of the outside world in sound, color, and relief.

As for the latter, the film historian P. Potoniée has even felt justified in maintaining that it was not the discovery of photography but of stereoscopy, which came onto the market just slightly before the first attempts at animated photography in 1851, that opened the eyes of the researchers. Seeing people immobile in space, the photographers realized that what they needed was movement if their photographs were to become a picture of life and a faithful copy of nature. In any case, there was not a single inventor who did not try to combine sound and relief with animation of the image—whether it be Edison with his kinetoscope made to be attached to a phonograph, or Demenay and his talking portraits, or even Nadar who shortly before producing the first photographic interview, on Chevreul, had written, "My dream is to see the photograph register the bodily movements and the facial expressions of a speaker while the phonograph is recording his speech" (February, 1887) If color had not yet appeared it was because the first experiments with the three-color process were slower in coming. But E. Reynaud had been painting his little figurines for some time and the first films of Méliès are colored by stencilling. There are numberless writings, all of them more or less wildly enthusiastic, in which inventors conjure up nothing less than a total cinema that is to provide that complete illusion of life which is still a long way away. Many are familiar with that passage from L'Ève Future in which Villiers de l'Isle-Adam, two years before Edison had begun his researches on animated photography, puts into the inventor's mouth the following description of a fantastic achievement: ". . . the vision, its transparent flesh miraculously photographed in color and wearing a spangled costume, danced a kind of popular Mexican dance. Her movements had the flow of life itself, thanks to the process of successive photography which can retain six minutes of movement on microscopic glass, which is subsequently reflected by means of a powerful lampascope.

Suddenly was heard a flat and unnatural voice, dull-sounding and harsh. The dancer was singing the *alza* and the *olé* that went with her *fandango*."

The guiding myth, then, inspiring the invention of cinema, is the accomplishment of that which dominated in a more or less vague fashion all the techniques of the mechanical reproduction of reality in the nineteenth century, from photography to the phonograph, namely an integral realism, a recreation of the world in its own image, an image unburdened by the freedom of interpretation of the artist or the irreversibility of time. If cinema in its cradle lacked all the attributes of the cinema to come, it was with reluctance and because its fairy guardians were unable to provide them however much they would have liked to.

If the origins of an art reveal something of its nature, then one may legitimately consider the silent and the sound film as stages of a technical development that little by little made a reality out of the original "myth." It is understandable from this point of view that it would be absurd to take the silent film as a state of primal perfection which has gradually been forsaken by the realism of sound and color. The primacy of the image is both historically and technically accidental. The nostalgia that some still feel for the silent screen does not go far enough back into the childhood of the seventh art. The real primitives of the cinema, existing only in the imaginations of a few men of the nineteenth century, are in complete imitation of nature. Every new development added to the cinema must, paradoxically, take it nearer and nearer to its origins. In short, cinema has not yet been invented!

It would be a reversal then of the concrete order of causality, at least psychologically, to place the scientific discoveries or the industrial techniques that have loomed so large in its development at the source of the cinema's invention. Those who had the least confidence in the future of the cinema were precisely the two industrialists Edison and Lumière. Edison was satisfied with just his kinetoscope and if Lumière judiciously refused to sell his patent to Méliès it was undoubtedly because he hoped to make a large profit out of it for himself, but only as a plaything of which the public would soon tire. As for the real savants such as Marey, they were only of indirect assistance to the cinema. They had a specific purpose in mind and were satisfied when they had accomplished it. The fanatics, the madmen, the disinterested pioneers, capable, as was Berard Palissy, of burning their furniture for a few seconds of shaky images, are neither industrialists nor savants, just men obsessed by their own imaginings. The cinema was born from the converging of these various obsessions, that is to say, out of a myth, the myth of total cinema. This likewise adequately explains the delay of Plateau in applying the optical principle of the persistence of the image on the retina, as also the continuous progress of the syntheses of movement as compared with the state of photographic techniques. The fact is that each alike was dominated by the imagination of the century. Undoubtedly there are other examples in the history of techniques and inventions of the convergence of research, but one must distinguish between those which come as a result precisely of scientific evolution and industrial or military requirements and those which quite clearly precede them. Thus, the myth of Icarus had to wait on the internal combustion engine before descending from the platonic heavens. But it had dwelt in the soul of everyman since he first thought about birds. To some extent, one could say the same thing about the myth of cinema, but its forerunners prior to the nineteenth century have only a remote connection with the myth which we share today and which has prompted the appearance of the mechanical arts that characterize today's world.

1946

RUDOLPH ARNHEIM
FROM FILM AS ART

THE COMPLETE FILM

The technical development of the motion picture will soon carry the mechanical imitation of nature to an extreme. The addition of sound was the first obvious step in this direction. The introduction of sound film must be considered as the imposition of a technical novelty that did not lie on the path the best film artists were pursuing. They were engaged in working out an explicit and pure style of silent film, using its restrictions to transform the peep show into an art. The introduction of sound film smashed many of the forms that the film artists were using in favor of the inartistic demand for the greatest possible "naturalness" (in the most superficial sense of the word). By sheer good luck, sound film is not only destructive but also offers artistic potentialities of its own. Owing to this accident alone the majority of art-lovers still do not realize the pitfalls in the road pursued by the movie producers. They do not see that the film is on its way to the victory of wax museum ideals over creative art.

The development of the silent film was arrested possibly forever when it had hardly begun to produce good results; but it has left us with a few splendidly mature films. In the future, no doubt, "progress" will be faster. We shall have color films and stereoscopic films, and the artistic potentialities of the sound film will be crushed at an even earlier stage of their development.

What will the color film have to offer when it reaches technical perfection? We know what we shall lose artistically by abandoning the black-and-white film. Will color ever allow us to achieve a similar compositional precision, a similar independence of "reality"?

The masterpieces of painting prove that color provides wider possibilities than black-and-white and at the same time permits of a very exact and genuine style. But can painting and color photography be compared? Whereas the painter has a perfectly free hand with color and form in presenting nature, photography is obliged to record mechanically the light values of physical reality. In achromatic photography the reduction of everything to the gray scale resulted in an art medium that was sufficiently independent and divergent from nature. There is not much likelihood of any such transpositon of reality into a qualitatively different range of colors in color film. To be sure, one can eliminate individual colors— one may, for example, cut out all blues, or, vice versa, one may cut out everything except the blues. Probably it is possible also to change one or more color tones qualitatively— for example, give all reds a cast of orange or make all the yellows greenish—or let colors change places with one another—turn all blues to red and all reds to blue—but all this would be, so to speak, only transposition of reality, mechanical shifts, whose usefulness as a formative medium may be doubted. Hence there remains only the possibility of controlling the color by clever choice of what is to be photographed. All kinds of fine procedures are conceivable, especially in the montage of colored pictures, but it must not be overlooked that in this way the subjective formative virtues of the camera, which are so distinctive a characteristic of film, will be more and more restricted, and the artistic part of the work will be more and more focused upon what is set up and enacted *before* the camera. The camera is thereby increasingly relegated to the position of a mere mechanical recording machine.

Above all, it is hardly realistic to speculate on the artistic possibilities of the color film without keeping in mind that at the same time we are likely to be presented with the three-dimensional film and the wide screen. Efforts in these directions are in progress. The illusion of reality will thereby have been increased to such a degree that the spectator will not be able to appreciate certain artistic color effects even if they should be feasible technically. It is quite conceivable that by a careful choice and arrangement of objects it might be possible to use the color on the projection surface artistically and harmoniously. But if the film image becomes stereoscopic there is no longer a plane surface within the confines of the screen, and therefore there can be no composition of that surface; what remains will be effects that are also possible on the stage. The increased size of the screen will render any two-dimensional or three-dimensional composition less compelling; and formative devices such as montage and changing camera angles will become unusable if the illusion of reality is so enormously strengthened. Obviously, montage will seem an intolerable accumulation of heterogeneous settings if the illusion of reality is very strong. Obviously also a change in the position of the camera will now be felt as an actual displacement within the space of the picture. The camera will have to become an immobile recording machine, every cut in the film strip will be mutilation. Scenes will have to be taken in their entire length and with a stationary camera, and they will have to be shown as they are. The artistic potentialities of this form of film will be exactly those of the stage. Film will no longer be able in any sense to be considered as a separate art. It will be thrown back to before its first beginnings—for it was with a fixed camera and an uncut strip that film started. The only difference will be that instead of having all before it film will have nothing to look forward to.

This curious development signifies to some extent the climax of that striving after likeness to nature which has hitherto permeated the whole history of the visual arts. Among the strivings that make human beings create faithful images is the primitive desire to get material objects into one's power by creating them afresh. Imitation also permits people to cope with significant experiences; it provides release, and makes for a kind of reciprocity between the self and the world. At the same time a reproduction that is true to nature provides the thrill that by the hand of man an image has been created which is astoundingly like some natural object. Nevertheless, various countertendencies—some of them purely perceptual—have prevented mechanically faithful imitation from being achieved hundreds of years ago. Apart from rare exceptions, only our modern age has succeeded in approaching this dangerous goal. In practice, there has always been the artistic urge not simply to copy but to originate, to interpret, to mold. We may, however, say that aesthetic theory has rarely sanctioned such activities. Even for artists like Leonardo da Vinci the demand for being as true to nature as possible was a matter of course when he talked theory, and Plato's attack on artists, in which he charged them with achieving nothing but reproductions of physical objects, is far from the general attitude.

To this very day some artists cherish this doctrine, and the general public does so to an even greater extent. In painting and sculpture it is only in recent decades that works have been appearing which show that their creators have broken with this principle intellectually and not merely practically. If a man considers that the artist should imitate nature, he may possibly paint like Van Gogh, but certainly not like Paul Klee. We know that the very powerful and widespread rejection of modern art is almost entirely supported by the argument that it is not true to nature.

The development of film shows clearly how all-powerful this ideal still is.

Photography and its offspring, film, are art media so near to nature that the general public looks upon them as superior to such old-fashioned and imperfect imitative techniques as drawing and painting. Since on economic grounds film is much more dependent on the general public than any other form of art, the "artistic" preferences of the public sweep everything before them. Some work of good quality can be smuggled in but it does not compensate for the more fundamental defeats of film art. The complete film is the fulfillment of the age-old striving for the complete illusion. The attempt to make the two-dimensional picture as nearly as possible like its solid model succeeds; original and copy become practically indistinguishable. Thereby all formative potentialities which were based on the differences between model and copy are eliminated and only what is inherent in the original in the way of significant form remains to art.

H. Baer in a remarkable little essay in the *Kunstblatt* has pointed out that color film represents the accomplishment of tendencies which have long been present in graphic art.

"Graphic art (he says)—of which photography is one branch—has always striven after color. The oldest woodcuts, the blockbooks, were finished off by being handpainted. Later, a second, colored, plate was added to the black-and-white—as in Dürer's portrait of 'Ulrich Varnbühler.' A magnificent picture of a knight in armor in black, silver, and gold, exists by Burgmair. In the eighteenth century multicolored etchings were produced. In the nineteenth the lithographs of Daumier and Gavarni are colored in mass production. . . . Color invaded the graphic arts as an increased attraction for the eye. Uncivilized man is not as a rule satisfied with black-and-white. Children, peasants and primitive peoples demand the highest degree of bright coloring. It is the primitives of the great cities who congregate before the film screen. Therefore film calls in the aid of bright colors. It is a fresh stimulus."

In itself, the perfection of the "complete" film need not be a catastrophe—if silent film, sound film, and colored sound film were allowed to exist alongside it. There is no objection to the "complete" film as an alternative to the stage—it might help to take into remote places fine performances of good works, as also of operas, musical comedies, ballets, the dance. Moreover, by its very existence it would probably have an excellent influence on the other—the real—film forms, by forcing them to advance along their own lines. Silent film, for example, would no longer provide dialogue in its titles, because then the absence of the spoken word would be felt as artificial and disturbing. In sound film, too, any vague intermediate form between it and the stage would be avoided.

Just as the stage will feel itself obliged by the very existence of film to emphasize its own characteristic—the predominance of dramatic speech—so the "complete" film could relegate the true film forms to their own sphere.

The fact is, however, that whereas aesthetically these categories of film could and should exist along with mechanically complete reproduction, they are inferior to it in the capacity to imitate nature. Therefore the "complete" film is certain to be considered an advance upon the preceding film forms, and will supplant them all.

1933

WILLIAM EARLE
REVOLT AGAINST REALISM
IN THE FILMS

Let us call *realist* a certain sensibility which feels most at home living among familiar things in their familiar places, or among persons with recognizable characters acting or suffering in comprehensible ways. I shall presently return to these adjectives, *familiar*, *recognizable*, and *comprehensible*, to define reality. Meanwhile, unquestionably there is some such sensibility; unquestionably its pleasures are genuine and widespread—why, otherwise, would most commercial films address themselves to it?—but equally unquestionably, there is another sensibility which finds any such *reality* the very home of the boring and a serious invitation to spiritual death. For its life consists not so much in revisiting the familiar, recognizing what had been seen before, or comprehending the familiar under generalizable concepts, as in encountering something never seen before, in the primary cognition of novel singularities which can not be comprehended under the universal, in short, in a primordial disclosure of what can only be called, in our present terms, *unreal*. For pleasure let each sensibility look at the films of its choice; but philosophically the two sensibilities and their respective arts are not exactly on such an equal footing. The realist satisfaction in seeing variations on what had already been seen and in the reconfirmation of its conviction in an eternal, known moral order by seeing things "come out right" is clearly of a *derived* order. Nothing can become familiar unless previously encountered originally; and a moral order can not be reconfirmed unless it has been threatened. Existentially, the satisfactions of realist art almost seem to be created precisely in order to extinguish the lurking anxiety that the real world is nothing in the first place but a delusive fiction. Any such contention must be supported by plausible evidence; so I will now turn to the general question, what is realism? in order to show its range and pervasiveness, and then consider three alternatives to it, sensory, surrealist, and ironic art. In this discussion, we shall try to keep our eyes on what might be pertinent to movies.

I. REALISM

If *realism* is taken simply as one aesthetic manner in painting, literature, and movies, an option, among others, like naturalism, expressionism, symbolism, etc., open to the artist's taste and defining a school, perhaps we shall be dealing only with certain ambiguous by-products which, whatever their use, hardly enable us to get at origins. In the case of realism, the simple truth is that it is hardly a peculiar aesthetic style at all. Every human being is already and forever *realist*; he has other potentialities but those other potentialities are necessarily rooted in a basic realism: *perception itself* is inherently realist, and *reality* is inherently defined in terms of possible perception. The simplest definition of a reality is obviously, "that which we can perceive," a definition not meant as a philosophical contention opposed, let us say, to Plato, Plotinus, Spinoza, or Hegel, who define an ultimate reality otherwise. It is a simple stipulation of meaning, and one which will, I hope, be useful to a consideration of realism as pertinent to movies. In a word, in everyday life we count something as a reality if we can perceive it; otherwise it has a dubious mode of being, best left to the philosophers. And *perception*, what does it mean? For the moment, it is enough if we consider it any continuing act of the senses, or better, all of them cooperatively, which grasps something individual. Hence the real world is composed of those things we can see, hear, touch, feel, bump into. Let us call all of this *perception*; and since movies are primarily seen and heard, the *real* for movies then will be what can be seen and heard. To this somewhat sterile beginning, I will add a few pages from the phenomenology of perception to define a little more clearly what any such perceptible reality must be. A definition is necessary since it is far from obvious what these ordinary perceptible realities are; by defining them, perhaps, we can see eventually what some radically different alternatives are to that realism which inherently adheres to perception. In short, by systematically altering every feature of perception, we can at the same time make sense of some of the origins of alternative sensibilities in contemporary cinema.

What then are some central features of perception and the real world? I will discuss them under three titles: A. The *referential* character of perception; B. its *public* character; C. the *meanings* of real things.

A. The Referential Character of Perception

Sensation, first of all, must be distinguished from *perception;* or, in the whole perceptual act, that aspect of it which is purely private to me, which is a literal part of my own flowing perceptual consciousness I call *sensation*, but insofar as these same sensations are taken by me as *referring* to something beyond myself, they are *perceptions* of that thing. Only I *sense* the ache of my tooth; yet, if I take that ache as issuing from my tooth, as "perceptive" of the tooth, then the sensation refers to a tooth which my dentist can also see. Or, as the phenomenologists say, perception "intends" a perceptual *object* which lies in a world open to all perceivers. It refers to identities beyond the sheer privacy of my own sensation.

Precisely how a stream of sensation can refer to or intend these identities beyond itself is a subtle and delicate problem, but for our purposes we can summarize some central features. The question is pertinent to movies since the realities which constitute the home of the realist sensibility are none other than these perceptual identities, things and people. And briefly, sensations will be interpreted by the perceiver as perceptions of an identity when in fact they exhibit a certain order or when they are bound together by a systematic repeatability. And so, if indeed I am perceiving a chair, then my sensations of it will change as I move nearer or farther away, but change systematically, following what we later call the *laws of perspective* but which operate informally in the very act of perception itself. Thus, if I should move closer to the chair, and my sensation of it got progressively smaller, or abruptly and nonsystematically changed at every instant, I should not then take my sensations as the perceptions of anything but rather as mere sensations, a dizziness in me. Or if every time I blinked my eye, what I saw absolutely changed in every one of its sensed qualities, I would not take my sensations as referential at all; and no real identities would be constituted in the process. A perceptual reality, therefore, can change very rapidly indeed; but every appearance of it can not be *wholly* disconnected from my previous perceptions or no reality would appear at all. My sensations would not refer to any identity and would therefore collapse into nonreferential and purely subjective sensings. In a word, real identities must be constituted through repeatability and familiarity; they are automatically built-up through recognition. If I perceive a man walking out of the door, an inherent part of that perception is the belief that *that same man could* walk back through, whether in fact he does or does not. And if he does not, then indeed he must be somewhere else, and not simply nowhere by virtue of his disappearance from my sensation.

A second aspect of perception and its world of realities is, namely, that these real identities are always taken by perception to be *in a world*. And, for perception, this world is not so much a sum total of things nor an infinite container, as it is a horizon which itself can never be perceived but which expresses the sense in perception that its realities are always somewhere even when not seen by me; that there could be other perceivers besides myself who could see the same things; and that things and persons themselves have perceptible properties even when those properties are not being actually perceived.

A reality then for perception is a recognizable identity with its own place in a world of similar identities.

B. Public Availability of Perceptual Realities

Closely connected with the above, a reality for my perception has the inherent meaning of something there *for other senses and other perceivers too*. Therefore, if I *see* something, I should in general be able to touch it, too; if these and the other senses do not yield coherent sensations, I doubt the *reality* of the thing; but also, if only *I* can perceive the thing, and no one else in my place could see it, I begin to doubt the reality of my perception. It was only a subjective sensation or perhaps a mere illusion. All the properties which I ascribe as "real properties" to the real thing must similarly be publicly available. If the public sees it as red and I see it as grey, its real property is red and I am color-blind.

C. The Meanings of Things

Finally, our whole description is hopelessly oversimplified. No one *merely* perceives things and persons. Philosophers as otherwise diverse as Dewey and Heidegger have shown the vacuity of mere perception if not its theoretical impossibility. Nietzsche called it "immaculate perception." All realities we encounter have a meaning for us, a significance which is not in the least reducible to mere perception. Automobiles, pencils, buildings, streets, and above all persons, are hardly to be understood as compositions of colors, shapes, sounds, etc. They are rather things and persons we are already living with, whose very essence is *what they are for us*: what we can do with them, what they can do to us, how we feel about them, in short, their role in our complete active emotional and not merely perceptual *life*. They are structured with values, if you like; their meaning for us is not experienced as something superadded to bare perception but inherent in that perception from the start. Some aestheticians like to think of this aspect as though it were a literary association; but there is nothing literary about it, nor is it necessarily an association brought to mere things from without; the identities in the first place are invariably things and persons for us, with that meaning already there. And that meaning implicates again a public world, where such things are already in their places. And their places in the world are their already familiar relations to other things and people, where those meanings emerge. The hammer is for hammering and its place is its proximity to the hand and the hammerable, or else it is displaced. A hammer flying from tree to tree loses its sense of hammer. Or it becomes a bird-hammer.

In summary then, perception is inherently realist; it constitutes its real things out of its own order, things which are in a world, related to their proper places, and in such a way that this real world of real things is there in more or less the same way for everyone. It is *necessarily* familiar, recognizable, comprehensible. A revolt in the cinema against realism would take each of these features and by its radical removal be in a position to exhibit what can never be realistically perceived, the unreal. From our present point of view, there would be two directions. One would proceed to remove system from sensation so that it *could* not constitute real identities; this I shall call sub-realist, sensory, or, following Marcel Duchamp, "retinal art." A second, moving in the opposite direction, would retain identities, but by *dislocation*, or removing them from their proper places, constitute an unreal world, no longer comprehensible in any realist sense, and, as André Breton said, would disclose the marvellous.

II. SENSORY OR RETINAL ART

Movies are in an excellent position to accomplish the first destruction of realism; for obviously, since the realities in question are given only through a medium in the form of images, by removing the imagistic character of the medium, we can easily in the same blow remove any possibility of perceiving real identities through them. Nothing need be done except reverse every excellence in the realist camera: if lens makers have finally designed optics with virtually no sensible distortion at all, we will use cracked lenses, lenses out of focus, smeared with vaseline, or covered with filters and screens; or if a zoom lens is best used for exact framing, by moving too close, or looking at the object from an odd angle, all trace of recognizability can be removed; or if the film transport of camera and projector are designed for perfect synchronization, we can easily run them so far out of synch that motions can be arrested or wholly altered, and so on through the usual bag of camera tricks. Triple and quadruple exposure can quickly reverse any world or obliterate foreground and background relationships. Editing can be so abrupt and quick that no recognizability, familiarity, or comprehensibility can occur. Briefly, what for the realist perception was an *image*, now loses that function and what is left approximates *sensation without perception;* we suffer perhaps for the first time a continuing experience of what some philosophers used to call "sense-data." LSD films move in this direction and, compared with them, dreams and hallucinations are hopelessly organized and significant of a world.

The senses, by themselves, of course quickly tire; they come alive only in change to such an extent that some animals can see nothing at all unless it moves. Sensation dies when stopped; it is perfectly natural that having deprived perception of the conditions of its operation, the sensation remaining must go faster and faster. Twenty-four absolutely diverse and unrelated frames per second seems far too slow for some; a number of projectors can, therefore, be brought to bear on the same or different screens. And if the senses left to themselves love speed, they also have an obvious longing for the *violent;* gentle changes of intensity will pass unnoticed, until the violence of light and sound approaches an assault on their very physiological limits. A friend of mine who makes films in this vein recently remarked that his ideal was a film that would "punch the audience squarely in the eyes"; oddly enough he felt that this was the best way to "teach people how to see," forgetting in his enthusiasm that no one either can or needs to be *taught* how to see: at very least, would we not have first to see the teacher who was to teach us how to see? What *can* be taught or induced by filmic conditions is *how not to see in order to sense;* and this surely is what the films presently under discussion aim at through the systematic defeat of every built-in expectation of perception.

Many of the same considerations must apply *mutatis mutandi* to the sound of sensory movies. There is a marked preference for electronic and aleatoric sound, and for *musique concrète*. For just as in realist perception, colors and shapes are the appearances of *something*, and sounds are the sounds and voices *of* things and persons, disclosing their qualities and character. Even in performance, the sounds are always the sounds of a violin, piano, singer, a real something or other giving out these sounds. If now the thing sounding or person speaking is suppressed or becomes unrecognizable, then something like a sounding which is not taken to be the sound *of anything* emerges, an aural sense-datum. Further, if all comprehensible pattern is removed, as in chance sound, then the result at last means nothing, announces nothing, expresses no one personality; we now have the perfect sound track for a sensory film.

III. SURREALISM

The revolt against realism can take an opposite direction, that of surrealism, and that surrealism and retinal or sensory art are indeed opposite directions was clear even in the twenties; surrealism was never friendly to purely abstract or non-representational painting. That the familiar and prefabricated perceptual reality is not the final horizon in which men must live can be shown best not by removing the conditions for all genuine perception, and thereby plunging the spirit into pure sensation, but rather by offering it what Breton repeatedly called the "marvellous." And, for Breton, the marvellous was never regarded as simply a new aesthetic style or excitement, but rather as a necessary means of liberating the spirit from any final engrossment in what passes for the real, what offers itself to perception and to comprehension. Against that world it offers another, the surreal, within which the real world is seen as but one minor variation, a variation moreover constructed by and correlative to our least admirable desires, the desire not to be oneself but rather a member of the public, the very public which defines reality.

Surrealism then is primarily an effort to effect a spiritual re-orientation; its theater of operations was never exclusively in works of art but rather in that very public reality which it wished to undermine: hence the necessity for its jokes, outrages, scandals, manifestoes, demonstrations, its temporary flirtation with revolutionary communism, and its love for gratuitous scandals such as Benjamin Peret's penchant for spitting at priests. Overflowing from this particular sentiment was its aesthetic, a sensibility directed to the irrational and magical.

The surreal world, unlike that of sensory art, is indeed a world and is populated by identities; its world is composed of things drawn from the real world but now de- or sur-realized; they are set free from their public or scientific connections and places in order to live a life of their own. Perhaps the most general name for such a freeing is dislocation; for if the very meanings of the things and persons we encounter derive from their relations to their proper places, a dislocation will show that object in a new light. The bringing together of distant realities can then strike off new sparks; the surrealists never tired of repeating from Lautréamont the "beauty of the chance encounter of a sewing machine and an umbrella on a dissecting table." The displacement of things and

persons from their own space and own time, from their own relative dimensions and public values is designed to offer the spirit
a world closer to its own desire. Its own desire was from the beginning understood in Freudian terms; it was the subconscious,
where contraries were identified, which knew nothing of the world
as redefined by science, which was at home in the magical, and
whose desires must be liberated from the expected, the public,
the predictable, the morality of public safety.

The techniques are well-known: automatic writing and free
association to eliminate reflection; collective works, where many
worked on a single object, no one knowing what the other was
doing, the so-called "exquisite corpse"; random trips around Paris;
coincidences through chance street encounters; found objects,
collage, frottage, the primitive, the insane, the erotic, the criminal,
the violent; each form of subjectivity disclosed its own domain of
the surreal, a world not accessible to ordinary action, perception,
or reason, and appearing to those faculties as marvellous and
magical.

To return to films, it is almost as though they were predestined
to be an excellent surrealist medium. For if we are already accustomed to the liberties which language and painting can take with
reality, moving pictures almost automatically make us expect some
sort of true camera reality; films remain a form of photography,
and while everyone *knows* the camera can lie, we do not look
initially at photographs as though they were lies. And so the force
of movies to wrench us out of our habitual realism is particularly
great. Further, the conditions of viewing a movie, in a darkened
room, are particularly conducive to a form of dreamy participation
where the marvellous would not appear simply as wrong, silly, or
outrageous. Similarly the liberties which can be taken in editing
and arranging, and the very same camera tricks which are used for
a wholly different effect by sensory art, can now serve surrealist
purposes admirably.

If the one real world and its reflection in movies provide us with
the satisfactions of recognizability and comprehension, the worlds
of surrealism are inherently private, plural, organizable into no
whole, and invariably either strange, marvellous, or funny. If
reality is not so much funny as serious, the systematic *disruption*
of the expectations generated by familiarity could be, if not serious
in their damage, hilarious, for example, in René Clair's *Entr'acte*.
And the surrealists always regarded humor, particularly black
humor, as especially liberating. Or, when serious, as in the early
Buñuel films, evocative of the revolutionary sentiment of indigna-
tion, as Buñuel says, in the "conviction that this is NOT the best of
all possible worlds"; or magical, as in. some of Man Ray's films,
where the bringing together of distant realities constructs a world

May Ray's *Étoile de Mer* (1928) and the slitting of the eyeball from Dali-Buñuel's *Un Chien Andalou* (1929). "In some of Man Ray's films, the bringing together of distant realities constructs a world closer to the hidden desires of the heart than the public reality could provide. . . ." Surrealism wishes to undermine the public reality, "hence the necessity for its jokes, outrages, scandals, manifestoes, demonstrations . . . and its love for gratuitous scandals . . ." (EARLE, pages 38, 37).

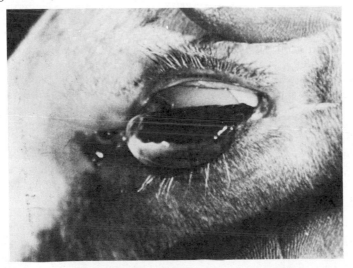

closer to the hidden desires of the heart than the public reality could provide. These sentiments, obviously, are modifications of the sentiments appropriate to perceptual public reality; nothing can be strange unless measured against the familiar, or have the unexpectedness of a joke unless there were expectations to be defeated. And yet the final intent of these surrealist worlds is not to be a mere derivation of the real public world so much as the disclosure of the domain of the possible, in the middle of which the real, public world is finally seen to be just as mysterious and arbitrary as any other possibility. The real perceptual world then could be finally experienced as a surrealist poem imagined by the *public in each of us*. At this point, realism and surrealism join hands in a poetic realism; but that particular meeting is only possible after the detour into the imaginary of surrealism and not before. It is here that the late Siegfried Kracauer's view of film as the "redemption of physical reality" might find its place.

IV. IRONIC FILMS

There remains from our present perspective one more alternative to realism in the film. Realist films of course do not offer us realities themselves, but rather *images of them*. If sensory art destroys images in their function of presenting us something else of which they are images, and if surrealism retains that function of presenting something else, but profoundly alters the character of the something else presented, a remaining alternative would be to develop films which *called attention* to the image, while still employing it as an image. Here, our experience would be an ironic one, doubly aware both of the scene passing before our eyes and of our seeing it through images. In a purely realist film, every effort is devoted to making the audience unaware of the camera, unaware that they are seeing only a reflected reality. The camera moves rarely, the sequences of what is shown agree with the order of showing it; everything is shown as we would see it if we were there in person. On the other hand, in ironic films we have the double awareness of seeing some action as it is refracted through an artificial medium. Now the camera will be hand held, so its jiggle will remind the audience that they are indeed looking at a movie; sometimes processing perforations are shown, and the trailers and leaders of film as they come back from the developer; sometimes the actors ham it up so we are aware they are acting. Or, as in the case of Jean-Luc Godard, the film will make references to other films, reminding the audience that this is a film, making a commentary on or spoofing other films. Sometimes the film or film-making itself becomes the subject of the action, as in *8½*, *Muriel*, or *Blow-Up*. Insofar as there is any suggestion in these ironic films that there is no public, stable reality at all, but only imaginary or *filmic versions* of it, they fall within the general revolt against any acquiescence to the real. Alain Resnais' films also proceed to dissolve any assurance in a public reality by demonstrating the ambiguity of the meaning of the present through its dependence on the past, a past moreover which is itself ambiguous through its significance for the present. Memory here becomes the artist whose materials are always on the verge of losing any independent reality whatsoever. But this carries us into other problems.

Finally, it should be understood that realism, sensory, surrealist, and ironic are only ideal types. No film perfectly exemplifies them, or could exemplify them. Not that this is the fault of the films or of the types; in any closer consideration, we should certainly find that each film most closely exemplified nothing but its own type, that is, no type at all. Each is what it is and asks not so much to be typed as simply seen.

1968

V. F. PERKINS
FROM FILM AS FILM

FORM AND DISCIPLINE

I do not believe that the film (or any other medium) has an essence which we can usefully invoke to justify our criteria. We do not deduce the standards relevant to Rembrandt from the essence of paint; nor does the nature of words impose a method of judging ballads and novels. Standards of judgement cannot be appropriate to a medium as such but only to particular ways of exploiting its opportunities. That is why the concept of the cinematic, presented in terms of demands, has stunted the useful growth of film theory. Helpful criteria are more likely to be based on positive statements of value than on prohibitions. To regard criticism positively, as a search for the most satisfactory definitions of function and value, allows an escape from academic systems of rules and requirements. Criteria then relate to claims which the critic can sustain rather than to demands which he must make. The clarification of standards should help to develop the disciplines of criticism without seeking to lay obligations on the film-maker. Criticism and its theory are concerned with the interplay of available resources and desirable functions. They attempt to establish what the medium is good for. They cannot determine what is good for the medium, because the question is senseless. The search for appropriate criteria leads us to observe limitations; it does not allow us to prescribe them. Anything possible is also permissible, but we still have to establish its value. We cannot assess worth without indicating function.

Hence we can evolve useful criteria only for specific types of film, not for the cinema. Our standards of judgement will have to follow from definitions of types in terms of both their possibilities and their limitations. We have to discover what values we can claim for, what functions it makes sense to assign to, particular applications of the moving picture's resources. Our major concern will be with the different opportunities which can be realized within the various forms of cinema. A theory of film which claims universal validity must provide either an exhaustive catalogue of film forms or a description of the medium in such general terms as to offer minimal guidance to the appreciation of any movie. The problem arises from the embarrassing richness of the cinema's aptitudes.

The movie offers two forms of magic, since its conquest of the visible world extends in two opposite directions. The first, on which the realist theory concentrates, gives it the power to "possess" the real world by capturing its appearance. The second, focus of the traditional aesthetic, permits the presentation of an ideal image, ordered by the film-maker's will and imagination. Since the cinema's mechanism incorporates both these tendencies, neither of them can be condemned on rational, technical or aesthetic grounds. A useful film theory must acknowledge the range and diversity of the film-maker's achievements. At one end of the scale we find the most rigorous forms of documentary, which aim to present the truth about an event with the minimum of human intervention between the real object and its film image; at the other end lies the abstract, cartoon or fantasy film which presents a totally controlled vision. This diversity of methods might be attributed to the movies' mixed parentage, the "objective," factual elements being derived from the camera and the "subjective," magical ones from the Phenakistascope and its relations.

Within the first few years of the cinema's existence the polarities were firmly established. The Lumière brothers' first movie-show presented short "actualities"—a train entering a station, baby eating breakfast and so on. In the earliest days the fact that a machine could present real situations in recognizable form was sufficient sensation to draw enthusiastic audiences throughout Europe and the United States. As soon as that magic lost its appeal, Georges Méliès was ready to step in with the other kind. A professional magician, Méliès took up film-making in 1896 and devoted himself to exploiting the cinema as a medium for fantasy. Using every form of camera trickery he could invent, he told a series of amusing and amazing stories. His two most famous pictures, *A Trip to the Moon* (1902) and *The Impossible Voyage* (1904), presented fantastic situations in fantastic settings. They are packed with magical appearances, disappearances and transformations. The arrival of Méliès and the subsequent development of the narrative film revived the public's waning interest in motion pictures.

Lumière's actualities represent one extreme of the cinema and Méliès's fantasies are quite near to the other. But few films confine themselves to either a purely reproductive or a purely imaginative technique. The cinema extends across the whole of the area between the two extremes. The photographic narrative film occupies a compromise position where a fictional "reality" is *created* in order to be *recorded*. Here the relationship between reality and illusion, object and image, becomes extremely complex; any attempt to isolate either in a "pure" state becomes correspondingly inept.

The fiction movie exploits the possibilities of synthesis between photographic realism and dramatic illusion. That synthesis, its value and implications, will be the major subject of this study. Unless a wider relevance is explicitly claimed, the reader should assume that arguments are meant to apply only to the cinema of photographic fiction. I hope to present criteria which will aid discussion of various kinds and degrees of excellence within this form. I shall offer no case about the usefulness of other forms, nor will my remarks be relevant to the qualities of works outside the range of my definitions. The chosen field to some extent reflects the limits of my familiarity and enthusiasm, but that is all. It would clearly be possible and useful to argue claims and criteria for cartoon, documentary, instructional and many other kinds of film which lie beyond the scope of this study. Nonetheless the fiction movie presents the most urgent claim to attention for two reasons: by almost any reasonable method of calculation, it must be granted the central role in the cinema's development; but it is also precisely the fictional element which existing film theories have most difficulty in accommodating.

A necessary consequence of adopting positive criteria is that we are better equipped to praise than to condemn. Discriminations will be possible within the type, in so far as we see one film as a more complete or skilful realization of its opportunities than another. But the claims we can make for a comedy by Howard Hawks will not yield ammunition for use against an Ingmar Bergman allegory, because they belong to types almost as distinct as cartoon and documentary. Even within the field of cine-fiction the range of possibilities remains enormous. The critical problem is to arrive at descriptions which are both specific and comprehensive enough to be useful. The critic cannot require a movie to fit his definitions; it's his task to find the description which best fits the movie. The most he can "demand" from a film is coherence: a structure which points consistently towards the performance of comprehensible functions. Without that, judgement becomes impossible. From this viewpoint the most significant limitations are those of the form rather than of the medium, the disciplines which the film-maker obeys in order to pursue a particular range of opportunities. For if there are no rules by which every movie can be bound, there are forms which, once adopted by the film-maker, impose their own logic both on him and on the intelligent spectator, since the opportunities of the form may be realized only at the expense of other, attractive but incompatible, possibilities. Yet the central issue remains: not what the film-maker may not do, but the value we can find in what he has done.

In a hybrid form the quest for purity is much less important than the achievement of an ideal compromise, a meaningful resolution of inherent conflict. The fictional film exploits, where purer forms attempt to negate, the conflict between reality and illusion. Instead of trying exclusively either to create or to record, the story film attempts a synthesis: it both records what has been created and creates by its manner of recording. At its most powerful it achieves a credibility which consummates the cinema's blend of actuality and fantasy.

The credibility of the movies comes, I believe, from our habit of placing more trust in the evidence of our eyes than in any other form of sense data. a film makes us feel like eye-witnesses of the events which it portrays. Moreover, our belief extends even to the least realistic forms of movie because movement so strongly connotes life. The source meaning of the term "animation" indicates that we regard a moving picture, even a cartoon, as a picture *brought to life*. In the early days of the movies words like cinematograph and kinetoscope, which meant *moving* picture, were interchangeable with words meaning *living* picture (vitascope, biograph, bioscope, etc.). The powerful combination of picture and movement tempts us to disregard the involvement of our imaginations in what we see. . . .

The most "realistic" films are the ones which convey the most complete illusion. The most obviously imaginative films, the "pure works of man"—cartoons and fantasies—lean heavily upon the cinema's realistic resources in order to make us see the impossible and believe the incredible. When the cartoon cat walks confidently off the edge of a skyscraper and stands paralysed for a couple of fearful seconds before falling, it is precisely our habit of believing our eyes that makes a piece of anti-Newtonian nonsense amusing.

Some abstract films make no use of the cinema's realism (the spectator's credulity). They do not pretend to show real objects but are an extension of non-representational painting. Yet even films in this genre—like Norman McLaren's "caprice in colour," *Begone, Dull Care*—seem to rely on our anthropomorphic tendencies. Whenever the opportunity arises movement becomes action (a round blob "bumps into" a vertical line: accident or aggression?) and shape becomes object (a coloured circle: a ball, a wheel, the sun?). Ernest Pintoff's cartoon *The Critic* comments joyfully on the abstract film's tendency to shed its abstract quality. The screen is filled with coloured shapes which apparently defy interpretation. After a few seconds we hear a Bronx-accented voice demanding "what the hell is this?" The question is momentarily resolved: "Must be a cartoon." Pause. Small blob emerges from "inside" larger blob and the interpretation begins: "Must be Birth." The shapes are rearranged and the spectator becomes confused again: "This is cute. This is cute. This is nice. What the hell *is* it?" Two black shapes converge from opposite sides of the screen: "Two Things! . . . They like each other." (Rhythmic movement of black shapes.) "Could this be the sex life of two Things?" As the commentary progresses (spiky black oval: "Uh-uh! It's a cockroach") it becomes increasingly contemptuous of the movie's imagined content ("Dirt! Dirt and filth!") until, after four minutes of "pure" abstraction the critic reaches his conclusion: "I don't know much about psychoanalysis, but I'd say this is a dirty picture." Pintoff's movie is funny because it is accurate. With any luck actual spectators can be heard commenting and interpreting before "the critic" starts to speak; the two sets of remarks are often very similar.

If abstract shapes in movement attract "realistic" interpretation as objects and actions, it is hardly surprising that the moving photograph carries such conviction. Photographic subjects, says Newhall, "can be misrepresented, distorted, faked . . . and [we] even delight in it occasionally, but the knowledge still cannot shake our implicit faith in the truth of a photographic record."[1]

In 1895 the Lumières' audience believed completely in the reality of a soundless, colourless, two-dimensional and rigidly enclosed image: the spectators feared for their lives when shown an oncoming train. Sixty years later, engulfed in Cin-

---

[1]Newhall, *The History of Photography from 1839 to the Present Day*, p. 91.

erama's huge screen and surrounded by a battery of realistic sound effects, people reacted to film taken from the front of a roller-coaster just as they would react to a ride on a real switchback. They gripped the arms of their seats, screamed and even felt the authentic stomach-tumbling effect. Still, we can hardly claim that *This Is Cinerama* offered a perfect illusion. Its picture, while not exactly flat, was less than three-dimensional. The joins between its three images were clearly visible. We were subject to none of the physical effects essential to a total illusion: no wind disturbed the spectator's hair as he rode the switchback, no smell reached his nostrils as he was conducted along the canals of Venice.

But although Cinerama provided only a partial illusion, it imposed the only sort of belief which we can regard as truly complete: the audience was made to react to the image as it would to the event. The trick here is just the same as it was with the Lumières' presentation and with the 3-D films whose audiences dived for cover under a barrage of arrows, axes and ping-pong balls: not to provide a perfect illusion, that is an integral reproduction of reality, but to offer enough of reality to make the spectator disregard what is missing.

This kind and degree of belief is inevitably short-lived since "enough" means "more than ever before." Audiences rapidly adjust to an extension of the cinema's realism. The primitive magic which creates belief in the real presence of the object shown soon loses its power. "Illusion wears off once . . . expectation is stepped up; we take it for granted and want more."[2] After less than ten minutes of *This Is Cinerama* the sense of being transported around the world began to be replaced by a more conscious appreciation of the techniques by which the world was so convincingly brought into the cinema. The illusory environment of the roller-coaster or the Venetian canal is too inconsistent with what we know about our actual situation for a lasting deception.

But even if we do not believe in the actual presence of the things we see, a film remains credible so long as we are not led to question the *reality* of the objects and events presented. Verbal statements and propositions are seen as either true or false: if we believe them, we believe them; if not, not. Sights, sounds and, particularly, stories—the things which we believe *in*—present a much more complex problem. Belief here can occur in so many ways and at so many levels.

Films are often described as existing in the present tense. Like most direct linguistic analogies this one promotes confu-

---

[2] F. H. Gombrich, *Art and Illusion*, Phaidon Press, 1962, pp. 52–4.

sion rather than enlightenment. It implies that we see a film as a series of events taking place for the first time. Usually we are well aware that this is not the case, just as we know that the conjurer has not magically transformed the queen of hearts into the king of spades. If films were really seen in the present tense cinema managers would have always to protect their screens against assault by gallant spectators rushing to the aid of embattled heroines. If we can describe the movie as existing in any tense at all then the nearest equivalent is probably the historic present which evokes the vividness of memory or fantasy: "There I am walking along the street, and there's this old man standing on the corner. And then he steps out into the road just as this lorry comes around . . ."

Our reaction to the cinema, when we are not caught unawares by some new development like Cinerama or 3-D, is conditioned by our awareness that the camera is a recording instrument and the projected film a method of reproduction. Just as we can talk of hearing Bessie Smith on a gramophone record despite our knowledge that the singer is long dead, so we can watch events taking place on the screen *now* while remaining aware that they actually occurred some time ago. In both cases we accept the accuracy of the illusion.

Ideally the sounds coming from the gramophone's loudspeaker are indistinguishable from the sounds which first went into the microphone. Even when a recorded performance falls spectacularly short of this ideal we have great difficulty in disentangling the sounds made by the artist from the noises made by the recording: it is impossible to be certain how much our concept of what Bessie Smith sounded like is derived from tones which should be attributed to primitive recording mechanisms, not to the singer. Our belief in the recording is not shaken by our knowledge that the "Bessie Smith sound" may not be a very faithful reproduction of the voice of Bessie Smith. It is hard not to feel, against reason, that the recording renders accurately the sounds made by the jazz-singer and her accompanists: if I ask myself to describe Bessie Smith's vocal quality, "scratchy" is one of the words which most immediately comes to mind.

Similarly I find it hard to form a mental picture of life in the first decade of this century which does not include people walking faster and more jauntily than they do nowadays. The image offered by accelerated projection of early films takes mental precedence over the recognized unlikelihood of an evolution towards slower walking.

It is the belief in the actual (if past) existence of the objects on the screen which enables us to discuss movies in terms of credibility. Clearly, one cannot record something which has never existed. Everything that happens on the screen in a live-action picture has happened in front of the camera. The particular magic of the narrative film is to make us put an inaccurate construction on an accurate series of images. The camera neither lies nor tells the truth, because the camera does not make statements. It is we who convert images into assertions. The cinema shows us a man holding a pistol at his head, squeezing the trigger and falling to the floor. This is precisely what happened. But we fictionalize this documentary image when we claim to have seen a man committing suicide. . . .

The camera does not discriminate between real events (which would have taken place even if it had not been on the spot to record them) and action created specifically in order to be recorded. In this respect, the movie simply extends the ambiguity present in any credible image; so long as it looks correct we have no way of telling whether a picture portrays an actual or an imagined subject. The blurred distinction between authentic and staged events helps to make the cinema a peculiarly vivid medium. It is absurd to claim that movies are like life; but it is certain that they can impress us as being more lifelike than any other form of narrative.

The moving image lends its immediacy and conviction, its concreteness of credible detail, to the fictional world. But at this point the film maker confronts the limitation that accompanies opportunity. If he chooses to exploit the credibility of the recording, he thereby sacrifices some of the freedom to invent and arrange which is offered by the celluloid strip. The discipline is inherent in the attempt to create from a succession of images an apparently solid world which exists in its own right.

In the fiction movie, reality becomes malleable but remains (or continues to seem) solid. The world is shaped by the filmmaker to reveal an order beyond chronology, in a system of time and space which is both natural and synthetic. The movie offers its reality in a sequence of privileged moments during which actions achieve a clarity and intensity seldom found in everyday life. Motive and gesture, action and reaction, cause and effect, are brought into a more immediate, dynamic and revealing relationship. The filmmaker fashions a world more concentrated and more shaped than that of our usual experience.

Movies are not distinguished from other forms of narrative by the fact that they isolate and mould aspects of experience in order to intensify our perception. But films are peculiar in performing this work primarily in the sphere of action and appearance rather than of reflection or debate.

The story-teller's freedom to create is inhibited by his two first requirements: clarity and credibility. In movies, the most direct and concrete method of narration, these aims impose a greater restraint than on any other medium. The audience has to know what is happening, of course, but it must also be convinced by what it sees. The organization of image and sound must usually defer to these interests. The narrative picture, in most of its forms, submits to the twin criteria of order and credibility. The movie itself creates these criteria whenever it proposes to be at the same time significant and convincing. The impurity of the medium is consummated by a decision to project a world which is both reproduced and imagined, a creation and a copy. Committed to this impurity, the film-maker is also committed to maintaining a balance between its elements. His aim is to organize the world to the point where it becomes most meaningful but to resist ordering it out of all resemblance to the real world which it attempts to evoke. . . .

1972

MAYA DEREN
CINEMATOGRAPHY: THE CREATIVE USE OF REALITY

The motion-picture camera is perhaps the most paradoxical of all machines, in that it can be at once independently active and infinitely passive. Kodak's early slogan, "You push the button, it does the rest," was not an exaggerated advertising claim, and, connected to any simple trigger device, a camera can even take pictures all by itself. At the same time, while a comparable development and refinement of other mechanisms has usually resulted in an increased specialization, the advances in the scope and sensitivity of lenses and emulsions have made the camera capable of infinite receptivity and in discriminate fidelity. To this must be added the fact that the medium deals, or can deal, in terms of the most elemental actuality. In sum, it can produce maximum results for virtually minimal effort: it requires of its operator only a modicum of aptitude and energy; of its subject matter, only that it exist; and of its audience, only that they can see. On this elementary level it functions ideally as a mass medium for communicating equally elementary ideas.

The photographic medium is, as a matter of fact, so amorphous that it is not merely unobtrusive but virtually transparent, and so becomes, more than any other medium, susceptible of servitude to any and all the others. The enormous value of such servitude suffices to justify the medium and to be generally accepted as its function. This has been a major obstacle to the definition and development of motion pictures as a creative fine-art form—capable of creative action in its own terms—for its own character is as a latent image which can become manifest only if no other image is imposed upon it to obscure it.

Those concerned with the emergence of this latent form must therefore assume a partially protective role, one which recalls the advice of an art instructor who said, "If you have trouble drawing the vase, try drawing the space around the vase." Indeed, for the time being, the definition of the creative form of film involves as careful attention to what it is not as to what it is.

ANIMATED PAINTINGS

In recent years, perceptible first on the experimental fringes of the film world and now in general evidence at the commercial art theaters, there has been an accelerated development of what might be called the "graphic arts school of animated film." Such films, which combine abstract backgrounds with recognizable but not realistic figures, are designed and painted by trained and talented graphic artists who make use of a sophisticated, fluent knowledge of the rich resources of plastic media, including even collage. A major factor in the emergence of this school has been the enormous technical and laboratory advance in color film and color processing, so that it is now possible for these artists to approach the two-dimensional, rectangular screen with all the graphic freedom they bring to a canvas.

The similarity between screen and canvas had long ago been recognized by artists such as Hans Richter, Oskar Fischinger, and others, who were attracted not by its graphic possibilities (so limited at that time) but rather by the excitements of the film medium, particularly the exploitation of its time dimension—rhythm, spatial depth created by a diminishing square, the three-dimensional illusion created by the revolutions of a spiral figure, etc. They put their graphic skills at the service of the film medium, as a means of extending film expression.*

The new graphic-arts school does not so much advance those

---

*It is significant that Hans Richter, a pioneer in such a use of film, soon abandoned this approach. All his later films, along with the films of Léger, Man Ray, Dali, and the painters who participated in Richter's later films (Ernst, Duchamp, etc.) indicate a profound appreciation of the distinction between the plastic and the photographic image and make enthusiastic and creative use of photographic reality.

early efforts as reverse them, for here the artists make use of the film medium as an extension of the plastic media. This is particularly clear when one analyzes the principle of movement employed, for it is usually no more than a sequential articulation—a kind of spelling out in time— of the dynamic ordinarily implicit in the design of an individual composition. The most appropriate term to describe such works, which are often interesting and witty, and which certainly have their place among visual arts, is "animated paintings."

This entry of painting into the film medium presents certain parallels with the introduction of sound. The silent film had attracted to it persons who had talent for and were inspired by the exploration and development of a new and unique form of visual expression. The addition of sound opened the doors for the verbalists and dramatists. Armed with the authority, power, laws, techniques, skills, and crafts which the venerable literary arts had accumulated over centuries, the writers hardly even paused to recognize the small resistance of the "indigenous" film-maker, who had had barely a decade in which to explore and evolve the creative potential of his medium.

The rapid success of the "animated painting" is similarly due to the fact that it comes armed with all the plastic traditions and techniques which are its impressive heritage. And just as the sound film interrupted the development of film form on the commercial level by providing a more finished substitute, so the "animated painting" is already being accepted as a form of film art in the few areas (the distribution of 16 mm. film shorts of film series and societies) where experiments in film form can still find an audience.

The motion-picture medium has an extraordinary range of expression. It has in common with the plastic arts the fact that it is a visual composition projected on a two-dimensional surface; with dance, that it can deal in the arrangement of movement; with theater, that it can create a dramatic intensity of events; with music, that it can compose in the rhythms and phrases of time and can be attended by song and instrument; with poetry, that it can juxtapose images; with literature generally, that it can encompass in its sound track the abstractions available only to language.

This very profusion of potentialities seems to create confusion in the minds of most film-makers, a confusion which is diminished by eliminating a major portion of those potentialities in favor of one or two, upon which the film is subsequently structured. An artist, however, should not seek security in a tidy mastery over the simplifications of deliberate poverty; he should, instead, have the creative courage to face the danger of being overwhelmed by fecundity in the effort to resolve it into simplicity and economy.

While the "animated painting" film has limited itself to a small area of film potential, it has gained acceptance on the basis of the fact that it *does* use an art form—the graphic art form—and that it does seem to meet the general condition of film: it makes its statement as an image in movement. This opens the entire question of whether a photograph is of the same order of image as all others. If not, is there a correspondingly different approach to it in a creative context? Although the photographic process is the basic building block of the motion-picture medium, it is a tribute to its self-effacement as a servant that virtually no consideration has been given to its own character and the creative implications thereof.

THE CLOSED CIRCUIT OF THE PHOTOGRAPHIC PROCESS

The term "image" (originally based on "imitation") means in its first sense the visual likeness of a real object or person, and in the very act of specifying resemblance it distinguishes and establishes the entire category of visual experience which is *not* a real object or person. In this specifically negative sense—in the sense that the photograph of a horse is not the horse itself—a photograph is an image.

But the term "image" also has positive implications: it presumes a mental activity, whether in its most passive form (the "mental images" of perception and memory) or, as in the arts, the creative action of the imagination realized by the art instrument. Here reality is first filtered by the selectivity of individual interests and modified by prejudicial perception to become experience; as such it is combined with similar, contrasting or modifying experiences, both forgotten and remembered, to become assimilated into a conceptual image; this in turn is subject to the manipulations of the art instrument; and what finally emerges is a plastic image which is a reality in its own right. A painting is not, fundamentally, a likeness or image of a horse; it is a likeness of a mental concept which may resemble a horse or which may, as in abstract painting, bear no visible relation to any real object.

Photography, however, is a process by which an object creates its own image by the action of its light or light-sensitive material. It thus presents a closed circuit precisely at the point where, in the traditional art forms, the creative process takes place as reality passes through the artist. This exclusion of the artist at that point is responsible both for the absolute fidelity of the photographic process and for the widespread conviction that a photographic medium cannot be, itself, a creative form. From these observations it is but a step to the conclusion that its use as a visual printing press or as an extension of another creative form represents a full realization of the potential of the medium. It is precisely in this manner that the photographic process is used in "animated paintings."

But in so far as the camera is applied to objects which are already accomplished images, is this really a more creative use of the instrument than when, in scientific films, its fidelity is applied to reality in conjunction with the revelatory functions of telescopic or microscopic lenses and a comparable use of the motor?

Just as the magnification of a lens trained upon matter shows us a mountainous, craggy landscape in an apparently smooth surface, so slow-motion can reveal the actual structure of movements or changes which either cannot be slowed down in actuality or whose nature would be changed by a change in tempo of performance. Applied to the flight of a bird, for example, slow-motion reveals the hitherto unseen sequence of the many separate strains and small movements of which it is compounded.

By a telescopic use of the motor, I mean the telescoping of time achieved by triggering a camera to take pictures of a vine at ten-minute intervals. When projected at regular speed, the film reveals the actual integrity, almost the intelligence, of the movement of the vine as it grows and turns with the sun. Such telescoped-time photography has been applied to chemical changes and to physical metamorphoses whose tempo is so slow as to be virtually imperceptible.

Although the motion-picture camera here functions as an instrument of discovery rather than of creativity, it does yield a kind of image which, unlike the images of "animated paintings" (animation itself is a use of the telescoped-time principle), is unique to the motion-picture medium. It may therefore be regarded as an even more valid basic element in a creative film form based on the singular properties of the medium.

REALITY AND RECOGNITION

The application of the photographic process to reality results in an image which is unique in several respects. For one thing, since a specific reality is the prior condition of the existence of a photograph, the photograph not only testifies to the existence of that reality (just as a drawing testifies to the existence of an artist) but is, to all intents and purposes, its equivalent. This equivalence is not at all a matter of fidelity but is of a different order altogether. If realism is the term of a graphic image which precisely simulates some real object, then a photograph must be differentiated from it as *a form of reality itself.*

This distinction plays an extremely important role in the address of these respective images. The intent of the plastic arts is to make meaning manifest. In creating an image for the express purpose of communicating, the artist primarily undertakes to create the most effective aspect possible out of the total resources of his medium. Photography, however, deals in a living reality which is structured primarily to edure, and whose configurations are designed to serve that purpose, not to communicate its meaning; they may even serve to conceal that purpose as a protective measure. In a photograph, then, we begin by recognizing a reality, and our attendant knowledges and attitudes are brought into play; only then does the aspect become meaningful in reference to it. The abstract shadow shape in a night scene is not understood at all until revealed and identified as a person; the bright red shape on a pale ground which might, in an abstract, graphic context, communicate a sense of gaiety, conveys something altogether different when recognized as a wound. As we watch a film, the continuous act of recognition in which we are involved is like a strip of memory unrolling beneath the images of the film itself, to form the invisible underlayer of an implicit double exposure.

The process by which we understand an abstract, graphic image is almost directly opposite, then, to that by which we understand a photograph. In the first case, the aspect leads us to meaning; in the second case the understanding which results from recognition is the key to our evaluation of the aspect.

PHOTOGRAPHIC AUTHORITY AND THE "CONTROLLED ACCIDENT"

As a reality, the photographic image confronts us with the innocent arrogance of an objective fact, one which exists as an independent presence, indifferent to our response. We may in turn view it with an indifference and detachment we do not have toward the man-made images of other arts, which invite and require our perception and demand our response in order to consummate the communication they initiate and which is their *raison d'être*. At the same time precisely because we are aware that our personal detachment does not in any way diminish the verity of the photographic image, it exercises an authority comparable in weight only to the authority of reality itself.

It is upon this authority that the entire school of the social documentary film is based. Although expert in the selection of the most effective reality and in the use of camera placement and angle to accentuate the pertinent and effective features of it, the documentarists operate on a principle of minimal intervention, in the interests of bringing the authority of reality to the support of the moral purpose of the film.

Obviously, the interest of a documentary film corresponds closely to the interest inherent in its subject matter. Such films enjoyed a period of particular pre-eminence during the war. This popularity served to make fiction-film producers more keenly aware of the effectiveness and authority of reality, an awareness which gave rise to the "neo-realist" style of film and contributed to the still growing trend toward location filming.

In the theater, the physical presence of the performers provides a sense of reality which induces us to accept the symbols of geography, the intermissions which represent the passage of time, and the other conventions which are part of the form. Films cannot include this physical presence of the performers. They can, however, replace the artifice of theater by the actuality of landscape, distances, and place; the interruptions of intermissions can be transposed into transitions which sustain and even intensify the momentum of dramatic development; while events and episodes which, within the context of theatrical artifice, might not have been convincing in their logic or aspect can be clothed in the verity which emanates from the reality of the surrounding landscape, the sun, the streets and buildings.

In certain respects, the very absence in motion pictures of the physical presence of the performer, which is so important to the theater, can even contribute to our sense of reality. We can, for example, believe in the existence of a monster if we are not asked to believe that it is present in the room with us. The intimacy imposed upon us by the physical reality of other art works presents us with alternative choices: either to identify with or to deny the experience they propose, or to withdraw altogether to a detached awareness of that reality as merely a metaphor. But the film image — whose intangible reality consists of lights and shadows beamed through the air and caught on the surface of a silver screen — comes to us as the reflection of another world. At that distance we can accept the reality of the most monumental and extreme of images, and from that perspective we can perceive and comprehend them in their full dimension.

The authority of reality is available even to the most artificial constructs if photography is understood as an art of the "controlled accident." By "controlled accident" I mean the maintenance of a delicate balance beween what is there spontaneously and naturally as evidence of the independent life of actuality, and the persons and activities which are deliberately introduced into the scene. A painter, relying primarily upon aspect as the means of communicating his intent, would take enormous care in the arrangement of every detail of, for example, a beach scene. The cinematographer, on the other hand, having selected a beach which, in general, has the desired aspect—whether grim or happy, deserted or crowded—must on the contrary refrain from overcontrolling the aspect if he is to retain the authority of reality. The filming of such a scene should be planned and framed so as to create a context of limits within which anything that occurs is compatible with the intent of the scene.

The invented event which is then introduced, though itself an artifice, borrows reality from the reality of the scene—from the natural blowing of the hair, the irregularity of the waves, the very texture of the stones and sand—in short, from all the uncontrolled, spontaneous elements which are the property of actuality itself. Only in photography—by the delicate manipulation which I call controlled accident—can natural phenomena be incorporated into our own creativity, to yield an image where the reality of a tree confers its truth upon the events we cause to transpire beneath it.

ABSTRACTIONS AND ARCHETYPES

Inasmuch as the other art forms are not constituted of reality itself, they create metaphors for reality. But photography, being itself the reality or the equivalent thereof, can use its own reality as a metaphor for ideas and abstractions. In painting, the image is an abstraction of the aspect; in photography, the abstraction of an idea produces the archetypal image.

This concept is not new to motion pictures, but its development was interrupted by the intrusions of theatrical traditions into the film medium. The early history of film is studded with archetypal figures: Theda Bara, Mary Pickford, Marlene Dietrich, Greta Garbo, Charles Chaplin, Buster Keaton, etc. These appeared as personages, not as people or personalities, and the films which were structured around them were like monumental myths which celebrated cosmic truths.

The invasion of the motion-picture medium by modern playwrights and actors introduced the concept of realism, which is at the root of theatrical metaphor and which, in the a priori reality of photography, is an absurd redundancy which has served merely to deprive the motion-picture medium of its creative dimension. It is significant that, despite every effort of pretentious producers, directors and film critics who seek to raise their professional status by adopting the methods, attitudes, and criteria of the established and respected art of theater, the major figures—both the most popular stars and the most creative directors (such as Orson Welles)—continue to operate in the earlier archetypal tradition. It was even possible, as Marlon Brando demonstrated, to transcend realism and to become an archetypal realist, but it would appear that his early intuition has been subsequently crushed under the pressures of the repertory complex, another carry-over from theater, where it functioned as the means by which a single company could offer a remunerative variety of plays to an audience while providing consistent employment for its members. There is no justification whatsoever for insisting on a repertory variety of roles for actors involved in the totally different circumstances of motion pictures.

PHOTOGRAPHY'S UNIQUE IMAGES

In all that I have said so far, the fidelity, reality, and author ity of the photographic image serve primarily to modify and to support. Actually, however, the sequence in which we perceive photography—an initial identification followed by an interpretation of the aspect according to that identification (rather than in primarily aspectual terms)—becomes irreversible and confers meaning upon aspect in a manner unique to the photographic medium.

I have previously referred to slow-motion as a time microscope, but it has its expressive uses as well as its revelatory ones. Depending upon the subject and the context, it can be a statement of either ideal ease or nagging frustration, a kind of intimate and loving meditation on a movement or a solemnity which adds ritual weight to an action; or it can bring into reality that dramatic image of anguished helplessness, otherwise experienced only in the nightmares of childhood, when our legs refused to move while the terror which pursues us comes ever closer.

Yet, slow-motion is not simply slowness of speed. It is, in

fact, something which exists in our minds, not on the screen, and can be created only in conjunction with the identifiable reality of the photographic image. When we see a man in the attitudes of running and identify the activity as a run, one of the knowledges which is part of that identification is the pulse normal to that activity. It is because we are aware of the known pulse of the identified action while we watch it occur at a slower rate of speed that we experience the double-exposure of time which we know as slow-motion. It cannot occur in an abstract film, where a triangle, for instance, may go fast or slow, but, having no necessary pulse, cannot go in slow-motion.

Another unique image which the camera can yield is reverse motion. When used meaningfully, it does not convey so much a sense of a backward movement spatially, but rather an undoing of time. One of the most memorable uses of this occurs in Cocteau's *Blood of a Poet*, where the peasant is executed by a volley of fire which also shatters the crucifix hanging on the wall behind him. This scene is followed by a reverse motion of the action—the dead peasant rising from the ground and the crucifix reassembling on the wall; then again the volley of fire, the peasant falling, the crucifix shattering; and again the filmic resurrection. Reverse motion also, for obvious reasons, does not exist in abstract films.

The photographic negative image is still another striking case in point. This is not a direct white-on-black statement but is understood as an inversion of values. When applied to a recognizable person or scene, it conveys a sense of a critically qualitative change, as in its use for the landscape on the other side of death in Cocteau's *Orpheus*.

Both such extreme images and the more familiar kind which I referred to earlier make use of the motion-picture medium as a form in which the meaning of the image originates in our recognition of a known reality and derives its authority from the direct relationship between reality and image in the photographic process. While the process permits some intrusion by the artist as a modifier of that image, the limits of its tolerance can be defined as that point at which the original reality becomes unrecognizable or is irrelevant (as when a red reflection in a pond is used for its shape and color only and without contextual concern for the water or the pond).

In such cases the camera itself has been conceived of as the artist, with distorting lenses, multiple superpositions, etc. used to simulate the creative action of the eye, the memory, etc. Such well-intentioned efforts to use the medium creatively, by forcibly inserting the creative act in the position it traditionally occupies in the visual arts, accomplish, instead, the destruction of the photographic image as reality. This image, with its unique ability to engage us simultaneously on several levels—by the objective authority of reality, by the knowledges and values which we attach to that reality, by the direct address of its aspect, and by a manipulated relationship between these—is the building block for the creative use of the medium.

THE PLACEMENT OF THE CREATIVE ACT AND TIME-SPACE MANIPULATIONS

Where does the film-maker then undertake his major creative action if, in the interests of preserving these qualities of the image, he restricts himself to the control of accident in the pre-photographic stage and accepts almost complete exclusion from the photographic process as well?

Once we abandon the concept of the image as the end product and consummation of the creative process (which it is in both the visual arts and the theater), we can take a larger view of the total medium and can see that the motion-picture instrument actually consists of two parts, which flank the artist on either side. The images with which the camera provides him are like fragments of a permanent, incorruptible memory; their individual reality is in no way dependent upon their sequence in actuality, and they can be assembled to compose any of several statements. In film, the image can and should be only the beginning, the basic material of the creative action.

All invention and creation consist primarily of a new relationship between known parts. The images of film deal in realities which, as I pointed out earlier, are structured to fulfill their various functions, not to communicate a specific meaning. Therefore they have several attributes simultaneously, as when a table may be, at once, old, red, and high. Seeing it as a separate entity, an antique dealer would appraise its age, an artist its color, and a child its inaccessible height. But in a film such a shot might be followed by one in which the table falls apart, and thus a particular aspect of its age would constitute its meaning and function in the sequence, with all other attributes becoming irrelevant. The editing of a film creates the sequential relationship which gives particular or new meaning to the images *according to their function;* it establishes a context, a form which transfigures them without distorting their aspect, diminishing their reality and authority, or impoverishing that variety of potential functions which is the characteristic dimension of reality.

Whether the images are related in terms of common or contrasting qualities, in the causal logic of events which is narrative, or in the logic of ideas and emotions which is the poetic mode, the structure of a film is sequential. The creative action in film, then, takes place in its time dimension; and for this reason the motion picture, though composed of spatial images, is primarily *a time form.*

A major portion of the creative action consists of a manipulation of time and space. By this I do not mean only such established filmic techniques as flashback, condensation of time, parallel action etc. These affect not the action itself but the method of revealing it. In a flashback there is no implication that the usual chronological integrity of the action itself is in any way affected by the process, however disrupted, of memory. Parallel action, as when we see alternately the hero who rushes to the rescue and the heroine whose situation becomes increasingly critical, is an omnipresence on the part of the camera as a witness of action, not as a creator of it.

The kind of manipulation of time and space to which I refer becomes itself part of the organic structure of a film. There is, for example, the extension of space by time and of time by space. The length of a stairway can be enormously extended if three different shots of the person ascending it (filmed from different angles so that it is not apparent that the identical area is being covered each time) are so edited together that the action is continuous and results in an image of enduring labor toward some elevated goal. A leap in the air can be extended by the same technique, but in this case, since the film action is sustained far beyond the normal duration of the real action itself, the effect is one of tension as we wait for the figure to return, finally, to earth.

Time may be extended by the reprinting of a single frame, which has the effect of freezing the figure in mid-action; here the frozen frame becomes a moment of suspended animation which, according to its contextual position, may convey either the sense of critical hesitation (as in the turning back of Lot's wife) or may constitute a comment on stillness and movement as the opposition of life and death. The reprinting of scenes of a casual situation involving several persons may be used either in a prophetic context, as a *déjà-vu;* or, again, precise reiteration, by inter-cutting reprints, of those spontaneous movements, expressions, and exchanges, can change the quality of the scene from one of informality to that of a stylization akin to dance; in so doing it confers dance upon non-dancers, by shifting emphasis from the purpose of the movement to the movement itself, and an informal social encounter then assumes the solemnity and dimension of ritual.

Similarly, it is possible to confer the movement of the camera upon the figures in the scene, for the large movement of a figure in a film is conveyed by the changing relationship between that figure and the frame of the screen. If, as I have done in my recent film *The Very Eye of Night,* one eliminates the horizon line and any background which would reveal the movement of the total field, then the eye accepts the frame as stable and ascribes all movement to the figure within it. The hand-held camera, moving and revolving over the white figures on a totally black ground, produces images in which their movement is as gravity-free and as three-dimensional as that of birds in air or fish in water. In the absence of any absolute orientation, the push and pull of their interrelationships becomes the major dialogue.

By manipulation of time and space, I mean also the creation of a relationship between separate times, places, and persons. A swing-pan—whereby a shot of one person is terminated by a rapid swing away and a shot of another person or place begins with a rapid swing of the camera, the two shots being subsequently joined in the blurred area of both swings—brings into dramatic proximity people, places, and actions which in actuality might be widely separated. One can film different people at different times and even in different places performing approximately the same gesture or movement, and, by a judicious joining of the shots in such a manner as to preserve the continuity of the movement, the action itself becomes the dominant dynamic which unifies all separateness.

Separate and distant places not only can be related but can be made continuous by a continuity of identity and of movement, as when a person begins a gesture in one setting, this shot being immediately followed by the hand entering another setting altogether to complete the gesture there. I have used this technique to make a dancer step from woods to apartment in a single stride, and similarly to transport him from location to location so that the world itself became his stage. In my *At Land,* it has been the technique by which the dynamic of the *Odyssey* is reversed and the protagonist, instead of undertaking the long voyage of search for adventure, finds instead that the universe itself has usurped the dynamic action which was once the prerogative of human will, and confronts her with a volatile and relentless metamorphosis in which her personal identity is the sole constancy.

These are but several indications of the variety of creative timespace relationships which can be accomplished by a meaningful manipulation of the sequence of film images. It is an order of creative action available only to the motion-picture medium because it is a photographic medium. The ideas of condensation and of extension, of separateness and continuity, in which it deals, exploit to the fullest degree the various attributes of the photographic image: its fidelity (which establishes the identity of the person who serves as a transcendant unifying force between all separate times and places), its reality (the basis of the recognition which activates our knowledges and values and without which the geography of location and dislocation could not exist), and its authority (which transcends the impersonality and intangibility of the image and endows it with independent and objective consequence).

THE TWENTIETH-CENTURY ART FORM

I initiated this discussion by referring to the effort to determine what creative film form is not, as a means by which we can arrive eventually at a determination of what it is. I recommend this as the only valid point of departure for all custodians of classifications, to the keepers of catalogues, and in particular to the harassed librarians, who, in their effort to force film into one or another of the performing or the plastic arts, are engaged in an endless Procrustean operation.

A radio is not a louder voice, an airplane is not a faster car, and the motion picture (an invention of the same period of history) should not be thought of as a faster painting or a more real play.

All of these forms are qualitatively different from those which preceded them. They must not be understood as unrelated developments, bound merely by coincidence, but as diverse aspects of a new way of thought and a new way of life—one in which an appreciation of time, movement, energy, and dynamics is more immediately meaningful than the familiar concept of matter as a static solid anchored to a stable cosmos. It is a change reflected in every field of human endeavor, for example, architecture, in which the notion of mass-upon-mass structure has given way to the lean strength of steel and the dynamics of cantilever balances.

It is almost as if the new age, fearful that whatever was there already would not be adequate, had undertaken to arrive completely equipped, even to the motion-picture medium, which, structured expressly to deal in movement and time-space relationships, would be the most propitious and appropriate art form for expressing, in terms of its own paradoxically intangible reality, the moral and metaphysical concepts of the citizen of this new age.

This is not to say that cinema should or could replace the other art forms, any more than flight is a substitute for the pleasures of walking or for the leisurely panorama of landscapes seen from a car or train window. Only when new things serve the same purpose better do they replace old things. Art, however, deals in ideas; time does not deny them, but may merely make them irrelevant. The truths of the Egyptians are no less true for failing to answer questions which they never raised. Culture is cumulative, and to it each age should make its proper contribution.

How can we justify the fact that it is the art instrument, among all that fraternity of twentieth-century inventions, which is still the least explored and exploited; and that it is the artist—of whom, traditionally, the culture expects the most prophetic and visionary statements—who is the most laggard in recognizing that the formal and philosophical concepts of his age are implicit in the actual structure of his instrument and the techniques of his medium?

If cinema is to take its place beside the others as a full-fledged art form, it must cease merely to record realities that owe nothing of their actual existence to the film instrument. Instead, it must create a total experience so much out of the very nature of the instrument as to be inseparable from its means. It must relinquish the narrative disciplines it has borrowed from literature and its timid imitation of the causal logic of narrative plots, a form which flowered as a celebration of the earth-bound, step-by-step concept of time, space and relationship which was part of the primitive materialism of the nineteenth century. Instead, it must develop the vocabulary of filmic images and evolve the syntax of filmic techniques which relate those. It must determine the disciplines inherent in the medium, discover its own structural modes, explore the new realms and dimensions accessible to it and so enrich our culture artistically as science has done in its own province.

1960

STAN BRAKHAGE
FROM METAPHORS ON VISION

Imagine an eye unruled by man-made laws of perspective, an eye unprejudiced by compositional logic, an eye which does not respond to the name of everything but which must know each object encountered in life through an adventure of perception. How many colors are there in a field of grass to the crawling baby unaware of "Green?" How many rainbows can light create for the untutored eye? How aware of variations in heat waves can that eye be? Imagine a world alive with incomprehensible objects and shimmering with an endless variety of movement and innumerable gradations of color. Imagine a world before the "beginning was the word."

To see is to retain—to behold. Elimination of all fear is in sight—which must be aimed for. Once vision may have been given—that which seems inherent in the infant's eye, an eye which reflects the loss of innocence more eloquently than any other human feature, an eye which soon learns to classify sights, an eye which mirrors the movement of the individual toward death by its increasing inability to see.

But one can never go back, not even in imagination. After the loss of innocence, only the ultimate of knowledge can balance the wobbling pivot. Yet I suggest that there is a pursuit of knowledge foreign to language and founded upon visual communication, demanding a development of the optical mind, and dependent upon perception in the original and deepest sense of the word.

Suppose the Vision of the saint and the artist to be an increased ability to see — vision. Allow so-called hallucination to enter the realm of perception, allowing that mankind always finds derogatory terminology for that which doesn't appear to be readily usable, accept dream visions, day-dreams or night-dreams, as you would so-called real scenes, even allowing that the abstractions which move so dynamically when closed eyelids are pressed are actually perceived. Become aware of the fact that you are not only influenced by the visual phenomenon which you are focused upon and attempt to sound the depths of all visual influence. There is no need for the mind's eye to be deadened after infancy, yet in these times the development of visual understanding is almost universally forsaken.

This is an age which has no symbol for death other than the skull and bones of one stage of decomposition . . . and it is an age which lives in fear of total annihilation. It is a time haunted by sexual sterility yet almost universally incapable of perceiving the phallic nature of every destructive manifestation of itself. It is an age which artificially seeks to project itself materialistically into abstract space and to fulfill itself mechanically because it has blinded itself to almost all external reality within eyesight and to the organic awareness of even the physical movement properties of its own perceptibility. The earliest cave paintings discoverd demonstrate that primitive man had a greater understanding than we do that the object of fear must be objectified. The entire history of erotic magic is one of possession of fear thru the beholding of it. The ultimate searching visualization has been directed toward God out of the deepest possible human understanding that there can be no ultimate love where there is fear. Yet in this contemporary time how many of us even struggle to deeply perceive our own children?

The artist has carried the tradition of vision and visualization down through the ages. In the present time a very few have continued the process of visual perception in its deepest sense and transformed their inspirations into cinematic experiences. They create a new language made possible by the moving picture image. They create where fear before them has created the greatest necessity. They are essentially preoccupied by and deal imagistically with — birth, sex, death, and the search for God.

CAMERA EYE

Oh transparent hallucination, superimposition of image on image, mirage of movement, heroine of a thousand and one nights (Scheherazade must surely be the muse of this art), you obstruct the light, muddie the pure white beaded screen (it perspires) with your shuffling patterns. Only the spectators (the unbelievers who attend the carpeted temples where coffee and paintings are served) think your spirit is in the illuminated occasion (mistaking your sweaty, flaring, rectangular body for more than it is). The devout, who break popcorn together in your humblest double-feature services, know that you are still being born, search for your spirit in their dreams, and dare only dream when in contact with your electrical reflection. Unknowingly, as innocent, they await the priests of this new religion, those who can stir cinematic entrails divinely. They await the prophets who can cast (with the precision of Confucian sticks) the characters of this new order across filmic mud. Being innocent, they do not consciously know that this church too is corrupt; but they react with counter hallucinations, believing in the stars, and cast themselves among these Los Angelic orders. Of themselves, they will never recognize what they are awaiting. Their footsteps, the dumb drum which destroys cinema, They are having the dream piped into their homes, the destruction of the romance thru marriage, etc.

So the money vendors have been at it again. To the catacombs then, or rather plant this seed deeper in the undergrounds beyond false nourishing of sewage waters. Let it draw nourishment from hidden uprising springs channeled by gods. Let there be no cavernous congregation but only the network of individual channels, that narrowed vision which splits beams beyond rainbow and into the unknown dimensions. (To those who think this is waxing poetic, squint, give the visual objects at hand their freedom, and allow the distant to come to you; and when mountains are moving, you will find no fat in this prose). Forget ideology, for film unborn as it is has no language and speaks like an aborigine—monotonous rhetoric. Abandon aesthetics—the moving picture image without religious foundations, let alone the cathedral, the art form, starts its search for God with only the danger of accepting an architectural inheritance from the categorized "seven," other arts its sins, and closing its circle, stylistic circle, therefore zero. Negate technique, for film, like America, has not been discovered yet, and mechanization, in the deepest possible sense of the word, traps both beyond measuring even chances—chances are these twined searches may someday orbit about the same central negation. Let film be. It is something . . . becoming. (The above being for creator and spectator alike in searching, an ideal of anarchic religion where all are priests both giving and receiving, or rather witch doctors, or better witches, or . . . O, for the unnamable).

And here, somewhere, we have an eye (I'll speak for myself) capable of any imagining (the only reality). And there (right there) we have the camera eye (the limitation the original liar); yet lyre sings to the mind so immediately (the exalted selectivity one wants to forget that its strings can so easily make puppetry of human motivation (for form as finality) dependent upon attunation, what it's turned to (ultimately death) or turned from (birth) or the way to get out of it (transformation). I'm not just speaking of that bird on fire (not thinking of circles) or of Spengler (spirals neither) or of any known progression (nor straight lines) logical formation (charted levels) or ideological formation (mapped for scenic points of interest); but I am speaking for possibilities (myself), infinite possibilities (preferring chaos).

And here, somewhere, we have an eye capable of any imagining. And then we have the camera eye, its lenses grounded to achieve 19th century Western compositional perspective (as best exemplified by the 19th century architectural conglomeration of details of the "classic" ruin) in bending the light and limiting the frame of the image just so, its standard camera and projector speed for recording movement geared to the feeling of the ideal slow Viennese waltz, and even its tripod head, being the neck it swings on, balled with bearings to permit it that Les Sylphides motion (ideal to the contemplative romantic) and virtually restricted to horizontal and vertical movements (pillars and horizon lines) a diagonal requiring a major adjustment, its lenses coated or provided with filters, its light meters balanced, and its color film manufactured, to produce that picture post card effect (salon painting) exemplified by those oh so blue skies and peachy skins.

By deliberately spitting on the lens or wrecking its focal intention, one can achieve the early stages of impressionism. One can make this prima donna heavy in performance of image movement by speeding up the motor, or one can break up movement, in a way that approaches a more direct inspiration of contemporary human eye perceptibility of movement, by slowing the motion while recording the image. One may hand hold the camera and inherit worlds of space. One may over- or under-expose the film. One may use the filters of the world, fog, downpours, unbalanced lights, neons with neurotic color temperatures, glass which was never designed for a camera, or even glass which was but which can be used against specifications, or one may photograph an hour after sunrise or an hour before sunset, those marvelous taboo hours when the film labs will guarantee nothing, or one may go into the night with a specified daylight film or vice versa. One may become the supreme trickster, with hatfuls of all the rabbits listed above breeding madly. One may, out of incredible courage, become Méliès, that marvelous man who gave even the "art of the film" its beginning in magic Yet Méliès was not witch, witch doctor, priest, or even sorcerer. He was a 19th-century stage magician. His films *are* rabbits.

What about the hat? the camera? or if you will, the stage, the page, the ink, the hieroglyphic itself, the pigment shaping that original drawing, the musical and/or all other instruments for copula-and-then-procreation? Kurt Sachs talks sex (which fits the hat neatly) in originating musical instruments, and Freud's revitalization of symbol charges all contemporary content in art. Yet possession thru visualization speaks for fear-of-death as motivating force—the tomb art of the Egyptian, etc. And then there's "In the beginning," "Once upon a time," or the very concept of a work of art being a "Creation." Religious motivation only reaches us thru the anthropologist these days—viz., Frazer on a golden bough. And so it goes—ring around the rosary, beating about the bush, describing. One thread runs clean thru the entire fabric of expression—the trick-and-effect. And between those two words, somewhere, magic . . . the brush of angel wings, even rabbits leaping heavenwards and, given some direction, language corresponding. Dante looks upon the face of God and Rilke is heard among the angelic orders. Still the Night Watch was tricked by Rembrandt and Pollack was out to produce an effect. The original word was a trick, and so were all the rules of the game that followed in its wake. Whether the instrument be musical or otherwise, it's still a hat with more rabbits yet inside the head wearing it—i.e., thought's a trick, etc. Even The Brains for whom thought's the world, and the word and visi-or-audibility of it, eventually end with a ferris wheel of a solar system in the middle of the amusement park of the universe. They know it without experiencing it, screw it lovelessly, find "trick" or "effect" derogatory terminology, too close for comfort, are utterly unable to comprehend "magic." We are either experiencing (copulating) or conceiving (procreating) or very rarely both are balancing in that moment of living, loving, and creating, giving and receiving, which is so close to the imagined divine as to be more unmentionable than "magic."

In the event you didn't know, "magic" is realmed in "the imaginable," the moment of it being when that which is imagined dies, is penetrated by mind and known rather than believed in. Thus "reality" extends its picketing fence and each is encouraged to sharpen his wits. The artist is one who leaps that fence at night, scatters his seeds among the cabbages, hybrid seeds inspired by both the garden and wits-end forest where only fools and madmen wander, seeds needing several generations to be . . . finally proven edible. Until then they remain invisible, to those with both feet on the ground, yet prominent enough to be tripped over. Yes, those unsightly bulges between those oh so even rows will find their flowering moment . . . and then be farmed. Are you really thrilled at the sight of a critic tentatively munching artichokes? Wouldn't you rather throw overalls in the eventual collegic chowder? Realize the garden as you will—the growing is mostly underground. Whatever daily care you may give it—all is planted only by moonlight. However you remember it—everything in it originates elsewhere. As for the unquotable magic—it's as indescribable as the unbound woods it comes from.

(A foot-on-the-ground-note: The sketches of T. E. Lawrence's "realist" artist companion were scratches to Lawrence's Arab friends. Flaherty's motion picture projection of NANOOK OF THE NORTH was only a play of lights and silhouettes to the Aleutian Islander Nanook himself. The schizophrenic does see symmetrically, does believe in the reality of Korschach, yet he will not yield to the suggestion that a pinpoint light in a darkened room will move, being the only one capable of perceiving its stasis correctly. Question any child as to his drawing and he will defend the "reality" of what you claim "scribbles." Answer any child's question and he will shun whatever quest he'd been beginning.)

Light, lens concentrated, either burns negative films to a chemical crisp which, when lab washed, exhibits the blackened pattern of its ruin or, reversal film, scratches the emulsion to eventually bleed it white. Light, again lens concentrated, pierces white and casts its shadow patterned self to reflect upon the spectator. When light strikes a color emulsion, multiple chemical layers restrict its various wave lengths, restrain its bruises to eventually produce a phenomenon unknown to dogs. Don't think of creatures of uncolored vision as restricted, but wonder, rather, and marvel at the known internal mirrors of the cat which catch each spark of light in the darkness and reflect it to an intensification. Speculate as to insect vision, such as the bee's sense of scent thru ultraviolet perceptibility. To search for human visual realities, man must, as in all other homo motivation, transcend the original physical restrictions and inherit worlds of eyes. The very narrow contemporary moving visual reality is exhausted. The belief in the sacredness of any man-achievement sets concrete about it, statues becoming statutes, needing both explosives, and earthquakes for disruption. As to the permanency of the present or any established reality, consider in this light and thru most individual eyes that without either illumination or photographic lens, any ideal animal might claw the black off a strip of film or walk ink-footed across transparent celluloid and produce an effect for projection identical to a photographed image. As to color, the earliest color films were entirely hand painted a frame at a time. The "absolute realism" of the motion picture image is a human invention.

What reflects from the screen is shadow play. Look, there's no real rabbit. Those ears are index fingers and the nose a knuckle interfering with the light. If the eye were more perceptive it would see the sleight of 24 individual pictures and an equal number of utter blacknesses every second of the show. What incredible films might ultimately be made for such an eye. But the machine has already been fashioned to outwit even that perceptibility, a projector which flashes advertisement at subliminal speed to up the sale of popcorn. Oh, slow-eyed spectator, this machine is grinding you out of existence. Its electrical storms are manufactured by pure white frames interrupting the flow of the photographed images, its real tensions are a dynamic interplay of two-dimensional shapes and lines, the horizon line and background shapes battering the form of the horseback rider as the camera moves with it, the curves of the tunnel exploding away from the pursued, camera following, and tunnel perspective converging on the pursuer, camera preceding, the dream of the close-up kiss being due to the linear purity of facial features after cluttersome background, the entire film's soothing syrup being the depressant of imagistic repetition, a feeling akin to counting sheep to sleep. Believe in it blindly, and it will fool you—mind wise, instead of sequins on cheesecloth or max-manu-factured make-up, you'll see stars. Believe in it eye-wise, and the very comet of its overhead throw from projector to screen will intrigue you so deeply that its fingering play will move integrally with what's reflected, a comet-tail integrity which would lead back finally to the film's creator. I am meaning, simply, that the rhythms of change in the beam of illumination which now goes entirely over the heads of the audience would, in the work of art, contain in itself some quality of a spiritual experience. As is, and at best, that hand spreading its touch toward the screen taps a neurotic chaos comparable to the doodles it produces for reflection. The "absolute realism" of the motion picture image is a 20th-century, essentially Western, illusion.

Nowhere in its mechanical process does the camera hold either mirror or candle to nature. Consider its history. Being machine, it has always been manufacturer of the medium, mass-producer of stilled abstract images, its virtue—related variance, the result—movement. Essentially, it remains fabricator of a visual language, no less a linguist than the typewriter. Yet in the beginning, each of an audience thought himself the camera, attending a play or, toward the end of the purely camera career, being run over by the unedited filmic image of a locomotive which had once rushed straight at the lens, screaming when a revolver seemed fired straight out of the screen, motion of picture being the original magic of the medium. Méliès is credited with the first splice. Since then, the strip of celluloid has increasingly revealed itself suited to transformations beyond those conditioned by the camera. Originally Méliès' trickery was dependent upon starting and stopping the photographic mechanism and between-times creating, adding objects to its field of vision, transformations, substituting one object for another, and disappearances, removing the objectionable. Once the celluloid could be cut, the editing of filmic images began its development toward Eisenteinian montage, the principle of 1 plus 2 making 3 in moving imagery as anywhere else. Meantime labs came into the picture, playing with the illumination of original film, balancing color temperature, juggling double imagery in superimposition, adding all the acrobatic grammar of the film inspired by D. W. Griffith's dance; fades to mark the montage sentenced motion picture paragraph, dissolves to indicate lapse of time between interrelated subject matter, variations in the framing for the epic horizontal composition, origin of Cinemascope, and vertical picture delineating character, or the circle exclamating a pictorial detail, etc. The camera itself taken off the pedestal, began to move, threading its way, in and around its source of material for the eventual intricately patterned fabric of the edited film. Yet editing is still in its 1, 2, 3 infancy, and the labs are essentially still just developing film, no less trapped by the standards they're bearing than the camera by its original mechanical determination. No very great effort has ever been made to interrelate these two or three processes, and already another is appearing possible, the projector as creative instrument with the film show a kind of performance, celluloid or tape merely source of material to the projectioning interpreter, this expression finding its origins in the color, or the scent, or even the musical organ, its most recent manifestations—the increased programming potential of the IBM and other electronic machines now capable of inventing imagery

from scratch. Considering then the camera eye as almost obsolete, it can at last be viewed objectively and, perhaps, view-
pointed with subjective depth as never before. Its life is truly
all before it. The future fabricating machine in performance
will invent images as patterned after cliché vision as those of
the camera, and its results will suffer a similar claim to "realism," IBM being no more God nor even a "Thinking machine"
than the camera eye all-seeing or capable of creative selectivity, both essentially restricted to "yes-no," "stop-go," "on-off,"
and instrumentally dedicated to communication of the simplest sort. Yet increased human intervention and control renders any process more capable of a balance between sub-and-
objective expression, and between those two concepts, somewhere, soul . . . The second stage of transformation of image
editing revealed the magic of the movement. Even though each
in the audience then proceeded to believe himself part of the
screen reflection, taking two-dimension visual characters as his
being within the drama, he could not become every celluloid
sight running thru the projector, therefore allowance of another viewpoint, and no attempt to make him believe his eye
to be where the camera eye once was has ever since proven
successful—excepting the novelty of three-dimension, audiences jumping when rocks seemed to avalanche out of the
screen and into the theatre. Most still imagine, however, the
camera a recording mechanism, a lunatic mirroring, now full
of sound and fury presenting its half of a symmetrical pattern,
a kaleidoscope with the original pieces of glass missing and
their movement removed in time. And the instrument is still
capable of winning Stanford's bet about horse-hooves never
all leaving the ground in galloping, though Stanford significantly enough used a number of still cameras with strings
across the track and thus inagurated the flip-pic of the penny
arcade, Hollywood still racing after the horse. Only when the
fans move on to another track can the course be cleared for
this eye to interpret the very ground, perhaps to discover its
non-solidity, to create a contemporary Pegasus, without wings,
to fly with its hooves, beyond any imagining, to become gallop, a creation. It can then inherit the freedom to agree or disagree with 2000 years of Western equine painting and attain
some comparable aesthetic stature. As is, the "absolute realism" of the motion picture image is a contemporary mechanical myth. Consider this prodigy for its virtually untapped talents, viewpoints it possesses more readily recognizable as
visually non-human yet within the realm of the humanly imaginable. I am speaking of its speed for receptivity which can
slow the fastest motion for detailed study, or its ability to cre-

ate a continuity for time compression, increasing the slowest motion to a comprehensibility. I am praising its cyclopean penetration of haze, its infra-red visual ability in darkness, its just-developed 360-degree view, its prismatic revelation of rainbows, its zooming potential for exploding space and its telephotic compression of same to flatten perspective, its micro- and macroscopic revelations. I am marvelling at its Schlaeran self capable of representing heat waves and the most invisible air pressures, and appraising its other still camera developments which may grow into motion, its rendering visible the illumination of bodily heat, its transformation of ultra-violets to human cognizance, its penetrating X-ray. I am dreaming of the mystery camera capable of graphically representing the form of an object after it's been removed from the photographic scene, etc. The "absolute realism" of the motion picture is unrealized, therefore potential, magic.

1963

II
Film Image and Film Language

The art of music did not arise as soon as man learned how to create pleasing sounds. It was necessary to arrange those sounds into scales, to organize them into harmonic systems, and to devise appropriate musical forms for them. Similarly, the art of poetry required more than the mere existence of a list of words. These words had to be arranged according to rules of grammar and organized into intelligible literary structures. When the poet writes an epic, his words must be capable of telling a story, and when he writes a sonnet, they must fall into specific rhyme schemes and structural patterns.

The great Soviet filmmakers, Sergei Eisenstein and Vsevolod Pudovkin, thought about the art of the cinema in a similar way. This art required more than the mere ability to make moving pictures of reality, and, therefore, it required more than the discovery of photography. But what more? What is it that transformed a new technical ability into a great new art? The answer was montage, the art of combining pieces of film or shots (film's "sounds" or "words") into larger units— first, the scene, then, the sequence, and, finally, the complete film. D. W. Griffith, the great American director of *The Birth of a Nation* and *Intolerance*, to whom the Soviet directors acknowledged a great debt, was not important because he took better pictures than anybody else. He was important for having discovered montage, the fluid integration of the camera's total range of shots, from extreme close-up to distant panorama, so as to produce the most coherent narrative sequence, the most systematic meaning, and most effective rhythmic pattern. In doing so, Griffith had, they thought, contributed to the development of a cinematic language and invented the distinctive art of the film.

The career of Sergei M. Eisenstein, the most brilliant figure in Soviet cinema, began as a stage director. The youthful Eisenstein then made four films in five years: *Strike* (1924), *Potemkin* (1925), *October* (1927), and *Old and New* (1928). In the 1930s and 1940s (until his death in 1948) Eisenstein worked primarily as a theorist and teacher, completing only *Alexander Nevsky* and *Ivan the Terrible, Parts I and II*. Eisenstein's conversion from an artist to a theorist is to be explained in part by political realities, for his emphasis on cinematic "form" was uncongenial to his government's official aesthetics. But it is equally true that his conception of montage did not easily accommodate itself to the use of synchronized dialogue and, therefore, to the kind of film which prevailed in the 1930s.

Eisenstein viewed montage as a kind of collision or conflict, especially between a shot and its successor. He sees each shot as having a kind of potential energy—in purely visual terms of its direction of movement, its volumes of shapes, its intensity of light, and so forth. This potential energy becomes kinetic when the first shot collides with the succeeding one. The two shots can produce a conflict in their emotional content (happy versus sad), in their use of light (dark versus light), in their rhythms (slow versus fast), in their objects (large versus small), in their directions of movement (right versus left), in their distances (close-up versus far shot) or in any combination thereof. In his films, this conflict produced the tense, violent rhythms that became an Eisenstein trademark. Conflict was also important to Eisenstein because he took it to be an expression, in the realm of images, of the Marxist's dialectical principle. Indeed, Eisenstein maintained that just as the meaning of a sentence arises from the interaction of its individual words, cinematic meaning is the result of the dialectical interplay of shots. His emphasis on the conflict of shots, as distinct from a mere linking of shots, distinguishes his conception from that of his colleague, Pudovkin. Pudovkin's view of montage as a method of building, of adding one thing to another, is not merely of theoretical interest. His theory produced his more realistic narratives (*Mother, Storm over Asia*), with their more deliberate, calmer pace.

Eisenstein, like most of the "first" generation theorists, was uncomfortable with the addition of synchronized dialogue. Because "silent" films had always used asynchronous sound effects and music, Eisenstein believed that the sound film could use these tools with even greater precision and complexity. But he positively rejected dialogue as being incompatible with the proper use of montage. By contrast André Bazin, a theorist of the "second" generation, while assenting to the incompatibility of dialogue and montage, regards synchronized speech as a necessary and proper development. For Bazin, dialogue returns film to the rightful path from which montage and silence diverted it. According to him, the film image ought to reveal nature whole, not present reality by cutting it into tiny bits. The cinematic methods Bazin endorses, which combines composing with the camera and staging an action in front of it, has, like montage, come to be known by a French term, mise-en-scène.

In Bazin's view the montage theorists did not in fact speak for all of the silent film, and he discerns in the work of von Stroheim, Murnau, and Flaherty an alternative, mise-en-scène tradition. Bazin sees this tradition as emphasizing not the ordering, but the content of images. The film's effect and meaning is not the product of a juxtaposition of images, but is inherent in the visual images themselves. For Bazin, the montage theorists' emphasis on the analogy between word and shot is false, and he rejects it along with their reluctance to employ sound as a source of cinematic meaning. Bazin argues that the mise-en-scène tradition within silent film actually looked toward the incorporation of synchronous sound as a fulfillment, not as a violation, of the film's destiny.

In the 1930s and 1940s Bazin sees German expressionism and Russian symbolism as having been superseded by a form of editing more appropriate to the dialogue film. This "analytic" editing, which characteristically manifests itself in the dramatic technique of shot and reverse shot, was an important innovation. Still more important, however, was the development of the shot-in-depth by Orson Welles and William Wyler in the early 1940s (anticipated in the 1930s by Jean Renoir), which made even the use of "analytic" montage unnecessary. Entire scenes could now be covered in one take, the camera remaining motionless. For Bazin, the shot-in-depth, like the use of synchronous sound, constituted a crucial advance toward total cinema.

Charles Barr, a contemporary English critic sympathetic to Bazin's ideas, defends the development of CinemaScope against those who reject it as a desecration of cinematic art. He notes the similarity of the attacks on the wide screen to those earlier attacks on synchronized sound, and he believes that both attacks are corollaries of the assumptions of the montage theorists. Barr therefore expands Bazin's attacks on montage theory, questioning even more vigorously the alleged analogy between word and shot. He also disputes Eisenstein's claim that associative montage gives a viewer the freedom to participate actively in the aesthetic experience. Barr finds it no accident that the rhetorical and coercive montage of Einstein, admittedly designed to serve propagandistic purposes, can now most frequently be found in television commercials. Barr in effect brings Bazin into the 1960s by viewing the wide screen as a refinement of the shot-in-depth method that Bazin endorsed and an advance in the representation of "nature whole" that "total" cinema seeks.

A very important new direction in contemporary film theory has arisen from this parallel concern with the way an image is understood and the way a sequence of such images might constitute a kind of "language." Christian Metz, a contemporary French theorist who was also influenced by André Bazin, believes that cinema is indeed a kind of language, although its signifying processes must be carefully distinguished from those of verbal languages. Using the linguistic science as a model, Metz's goal is to discover and establish the semiotics of the cinema—a theory of cinema as a system of signs. Many contemporary film theorists wish to put film theory and criticism on a firmer scientific basis. To consider film as a semiological system would permit film study—which suffers (in the opinion of many besides semiologists) from impressionism, subjectivity, and vagueness—to attain a scientific precision and rigor.

Metz believes that the concept of a "code," of encoded signs whose meanings we have learned to translate, is central to the development of a theory of film language. In the beginning, film was purely iconic—it signified exclusively by means of the resemblance of its imagery to objects in the visible world. But the development of narrative techniques required the development of various codes to denote the narrative progression. These rules and conventions, which were more or less complete by the time of D. W. Griffith, constitute the essence of film language and permit us to explain the procedures by which cinema denotes such narrative phenomena as successivity, priority, temporal breaks, and spatial continuity. As he shows in his analysis of what he calls the alternating *syntagma*, the order in which the signifying images occur may or may not be the same as that in which the realities they signify occur. The student of the language of cinema must therefore account for the processes and mechanisms which make it possible for the viewer to interpret them correctly. For Metz, the film does not simply reveal reality; it describes it in a language whose features we are only beginning to understand.

In his explication and critique of Metz, Alfred Guzzetti, an American critic, theorist, and filmmaker, explains Metz's central distinctions—between *langue* and language, code and message, syntagm and paradigm. At the same time, Guzzetti questions the alleged scientific neutrality of Metz's reliance on narrative film—and a particular type of narrative film—to develop his theory: Metz's dependence on the "classical Hollywood mode" of film narration. Guzzetti shows that such a model (derived from Bazin's notions of film realism) not only guarantees certain kinds of questions (and, therefore, answers) but also fails to describe any of the modernist experiments with film narrative of the last three decades.

More generally, Guzzetti criticizes Metz's theory for arbitrarily differentiating between cinematic codes (those signifying processes which are unique to cinema) and filmic codes (those signs which function in cinema but also exist elsewhere in a culture or in nature). For Guzzetti, all signs in a film have been "cinematified," have acquired unique cinematic meaning; our relation to a sign in cinema is not the same as it would be to the same object outside the theater, for our response to it (and, therefore, perception of it) has been determined by both its precise cinematic context and the general fact that we have no responsibility in responding to such a sign except as viewers of cinema.

The kind of problems raised by Metz also lead Umberto Eco, the influential Italian semiologist and critic, to the Peircian theory of signs, rather than Saussure's linguistics, for his model in developing a contrasting theory of semiotics. According to the Peircian system, a sign can relate to what it signifies in three ways: as an icon (the sign resembles the signified, as a picture of a dog resembles a dog), as an index (the significance of the sign depends on a real connection between the sign and what it signifies, as when the footprint of a dog signifies a dog), or as a symbol (the sign bears a purely arbitrary or conventional relationship to the signified, as the sign "dog" does to the animal it signifies). Like Guzzetti, and unlike Metz, Eco insists that iconic resemblances of the film image to real objects cannot be exempt from further analysis. Iconic signs are governed by codes and conventions; the semiologist must analyze these if he wishes to understand how film communicates and if he wants to further the Marxist project of demonstrating that there is no such thing as a "spontaneous" or "natural" reproduction of reality. Eco believes that all representation can be shown to reveal "plots of culture." For this reason, Eco would not be content with Metz's decision to examine only the denotative signifying processes of cinema; to eliminate the semiotic study of connotation would both impoverish the potential richness of the semiotic undertaking and would leave the most complex methods of film manipulation unexamined.

VSEVOLOD PUDOVKIN
FROM FILM TECHNIQUE

[ON EDITING]

METHODS OF TREATMENT OF THE MATERIAL

(Structural Editing)

A cinematograph film, and consequently also a scenario, is always divided into a great number of separate pieces (more correctly, it is built out of these pieces). The sum of the shooting-script is divided into sequences, each sequence into scenes, and, finally, the scenes themselves are constructed from a whole series of pieces (script-scenes) shot from various angles. An actual scenario, ready for use in shooting, must take into account this basic property of the film. The scenarist must be able to write his material on paper exactly as it will appear upon the screen, thus giving exactly the content of each shot as well as its position in sequence. The construction of a scene from pieces, a sequence from scenes, and reel from sequences, and so forth, is called *editing*. Editing is one of the most significant instruments of effect possessed by the film technician and, therefore, by the scenarist also. Let us now become acquainted with its methods one by one.

Editing of the Scene

Everyone familiar with a film is familiar with the expression "close-up." The alternating representation of the faces of the characters during a dialogue; the representation of hands, or feet, filling the whole screen—all this is familiar to everyone. But in order to know how properly to use the close-up, one must understand its significance, which is as follows: the close-up directs the attention of the spectator to that detail which is, at the moment, important to the course of the action. For instance, three persons are taking part in a scene. Suppose the significance of this scene consist in the *general* course of the action (if, for example, all three are lifting some heavy object), then they are taken simultaneously in a *general* view, the so-called long-shot. But suppose any one of them change to an independent action having significance in the scenario (for example, separating himself from the others, he draws a revolver cautiously from his pocket), then the camera is directed on him alone. His action is recorded separately.

What is said above applies not only to persons, but also to separate parts of a person, and objects. Let us suppose a man is to be taken apparently listening calmly to the conversation of someone else, but actually restraining his anger with difficulty. The man crushes the cigarette he holds in his hand, a gesture unnoticed by the other. This hand will always be shown on the screen separately, in close-up, otherwise the spectator will not notice it and a characteristic detail will be missed. The view formerly obtained (and is still held by some) that the close-up is an "interruption" of the long-shot. This idea is entirely false. It is no sort of interruption. It represents a proper form of construction.

In order to make clear to oneself the nature of the process of editing a scene, one may draw the following analogy. Imagine yourself observing a scene unfolded in front of you, thus: a man stands near the wall of a house and turns his head to the left; there appears another man slinking cautiously through the gate. The two are fairly widely distant from one another—they stop. The first takes some object and shows it to the other, mocking him. The latter clenches his fists in a rage and throws himself at the former. At this moment a woman looks out of a window on the third floor and calls, "Police!" The antagonists run off in opposite directions. Now, how would this have been observed?

1. The observer looks at the first man. He turns his head.

2. What is he looking at? The observer turns his glance in the same direction and sees the man entering the gate. The latter stops.

3. How does the first react to the appearance on the scene of the second? A new turn by the observer; the first takes out an object and mocks the second.

4. How does the second react? Another turn; he clenches his fists and throws himself on his opponent.

5. The observer draws aside to watch how both opponents roll about fighting.

6. A shout from above. The observer raises his head and sees the woman shouting at the window.

7. The observer lowers his head and sees the result of her warning—the antagonists running off in opposite directions.

The observer happened to be standing near and saw every detail,
saw it clearly, but to do so he had to turn his head, first left, then
right, then upwards, whithersoever his attention was attracted
by the interest of observation and the sequence of the developing
scene. Suppose he had been standing farther away from the action,
taking in the two persons and the window on the third floor simultaneously, he would have received only a general impression, without being able to look separately at the first, the second, or the
woman. Here we have approached closely the basic significance
of editing. Its object is the showing of the development of the scene
in relief, as it were, by guiding the attention of the spectator now
to one, now to the other separate element. The lens of the camera
replaces the eye of the observer, and the changes of angle of the
camera—directed now on one person, now on another, now on
one detail, now on another—must be subject to the same conditions
as those of the eyes of the observer. The film technician, in order
to secure the greatest clarity, emphasis, and vividness, shoots the
scene in separate pieces and, joining them and showing them, directs the attention of the spectator to the separate elements, compelling him to see as the attentive observer saw. From the above
is clear the manner in which editing can even work upon the emotions. Imagine to yourself the excited observer of some rapidly
developing scene. His agitated glance is thrown rapidly from one
spot to another. If we imitate this glance with the camera we get
a series of pictures, rapidly alternating pieces, creating a *stirring
scenario editing-construction*. The reverse would be long pieces
changing by mixes, conditioning a calm and slow editing-construction (as one may shoot, for example, a herd of cattle wandering
along a road, taken from the viewpoint of a pedestrian on the same
road).

We have established, by these instances, the basic significance
of the constructive editing of scenes. It builds the scenes from separate pieces, of which each concentrates the attention of the spectator only on that element important to the action. The sequence
of these pieces must not be uncontrolled, but must correspond
to the natural transference of attention of an imaginary observer
(who, in the end, is represented by the spectator). In this sequence
must be expressed a special logic that will be apparent only if each
shot contain an impulse towards transference of the attention to
the next. For example (1) A man turns his head and looks; (2) What
he looks at is shown.

Editing of the Sequence

The guidance of the attention of the spectator to different elements of the developing action in succession is, in general, characteristic of the film. It is its basic method. We have seen that the separate scene, and often even the movement of one man, is built up upon the screen from separate pieces. Now, the film is not simply a collection of different scenes. Just as the pieces are built up into scenes endowed, as it were, with a connected action, so the separate scenes are assembled into groups forming whole sequences. The sequence is constructed (edited) from scenes. Let us suppose ourselves faced with the task of constructing the following sequence: two spies are creeping forward to blow up a powder magazine; on the way one of them loses a letter with instructions. Someone else finds the letter and warns the guard, who appears in time to arrest the spies and save the magazine. Here the scenarist has to deal with simultaneity of various actions in several different places. While the spies are crawling towards the magazine, someone else finds the letter and hastens to warn the guard. The spies have nearly reached their objective; the guards are warned and rushing towards the magazine. The spies have completed their preparations; the guard arrives in time. If we pursue the previous analogy between the camera and an observer, we now not only have to turn it from side to side, but also to move it from place to place. The observer (the camera) is now on the road shadowing the spies, now in the guardroom recording the confusion, now back at the magazine showing the spies at work, and so forth. But, in combination of the separate scenes (editing), the former law of sequence succession remains in force. A consecutive sequence will appear upon the screen only if the attention of the spectator be transferred correctly from scene to scene. And this correctness is conditioned as follows: the spectator sees the creeping spies, the loss of the letter, and finally the person who finds the letter. The person with the letter rushes for help. The spectator is seized with inevitable excitement—Will the man who found the letter be able to forestall the explosion? The scenarist immediately answers by showing the spies nearing the magazine—his answer has the effect of a warning "Time is short." The excitement of the spectator—Will they be in time?—continues; the scenarist shows the guard turning out. Time is very short—the spies are shown beginning their work. Thus, transferring attention now to the rescuers, now to the spies, the scenarist answers with actual impulses to increase of the spectator's interest, and the construction (editing) of the sequence is correctly achieved.

There is a law in psychology that lays it down that if an emotion give birth to a certain movement, by imitation of this movement the corresponding emotion can be called forth. If the scenarist can effect in even rhythm the transference of interest of the intent spectator, if he can so construct the elements of increasing interest that the question, "What is happening at the other place?" arises and at the same moment the spectator is transferred whither he wishes to go, then the editing thus created can really excite the spectator. One must learn to understand that editing is in actual fact a compulsory and deliberate guidance of the thoughts and associations of the spectator. If the editing be merely an uncontrolled combination of the various pieces, the spectator will understand (apprehend) nothing from it; but if it be co-ordinated according to a definitely selected course of events or conceptual line, either agitated or calm, it will either excite or soothe the spectator.

Editing of the Scenario

The film is divided into reels. The reels are usually equal in length, on an average from 900 to 1,200 feet long. The combination of the reels forms the picture. The usual length of a picture should not be more than from 6,500 to 7,500 feet. This length, as yet, involves no unnecessary exhaustion of the spectator. The film is usually divided into from six to eight reels. It should be noted here, as a practical hint, that the average length of a piece (remember the editing of scenes) is from 6 to 10 feet, and consequently from 100 to 150 pieces go to a reel. By orientating himself on these figures, the scenarist can visualise how much material can be fitted into the scenario. The scenario is composed of a series of sequences. In discussing the construction (editing) of the scenario from sequences, we introduce a new element into the scenarist's work — the element of so-called dramatic continuity of action that was discussed at the beginning of this sketch. The continuity of the separate sequences when joined together depends not merely upon the simple transference of attention from one place to another, but is conditioned by the development of the action forming the foundation of the scenario. It is important, however, to remind the scenarist of the following point: a scenario has always in its development a moment of greatest tension, found nearly always at the end of the film. To prepare the spectator, or, more correctly, preserve him, for this final tension, it is especially important to see that he is not affected by unnecessary exhaustion during the course of the film. A method . . . that the scenarist can employ to this end is the careful distribution of the titles (which always distract the spectator), securing compression of the greater quantity of them into the first reels, and leaving the last one for uninterrupted action.

Thus, first is worked out the action of the scenario, the action is then worked out into sequences, the sequences into scenes, and these constructed by editing from the pieces, each corresponding to a camera angle.

EDITING AS AN INSTRUMENT OF IMPRESSION

(Relational Editing)

We have already mentioned, in the section on editing of sequences, that editing is not merely a method of the junction of separate scenes or pieces, but is a method that controls the "psychological guidance" of the spectator. We should now acquaint ourselves with the main special editing methods having as their aim the impression of the spectator.

Contrast.—Suppose it be our task to tell of the miserable situation of a starving man; the story will impress the more vividly if associated with mention of the senseless gluttony of a well-to-do man.

On just such a simple contrast relation is based the corresponding editing method. On the screen the impression of this contrast is yet increased, for it is possible not only to relate the starving sequence to the gluttony sequence, but also to relate separate scenes and even separate shots of the scenes to one another, thus, as it were, forcing the spectator to compare the two actions all the time, one strengthening the other. The editing of contrast is one of the most effective, but also one of the commonest and most standardised, of methods, and so care should be taken not to overdo it.

Parallelism.—This method resembles contrast, but is considerably wider. Its substance can be explained more clearly by an example. In a scenario as yet unproduced a section occurs as follows: a working man, one of the leaders of a strike, is condemned to death; the execution is fixed for 5 a.m. The sequence is edited thus: a factory-owner, employer of the condemned man, is leaving a restaurant drunk, he looks at his wrist-watch: 4 o'clock. The accused is shown—he is being made ready to be led out. Again the manufacturer, he rings a door-bell to ask the time: 4.30. The prison waggon drives along the street under heavy guard. The maid who opens the door—the wife of the condemned—is subjected to a sudden senseless assault. The drunken factory-owner snores on a bed, his leg with trouser-end upturned, his hand hanging down with wrist-watch visible, the hands of the watch crawl slowly to 5 o'clock. The workman is being hanged. In this instance two thematically unconnected incidents develop in parallel by means of the watch that tells of the approaching execution. The watch on the wrist of the callous brute, as it were connects him with the chief protagonist of the approaching tragic *dénouement*, thus ever present in the consciousness of the spectator. This is undoubtedly an interesting method, capable of considerable development.

Symbolism. — In the final scenes of the film *Strike* the shooting down of workmen is punctuated by shots of the slaughter of a bull in a stockyard. The scenarist, as it were, desires to say: just as a butcher fells a bull with the swing of a pole-axe, so, cruelly and in cold blood, were shot down the workers. This method is especially interesting because, by means of editing, it introduces an abstract concept into the consciousness of the spectator without use of a title.

Simultaneity. — In American films the final section is constructed from the simultaneous rapid development of two actions, in which the outcome of one depends on the outcome of the other. The end of the present-day section of *Intolerance* . . . is thus constructed. The whole aim of this method is to create in the spectator a maximum tension of excitement by the constant forcing of a question, such as, in this case: Will they be in time? — will they be in time?

The method is a purely emotional one, and nowadays overdone almost to the point of boredom, but it cannot be denied that of all the methods of constructing the end hitherto devised it is the most effective.

Leit-motif (reiteration of theme). — Often it is interesting for the scenarist especially to emphasise the basic theme of the scenario. For this purpose exists the method of reiteration. Its nature can easily be demonstrated by an example. In an anti-religious scenario that aimed at exposing the cruelty and hypocrisy of the Church in employ of the Tsarist régime the same shot was several times repeated: a church-bell slowly ringing and, superimposed on it, the title: "The sound of bells sends into the world a message of patience and love." This piece appeared whenever the scenarist desired to emphasise the stupidity of patience, or the hypocrisy of the love thus preached.

The little that has been said above of relational editing naturally by no means exhausts the whole abundance of its methods. It has merely been important to show that constructional editing, a method specifically and peculiarly filmic, is, in the hands of the scenarist, an important instrument of impression. Careful study of its use in pictures, combined with talent, will undoubtedly lead to the discovery of new possibilities and, in conjunction with them, to the creation of new forms.

1926

SERGEI EISENSTEIN
FROM FILM FORM

THE CINEMATOGRAPHIC
PRINCIPLE AND THE IDEOGRAM

It is a weird and wonderful feat to have written a pamphlet on something that in reality does not exist. There is, for example, no such thing as a cinema without cinematography. And yet the author of the pamphlet preceding this essay* has contrived to write a book about the *cinema* of a country that has no *cinematography*. About the cinema of a country that has, in its culture, an infinite number of cinematographic traits, strewn everywhere with the sole exception of—its cinema.

This essay is on the cinematographic traits of Japanese culture that lie outside the Japanese cinema, and is itself as apart from the preceding pamphlet as these traits are apart from the Japanese cinema.

Cinema is: so many corporations, such and such turnovers of capital, so and so many stars, such and such dramas.

Cinematography is, first and foremost, montage.

The Japanese cinema is excellently equipped with corporations, actors, and stories. But the Japanese cinema is completely unaware of montage. Nevertheless the principle of montage can be identified as the basic element of Japanese representational culture.

---

*Eisenstein's essay was originally published as an "afterword" to N. Kaufman's pamphlet, *Japanese Cinema* (Moscow, 1929).

Writing—for their writing is primarily representational.
The hieroglyph.

The naturalistic image of an object, as portrayed by the skilful Chinese hand of Ts'ang Chieh 2650 years before our era, becomes slightly formalized and, with its 539 fellows, forms the first "contingent" of hieroglyphs. Scratched out with a stylus on a slip of bamboo, the portrait of an object maintained a resemblance to its original in every respect.

But then, by the end of the third century, the brush is invented. In the first century after the "joyous event" (A.D.)—paper. And, lastly, in the year 220—India ink.

A complete upheaval. A revolution in draughtsmanship. And, after having undergone in the course of history no fewer than fourteen different styles of handwriting, the hieroglyph crystallized in its present form. The, means of production (brush and India ink) determined the form.

The fourteen reforms had their way. As a result:

In the fierily cavorting hieroglyph *ma* (a horse) it is already impossible to recognize the features of the dear little horse sagging pathetically in its hindquarters, in the writing style of Ts'ang Chieh, so well-known from ancient Chinese bronzes.

But let it rest in the Lord, this dear little horse, together with the other 607 remaining *hsiang cheng* symbols—the earliest extant category of hieroglyphs.

The real interest begins with the second category of hieroglyphs—the *huei-i*, i.e., "copulative."

The point is that the copulation (perhaps we had better say, the combination) of two hieroglyphs of the simplest series is to be regarded not as their sum, but as their product, i.e., as a value of another dimension, another degree; each, separately, corresponds to an *object*, to a fact, but their combination corresponds to a *concept*. From separate hieroglyphs has been fused—the ideogram. By the combination of two "depictables" is achieved the representation of something that is graphically undepictable.

For example: the picture for water and the picture of an eye signifies "to weep"; the picture of an ear nearing the drawing of

a dog = "to listen";
a dog + a mouth = "to bark";
a mouth + a child = "to scream";
a mouth + a bird = "to sing";
a knife + a heart = "sorrow," and so on.

But this is—montage!

Yes. It is exactly what we do in the cinema, combining shots that are *depictive*, single in meaning, neutral in content—into *intellectual* contexts and series.

This is a means and method inevitable in any cinematographic exposition. And, in a condensed and purified form, the starting point for the "intellectual cinema."

For a cinema seeking a maximum laconism for the visual representation of abstract concepts.

And we hail the method of the long-lamented Ts'ang Chieh as a first step along these paths.

We have mentioned laconism. Laconism furnishes us a transition to another point. Japan possesses the most laconic form of poetry: the *haikai* (appearing at the beginning of the thirteenth century and known today as "haiku" or "hokku") and the even earlier *tanka* (mythologically assumed to have been created along with heaven and earth).

Both are little more than hieroglyphs transposed into phrases. So much so that half their quality is appraised by their calligraphy. The method of their resolution is completely analogous to the structure of the ideogram.

As the ideogram provides a means for the laconic imprinting of an abstract concept, the same method, when transposed into literary exposition, gives rise to an identical laconism of pointed imagery.

Applied to the collision of an austere combination of symbols this method results in a dry definition of abstract concepts. The same method, expanded into the luxury of a group of already formed verbal combinations, swells into a splendor of *imagist* effect.

The concept is a bare formula; its adornment (an expansion by additional material) transforms the formula into an image—a finished form.

Exactly, though in reverse, as a primitive thought process—

imagist thinking, displaced to a definite degree, becomes transformed to conceptual thinking.

But let us turn to examples.

The *haiku* is a concentrated impressionist sketch:

> A lonely crow
>   On leafless bough,
>   One autumn eve.
>
> BASHO

> What a resplendent moon!
>   It casts the shadow of pine boughs
>   Upon the mats.
>
> KIKAKU

> An evening breeze blows.
>   The water ripples
>   Against the blue heron's legs.
>
> BUSON

> It is early dawn.
>   The castle is surrounded
>   By the cries of wild ducks.
>
> KYOROKU

The earlier *tanka* is slightly longer (by two lines):

> O mountain pheasant
> long are the feathers trail'st thou
> on the wooded hill-side—
> as long the nights seem to me
> on lonely couch sleep seeking.
>
> HITOMARO[?]

From our point of view, these are montage phrases. Shot lists. The simple combination of two or three details of a material kind yields a perfectly finished representation of another kind—psychological.

And if the finely ground edges of the intellectually defined concepts formed by the combined ideograms are blurred in these poems, yet, in *emotional quality*, the concepts have blossomed forth immeasurably. We should observe that the emotion is directed towards the reader, for, as Yone Nobuchi has said, "it is the readers who make the *haiku's* imperfection a perfection of art."

It is uncertain in Japanese writing whether its predominating aspect is as a system of characters (denotative), or as an independent creation of graphics (depictive). In any case, born of the dual mating of the depictive by method, and the denotative by purpose, the ideogram continued both these lines (not consecutive historically but consecutive in principle in the minds of those developing the method).

Not only did the denotative line continue into literature, in the *tanka,* as we have shown, but exactly the same method (in its depictive aspect) operates also in the most perfect examples of Japanese pictorial art.

Sharaku—creator of the finest prints of the eighteenth century, and especially of an immortal gallery of actors' portraits. The Japanese Daumier. Despite this, almost unknown to us. The characteristic traits of his work have been analyzed only in our century. One of these critics, Julius Kurth, in discussing the question of the influence on Sharaku of sculpture, draws a parallel between his wood-cut portrait of the actor Nakayama Tomisaburō and an antique mask of the semi-religious Nō theater, the mask of a Rozo.

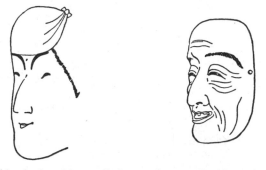

The faces of both the print and the mask wear an *identical expression.* . . . Features and masses are similarly arranged although the mask represents an old priest, and the print a young woman. This relationship is striking, yet these two works are otherwise totally dissimilar; this in itself is a demonstration of Sharaku's originality. While the carved mask was constructed according to fairly accurate anatomical proportions, the proportions of the portrait print are simply impossible. The space between the eyes comprises a width that makes mock of all good sense. The nose is almost twice as long in relation to the eyes as any normal nose would dare to be, and the chin stands in no sort of relation to the mouth; the brows, the mouth, and every feature—is hopelessly misrelated. *This observation may be made in all the large heads by Sharaku.* That the artist was unaware that all these proportions are false is, of course, out of the question. It was with a full awareness that he repudiated normalcy, and, while the drawing of the separate features depends on severely concentrated naturalism, their proportions have been subordinated to purely intellectual considerations. *He set up the essence of the psychic expression as the norm for the proportions of the single features.*

Is not this process that of the ideogram, combining the independent "mouth" and the dissociated symbol of "child" to form the significance of "scream"?

Is this not exactly what we of the cinema do temporally, just as Sharaku in simultaneity, when we cause a monstrous disproportion of the parts of a normally flowing event, and suddenly dismember the event into "close-up of clutching hands," "medium shots of the struggle," and "extreme close-up of bulging eyes," in making a montage disintegration of the event in various planes? In making an eye twice as large as a man's full figure?! By combining these monstrous incongruities we newly collect the disintegrated event into one whole, but in *our* aspect. According to the treatment of our relation to the event.

The disproportionate depiction of an event is organically natural to us from the beginning. Professor Luriya, of the Psychological Institute in Moscow, has shown me a drawing by a child of "lighting a stove." Everything is represented in passably accurate relationship and with great care. Firewood. Stove. Chimney. But what are those zigzags in that huge central rectangle? They turn out to be—matches. Taking into account the crucial importance of these matches for the depicted process, the child provides a proper scale for them.*

The representation of objects in the actual (absolute) proportions proper to them is, of course, merely a tribute to orthodox formal logic. A subordination to an inviolable order of things.

---

*It is possible to trace this particular tendency from its ancient, almost prehistorical source (". . . in all ideational art, objects are given size according to their importance, the king being twice as large as his subjects, or a tree half the size of a man when it merely informs us that the scene is out-of-doors. Something of this principle of size according to significance persisted in the Chinese tradition. The favorite disciple of Confucius looked like a little boy beside him and the most important figure in any group was usually the largest." [George Rowley, *Principles of Chinese Painting*. Princeton University Press, 1947, p. 56.]) through the highest development of Chinese art, parent of Japanese graphic arts: ". . . natural scale always had to bow to pictorial scale . . . size according to distance never followed the laws of geometric perspective but the needs of the design. Foreground features might be diminished to avoid obstruction and overemphasis, and far distant objects, which were too minute to count pictorially, might be enlarged to act as a counterpoint to the middle distance or foreground." [Rowley, p. 66.]

Both in painting and sculpture there is a periodic and invariable return to periods of the establishment of absolutism. Displacing the expressiveness of archaic disproportion for regulated "stone tables" of officially decreed harmony.

Absolute realism is by no means the correct form of perception. It is simply the function of a certain form of social structure. Following a state monarchy, a state uniformity of thought is implanted. Ideological uniformity of a sort that can be developed pictorially in the ranks of colors and designs of the Guards regiments . . .

Thus we have seen how the principle of the hieroglyph—"denotation by depiction"—split in two: along the line of its purpose (the principle of "denotation"), into the principles of creating literary imagery; along the line of its method of realizing this purpose (the principle of "depiction"), into the striking methods of expressiveness used by Sharaku.*

And, just as the two outspreading wings of a hyperbola meet, as we say, at infinity (though no one has visited so distant a region!), so the principle of hieroglyphics, infinitely splitting into two parts (in accordance with the function of symbols), unexpectedly unites again from this dual estrangement, in yet a fourth sphere—in the theater.

Estranged for so long, they are once again—in the cradle period of the drama—present in a *parallel* form, in a curious dualism.

The *significance* (denotation) of the action is effected by the reciting of the *Jōruri* by a voice behind the stage—the *representation* (depiction) of the action is effected by silent marionettes on the stage. Along with a specific manner of movement this archaism migrated into the early Kabuki theater, as well. To this day it is preserved, as a partial method, in the classical repertory (where certain parts of the action are narrated from behind the stage while the actor mimes).

But this is not the point. The most important fact is that into the technique of acting itself the ideographic (montage) method has been wedged in the most interesting ways.

However, before discussing this, let us be allowed the luxury of a digression—on the matter of the shot, to settle the debated question of its nature, once and for all.

A shot. A single piece of celluloid. A tiny rectangular frame in which there is, organized in some way, a piece of an event.

---

*It has been left to James Joyce to develop in *literature* the depictive line of the Japanese hieroglyph. Every word of Kurth's analysis of Sharaku may be applied, neatly and easily, to Joyce.

"Cemented together, these shots form montage. When this is done in an appropriate rhythm, *of course!*"

This, roughly, is what is taught by the old, old school of film-making, that sang:

> "Screw by screw,
> Brick by brick . . ."

Kuleshov, for example, even writes with a brick:

If you have an idea-phrase, a particle of the story, a link in the whole dramatic chain, then that idea is to be expressed and accumulated from shot-ciphers, just like bricks.

"The shot is an element of montage. Montage is an assembly of these elements." This is a most pernicious make-shift analysis.

Here the understanding of the process as a whole (connection, shot-montage) derives only from the external indications of its flow (a piece cemented to another piece). Thus it would be possible, for instance, to arrive at the well-known conclusion that street-cars exist in order to be laid across streets. An entirely logical deduction, if one limits oneself to the external indications of the functions they performed during the street-fighting of February 1917, here in Russia. But the materialist conception of history interprets it otherwise.

The worst of it is that an approach of this kind does actually lie, like an insurmountable street-car, across the potentialities of formal development. Such an approach overrules dialectical development, and dooms one to mere evolutionary "perfecting," in so far as it gives no bite into the dialectical substance of events.

In the long run, such evolutionizing leads either through refinement to decadence or, on the other hand, to a simple withering away due to stagnation of the blood.

Strange as it may seem, a melodious witness to both these distressing eventualities, simultaneously, is Kuleshov's latest film, *The Gay Canary* [1929].

The shot is by no means an *element* of montage.
The shot is a montage *cell.*

Just as cells in their division form a phenomenon of another order, the organism or embryo, so, on the other side of the dialectical leap from the shot, there is montage.

By what, then, is montage characterized and, consequently, its cell—the shot?

By collision. By the conflict of two pieces in opposition to each other. By conflict. By collision.

In front of me lies a crumpled yellowed sheet of paper. On it is a mysterious note:

"Linkage—P" and "Collision—E."

This is a substantial trace of a heated bout on the subject of montage between P (Pudovkin) and E (myself).

This has become a habit. At regular intervals he visits me late at night and behind closed doors we wrangle over matters of principle. A graduate of the Kuleshov school, he loudly defends an understanding of montage as a *linkage* of pieces. Into a chain. Again, "bricks." Bricks, arranged in series to *expound* an idea.

I confronted him with my viewpoint on montage as a *collision*. A view that from the collision of two given factors *arises* a concept.

From my point of view, linkage is merely a possible *special* case.

Recall what an infinite number of combinations is known in physics to be capable of arising from the impact (collision) of spheres. Depending on whether the spheres be resilient, non-resilient, or mingled. Amongst all these combinations there is one in which the impact is so weak that the collision is degraded to an even movement of both in the same direction.

This is the one combination which would correspond with Pudovkin's view.

Not long ago we had another talk. Today he agrees with my point of view. True, during the interval he took the opportunity to acquaint himself with the series of lectures I gave during that period at the State Cinema Institute. . . .

So, montage is conflict.

As the basis of every art is conflict (an "imagist" transformation of the dialectical principle). The shot appears as the *cell* of montage. Therefore it also must be considered from the viewpoint of *conflict*.

Conflict within the shot is potential montage, in the development of its intensity shattering the quadrilateral cage of the shot and exploding its conflict into montage impulses *between* the montage pieces. As, in a zigzag of mimicry, the *mise-en-scène* splashes out into a spatial zigzag with the *same* shattering. As the slogan, "All obstacles are vain before Russians," bursts out in the multitude of incident of *War and Peace*.

If montage is to be compared with something, then a phalanx of montage pieces, of shots, should be compared to the series of explosions of an internal combustion engine, driving forward its automobile or tractor: for, similarly, the dynamics of montage serve as impulses driving forward the total film.

Conflict within the frame. This can be very varied in charac-

ter: it even can be a conflict in—the story. As in that "prehistoric" period in films (although there are plenty of instances in
the present, as well), when entire scenes would be photographed in a single, uncut shot. This, however, is outside the
strict jurisdiction of the film-form.

These are the "cinematographic" conflicts within the frame:
Conflict of graphic directions.

(Lines—either static or dynamic)

Conflict of scales.
Conflict of volumes.
Conflict of masses.

(Volumes filled with various intensities of light)

Conflict of depths.

And the following conflicts, requiring only one further impulse of intensification before flying into antagonistic pairs of
pieces:

Close shots and long shots.
Pieces of graphically varied directions. Pieces resolved in vol-
ume, with pieces resolved in area.
Pieces of darkness and pieces of lightness.

And, lastly, there are such unexpected conflicts as:
Conflicts between an object and its dimension—and conflicts between an event and its duration.

These may sound strange, but both are familiar to us. The
first is accomplished by an optically distorted lens, and the
second by stop-motion or slow-motion.

The compression of all cinematographic factors and properties within a single dialectical formula of conflict is no empty
rhetorical diversion.

We are now seeking a unified system for methods of cinematographic expressiveness that shall hold good for all its elements. The assembly of these into series of common indications will solve the task as a whole.

Experience in the separate elements of the cinema cannot be
absolutely measured.

Whereas we know a good deal about montage, in the theory
of the shot we are still floundering about amidst the most academic attitudes, some vague tentatives, and the sort of harsh
radicalism that sets one's teeth on edge.

To regard the frame as a particular, as it were, molecular
case of montage makes possible the direct application of montage practice to the theory of the shot.

And similarly with the theory of lighting. To sense this as a
collision between a stream of light and an obstacle, like the
impact of a stream from a fire-hose striking a concrete object,
or of the wind buffeting a human figure, must result in a
usage of light entirely different in comprehension from that

employed in playing with various combinations of "gauzes" and "spots."

Thus far we have one such significant principle of conflict: *the principle of optical counterpoint.*

And let us not now forget that soon we shall face another and less simple problem in counterpoint: *the conflict in the sound film of acoustics and optics.*

Let us return to one of the most fascinating of optical conflicts: the conflict between the frame of the shot and the object!

The camera position, as a materialization of the conflict between organizing logic of the director and the inert logic of the object, in collision, reflects the dialectic of the camera-angle.

In this matter we are still impressionistic and lacking in principle to a sickening degree. Nevertheless, a sharpness of principle can be had in the technique of this, too. The dry quadrilateral, plunging into the hazards of nature's diffuseness . . .

And once again we are in Japan! For the cinematographic method is used in teaching drawing in Japanese schools.

What is our method of teaching drawing? Take any piece of white paper with four corners to it. Then cram onto it, usually even without using the edges (mostly greasy from the long drudgery!), some bored caryatid, some conceited Corinthian capital, or a plaster Dante (not the magician performing at the Moscow Hermitage, but the other one—Alighieri, the comedy writer).

The Japanese approach this from a quite different direction: Here's the branch of a cherry-tree. And the pupils cuts out from this whole, with a square, and a circle, and a rectangle—compositional units:

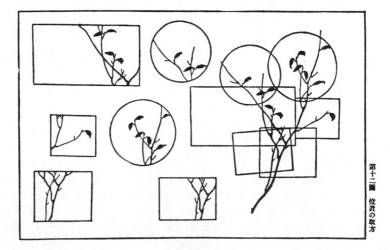

第十二圖　位置の取方

He frames a shot!

These two ways of teaching drawing can characterize the two basic tendencies struggling within the cinema of today. One—the expiring method of artificial spatial organization of an event in front of the lens. From the "direction" of a sequence, to the erection of a Tower of Babel in front of the lens. The other—a "picking-out" by the camera: organization by means of the camera. Hewing out a piece of actuality with the ax of the lens.

However, at the present moment, when the center of attention is finally beginning, in the intellectual cinema, to be transferred from the materials of cinema, as such, to "deductions and conclusions," to "slogans" based on the material, both schools of thought are losing distinction in their differences and can quickly blend into a synthesis.

Several pages back we lost, like an overshoe in a street-car, the question of the theater. Let us turn back to the question of methods of montage in the Japanese theater, particularly in acting.

The first and most striking example, of course, is the purely cinemetographic method of "acting without transitions." Along with mimic transitions carried to a limit of refinement, the Japanese actor uses an exactly contrary method as well. At a certain moment of his performance he halts; the black-shrouded *kurogo* obligingly conceals him from the spectators. And lo!—he is resurrected in a new make-up. And in a new wig. Now characterizing another stage (degree) of his emotional state.

Thus, for example, in the Kabuki play *Narukami*, the actor Sadanji must change from drunkenness to madness. This transition is solved by a mechanical cut. And a change in the arsenal of grease-paint colors on his face, emphasizing those streaks whose duty it is to fulfill the expression of a higher intensity than those used in his previous make-up.

This method is organic to the film. The forced introduction into the film, by European acting traditions, of pieces of "emotional transitions" is yet another influence forcing the cinema to mark time. Whereas the method of "cut" acting makes possible the construction of entirely new methods. Replacing one changing face with a whole scale of facial types of varying moods affords a far more acutely expressive result than does the changing surface, too receptive and devoid of organic resistance, of any single professional actor's face.

In our new film [*Old and New*] I have eliminated the intervals between the sharply contrasting polar stages of a face's expression. Thus is achieved a greater sharpness in the "play of doubts" around the new cream separator. Will the milk thicken or no? Trickery? Wealth? Here the psychological process of mingled faith and doubt is broken up into its two extreme states of joy (confidence) and gloom (disillusionment). Furthermore, this is sharply emphasized by light—illumination in no wise conforming to actual light conditions. This brings a distinct strengthening of the tension.

Another remarkable characteristic of the Kabuki theater is the principle of "disintegrated" acting. Shocho, who played the leading female rôles in the Kabuki theater that visited Moscow, in depicting the dying daughter in *Yashaō* (*The Mask-Maker*), performed his rôle in pieces of acting completely detached from each other: Acting with only the right arm. Acting with one leg. Acting with the neck and head only. (The whole process of the death agony was disintegrated into solo performances of each member playing its own rôle: the rôle of the leg, the rôle of the arms, the rôle of the head.) A breaking-up into shots. With a gradual shortening of these separate, successive pieces of acting as the tragic end approached.

Freed from the yoke of primitive naturalism, the actor is enabled by this method to fully grip the spectator by "rhythms," making not only acceptable, but definitely attractive, a stage built on the most consecutive and detailed flesh and blood of naturalism.

Since we no longer distinguish in principle between questions of shot-content and montage, we may here cite a third example:

The Japanese theater makes use of a slow tempo to a degree unknown to our stage. The famous scene of hara-kiri in *Chushingura* is based on an unprecedented slowing down of all movement—beyond any point we have ever seen. Whereas, in the previous example, we observed a disintegration of the transitions between movements, here we see disintegration of the process of movement, viz., slow-motion. I have heard of only one example of a thorough application of this method, using the technical possibility of the film with a compositionally reasoned plan. It is usually employed with some purely pictorial aim, such as the "submarine kingdom" in *The Thief of Bagdad,* or to represent a dream, as in *Zvenigora*. Or, more often, it is used simply for formalist jackstraws and unmotivated camera mischief as in Vertov's *Man with the Movie-Camera*. The more commendable example appears to be in Jean Epstein's *La chute de la Maison Usher*—at least according to the press reports. In this film, normally acted emotions filmed with a speeded-up camera are said to give unusual emotional pressure by their unrealistic slowness on the screen. If it be borne in mind that the effect of an actor's performance on the audience is based on its identification by each spectator, it will be easy to relate both examples (the Kabuki play and the Epstein film) to an identical causal explanation. The intensity of perception increases as the didactic process of identification proceeds more easily along a disintegrated action.

Even instruction in handling a rifle can be hammered into the tightest motor-mentality among a group of raw recruits if the instructor uses a "break-down" method.

The most interesting link of the Japanese theater is, of course, its link with the sound film, which can and must learn its fundamentals from the Japanese—the reduction of visual and aural sensations to a common physiological denominator.

So, it has been possible to establish (cursorily) the permeation of the most varied branches of Japanese culture by a pure cinematographic element—its basic nerve, montage.

And it is only the Japanese cinema that falls into the same error as the "leftward drifting" Kabuki. Instead of learning how to extract the principles and technique of their remarkable acting from the traditional feudal forms of their materials, the most progressive leaders of the Japanese theater throw their energies into an adaptation of the spongy shapelessness of our own "inner" naturalism. The results are tearful and saddening. In its cinema Japan similarly pursues imitations of the most revolting examples of American and European entries in the international commercial film race.

To understand and apply her cultural peculiarities to the cinema, this is the task of Japan! Colleagues of Japan, are you really going to leave this for us to do?

1929

A DIALECTIC APPROACH
TO FILM FORM

In nature we never see anything isolated, but everything in connection with something else which is before it, beside it, under it, and over it.

GOETHE

According to Marx and Engels the dialectic system is only the conscious reproduction of the dialectic course (substance) of the external events of the world.

Thus:

The projection of the dialectic system of things
into the brain
into creating abstractly
into the process of thinking
yields: dialectic methods of thinking;
dialectic materialism—   PHILOSOPHY.

And also:

The projection of the same system of things
while creating concretely
while giving form
yields: ART.

The foundation for this philosophy is a *dynamic* concept of things:

Being—as a constant evolution from the interaction of two contradictory opposites.

Synthesis—arising from the opposition between thesis and antithesis.

A dynamic comprehension of things is also basic to the same degree, for a correct understanding of art and of all art-forms. In the realm of art this dialectic principle of dynamics is embodied in

CONFLICT

as the fundamental principle for the existence of every art-work and every art-form.

For art is always conflict:
(1) according to its social mission,
(2) according to its nature,
(3) according to its methodology.

According to its social mission *because:* It is art's task to make manifest the contradictions of Being. To form equitable views by stirring up contradictions within the spectator's mind, and to forge accurate intellectual concepts from the dynamic clash of opposing passions.

According to its nature *because:* Its nature is a conflict between natural existence and creative tendency. Between organic inertia and purposeful initiative. Hypertrophy of the purposive initiative—the principles of rational logic—ossifies art into mathematical technicalism. (A painted landscape becomes a topographical map, a painted Saint Sebastian becomes an anatomical chart.) Hypertrophy of organic natural-ness—of organic logic—dilutes art into formlessness. (A

Malevich becomes a Kaulbach, an Archipenko becomes a wax-works side-show.)

Because the limit of organic form (the passive principle of being) is *Nature*. The limit of rational form (the active principle of production) is *Industry*. At the intersection of Nature and Industry stands *Art*.

The logic of organic form *vs.* the logic of rational form yields, in collision,

the dialectic of the art-form.

The interaction of the two produces and determines Dynamism. (Not only in the sense of a space-time continuum, but also in the field of absolute thinking. I also regard the inception of new concepts and viewpoints in the conflict between customary conception and particular representation as dynamic—as a dynamization of the inertia of perception—as a dynamization of the "traditional view" into a new one.)

The quantity of interval determines the pressure of the tension. (See in music, for example, the concept of intervals. There can be cases where the distance of separation is so wide that it leads to a break—to a collapse of the homogeneous concept of art. For instance, the "inaudibility" of certain intervals.)

> *The spatial form of this dynamism is expression.*
> *The phrases of its tension: rhythm.*

This is true for every art-form, and, indeed, for every kind of expression.

Similarly, human expression is a conflict between conditioned and unconditioned reflexes. (In this I cannot agree with Klages, who, a) does not consider human expression dynamically as a process, but statically as a result, and who, b) attributes everything in motion to the field of the "soul," and only the hindering element to "reason." ["Reason" and "Soul" of the idealistic concept here correspond remotely with the ideas of conditioned and unconditioned reflexes.])

This is true in every field that can be understood as an art. For example, logical thought, considered as an art, shows the same dynamic mechanism:

> . . . the intellectual lives of Plato or Dante or Spinoza or Newton were largely guided and sustained by their delight in the sheer beauty of the rhythmic relation between law and instance, species and individual, or cause and effect.

This holds in other fields, as well, e.g., in speech, where all its sap, vitality, and dynamism arise from the irregularity of the part in relation to the laws of the system as a whole.

In contrast we can observe the sterility of expression in such artificial, totally regulated languages as Esperanto.

It is from this principle that the whole charm of poetry derives. Its rhythm arises as a conflict between the metric measure employed and the distribution of accents, over-riding this measure.

The concept of a formally static phenomenon as a dynamic function is dialectically imaged in the wise words of Goethe:

> Die Baukunst ist eine ertarrte Musik.
> (Architecture is frozen music.)

Just as in the case of a homogeneous ideology (a monistic viewpoint), the whole, as well as the least detail, must be penetrated by a sole principle. So, ranged alongside the conflict of *social conditionality*, and the conflict of *existing nature*, the *methodology* of an art reveals this same principle of conflict.

As the basic principle of the rhythm to be created and the inception of the art-form.

Art is always conflict, according to its methodology.

Here we shall consider the general problem of art in the specific example of its highest form—film.

Shot and montage are the basic elements of cinema.

Montage

has been established by the Soviet film as the nerve of cinema.

To determine the nature of montage is to solve the specific problem of cinema. The earliest conscious film-makers, and our first film theoreticians, regarded montage as a means of description by placing single shots one after the other like building-blocks. The movement within these building-block shots, and the consequent length of the component pieces, was then considered as rhythm.

A completely false concept!

This would mean the defining of a given object solely in relation to the nature of its external course. The mechanical process of splicing would be made a principle. We cannot describe such a relationship of lengths as rhythm. From this comes metric rather than rhythmic relationships, as opposed to one another as the mechanical-metric system of Mensendieck is to the organic-rhythmic school of Bode in matters of body exercise.

According to this definition, shared even by Pudovkin as a theoretician, montage is the means of *unrolling* an idea with the help of single shots: the "epic" principle.

In my opinion, however, montage is an idea that arises from

the collision of independent shots—shots even opposite to one another: the "dramatic" principle.*

A sophism? Certainly not. For we are seeking a definition of the whole nature, the principal style and spirit of cinema from its technical (optical) basis.

We know that the phenomenon of movement in film resides in the fact that two motionless images of a moving body, following one another, blend into an appearance of motion by showing them sequentially at a required speed.

This popularized description of what happens as a *blending* has its share of responsibility for the popular miscomprehension of the nature of montage that we have quoted above.

Let us examine more exactly the course of the phenomenon we are discussing—how it really occurs—and draw our conclusion from this. Placed next to each other, two photographed immobile images result in the appearance of movement. Is this accurate? Pictorially—and phraseologically, yes.

But mechanically, it is not. For, in fact, each sequential element is perceived not *next* to the other, but on *top* of the other. For the idea (or sensation) of movement arises from the process of superimposing on the retained impression of the object's first position, a newly visible further position of the object. This is, by the way, the reason for the phenomenon of spatial depth, in the optical superimposition of two planes in stereoscopy. From the superimposition of two elements of the same dimension always arises a new, higher dimension. In the case of stereoscopy the superimposition of two nonidentical two dimensionalities results in stereoscopic three-dimensionality.

In another field; a concrete word (a denotation) set beside a concrete word yields an abstract concept—as in the Chinese and Japanese languages,* where a material ideogram can indicate a transcendental (conceptual) result.

The incongruence in contour of the first picture—already impressed on the mind—with the subsequently perceived second picture engenders, in conflict, the feeling of motion. Degree of incongruence determines intensity of impression, and determines that tension which becomes the real element of authentic rhythm.

Here we have, temporally, what we see arising spatially on a graphic or painted plane.

What comprises the dynamic effect of a painting? The eye

---

*"Epic" and "dramatic" are used here in regard to methodology of form—not to *content* or *plot!*

*See discussion in preceding essay.

follows the direction of an element in the painting. It retains a
visual impression, which then collides with the impression
derived from following the direction of a second element. The
conflict of these directions forms the dynamic effect in apprehending the whole.

I. It may be purely linear: Fernand Léger, or Suprematism.

II. It may be "anecdotal." The secret of the marvelous mobility of Daumier's and Lautrec's figures dwells in the fact that
the various anatomical parts of a body are represented in spatial circumstances (positions) that are temporally various, disjunctive. For example, in Toulouse-Lautrec's lithograph of
Miss Cissy Loftus, if one logically develops position A of the
foot, one builds a body in position A corresponding to it. But
the body is represented from knee up already in position
A + a. The cinematic effect of joined motionless pictures is already established here! From hips to shoulders we can see
A + a + a. The figure comes alive and kicking!

III. Between I and II lies primitive Italian futurism—such as
in Balla's "Man with Six Legs in Six Positions"—for II obtains
its effect by retaining natural unity and anatomical correctness, while I, on the other hand, does this with purely elementary elements. III, although destroying naturalness, has
not yet pressed forward to abstraction.

IV. The conflict of directions may also be of an ideographic
kind. It was in this way that we have gained the pregnant
characterizations of a Sharaku, for example. The secret of his
extremely perfected strength of expression lies in the anatomical and *spatial disproportion* of the parts—in comparison with
which, our I might be termed *temporal disproportion.*

Generally termed "irregularity," this *spatial disproportion* has
been a constant attraction and instrument for artists. In writing of Rodin's drawings, Camille Mauclair indicated one explanation for this search:

> The greatest artists, Michelangelo, Rembrandt, Delacroix, all, at
> a certain moment of the upthrusting of their genius, threw
> aside, as it were, the ballast of exactitude as conceived by our
> simplifying reason and our ordinary eyes, in order to attain the
> fixation of ideas, the synthesis, the *pictorial handwriting* of their
> dreams.

Two experimental artists of the nineteenth century—a painter
and a poet—attempted esthetic formulations of this "irregularity." Renoir advanced this thesis:

> Beauty of every description finds its charm in variety. Nature
> abhors both vacuum and regularity. For the same reason, no
> work of art can really be called such if it has not been created by

an artist who believes in irregularity and rejects any set form. Regularity, order, desire for perfection (which is always a false perfection) destroy art. The only possibility of maintaining taste in art is to impress on artists and the public the importance of irregularity. Irregularity is the basis of all art.

And Baudelaire wrote in his journal:

That which is not slightly distorted lacks sensible appeal; from which it follows that irregularity—that is to say, the unexpected, surprise and astonishment, are an essential part and characteristic of beauty.

Upon closer examination of the particular beauty of irregularity as employed in painting, whether by Grünewald or by Renoir, it will be seen that it is a disproportion in the relation of a detail in one dimension to another detail in a different dimension.

The spatial development of the relative size of one detail in correspondence with another, and the consequent collision between the proportions designed by the artist for that purpose, result in a characterization—a definition of the represented matter.

Finally, color. Any shade of a color imparts to our vision a given rhythm of vibration. This is not said figuratively, but purely physiologically, for colors are distinguished from one another by their number of light vibrations.

The adjacent shade or tone of color is in another rate of vibration. The counterpoint (conflict) of the two—the retained rate of vibration against the newly perceived one—yields the dynamism of our apprehension of the interplay of color.

Hence, with only one step from visual vibrations to acoustic vibrations, we find ourselves in the field of music. From the domain of the spatial-pictorial—to the domain of the temporal-pictorial—where the same law rules. For counterpoint is to music not only a form of composition, but is altogether the basic factor for the possibility of tone perception and tone differentiation.

It may almost be said that in every case we have cited we have seen in operation the same *Principle of Comparison* that makes possible for us perception and definition in every field.

In the moving image (cinema) we have, so to speak, a synthesis of two counterpoints—the spatial counterpoint of graphic art, and the temporal counterpoint of music.

Within cinema, and characterizing it, occurs what may be described as:

visual counterpoint

In applying this concept to the film, we gain several leads to the problem of film grammar. As well as a *syntax* of film manifestations, in which visual counterpoint may determine a whole new system of forms of manifestation.

For all this, the *basic premise* is:

> *The shot is by no means an element of montage.*
> *The shot is a montage cell (or molecule).*

In this formulation the dualistic division of

Sub-title and shot
and
Shot and montage

leaps forward in analysis to a dialectic consideration as three different phases of one homogeneous task of expression, its homogeneous characteristics determining the homogeneity of their structural laws.

Inter-relation of the three phases:

Conflict within a thesis (an abstract idea)—*formulates* itself in the dialectics of the sub-title—*forms* itself spatially in the conflict within the shot—and *explodes* with increasing intensity in montage-conflict among the separate shots.

This is fully analogous to human, psychological expression. This is a conflict of motives, which can also be comprehended in three phases:

1. Purely verbal utterance. Without intonation—expression in speech.
2. Gesticulatory (mimic-intonational) expression. Projection of the conflict onto the whole expressive bodily system of man. Gesture of bodily movement and gesture of intonation.
3. Projection of the conflict into space. With an intensification of motives, the zigzag of mimic expression is propelled into the surrounding space following the same formula of distortion. A zigzag of expression arising from the spatial division caused by man moving in space. *Mise-en-scène.*

This gives us the basis for an entirely new understanding of the problem of film form.

We can list, as examples of types of conflicts within the form—characteristic for the conflict within the shot, as well as for the conflict between colliding shots, or, montage:

1. Graphic conflict.
2. Conflict of planes.
3. Conflict of volumes.
4. Spatial conflict.

5. Light conflict.
6. Tempo conflict, and so on.

Nota bene: This list is of principal features, of *dominants.* It is naturally understood that they occur chiefly as complexes.

For a transition to montage, it will be sufficient to divide any example into two independent primary pieces, as in the case of graphic conflict, although all other cases can be similarly divided:

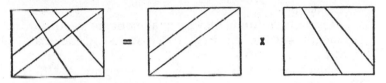

Some further examples:

7. Conflict between matter and viewpoint (achieved by spatial distortion through camera-angle).
8. Conflict between matter and its spatial nature (achieved by *optical distortion* by the lens).
9. Conflict between an event and its temporal nature (achieved by *slow-motion* and *stop-motion*)
   and finally
10. Conflict between the whole *optical* complex and a quite different sphere.

Thus does conflict between optical and acoustical experience produce:

sound-film,

which is capable of being realized as

audio-visual counterpoint.

Formulation and investigation of the phenomenon of cinema as forms of conflict yield the first possibility of devising a homogeneous system of *visual dramaturgy* for all general and particular cases of the film problem.

Of devising a *dramaturgy of the visual film-form* as regulated and precise as the existing *dramaturgy of the film-story.*

From this viewpoint on the film medium, the following forms and potentialities of style may be summed up as a film syntax, or it may be more exact to describe the following as:

a tentative film-syntax.

We shall list here a number of potentialities of dialectical development to be derived from this proposition: The concept of the moving (time-consuming) image arises from the superimposition—or counterpoint—of two differing immobile images.

I. Each *moving fragment of montage*. Each photographed piece. Technical definition of the phenomenon of movement. *No composition as yet*. (A running man. A rifle fired. A splash of water.)

II. *An artificially produced image of motion*. The basic optical element is used for deliberate compositions:

A. *Logical*

Example 1 (from *October*): a montage rendition of a machine-gun being fired, by cross-cutting details of the firing.

Combination A: a brightly lit machine-gun. A different shot in a low key. Double burst: graphic burst + light burst. Closeup of machine-gunner.

Combination B: Effect almost of double exposure achieved by *clatter* montage effect. Length of montage pieces—two frames each.

Example 2 (from *Potemkin*): an illustration of instantaneous action. Woman with pince-nez. Followed immediately—without transition—by the same woman with shattered pince-nez and bleeding eye: impression of a shot hitting the eye.

B. *Illogical*

Example 3 (from *Potemkin*): the same device used for pictorial symbolism. In the thunder of the *Potemkin's* guns, a marble lion leaps up, in protest against the bloodshed on the Odessa steps. Composed of three shots of three stationary marble lions at the Alupka Palace in the Crimea: a sleeping lion, an awakening lion, a rising lion. The effect is achieved by a correct calculation of the length of the second shot. Its superimposition on the first shot produces the first action. This establishes time to impress the second position on the mind. Superimposition of the third position on the second produces the second action: the lion finally rises.

Example 4 (from *October*): Example 1 showed how the firing was manufactured symbolically from elements outside the process of firing itself. In illustrating the monarchist *putsch* attempted by General Kornilov, it occurred to me that his militarist *tendency* could be shown in a montage that would employ religious details for its material. For Kornilov had revealed his intention in the guise of a peculiar "Crusade" of Moslems (!), his Caucasian "Wild Division," together with some Christ-

From *Potemkin* (1925). "An illustration of instantaneous action. Woman with pince-nez. Followed immediately—without transition—by the same woman with shattered pince-nez and bleeding eye: impression of a shot hitting the eye" (EISENSTEIN, page 112).

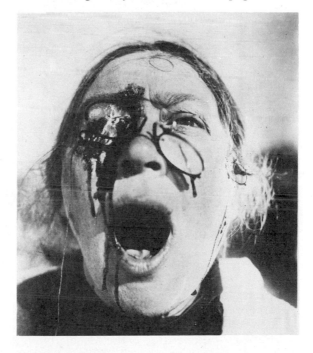

ians, against the Bolsheviki. So we intercut shots of a Baroque Christ (apparently exploding in the radiant beams of his halo) with shots of an egg-shaped mask of Uzume, Goddess of Mirth, completely self-contained. The temporal conflict between the closed egg-form and the graphic star-form produced the effect of an instantaneous *burst*—of a bomb, or shrapnel. . . .

Thus far the examples have shown *primitive-physiological* cases—employing superimposition of optical motion *exclusively*.

III. *Emotional* combinations, not only with the visible elements of the shots, but chiefly with chains of psychological associations. *Association montage*. As a means for pointing up a situation emotionally.

In Example 1, we had two successive shots A and B, identical in subject. However, they were not identical in respect to the position of the subject within the frame:

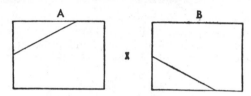

producing *dynamization in space*—an impression of spatial dynamics:

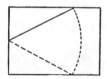

The degree of difference between the positions A and B determines the tension of the movement.

For a new case, let us suppose that the subjects of Shots A and B are not *identical*. Although the associations of the two shots are identical, that is, associatively identical.

This *dynamization of the subject,* not in the field of space but of psychology, i.e., *emotion,* thus produces:

emotional dynamization.

Example 1 (in *Strike*): the montage of the killing of the workers is actually a cross montage of this carnage with the butchering of a bull in an abattoir. Though the subjects are different, "butchering" is the associative link. This made for a powerful emotional intensification of the scene. As a matter of fact, homogeneity of gesture plays an important part in this case in achieving the effect—both the movement of the dynamic gesture within the frame, and the static gesture dividing the frame graphically.

This is a principle subsequently used by Pudovkin in *The End of St. Petersburg*, in his powerful sequence intercutting shots of stock exchange and battlefield. His previous film, *Mother*, had a similar sequence: the ice-break on the river, paralleled with the workers' demonstration.

Such a means may decay pathologically if the essential viewpoint—emotional dynamization of the subject—is lost. As soon as the film-maker loses sight of this essence the means ossifies into lifeless literary symbolism and stylistic mannerism. Two examples of such hollow use of this means occur to me:

Example 2 (in *October*): the sugary chants of compromise by the Mensheviki at the Second Congress of Soviets—during the storming of the Winter Palace—are intercut with hands playing harps. This was a purely literary parallelism that by no means dynamized the subject matter. Similarly in Otzep's *Living Corpse*, church spires (in imitation of those in *October*) and lyrical landscapes are intercut with the courtroom speeches of the prosecutor and defense lawyer. This error was the same as in the "harp" sequence.

On the other hand, a majority of *purely dynamic* effects can produce positive results:

Example 3 (in *October*): the dramatic moment of the union of the Motorcycle Battalion with the Congress of Soviets was dynamized by shots of abstractly spinning bicycle wheels, in association with the entrance of the new delegates. In this way the large-scale emotional content of the event was transformed into actual dynamics.

This same principle—giving birth to concepts, to emotions, by juxtaposing two disparate events—led to:
IV. *Liberation of the whole action from the definition of time and space*. My first attempts at this were in *October*.

Example 1: a trench crowded with soldiers appears to be crushed by an enormous gun-base that comes down inexorably. As an anti-militarist symbol seen from the viewpoint of subject alone, the effect is achieved by an apparent bringing together of an independently existing trench and an overwhelming military product, just as physically independent.

Example 2: in the scene of Kornilov's *putsch*, which puts an end to Kerensky's Bonapartist dreams. Here one of Kornilov's tanks climbs up and crushes a plaster-of-Paris Napoleon standing on Kerensky's desk in the Winter Palace, a juxtaposition of purely symbolic significance.

This method has now been used by Dovzhenko in *Arsenal* to shape whole sequences, as well as by Esther Schub in her use of library footage in *The Russia of Nikolai II and Lev Tolstoy*.

I wish to offer another example of this method, to upset the traditional ways of handling plot—although it has not yet been put into practice.

In 1924–1925 I was mulling over the idea of a filmic portrait of *actual* man. At that time, there prevailed a tendency to show actual man in films only in *long* uncut dramatic scenes. It was believed that cutting (montage) would destroy the idea of actual man. Abram Room established something of a record in this respect when he used in *The Death Ship* uncut dramatic shots as long as 40 meters or 135 feet. I considered (and still do) such a concept to be utterly unfilmic.

Very well—what would be a linguistically accurate characterization of a man?

> His raven-black hair . . .
> The waves of his hair . . .
> . His eyes radiating azure beams . . .
> His steely muscles . . .

Even in a less exaggerated description, any verbal account of a person is bound to find itself employing an assortment of waterfalls, lightning-rods, landscapes, birds, etc.

Now why should the cinema follow the forms of theater and painting rather than the methodology of language, which allows wholly new concepts of ideas to arise from the combination of two concrete denotations of two concrete objects? Language is much closer to film than painting is. For example, in painting the form arises from *abstract* elements of line and color, while in cinema the material *concreteness* of the image within the frame presents—as an element—the greatest difficulty in manipulation. So why not rather lean towards the system of language, which is forced to use the same mechanics in inventing words and word-complexes?

On the other hand, why is it that montage cannot be dispensed with in orthodox films?

The differentiation in montage-pieces lies in their lack of existence as single units. Each piece can evoke no more than a certain association. The accumulation of such associations can achieve the same effect as is provided for the spectator by purely physiological means in the plot of a realistically produced play.

For instance, murder on the stage has a purely physiological effect. Photographed in *one* montage-piece, it can function simply as *information*, as a sub-title. *Emotional* effect begins only with the reconstruction of the event in montage fragments, each of which will summon a certain association—the sum of which will be an all-embracing complex of emotional feeling. Traditionally:

1. A hand lifts a knife.
2. The eyes of the victim open suddenly.
3. His hands clutch the table.
4. The knife is jerked up.
5. The eyes blink involuntarily.
6. Blood gushes.
7. A mouth shrieks.
8. Something drips onto a shoe . . .

and similar film clichés. Nevertheless, in regard to the *action as a whole, each fragment-piece* is almost *abstract*. The more differentiated they are the more abstract they become, provoking no more than a certain association.

Quite logically the thought occurs: could not the same thing be accomplished more productively by not following the plot so slavishly, but by materializing the idea, the impression, of *Murder* through a free accumulation of associative matter? For the most important task is still to restablish the idea of murder—the feeling of murder, as such. The plot is no more than a device without which one isn't yet capable of telling something to the spectator! In any case, effort in this direction would certainly produce the most interesting variety of forms.

Someone should try, at least! Since this thought occurred to me, I have not had time to make this experiment. And today I am more concerned with quite different problems. But, returning to the main line of our syntax, something there may bring us closer to these tasks.

While, with I, II, and III, tension was calculated for purely physiological effect—from the purely optical to the emotional,

Ten shots from the montage sequence on the "Odessa Steps" from *Potemkin* (1925). "Step by step, by a process of comparing each new image with the common denotation, power is accumulated behind a process that can be formally identified with that of logical deduction" (EISENSTEIN, page 122). "The creation of a sense or meaning not proper to the images themselves but derived exclusively from their juxtaposition" (BAZIN, page 127).

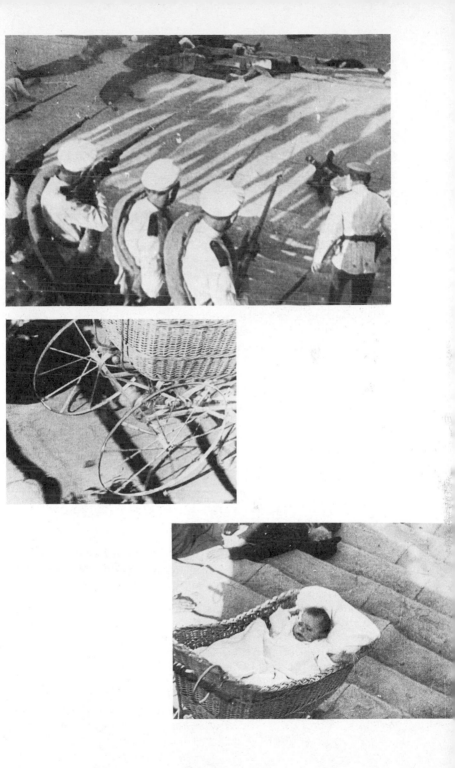

we must mention here also the case of the same conflict-tension serving the ends of new concepts—of new attitudes, that is, of purely intellectual aims.

Example 1 (in *October*): Kerensky's rise to power and dictatorship after the July uprising of 1917. A comic effect was gained by sub-titles indicating regular ascending ranks ("*Dictator*"—"*Generalissimo*"—"*Minister of Navy—and of Army*"—etc.) climbing higher and higher—cut into five or six shots of Kerensky, climbing the stairs of the Winter Palace, all with exactly the *same* pace. Here a conflict between the flummery of the ascending ranks and the "hero's" trotting up the same unchanging flight of stairs yields an intellectual result: Kerensky's essential nonentity is shown satirically. We have the counterpoint of a literally expressed conventional idea with the *pictured* action of a particular person who is unequal to his swiftly increasing duties. The incongruence of these two factors results in the spectator's purely *intellectual* decision at the expense of this particular person. Intellectual dynamization.

Example 2 (in *October*): Kornilov's march on Petrograd was under the banner of "In the Name of God and Country." Here we attempted to reveal the religious significance of this episode in a rationalistic way. A number of religious images, from a magnificient Baroque Christ to an Eskimo idol, were cut together. The conflict in this case was between the concept and the symbolization of God. While idea and image appear to accord completely in the first statue shown, the two elements move further from each other with each successive image. Maintaining the denotation of "God," the images increasingly disagree with our concept of God, inevitably leading to individual conclusions about the true nature of all deities. In this case, too, a chain of images attempted to achieve a purely intellectual resolution, resulting from a conflict between a preconception and a *gradual discrediting of it in purposeful steps.*

Step by step, by a process of comparing each new image with the common denotation, power is accumulated behind a process that can be formally identified with that of logical deduction. The decision to release these ideas, as well as the method used, is already *intellectually* conceived.

The conventional *descriptive* form for film leads to the formal possibility of a kind of filmic reasoning. While the conventional film directs the *emotions*, this suggests an opportunity to encourage and direct the whole *thought process*, as well.

These two particular sequences of experiment were very much opposed by the majority of critics. Because they were understood as purely political. I would not attempt to deny that *this form is most suitable for the expression of ideologically pointed theses*, but it is a pity that the critics completely overlooked the purely filmic potentialities of this approach.

In these two experiments we have taken the first embryonic step towards a totally new form of film expression. Towards a purely intellectual film, freed from traditional limitations, achieving direct forms for ideas, systems, and concepts, without any need for transitions and paraphrases. We may yet have a

synthesis of art and science.

This would be the proper name for our new epoch in the field of art. This would be the final justification for Lenin's words, that "the cinema is the most important of all the arts."

1929

ANDRÉ BAZIN
FROM WHAT IS CINEMA?

THE EVOLUTION OF
THE LANGUAGE OF CINEMA

By 1928 the silent film had reached its artistic peak. The despair of its elite as they witnessed the dismantling of this ideal city, while it may not have been justified, is at least understandable. As they followed their chosen aesthetic path it seemed to them that the cinema had developed into an art most perfectly accommodated to the "exquisite embarrassment" of silence and that the realism that sound would bring could only mean a surrender to chaos.

In point of fact, now that sound has given proof that it came not to destroy but to fulfill the Old Testament of the cinema, we may most properly ask if the technical revolution created by the sound track was in any sense an aesthetic revolution. In other words, did the years from 1928 to 1930 actually witness the birth of a new cinema? Certainly, as regards editing, history does not actually show as wide a breach as might be expected between the silent and the sound film. On the contrary there is discernible evidence of a close relationship between certain directors of 1925 and 1935 and especially of the 1940's through the 1950's. Compare for example Erich von Stroheim and Jean Renoir or Orson Welles, or again Carl Theodore Dreyer and Robert Bresson. These more or less clear-cut affinities demonstrate first of all that the gap separating the 1920's and the 1930's can be bridged, and secondly that certain cinematic values actually carry over from the silent to the sound film and, above all, that it is less a matter of setting silence over against sound than of contrasting certain families of styles, certain basically different concepts of cinematographic expression.

Aware as I am that the limitations imposed on this study restrict me to a simplified and to that extent enfeebled presentation of my argument, and holding it to be less an objective statement than a working hypothesis, I will distinguish, in the cinema between 1920 and 1940, between two broad and opposing trends: those directors who put their faith in the image and those who put their faith in reality. By "image" I here mean, very broadly speaking, everything that the representation on the screen adds to the object there represented. This is a complex inheritance but it can be reduced essentially to two categories: those that relate to the plastics of the image and those that relate to the resources of montage, which after all, is simply the ordering of images in time.

Under the heading "plastics" must be included the style of the sets, of the make-up, and, up to a point, even of the performance, to which we naturally add the lighting and, finally, the framing of the shot which gives us its composition. As regards montage, derived initially as we all know from the masterpieces of Griffith, we have the statement of Malraux in his *Psychologie du cinéma* that it was montage that gave birth to film as an art, setting it apart from mere animated photography, in short, creating a language.

The use of montage can be "invisible" and this was generally the case in the prewar classics of the American screen. Scenes were broken down just for one purpose, namely, to analyze an episode according to the material or dramatic logic of the scene. It is this logic which conceals the fact of the analysis, the mind of the spectator quite naturally accepting the viewpoints of the director which are justified by the geography of the action or the shifting emphasis of dramatic interest.

But the neutral quality of this "invisible" editing fails to make use of the full potential of montage. On the other hand these potentialities are clearly evident from the three processes generally known as parallel montage, accelerated montage, montage by attraction. In creating parallel montage, Griffith succeeded in conveying a sense of the simultaneity of two actions taking place at a geographical distance by means of alternating shots from each. In *La Roue* Abel Gance created the illusion of the steadily increasing speed of a locomotive without actually using any images of speed (indeed the wheel could have been turning on one spot) simply by a multiplicity of shots of ever-decreasing length.

Finally there is "montage by attraction," the creation of S. M. Eisenstein, and not so easily described as the others, but which may be roughly defined as the reenforcing of the meaning of one image by association with another image not necessarily part of

McTeague (Gibson Gowland) confronting Marcus Schouler (Jean Hersholt) in the wastes of Death Valley in *Greed* (1923); Nanook building his igloo in *Nanook of the North* (1922). Von Stroheim and Flaherty were two of "those who put their faith in reality" (BAZIN, page 125).

the same episode—for example the fireworks display in *The General Line* following the image of the bull. In this extreme form, montage by attraction was rarely used even by its creator but one may consider as very near to it in principle the more commonly used ellipsis, comparison, or metaphor, examples of which are the throwing of stockings onto a chair at the foot of a bed, or the milk overflowing in H.G. Clouzot's *Quai des orfèvres*. There are of course a variety of possible combinations of these three processes.

Whatever these may be, one can say that they share that trait in common which constitutes the very definition of montage, namely, the creation of a sense or meaning not proper to the images themselves but derived exclusively from their juxtaposition. The well-known experiment of Kuleshov with the shot of Mozhukhin in which a smile was seen to change its significance according to the image that preceded it, sums up perfectly the properties of montage.

Montage as used by Kuleshov, Eisenstein, or Gance did not give us the event; it alluded to it. Undoubtedly they derived at least the greater part of the constituent elements from the reality they were describing but the final significance of the film was found to reside in the ordering of these elements much more than in their objective content.

The matter under recital, whatever the realism of the individual image, is born essentially from these relationships—Mozhukhin plus dead child equal pity—that is to say an abstract result, none of the concrete elements of which are to be found in the premises; maidens plus appletrees in bloom equal hope. The combinations are infinite. But the only thing they have in common is the fact that they suggest an idea by means of a metaphor or by an association of ideas. Thus between the scenario properly so-called, the ultimate object of the recital, and the image pure and simple, there is a relay station, a sort of aesthetic "transformer." The meaning is not in the image, it is in the shadow of the image projected by montage onto the field of consciousness of the spectator.

Let us sum up. Through the contents of the image and the resources of montage, the cinema has at its disposal a whole arsenal of means whereby to impose its interpretation of an event on the spectator. By the end of the silent film we can consider this arsenal to have been full. On the one side the Soviet cinema carried to its ultimate consequences the theory and practice of montage while the German school did every kind of violence to the plastics of the image by way of sets and lighting. Other cinemas count too besides the Russian and German, but whether in France or Sweden or the United States, it does not appear that the language of cinema was at a loss for ways of saying what it wanted to say.

If the art of cinema consists in everything that plastics and montage can add to a given reality, the silent film was an art on its own. Sound could only play at best a subordinate and supplementary role: a counterpoint to the visual image. But this possible enhancement—at best only a minor one—is likely not to weigh much in comparison with the additional bargain-rate reality introduced at the same time by sound.

Thus far we have put forward the view that expressionism of montage and image constitute the essence of cinema. And it is precisely on this generally accepted notion that directors from silent days, such as Erich von Stroheim, F.W. Murnau, and Robert Flaherty, have by implication cast a doubt. In their films, montage plays no part, unless it be the negative one of inevitable elimination where reality superabounds. The camera cannot see everything at once but it makes sure not to lose any part of what it chooses to see. What matters to Flaherty, confronted with Nanook hunting the seal, is the relation between Nanook and the animal; the actual length of the waiting period. Montage could suggest the time involved. Flaherty however confines himself to showing the actual waiting period; the length of the hunt is the very substance of the image, its true object. Thus in the film this episode requires one set-up. Will anyone deny that it is thereby much more moving than a montage by attraction?

Murnau is interested not so much in time as in the reality of dramatic space. Montage plays no more of a decisive part in *Nosferatu* than in *Sunrise*. One might be inclined to think that the plastics of his image are impressionistic. But this would be a superficial view. The composition of his image is in no sense pictorial. It adds nothing to the reality, it does not deform it, it forces it to reveal its structural depth, to bring out the preexisting relations which become constitutive of the drama. For example, in *Tabu*, the arrival of a ship from left screen gives an immediate sense of destiny at work so that Murnau has no need to cheat in any way on the uncompromising realism of a film whose settings are completely natural.

But it is most of all Stroheim who rejects photographic expressionism and the tricks of montage. In his films reality lays itself bare like a suspect confessing under the relentless examination of the commissioner of police. He has one simple rule for direction. Take a close look at the world, keep on doing so, and in the end it will lay bare for you all its cruelty and its ugliness. One could easily imagine as a matter of fact a film by Stroheim composed of a single shot as long-lasting and as close-up as you like. These three directors do not exhaust the possibilities. We would undoubtedly find scattered among the works of others elements of nonexpressionistic cinema in which montage plays no part—even including Griffith. But these examples suffice to reveal, at the very heart of the silent film, a cinematographic art the very opposite of that which has been identified as "*cinéma par excellence*," a language the semantic and syntactical unit of which is in no sense the Shot; in which the image is evaluated not according to what it adds to reality but what it reveals of it. In the latter art the silence of the screen was a drawback, that is to say, it deprived reality of one of its elements. *Greed*, like Dreyer's *Jeanne d' Arc*, is already virtually a talking film. The moment that you cease to maintain that montage and the plastic composition of the image are the very essence of the language of cinema, sound is no longer the aesthetic crevasse dividing two radically different aspects of the seventh art. The cinema that is believed to have died of the soundtrack is in no sense "*the* cinema." The real dividing line is elsewhere. It was operative in the past and continues to be through thirty-five years of the history of the language of the film.

Having challenged the aesthetic unity of the silent film and divided it off into two opposing tendencies, now let us take a look at the history of the last twenty years.

From 1930 to 1940 there seems to have grown up in the world, originating largely in the United States, a common form of cinematic language. It was the triumph in Hollywood, during that time, of five or six major kinds of film that gave it its overwhelming superiority: (1) American comedy (*Mr. Smith Goes to Washington*, 1936); (2) The burlesque film (The Marx Brothers); (3) The dance and vaudeville film (Fred Astaire and Ginger Rogers and the Ziegfield Follies); (4) The crime and gangster film (*Scarface, I Am a Fugitive from a Chain Gang, The Informer*); (5) Psychological and social dramas (*Back Street, Jezebel*); (6) Horror or fantasy films (*Dr. Jekyll and Mr. Hyde, The Invisible Man, Frankenstein*); (7) The western (*Stagecoach*, 1939). During that time the French cinema undoubtedly ranked next. Its superiority was gradually manifested by way of a trend towards what might be roughly called stark somber realism, or poetic realism, in which four names stand out: Jacques Feyder, Jean Renoir, Marcel Carné, and Julien Duvivier. My intention not being to draw up a list of prize-winners, there is little use in dwelling on the Soviet, British, German, or Italian films for which these years were less significant than the ten that were to follow. In any case, American and French production sufficiently clearly indicate that the sound film, prior to World War II, had reached a well-balanced stage of maturity.

First as to content: Major varieties with clearly defined rules capable of pleasing a worldwide public, as well as a cultured elite, provided it was not inherently hostile to the cinema.

Secondly as to form: well-defined styles of photography and editing perfectly adapted to their subject matter; a complete harmony of image and sound. In seeing again today such films as *Jezebel* by William Wyler, *Stagecoach* by John Ford, or *Le Jour se lève* by Marcel Carné, one has the feeling that in them an art has found its perfect balance, its ideal form of expression, and reciprocally one admires them for dramatic and moral themes to which the cinema, while it may not have created them, has given a grandeur, an artistic effectiveness, that they would not otherwise have had. In short, here are all the characteristics of the ripeness of a classical art.

I am quite aware that one can justifiably argue that the originality of the postwar cinema as compared with that of 1938 derives from the growth of certain national schools, in particular the dazzling display of the Italian cinema and of a native English cinema freed from the influence of Hollywood. From this one might conclude that the really important phenomenon of the years 1940–1950 is the introduction of new blood, of hitherto unexplored themes. That is to say, the real revolution took place more on the level of subject matter than of style. Is not neorealism primarily a kind of humanism and only secondarily a style of film-making? Then as to the style itself, is it not essentially a form of self-effacement before reality?

Our intention is certainly not to preach the glory of form over content. Art for art's sake is just as heretical in cinema as elsewhere, probably more so. On the other hand, a new subject matter demands new form, and as good a way as any towards understanding what a film is trying to say to us is to know how it is saying it.

Thus by 1938 or 1939 the talking film, particularly in France and in the United States, had reached a level of classical perfection as a result, on the one hand, of the maturing of different kinds of drama developed in part over the past ten years and in part inherited from the silent film, and, on the other, of the stabilization of technical progress. The 1930's were the years, at once, of sound and of panchromatic film. Undoubtedly studio equipment had continued to improve but only in matters of detail, none of them opening up new, radical possibilities for direction. The only changes in this situation since 1940 have been in photography, thanks to the increased sensitivity of the film stock. Panchromatic stock turned visual values upside down, ultrasensitive emulsions have made a modification in their structure possible. Free to shoot in the studio with a much smaller aperture, the operator could, when necessary, eliminate the soft-focus background once considered essential. Still there are a number of examples of the prior use of deep focus, for example in the work of Jean Renoir. This had always been possible on exteriors, and given a measure of skill, even in the studios. Anyone could do it who really wanted to. So that it is less a question basically of a technical problem, the solution of which has admittedly been made easier, than of a search after a style—a point to which we will come back. In short, with panchromatic stock in common use, with an understanding of the potentials of the microphone, and with the crane as standard studio equipment, one can really say that since 1930 all the technical requirements for the art of cinema have been available.

Since the determining technical factors were practically eliminated, we must look elsewhere for the signs and principles of the evolution of film language, that is to say by challenging the subject matter and as a consequence the styles necessary for its expression.

By 1939 the cinema had arrived at what geographers call the equilibrium-profile of a river. By this is meant that ideal mathematical curve which results from the requisite amount of erosion. Having reached this equilibrium-profile, the river flows effortlessly from its source to its mouth without further deepening of its bed. But if any geological movement occurs which raises the erosion level and modifies the height of the source, the water sets to work again, seeps into the surrounding land, goes deeper, burrowing and digging. Sometimes when it is a chalk bed, a new pattern is dug across the plain, almost invisible but found to be complex and winding, if one follows the flow of the water.

THE EVOLUTION OF EDITING SINCE THE ADVENT OF SOUND

In 1938 there was an almost universal standard pattern of editing. If, somewhat conventionally, we call the kind of silent films based on the plastics of the image and the artifices of montage, "expressionist" or "symbolistic," we can describe the new form of storytelling "analytic" and "dramatic." Let us suppose, by way of reviewing one of the elements of the experiment of Kuleshov, that we have a table covered with food and a hungry tramp. One can imagine that in 1936 it would have been edited as follows:

(1) Full shot of the actor and the table.
(2) Camera moves forward into a close-up of a face expressing a mixture of amazement and longing.
(3) Series of close-ups of food.
(4) Back to full shot of person who starts slowly towards the camera.
(5) Camera pulls slowly back to a three-quarter shot of the actor seizing a chicken wing.

Whatever variants one could think of for this scene, they would all have certain points in common:

(1) The verisimilitude of space in which the position of the actor is always determined, even when a close-up eliminates the decor.

(2) The purpose and the effects of the cutting are exclusively dramatic or psychological.

In other words, if the scene were played on a stage and seen from a seat in the orchestra, it would have the same meaning, the episode would continue to exist objectively. The changes of point of view provided by the camera would add nothing. They would present the reality a little more forcefully, first by allowing a better view and then by putting the emphasis where it belongs.

It is true that the stage director like the film director has at his disposal a margin within which he is free to vary the interpretation of the action but it is only a margin and allows for no modification of the inner logic of the event. Now, by way of contrast, let us take the montage of the stone lions in *The End of St. Petersburg*. By skillful juxtaposition a group of sculptured lions are made to look like a single lion getting to its feet, a symbol of the aroused masses. This clever device would be unthinkable in any film after 1932. As late as 1935 Fritz Lang, in *Fury*, followed a series of shots of women dancing the can-can with shots of clucking chickens in a farmyard. This relic of associative montage came as a shock even at the time, and today seems entirely out of keeping with the rest of the film. However decisive the art of Marcel Carné, for example, in our estimate of the respective values of *Quai des Brumes* or of *Le Jour se lève* his editing remains on the level of the reality he is analyzing. There is only one proper way of looking at it. That is why we are witnessing the almost complete disappearance of optical effects such as superimpositions, and even, especially in the United States, of the close-up, the too violent impact of which would make the audience conscious of the cutting. In the typical American comedy the director returns as often as he can to a shot of the characters from the knees up, which is said to be best suited to catch the spontaneous attention of the viewer — the natural point of balance of his mental adjustment.

Actually this use of montage originated with the silent movies. This is more or less the part it plays in Griffith's films, for example in *Broken Blossoms*, because with *Intolerance* he had already introduced that synthetic concept of montage which the Soviet cinema was to carry to its ultimate conclusion and which is to be found again, although less exclusively, at the end of the silent era. It is understandable, as a matter of fact, that the sound image, far less flexible than the visual image, would carry montage in the direction of realism, increasingly eliminating both plastic impressionism and the symbolic relation between images.

Thus around 1938 films were edited, almost without exception, according to the same principle. The story was unfolded in a series of set-ups numbering as a rule about 600. The characteristic procedure was by shot-reverse-shot, that is to say, in a dialogue scene, the camera followed the order of the text, alternating the character shown with each speech.

It was this fashion of editing, so admirably suitable for the best films made between 1930 and 1939, that was challenged by the shot in depth introduced by Orson Welles and William Wyler. *Citizen Kane* can never be too highly praised. Thanks to the depth of field, whole scenes are covered in one take, the camera remaining motionless. Dramatic effects for which we had formerly relied on montage were created out of the movements of the actors within a fixed framework. Of course Welles did not invent the in-depth shot any more than Griffith invented the close-up. All the pioneers used it and for a very good reason. Soft focus only appeared with montage. It was not only a technical must consequent upon the use of images in juxtaposition, it was a logical consequence of montage, its plastic equivalent. If at a given moment in the action the director, as in the scene imagined above, goes to a close-up of a bowl of fruit, it follows naturally that he also isolates it in space through the focusing of the lens. The soft focus of the background confirms therefore the effect of montage, that is to say, while it is of the essence of the storytelling, it is only an accessory of the style of the photography. Jean Renoir had already clearly understood this, as we see from a statement of his made in 1938 just after he had made *La Bête humaine* and *La Grande illusion* and just prior to *La Règle du jeu:* "The more I learn about my trade the more I incline to direction in depth relative to the screen. The better it works, the less I use the kind of set-up that shows two actors facing the camera, like two well-behaved subjects posing for a still portrait." The truth of the matter is, that if you are looking for the precursor of Orson Welles, it is not Louis Lumière or Zecca, but rather Jean Renoir. In his films, the search after composition in depth is, in effect, a partial replacement of montage by frequent panning shots and entrances. It is based on a respect for the continuity of dramatic space and, of course, of its duration.

To anybody with eyes in his head, it is quite evident that the sequence of shots used by Welles in *The Magnificent Ambersons* is in no sense the purely passive recording of an action shot within the same framing. On the contrary, his refusal to break up the action, to analyze the dramatic field in time, is a positive action the results of which are far superior to anything that could be achieved by the classical "cut."

All you need to do is compare two frames shot in depth, one from 1910, the other from a film by Wyler or Welles, to under-

The shot-in-depth from *Citizen Kane* (1941). (Note the perfect focus of the image on all three planes—the three faces extremely close to the camera, the face in the middle distance, and the letters on the sign in the far distance.) "Thanks to the depth of field, whole scenes are covered in one take, the camera remaining motionless. . . . Director and cameraman have converted the screen into a dramatic checkerboard, planned down to the last detail" (BAZIN, pages 133, 135).

stand just by looking at the image, even apart from the context of the film, how different their functions are. The framing in the 1910 film is intended, to all intents and purposes, as a substitute for the missing fourth wall of the theatrical stage, or at least in exterior shots, for the best vantage point to view the action, whereas in the second case the setting, the lighting, and the camera angles give an entirely different reading. Between them, director and cameraman have converted the screen into a dramatic checker-board, planned down to the last detail. The clearest if not the most original examples of this are to be found in *The Little Foxes* where the *mise-en-scène* takes on the severity of a working drawing. Welles' pictures are more difficult to analyze because of his over-fondness for the baroque. Objects and characters are related in such a fashion that it is impossible for the spectator to miss the significance of the scene. To get the same results by way of montage would have necessitated a detailed succession of shots.

What we are saying then is that the sequence of shots "in depth" of the contemporary director does not exclude the use of montage —how could he, without reverting to a primitive babbling?—he makes it an integral part of his "plastic." The storytelling of Welles or Wyler is no less explicit that John Ford's but theirs has the advantage over his that it does not sacrifice the specific effects that can be derived from unity of image in space and time. Whether an episode is analyzed bit by bit or presented in its physical entirety cannot surely remain a matter of indifference, at least in a work with some pretensions to style. It would obviously be absurd to deny that montage has added considerably to the progress of film language, but this has happened at the cost of other values, no less definitely cinematic.

This is why depth of field is not just a stock in trade of the cameraman like the use of a series of filters or of such-and-such a style of lighting, it is a capital gain in the field of direction—a dialectical step forward in the history of film language.

Nor is it just a formal step forward. Well used, shooting in depth is not just a more economical, a simpler, and at the same time a more subtle way of getting the most out of a scene. In addition to affecting the structure of film language, it also affects the relation-ships of the minds of the spectators to the image, and in consequence it influences the interpretation of the spectacle.

It would lie outside the scope of this article to analyze the psychological modalities of these relations, as also their aesthetic consequences, but it might be enough here to note, in general terms:

(1) That depth of focus brings the spectator into a relation with the image closer to that which he enjoys with reality. Therefore it is correct to say that, independently of the contents of the image, its structure is more realistic;

(2) That it implies, consequently, both a more active mental attitude on the part of the spectator and a more positive contribution on his part to the action in progress. While analytical montage only calls for him to follow his guide, to let his attention follow along smoothly with that of the director who will choose what he should see, here he is called upon to exercise at least a minimum of personal choice. It is from his attention and his will that the meaning of the image in part derives.

(3) From the two preceding propositions, which belong to the realm of psychology, there follows a third which may be described as metaphysical. In analyzing reality, montage presupposes of its very nature the unity of meaning of the dramatic event. Some other form of analysis is undoubtedly possible but then it would be another film. In short, montage by its very nature rules out ambiguity of expression. Kuleshov's experiment proves this *per absurdum* in giving on each occasion a precise meaning to the expression on a face, the ambiguity of which alone makes the three successively exclusive expressions possible.

On the other hand, depth of focus reintroduced ambiguity into the structure of the image if not of necessity—Wyler's films are never ambiguous—at least as a possibility. Hence it is no exaggeration to say that *Citizen Kane* is unthinkable shot in any other way but in depth. The uncertainty in which we find ourselves as to the spiritual key or the interpretation we should put on the film is built into the very design of the image.

It is not that Welles denies himself any recourse whatsoever to the expressionistic procedures of montage, but just that their use from time to time in between sequences of shots in depth gives them a new meaning. Formerly montage was the very stuff of cinema, the texture of the scenario. In *Citizen Kane* a series of superimpositions is contrasted with a scene presented in a single take, constituting another and deliberately abstract mode of story-telling. Accelerated montage played tricks with time and space while that of Welles, on the other hand, is not trying to deceive us; it offers us a contrast, condensing time, and hence is the equivalent for example of the French imperfect or the English frequentative tense. Like accelerated montage and montage of attractions these superimpositions, which the talking film had not used for ten years, rediscovered a possible use related to temporal realism in a film without montage.

If we have dwelt at some length on Orson Welles it is because the date of his appearance in the filmic firmament (1941) marks more or less the beginning of a new period and also because his case is the most spectacular and, by virtue of his very excesses, the most significant.

Yet *Citizen Kane* is part of a general movement, of a vast stirring of the geological bed of cinema, confirming that everywhere up to a point there had been a revolution in the language of the screen.

I could show the same to be true, although by different methods, of the Italian cinema. In Roberto Rossellini's *Paisà* and *Allemania Anno Zero* and Vittorio de Sica's *Ladri de Biciclette*, Italian neo-realism contrasts with previous forms of film realism in its stripping away of all expressionism and in particular in the total absence of the effects of montage. As in the films of Welles and in spite of conflicts of style, neorealism tends to give back to the cinema a sense of the ambiguity of reality. The preoccupation of Rossellini when dealing with the face of the child in *Allemania Anno Zero* is the exact opposite of that of Kuleshov with the close-up of Mozhukhin. Rossellini is concerned to preserve its mystery. We should not be misled by the fact that the evolution of neorealism is not manifest, as in the United States, in any form of revolution in editing. They are both aiming at the same results by different methods. The means used by Rossellini and de Sica are less spectacular but they are no less determined to do away with montage and to transfer to the screen the *continuum* of reality. The dream of Zavattini is just to make a ninety-minute film of the life of a man to whom nothing ever happens. The most "aesthetic" of the neorealists, Luchino Visconti, gives just as clear a picture as Welles of the basic aim of his directorial art in *La Terra Trema*, a film almost entirely composed of one-shot sequences, thus clearly showing his concern to cover the entire action in interminable deep-focus panning shots.

However we cannot pass in review all the films that have shared in this revolution in film language since 1940. Now is the moment to attempt a synthesis of our reflections on the subject.

It seems to us that the decade from 1940 to 1950 marks a decisive step forward in the development of the language of the film. If we have appeared since 1930 to have lost sight of the trend of the silent film as illustrated particularly by Stroheim, F. W. Murnau, Robert Flaherty, and Dreyer, it is for a purpose. It is not that this trend seems to us to have been halted by the talking film. On the contrary, we believe that it represented the richest vein of the so-called silent film and, precisely because it was not aesthetically tied to montage, but was indeed the only tendency that looked to the realism of sound as a natural development. On the other hand it is a fact that the talking film between 1930 and 1940 owes it virtually nothing save for the glorious and retrospectively prophetic exception of Jean Renoir. He alone in his searchings as a director prior to *La Règle du jeu* forced himself to look back beyond the resources provided by montage and so uncovered the secret of a film form that would permit everything to be said without chopping the world up into little fragments, that would reveal the hidden meanings in people and things without disturbing the unity natural to them.

It is not a question of thereby belittling the films of 1930 to 1940, a criticism that would not stand up in the face of the number of masterpieces, it is simply an attempt to establish the notion of a dialectic progress, the highest expression of which was found in the films of the 1940's. Undoubtedly, the talkie sounded the knell of a certain aesthetic of the language of film, but only wherever it had turned its back on its vocation in the service of realism. The sound film nevertheless did preserve the essentials of montage, namely discontinuous description and the dramatic analysis of action. What it turned its back on was metaphor and symbol in exchange for the illusion of objective presentation. The expressionism of montage has virtually disappeared but the relative realism of the kind of cutting that flourished around 1937 implied a congenital limitation which escaped us so long as it was perfectly suited to its subject matter. Thus American comedy reached its peak within the framework of a form of editing in which the realism of the time played no part. Dependent on logic for its effects, like vaudeville and plays on words, entirely conventional in its moral and sociological content, American comedy had everything to gain, in strict line-by-line progression, from the rhythmic resources of classical editing.

Undoubtedly it is primarily with the Stroheim-Murnau trend—almost totally eclipsed from 1930 to 1940—that the cinema has more or less consciously linked up once more over the last ten years. But it has no intention of limiting itself simply to keeping this trend alive. It draws from it the secret of the regeneration of realism in storytelling and thus of becoming capable once more of bringing together real time, in which things exist, along with the duration of the action, for which classical editing had insidiously substituted mental and abstract time. On the other hand, so far from wiping out once and for all the conquests of montage, this reborn realism gives them a body of reference and a meaning. It is only an increased realism of the image that can support the abstraction of montage. The stylistic repertory of a director such as Hitchcock, for example, ranged from the power inherent in the basic document as such, to superimpositions, to large close-ups. But the close-ups of Hitchcock are not the same as those of C. B. de Mille in *The Cheat* [1915]. They are just one type of figure, among others, of his style. In other words, in the silent days, montage evoked what the director wanted to say; in the editing of 1938, it described it. Today we can say that at last the director writes in film. The image—its plastic composition and the way it is set in time, because it is founded on a much higher degree of realism—has at its disposal more means of manipulating reality and of modifying it from within. The film-maker is no longer the competitor of the painter and the playwright, he is, at last, the equal of the novelist.

1950—55

CHARLES BARR
CINEMASCOPE: BEFORE AND AFTER

CinemaScope was introduced by 20th Century-Fox in 1953. It confused a lot of people, and has continued to do so. It was assumed that its value was purely a sensational one, that it was self-evidently "inartistic," and that once the novelty wore off the companies would be forced to drop it as abruptly as they had dropped 3-D, Hollywood's previous answer to the Television Menace. A decade later, however, the CinemaScope revolution is a fait accompli. Not only are a large proportion of Hollywood films in CinemaScope or similar processes, but other countries too make Scope films in increasing numbers. Most theaters have been adapted for Scope projection without changing the old pattern of exhibition, as it had been forecast they would have to. Cinema-Scope scarcely makes an impact any longer for its own sake: most of the really big pictures today are made on 70mm film or in Cinerama. It is even possible now to be disappointed when a block-buster *(The Guns of Navarone, The Longest Day)* is "only" in CinemaScope.

I will assume that the technical details are familiar. Since Fox holds the rights to CinemaScope itself, other companies have preferred to develop their own variants, some of which use different methods, and are arguably superior but which are similar in essentials, with an aspect ratio (height to width) of 1:2.35. All of these can be classed together, as indeed they usually are, as "CinemaScope" or just as "Scope."

CinemaScope has had a more general indirect influence: although non-Scope productions still use 35mm nonanamorphic film, very few of them are still designed for projection in the old 1:1.33 ratio. Instead, the top and bottom are masked off, and the image thrown over a wider area. This ratio is, it seems, becoming settled at 1:1.85. Thus all films, with the occasional foreign-language exception, are now widescreen films; this format will clearly share, in a minor way, some of the characteristics of CinemaScope, and normally when I talk of the effects of the "CinemaScope" ratio this can be taken to mean something like "Scope; and even more so the 70mm systems; and to a lesser extent the wide screen."

The commercial survival of Cinemascope has disconcerted critics, especially English-speaking ones. So far as I can see, all of them had condemned it from the start as a medium for anything other than the spectacular and the trivial. Its shape was apparently wrong for "serious" or "intimate" drama, for the kind of film and the kind of effects which a sensitive director aims at. Now Cinema-Scope was, obviously, a commercial innovation designed purely to save the finances of Fox, whose executives were evasive and hypocritical in their pretense that they were doing this for Art's sake. Most of the early Scope films were indeed crude. Fox was enlightened neither in choice of subjects nor of directors: among those who made the first of these films were Koster, Dunne, Johnson, Dmytryk, and Negulesco. However, since then a great number of serious and or intimate films have been made in Scope, too many to catalogue, and too many for it to be worth remarking on any longer, when each comes out. The early ones included *A Star is Born* (Cukor), *East of Eden* (Kazan), and *River of No Return* (Preminger); then, among others, all Truffaut's features; *La Dolce Vita, The Island, Trials of Oscar Wilde, Lola, Lola Montes, Rebel Without a Cause, Bitter Victory, Tarnished Angels, Man of the West, The Tall Men, Some Came Running, The Courtship of Eddie's Father* . . . not forgetting *L'Année Dernière à Marienbad* and, on 70 mm film, *Lawrence of Arabia* and *Exodus*.

The cycle of events has been very close to that which followed the introduction of sound. That too was a commercial move, designed to save Warner Brothers, and it led to a comparable, temporary chaos. Most commentators were misled into thinking that sound must be in itself inartistic, and a betrayal of "pure" cinema, but gradually it became accepted as a useful development, and one could say that Scope too is coming, tacitly, to be accepted, because there is really no alternative. . . .

The point is this: the rejection of CinemaScope was, and is, based on certain familiar, but in fact highly disputable, assumptions, the fundamental one being that the film image consists of a *frame* into which a number of things are successively *fitted*, and that a film is made by sticking such images together in a creative way. The old 1:1.33 ratio screen was compatible with this aesthetic, and the

CinemaScope screen is not, but instead of considering afresh whether these preconceptions were valid the critics simply used them to make an a priori condemnation of a format which is, one admits, manifestly unsuitable for "framing" things.

One can call this the "traditional" aesthetic: it is the one which is found in books. It puts the emphasis on framing, the close-up, camera angles, and montage. Montage is only the French word for editing, and is clearly indispensable to any director; the difference is that here this stage is made into the crucial one in a process which consists of selecting details and "showing them one by one" (Pudovkin in *Film Technique*).

I believe this aesthetic was always misguided, at least in the dogmatic form in which it was applied, and that the most valuable and forward-looking films at any time have been made to some extent outside it. Ideally, Scope could have been the occasion for its ceremonial abandonment. It was no longer workable, but then it was no longer necessary. It is a hangover from the silent cinema, but people still try to muddle through using it as an implicit basis for their judgment even of Scope films: it is not surprising if they can't cope. You still get films evaluated according to whether the "set-ups" are "imaginative" or not, and a film which uses long takes and few close-ups is liable to be dismissed automatically as unfilmic or as visually dull. Any summary of the development of style is bound to be schematic, but if one bears in mind that there can be no clear-cut division between sound and silent, and between post- and pre-Scope, I think it is useful to go back and estimate how this "traditional" aesthetic was established, and became ingrained.

There were four main factors:

(1) The image was narrow and unaccompanied by sound; it was therefore difficult to make a full impact within a single shot, and without cutting. Naturally, this objection applies less and less after the introduction of, in turn, the moving camera, sound, composition in depth, and CinemaScope.

The film was a new and bewildering medium; this aesthetic made it easy to assimilate to the pattern of other arts, notably painting and literature:

(2) It played down the film's basis in "reality," which was felt to be incompatible with art.

(3) It took the shot as a "unit," like the ideogram or the word: this made it more easily manageable and gave it the prestige of a "language" of its own.*

---

*"In the silent cinema, montage had a precise meaning, because it represented language. From the silent cinema we have inherited this myth of montage, though it has lost most of its meaning."

— Roberto Rossellini

Finally, (4) it was formulated and applied chiefly by certain Russian directors; theirs is one kind of film, and of temperament, which it really suits.

These points merge into one another, and need to be elaborated more fully.

The first films were straightforward records of everyday reality. As such, they gave audiences a big thrill. Lumière set up his camera to take a scene in a single, static shot: workers leaving a factory, a train entering a station, a family eating out of doors, etc. The spectators' first instinct was to scramble out of the way of the approaching train, and in the background of the shot of the family eating *(Bébé Mange sa Soupe)* they noticed the detail of leaves blowing in the wind, and called out excitedly.

However, once the novelty of such shots wore off, it became apparent that the impact of a single image was limited. You do not, in fact, get a very strong sense of actuality from a narrow, silent image; it is too much of an abstraction, the picture too remote. For the same reason, there is not much scope for the integration of background detail. It was difficult to cover a scene of any complexity, as film-makers discovered when they began to extend their range and to tell stories. Few of them thought to move the camera, or to move and group people with any precision, within the frame. The usual solution would be to photograph the action in long shot, in order to get it all in, or to huddle actors and décor unrealistically close together. Then came montage, and the close-up, and this was of course a great advance. But although Griffith is associated with their development, he was already very skillful in controlling, when appropriate, all the elements of a scene within the same shot; indeed, the most striking thing today about *Birth of a Nation* is the number of scenes which are played in a remarkably modern, integral style (for instance: the scenes in the hospital; at the Camerons' home; in Lincoln's office). To judge from the few films of his that I have seen, and particularly *The Coward* (1915), Thomas Ince was working in the same way.

Meanwhile, however, pundits had decided that the film could not be art if it confined itself to recording "reality," and they extended this to mean that an uncut piece of film was nothing, that montage was all. Now "reality" is a word which has to be handled carefully. Nabokov nicely describes it as "one of the few words which mean nothing without quotes."

Both the still and the movie camera make a record of "reality" in the sense that they record, objectively, what is put in front of them. As Helmut Gernsheim (*Creative Photography*, 1960) expresses it: "The camera intercepts images, the paintbrush reconstructs them." This worried theorists from the start. No other art presented this problem, and no other art, furthermore, had ever been suddenly invented like this, rootless, instead of evolving slowly, and evolving a function as it did so. A decision had to be made. One interpretation was this: the camera records reality, but reality is not art, therefore photography cannot be art. And later: the cinema cannot be art. The second interpretation arises from this and is complementary to it: agreed, reality is not art, but we improve upon it by treating it in a creative way. In practice, this meant getting as far away as possible from objectivity, and it produced, in the first decades of photography, some quite ludicrous results, prints being posed and processed and stuck together in a form of "montage" in such a way as to be indistinguishable from painting. The "masterpieces" of this art look grotesque today, and I think warn us against dismissing as irrelevant the objective basis of the cinema. Gernsheim *(op. cit.)* puts this phase into perspective: "The mistaken ambition to compete with painting drove a minority to artificial picture-making alien to the nature of photography . . . to appreciate photography requires above all understanding of the qualities and limitations peculiar to it."

This is what André Bazin — the Gernsheim of the cinema — means when he says "Les virtualités esthétiques de la photographie résident dans la révélation du réel." In this essay* Bazin makes a far more useful analysis of the nature of film and its implications for film style, than Kracauer does in the whole of his book.

The film image is taken direct from "reality" and the spectator perceives and "recognizes" it direct; there is no intermediate process as there is when the writer "translates" his material into words which are in turn translated back by the imagination of the reader. This is a major difference which conditions the whole of the respective media, and the attempt to draw literal analogies between the two (for instance between the word and the shot) is as much of a dead end as the attempt to assimilate photography to the rules of painting.

However, to say that the camera records "reality" is not to advocate that the cinema should remain at the level of Lumière. The experience of seeing even a film like *Exodus*, which is about the furthest the cinema has gone in the direction of "reality" — 70mm film, long static takes, complete surface authenticity — is not something we get each day when we go out into the street. It is *a* reality, organized by the director; and in any case a record of reality is not the same thing as reality itself. The director selects or stages his "reality," and photographs it; we perceive the image, on the screen, in the course of the film. This process *in itself* means that the experience belongs to the "imaginative" as opposed to the "actual" life to use the categories distinguished by the art critic Roger Fry

---

*"Ontology of the Photographic Image," *What is Cinema?*

(*An Essay in Aesthetics*, 1909). Fry was talking about differences in our perception of life and of paintings, but the distinction applies equally to film, and he did in fact cite the examples of the elementary newsreel-type films of his time to illustrate how even a "transparent" recording of an everyday scene was perceived in a radically different way from actuality. This distinction, which is basic to our responses to any art, is summed up thus by I. A. Richards *(Principles of Literary Criticism)*: "In ordinary life a thousand considerations prohibit for most of us any complete working-out of our response; the range and complexity of the impulse-systems involved is less; the need for action, the comparative uncertainty and vagueness of the situation, the intrusion of accidental irrelevancies, inconvenient temporal spacing—the action being too slow or too fast —all these obscure the issue and prevent the full development of the experience. But in the "imaginative experience" these obstacles are removed. . . . As a chemist's balance to a grocer's scales, so is the mind in the imaginative moment to the mind engaged in ordinary intercourse or in practical affairs."

The crucial point is that in the cinema this distinction operates *before* the montage stage, and independently of it.

Art does indeed involve organization, but this is just as possible within a complex image as in a montage sequence: it can in many ways be more subtle. I will analyze these possibilities more specifically later on. For a number of reasons, as I say, they had not been explored very fully in the early days of the cinema. The cutting together of separate shots is a more obviously "creative" method, and a more straightforward one.

Even if it's true, as I think it is, that those who first imagined and developed the cinematograph thought in terms of a *total* illusion, with sound, color and depth† and that the restricted form it temporarily took was in this sense accidental, it is still possible to see the history of the cinema as a nicely arranged series of advances, each one coming when directors, and audiences, were ready for it. First they learned to cope with the camera alone, then gradually with more and more of the ingredients of reality: they could hardly have controlled all of them at once, from the start, without practice or precedent, any more than primitive musicians would have been able to cope immediately with a symphony orchestra—or audiences to respond to it. The greater density of the sound-Scope-color image requires a more precise control than the simple "unit" image does. One has to ascend by stages. The idea of predetermined advance should not be applied too rigidly, for the immediate instrument of each advance has after all been financial pressure, and

---

† Cf. Bazin's essay "The Myth of Total Cinema," also published in the first volume of *What is Cinema?*

Warners' crisis, and therefore their introduction of the sound film, could have come a few years earlier or later; similarly with Fox and the introduction of CinemaScope. But this does not make the whole thing fortuitous, as Macgowan seems to imply when he says that we might easily have had Todd-AO thirty years ago, at the same time as sound, only support was withheld. The cinema evolves by a form of Natural Selection: technicians and financiers provide the "mutations," and their survival depends upon whether they can be usefully assimilated at the time.

Often when "use of CinemaScope" is picked out by a critic it indicates an obtrusive style, with the director striving to "compensate" for the openness of the frame, or indulging in flashy compositional effects—as in, say, Kurosawa's *The Hidden Fortress*, or *Vera-Cruz*, the first half-hour of which Robert Aldrich makes into an absolute orgy of formalism, composing frames within frames, and blocking up the sides of the image with rocks, trees, etc. In general, what they say about the camera makes a good working rule for Scope: if you notice it, it's bad. Or, more reasonably: you don't have to notice it for it to be good. This is not to forbid the critic the phrase "use of Scope," which may be useful to avoid periphrasis, provided that it's not made into a criterion in itself, unrelated to the work as a whole.

In their book *Hitchcock*, Chabrol and Rohmer mention that in CinemaScope "the extreme edges of the screen are virtually unusable": that the edges are by no means useless, but that they will not be used for the placing of details meaningful for their own sake.

While the chief advantage of Scope is, as they maintain, its opening-up of the frame, the greater sense it gives us of a continuous space—and this is where it relates to the film they are discussing here, namely *Rope*—this is a slight over-simplification. Sometimes people can be placed at the extreme edges for perfectly legitimate effect: as in *The Tall Men* (Walsh, 1955): Jane Russell and Clark Gable play a long, intimate scene together; it ends in a fight, and they retire sulking to opposite corners of the room—and of the Scope frame, leaving a great gulf between them. A different effect: near the end of *The True Story of Jesse James* (Nicholas Ray, 1957) Jesse decides to retire: he goes out into the garden to play with his children: a green and white image, Jesse on the right: a man walks past, glimpsed on the extreme left of the frame, and calls out a greeting: the strong "horizontal" effect here reinforces the feeling of a new freedom. In *Spartacus* Kubrick uses a similar technique for the shots of Crassus and his entourage visiting the training camp; the contrast between this openness and the cooped-up images showing the gladiators' existence helps express the general contrast between luxury and oppression.

But it is not only the horizontal line which is emphasized in CinemaScope (this was implied by critics who concentrated on the *shape* of the frame qua shape—as though it were the frame of a painting—and concluded that the format was suitable only for showing/framing horizontal things like crocodiles and processions). The more open the frame, the greater the impression of depth: the image is more vivid, and involves us more directly. The most striking effect in Cinerama is the roller-coaster shot, which gives us a very strong sensation of movement forward. Even though at the crucial moment we may be focussing only on the very center of the image, i.e., the area of track directly in front of the roller-coaster—an area, in fact, no larger than the standard frame—the rest of the image is not useless. We may not be conscious of what exactly is there, but we are marginally aware of the objects and the space on either side. It is this peripheral vision which orients us and makes the experience so vivid. Similar effects were tried in the early films in Todd-AO (roller-coaster; train ride) and CinemaScope (the shots from the nose of the plane in *How to Marry a Millionaire*). In Scope the involvement is less strong, but it is still considerable: so are its implications. Although the shots quoted aim at nothing more than a circus effect, *physical* sensation of this kind can be dramatically useful (elementary form-and-content). This power was there even in the 1:1.33 image, but for the most part (after Lumière's train) remained latent. But there are classic examples of movement in this plane in Renoir's *Partie de Campagne:* the long-held shot at the end, taken from the stern of the boat being rowed home; rain on the water: an overwhelming sense of nostalgia conveyed by the movement. And in Wyler's *The Best Years of Our Lives*, the shots from the nose of the plane in which the three servicemen are returning home. The movement gives us a direct insight into their sensations and through this into "what it is like" generally for them.

Scope automatically gives images like these more "weight," and it also of course enhances the effect of lateral movement.

In *Rebel Without a Cause* (Ray, 1956) a shot of extraordinary beauty comes after the first twenty minutes of the film, during which the surroundings have been uniformly cramped and depressing, the images physically cluttered-up and dominated by blacks and browns. Now, James Dean is about to set out for school; he looks out of the window. He recognizes a girl (Natalie Wood) walking past in the distance. Cut to the first day/exterior shot, the first bright one, the first "horizontal" one. A close shot of Natalie Wood, in a light-green cardigan, against a background of green bushes. As she walks the camera moves laterally with her. This makes a direct, sensual impression which gives us an insight into Dean's experience, while at the same time remaining completely natural and unforced. On the small screen, such an image could not conceivably have had a comparable weight.

One of the climaxes of *Jesse James* is Jesse's revenge killing of a farmer. This is important to the story because it ruins Jesse's chance of an amnesty, and it is equally important to the understanding of his character in that it illustrates his pride, and his thoughtlessness. The crucial shot here has the farmer ploughing his land. Jesse rides up behind him, stops, and lifts his rifle. The man starts to run but Jesse keeps with him. The camera tracks back with them, holding this composition—the farmer in the foreground, running into the camera, Jesse inexorably behind, aiming—until finally Jesse shoots him dead. This is over in a moment but has a hypnotic, almost a slow-motion impact, which again is the result of the greater physical involvement achieved by Scope, its more vivid sense of space. The impact is direct, and there is no need to emphasize it by putting it into literal slow-motion, or making a significant "pattern."

Rudolf Arnheim, in *Film as Art*, claims that any such sensation of depth will be undesirable: compositional patterns which in the more abstract image would come across as being deliberate will, if the image is more vivid, seem natural, even accidental, so that the spectator may fail to note their symbolic force.*

From this point of view, an even more relevant Scope scene is this one from *River of No Return*, analyzed by V. F. Perkins in *Movie*. I think the narrative is clear enough from his description:

"As Harry lifts Kay from the raft, she drops the bundle which contains most of her 'things' into the water. Kay's gradual loss of the physical tokens of her way of life has great symbolic significance. But Preminger is not over-impressed. The bundle simply floats away off-screen while Harry brings Kay ashore. It would be wrong to describe this as understatement. The symbolism is in the event, not in the visual pattern, so the director presents the action clearly and leaves the interpretation to the spectator."

Arnheim would no doubt regard this as a reductio ad absurdum. His attitude, which is shared, deep down, by most critics, is based on his phobia of using the camera as a "recording machine" (reality is not art). It further reflects an unwillingness to leave the spectator any freedom to interpret action or behavior, or to make connections. This concept of "freedom" has been distorted as much

---

* Arnheim also wrote, and I am not making it up: "Silent laughter is often more effective than if the sound is actually heard. The gaping of the open mouth gives a vivid, highly artistic interpretation of the phenomenon 'laughter.' If, however, the sound is also heard, the opening of the mouth appears obvious and its value as a means of expression is almost entirely lost." But I don't know that this argument against sound is any more unconvincing than that against Scope—the logic is identical.

as that of "reality." It's taken to be absurd that a director should allow a viewer any freedom of interpretation, for he may then notice things that he isn't meant to, or fail to notice things that he should; he may get the wrong point altogether. This is in line with the idea that the test of a good film is whether it "makes statements."

Now in this scene from *River of No Return*, the spectator is "free" to notice the bundle, and, when he does so, free to interpret it as significant. But there is nothing random about the shot. The detail is placed in the background of the shot, and integrated naturally, so that we have to make a positive act of interpreting, of "reading," the shot. The act of interpreting the visual field—and through that the action—is in itself valuable. The significance of the detail is not announced, it is allowed to speak for itself. An alert spectator will notice the bundle, and "follow" it as it floats off screen.

The traditional method would be to make its significance unmistakable by cutting in close-ups. In this case we would gather that the bundle is meaningful *because* it is picked out for us. In Preminger's film, the process is reversed: we pick it out *because* it is meaningful. The emphasis arises organically out of the whole action; it is not imposed.

"The symbolism is in the event not in the visual pattern." Before Scope, it was difficult to show the "event" lucidly, with each detail given its appropriate weight. It wasn't impossible: many Renoir films, as well as Mizoguchi's *Ugetsu Monogatari*, are superlative examples of the "opening-up" of the 1:1.33 frame to achieve this kind of fluidity. But on the whole the tendency was to split up the event into its component parts, and to impose, whether deliberately or not, a "visual pattern," a pattern of montage and/or of obtrusively "composed" images. And a *visual* pattern involves a pattern of motivation, a pattern of significance, which in certain films is appropriate, but is more often damagingly crude.

At this stage one can hardly avoid talking of "participation," which is another much-abused word. Everyone agrees, in principle, that art should not so much state as reveal, and that we should not just register its meaning but understand it. Our experience of a work should involve active participation more than passive assimilation.

The Russians, in their theoretical work, appropriated this idea, and applied it in a somewhat outrageous way; but critics, even intelligent ones, have continued to accept what they said. The confusion rests on a misunderstanding of the relation between film and the other arts, notably literature. Eisenstein said that "participation" took place in the association of successive images (as in the association of juxtaposed images in poetry)—that it depended purely on montage. In *October* he had intercut shots of

Kerensky with ironic titles, and then with shots of a peacock preening itself. These images in themselves are fairly neutral, but the spectator fuses them together freely, he "participates," and arrives at an "intellectual decision" at the expense of Kerensky. In *Strike* we are shown, alternately, shots of workmen being massacred and of bulls being slaughtered: again, the two sets of images are independent of each other and we have to make the imaginative link between the two. Commenting recently on passages like these, an English critic said, "Thus, Eisenstein's 'intellectual cinema' proves itself a superior means of communication by demanding the co-operation of the spectator in consideration of the conflicting ideologies that Eisenstein chose to convey."

This seems to me so much solemn nonsense. The whole is more than the sum of its parts; but then the whole is *always* more than the sum of its parts. The spectator "interprets" but there is no genuine freedom of association. A montage link of this kind reminds one of the children's puzzle which consists of a series of numbered dots: when they are joined together correctly, the outline of an animal appears. We participate in solving these, but only in a mechanical way, and there is only one correct solution. The very last thing Eisenstein really wants us to do is to evaluate for ourselves, or even experience for ourselves, what we are shown. He does not show us heroic actions—which we can recognize or judge to be heroic—he shows actions (not even that, but only *bits* of actions) and tells us that they are heroic (or alternatively brutal). Vakoulintchouk, in *Potemkin*, is "defined" by the shots which are intercut with shots of his dead body: close-ups of weeping women, sympathetic titles. Similarly we are *told* how to react to Kerensky and to the killing of the workmen—told obliquely, it is true, by a form of visual code, but still told; nothing is in any useful sense communicated. It is revealing that the whole meaning of these films can be reversed, as happened apparently in places with *Potemkin*, by merely re-arranging certain shots and titles, just as one can reverse the meaning of a slogan by replacing one name with another. (This would be inconceivable with *Birth of a Nation*.)

What is in question is not Eisenstein's artistry, within his chosen field, but rather the way his technique has been rationalized, by him and by others, and a universal validity claimed for it. The style is appropriate to what he was aiming to do, namely to make propaganda. He was not interested (in the silent films) in characterization or in shades of meaning, nor did he want to leave the spectator any freedom of response. The struggle of authority against revolution, and of Old against New, is one of Black and White. Andrew Sarris, in an excellent article on Rossellini in the *New York Film Bulletin*, contrasts this extreme montage style—"Eisenstein's conceptual editing extracts a truth from the collision of two mechanistic forces in history"—with "Rossellini's visual conception of a unified cosmos undivided by the conceptual detail of montage," and he implies one should accept each on its own terms. I think it's legitimate to say that, even if the style reflects the vision accurately, the vision is crude, and the style, although powerful, crude likewise. The words Eisenstein and his contemporaries use in describing it are significant: impact, collision, clash, the juxtaposition of "concepts"; the approach is essentially a rhetorical one. What is obvious anyway from this is that Eisenstein is a special case, that few directors see things his way, and that few subjects are amenable to this treatment. Drama is not normally reducible to concepts, clashes and collisions. (This is quite apart from the implications of the change to the sound film, after which the technique becomes still less relevant.)

People complain sometimes that Eisenstein's methods of intellectual and ideological montage have been forgotten, as have the associative techniques of Pudovkin's *Mother*, and imply that directors today must be deficient in imagination: but insofar as they reject these techniques they are more subtle. And a field where they do notably survive is that of the filmed commercial. The product may not in itself look very special (a "dead object") but it takes on associations when intercut with a smiling mother holding a smiling baby. The montage-unit style no doubt sells products, and puts over propaganda, more effectively than would a more fluid one, and there are other films too for which it is perfectly appropriate: educational work, certain documentaries, anything which aims to put over a message concisely. One would not advocate CinemaScope for these.

Jean Mitry, in his interesting book *Eisenstein* criticizes him for at times indulging in arbitrary symbolism (the slaughterhouse in *Strike*), but he accepts Eisenstein's analogies between the interpretation of film and poetic images: the film-maker juxtaposing unrelated images by montage is like the poet juxtaposing words. But the reader genuinely "participates" in the associations he makes from the words, in building them up into a fused whole: words are allusive whereas the film image is concrete. Film images follow each other in rigid sequence, which we cannot vary; the interaction of words is much more flexible. The more one goes into the differences between word and shot, and between the literary and filmic sequences of description, the more shaky do all the analogies made by the Russians seem.

There is no literary equivalent for "getting things in the same shot." This seems never to have struck them. Both Eisenstein and Pudovkin made laborious comparisons between the word or ideogram and the individual shot, and between the sentence and the montage-sequence. This seems fantastically naïve. How else can you translate "the cat sat on the mat" into film except in a single shot? Disciples tend to admit that these theories went a bit far—after all, they never went quite so far in their films—but without realizing that the rest of their aesthetic, which sounds more plausible, is in fact equally shaky, and for similar reasons.

For instance: a writer has to describe details successively, even though they may exist together. In this case he will aim, by his description, to evoke a "total" simultaneous reality in the reader's mind. Because of the indirect, allusive quality of language this is not really a handicap. Thackeray, in his *Irish Sketchbook*, gives a description of a mountain scene, evoking it by a series of details and of comparisons: he adds, "Printer's ink cannot give these wonderful hues, and *the reader will make his picture at his leisure*" (my italics). But the film image is direct, it *shows* things.

In *Lolita* (the book) there is a scene which, had it been presented without comment, might have seemed a perfect vindication of the rules laid down by Pudovkin in *Film Technique*, in that it consists of a series of details, which Nabokov describes successively, and which Pudovkin would have filmed successively ("showing them one by one, just as we would describe them in separate sequence in literary work"). It is the scene of the death of Humbert's wife: "I rushed out. The far side of our steep little street presented a peculiar sight. . . . *I have to put the impact of an instantaneous vision into a sequence of words; their physical accumulation on the page impairs the actual flash, the sharp unity of impression.* Rug-heap, old-man doll, Miss O's nurse running with a rustle back to the screened porch . . ." (my italics).

It's naïve to suppose that even the most fragmented lines—"ships, towers, domes, theatres and temples lie/open unto the fields and to the sky" can be given an exact cinematic equivalent by a montage of ships, towers, domes, and so on. Eisenstein makes much of the fragmentary narrative of Dickens; this is fair enough in that a change of scene would correspond to a cut in film, but it does not hold for the *texture* of a narrative. Thomas Hardy makes a useful reference here, and at the risk of seeming repetitive I'd like to consider some passages from his novels.

Often he will introduce a character by, as it were, discovering him within a landscape. Being a writer, he describes things one by one, but they all contribute to the creation of a broad, total environment. His protagonists emerge from this, and are in turn absorbed into it; they are never detached; we retain a mental picture of them as a part of it. The film equivalent is to *show* them as a part of it, to engulf them in it. Boetticher's *Ride Lonesome* and Ray's *The Savage Innocents* are two films which portray people dominated by, almost defined by, their natural environment, and this connection is perfectly conveyed in their first images.

In *Ride Lonesome*, the camera is held on a shot of a vast plain, stretching away to mountains in the distance; then it tilts down slowly and we become aware of a rider coming toward us from deep among the rocks below. *The Savage Innocents* has a long, empty snowscape: the camera is still: a sledge enters frame left, deep within the shot, and is drawn gradually toward us. One can contrast this with the opening of *Scott of the Antarctic:* a montage of snow vistas, evocative music. We look *at* the scene instead of being involved in it, as we are in *The Savage Innocents;* and we accept, intellectually, for the purposes of the narrative, that the characters are there, instead of genuinely feeling it. Both Boetticher's and Ray's films are in Scope, and this helps enormously: it increases the involvement of the spectator and the physical integration of the characters.

It might be said that these are "landscape" films, that Scope is suitable for them but not for more confined drama. But the same principles hold; the dichotomy often expressed between interior and exterior drama is a false one.

Consider this passage from *Tess of the d'Urbervilles*. On her wedding night, Tess confesses to her husband about the child she had by Alec:

"Her narrative had ended; even its reassertions and secondary explanations were done. Tess's voice throughout had hardly risen higher than its opening tone; there had been no exculpatory phrase of any kind, and she had not wept.

"But the complexion even of external things seemed to suffer transmutation as her announcement proceeded. The fire in the grate looked impish—demoniacally funny, as if it did not care in the least about her strait. The fender grinned idly, as if it too did not care. The light from the water-bottle was merely engaged in a chromatic problem. All material objects around announced their irresponsibility with terrible iteration. And yet nothing had changed since the moments when he had been kissing her; or rather, nothing in the substance of things. But the essence of things had changed."

The Russians, again, might interpret this their own way: fragmentation, subjectivity, justifying a similar technique for film. But in film everything is concrete. Film shows the substance, it cannot *show* the essence, but it can *suggest* the essence by *showing* the substance. It suggests inner reality by showing outer reality with the greatest possible intensity. The writer has to build up a scene by description and allusion: images and metaphors, however fanciful, can help to strengthen our *objective* picture of the scene, whereas if transposed to film they would distract, and distort (imagine a close-up of the fender, grinning idly). For filming this passage from *Tess* I can't imagine a better method than to keep both of them in the frame the whole time, with the "material objects" around and between them, and to have her explanation, and then his silence, and reactions, in a single take, without any overt emphasis from the camera. Ideally, in CinemaScope, which makes the surroundings more palpable, and enables you to get close to one or both of the characters without shutting out the rest of the scene. The more precisely the camera charts the substance of things, the external movement of words, expressions, gestures, the more subtly can it express the internal movement: the essence of things.

Such a sequence would be condemned a priori by Arnheim ("immobile recording machine") and by Eisenstein, who laid down that *any* scene where a transition in feeling was observed, without a cut, was "theatrical." Need one point out that you can get a far greater control, on film, of all the elements of the scene, and of how each spectator sees them? And that the division of change into before and after can often be crudely mechanical? There could be no more eloquent illustration of this danger than the scene which Eisenstein holds up as an example of how to handle such a change in feeling: the cream-separator episode from the *The General Line*.

A great comfort to upholders of the "traditional" aesthetic has always been the Kuleshov/Pudovkin experiment (three neutral CUs of an actor, Mosjoukine, intercut with three different shots, to give the impression of three different emotions). This was felt to define the cinema for all time, and to establish that its essence was montage. If the same effect was difficult to achieve with sound, and then CinemaScope, that must prove that they were a bad thing. I do not honestly think that the effect on spectators of these sequences, presented as Pudovkin relates, can have been quite so overwhelming as he claims (is there any evidence, I wonder, that the experiment was done, and does not represent wishful thinking?), but one can accept that they do, up to a point, work: we understand what is being depicted, we complete the equations. Later experiments by psychologists have confirmed that one expression abstracted from its context looks very much like another. But this can far more reasonably be seen, I think, as an argument for not abstracting it in the first place.

The experiment illustrates that each act of perception automatically conditions succeeding ones; this is something which applies continuously, to life as well as to art, and which any intelligent artist will have taken into account in working out a style—not, however, to the extent of making it the cornerstone of his method. Pudovkin here reminds one of the bakers who first extract the nourishing parts of the flour, process it, and then put some back as "extra goodness": the result may be eatable, but it is hardly the only way to make bread, and one can criticize it for being unnecessary and "synthetic." Indeed one could extend the culinary analogy and say that the experience put over by the traditional aesthetic is essentially a *predigested* one. These two epithets have in ordinary usage a literal meaning and, by extension, a metaphorical one, applied pejoratively; the same correlation is valid here.

Writers like Manvell, Reisz, and Lindgren (all of whom base their aesthetic more or less closely on the Russians') advocate a method which gives us a *digest* of what we might see, in real life, if we were experiencing a given scene. Lindgren, in *The Art of the Film*, goes into this in most detail. He makes the usual comparisons with literary fragmentation, and then between what we see in life and in films. Sometimes we consciously see things as a whole, in their interrelationship (general shot). Sometimes we look round (pan) or walk (tracking shot). Normally we focus on one thing at a time (close-up or close-shot) and we look from one thing to another (cutting). Now it should be clear that the correspondence is by no means exact. In a film we sit facing the same direction all the time, looking at a screen which is set at a finite distance. In life we are oriented in our surroundings and our perception of them is continuous—continuous in time and space. But Lindgren claims that "in so far as the film is photographic and reproduces movement, it can give us a lifelike semblance of what we see; in so far as it employs editing, it can exactly [sic] reproduce the *manner* in which we see it."

At any time we see "central" things and "marginal" things; of the latter we may be aware, or half-aware, or they may serve merely to orient us. The traditional aesthetic separates out the central things: the marginal ones it either omits as inessential and distracting, or intercuts in close shot—in which case they are no longer marginal but central.

So an alternative method, a more strictly realistic one, which Lindgren and company pass over, is to present a complex image organized in such a way that we are induced to interpret it for ourselves. This is where genuine participation comes in, as in the sequence quoted from *River of No Return*.

Manvell *(The Film and the Public)* writes that "the comparatively narrow bounds of the normal screen shape sharpen perception by closing it in, giving the director full control of every detail which the audience should perceive." Conversely in CinemaScope "the sharpened perception of the normal film will be lost." In his aesthetic, we either see a thing or we don't. If a detail is important, the director singles it out for us; if there is a symbol or a meaningful connection to be noted, the director again does it for us, emphasizing it by close-ups. (Cf. Eisenstein's criticism of Dovshenko's *Earth*, on the grounds that he had not made the symbolism explicit enough —i.e., he had not brought the symbolic detail into close-up but had left it integrated, so that it might appear accidental.) We do not have to bother about noticing it for ourselves, or estimating whether it is significant. On the other hand when the image is complex we *have* to be alert to interpret it and the details within it. The difference between the Preminger method cited from *River of No Return* and the explicit close-up/montage style which he could have used, but didn't, corresponds to the difference between reading the meaning for ourselves and having it spelled out for us.*

"I don't think CinemaScope is a good medium. It's good only for showing great masses of movement. For other things, it's distracting, it's hard to focus attention, and it's very difficult to cut. Some people just go ahead and cut it and let people's eyes jump around and find what they want to find. It's very hard for an audience to focus—they have too much to look at—they can't see the whole thing." (Howard Hawks in an interview with Peter Bogdanovich.)

This is the danger; it was more worrying at the introduction of Scope, when audiences did apparently have to get used to "exploring" the more open image, but this I think was temporary. If a Scope image is decently organized the eyes will not just "jump around and find what they want to find," purely at random — they can be led to focus on detail, and to look from one thing to another within the frame with the emphasis which the director intends: that is, if the spectator is alert. Hawks may not like Scope (he had an apparently traumatic experience using it for *Land of the Pharaohs*, perhaps his worst film), but he approves of the 1:1.85 screen, and his style has always been one which allows the spectator freedom; in this sense he does not need Scope. One of the best of all examples of the alternative style to Lindgren's is from his *Hatari!* (wide screen). General shot of a bedroom: right of frame, in bed, waiting for her supper, Elsa Martinelli (back to camera); on the bed, John Wayne. Centre of frame, background, a tame cheetah. Left of frame, enter Red Buttons, carrying a tray; he trips over the cheetah's tail and the supper lands on Wayne, Martinelli, and the floor. Typically, Hawks takes this (exceedingly funny) scene in one static shot. It is done with a beautiful directness and lucidity, and without any of the usual look-this-is-funny comedy emphasis. The scene exists autonomously, action and reaction being integrated: Martinelli suddenly collapses with the giggles but we can only just see her at the edge of the frame. The nicest

---

*Cf. also in *Citizen Kane* Welles's extremely subtle handling of the Rosebud/snow-glass paperweight imagery, which he often leaves naturally in the background of the shot for us to notice, and to make the connections. Pages could be written on this.

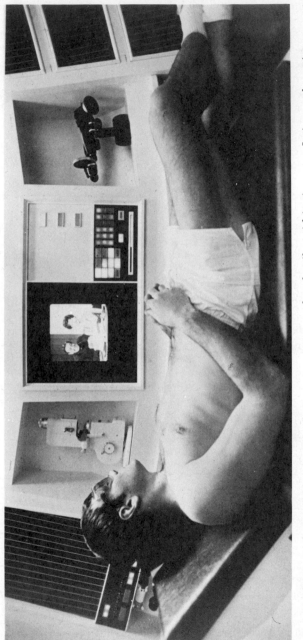

Composition in the wide screen. The astronaut (Gary Lockwood) receives birthday greetings from his parents in *2001: A Space Odyssey* (1968). "When the image is complex we *have* to be able to interpret it and the details within it. . . . It is much easier to put together a complex scene synthetically out of separate details . . . but you sacrifice the possibility of real conviction, of real subtlety" (BARR, pages 155, 157).

thing of all is the cheetah's reaction. He is obviously quite bewildered by the whole episode. We can see him in the background, looking up in pained manner at Red Buttons, and Hawks leaves him there, fading out the scene after a brief moment. Contrast the almost invariable procedure in other films for handling animal performers: that of extracting a certain laugh by cutting in their cute reactions in close-up. We are left "free" to interpret the scene visually, and this means we are free to respond. Our responses are not "signposted" by successive close-ups—foot tripping over tail, result, various reactions. No single reading of the scene is imposed. One could put it another way: the scene, as directed, is at once more subtle and more *authentic*. The reason why animals' reactions are normally cut in separately is not only that they thus get a surer laugh but that it's difficult to direct an animal so that it genuinely does what it is represented to be doing. It is sometimes held to be the chief glory of the cinema that you can, by montage, "create" an event like this which never happened. But the result (leaving aside certain kinds of film where the convention obviously allows this) is mechanical.*

The same applies in a less obvious way to other details of action and acting. It is much easier to put together a complex scene synthetically out of separate details—especially when you have an incompetent actor, or a child—than to organize and film the scene in its integrity. But you sacrifice the possibility of real conviction, of real subtlety.

The advantage of Scope over even the wide screen of *Hatari!* is that it enables complex scenes to be covered even more naturally: detail can be integrated, and therefore perceived, in a still more realistic way. If I had to sum up its implications I would say that it gives a greater range for *gradation of emphasis*. George Kaplan wrote in *Scene* that "there is no room for subtlety on 70mm film"; on the contrary, there is twice as much room, as is clear both from arithmetic and from *Exodus*. The 1:1.33 screen is too much of an abstraction, compared with the way we normally see things, to admit easily the detail which can only be really effective if it is perceived *qua* casual detail. There are innumerable applications of this (the whole question of significant imagery is affected by it): one quite common one is the scene where two people talk, and a third watches, or just appears in the background unobtrusively— he might be a person who is relevant to the others in some way, or who is affected by what they say, and it is useful for us to be "reminded" of his presence. The simple cutaway shot coarsens the

---

*Bazin analyzed this issue—the existence of which no one before him seems to have realized—in another definitive essay, "The Virtues and Limitations of Montage."

effect by being too obvious a directorial aside (Look who's watching) and on the smaller screen it's difficult to play off foreground and background within the frame: the detail tends to look too obviously planted. The frame is so closed-in that any detail which is placed there *must* be deliberate — at some level we both feel this and know it intellectually.* Greater flexibility was achieved long before Scope by certain directors using depth of focus and the moving camera (one of whose main advantages, as Dai Vaughan pointed out in *Definition* 1, is that it allows points to be made literally "in passing"). Scope as always does not create a new method, it encourages, and refines, an old one. The most beautiful example of this "gradation of emphasis" point is I think *The Courtship of Eddie's Father*; others include *The True Story of Jesse James*, *Ride the High Country* (all Scope) and *Exodus* (70mm). This is not something which can be isolated from the excellence of the films as a whole, nor can it be satisfactorily documented — one just has to sit in front of the films and see how space and décor and relationships are organized, and the eye led from one point to another within the image; how connections are made, and characters introduced, not being "added on" to the rest of the context but developing *out of* it.

Few of the films like these which I'd regard as being the richest of all are liked by critics; to praise Ray, Preminger, Hawks, or Minnelli makes one liable to the charge of subscribing to a "cult," a common defense mechanism which enables critics to avoid any challenge to their preconceptions. While it's possible, of course, to reject any of these films in the last analysis, I think the disagreement is more basic than this. Mainstream critics have been conditioned to recognize only a style based on montage and the close-up, and on "signposting" of effects, as valid, and may be in effect physically unable to respond to a film which requires an active interpretation on every level. I mean by this that, as we become more sophisticated and get more familiar with ideas and concepts, we tend to interpret films in literary terms, and our visual acuteness atrophies. Norman Fruchter, conducting a Film Appreciation course for unsophisticated teenagers, found that "the cadets' visual

---

*In Antonioni's *Il Grido* there is a shot taken from inside a house: a woman goes out of the door and walks away. The door stays slightly ajar and through this very narrow aperture we continue to see her walking in a dead straight line away from the camera. This is a far too neat continued effect, and audiences groan. It is too good to be true that she should have walked along exactly the one line which would have kept her visible. On the other hand if the aperture had been wider, she would have been "free" to deviate, and even if she had in fact taken precisely the same path the shot would have been more acceptable — not in spite of but *because* of the "frame" of the door "fitting" her less well. I don't think it is fanciful to compare the door that frames her with the frame of the film image in general.

responses were far more acute than anyone might have given them credit for. I had to watch a film at least three times to see as much as they caught in a single viewing. They rarely missed detail. . . ." (*Sight and Sound*, Autumn, 1962). Now the traditional aesthetic allows for, and encourages, our more sophisticated tendencies by, as I described, "predigesting" a scene and serving it up in separate units, each one of which we can read like a sign. Critics who are conditioned by this will keep on (consciously or subconsciously) trying to separate out the "subject" of each shot, the "content" of each sequence, even when the film is made in a denser and more fluid style which does not admit this kind of treatment. They resent, or more commonly fail to understand, directors who give them too much work to do, and they naturally resent CinemaScope, which automatically makes for a more open, complex image.

The specific objections made to CinemaScope now, I hope, fall into place: they are really no objections at all. Sidney Lumet in an interview (*Film Quarterly*, Winter, 1960) was asked about the new screen processes and answered "I think they're ridiculous, I think they're pointless, I think they're typical Hollywood products. And typical Hollywood mentality, because the essence of any dramatic piece is people, and it is symptomatic that Hollywood finds a way of photographing people directly opposite to the way they are built. CinemaScope makes no sense until people are fatter than they are taller."

This is about as logical as to say that a book should be the shape of what it's about. If the screen is to correspond exactly to the human build then we should have vertical CinemaScope. If to the human face, it should be square (if not oval), and the most common criticism of Scope was, indeed, that it made the close-up impossible: it no longer "fits" the screen. As Gavin Lambert said, "A face squashed across a concave screen is clearly an unedifying prospect." (In CinemaScope, unlike Cinerama, the screen is seldom noticeably curved, and clearly the objection is more to the dimensions than to the curvature itself.)

The argument is effectively a circular one. I think one can sum up the development of the close-up roughly like this: the natural subject for the film is man-in-a-situation. But the frame was too narrow for this to be shown comfortably: also, it was difficult to organize from scratch, without some experience of the cinema and what could be done with it. So man-in-situation came to be conveyed by man + situation: close-up of a face, intercut with shots defining his experience and/or surroundings.

Certain film-makers welcomed this because it was more manageable and also more clearly "creative." At the same time, the process was rejected by others as being mechanical. One can look at this first from the point of view of actor and director. There

is a loss of spontaneity, which is reflected in the film. "If you isolate a detail, that means that you have to take it up again from
cold, to resuscitate the emotion" (Vincente Minnelli). "The close-up
in the cinema is essentially a reconstruction, something pre-fabri-
cated, carefully worked up" (Jean Renoir).

This in turn affects the spectator, who has to take on trust the
connection between the close-up and the rest of the scene; man
+ situation tends to become a formula, a cruder digest of a reality
which is continuous and complex. "If I were to throw in ten more
details, everything in my films would suddenly become extremely
clear. But those ten details are just what I don't want to add.
Nothing could be easier than to take a close-up; I don't take any,
lest I be tempted to use them" (Roberto Rossellini).

Directors like these worked out a more integral style presenting
man-*in*-situation. This involved compensating for the narrowness
of the frame by moving the camera laterally and composing the
scene in depth. If the actors were brought close to the camera they
would fill the screen, and blot out the background; therefore they
were seldom brought close. This style is associated mainly with
Renoir, who in 1938 wrote: "The more I advance in my craft, the
more I feel it necessary to have the scene set in depth in relation
to the screen; and the less can I stand actors placed carefully before
the camera, as if they were posing for their photograph. It suits
me rather to set my actors freely at different distances from the
camera, to make them move about." This can be traced back to
Boudu Sauvé des Eaux (1932) and even to his silent films; and there
are others in the 'thirties like Hawks and Ophuls who, while not
applying any formal principle of composition in depth, concentrate
on the organization of the space within the image, and avoid the
detached close-up — see especially *The Criminal Code* and *Liebelei*.
These, together with *Boudu*, make up a marvelous trio of early
sound films, which if one relied upon historians one would scarcely
know existed, for according to most theories they oughtn't to.

The most spectacular application of these ideas is undoubtedly
Antonioni's *Le Amiche* (made in 1955 but in the 1:1.33 ratio), of
which he said: "I wanted to show my characters in their context,
not to separate them, by montage, from their daily environment.
You will find no cross-cutting whatever in *Le Amiche:* this technique expresses nothing." There are no close-ups in this film, and
the average length of shot is 30 seconds, which is a lot. Antonioni
realizes, and demonstrates, that the interaction of people with
each other and with their surroundings is much more subtly expressed by showing them simultaneously. To dissociate them by
montage tends to dissociate them altogether. The difference is
not one of degree but of kind.

How does this relate to CinemaScope? Many of the directors

who thus "anticipate" it do not in fact use it; partly this is chance, partly that they can get along without. But while I would not quite agree with the magazine *Présence du Cinéma*, which states that everything is automatically better in Scope, I think that, other things being equal, Scope refines this style. The director can now afford to bring a character closer to the lens without shutting out the context, and this flexibility is useful. He can have two faces in close shot together, instead of having to cut from one to the other, or to squeeze them in unnaturally close together. (Antonioni, although he has not worked in Scope, has taken advantage of the 1:1.85 screen in this way. Ian Cameron discusses this apropos of *L'Avventura* in *Film Quarterly*, Fall, 1962).

In CinemaScope the close-up, so far from being impossible, is for the first time fully acceptable: it *cannot* be a mechanical, all-purpose CU like the one of Mosjoukine, and it cannot be detached, it must include a genuine and not just a token background. I say "cannot": at least, if it is done this way, it is patently absurd. The image is too open, its space too palpable, to accommodate the "dead object" and give it spurious life. A lifeless film is twice as lifeless in Scope, as certain directors continue to demonstrate by building up scenes in the cutting-room out of the most perfunctory of component-shots. The most grotesque example is *The Lion*, but *The Left Hand of God*, *The Barbarian and the Geisha*, *Bus Stop*, and *The Deep Blue Sea* are also instructively inept. (I don't suggest that Scope *makes* them bad; they would have been anyway, but Scope shows them up more clearly. Over-all, and with certain clear exceptions like the didactic and the animated film, Scope makes the bad film worse and the good film better· it should gradually separate the sheep among directors from the goats.)

Look at the Scope close-up, as before, from both angles, how it is shot, and how we see it. If it is to pass, it must be analytic rather than synthetic: instead of taking an insert CU, then, against a neutral background, the director will have to recreate the ambience of the whole, and this helps the actor. The actor at the same time is freer to move within the frame, and thus within his surroundings, instead of being "placed carefully before the camera". Mariette Hartley, the girl in *Ride the High Country*, stands at the window of her house, talking to a boy: Scope close-up: she moves around nervously while she talks, and the director (Sam Peckinpah) doesn't have to worry about keeping her fixed to any chalk-marks because there is room enough within the frame; the effect is marvelously spontaneous.

Kazan's *Wild River* (about the evacuation of a remote community by the Tennessee Valley Authority) is a film where environment, and its effect on different people, is as significant as in *Le Amiche* and *The Magnificent Ambersons*. Because it is in Scope

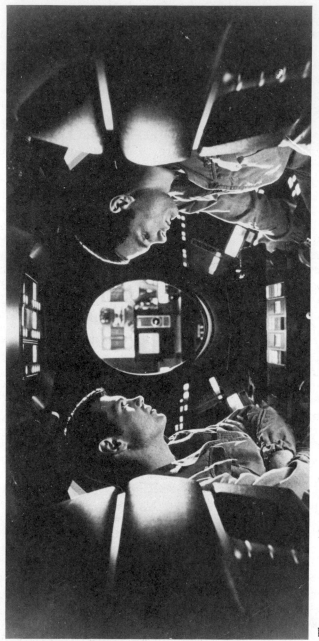

The astronauts (Gary Lockwood and Keir Dullea) discuss Hal's problems while Hal listens in the rear-ground in *2001: A Space Odyssey* (1968). "The director . . . can have two faces in close shot together, instead of having to cut from one to the other, or to squeeze them in unnaturally close together" (BARR, page 161).

it doesn't matter that it is full of close-ups and crosscut sequences. Antonioni's reservations no longer apply; Kazan can concentrate on a single face without dissociating it from its context and "dislocating" the spectator.

Finally, a not unusual CinemaScope scene (from Ray's *Bitter Victory*) which contradicts most of the facile generalizations about Scope, made alike by those against and those in favor. The three main characters sit around a table, talking. The atmosphere is important — a military club in Africa, during the war, a nervous, falsely cheerful environment. The scene is taken in a series of full or medium close-ups, each of the three in turn, as they talk, sometimes two together. The normal theoretical attitude is that this would be fine on the old-ratio screen but clumsy if not impossible in Scope. If anything, the reverse is true, and it works brilliantly *because* it is in Scope: the cutting does not disorient us, the close-ups do not wholly isolate the characters, we know where we are all through. At the edges of the frame there is décor and space and perhaps some casual detail; thus when the camera is on one of the men, Richard Burton, we can see a couple dancing, and an Arab guard, and a general background of the room; we are completely situated at each moment, and accept the scene as real, while getting the full concentration on each face which Ray intends. So far from distracting this awareness of environment and of the characters' relation in space is necessary.

In talking about the close-ups in *Bitter Victory* I am talking about the montage. The two have always been lumped together, by people condemning Scope ("the close-up and montage become impossible") and by those welcoming it ("but montage and the close up are not essential anyway"); the implications of Scope are identical for both. Montage is at once less necessary and more acceptable. Bazin and Roger Leenhardt, two of the few who approved of Scope from the start, imagined it would come to eliminate cutting within a sequence, and that this was no bad thing, but fortunately the medium is more flexible: some directors cut more in Scope, some less. There is no need to fragment reality, but there is less harm in fragmenting it because the different bits can be fitted together more satisfactorily. . . .

1963

CHRISTIAN METZ
FROM FILM LANGUAGE

SOME POINTS IN
THE SEMIOTICS OF THE CINEMA

The purpose of this text is to examine some of the problems and difficulties confronting the person who wants to begin undertaking, in the field of "cinematographic language," de Saussure's project of a general semiotics: to study the ordering and functionings of the main signifying units used in the filmic message. Semiotics, as de Saussure conceived it, is still in its childhood, but any work bearing on one of the nonverbal "languages," provided that it assumes a resolutely semiological relevance and does not remain satisfied with vague considerations of "substance," brings its contribution, whether modest or important, to that great enterprise, the general study of significations.

The very term "cinematographic *language*" already poses the whole problem of the semiotics of film. It would require a long justification, and strictly speaking it should be used only after the in-depth study of the semiological mechanisms at work in the filmic message had been fairly well advanced. Convenience, however, makes us retain, right from the start, that frozen syntagma—"language"—which has gradually assumed a place in the special vocabulary of film theoreticians and aestheticians. Even from a strictly semiological point of view, one can perhaps at this time give a preliminary justification for the expression "cinematographic language" (not to be confused with "cinematographic *langue*" (language system), which does not seem to me acceptable)—a justification that, in the present state of semiological investigations, can only be very general. I hope to outline it in this essay. . . .

CINEMA AND NARRATIVITY

A first choice confronts the "film semiologist": Is the corpus to be made up of feature films *(narrative films)* or, on the contrary, of short films, documentaries, technological, pedagogical, or advertising films, etc.? It could be answered that it depends simply on what one wants to study—that the cinema possesses various "dialects," and that each one of these "dialects" can become the subject of a specific analysis. This is undoubtedly true. Nevertheless, there is a hierarchy of concerns (or, better yet, a methodological urgency) that favors—in the beginning at least—the study of the narrative film. We know that, in the few years immediately before and after the Lumière brothers' invention in 1895, critics, journalists, and the pioneer cinematographers disagreed considerably among themselves as to the *social function* that they attributed to, or predicted for, the new machine: whether it was a means of preservation or of making archives, whether it was an auxiliary technography for research and teaching in sciences like botany or surgery, whether it was a new form of journalism, or an instrument of sentimental devotion, either private or public, which could perpetuate the living image of the dear departed one, and so on. That, over all these possibilities, the cinema could evolve into a machine for telling stories had never been really considered. From the very beginnings of the cinematograph there were various indications and statements that suggested such an evolution, but they had no common measure with the magnitude that the narrative phenomenon was to assume. The merging of the cinema and of narrativity was a great fact, which was by no means predestined—nor was it strictly fortuitous. It was a historical and social fact, a fact of civilization (to use a formula dear to the sociologist Marcel Mauss), a fact that in turn conditioned the later evolution of the film as a semiological reality, somewhat in the same way—indirect and general,* though effective —that "external" linguistic events (conquests, colonizations, transformations of language) influence the "internal" functioning of idioms. In the realm of the cinema, all nonnarrative genres—the documentary, the technical film, etc.—have become marginal provinces, border regions so to speak, while the *feature-length film of novelistic fiction*, which is simply called a "film"—the usage is significant†—has traced more and more clearly the king's highway of filmic expression.

This purely numerical and social superiority is not the only fact concerned. Added to it is a more "internal" consideration: Non-

---

*Except, of course, for specific lexical facts.

†As in statements like "The short was terrible, but the film was great" or "What are they showing tonight? a series of shorts or a film?" etc.

narrative films for the most part are distinguished from "real" films by their social purpose and by their content much more than by their "language processes." The basic figures of the semiotics of the cinema—montage, camera movements, scale of the shots, relationships between the image and speech, sequences, and other large syntagmatic units—are on the whole the same in "small" films and in "big" films. It is by no means certain that an independent semiotics of the various nonnarrative genres is possible other than in the form of a series of discontinuous remarks on the points of difference between these films and "ordinary" films. To examine fiction films is to proceed more directly and more rapidly to the heart of the problem.

There is, moreover, an encouraging diachronic consideration. We know, since the observations of Béla Balázs, André Malraux, Edgar Morin, Jean Mitry, and many others, that the cinema was not a specific "language" from its inception. Before becoming the means of expression familiar to us, it was a simple means of mechanical recording, preserving, and reproducing moving visual spectacles— whether of life, of the theater, or even of small *mises-en-scène*, which were specially prepared and which, in the final analysis, remained theatrical—in short, a "means of reproduction," to use André Malraux's term. Now, *it was precisely to the extent that the cinema confronted the problems of narration* that, in the course of successive gropings, it came to produce a body of specific signifying procedures. Historians of the cinema generally agree in dating the beginning of the "cinema" as we know it in the period 1910–15. Films like *Enoch Arden, Life for the Czar, Quo Vadis?, Fantômas, Cabiria, The Golem, The Battle of Gettysburg*, and above all *Birth of a Nation* were among the first films, in the acceptation we now give this word when we use it without a determinant: Narration of a certain magnitude based on procedures that are supposed to be specifically cinematographic. It so happens that these procedures were perfected in the wake of the narrative endeavor. The pioneers of "cinematographic language"—Méliès, Porter, Griffith— couldn't care less about "formal" research conducted for its own sake; what is more (except for occasional naïve and confused attempts), they cared little about the symbolic, philosophical or human "message" of their films. Men of denotation rather than of connotation, they wanted above all to tell a story; they were not content unless they could subject the continuous, analogical material of photographic duplication to the *articulations*—however rudimentary—of a narrative discourse. Georges Sadoul has indeed shown how Méliès, in his story-teller's naïveté, was led to invent double exposure, the device of multiple exposures with a mask and a dark backdrop, the dissolve and the fade-in, and the pan shot. Jean Mitry, who has written a very precise synthesis of these problems, examines the first occurrences of a certain number of procedures of filmic language—the close-up, the pan shot, the tracking shot, parallel montage, and interlaced, or alternate, montage—among the film primitives. I will summarize the conclusions he reaches: The principal "inventions" are credited to the Frenchmen Méliès and Promio, to the Englishmen G. A. Smith and J. Williamson, and to the American E. S. Porter; it was Griffith's role to define and to stabilize—we would say, to codify—the *function* of these different procedures in relation to the filmic *narrative*, and thereby unify them up to a certain point in a coherent "syntax" (note that it would be better to use the term *syntagmatic category;* Jean Mitry himself avoids the word syntax). Between 1911 and 1915, Griffith made a whole series of films having, more or less consciously, the value of experimental probings, and *Birth of a Nation,* released in 1915, appears as the crowning work, the sum and the public demonstration of investigations that, however naïve they may have been, were nonetheless systematic and fundamental. Thus, it was in a single motion that the cinema became narrative and took over some of the attributes of a language.

Today, still, the so-called filmic procedures are in fact filmic-narrative. This, to my mind, justifies the priority of the narrative film in the filmosemiological enterprise—a priority that must not of course become an exclusivity.

STUDIES OF DENOTATION AND STUDIES OF CONNOTATION IN THE SEMIOTICS OF THE CINEMA

The facts I have just reviewed lead to another consequence. The semiotics of the cinema can be conceived of either as a semiotics of connotation or as a semiotics of denotation. Both directions are interesting, and it is obvious that on the day when the semiological study of film makes some progress and begins to form a body of knowledge, it will have considered connotative and denotative significations together. The study of connotation brings us closer to the notion of the cinema as an art (the "seventh art"). As I have indicated elsewhere in more detail, the art of film is located on the same semiological "plane" as literary art: The properly aesthetic orderings and constraints—versification, composition, and tropes in the first case; framing, camera movements, and light "effects" in the second—serve as the connoted instance, which is superimposed over the denoted meaning. In literature, the latter appears as the purely linguistic signification, which is linked, in the employed idiom, to the units used by the author. In the cinema, it is represented by the literal (that is, perceptual) meaning of the spectacle reproduced in the image, or of the sounds duplicated by the sound-track. As for connotation, which plays a major role in all aesthetic languages,* its significate is the literary or cinematographic "style," "genre" (the epic, the western, etc.), "symbol" (philosophical, humanitarian, ideological, and so on), or "poetic atmosphere"— and its signifier is the whole denoted semiological material, whether signified or signifying. In American gangster movies, where, for example, the slick pavement of the waterfront distills an impression of anxiety and hardness (significate of the connotation), the scene represented (dimly lit, deserted wharves, with stacks of crates and overhead cranes, the significate of denotation), and the technique of the shooting, which is dependent on the effects of lighting in order to produce a certain *picture* of the docks (signifier of denotation), converge to form the signifier of connotation. The same scene filmed in a different light would produce a different impression; and so would the same technique used on a different subject (for example, a child's smiling face). Film aestheticians have often remarked that filmic effects must not be "gratuitous," but must remain "subordinate to the plot." This is another way of say-ing that the significate of connotation can establish itself only when the corresponding signifier brings into play *both* the signifier and the significate of denotation.

The study of the cinema as an art—the study of cinematographic expressiveness—can therefore be conducted according to methods derived from linguistics. For instance, there is no doubt that films are amenable to analyses comparable *(mutatis mutandis)* to those Thomas A. Sebeok has applied to Cheremis songs, or to those Samuel R. Levin has proposed. But there is another task that re-quires the careful attention of the film semiologist. For also, and even first of all, through its procedures of *denotation*, the cinema is a specific language. The concept of *diegesis* is as important for the film semiologist as the idea of art. The word is derived from the Greek δίήγησις, "narration" and was used particularly to designate one of the obligatory parts of judiciary discourse, the recital of facts. The term was introduced into the framework of the cinema by Étienne Souriau. It designates the film's *represented* instance (which Mikel Dufrenne contrasts to the expressed, properly aesthet-ic, instance)—that is to say, the sum of a film's denotation: the nar-ration itself, but also the fictional space and time dimensions implied in and by the narrative, and consequently the characters, the landscapes, the events, and other narrative elements, in so far

---

* Aesthetic language practices a kind of promotion of connotation, but connota-tion occurs as well in various phenomena of expressiveness proper to ordinary lan-guage, like those studied by Charles Bally (*Le Langage et la vie*, Geneva, Payot, 1926).

as they are considered in their denoted aspect. How does the cinema indicate successivity, precession, temporal breaks, causality, adversative relationships, consequence, spatial proximity, or distance, etc.? These are central questions to the semiotics of the cinema.

One must not indeed forget that, from the semiological point of view, the cinema is very different from still photography whence its technique is derived. In photography, as Roland Barthes has clearly shown, the denoted meaning is secured entirely through the automatic process of photochemical reproduction; denotation is a visual transfer,* which is not codified and has no inherent organization. Human intervention, which carries some elements of a proper semiotics, affects only the level of connotation (lighting, camera angle, "photographic effects," and so on). And, in point of fact, there is no specifically photographic procedure for designating the significate "house" in its denoted aspect, unless it is by showing a house. In the cinema, on the other hand, a whole semiotics of denotation is possible and necessary, for a film is composed of *many* photographs (the concept of montage, with its myriad consequences)—photographs that give us mostly only partial views of the diegetic referent. In film a "house" would be a shot of a staircase, a shot of one of the walls taken from the outside, a close-up of a window, a brief establishing shot of the building,† etc. Thus a kind of filmic *articulation* appears, which has no equivalent in photography: It is the denotation itself that is being constructed, organized, and to a certain extent codified (*codified, not necessarily encoded*). Lacking absolute laws, filmic intelligibility nevertheless depends on a certain number of dominant habits: A film put together haphazardly would not be understood.

I return to my initial observations: "Cinematographic language" is first of all the literalness of a plot. Artistic effects, even when they are substantially inseparable from the semic act by which the film tells us its story, nevertheless constitute another level of significa-

---

*I am speaking here as a semiologist and not as a psychologist. Comparative studies of visual perception, both in "real" and in filmic conditions, have indeed isolated all the optical distortions that differentiate between the photograph and the object. But these transformations, which obey the laws of optical physics, of the chemistry of emulsions and of retinal physiology, do not constitute a signifying system.

†Even if this over-all view is the only one shown us in the film, it is still the result of a choice. We know that the modern cinema has partially abandoned the practices of visual fragmentation and excessive montage in favor of the continuous shot (cf. the famous "shot-sequence" controversy). This condition *modifies* to the same extent the semiotics of filmic denotation, but it in no way dismisses it. Simply, cinematographic language, like other languages, has a diachronic side. A single "shot" itself contains several elements (example: switching from one view to another through a camera movement, and without montage).

tion, which from the methodological point of view must come "later."

PARADIGMATIC AND SYNTAGMATIC CATEGORIES

There is a danger that the semiotics of the cinema will tend to develop along the syntagmatic rather than along the paradigmatic axis. It is not that there is no filmic paradigm: At specific points along the chain of images the number of units liable to occur is limited, so that, in these circumstances, the unit that does appear derives its meaning in relation to the other members of the paradigm. This is the case with the "fade-dissolve" duality within the framework of the "conjunction of two sequences":* a simple commutation, which the users—that is to say, the spectators—perform spontaneously, makes it possible to isolate the corresponding significates: a spatiotemporal break with the establishing of an underlying transitive link (dissolve), and a straightforward spatiotemporal break (fade). But in most of the *positions* of the filmic chain, the number of units liable to appear is very much open (though not infinite). Much more open, in any case, than the series of lexemes that, by their nonfinite nature, are nonetheless opposed to the series of grammatical monemes in linguistics. For, despite the difficulty, already emphasized by Joseph Vendryes in *Le Langage*, of accurately enumerating the words of an idiom, it is at least possible to indicate the maximum and minimum limits, thus arriving at the approximate order of magnitude (for example, in French the lexeme *"lav-"* exists, but the lexeme *"patouf"* does not†). The case is different in the cinema, where the number of images is indefinite. Several times indefinite, one should say. For the "pro-filmic" spectacles‡ are themselves unlimited in number; the exact nature of lighting can be varied infinitely and by quantities that are nondiscrete; the same applies to the axial distance between the subject and the camera (in variations which are said to be scalar—that is, scale of the shot),§ to the camera angle, to the properties of the film and

---

*Fades, or dissolves, can also occur in other settings, especially at the center of sequences. In such cases, their value is different.

†The lexemic unit *"lav-"* corresponds to *"wash-"* in English; *"patouf"* is no more of a lexeme in English than it is in French.—TRANSLATOR.

‡As defined by Étienne Souriau. The "profilmic" spectacle is whatever is placed in front of the camera, or whatever one places the camera in front of, in order to "shoot" it.

§In *Le Langage cinématographique* (Paris, 1962), Francois Chevassu maintains (p. 14) that the "scale of shots" is coded. I would say instead that it is the technical terminology ("close-up," "thirty-degree angle shot," "medium shot," etc.) that is coded. The actual scale of the shots constitutes a continuous gradation, from the

the focal length of the lens, and to the exact trajectory of the camera movements (including the stationary shot, which represents zero degree in this case). It suffices to vary one of these elements by a perceptible quantity to obtain *another* image. The shot is therefore not comparable to the word in a lexicon; rather it resembles a complete statement (of one or more sentences), in that it is already the result of an essentially free combination, a "speech" arrangement. On the other hand the word is a syntagma that is precast by code — a "vertical" syntagma, as R. F. Mikus would say. Let us note in this connection that there is another similarity between the image and the statement: Both are actualized units, whereas the word in itself is a purely potential unit of code. The image is almost always assertive — and assertion is one of the great "modalities" of actualization, of the semic act. It appears therefore that the paradigmatic category in film is condemned to remain partial and fragmentary, at least as long as one tries to isolate it on the level of the *image*. This is naturally derived from the fact that *creation* plays a larger role in cinematographic language than it does in the handling of idioms: To "speak" a language is to use it, but to "speak" cinematographic language is to a certain extent to invent it. The speakers of ordinary language constitute a group of users; film-makers are a group of creators. On the other hand, movie *spectators* in turn constitute a group of users. That is why the semiotics of the cinema must frequently consider things from the point of view of the spectator rather than of the film-maker. Étienne Souriau's distinction between the filmic point of view and the "*cinéastique*," or film-making, point of view is a very useful concept; film semiotics is mainly a *filmic* study. The situation has a rough equivalent in linguistics: Some linguists connect the speaker with the message, while the listener in some way "represents" the code, since he requires it to understand what is being said to him, while the speaker is presumed to know beforehand what he wants to say.

But, more than paradigmatic studies, it is the syntagmatic considerations that are at the center of the problems of filmic denotation. Although each image is a free creation, the arrangement of these images into an intelligible sequence — cutting and montage — brings us to the heart of the semiological dimension of film. It is a rather paradoxical situation: Those proliferating (and not very discrete!) units — the *images* — when it is a matter of composing a film, suddenly accept with reasonably good grace the constraint of a few large syntagmatic structures. While no image ever entirely resembles another image, the great majority of narrative films

---

closest to the furthest shot. Codification intervenes at the metalinguistic level (studio jargon) in this case, and not on that of the language object (that is, cinematographic language).

resemble each other in their principal syntagmatic figures. *Filmic narrativity*—since it has again crossed our path—by becoming stable through convention and repetition over innumerable films, has gradually shaped itself into forms that are more or less fixed, but certainly not immutable. These forms represent a synchronic "state" (that of the present cinema), but if they were to change, it could only be through a complete positive evolution, liable to be challenged—like those that, in spoken languages, produce dia-chronic transformations in the distribution of aspects and tenses. Applying de Saussure's thought to the cinema, one could say that the large syntagmatic category of the narrative film *can change*, but that no single person can make it change over night.* A failure of intellection among the viewers would be the automatic sanction-ing of a purely individual innovation, which the system would re-fuse to confirm. The originality of creative artists consists, here as elsewhere, in tricking the code, or at least in *using* it ingeniously, rather than in attacking it directly or in violating it—and still less in ignoring it.

AN EXAMPLE: THE ALTERNATING SYNTAGMA

It is not within the scope of this paper to analyze the principal types of *large* filmic *syntagma*. Instead, as an example, I will simply indicate some of the characteristics of one type, the *alternating syntagma* (for example, image of a mother-image of her daughter-image of the mother, etc.). The alternating syntagma rests on the principle of alternating distribution of two or more diegetic ele-ments. The images thus fall into two or more *series*, each one of which, if shown continuously, would constitute a normal sequence. The alternating syntagma is, precisely, a rejection of the grouping by continuous series (which remains potential), for reasons of connotation—the search for a certain "construction" or a certain "effect." This type of syntagma apparently made its first appear-ance in 1901 in England, in a film by Williamson, *Attack on a Mission in China*, one of those "re-enacted news reels" that were popular at the time. In it, one saw images of a mission surrounded by Boxers (during the rebellion of that name) alternating with shots of marines coming to the rescue.* Subsequently the procedure becomes more or less usual.

The alternation defines the form of the signifier, but not neces-

---

* But then, I should have added, by the same token, that this syntagmatic category contains a paradigmatic category, and consequently I should have shown less skepti-cism as to the possibilities of a paradigmatic category in the cinema.

* "Alternation" means simultaneity here. It pertains therefore to the alternate *syntagma*, as I am about to define that term.

sarily, as we shall see, that of the significate—which amounts to saying that the relationship between the signifier and the significate is not always analogous in the alternating syntagma. If one takes the nature of the *significate of temporal denotation* as a relevant basis, one can distinguish three cases of alternating syntagma. In the first case (which might be called the *alternator*), the alternation of the signifiers refers to a parallel alternation of the significates (analogous relationship). Example: two tennis players framed alternately, at the moment each one is returning the ball. In the second case (which would be the *alternate syntagma*), the alternating of the signifiers corresponds to a simultaneity of the significates. Example: the pursuers and the pursued. Every spectator understands that he is seeing two chronological series which are contemporaneous at each instant, and that, while he is seeing the pursued galloping away (locus of the signifier, on the screen), the pursuers are nonetheless continuing the chase (locus of the signifier, in the diegesis). Thus the semiotic *nexus*—alternating simultaneity—is no longer analogous. But it does not become "arbitrary" because of that: It remains motivated (remember that analogy is one of the forms of motivation), and the understanding of this kind of syntagma by the viewer is relatively "natural." The motivation must be explained by the spontaneous psychological mechanisms of filmic perception. Anne Souriau has shown that sequences of the "pursued-pursuing" variety are readily understood, with little previous exposure, by the spectator (on the condition, only, that the rhythm of the alternation not be too slow), for he "interpolates spontaneously" the visual material that the film presents. He guesses that series 1 continues to unfold in the plot while he is seeing series 2 in the image. The third case could be called *parallel syntagma*. Two series of events are mixed together through montage without having any relevant temporal relationships on the level of the significate (diegesis), at least with respect to denotation. It is this variety of syntagma that film theoreticians sometimes refer to with expressions like "neutral temporal relationships." Example: a sinister urban landscape at night, alternating with a sunny pastoral view. There is nothing to indicate whether the two scenes are simultaneous or not (and if not, which precedes and which follows). It is simply a matter of two motifs brought together for "symbolic" reasons by montage (the rich and the poor, life and death, reaction and revolution, etc.) and without their literal location in time as a pertinent factor. It is as if the denoted temporal relationship had yielded to the rich, multiple values of connotation, which depend on the context as well as on the substance of the significate.

The three varieties of alternating syntagma constitute a small system whose internal configuration recalls somewhat the structure of verbal grammatical persons as conceived by Émile Benveniste.

A first correlation (presence or absence of relevant temporal denotation) allows us to distribute parallel montage to one side (absence), and alternate and alternator montage to the other (presence). Within the second term, another correlation (nature of the
significate of temporal denotation) distinguishes between the alternate (significate equals simultaneity) and the alternator (significate
equals alternation).*

OTHER PROBLEMS

These very brief remarks provided an example of what the syntagmatic study of filmic denotation could be. There are important
differences between the semiotics of the cinema and linguistics itself. Without repeating those mentioned elsewhere, let me recall
some of the main points: Film contains nothing corresponding to
the purely distinctive units of the second articulation; all of its
units—even the simplest, like the dissolve and the wipe—are directly significant (and moreover, as I have already pointed out,
they only occur in the actualized state). The commutations and
other manipulations by which the semiotics of the cinema proceeds
therefore affect the large significatory units. The "laws" of cinematographic language call for *statements* within a narrative, and
not monemes within a statement, or still less phonemes within a
moneme.

Contrary to what many of the theoreticians of the silent film

---

*I have retained this passage because it gives a simple example of what commuta-
tion can be in the filmic corpus, but the factual conclusions presented here no longer
correspond to the current state of my investigations of the considered point. First
of all, the study of various passages of films has made it appear that the "alternator"
cannot always be distinguished from the "alternate" syntagma (or, in rarer cases,
from the parallel syntagma) by any really probing difference: In the example of the
tennis players, it can also be considered that the two partners are both supposed to
be engaged in action continuously and simultaneously (i.e., alternate syntagma).
Thus—and although certain cases seem to subsist where the alternate syntagma
appears, more clearly than in other cases, as a *variant* similar to what I have called
here the "alternator"—I have not retained the alternator as a separate type or sub-
type. Then, there are cases where the alternating of images on the screen corresponds
to temporal relationships not mentioned in this article: For example, one finds "alternating syntagmas" that interweave a "present" series with a "past" series (a kind of
alternating flashback), and in which consequently the relationship of the two series
can be defined neither by simultaneity nor by the term "neutral temporal relationship." One will note also that the concept of "alternating syntagma" has a certain
obscure correspondence to that of the "frequentative syntagma." . . . In the final
analysis, however, the reason I have dropped the "alternator" *as a general category
of classification* is less because of the drawbacks I have just pointed out (and which
various adjustments could suppress) than because of an over-all *reformulation* of
the table of the main types of filmic arrangement. Taken separately, the analysis
developed above remains partially valid.

declared or suggested ("*Ciné langue*," "visual Esperanto," etc.), the cinema is certainly not a language system *(langue)*. It can, however, be considered as a *languuge*, to the extent that it orders signifying elements within ordered arrangements different from those of spoken idioms—and to the extent that these elements are not traced on the perceptual configurations of reality itself (which does not tell stories). Filmic manipulation transforms what might have been a mere visual transfer of reality into discourse. Derived from a kind of signification that is purely analogous and continuous —animated photography, cinematography—the cinema gradually shaped, in the course of its diachronic maturation, some elements of a proper semiotics, which remain scattered and fragmentary within the open field of simple visual duplication.*

The "shot"—an already complex unit, which must be studied— remains an indispensable reference for the time being, in somewhat the same way that the "word" was during a period of linguistic research. It might be somewhat adventurous to compare the shot to the *taxeme*, in Louis Hjelmslev's sense, but one can consider that it constitutes the largest *minimum segment* (the expression is borrowed from André Martinet), since at least one shot is required to make a film, or part of a film—in the same way, a linguistic statement must be made up of at least one phoneme. To isolate several shots from a sequence is still, perhaps, to analyze the sequence; to remove several frames from a shot is to destroy the shot. If the shot is not the smallest unit of filmic *signification* (for a single shot may convey several informational elements), it is at least the smallest unit of the filmic chain.*

One cannot conclude, however, that every minimum filmic segment is a shot. Besides shots, there are other minimum segments, *optical devices* various dissolves, wipes, and so on—that can be defined as visual but not photographic elements. Whereas images have the objects of reality as referents, optical procedures, which do not represent anything, have images as referents (those contiguous in the syntagma). The relationship of these procedures to the actual shooting of the film is somewhat like that of morphemes to lexemes; depending on the context, they have two main functions: as "trick" devices (in this instance, they are sorts of semiological exponents influencing contiguous images), or as "punctu-

---

*But I should have added here that the significations that analogy and mechanical duplication yield—although they do not pertain to *cinematographic* language as a specific system—nevertheless do have the effect of bringing structures and elements that belong to *other* systems which are also cultural, which also carry meaning and which are also more or less organized, into the cinema (as a whole).

*Similarly, the phoneme is not the minimum distinctive unit, since the latter is the "feature," but it is the minimum element of the spoken *sequence*, the threshold below which an order of consecutiveness yields to an order of simultaneity.

ation." The expression "filmic punctuation," which use has ratified, must not make us forget that optical procedures separate large, complex statements and thus correspond to the articulations of the literary narrative (with its pages and paragraphs, for example), whereas actual punctuation—that is to say, typographical punctuation—separates sentences (period, exclamation mark, question mark, semicolon), and clauses (comma, semicolon, dash), possibly even "verbal bases," with or without characteristics (apostrophe, or dash, between two "words," and so on).

IN CONCLUSION

The concepts of linguistics can be applied to the semiotics of the cinema only with the greatest caution. On the other hand, the methods of linguistics—commutation, analytical breakdown, strict distinction between the significate and the signifier, between substance and form, between the relevant and the irrelevant, etc.—provide the semiotics of the cinema with a constant and precious aid in establishing units that, though they are still very approximate, are liable over time (and, one hopes, through the work of many scholars) to become progressively refined. . . .

1968

ALFRED GUZZETTI
CHRISTIAN METZ
AND THE SEMIOLOGY
OF THE CINEMA

The three books[1] and numerous articles that Christian Metz
has written since 1964 give him fair claim to be considered the
most important film theorist since André Bazin. To Bazin's
question *What is Cinema?* he has replied cinema is a language
Though he is not the first to give this answer, he is the first to
inform it with a sophisticated understanding of modern
linguistics. Using models drawn from this discipline, his work
attempts to confer on film theory the virtues of system
atization, objectivity, and precision.

Metz is, to use his own term, a semiologist, and, as such,
groups natural language with signifying systems as diverse as
those of myth, dress, food, cinema, kinship, politeness, painting, poetry, and cartography. These systems are taken not
simply to serve a function analogous to natural language but to
be open to the sort of analysis developed in its study. For
these reasons, linguistics plays a double role in semiology. As
the source of method, it is the parent discipline; and as the
study of a single signifying system, it is a branch of the more
general, though still embryonic, science.

Since neither semiology nor the school of linguistics on
which it is based is very well known in the United States, I

---

[1]These are *Essais sur la Signification au Cinéma* (Paris, 1968), *Langage et
Cinéma* (Paris, 1971), and *Propositions Methodologiques pour l'analyse du Film*
(Universitatsverlag Boehum, Germany, 1970), the last of which I have not been
able to locate. My translations of quotations from the first two of these books
(abbreviated as *Essais* and *Langage*) are incorporated in the text of this essay.

shall try to give a brief outline of its premises and the place of Metz's work with relation to them. Semiology derives its linguistic framework from Ferdinand de Saussure, who furnished the indispensable distinction between the general term *langage* (e.g., French, English, Russian, etc.) and *langue*, the system within a *langage* that comprises such elements as the phonetic, syntactic, and semantic sub-systems, which together permit the intelligibility and multiplicity of utterances. For the term *langue*, which refers specifically to natural language, Metz substitutes the less prejudicial word "code," which is defined in opposition to the complementary term "message." The code is composed of signifying elements and the message of signified elements, called respectively *signifiers* and *signifieds*. A code, to merit the name, must be instanced in more than one *texte*, a word that I shall leave in French in order to indicate its pertinence to any division of any discourse, whether a poem, a painting, or all the films of Jerry Lewis. A *texte* may embody a single code, many codes, or no code at all. In any case, the respective messages will be the counterparts of the codes and not coextensive with the *texte*. Although code and message are complementary terms, their signifiers and signified may not be isomorphic. Metz illustrates this point by citing Gilbert Ryle's observation that the division of the verbal signifier "Fido" into its four constituent phonemes does not entail a corresponding division of the signified, which is, of course, a mental response to the signifier, not the real animal. By contrast, in the case of the cinematic image, a signifier which shows a dog will, if divided, effect a corresponding division of the signified; that is, it will signify a portion of a dog. Thus the relation of signifier to signified, and of code to message is a complex matter informed by problems specific to particular *textes* and languages.

Finally, there is the distinction between *syntagm* and *paradigm*. Following Roland Barthes's suggestion in *Elements of Semiology*, this may be envisioned as a pair of Cartesian coordinates in which the syntagm is the horizontal dimension and the paradigm the vertical. The syntagm is the dimension, whether temporal as in the case of music or a-temporal as in painting, along which the message unfolds, and the paradigm is the system of alternatives that comprise the code. The paradigm portrays the code as a system in which a given signifier takes its meaning through opposition to others which are possible but absent in a given place on the syntagm. Semiologists prefer to organize these oppositions in binary or bifurcating structures.

Metz's use of this general theory is characterized by his

resistance to a literal interpretation of the analogy between natural and cinematic language. From the outset he has denied that there is anything in cinema resembling a *langue*. However, he also denies that the intelligibility of the cinema can be entirely explained through its iconicity, that is, the resemblance of the sound and image to the perceived world. Cinema is a discourse and as such must depend on codes. Metz has tried to show that these codes are irreducibly multiple and that no one of them occupies a central or definitive place. Yet they can be, at least initially, divided into those which are found only in films and those which are also found elsewhere. The first group he calls cinematic ("cinématographique") and the second filmic ("filmique"). Among the second group there is a sort of hierarchy, since there exist codes that cinema shares with its double, television, and others with the novel, and still others which it embodies uniquely. Metz denies, however, that this hierarchy suffices to give any of the codes a place like that of the *langue* in natural language.

This position has consequences both for the semiologic study of the cinema and for non-semiologic efforts at theory and criticism. In the first case, it puts a decisive end to fruitless attempts to identify the *langue* of cinema, to isolate its minimal units, and to enumerate the cinematic equivalents of the phoneme, morpheme, sentence, and grammar. In the second, it shows the futility of trying to base normative definitions of the cinema on arguments about the nature of the medium. Metz is firm in his insistence that the medium, or in his terms the *matière de l'expression*, is manifest only through the codes it will support and permit, and that it is only in terms of these codes that cinema as a signifying system can be defined. Since no one or group of these occupies a controlling position, the semiologic study of the cinema will not authorize a normative position, thus superseding "theories" like Eisenstein's and Bazin's, which are at best criticism in disguise.

More now needs to be said about the seminal concepts *code* and *système*. The code is defined in relation to the message: "The code is that which is not the message" (*Langage* . . . , p. 65). The opposition *code/message* is parallel to *système/texte*: "The word 'système' for us has no sense other than that given by its opposition to 'texte' " (*Langage* . . . , p. 65). The *système* is the code-like configuration, the formal principle of a *texte*. Every code is a *système* and every message a *texte*, but not the reverse, since a *système* is a singular instance bound to a given *texte* while the code occurs in more than one *texte*. Both *système* and code are abstract entities: "A code (in theory) is defined exclusively as a relationship of logic, as pure form" (*Langage* . . . , p. 165). The "relationship of logic" obtains between the elements of the paradigm, the signifiers. The *système* has a similar definition: "What defines the *systématique* (that is, the non-textual) is its character as an ideal object constructed by analysis; the *système* has no material existence, it is nothing more than a logic, a principle of coherence; it is the intelligibility of the *texte:* what one must suppose in order that the *texte* be comprehensible" (*Langage* . . . , p. 57).

Using this vocabulary, Metz distinguishes the work of the semiologist from that of both film-maker and viewer. The semiologist's task begins where the film-maker's finishes; it does not lead toward the film, but away from it, toward its *systèmes*. This movement parallels that of the viewer but differs in one respect: while the viewer wishes to understand the film, the semiologist wishes to know in addition how the film is understood ("en outre comprehendre comment le film est compris"). His reading is a "méta-lecture" as opposed to the "lecture 'naïve' (en fait: à la lecture *culturelle*)" of the viewer.

In the passages quoted, Metz's own text supports two distinct readings. In the first, *système* is the name given to the fact of intelligibility in the *texte*. It is the process of comprehension ("comment le film est compris") and is pictured as the interaction of reader and *texte* within the culture that they share. The semiologist makes a naive—that is, cultural—reading and a simultaneous *méta-lecture*; he is the reader who, as he comprehends, enunciates the process of comprehension. This enunciation is the *système* or, in the case of multiple *textes*, the code. Both terms refer not to the *texte*, which can be isolated from its cultural context, but to the *lecture*, which cannot. The *méta-lecture* does not displace but rather subsumes the *lecture*. Therefore, the analysis remains *culturelle*, and the propositions of the semiologist are linked on some level to psychology, sociology, or political theory, as Chomsky's linguistics is to psychology.

In the second reading, the *système* is a fact logically (though not chronologically) prior to the intelligibility and comprehension of the *texte*. It is not implied by the *texte* but constructed ("construit") by the analyst in opposition to the *texte*. To accomplish this, the semiologist must first pass through and discard a cultural *lecture* in order to achieve an analytical *méta-lecture*, the *système*. Thus the *système*, and the code along with it, liberated from its cultural circumstances, becomes an "objet idéal."

Despite hints of the first interpretation, it is the second that prevails in *Langage et Cinéma*. Whatever the validity of this

position, it has several inescapable consequences for the cen
tral concepts code and *système*. First, it weakens the meaning
of "intelligibilité," "lecture," and comprehension by locating
these processes exclusively within the *texte*. Though the *lecture*
is required and presupposed, only the *méta-lecture* is expressed, or even reflected, at the level of the achieved theory.
This isolation of *méta-lecture* from *lecture* requires an opposition that Metz willingly accepts of "analytique" to "culturelle." The analytic statement, the *système* or code, can therefore be tested only against the *texte*, within which the
processes of the *lecture* have, somehow, been subsumed. In
addressing the *texte*, the semiologist can dismiss as "cultural"
the problems of how its messages were encoded and how they
are to be decoded. The process of signification thus becomes a
synchronic textual fact whose author is superfluous, his work
finished, and whose "reader" is demoted to the role of witness.

The abstract, difficult concept of a code that emerges from
this analysis can perhaps be better understood through two
examples. The first, drawn from the *Essais sur la Signification au
Cinéma* (pp. 121–146 and 105–107), is Metz's most ambitious
attempt to describe a particular cinematic code. According to
his scheme, the image in fiction film can be sorted into eight
categories, or syntagms.[2] One of these, the *montage alterné* or
alternating syntagm, is sufficient here to suggest the character
and structure of the code as a whole. It is defined at the level
of the signifier by two types of shots, called, in *Langage et
Cinéma*, A and B. The alternating of the signifiers A and B
yields at least three signifieds with respect to temporal denotation. It may indicate that the two signifieds are continuous in
time (e.g., alternating views of the two tennis players in a
game of singles), or simultaneous (alternating views of fugi-
tives and their pursuers in a chase), or a-temporal (the alternating shots of the situation comedy and singing auditions in
Milos Forman's *Taking Off*). The syntagm "A^1-B^1-A^2-B^2-A^1-B^1-
etc." is made possible by the sorting of the shots into two
classes according to a criterion like "pursuer versus pursued,"
that is, by a paradigmatic relation "*A/B*." This relation obtains
not between shots or types of shots but between two classes
defined by their mutual opposition. Its basis is logic, not the
texte of a given sequence.

The second example, described in *Langage et Cinéma* (pp.
149–150), is based on Bazin's essay "La meilleure femme ne

[2] The eight syntagms are described in "Film and Language, Film and Literature," JML 11 (September 1971), 154–160.

vaut pas un bon cheval." Bazin describes the well-known pattern in Westerns in which the figures of woman and horse are
charged with symbolic meanings (domesticity versus freedom,
for example) and presented to the hero for choice. This configuration, according to Metz, is a genuine code since it is common to numerous texts and depends not simply on the presence of a woman and a horse in the story but on the condition
of their co-presence, which qualifies the opposition wom-
an/horse as a paradigm. The modest code thus formed, unlike
that of the eight syntagmatic categories, is extra-cinematic, or
filmic, because it occurs in novels and songs as well as films.

It is true by definition that a code is common to multiple
textes, but the claim that those *textes* may belong to different
"languages"—one a song and another a film—requires some
discussion, particularly concerning the concepts of the message and the signified. It should be recalled that the message is
not the global meaning of the *texte*, but the set of meanings
produced by a single code. A *texte* may be the locus of more
than one code (for example, as Metz points out, the sentence
"Voudriez-vous tenir ceci, s'il vous plaît?" ["would you hold
this please?"] displays, among others, a code of phonemes and
a code of politeness) and hence of more than one message. In
this respect the message, like the code, is a function of the
point of view of the analysis.

I admit to some confusion on the question of exactly where
or what the signified and message are. In the case of the alternating syntagm one of the possible signifieds is "simultaneity." But it is not, evidently, the word I have written on
the page nor what was projected on the screen to provoke it—
since these can only be signifiers. It is rather the *idea* of simultaneity within what Metz calls the *diegesis*, that is, the fictional world of the film. Metz assures us that one cannot speak
of the *diegesis* or its constituent signifieds directly or in isolation from their signifiers. In other words, the message and its
signifieds belong neither to the *texte* nor in the head of its
reader, but to the explanatory abstraction of the *lecture*.

Since the signified can be approached only through its signifiers, which are, in turn, bound to a particular signifying
system, how can it be said that two or more languages may
embody one and the same code? This problem is approached
through a complex argument entitled "Interférences Sémio-
logiques entre Langages" (*Langage* . . . , p. 160ff). Its premise
is that a code, and hence a message, is by definition a logical
relation without physical existence. However, this premise has
a limiting condition: namely, that codes always occur in a *matière de l'expression*, a physical material, which affects and re-

stricts their possible configuration. Thus it is impossible for a code with temporal signifiers (though not temporal signifieds) to exist in a *matière* like painted canvas which does not extend through time. This limiting condition is outlined by three paradigm cases. The first, relatively inconsequential for semiology, concerns the borrowing by one language of a fragment of a code belonging to another. Metz's example is Faulkner's use in prose fiction of a narrative technique resembling *montage alterné*, which is, as explained earlier, a fragment of the code of the image in narrative cinema. The second, and most important case is the manifestation of one and the same code in two languages (or arts). Metz's example is the code of chiaroscuro, light and dark, in painting and color photography. These languages, like any two, necessarily differ with respect to their sensory base, or *matière de l'expression*. The critical point—and the one that distinguishes this category from the third—is "that the differences between the two *matières* concern traits not pertinent to the code in question" (*Langage*, p. 163). The third category fails to meet this condition and hence is a weaker version of the second; it concerns two languages (or arts) whose differences of *matière* will not permit the manifestation of the same code, but only of similar, or "isomorphic," codes. For example, the code of light versus dark may be shown directly in a painting, but in a novel its signifiers must be translated into words, which render the code in a similar, though by no means identical, form.

Can the condition of the second category be met in reality? I have difficulty considering this in the context of Metz's example, since I do not know precisely what the code of chiaroscuro is, unless it is the opposition between light and dark. It seems true enough that such an opposition is possible equally in a color photograph and a painting. Yet the two languages cannot have the same signifiers, since analine dye is not the same as oil paint, nor therefore the same signifieds. Metz's contention, I think, would be either that the differences between these *matières* would not truly change the signifiers (any more than speaking French with an American accent does) or that the opposition of signifiers, which is *logique relationnelle*, remains identical *despite* changes in the signifiers. This identity, however, is postulated, rather than proved; hence the argument is circular. As logic, codes may be exempted from the material conditions which embody them, but is it true that one may perform analogous surgery on the *matière de l'expression*, taking from it only the traits relevant to the codes? Standing before a particular painting and a particular color photograph, is it possible to regard the two systems of light-dark opposition apart from their material context? This may be conceivable as a mental operation, but is this operation other than a thesis whose meaning consists in a continuing relation and return to the *matière*? In the absence of this relation, how is the code capable of signifying? If the code is severed by definition from the *matière*, this does indeed authorize the erection of the second category, but does it not at the same time annul its power as an analytic tool?

Perhaps a more central question is why Metz needs such a category in the first place. His position in the *Essais* is that cinema is a *langage* without a *langue*, and his argument throughout is keyed to this denial. Apart from a few hesitant hypotheses, the work is unremittingly critical and distrustful of any wide-reaching claims for the role of codes in cinema. Cinematic imagery is "a rich message with a poor code, a rich *texte* with a poor *système*" (*Essais*, p. 74). Or "Goodbye, paradigm! Its poverty is the counterpart of a richness distributed elsewhere: the film-maker, different in this respect from the speaker of a language, can express himself by showing us directly the variety of the world; in this way the paradigm is quickly overwhelmed" (*Essais*, p. 75).

Langage et Cinéma gives these denials the positive terms of a theory by pursuing to its conclusion the definition of cinematic language as an "ensemble" of codes. To do this, the three categories of "interférence" are by themselves insufficient, since they only serve to indicate the further problem of describing the limiting conditions imposed by the *matière de l'expression*. Metz's response is to classify the languages bordering on cinema—still photography, painting, the photoroman, comic strip, radio and television—according to such traits of *matière* as iconicity, temporality, and provenance of the image. The resulting taxonomy, in conjunction with the crucial second category of "interférence," suggests a method of defining the relations between languages in terms of their shared codes. In this way, it is possible to identify the set of codes common to, say, cinema and the photo-roman and distinguish it from the set common to cinema and still photography. This network of inter-relations replaces the dichotomy "specific/non-specific," which is the descriptive basis for such normative statements as "Cinema is the art of movement." The analysis also implies that the "ensemble" of codes comprising a given language is not simply an inventory, but has a structure that may, Metz suggests, itself be code-like. Thus, one could complete the definition of cinematic language by writing the "formule codique de sa spécificité"—a prospect that both resolves and reflects the skepticism of the *Essais* concerning the explanatory power of codes regarded individually. However, *Langage et Cinéma* stops short of attempting such a definition since Metz's position is sufficiently established simply by indicating the possibility.

Is this theory truly without norms? To approach this question, I want to sketch an alternative explanation of the syntagm of the film image and compare Metz's to it. In my account, the telecast image of a football game may stand as a paradigm case. In order to understand what he sees, the viewer must know that the syntagm on his TV screen alternates among the views of a small, fixed number of cameras. It is—with apologies to Chomsky—a surface-structure whose deep structure may be visualized as the configuration of monitors in the control room, each of which displays the view of a single camera. It is unnecessary for the viewer to have the slightest knowledge of the circumstances of production in order to understand either this structure or the rules that link it with what appears on his screen at home—just as the native speaker of a language is said to know its deep structures even if he cannot describe them. The proof that this understanding is at work is that when the program deviates from the rules that transform the deep structure into the surface structure, this must be signalled; for instance, an instant replay must be identified either with superimposed titles, spoken comment, or the clear presence of slow motion, so as not to be confused with the live transmission; otherwise, the telecast lapses into unintelligibility.

The film-image is a more complex, but similar case. Again, the structure has two layers: one which appears on the screen, and its deeper counterpart, which may be represented by the unedited footage. Here too it may be said that the viewer understands the deeper structure even if he knows nothing about the production of motion pictures. If he did not infer it while watching films, he would, like certain early audiences, be confused and disoriented by every disjuncture of time and space, even when they are masked by the continuity of action within the *diegesis*. To understand the deep structure means, in part, to know that the syntagm is not a transmission, but an assemblage of pieces filmed discontinuously in time and space. This knowledge is reflected in the word "cut," which signifies not simply a change like the switch between television cameras, but a joint. To object that the deep structure is here a superfluous concept because the viewer only "knows" the portions of it that reach the surface is to miss the point; the viewer's ability to comprehend consists of his knowledge of the rules that connect the two. The *lecture*, therefore, in certain respects parallels the composition of the film, rather than occurring after it, as in Metz's model.

To take the simplest example, consider a dialogue scene in which bits of two camera-shots, or takes, *A* and *B*, alternate. Undoubtedly the viewer infers, as Metz maintains, on the basis of continuity in the dialogue that the alternating image signifies continuity in time. However, neither this observation nor its implied oppositions between temporal continuity and simultaneity and between alternating and linear syntagms accounts for the structure of alternation. It explains, so to speak, how the structure is absent, but not how it is present. One must add that the viewer also understands the provenance of the alternating shots, the model of which is the unedited takes *A* and *B*. If this were not so, dialogue scenes articulated by jump-cuts, like those in *Breathless*, would be, at least for the original audience, not simply novel or shocking, but unintelligible, or—what comes to the same thing—they would require a new category in the taxonomy of the image-syntagm. In fact, they are intelligible because their relation to the deep structure is intelligible. The role of this deep structure in the specific case of the alternating syntagm is demonstrated clearly by the "dialogue" scene in *Persona* in which the camera-takes *A* and *B*, which show in one-shot Liv Ullmann and Bibi Andersson respectively, are not intercut and do not alternate, but run in their entirety one after the other: *A*, then *B*. This repetition in the *diegesis* does not, however, impair the intelligibility of the sequence. Rather, its effect is to point to and illuminate the deep structure in a way that is not only locally intelligible, but indicative of the director's concern elsewhere in this work with the processes of cinema and representation.

Metz is also aware that exceptions test the rule, and in the *Essais* (pp. 213–215) he cites an image-sequence from *Pierrot le Fou* which does not fit any of his eight categories; it is the sequence, consisting of many short shots, in which the protagonists, Jean-Paul Belmondo and Anna Karina, flee Paris. For Metz, the problem is two-fold: first, the shots are out of chronological order, though the glimpses of the action that they permit allows the viewer to reconstruct the likely chronology, and second, they show some bits of the action more than once and in slightly differing versions. Metz takes the sequence to be an instance of the diachronic processes of history at work, altering and adding to one of the codes of cinema. His response as a semiologist is to give the excerpt the provisional name of a "potential" syntagm, since it allows neither a definitive nor chronological version of the action.

Whatever the paraphrasable meaning of its structure, the sequence is intelligible. As in the much simpler scene from *Persona*, the viewer is referred to the deep structure of the shots, which is, as always, open to an organization that contradicts the chronology of the diegesis. Godard goes further than Bergman, however, when he includes corresponding bits from different camera-takes in which the action happens to differ slightly. Though few viewers would describe this process as I have, in terms of shooting and cutting, everyone would, I think, recognize the director's gesture toward the deep structure and would understand that our normally unconscious knowledge of it is here being invoked. Presumably Godard makes such a gesture because at this moment he sees no alternative but to ask us to participate in his work of examining the world by means of the cinema, not because he is unsure how things happened and can give only a "potential" account. For after all, nothing "happened"; the story is made up, and its author would seem intolerably pretentious if he demanded that we forget this fact in the midst of a sequence that so clearly shows his hand.

The differences between my account of this sequence and Metz's suggest, among other things, the extent to which his thinking is bound to the narrative film. In all of his writing, I could not cite a single example from another source. In the *Essais* (pp. 96ff.) he defends the historical basis of this commitment. His recognition of the relevance of this diachronic question is remarkable in light of his usual contention that his is an exclusively synchronic discipline. His attitude elsewhere toward writing history is the same as toward the creation of individual *textes:* the semiologist begins his work where the film-maker, and likewise the film-historian, finish theirs. He minimizes the importance of the movements at which the work of production, history, and semiology must touch a common point; he maintains, for example, that the semiologist's choice of a *texte* for study may be influenced by the problems currently seen as urgent within his discipline, but is in itself as indifferent as the linguist's decision to study a particular dialect; and, as I have tried to show, his notion of significance neither incorporates nor permits reference to the composition of the *texte*.

The version of film history given in the *Essais* stresses the centrality of "la rencontre du cinéma et de la narrativité," the meeting of cinema and narrative. It holds that in the beginning film was purely iconic—that is, it signified exclusively by means of the resemblance between its imagery and the visible world—and that its association with narrative resulted in the gradual invention and superimposition of various codes over its iconic mechanisms. The repertory of codes pertaining to the image was complete by the time of D. W. Griffith, and those of image and sound formulated during the thirties, stabilizing in the style Bazin called "découpage classique." In this view, the Soviet school of the twenties, despite the magnificence of its production, is a cul-de-sac. Metz is clearly hostile (though respectful) both to Eisenstein's attempt to give montage the status of a "langue" (though, of course, Eisenstein would not use the term) and to his reading of film history, which groups Griffith with the Soviets as the dominant school. In short, Metz's history is like Bazin's, except that he does not acknowledge Bazin's characterization of the two warring tendencies in film history. Nor does he concede that the reliance of his synchronic theory on this version of history in any way compromises its claim of objectivity.

What is at stake here is not simply the importance of narrative film but the controlling place of narrative within film theory. The contrast between Metz's account of the articulation of the image and the alternative that I sketched should make this clear. The basis of his analytical method is to refer the structure of the image to the narrative. In cases where the practice of the cinema itself challenges the explanatory power of the narrative, as does the sequence from *Pierrot le Fou*, his response is to avoid the problem by inventing a new narrative category. The history of film as he rehearses it conveniently minimizes examples of this kind and at the same time authorizes his methods of dealing with them. Supported by this version of history, his synchronic theory affirms a notion of signification in which the spectator, in order to understand the structure of the image, refers not to the real world where films are financed, shot, cut, printed, sold, projected and criticized, but to the fantasy world that the films present—what is clinically called the "diegesis."

At first glance, this tendency is less clear in the vastly more abstract text of *Langage et Cinéma*. There (pp. 142–143) Metz denies that the syntagmatic categories of the image in narrative film merit the status of a *langue*, or even an especially important code, of the cinema. The denial harmonizes with the book's argument that the codes of cinema form an "ensemble," to which the notions of hierarchy, centrality, or specificity are simply not applicable. On the surface, this seems a neutral, a-historical, and objective definition. Yet on examination it turns out, I believe, to be only the position of the *Essais* slightly modified and projected into more abstract terms.

To support this contention, let me reopen the discussion of

the crucial second category of "interférence," the instance of one code in two languages, by adducing an example from the *Essais*. Though in context the example relates to some notions of Pasolini's that seem remote from "interférence," it presents issues that are, I think, easier to grasp than those of the light-dark code in paintings and color photographs:

> Certainly, the total comprehension of any film would be impossible if we did not carry within us this vague but quite real dictionary of "im-segni" of which Pasolini speaks, if we did not know—to take only one example—that Jean Claude Brialy's car in *Les Cousins* is a sports-car, with everything that this signifies in twentieth-century France, the diegetic period of the film. But we would know all the same, because we would see it, that it is a car, and this would be sufficient for the comprehension of the *denoted* meaning of the passage. One may not object that an Eskimo with no prior contact with industrial civilization would not even recognize it as a car! For what that Eskimo would need is acculturation, not translation . . . (*Essais*, pp. 209–210)

To analyze this example in terms of Metz's scheme of "interférence," we may note that the sports-car belongs both to a "language" of consumer items in twentieth-century France, like those described by Roland Barthes in *Mythologies*, and to the filmic language of *Les Cousins*. The *matières de l'expression* of these two languages, in the first case the visual, three-dimensional presence of the real objects and in the second their two-dimensional image on film, do not differ in the traits relevant to the code in question. For example, the paradigm sports-car/sedan, in which the sports-car signifies luxury, is possible equally in twentieth-century France and in a film. Like most of the visual codes of culture, the one that includes this paradigm can be rendered in the iconic terms of the cinematic image, and thus is an instance of the second category of "interférence": the manifestation of one and the same code in two languages.

The argument that establishes this instance also—and more importantly—opposes the notion that Metz calls "cinématographisation." His analysis of "interférence" implies that a code like the one of our example does not become "cinematic" by virtue of its mere presence in a film; it is an instance of the second category, not the third. The sports-car in *Les Cousins* not only has the significance it would also have in twentieth-century France—at least in part—but obtains this significance by the same means: "Thus is it necessary to insist on the fact that filmic code is not necessarily cinematic, since a code (in theory) is defined exclusively as a relationship of logic, as pure form, and is therefore not tied to a particular *matière de l'ex-*

pression, for example, the cinema's" (*Langage* . . . , p. 165).

Although it is a subtle and difficult matter to say how looking at a painting differs from looking at a color photograph, everyone can tell the difference between a sports-car and a picture of one. Metz does not deny this difference. Rather, he passes over it in silence, speaking only about the place the object occupies in a discourse. This silence is the counterpart of his contention elsewhere that one can sever the code from its *matière* and hence that none of its meaning consists in, or arises from, its situation in the *matière*. Here the difficulties begin. For—to return to the example—when we are before the actual automobile, the paradigm sports-car/sedan and the code which subsumes it can hardly be said to inhere exclusively in "logique relationnelle," but belongs at least partly to the concrete relation between the object and us. We are in the world where we may not address the object except as, say, an owner, customer, envier, producer or viewer—all relations in which the code, admittedly abstract, is at work. None of these relationships can enter unaltered into a film, where there is no longer the possibility of—to keep to the example—an economic relation between us and the object, but only the quite different opportunity to project this relationship onto, or extract it from, the world that is represented.

Yet filming is not simply the loss of a certain sort of relationship. The object filmed, it is true, is in one sense reduced to a phantom. But at the same time it becomes another sort of object—a picture. The code that describes our relation to an actual automobile has a proper analogy only in our relation to the commodity we call a movie, not to what is signified by the movie. Going to the movies and buying a sports-car can even be said to form a paradigm, since they have, as an opposition, the power to signify, and there exist situations in which such a choice may be read as a discourse. I do not mean to insist on the economic basis of this analysis (it is only an illustration chosen to suit Metz's example), but rather on the centrality in signification of the relation between the viewer and the *matière*, from which the code as a signifying mechanism is not detachable. Consequently, all codes, even those of natural language, are "cinematographized" when they pass into films; hence Metz's second category is without true examples.

This argument does not deny the points of similarity between, say, a film and a song that share the theme "The best woman isn't worth a good horse." Rather, it refuses such similarities the status of language, as that term is understood by Metz. This disagreement is reproduced and elaborated in Metz's critique of Pasolini's semiotics, from which the discussion of *Les Cousins* is taken. Pasolini maintains that cinematic language has two articulations, the second more or less equivalent to Metz's specific codes, and the first a rather ill-defined and partly to be-invented lexicon of "im-segni" (image-signs), which have meanings within culture and therefore comprise a kind of language prior to the intervention of the film-maker. Metz argues that this first articulation is not only questionable but superfluous, since it can be adequately replaced by the concept of iconic analogy; he insists on "the *perceptual* and *cultural* status of these 'im segni,' opposing it to the language-like character of the codes that are properly cinematic" (*Essais* . . . , p. 210n).

I do not wish to associate myself with Pasolini's position, least of all with the problematical concept of the "im-segno." But I do sympathize with Pasolini's motive, which is, I think, less to introduce economies into the semiologic study of cinema than to place its most fundamental premise, and hence the discipline itself, within a perceptual, cultural, and ultimately political context. Metz is not only unpersuaded of the necessity of this step, but sees an antithesis between the terms "cultural and perceptual" on the one hand and "language" on the other.

In thus opposing the signifying process to its cultural and perceptual setting, Metz exposes the basic of his conception of the cinema. Though his approach to particular questions is always distinguished by the sophisticated application of linguistic methodology, the effect of these methods is to attribute to the cinema a sort of transparency, to imagine it as a glass distinct from culture but through which culture is visible. Cinema emerges in his portrait as an instrument that is as indifferent to ideology and value as he supposes natural language to be, as a system whose workings are logical rather than material and whose history is the immaterial accretion of these processes in the realm of pure logic and pure form. It is a conception that, despite the linguistic vocabulary in which it is stated, recalls Bazin. For Bazin bequeathed to Metz not simply the question *What is Cinema?* but an answer of his own, namely that cinema is an image and substitute for reality, whose history is the gradual aesthetic and technological perfection of the power of illusion. He discards its normative arguments, fills in its silences on the structure of cinematic discourse, and banishes its aesthetic of illusionism if not from the description of particular codes, then at least from the higher, more abstract levels of the theory. Yet, despite all this, he preserves and elaborates Bazin's assumption that the cinema is something one looks through but not at and studies in

192 FILM IMAGE AND FILM LANGUAGE

isolation from the circumstances where it is made and seen.

This shared assumption indicates what is truly at issue in Metz's distinction of his work from that of other theorists and critics. For example, Eisenstein's concept of *montage*, which Metz patronizingly calls, "montage-roi," is, unlike any of the seminal concepts of Metz's theory, rooted in the material world of culture and perception. It locates the process of signification in the interaction of spectator and screen. The relation of frame to frame, of image to image, and of the parts of an image to each other is not merely a fact of the *texte*, but a relation which the film-maker creates and which produces ideas, emotions, and comprehension only by acting on, and being re-enacted by, the viewer. In a comparable way, Pasolini, whose conception is in other respects close to Metz's own, maintains that from the outset the discourse of cinema is entangled in its cultural origins, from which not even the image, for all its iconicity, can be entirely extricated.

Faced with such profound and consequential disagreements, no reader can ignore either the need for judgment or the search for criteria on which a judgment may be based. Despite the subordinate place habitually given to the discussion of particular films and parts of films in Metz's writing, and despite his repeated denial that such discussions are either urgent or germane to his work as a semiologist, I would argue that it is not only inevitable but fair that they should stand as a measure of his theory. Must one not ask what light is shed on the sequence from *Pierrot le Fou* by giving it the name of "potential" or by testing it against the eight supposed syntagmatic categories one at a time? Are we told any more about *The Outlaw* by calling its theme of woman-versus-horse a code? Or can any plausible rationale be conceived for preferring the long analysis of *Intolerance* in *Langage et Cinéma* (pp. 81ff.) to Eisenstein's supposedly unscientific and normative discussion of the same work in "Dickens, Griffith, and the Film Today"? Can one deny that Metz's detailed description of Griffith's parallel montage is simply *less* than Eisenstein's effort to relate it to the film's ideology, than to submit that ideology to a critique based on a reading of history? Whatever the talent of these two men as critics, and whatever one's attitude toward what they value, is there any possible conclusion but that Metz's ideas produce what is by comparison to Eisenstein a diminution and abortion?

But Eisenstein is not to be taken as the measure of Metz's writing. The point is rather that Metz's effort to excise from cinema the process of signification and, in the name of language, to set it in a realm of abstract logical relations is in the end both meaningless and futile. The analogy between natural and cinematic language is not perfect enough in itself to authorize or sustain such an effort. Cinema as a signifying system lacks, as Metz concedes, both arbitrariness in Saussure's sense and the paired systems that permit both distinctive and significative articulation. Moreover, it is, unlike natural language, the outcome of industrial production—a fact with inescapable consequences for its means of signification. When the world, whether coded or not, passes into the sounds and images of cinema, it is not merely reduced to the configurations of an abstract system, but transformed into a concrete object of another kind. The difference between these sounds and images and the objects and codes that they reflect, though it has no stable meaning, nonetheless always and of necessity enters into the process of signification. It is not within the power of the film-maker's intentions, or of their reflection in the film's style, to dissolve this difference. Even if it were, we as spectators are not simply prisoners of those intentions, but are free and co-present in the world where the images and sounds exist as objects. The conditions of this world, its social, economic, and political structure, impose on us, spectators, critics, theorists, and film-makers alike, the obligation to analyze, interpret, and criticize the cinema as it reflects and embodies these conditions. In this light, Metz's retreat to the realm of logic and abstraction that he calls "language" can be seen as not simply anti-normative, but, despite its methodological precision, anti-critical and anti-analytical as well.

1973

UMBERTO ECO
ON THE CONTRIBUTION
OF FILM TO SEMIOTICS

Many discussions of the semiotics of film (as well as the semiotics of music or of painting) are confused because they try to answer two different questions. First question: "To what extent can semiotics help one to understand film?" Second question: "To what extent can filmic experience help one better understand semiotic problems?" Frequently such confusion has been increased by another ambiguity. Is one studying the elementary mechanisms of film as a medium of communication or rather the complex mechanisms of a movie as a work of art?

I shall want to make just a few statements about the contribution of filmic experience to a semiotic enquiry and about the semiotic nature of film images. It goes without saying that I believe that any film student could rely on those remarks in order to insert them into the framework of his own specific methodology, but I refuse the responsibility of proposing to someone a new key for the understanding of the artistic problems of film. Let me only surreptitiously add that I do not believe it is possible to understand the social relevance and the aesthetic functioning of a movie without focusing on it from a semiotic point of view. But, according to a popular Italiian joke, "qui l'ho detto e qui lo nego," in this precise moment I say this and in this precise moment I deny having said it.

Nobody here has denied the existence of such a phenomenon as cinema, and nobody has denied that good movies exist. But Professor Harman says that he is not sure that a science of signs exists and that, if this science has to be identified with Peirce's trichotomies, this "can be fun, for a while, but it does not constitute a science." Since I believe that there does exist a discipline studying the various types of signs, that many of the things said by Peirce constitute a science, and that those things are not fun at all, let me try to outline some basic requirements of a general approach and to illustrate them by some examples referring to the filmic experience. Naturally I cannot propose a satisfactory semiotic theory within present limitations. Therefore I ask you to consider my statements as a tentative summary of a more elaborated approach. By accident it happens that this approach is outlined in my book *A Theory of Semiotics.* Since there are of course other semiotic theories, I suggest that the organizers of the symposium on Film and the University devote the next one to Semiotics and the University. There has recently been a Charles Sanders Peirce Symposium in Baltimore. By the way, some one hundred years ago, someone in Baltimore considered Peirce neither scientific nor fun, and they fired him. Fortunately people in Baltimore have changed their minds and I hope the same thing will happen in New York.

According to Peirce, a sign is something which stands for something (else) to somebody in some respect or capacity. This definition has some consequences:

1. We have a sign when a material occurrence stands for something else to us. Since a word, a medical symptom, and a movie image are material occurrences sending us back to something else, all those phenomena are signs.

2. In order for an occurrence to be a sign, it is not necessary that the occurrence be intentionally produced by a human agent. According to Morris "something is a sign only because it is interpreted as a sign of something else by some interpreter. . . . Semiotics, then, is not concerned with the study of a particular kind of object, but with ordinary objects insofar (and only insofar) as they participate in semiosis." It is true that the word "smoke" and smoke are not the same kind of entity (and in fact the word sends us back to smoke while smoke sends us back to fire) and it is true that the way the word stands for smoke is not the way smoke stands for fire: but a science has to choose its own level of pertinence. Physical differences between the word "smoke" and smoke are pertinent to a phonologist and to a fireman; from the semiotic point of view one is obliged to realize that they have at least one feature in common: a physical occurrence sends us back to

something which is not present. Any further difference should be isolated on the basis of this identity. To ignore a deep functional identity because of superficial evidence of differences displays a poor scientific attitude. Therefore, between a drawing (intentionally produced by a human being) and an imprint (unintentionally left by an animal agent) there is no semiotic difference as far as a human receiver connects both of them with an absent entity.

3. Signs stand for something else in some respect or capacity. "In some respect" means that they are not a mere duplicate of the thing they stand for; "in some capacity" means that signs represent something else because of some correlated features that must be thoroughly described. Let me say for the moment that signs are correlated with what they stand for on the basis of a rule or a convention. [I shall demonstrate that even the so called natural, iconic, analogic signs, like movie images (supposedly possessing some of the properties of the things they represent) are ruled by conventions.] A conventional relationship is not necessarily an arbitrary one. A sign can be motivated by something else and nevertheless be conventionally correlated with it.

4. The notion of "sign" is an oversimplification. Let me substitute for it, following Hjelmslev, the notion of sign-function. A sign-function is the correlation, posited by a rule of equivalence, between an expression (that is a material occurrence) and its content.

5. A repertoire or a system of sign-functions is a code.

6. Since a sign-function is a posited correlation, its functives (expression and content) are independent of each other. This means that the same expression, on the basis of another rule, can be correlated with a different content. A gold star on the epaulet of a soldier means "lieutenant," while on a striped flag it means "state of the Union." It could be the same star, graphically realized in the same way, at the interior of a frame, twice inserted in two different contexts (image of the soldier and image of the flag).

This shows that a particular iconological system of correlation (or code) establishes, among its rules, some contextual principles of the type "when inserted in the context x it means. . . ."

7. A sign function becomes possible when both its functives are produced by a system of variously articulated pertinent elements. There are various ways of articulating expressions and the way followed by verbal languages is only one of them. The articulation of content is the one provided by the cultural system of a given society and in principle it does not vary

through the possible substitutions of the expression system. In other words, our culture makes available the entity "star" defined as a shining heavenly body and opposed to other bodies such as the planets: this available element of the content system can be expressed either by the words /star/, /étoile/, or /stella/ or by the conventional drawing resulting from different arrangements of intersecting triangles (naturally other types of expression are available).

Different expression systems can have one, two, or more articulations. As we shall see later, so called iconic signs do not have the same kind of articulation as verbal languages.

8. Sign-functions are used in order to mention things or states of the world (in other words we take signs to refer to objects or other entities); but the referential use of a sign-function does not constitute the sign-function as such. This means that the content of an expression is not the referent of the sign. Signs can refer to their possible referent just because they are expressions sending us back to a content. The content of expressions can be analyzed and described by means of a semantic compositional analysis independent of the corresponding referent and also of the correlated expression. Only in this way is it possible to justify theoretically the double phenomenon of signs referring to nonexistent entities and of the use of languages in order to lie. The possibility of signifying nonexistent objects (and therefore of lying) is not only connected with the existence of highly conventionalized and arbitrary sign-functions, as happens with verbal language: drawings, photographs, and cinematographic icons can also signify nonexistent entities, so they cannot be referential indices. As for filmic expressions, through montage two persons can be shown as if they were meeting each other even though this event has never happened. Through various modes of trucage images can be alternated so as to display nonexistent or aberrant shapes; ghosts can appear between real men; a fictitious character can appear to be pointing towards a precise person existing in our physical world while the signified content belongs only to a "possible" world; etc. (One could object that there is at least one instance in which the movie image not only sends back to, but also points directly to, and is motivated by, the real presence of a physical entity: that the image is a sort of imprint of the human body of the actor. I shall discuss the complexities involved here later, when speaking of the semiotic nature of imprints.)

9. When speaking of the coded correlation between an expression and a content we are not obliged to think of a unit-to-unit correlation. In verbal language units of second articula-

tion, phonemes, are combined in order to form units of first articulation, morphemes; these morphemes are usually correlated to cultural units, i.e., to units of content which can in their turn be analyzed into minor semantic units (a "star" is a unit of content that can be analyzed as a "body," as "celestial," as "shining" or "burning," as "rotating," and so on). However, the minor units of the corresponding morpheme, the phonemes, do not refer back to the minor units of the cultural units of sememe—in other words, the elementary components of the word /star/ do not represent the elementary components of the sememe "star." Thus language does not represent a code in which the correlation is posited unit to unit: one could rather speak of a cluster-to-cluster correlation. Morse code represents a case of correlation string to unit (a series of dots and dashes is referred to a precise alphabetic unit not otherwise decomposable). On the contrary, on a watch every movement of the main hand corresponds to a step of the apparent movement of the sun around the earth (or vice versa). Notice that even in this case the movement of the hand does not directly refer back to the real movement of the real celestial body but rather to the way in which our culture has rendered it evident and pertinent: the organization of the expression sends us back to an organization of the content and only in this way can it be used as something pointing towards a real state of the world. (The problem of how the organization of the content has been motivated by the real state of the world is at this stage an extra-semiotic one.) In any case, one should admit that the code of the measurement of time is different from the one of verbal language. We can say that in the former the features of the expression are in some way determined or motivated by the features of the content, while in the latter they are not. Nevertheless, a watch could exist and function even if our astronomic system were by chance totally different. This cannot be said of the sundial: here not only the movements of the shadow reproduce (or are made pertinent in the same way as) the movements of the sun, but the movement of the sun directly causes the movement of the shadow. In this sense one can say that the shadow is an index of the sun. I would like, however, to stress the fact that even in this case there is a sign-function correlating an expression to a content, and the proof is that I can lie with a sundial, producing the shadow by means of an artificial light source. (I can undoubtedly do it in a movie but in principle I can also do it in everyday life, provided that the one I want to cheat is sufficiently naive.) The conclusion of the preceding tentative typology of different sign-functions shows in any case that it is impossible to apply the laws of verbal language to every system of sign-function. The rules of semiotics are not necessarily the same as the rules of linguistics.

10. An expression is correlated to a first content which is denoted by it. I mean by denotation (in a nonreferential framework) the immediate posited correlation between an expression and a given content. I mean by connotation any other content that finds a vehicle only in a preceding sign-function, i.e., that can be expressed through the mediation of a previous content. Consider the word /murderer/: it denotes a man who has killed, or who is killing, another man; by means of this denotation it also connotes a "bad" man or a man doing something against the law. The connotation is associated with the previous denotation by another convention or a subcode. To a secret service planning the assassination of a foreign leader, the word /murderer/ still denotes a man who is killing another man but does not necessarily connote "bad guy." Secret services have connotative codes different from ours. Suppose now that a movie, let us say *War and Peace* shows a small fat man, but does not necessarily show his face; the image denotes "man." But if this man wears a particular coat and a particular hat, and if he is polishing his ears with his little finger, we detect the connotation "Napoleon Bonaparte." A certain iconographic subcode establishes the right connotation. Suppose now that we see another man who, from a window, tries to shoot Napoleon with a gun; denotatively speaking the image tells us no more than that. Nevertheless, a previous verbal denotation has told us that this possible murderer is a Russian nobleman called Pierre Besuchov. Through other indications in the context we know that Pierre connotes some psychological and sociological values (for instance the enlightened liberal aristocracy). Through the contextual pressure, by means of inferences and presuppositions which have not been previously coded, we can arrive at an interpretation of the gesture of Pierre as the manifestation of a wish for justice. We are therefore tempted to dissociate from the denotation of murdering the usual connotation of "bad guy" and to add to the gesture (and to the person who performs it) other and more complex connotations. These connotations are not culturally coded. They represent a sort of semiotic initiative taken by the addressee of such a complex message. The addressee tries to institute a new subcode. This subcode lasts "l'espace d'un matin," the message itself represses, so to speak, the initiative of the addressee, since it tells him that Pierre gives up. But when a different text introduces and reinforces a new connotation (for instance, when in "Citizen Kane" the word—and the

sled— /rosebud/ succeeds in connoting the memory of child-hood and maternal tenderness) this connotation can last beyond the text that has imposed it and gain acceptance by a cultural milieu as an established metaphor or an emblem.

Please note that in the preceding example I have cited a case in which:

a) the filmic image has no referential index (in any case the real world in which Napoleon has lived is not the possible world in which Pierre lives) and what has been denoted by the message is not a real state of the world (a referent) but pure content;

b) what is connoted has no less consistency (from the re-ferential point of view) than what has been denoted: simply, connotations need previous denotations in order to be grasped;

c) something is directly denoted by the images, something else acquires its denotative consistency through the support of other signs, words, or noises;

d) something is denoted not only by a simple image or a frame but also by a continuous chain of events.

Sometimes signs, that from the iconic point of view are highly imprecise, acquire their denotative power through the impact of the narrative context and of other denotations.

In Antonioni's *Blow Up*, for example, a photographer, after having taken numerous photos in a park, returns to his studio where he succeeds, by means of successive enlargements, in identifying a human form stretched out behind a tree: a man killed by a hand armed with a revolver which, in another sec-tion of the enlargement, appears in the middle of the foliage of a hedge.

But this narrative element (which, in the film—and in the critical commentaries about it—assumes the weight of a recall-ing to reality, and to the total and implacable stare of the pho-tographic lens) only functions if the iconic code interacts with a code of narrative functions. In fact, if the enlargement were shown to someone unfamiliar with its context in the film, it would be very difficult for him to recognize the distorted and granular areas which supposedly denote "a stretched out human form" and "a hand with revolver." The signified "corpse" and "hand with revolver" are only attributed to the signifying form on the basis of the narrative context of the film which, by building the suspense, prepares the spectator (and the protagonist in the film) *to see those things*. The context functions as an ideolect, assigning given values within the code to signals which might otherwise appear as mere noise.

Another example taken from an Antonioni movie can clarify

the difference between denotative and connotative conventions. You probably know that Antonioni's *China-Chung Kuo*, a movie the artist directed in a genuinely sympathetic mood, has been interpreted by Chinese critics as an unbearably denigratory pamphlet directed against the Chinese people. Now if one analyzes frame by frame and sequence by sequence all the cases in which Chinese critics and authorities charge Antonioni with unfriendly attitudes, one realizes that they are all cases in which Chinese addressees have superimposed different connotative subcodes on the ones foreseen by the author. Among the sequences which have most offended Chinese audiences is one in which the camera shows the Nanking Bridge. The Chinese say that Antonioni has tried to give the impression that the bridge is unstable and on the verge of collapsing. If you look at the movie you can see that the director has shown the bridge, by passing underneath it moving the camera in a circular manner, from a sort of "expressionistic" point of view. This has the effect of privileging oblique angles, transverse perspectives, and asymmetric frames, as any western movie-maker does when he wants to suggest power and architectural impact. But present Chinese iconographic subcodes are obviously different, as anybody can see when looking at a Chinese movie like *The Girl of the Red Guards Detachment*, or a propaganda mural painting: Chinese iconography is based on symmetrical and frontal frames with a sort of neoclassical mood and they express power, stability, monumentality only by frontal and symmetric shots. The denotation was the same (it was for the Nanking Bridge) but the connotations were based on different subcodes.

11. I have so far outlined some basic definitions of a semiotic discipline and I have given some examples taken from cinematographic practice. But a possible unanswered objection is the following: there is no homology between the definition of sign-function as applied to the arbitrary correlation between a word and its content and as applied to the motivated or iconic correlation between an image and the corresponding object. Cinema can make people believe that a given person is Napoleon or that Pierre Besuchov has the same kind of referentiality as Napoleon, but in order to do so it has nevertheless to start from physically existing bodies of which it "reflects" some properties at the same time acting as an index, since the traces on the screen demonstrate that there was something which has motivated them. Is this relationship a coded one? And if it is can one speak of "code" both in the case of a word and of an icon without resorting to a mere metaphorical transference?

Since a discipline can control many objects provided it can

describe them using the same categories, if the categories of code and sign-function show a lack of univocity, then semiotics is not entitled to speak of such diverse phenomena.

We have said that the proper object of semiotics is the relationship of standing for or of sending-back-to, and it is evident that the cinematographic image of a train stands for a train just as the word /train/ stands for the same content-unit, or sememe. But one could observe that the way in which a word stands for the sememe is not the same as the way in which an image does. What I have to demonstrate (or at least to suggest) is that those different ways of standing for can be methodologically defined by resorting to the same precise set of theoretical tools. The Peircian trichotomy of symbol, index, and icon describes very well the fact that there are different modes of sending-back-to, but it fails in its attempt to unify those three modes. At most, Peirce shows, *et pour cause*, that in every sign phenomenon those three modes interact and that there is never a pure iconic or a pure indexical sign, but that every concrete occurrence of an act of signification relies on all these three modes. But in doing so he stops at the observation that every sign is composed of three mutually incompatible semiotic features. And he does not answer the objection that iconic and indexical signs are in fact uncoded signs (therefore escaping our definition of sign-function) which obey natural rather than cultural laws.

If one undertakes a careful analysis of the notion of iconism and indexicality one can easily see that these are umbrella-notions covering a disparate range of different semiotic phenomena. (I have undertaken this task in two of my books and the critical revision of the notion of iconism is presently being pursued in many semiotic circles. I am obliged to spare you such a complicated argument. Let me only suggest a possible line of solution.) I think that the entire problem becomes clearer if, instead of listing types of signs, one lists the different modalities in which a sign-function is established, that is, the different ways in which one can manipulate a given material continuum in order to produce expressions and to correlate them to a given content. In *A Theory of Semiotics* I have therefore proposed a typology of modes of sign-production according to four parameters, namely a) the material continuum used, b) the complexity of its articulation, c) the arbitrary or the motivated relationship between the form of the expression and the form of the content and, d) the kind of physical labor performed in order to generate the expression. Let me consider for the moment only the last two parameters. From the point of view of physical labor an expression can be produced starting from the minimal physical effort and proceeding to the maximum one: thus we can list *recognition, ostension, combination,* and *invention.*

In *recognition*, on the basis of a cultural convention, I use a natural event (or a mechanical result) as the expression of a given content: instances of this type of labor are imprints, medical symptoms, and clues. In *ostension* I can use an existing object, isolating it and showing it as the representative of the class to which it belongs: I can show a cigarette or its image as the *example* of all existing cigarettes: I can show a handful of tobacco as a *sample* of the entire product of a tobacco factory; and I can reproduce the gesture of a man smoking a cigarette as the *fictive sample* sending us back either to "cigarette" or to "smoking" (according to some previous indications or contextual clues). In *combination* I can reproduce ready-made types of expression in order to compose them in major strings (as it happens with the pre-established expression proposed by any structured verbal language). In all those three cases (recognition, ostension, and combination) the expressions can be chosen or produced according to a preestablished type and are correlated to a content which is already known. The fourth case is the one of *inventions:* one has to invent a sign-function when the broken expression has to be elaborated along with its type since a given culture has not provided a workable model; and it has not been produced because the content to be expressed has not yet been defined. Thus the sign producer has at the same time to propose a new expression, a new content, and a new way of correlating both. Cases of invention are not cases of performance of a given code but rather cases of invention of a new code.

I shift on many minor distinctions and subcategories, but I would like to stress the fact that these modes of sign production do not correspond to different types of signs. Rather, in every sign-function two or more of these productive modes are at work.

Let me now consider a typical instance of imprint, the trace left on the ground by the hoof of a horse. Apparently the imprint, insofar as it has been physically motivated by the passage of the horse, is an index of its passage and an icon of its horseshoe.

One has now to answer the following questions: how can such a hoof be falsified so as to lie? Why is it recognizable even if reproduced on a reduced scale? Why is the horseshoe recognizable although the hoof reproduces, among its properties, only its outline and although the imprint is larger than the horseshoe? The answer is that imprints also send us back to a cultural content; they are produced by individual agents but stand for a cultural notion ("horse," or "hoof," or "a horse has passed here going in that direction"). When the expression is falsely produced by means of a vicarious imprinter and has no real indexical properties, the process of signification takes place equally; the so called similarity between the trace on the ground and the cultural notion of a hoof is recognized only on the basis of some rules of *similitude*. I am expressly using the geometrical term: similitude is not a vague resemblance, it is a system of geometrical transformation ruled by laws of proportionality and by a precise selection of features to be transformed or projected, while other features are completely disregarded. Therefore the correlation between expression and content is governed by some technical conventions. Moreover if one has no previous knowledge of the features characterizing a horseshoe one will never be able to project backward from the imprint to the imprinter.

To speak of rules of similitude and of projection devices means to recognize that the expression must realize or embody certain pertinent features by articulation of which a significant shape takes place. Articulations in imprints are not the same as in language: they are not combined in a temporal succession but in a spatial coexistence; they projectively reproduce the articulations of the content type to which they refer, so that the correlation is not only unit to unit, but point to point. But there are nevertheless features and articulations. Suppose I want to produce (perhaps in order to cheat someone) the imprint of a glass of wine upon a table. There are four and no more than four pertinent features: a circular form, the length of the radius, a cue of red, and the characteristic of being wet. Only by familiarity with previous imprints of this type can one detect from this one the past presence of a glass of wine. And only if one knows the transformation rule for passing from the size of the imprint to the supposed size of the glass, can the detection be correct. At the end of such a process what one has detected is not the referent (this or that glass of wine) but only the content "glass of wine." Only by a work of circumstantial inference (for instance, the presence of a given glass on another table) can one use this imprint to refer to that precise glass of wine.

We can undoubtedly consider an imprint as the functive of a sign-function where the correlation has been posited on the basis of some rules. Since a sign-function is the atomic element of a code, we can speak of a code of imprints, a code that for instance is more familiar to hunters and boy scouts than to philosophy professors. Despite their presumed iconism, I would be pretty embarrassed in distinguishing the paw of a dog from the paw of a wolf. Now, the difference between the way in which a word and a hoof are correlated to their content consists in their *type-token* ratio. As for the word, the expression type is independent of the content type; as for the hoof, both types realize the same features. I call those two different cases of type-token ratio, *ratio facilis*, and *ratio difficilis*. But in many cases this opposition is not so straight. A medical symptom is a case of recognition as well as an imprint, but while the imprint relies on a *ratio difficilis* the symptom relies on a *ratio facilis* (like a word): in fact, a symptom is motivated by the corresponding organic disease but has not the form of the disease it signifies. So we could isolate a sort of continuum of differences in the mode of correlation, but all these cases are definable in the terms I have proposed to define a standard sign-function.

Now, what kind of sign-function is realized by the graphic film image of a human being who stands for Napoleon? The reproduction of the form of a human body is an *imprint*. The imprint disregards a lot of the features of the real body (color, third dimension, texture of the skin, and so on) and retains only those which are considered pertinent for a recognizable transformation. As in geometrical similitude, size is not pertinent (we are able to recognize a man projected upon a cinerama screen without believing he is a giant). Understanding images must be learned. But let us consider the man himself, the actor acting in front of the camera. As such it is an *ostensive* sign, a prepared material for the shooting: he and all the surrounding objects stand for the class to which they belong. This man acts and makes gestures: these gestures are elements of a kinesic code and as such they are the significant result of the *combination* of preestablished units. The man moves left to right meeting another man: there are at work *"vectorial"* features (that can be classified half way between imprints and combinational units); by these features the expression sends us back to vectorial features of the content for which it serves as the vehicle. In the same way the verbal difference between /Mary gives something to John/ and /John gives something to Mary/ is given by another vectorial feature, the temporal or spatial succession (before-after, or left-right) embodied in the uttered or written phrase. Since the real purport of the movement of men is reinforced, usually, by words and other sounds, the global denotation of the sequence is supported by many modes of sign production and by many sign-functions. Perhaps at a certain point the actor expresses something by an unheard-of expression of the face or an uncoded gesture: we are witnessing in this case an instance of *invention*. But the acceptance of this new way of coding is undoubtedly supported by the contextual pressure of other already coded sign-functions.

I could continue in this kind of analysis, but a typology of modes of sign production is just at its beginning. I think that it can prove itself very useful in the definition of filmic signification. It could destroy the temptation to analyze movie images as if they were words, duly articulated in minor recognizable units. Someone has, in fact, naively tried to say that the image of a man is the equivalent of a verbal sentence, his eyes and his nose being the equivalent of words, and so on, desperately fishing for nosemes, mouthemes, beardemes, footemes, and so on.

A semiotic of film is possible if one accepts that semiotics is neither a province nor a byproduct of linguistics. But one should at the same time accept the hypothesis that movie images "say" something and, since not everybody understands them, there must be semiotic rules governing this kind of communication.

Once this is accepted, many other problems arise. A movie is a text. As such it is governed by textual rules. All the paraphernalia of a text grammar, presently elaborated mainly at a level of verbal communication, should be applied to the study of film. All the problems approached by the study of cultural interaction, the conversational rules studied by ethnomethodology and sociolinguistics, all interactional laws approached by proxemics and kinesics, should support the study of those visual texts called films. In the same sense the logic of narrative function and the logic of presuppositions should become indispensable tools for the right understanding of the narrative arrangement of a film.

One should indicate, at this stage, when something is understood by means of coded denotation; or by means of a complex inferential labor, which partially relies on coded narrative rules (therefore releasing presuppositions, anaphors, narrative syllogisms, and enthymemes); or when something becomes conventionally coded by force of the contextual pressure of the text itself. When Metz observes that in *M* a loose balloon caught in overhead wires symbolizes the death of the girl whom we earlier saw holding a balloon, I would analyze this in a way which partially differs from the one proposed by Gilbert Harman. The earlier photographic image of the girl holding the balloon *denotes* a girl holding a balloon; at this stage I would draw no distinction between "depicting" a girl and "standing for a girl": on the basis of some conventions the addressee understands that those traces upon the screen send us back to the content "a girl holding a balloon." Until the word "depicts" or some other expression like it has been scientifically analyzed, I prefer to rely on my own definition of the so called iconic relationship: a sign-function based on a visual transformation, a coded projection. When the balloon is seen in isolation, among wires, it is taken as a metonymy for the girl and the correlation girl-balloon is *posited* by the context, it is inferred by the addressee, and it is not necessarily inserted into a code: it represents the provisional and transitory positing of a sign-function, ready to dissolve as soon as the film has accomplished its communicative task. The image of the balloon is ready, so to speak, to become the functive of other sign-functions, and at the end of the movie it is restored to its immediate denotative function: a balloon is a balloon is a balloon is a balloon. It is a girl only for a moment and within a precise context.

The capture of the balloon by the wires may or may not stand for the capture of the girl. Probably the director wished the image to be understood in this way: it was a form of semiotic gambling. Since we are speaking of this interpretation, Fritz Lang has won. The relationship between capture and murder is another metonymy. It too is not coded: this means that outside the film wires do not represent murderers. But culturally speaking wires recall ropes, ropes capture, and so on. The film is playing a risky game between the coded and the uncoded. It supports daring suggestions by coded connotations. Culture acts as a glue to amalgamate the invention of unheard-of relationships. In all this nothing is really "natural." Semiotic laws are at work at every level. A movie is the meeting point of many semiotic phenomena. It carries preexisting codes and it is carried by its own specific codes. Sometimes it establishes new codes and often these new correlations produced by a given film will not be accepted by cinema. A semiotics of cinema and film is still to be completely outlined. But its laws lie outside cinema and film, they are the laws of signification in general.

But nobody can discover laws unless he is guided by the hypothesis that there are laws. It is very dangerous to refuse to recognize semiotic laws acting in cinematographic and filmic phenomena. In this way films are believed to be the spontaneous reproduction of reality, they are polluted by a sort of referential and indexical fallacy and it becomes impossible to detect the plots of culture under the supposed spontaneity of nature. Without a semiotic awareness films are viewed as magic spells. One believes that things make films. On the contrary, frequently, films make things. The semiotic approach is not only a criticism of the illusions of reality, it is also a continuous criticism of the ideological shaping of the reality on the part of the processes of semiosis.

1975

III

The Film Medium

Film theory and film criticism have been largely concerned with one central issue: What is "cinematic?" Which paths should the cinema follow? Which should it reject? Attempts to answer this question inevitably take their lead from Lessing's classic essay, *Laocoon*, in which the eighteenth century German dramatist and essayist attempted to demonstrate that the visual arts organize their materials spatially while the poetic arts organize their materials temporally. The materials, procedures, subjects, and effects of these two different forms (or "media") of artistic organization are therefore necessarily different. In this spirit, film theorists have attempted to discover the characteristics of the film medium, declaring those subjects, materials, procedures, and effects that "exploit" the characteristics of the medium proper, legitimate, and truly cinematic and those subjects, materials, procedures, and effects that "violate" the characteristics of the medium barren, misleading and fundamentally uncinematic.

The concept of a medium is, of course, a difficult one. Is the medium to be defined in purely physical terms (that is, the projection of images at twenty-four frames per second on a screen) or rather in terms of an artistic language (angle and distance of shots, rhythms and patterns of editing, and so forth)? Does it include the main structural features of the art (such as plot) and its main historical conventions (say, its genres)? And how are we to determine which possibilities of the medium are legitimate? Is it legitimate to pursue any possibility inherent in the medium, or only those for which the medium has a special affinity? And how are we to judge what those special affinities are? May two different artistic media share those affinities or must an art confine itself, as certain purists urge, to realizing only those possibilities that it shares with no other art?

Erwin Panofsky, the great art historian who was a contemporary of both Arnheim and Kracauer, has written the most influential discussion of the subject. He argues that an art ought to exploit the "unique and specific" possibilities of its medium; and in the film medium these can be defined as the "dynamization of space" and the "spatialization of time." Both these features are visual ones, and Panofsky's primarily visual conception of the film medium is vulnerable to the objection that it accords an undue priority to the silent film, placing unwise restrictions on the use of speech in films. According to Panofsky's principle of "co-expressibility," "the sound, articulate or not, cannot express any more than is expressed, at the same time, by visible movement." Panofsky claims that the Shavian dialogue in the film version of Shaw's *Pygmalion* falls flat and suggests that Olivier's monologues in *Henry V* are successful only to the extent that Olivier's face becomes "a huge field of action" in oblique "close-up." But those who admire the brilliant Hollywood "dialogue" comedies of the 30s and early 40s and who recall that Olivier does not deliver the "St. Crispin's Day" speech in *Henry V* in close-up will receive these views with a measure of skepticism. Indeed, Panofsky modified them in the revised version of his essay that appears in this anthology.

Siegfried Kracauer acknowledges the difficulty of defining the film medium but believes, nevertheless, that cinema has certain "inherent affinities." There are, in particular, certain subjects in the physical world that may be termed "cinematic" because they exert a peculiar attraction on the medium. Kracauer argues that cinema is predestined and even eager to exhibit them. Like Panofsky, Kracauer accepts the use of sound in films only under certain very restrictive conditions, and he especially dislikes the development of the "theatrical" film: "What even the most theatrical minded silent film could not incorporate—pointed controversies, Shavian witticisms, Hamlet's soliloquies—has been annexed to the screen." But Kracauer finds this annexation unfortunate; it in no way proves that such theatrical speeches are legitimate possibilities of the cinematic medium, for "popularity," in Kracauer's view, has no bearing on questions of aesthetic legitimacy.

Kracauer calls the comedies of Frank Capra and Preston Sturges border-line cases, but only on the ground that their witty dialogue is "complemented and compensated for" by "visuals of independent interest" (he means that they include slapstick sequences). Just as witty dialogue violates the visual requirements of the medium and requires "compensation," surrealistic projections of inner realities, expressionist dreams and visions, and experimental abstractions violate the realist requirements of the medium. On the other hand, certain types of movement—the chase and dancing—and certain types of objects—those that are normally too big or too small to be seen—are peculiarly appropriate subjects of cinema. But does the dance really have a greater affinity for the film than it does for the stage? Must the film avoid what is normally seen simply because it is the subject matter of other arts? One can agree with Kracauer that the close-up is a peculiarly cinematic technique, and even with the influential Hungarian theorist, scenarist, and filmmaker, Béla Balázs, that the close-up is responsible for the "discovery of the human face," without supposing that the film must devote itself exclusively to the exploitation of these "unique" potentialities.

Rudolph Arnheim shares Panofsky's and Kracauer's view that the film ought to stress the peculiar possibilities of the cinematic medium. But he feels obligated to refute the view that cinema is a mere mechanical reproduction of physical reality. If it were, it would not be an art. Arnheim therefore insists on the various discrepancies between the film image and the standard perception of physical reality. The film image suffers a reduction of depth, a distortion of perspective, an accentuation of perspective overlapping and, in the past, an absence of color and articulate speech. Arnheim asserts that the true task of cinema is to exploit these very "defects" and turn them to an advantage, just as painting exploits the fact that it is a two-dimensional, enclosed object. Perhaps a great art can be devised that confines itself to exploiting these defects (the silent film may have been such an art), but can we accept the suggestion that film must avoid exploiting the affinities with physical reality that Kracauer mentions, just because they conform to, rather than deviate from, reality? And should we regret the fact that we can remedy some of the "defects" of a medium rather than exploit them? Should we regret the development of sound, as all three of these theorists do?

Gerald Mast rejects the problem of defining the distinctively cinematic medium as any function of the method of recording moving images—photographic or otherwise. Instead, he regards the projection of images by light as the essential feature of any cinematic work. And the fact of projection permits him to distinguish the experience of cinema from that of theater, television, and painting. He also argues that a careful investigation of the characteristics of projected images undermines a number of commonly held opinions, among them the view that one must project photographic images—upon which Kracauer's theory (and that of all realist cinema theory) is founded, and the view that the projected image is two-dimensional and perceived as flat—claims upon which Arnheim's theory (and that of most puristic and modernistic cinema theory) is based.

Stanley Cavell, the American philosopher and aesthetician, also places great emphasis on the importance of projection and, more particularly, on the fact of projection onto a screen. The projected image is the image of a world, and of a world which, in contrast to the world of a painting, exists beyond the frame. Indeed, the only difference between the projected world and reality is that the projected world does not exist now. It is simultaneously absent and present. One function of the movie screen, then, is to screen that world from the audience. Another is to screen the audience from the projected world. Unlike the audience in a theater which is not present to the actors on stage by convention, the film medium renders the audience absent mechanically and automatically. By this enforced invisibility, movies give expression to our modern experience of privacy and anonymity. Man has longed for invisibility and the absence of responsibility it confers, and film satisfies precisely this wish. In watching a film we view a magically reproduced world while remaining invisible to it. This condition makes the experience of film essentially voyeuristic and even pornographic. It permits the audience a magical-sexual contact with the hypnotic Garbos, Dietrichs, and Gables of the screen.

However, unlike Panofsky and many other theorists, Cavell does not think that the aesthetic possibilities of the movie medium can be deduced from its physical or technical properties. A medium, in his unconventional construal, is simply something through which or by means of which something specific gets said or done in particular ways. In his view, only the art itself, and not a mere consideration of its physical medium, can discover its aesthetic possibilities.

Cavell argues that the issues of genre and of medium are inseparable, and that the classical Hollywood world was composed of three such media—stories or structures that revolve about the Military Man, the Dandy, and the Woman. The Military Man conquers evil for the sake of society (James Stewart in *The Man Who Shot Liberty Valance*, Gary Cooper in *Mr. Deeds Goes to Town*); the Dandy pursues his own interests, values, and self-respect (John Wayne in *Red River*, Cary Grant in anything); and the Woman attracts men as flames attract the moth (Garbo, Dietrich, Davis). With the loss of conviction in these genres, film reached (very belatedly in comparison to the other arts of the twentieth century) the condition of modernism, in which the self-conscious artist seeks to produce a new genre, a new medium, rather than simply producing more instances of a familiar one.

Francis Sparshott, a contemporary philosopher and aesthetician, challenges the assumptions to which the Lessing tradition has given rise. Sparshott regards many of the views expressed by Panofsky, Kracauer, and Arnheim as dogmas. "Whatever can be done with a medium is among its possibilities and hence 'true to' it in a sense that has yet to be shown to be illegitimate." Sparshott offers an account of the film medium which indicates both its great range and its special features—its unique way of representing space, time, and motion. This analysis provides the foundation for his conclusion: "Film is unique in its capacity for visual recording and analysis, in its ability to convey the unique present reality of things, in its ability to reveal the qualities of lives; but also in its formal freedom, its capacity for realizing fantasy and developing abstract forms." Sparshott's essay implies that a definition of the film medium ought not to be some simple assertion of dogma or a naked attempt to establish as law the dictates of individual taste or the surmises of personal experience.

David Antin, the poet and art critic, formulates his views about video art and its relation to television in the language of the Lessing tradition. But he argues that the distinctive features of the television medium reflect the realities of social and economic control, not the technical possibilities of the physical medium. The tempo of presentation, the style of performance, the visual syntax of editing all manifest the television industry's "money metric," which transforms a "quasi-recording medium" into one that conveys little sense of reality. It is the distinctive mark of video art to take television's representation of reality and, especially, its presentation of time as its own subject. For the segmentation and pace of television time has more to do with the commercial realities of the television industry than it does with the technical possibilities of representation by the cathode ray tube. In fact, the signficance of all types of video art derives from their attitude toward some characteristic of television itself, which in turn reflects both the state of our society and the power relations within it. In this way, video art embarks on a curiously mediated but serious critique of our culture.

ERWIN PANOFSKY
STYLE AND MEDIUM
IN THE MOTION PICTURES

Film art is the only art the development of which men now living have witnessed from the very beginnings; and this development is all the more interesting as it took place under conditions contrary to precedent. It was not an artistic urge that gave rise to the discovery and gradual perfection of a new technique; it was a technical invention that gave rise to the discovery and gradual perfection of a new art.

From this we understand two fundamental facts. First, that the primordial basis of the enjoyment of moving pictures was not an objective interest in a specific subject matter, much less an aesthetic interest in the formal presentation of subject matter, but the sheer delight in the fact that things seemed to move, no matter what things they were. Second, that films—first exhibited in "kinetoscopes," viz., cinematographic peep shows, but projectable to a screen since as early as 1894—are, originally, a product of genuine folk art (whereas, as a rule, folk art derives from what is known as "higher art"). At the very beginning of things we find the simple recording of movements: galloping horses, railroad trains, fire engines, sporting events, street scenes. And when it had come to the making of narrative films these were produced by photographers who were anything but "producers" or "directors," performed by people who were anything but actors, and enjoyed by people who would have been much offended had anyone called them "art lovers."

The casts of these archaic films were usually collected in a "café" where unemployed supers or ordinary citizens possessed of a suitable exterior were wont to assemble at a given hour. An enterprising photographer would walk in, hire four or five convenient characters and make the picture while carefully instructing them what to do: "Now, you pretend to hit this lady over the head"; and (to the lady): "And you pretend to fall down in a heap." Productions like these were shown, together with those purely factual recordings of "movement for movement's sake," in a few small and dingy cinemas mostly frequented by the "lower classes" and a sprinkling of youngsters in quest of adventure (about 1905, I happen to remember, there was only one obscure and faintly disreputable *kino* in the whole city of Berlin, bearing, for some unfathomable reason, the English name of "The Meeting Room"). Small wonder that the "better classes," when they slowly began to venture into these early picture theaters, did so, not by way of seeking normal and possibly serious entertainment, but with that characteristic sensation of self-conscious condescension with which we may plunge, in gay company, into the folkloristic depths of Coney Island or a European kermis; even a few years ago it was the regulation attitude of the socially or intellectually prominent that one could confess to enjoying such austerely educational films as *The Sex Life of the Starfish* or films with "beautiful scenery," but never to a serious liking for narratives.

Today there is no denying that narrative films are not only "art" —not often good art, to be sure, but this applies to other media as well—but also, besides architecture, cartooning and "commercial design," the only visual art entirely alive. The "movies" have reestablished that dynamic contact between art production and art consumption which, for reasons too complex to be considered here, is sorely attenuated, if not entirely interrupted, in many other fields of artistic endeavor. Whether we like it or not, it is the movies that mold, more than any other single force, the opinions, the taste, the language, the dress, the behavior, and even the physical appearance of a public comprising more than 60 per cent of the population of the earth. If all the serious lyrical poets, composers, painters and sculptors were forced by law to stop their activities, a rather small fraction of the general public would become aware of the fact and a still smaller fraction would seriously regret it. If the same thing were to happen with the movies the social consequences would be catastrophic.

In the beginning, then, there were the straight recordings of movement no matter what moved, viz., the prehistoric ancestors of our "documentaries"; and, soon after, the early narratives, viz., the prehistoric ancestors of our "feature films." The craving for a narrative element could be satisfied only by borrowing from older arts, and one should expect that the natural thing would have been to borrow from the theater, a theater play being apparently the *genus proximum* to a narrative film in that it consists of a narrative enacted by persons that move. But in reality the imitation of stage performances was a comparatively late and thoroughly frustrated development. What happened at the start was a very different thing. Instead of imitating a theatrical performance already endowed with a certain amount of motion, the earliest films added movement to works of art originally stationary, so that the dazzling technical invention might achieve a triumph of its own without intruding upon the sphere of higher culture. The living language, which is always right, has endorsed this sensible choice when it still speaks of a "moving picture" or, simply, a "picture," instead of accepting the pretentious and fundamentally erroneous "screen play."

The stationary works enlivened in the earliest movies were indeed pictures: bad nineteenth-century paintings and postcards (or waxworks à la Madame Tussaud's), supplemented by the comic strips—a most important root of cinematic art—and the subject matter of popular songs, pulp magazines and dime novels; and the films descending from this ancestry appealed directly and very intensely to a folk art mentality. They gratified—often simultaneously—first, a primitive sense of justice and decorum when virtue and industry were rewarded while vice and laziness were punished; second, plain sentimentality when "the thin trickle of a fictive love interest" took its course "through somewhat serpentine channels," or when Father, dear Father returned from the saloon to find his child dying of diphtheria; third, a primordial instinct for bloodshed and cruelty when Andreas Hofer faced the firing squad, or when (in a film of 1893–94) the head of Mary Queen of Scots actually came off; fourth, a taste for mild pornography (I remember with great pleasure a French film of ca. 1900 wherein a seemingly but not really well-rounded lady as well as a seemingly but not really slender one were shown changing to bathing suits—an honest, straightforward *porcheria* much less objectionable than the now extinct Betty Boop films and, I am sorry to say, some of the more recent Walt Disney productions); and, finally, that crude sense of humor, graphically described as "slapstick," which feeds upon the sadistic and the pornographic instinct, either singly or in combination.

Not until as late as ca. 1905 was a film adaptation of *Faust* ventured upon (cast still "unknown," characteristically enough), and not until 1911 did Sarah Bernhardt lend her prestige to an unbelievably funny film tragedy, *Queen Elizabeth of England*. These films represent the first conscious attempt at transplanting the movies from the folk art level to that of "real art"; but they also bear witness to the fact that this commendable goal could not be reached in so simple a manner. It was soon realized that the imitation of a theater performance with a set stage, fixed entries and exits, and distinctly literary ambitions is the one thing the film must avoid.

The legitimate paths of evolution were opened, not by running away from the folk art character of the primitive film but by developing it within the limits of its own possibilities. Those primordial archetypes of film productions on the folk art level—success or retribution, sentiment, sensation, pornography, and crude humor—could blossom forth into genuine history, tragedy and romance, crime and adventure, and comedy, as soon as it was realized that they could be transfigured—not by an artificial injection of literary values but by the exploitation of the unique and specific possibilities of the new medium. Significantly, the beginnings of this legitimate development antedate the attempts at endowing the film with higher values of a foreign order (the crucial period being the years from 1902 to *ca.* 1905), and the decisive steps were taken by people who were laymen or outsiders from the viewpoint of the serious stage.

These unique and specific possibilities can be defined as *dynamization of space* and, accordingly, *spatialization of time.* This statement is self-evident to the point of triviality but it belongs to that kind of truths which, just because of their triviality, are easily forgotten or neglected.

In a theater, space is static, that is, the space represented on the stage, as well as the spatial relation of the beholder to the spectacle, is unalterably fixed. The spectator cannot leave his seat, and the setting of the stage cannot change, during one act (except for such incidentals as rising moons or gathering clouds and such illegitimate reborrowings from the film as turning wings or gliding backdrops). But, in return for this restriction, the theater has the advantage that time, the medium of emotion and thought conveyable by speech, is free and independent of anything that may happen in visible space. Hamlet may deliver his famous monologue lying on a couch in the middle distance, doing nothing and only dimly discernible to the spectator and listener, and yet by his mere words enthrall him with a feeling of intensest emotional action.

With the movies the situation is reversed. Here, too, the spectator occupies a fixed seat, but only physically, not as the subject of an aesthetic experience. Aesthetically, he is in permanent motion as his eye identifies itself with the lens of the camera, which permanently shifts in distance and direction. And as movable as the spectator is, as movable is, for the same reason, the space presented to him. Not only bodies move in space, but space itself does, approaching, receding, turning, dissolving and recrystallizing as it appears through the controlled locomotion and focusing of the camera and through the cutting and editing of the various shots — not to mention such special effects as visions, transformations, disappearances, slow-motion and fast-motion shots, reversals and trick films. This opens up a world of possibilities of which the stage can never dream. Quite apart from such photographic tricks as the participation of disembodied spirits in the action of the *Topper* series, or the more effective wonders wrought by Roland Young in *The Man Who Could Work Miracles*, there is, on the purely factual level, an untold wealth of themes as inaccessible to the "legitimate" stage as a fog or a snowstorm is to the sculptor; all sorts of violent elemental phenomena and, conversely, events too microscopic to be visible under normal conditions (such as the life-saving injection with the serum flown in at the very last moment, or the fatal bite of the yellow-fever mosquito); full-scale battle scenes; all kinds of operations, not only in the surgical sense but also in the sense of any actual construction, destruction or experimentation, as in *Louis Pasteur* or *Madame Curie*; a really grand party, moving through many rooms of a mansion or a palace. Features like these, even the mere shifting of the scene from one place to another by means of a car perilously negotiating heavy traffic or a motorboat steered through a nocturnal harbor, will not only always retain their primitive cinematic appeal but also remain enormously effective as a means of stirring the emotions and creating suspense. In addition, the movies have the power, entirely denied to the theater, to convey psychological experiences by directly projecting their content to the screen, substituting, as it were, the eye of the beholder for the consciousness of the character (as when the imaginings and hallucinations of the drunkard in the otherwise overrated *Lost Weekend* appear as stark realities instead of being described by mere words). But any attempt to convey thought and feelings exclusively, or even primarily, by speech leaves us with a feeling of embarrassment, boredom, or both.

What I mean by thoughts and feelings "conveyed exclusively, or even primarily, by speech" is simply this: Contrary to naïve expectation, the invention of the sound track in 1928 has been unable to change the basic fact that a moving picture, even when it has learned to talk, remains a picture that moves and does not convert itself into a piece of writing that is enacted. Its substance remains a series of visual sequences held together by an uninterrupted flow of movement in space (except, of course, for such checks and pauses as have the same compositional value as a rest in music), and not a sustained study in human character and destiny transmitted by effective, let alone "beautiful," diction. I cannot remember a more misleading statement about the movies than Mr. Eric Russell Bentley's in the spring number of the *Kenyon Review*,

1945: "The potentialities of the talking screen differ from those of the silent screen in adding the dimension of dialogue—which could be poetry." I would suggest: "The potentialities of the talking screen differ from those of the silent screen in integrating visible movement with dialogue which, therefore, had better not be poetry."

All of us, if we are old enough to remember the period prior to 1928, recall the old-time pianist who, with his eyes glued on the screen, would accompany the events with music adapted to their mood and rhythm; and we also recall the weird and spectral feeling overtaking us when this pianist left his post for a few minutes and the film was allowed to run by itself, the darkness haunted by the monotonous rattle of the machinery. Even the silent film, then, was never mute. The visible spectacle always required, and received, an audible accompaniment which, from the very beginning, distinguished the film from simple pantomime and rather classed it — *mutatis mutandis*—with the ballet. The advent of the talkie meant not so much an "addition" as a transformation: the transformation of musical sound into articulate speech and, therefore, of quasi pantomime into an entirely new species of spectacle which differs from the ballet, and agrees with the stage play, in that its acoustic component consists of intelligible words, but differs from the stage play and agrees with the ballet in that this acoustic component is not detachable from the visual. In a film, that which we hear remains, for good or worse, inextricably fused with that which we see; the sound, articulate or not, cannot express any more than is expressed, at the same time, by visible movement; and in a good film it does not even attempt to do so. To put it briefly, the play— or, as it is very properly called, the "script"—of a moving picture is subject to what might be termed the *principle of coexpressibility*.

Empirical proof of this principle is furnished by the fact that, wherever the dialogical or monological element gains temporary prominence, there appears, with the inevitability of a natural law, the "close-up." What does the close-up achieve? In showing us, in magnification, either the face of the speaker or the face of the listeners or both in alternation, the camera transforms the human physiognomy into a huge field of action where—given the qualification of the performers—every subtle movement of the features, almost imperceptible from a natural distance, becomes an expressive event in visible space and thereby completely integrates itself with the expressive content of the spoken word; whereas, on the stage, the spoken word makes a stronger rather than a weaker impression if we are not permitted to count the hairs in Romeo's mustache.

This does not mean that the scenario is a negligible factor in the making of a moving picture. It only means that its artistic intention differs in kind from that of a stage play, and much more from that of a novel or a piece of poetry. As the success of a Gothic jamb figure depends not only upon its quality as a piece of sculpture but also, or even more so, upon its integrability with the architecture of the portal, so does the success of a movie script—not unlike that of an opera libretto—depend, not only upon its quality as a piece of literature but also, or even more so, upon its integrability with the events on the screen.

As a result—another empirical proof of the coexpressibility principle—good movie scripts are unlikely to make good reading and have seldom been published in book form; whereas, conversely, good stage plays have to be severely altered, cut, and, on the other hand, enriched by interpolations to make good movie scripts. In Shaw's Pygmalion, for instance, the actual process of Eliza's phonetic education and, still more important, her final triumph at the grand party, are wisely omitted; we see—or, rather, hear—some samples of her gradual linguistic improvement and finally encounter her, upon her return from the reception, victorious and splendidly arrayed but deeply hurt for want of recognition and sympathy. In the film adaptation, precisely these two scenes are not only supplied but also strongly emphasized; we witness the fascinating activities in the laboratory with its array of spinning disks and mirrors, organ pipes and dancing flames, and we participate in the ambassadorial party, with many moments of impending catastrophe and a little counterintrigue thrown in for suspense. Unquestionably these two scenes, entirely absent from the play, and indeed unachievable upon the stage, were the highlights of the film; whereas the Shavian dialogue, however severely cut, turned out to fall a little flat in certain moments. And wherever, as in so many other films, a poetic emotion, a musical outburst, or a literary conceit (even, I am grieved to say, some of the wisecracks of Groucho Marx) entirely lose contact with visible movement, they strike the sensitive spectator as, literally, out of place. It is certainly terrible when a soft-boiled he-man, after the suicide of his mistress, casts a twelve-foot glance upon her photograph and says something less-than-coexpressible to the effect that he will never forget her. But when he recites, instead, a piece of poetry as sublimely more-than-coexpressible as Romeo's monologue at the bier of Juliet, it is still worse. Reinhardt's *Midsummer Night's Dream* is probably the most unfortunate major film ever produced; and Olivier's *Henry V* owes its comparative success, apart from the all but providential adaptability of this particular play, to so many *tours de force* that it will, God willing, remain an exception rather than set a pattern. It combines "judicious pruning" with the interpolation of pageantry, nonverbal comedy and melodrama; it uses a device perhaps best designated as "oblique close-up"

(Mr. Olivier's beautiful face inwardly listening to but not pronouncing the great soliloquy); and, most notably, it shifts between
three levels of archaeological reality: a reconstruction of Elizabethan London, a reconstruction of the events of 1415 as laid down
in Shakespeare's play, and the reconstruction of a performance of
this play on Shakespeare's own stage. All this is perfectly legitimate;
but, even so, the highest praise of the film will always come from
those who, like the critic of the *New Yorker*, are not quite in sympathy with either the movies *au naturel* or Shakespeare *au naturel*.

As the writings of Conan Doyle potentially contain all modern
mystery stories (except for the tough specimens of the Dashiell
Hammett school), so do the films produced between 1900 and 1910
pre-establish the subject matter and methods of the moving picture
as we know it. This period produced the incunabula of the Western
and the crime film (Edwin S. Porter's amazing *Great Train Robbery*
of 1903) from which developed the modern gangster, adventure,
and mystery pictures (the latter, if well done, is still one of the
most honest and genuine forms of film entertainment, space being
doubly charged with time as the beholder asks himself not only
"What is going to happen?" but also "What has happened before?"). The same period saw the emergence of the fantastically
imaginative film (Méliès) which was to lead to the expressionist
and surrealist experiments (*The Cabinet of Dr. Caligari, Sang d'un
Poète*, etc.), on the one hand, and to the more superficial and spectacular fairy tales à la Arabian Nights, on the other. Comedy, later
to triumph in Charlie Chaplin, the still insufficiently appreciated
Buster Keaton, the Marx Brothers and the pre-Hollywood creations
of René Clair, reached a respectable level in Max Linder and others.
In historical and melodramatic films the foundations were laid for
movie iconography and movie symbolism, and in the early work of
D. W. Griffith we find, not only remarkable attempts at psychological analysis *(Edgar Allan Poe)* and social criticism *(A Corner
in Wheat)* but also such basic technical innovations as the long shot,
the flashback and the close-up. And modest trick films and cartoons
paved the way to Felix the Cat, Popeye the Sailor, and Felix's prodigious offspring, Mickey Mouse.

Within their self-imposed limitations the earlier Disney films,
and certain sequences in the later ones,* represent, as it were, a

---

*I make this distinction because it was, in my opinion, a fall from grace when
Snow White introduced the human figure and when *Fantasia* attempted to pictur-
alize The World's Great Music. The very virtue of the animated cartoon is to ani-
mate, that is to say endow lifeless things with life, or living things with a different
kind of life. It effects a metamorphosis, and such a metamorphosis is wonderfully
present in Disney's animals, plants, thunderclouds and railroad trains. Whereas his
dwarfs, glamourized princesses, hillbillies, baseball players, rouged centaurs and

chemically pure distillation of cinematic possibilities. They retain the most important folkloristic elements—sadism, pornography, the humor engendered by both, and moral justice—almost without dilution and often fuse these elements into a variation on the primitive and inexhaustible David-and-Goliath motif, the triumph of the seemingly weak over the seemingly strong; and their fantastic independence of the natural laws gives them the power to integrate space with time to such perfection that the spatial and temporal experiences of sight and hearing come to be almost interconvertible. A series of soap bubbles, successively punctured, emits a series of sounds exactly corresponding in pitch and volume to the size of the bubbles; the three uvulae of Willie the Whale—small, large and medium—vibrate in consonance with tenor, bass and baritone notes; and the very concept of stationary existence is completely abolished. No object in creation, whether it be a house, a piano, a tree or an alarm clock, lacks the faculties of organic, in fact anthropomorphic, movement, facial expression and phonetic articulation. Incidentally, even in normal, "realistic" films the inanimate object, provided that it is dynamizable, can play the role of a leading character as do the ancient railroad engines in Buster Keaton's *General* and *Niagara Falls*. How the earlier Russian films exploited the possibility of heroizing all sorts of machinery lives in everybody's memory; and it is perhaps more than an accident that the two films which will go down in history as the great comical and the great serious masterpiece of the silent period bear the names and immortalize the personalities of two big ships: Keaton's *Navigator* (1924) and Eisenstein's *Potemkin* (1925).

amigos from South America are not transformations but caricatures at best, and fakes or vulgarities at worst. Concerning music, however, it should be borne in mind that its cinematic use is no less predicated upon the principle of coexpressibility than is the cinematic use of the spoken word. There is music permitting or even requiring the accompaniment of visible action (such as dances, ballet music and any kind of operatic compositions) and music of which the opposite is true; and this is, again, not a question of quality (most of us rightly prefer a waltz by Johann Strauss to a symphony by Sibelius) but one of intention. In *Fantasia* the hippopotamus ballet was wonderful, and the Pastoral Symphony and "Ave Maria" sequences were deplorable, not because the cartooning in the first case was infinitely better than in the two others (*cf.* above), and certainly not because Beethoven and Schubert are too sacred for picturalization, but simply because Ponchielli's "Dance of the Hours" is coexpressible while the Pastoral Symphony and the "Ave Maria" are not. In cases like these even the best imaginable music and the best imaginable cartoon will impair rather than enhance each other's effectiveness.

Experimental proof of all this was furnished by Disney's recent *Make Mine Music* where The World's Great Music was fortunately restricted to Prokofieff. Even among the other sequences the most successful ones were those in which the human element was either absent or reduced to a minimum; Willie the Whale, the Ballad of Johnny Fedora and Alice Blue-Bonnet, and, above all, the truly magnificent Goodman Quartet.

The evolution from the jerky beginnings to this grand climax offers the fascinating spectacle of a new artistic medium gradually becoming conscious of its legitimate, that is, exclusive, possibilities and limitations—a spectacle not unlike the development of the mosaic, which started out with transposing illusionistic genre pictures into a more durable material and culminated in the hieratic supernaturalism of Ravenna; or the development of line engraving, which started out as a cheap and handy substitute for book illumination and culminated in the purely "graphic" style of Dürer.

Just so the silent movies developed a definite style of their own, adapted to the specific conditions of the medium. A hitherto unknown language was forced upon a public not yet capable of reading it, and the more proficient the public became the more refinement could develop in the language. For a Saxon peasant of around 800 it was not easy to understand the meaning of a picture showing a man as he pours water over the head of another man, and even later many people found it difficult to grasp the significance of two ladies standing behind the throne of an emperor. For the public of around 1910 it was no less difficult to understand the meaning of the speechless action in a moving picture, and the producers employed means of clarification similar to those we find in medieval art. One of these were printed titles or letters, striking equivalents of the medieval *tituli* and scrolls (at a still earlier date there even used to be explainers who would say, *viva voce*, "Now he thinks his wife is dead but she isn't" or "I don't wish to offend the ladies in the audience but I doubt that any of them would have done that much for her child"). Another, less obtrusive method of explanation was the introduction of a fixed iconography which from the outset informed the spectator about the basic facts and characters, much as the two ladies behind the emperor, when carrying a sword and a cross respectively, were uniquely determined as Fortitude and Faith. There arose, identifiable by standardized appearance, behavior and attributes, the well-remembered types of the Vamp and the Straight Girl (perhaps the most convincing modern equivalents of the medieval personifications of the Vices and Virtues), the Family Man, and the Villain, the latter marked by a black mustache and walking stick. Nocturnal scenes were printed on blue or green film. A checkered tablecloth meant, once for all, a "poor but honest" milieu; a happy marriage, soon to be endangered by the shadows from the past, was symbolized by the young wife's pouring the breakfast coffee for her husband; the first kiss was invariably announced by the lady's gently playing with her partner's necktie and was invariably accompanied by her kicking out with her left foot. The conduct of the characters was predetermined accordingly. The poor but honest laborer who, after leaving his little house with the checkered tablecloth, came upon an abandoned baby could not but take it to his home and bring it up as best he could; the Family Man could not but yield, however temporarily, to the temptations of the Vamp. As a result these early melodramas had a highly gratifying and soothing quality in that events took shape, without the complications of individual psychology, according to a pure Aristotelian logic so badly missed in real life.

Devices like these became gradually less necessary as the public grew accustomed to interpret the action by itself and were virtually abolished by the invention of the talking film. But even now there survive—quite legitimately, I think—the remnants of a "fixed attitude and attribute" principle and, more basic, a primitive or folkloristic concept of plot construction. Even today we take it for granted that the diphtheria of a baby tends to occur when the parents are out and, having occurred, solves all their matrimonial problems. Even today we demand of a decent mystery film that the butler, though he may be anything from an agent of the British Secret Service to the real father of the daughter of the house, must not turn out to be the murderer. Even today we love to see Pasteur, Zola or Ehrlich win out against stupidity and wickedness, with their respective wives trusting and trusting all the time. Even today we much prefer a happy finale to a gloomy one and insist, at the very least, on the observance of the Aristotelian rule that the story have a beginning, a middle and an ending—a rule the abrogation of which has done so much to estrange the general public from the more elevated spheres of modern writing. Primitive symbolism, too, survives in such amusing details as the last sequence of *Casablanca* where the delightfully crooked and right-minded *préfet de police* casts an empty bottle of Vichy water into the wastepaper basket; and in such telling symbols of the supernatural as Sir Cedric Hardwicke's Death in the guise of a "gentleman in a dustcoat trying" *(On Borrowed Time)* or Claude Rains's Hermes Psychopompos in the striped trousers of an airline manager *(Here Comes Mister Jordan)*.

The most conspicuous advances were made in directing, lighting, camera work, cutting and acting proper. But while in most of these fields the evolution proceeded continuously—though, of course, not without detours, breakdowns and archaic relapses—the development of acting suffered a sudden interruption by the invention of the talking film; so that the style of acting in the silents can already be evaluated in retrospect, as a lost art not unlike the painting technique of Jan van Eyck or, to take up our previous simile, the burin technique of Dürer. It was soon realized that acting in a silent film neither meant a pantomimic exaggeration of stage acting (as was generally and erroneously assumed by professional stage actors who more and more frequently condescended to perform in the movies), nor could dispense with stylization altogether; a man photographed while walking down a gangway in ordinary, every-day-life fashion looked like anything but a man walking down a gangway when the result appeared on the screen. If the picture was to look both natural and meaningful the acting had to be done in a manner equally different from the style of the stage and the re-ality of ordinary life; speech had to be made dispensable by estab-lishing an organic relation between the acting and the technical procedure of cinephotography—much as in Dürer's prints color had been made dispensable by establishing an organic relation be-tween the design and the technical procedure of line engraving.

This was precisely what the great actors of the silent period ac-complished, and it is a significant fact that the best of them did not come from the stage, whose crystallized tradition prevented Duse's only film, *Cenere*, from being more than a priceless record of Duse. They came instead from the circus or the variety, as was the case of Chaplin, Keaton and Will Rogers; from nothing in particular, as was the case of Theda Bara, of her greater European parallel, the Danish actress Asta Nielsen, and of Garbo; or from everything under the sun, as was the case of Douglas Fairbanks. The style of these "old masters" was indeed comparable to the style of line en-graving in that it was, and had to be, exaggerated in comparison with stage acting (just as the sharply incised and vigorously curved *tailles* of the burin are exaggerated in comparison with pencil strokes or brushwork), but richer, subtler and infinitely more pre-cise. The advent of the talkies, reducing if not abolishing this dif-ference between screen acting and stage acting, thus confronted the actors and actresses of the silent screen with a serious problem. Buster Keaton yielded to temptation and fell. Chaplin first tried to stand his ground and to remain an exquisite archaist but finally gave in, with only moderate success *(The Great Dictator)*. Only the glorious Harpo has thus far successfully refused to utter a single articulate sound; and only Greta Garbo succeeded, in a measure, in transforming her style in principle. But even in her case one can-not help feeling that her first talking picture, *Anna Christie*, where she could ensconce herself, most of the time, in mute or monosyl-labic sullenness, was better than her later performances; and in the second, talking version of *Anna Karenina*, the weakest moment is certainly when she delivers a big Ibsenian speech to her husband, and the strongest when she silently moves along the platform of the railroad station while her despair takes shape in the consonance of her movement (and expression) with the movement of the noc-turnal space around her, filled with the real noises of the trains and the imaginary sound of the "little men with the iron hammers" that drives her, relentlessly and almost without her realizing it, under the wheels.

Small wonder that there is sometimes felt a kind of nostalgia for the silent period and that devices have been worked out to combine the virtues of sound and speech with those of silent acting, such as the "oblique close-up" already mentioned in connection with *Henry V*; the dance behind glass doors in *Sous les Toits de Paris*; or, in the *Histoire d'un Tricheur*, Sacha Guitry's recital of the events of his youth while the events themselves are "silently" enacted on the screen. However, this nostalgic feeling is no argument against the talkies as such. Their evolution has shown that, in art, every gain entails a certain loss on the other side of the ledger; but that the gain remains a gain, provided that the basic nature of the medium is realized and respected. One can imagine that, when the cavemen of Altamira began to paint their buffaloes in natural colors instead of merely incising the contours, the more conservative cavemen foretold the end of paleolithic art. But paleolithic art went on, and so will the movies. New technical inventions always tend to dwarf the values already attained, especially in a medium that owes its very existence to technical experimentation. The earliest talkies were infinitely inferior to the then mature silents, and most of the present technicolor films are still inferior to the now mature talkies in black and white. But even if Aldous Huxley's nightmare should come true and the experiences of taste, smell and touch should be added to those of sight and hearing, even then we may say with the Apostle, as we have said when first confronted with the sound track and the technicolor film, "We are troubled on every side, yet not distressed; we are perplexed, but not in despair."

From the law of time-charged space and space-bound time, there follows the fact that the screenplay, in contrast to the theater play, *has no aesthetic existence independent of its performance, and that its characters have no aesthetic existence outside the actors.*

The playwright writes in the fond hope that his work will be an imperishable jewel in the treasure house of civilization and will be presented in hundreds of performances that are but transient variations on a "work" that is constant. The script-writer, on the other hand, writes for one producer, one director and one cast. Their work achieves the same degree of permanence as does his; and should the same or a similar scenario ever be filmed by a different director and a different cast there will result an altogether different "play."

Othello or Nora are definite, substantial figures created by the playwright. They can be played well or badly, and they can be "interpreted" in one way or another; but they most definitely exist, no matter who plays them or even whether they are played at all. The character in a film, however, lives and dies with the actor. It is not the entity "Othello" interpreted by Robeson or the entity "Nora" interpreted by Duse; it is the entity "Greta Garbo" incarnate in a figure called Anna Christie or the entity "Robert Montgomery" incarnate in a murderer who, for all we know or care to know, may forever remain anonymous but will never cease to haunt our memories. Even when the names of the characters happen to be Henry VIII or Anna Karenina, the king who ruled England from 1509 to 1547 and the woman created by Tolstoy, they do not exist outside the being of Garbo and Laughton. They are but empty and incorporeal outlines like the shadows in Homer's Hades, assuming the character of reality only when filled with the lifeblood of an actor. Conversely, if a movie role is badly played there remains literally nothing of it, no matter how interesting the character's psychology or how elaborate the words.

What applies to the actor applies, *mutatis mutandis*, to most of the other artists, or artisans, who contribute to the making of a film: the director, the sound man, the enormously important cameraman, even the make-up man. A stage production is rehearsed until everything is ready, and then it is repeatedly performed in three consecutive hours. At each performance everybody has to be on hand and does his work; and afterward he goes home and to bed. The work of the stage actor may thus be likened to that of a musician, and that of the stage director to that of a conductor. Like these, they have a certain repertoire which they have studied and present in a number of complete but transitory performances, be it *Hamlet* today and *Ghosts* tomorrow, or *Life with Father per saecula saeculorum*. The activities of the film actor and the film director, however, are comparable, respectively, to those of the plastic artist and the architect, rather than to those of the musician and the conductor. Stage work is continuous but transitory; film work is discontinuous but permanent. Individual sequences are done piecemeal and out of order according to the most efficient use of sets and personnel. Each bit is done over and over again until it stands; and when the whole has been cut and composed everyone is through with it forever. Needless to say that this very procedure cannot but emphasize the curious consubstantiality that exists between the person of the movie actor and his role. Coming into existence piece by piece, regardless of the natural sequence of events, the "character" can grow into a unified whole only if the actor manages to be, not merely to play, Henry VIII or Anna Karenina throughout the entire wearisome period of shooting. I have it on the best of authorities that Laughton was really difficult to live with in the particular six or eight weeks during which he was doing—or rather being—Captain Bligh.

It might be said that a film, called into being by a co-operative effort in which all contributions have the same degree of permanence, is the nearest modern equivalent of a medieval cathedral; the role of the producer corresponding, more or less, to that of the

Laurence Olivier in *Henry V* (1944). The film "uses a device perhaps best designated as 'oblique close-up' (Mr. Olivier's beautiful face inwardly listening to but not pronouncing the great soliloquy)." (PANOFSKY, page 221).

Caligari (Werner Krauss) feeding Cesare (Conrad Veidt) in *The Cabinet of Doctor Caligari* (1919). "The expressionist settings . . . could exert but little influence upon the general course of events. To prestylize reality prior to tackling it amounts to dodging the problem" (PANOFSKY, page 233). "Films of this type are not only intended as autonomous wholes but frequently ignore physical reality or exploit it for purposes alien to photographic veracity" (KRACAUER, page 19).

bishop or archbishop; that of the director to that of the architect in chief; that of the scenario writers to that of the scholastic advisers establishing the iconographical program; and that of the actors, cameramen, cutters, sound men, make-up men and the divers technicians to that of those whose work provided the physical entity of the finished product, from the sculptors, glass painters, bronze casters, carpenters and skilled masons down to the quarry men and woodsmen. And if you speak to any one of these collaborators he will tell you, with perfect *bona fides*, that his is really the most important job—which is quite true to the extent that it is indispensable.

This comparison may seem sacrilegious, not only because there are, proportionally, fewer good films than there are good cathedrals, but also because the movies are commercial. However, if commercial art be defined as all art not primarily produced in order to gratify the creative urge of its maker but primarily intended to meet the requirements of a patron or a buying public, it must be said that noncommercial art is the exception rather than the rule, and a fairly recent and not always felicitous exception at that. While it is true that commercial art is always in danger of ending up as a prostitute, it is equally true that noncommercial art is always in danger of ending up as an old maid. Noncommercial art has given us Seurat's "Grande Jatte" and Shakespeare's sonnets, but also much that is esoteric to the point of incommunicability. Conversely, commercial art has given us much that is vulgar or snobbish (two aspects of the same thing) to the point of loathsomeness, but also Dürer's prints and Shakespeare's plays. For, we must not forget that Dürer's prints were partly made on commission and partly intended to be sold in the open market; and that Shakespeare's plays—in contrast to the earlier masques and intermezzi which were produced at court by aristocratic amateurs and could afford to be so incomprehensible that even those who described them in printed monographs occasionally failed to grasp their intended significance—were meant to appeal, and did appeal, not only to the select few but also to everyone who was prepared to pay a shilling for admission.

It is this requirement of communicability that makes commercial art more vital than noncommercial, and therefore potentially much more effective for better or for worse. The commercial producer can both educate and pervert the general public, and can allow the general public—or rather his idea of the general public—both to educate and to pervert himself. As is demonstrated by a number of excellent films that proved to be great box office successes, the public does not refuse to accept good products if it gets them. That it does not get them very often is caused not so much by commercialism as such as by too little discernment and, paradoxical though it may seem, too much timidity in its application. Hollywood believes that it must produce "what the public wants" while the public would take whatever Hollywood produces. If Hollywood were to decide for itself what it wants it would get away with it—even if it should decide to "depart from evil and do good." For, to revert to whence we started, in modern life the movies are what most other forms of art have ceased to be, not an adornment but a necessity.

That this should be so is understandable, not only from a sociological but also from an art-historical point of view. The processes of all the earlier representational arts conform, in a higher or lesser degree, to an idealistic conception of the world. These arts operate from top to bottom, so to speak, and not from bottom to top; they start with an idea to be projected into shapeless matter and not with the objects that constitute the physical world. The painter works on a blank wall or canvas which he organizes into a likeness of things and persons according to his idea (however much this idea may have been nourished by reality); he does not work with the things and persons themselves even if he works "from the model." The same is true of the sculptor with his shapeless mass of clay or his untooled block of stone or wood; of the writer with his sheet of paper or his dictaphone; and even of the stage designer with his empty and sorely limited section of space. It is the movies, and only the movies, that do justice to that materialistic interpretation of the universe which, whether we like it or not, pervades contemporary civilization. Excepting the very special case of the animated cartoon, the movies organize material things and persons, not a neutral medium, into a composition that receives its style, and may even become fantastic or pretervoluntarily symbolic, not so much by an interpretation in the artist's mind as by the actual manipulation of physical objects and recording machinery. The medium of the movies is physical reality as such: the physical reality of eighteenth-century Versailles—no matter whether it be the original or a Hollywood facsimile indistinguishable therefrom for all aesthetic intents and purposes—or of a suburban home in Westchester; the physical reality of the Rue de Lappe in Paris or of the Gobi Desert, of Paul Ehrlich's apartment in Frankfurt or of the streets of New York in the rain; the physical reality of engines and animals, of Edward G. Robinson and Jimmy Cagney. All these objects and persons must be organized into a work of art. They can be arranged in all sorts of ways ("arrangement" comprising, of course, such things as make-up, lighting and camera work); but there is no running away from them. From this point of view it becomes evident that an attempt at subjecting the world to artistic prestylization, as in the expressionist settings of *The Cabinet of Dr. Caligari* (1919), could be no more than an exciting experiment that could exert but little influence upon the general course of events. To prestylize reality prior to tackling it amounts to dodging the problem. The problem is to manipulate and shoot unstylized reality in such a way that the result has style. This is a proposition no less legitimate and no less difficult than any proposition in the older arts.

1934; revised 1947

SIEGFRIED KRACAUER
FROM THEORY OF FILM

THE ESTABLISHMENT OF PHYSICAL EXISTENCE

In establishing physical existence, films differ from photographs in two respects: they represent reality as it evolves in time; and they do so with the aid of cinematic techniques and devices.

Consequently, the recording and revealing duties of the two kindred media coincide only in part. And what do they imply for film in particular? The hunting ground of the motion picture camera is in principle unlimited; it is the external world expanding in all directions. Yet there are certain subjects within that world which may be termed "cinematic" because they seem to exert a peculiar attraction on the medium. It is as if the medium were predestined (and eager) to exhibit them. The following pages are devoted to a close examination of these cinematic subjects. Several lie, so to speak, on the surface; they will be dealt with under the title "recording functions." Others would hardly come to our attention or be perceptible were it not for the film camera and/or the intervention of cinematic techniques; they will be discussed in the subsequent section "revealing functions." To be sure, any camera revelation involves recording, but recording on its part need not be revealing.

RECORDING FUNCTIONS

Movement

At least two groups of quite common external phenomena are naturals for the screen. As might be expected, one is made up of all kinds of movements, these being cinematic because only the motion picture camera is able to record them. Among them are three types which can be considered cinematic subjects par excellence.

The Chase

"The chase," says Hitchcock, "seems to me the final expression of the motion picture medium." This complex of interrelated movements is motion at its extreme, one might almost say, motion as such—and of course it is immensely serviceable for establishing a continuity of suspenseful physical action. Hence the fascination the chase has held since the beginning of the century. The primitive French comedies availed themselves of it to frame their space-devouring adventures. Gendarmes pursued a dog who eventually turned the tables on them (*Course des sergeants de ville*); pumpkins gliding from a cart were chased by the grocer, his donkey, and passers-by through sewers and over roofs (*La Course des potirons, 1907*; English title: *The Pumpkin Race*). For any Keystone comedy to forgo the chase would have been an unpardonable crime. It was the climax of the whole, its orgiastic finale—a pandemonium, with onrushing trains telescoping into automobiles and narrow escapes down ropes that dangled above a lion's den.

But perhaps nothing reveals the cinematic significance of this reveling in speed more drastically than D. W. Griffith's determination to transfer, at the end of all his great films, the action from the ideological plane to that of his famous "last-minute rescue," which was a chase pure and simple. Or should one say, a race? In any case, the rescuers rush ahead to overwhelm the villains or free their victims at the very last moment, while simultaneously the inner emotion which the dramatic conflict has aroused yields to a state of acute physiological suspense called forth by exuberant physical motion and its immediate implications. Nor is a genuine Western imaginable without a pursuit or a race on horseback. As Flaherty put it, Westerns are popular "because people never get tired of seeing a horse gallop across the plains." Its gallop seems still to gain momentum by contrast with the immense tranquility of the far-away horizon.

Dancing

The second type of specifically cinematic movement is dancing. This does not apply, of course, to the stage ballet which evolves in a space-time outside actuality proper. Interestingly enough, all attempts at "canning" it adequately have so far failed. Screen reproductions of theatrical dancing either indulge in a completeness which is boring or offer a selection of attractive details which confuse in that they dismember rather than preserve the original. Dancing attains to cinematic eminence only if it is part and parcel of physical reality. René Clair's early sound films have judiciously been called ballets. True, they are, but the performers are real-life Parisians who just cannot help executing dance movements when going about their love adventures and minor quarrels. With infinite subtlety Clair guides them along the divide between the real and unreal. Sometimes it appears as though these delivery boys, taxi drivers, girls, clerks, shopkeepers, and nondescript figures are marionettes banding together and parting from each other according to designs as delicate as lacework; and then again they are made to look and behave like ordinary people in Paris streets and bistros. And the latter impression prevails. For, even granted that they are drawn into an imaginary universe, this universe itself reflects throughout our real world in stylizing it. What dancing there is, seems to occur on the spur of the moment; it is the vicissitudes of life from which these ballets issue.

Fred Astaire too prefers apparent impromptu performances to stage choreography; he is quite aware that this type of performance is appropriate to the medium. "Each dance," says he, "ought to spring somehow out of character or situation, otherwise it is simply a vaudeville act." This does not mean that he would dispense with theatrical production numbers. But no sooner does he perform in vaudeville fashion than he breaks out of the prison of prearranged stage patterns and, with a genius for improvisation, dances over tables and gravel paths into the everyday world. It is a one-way route which invariably leads from the footlights to the heart of camera-reality. Astaire's consummate dancing is meant to belong among the real-life events with which he toys in his musicals; and it is so organized that it imperceptibly emerges from, and disappears, in the flow of these happenings. . . .

Nascent Motion

The third type of motion which offers special interest cinematically is not just another group of interrelated movements but movement as contrasted with motionlessness. In focusing upon this contrast, films strikingly demonstrate that objective movement—any movement, for that matter—is one of their choice subjects. Alexander Dovzhenko in both *Arsenal* and *Earth* frequently stops the action to resume it after a short lull. The first phase of this procedure—characters or parts of them abruptly ceasing to move— produces a shock effect, as if all of a sudden we found ourselves in a vacuum. The immediate consequence is that we acutely realize the significance of movement as an integral element of the external world as well as film.

But this is only part of the story. Even though the moving images on the screen come to a standstill, the thrust of their movement is too powerful to be discontinued simultaneously. Accordingly, when the people in *Arsenal* or *Earth* are shown in the form of stills,

the suspended movement nevertheless perpetuates itself by changing from outer motion into inner motion. Dovzhenko has known
how to make this metamorphosis benefit his penetrations of reality.
The immobile lovers in *Earth* become transparent; the deep happiness which is moving them turns inside out. And the spectator on
his part grasps their inward agitation because the cessation of external motion moves him all the more intensely to commune with
them. Yet despite these rewarding experiences he cannot help feeling a certain relief when eventually the characters take on life again
—an event which marks the second and final phase of the procedure. It is a return to the world of film, whose inherent motion
alone renders possible such excursions into the whirlpool of the
motionless. . . .

Inanimate Objects

Since the inanimate is featured in many paintings, one might
question the legitimacy of characterizing it as a cinematic subject.
Yet it is a painter—Fernand Léger—who judiciously insists that
only film is equipped to sensitize us, by way of big close-ups, to the
possibilities that lie dormant in a hat, a chair, a hand, and a foot.
Similarly Cohen-Séat: "And I? says the leaf which is falling.—And
we? say the orange peel, the gust of wind. . . . Film, whether intentionally or not, is their mouthpiece." Nor should it be forgotten that
the camera's ability to single out and record the orange peel or the
hand marks a decisive difference between screen and stage, so close
to each other in some respects. Stage imagery inevitably centers on
the actor, whereas film is free to dwell on parts of his appearance
and detail the objects about him. In using its freedom to bring the
inanimate to the fore and make it a carrier of action, film only
protests its peculiar requirement to explore all of physical existence,
human or nonhuman. Within this context it is of interest that in the
early 'twenties, when the French cinema was swamped with theatrical adaptations and stage-minded dramas, Louis Delluc tried to put
the medium on its own feet by stressing the tremendous importance
of objects. If they are assigned the role due to them, he argued, the
actor too "is no more than a detail, a fragment of the matter of the
world."

Actually, the urge to raise hats and chairs to the status of full-
fledged actors has never completely atrophied. From the malicious
escalators, the unruly Murphy beds, and the mad automobiles in
silent comedy to the cruiser Potemkin, the oil derrick in *Louisiana
Story* and the dilapidated kitchen in *Umberto D.*, a long procession
of unforgettable objects has passed across the screen—objects
which stand out as protagonists and all but overshadow the rest of
the cast. Or remember the powerful presence of environmental in-

fluences in *The Grapes of Wrath*, the part played by nocturnal Coney Island in *Little Fugitive*, the interaction between the marshland and the guerilla fighters in the last episode of *Paisan*. Of course, the reverse holds true also: films in which the inanimate merely serves as a background to self-contained dialogue and the closed circuit of human relationships are essentially uncinematic.

REVEALING FUNCTIONS

"I ask that a film *discover* something for me" declares Luis Buñuel, who is himself a fiery pathfinder of the screen. And what are films likely to discover? The evidence available suggests that they assume three kinds of revealing functions. They tend to reveal things normally unseen; phenomena overwhelming consciousness; and certain aspects of the outer world which may be called "special modes of reality."

Things Normally Unseen

The many material phenomena which elude observation under normal circumstances can be divided into three groups. The first includes objects too small to be readily noticed or even perceived by the naked eye and objects so big that they will not be fully taken in either.

The Small and the Big

The small.   The small is conveyed in the form of close-ups. D. W. Griffith was among the first to realize that they are indispensable for cinematic narration. He initiated their use, as we now know it, in *After Many Years* (1908), an adaptation of Tennyson's *Enoch Arden*. There his memorable first close-up appeared within contexts which Lewis Jacobs describes as follows: "Going further than he had ventured before, in a scene showing Annie Lee brooding and waiting for her husband's return, Griffith daringly used a large close-up of her face. . . . He had another surprise, even more radical, to offer. Immediately following the close-up of Annie, he inserted a picture of the object of her thoughts—her husband cast away on a desert isle."

On the surface, this succession of shots seems simply designed to lure the spectator into the dimension of her intimate preoccupations. He first watches Annie from a distance and then approaches her so closely that he sees only her face; if he moves on in the same direction, as the film invites him to do, it is logical that he should penetrate Annie's appearance and land inside her mind. Granting the validity of this interpretation, the close-up of her face is not an end in itself; rather, along with the subsequent shots, it serves to suggest what is going on behind that face—Annie's longing for re-union with her husband. A knowingly chosen detail of her physique thus would help establish the whole of her being in a dramatic interest.

The same obviously holds true of another famous Griffith close-up: Mae Marsh's clasped hands in the trial episode of *Intolerance*. It almost looks as if her huge hands with the convulsively moving fingers were inserted for the sole purpose of illustrating eloquently her anguish at the most crucial moment of the trial; as if, generally speaking, the function of any such detail exhausted itself in intensifying our participation in the total situation. This is how Eisenstein conceives of the close-up. Its main function, says he, is "not so much to *show* or to *present* as to *signify*, to *give meaning*, to *designate*." To designate what? Evidently something of importance to the narrative. And montage-minded as he is, he immediately adds that the significance of the close-up for the plot accrues to it less from its own content than from the manner in which it is juxtaposed with the surrounding shots. According to him, the close-up is primarily a montage unit.

But is this really its only function? Consider again the combination of shots with the close-up of Annie's face: the place assigned to the latter in the sequence intimates that Griffith wanted us also to absorb the face for its own sake instead of just passing through and beyond it; the face appears before the desires and emotions to which it refers have been completely defined, thus tempting us to get lost in its puzzling indeterminacy. Annie's face is also an end in itself. And so is the image of Mae Marsh's hands. No doubt it is to impress upon us her inner condition, but besides making us experience what we would in a measure have experienced anyway because of our familiarity with the characters involved, this close-up contributes something momentous and unique—it reveals how her hands behave under the impact of utter despair.

Eisenstein criticizes the close-ups in Griffith films precisely for their relative independence of the contexts in which they occur. He calls them isolated units which tend "to show or to present"; and he insists that to the extent that they indulge in isolation they fail to yield the meanings which the interweaving processes of montage may elicit from them. Had Eisenstein been less possessed with the magic powers of montage he would certainly have acknowledged the cinematic superiority of the Griffith close-up. To Griffith such huge images of small material phenomena are not only integral components of the narrative but disclosures of new aspects of physical reality. In representing them the way he does, he seems to have been guided by the conviction that the cinema is all the more cinematic if it acquaints us with the physical origins, ramifications, and connotations of all the emotional and intellectual events which comprise the plot; that it cannot adequately account for these inner developments unless it leads us through the thicket of material life from which they emerge and in which they are embedded. . . .

The big.   Among the large objects, such as vast plains or panoramas of any kind, one deserves special attention: the masses. No doubt imperial Rome already teemed with them. But masses of people in the modern sense entered the historical scene only in the wake of the industrial revolution. Then they became a social force of first magnitude. Warring nations resorted to levies on an unheard-of scale and identifiable groups yielded to the anonymous multitude which filled the big cities in the form of amorphous crowds. Walter Benjamin observes that in the period marked by the rise of photography the daily sight of moving crowds was still a spectacle to which eyes and nerves had to get adjusted. The testimony of sensitive contemporaries would seem to corroborate this sagacious observation: The Paris crowds omnipresent in Baudelaire's *Les Fleurs du mal* function as stimuli which call forth irritating kaleidoscopic sensations; the jostling and shoving passers-by who, in Poe's *Man of the Crowd*, throng gas-lit London provoke a succession of electric shocks.

At the time of its emergence the mass, this giant animal, was a new and upsetting experience. As might be expected, the traditional arts proved unable to encompass and render it. Where they failed, photography easily succeeded; it was technically equipped to portray crowds as the accidental agglomerations they are. Yet only film, the fulfillment of photography in a sense, was equal to the task of capturing them in motion. In this case the instrument of reproduction came into being almost simultaneously with one of its main subjects. Hence the attraction which masses exerted on still and motion picture cameras from the outset. It is certainly more than sheer coincidence that the very first Lumière films featured a crowd of workers and the confusion of arrival and departure at a railway station. Early Italian films elaborated upon the theme; and D. W. Griffith, inspired by them, showed how masses can be represented cinematically. The Russians absorbed his lesson, applying it in ways of their own. . . .

The Transient

The second group of things normally unseen comprises the transient. Here belong, first, fleeting impressions—"the shadow of a cloud passing across the plain, a leaf which yields to the wind." Evanescent, like dream elements, such impressions may haunt the moviegoer long after the story they are called upon to implement has sunk into oblivion. The manes of the galloping horses— flying threads or streamers rather than manes—in the chariot race episode of Fred Niblo's *Ben Hur* are as unforgettable as the fiery traces of the projectiles that tear the night in *Desert Victory*. The motion picture camera seems to be partial to the least permanent components of our environment. It may be anticipated that the street in the broadest sense of the word is a place where impressions of this kind are bound to occur. "The cinema," says Aragon, delighting in its snapshot-like predilection for the ephemeral, "has taught us more about man in a few years than centuries of painting have taught: fugitive expressions, attitudes scarcely credible yet real, charm and hideousness"

Second, there are movements of so transitory a nature that they would be imperceptible were it not for two cinematic techniques: accelerated-motion, which condenses extremely slow and, hence, unobservable developments, such as the growth of plants, and slow-motion, which expands movements too fast to be registered. Like the big close-up, these correlated techniques lead straight into "reality of another dimension." Pictures of stalks piercing the soil in the process of growing open up imaginary areas, and racing legs shown in slow-motion do not just slow down but change in appearance and perform bizarre evolutions—patterns remote from reality as we know it. Slow-motion shots parallel the regular close-ups; they are, so to speak, temporal close-ups achieving in time what the close-up proper is achieving in space. That, unlike the latter, they are used rather infrequently, may be traced to the fact that the enlargement of spatial phenomena, as effected by the close-up, seems more "natural" to us than the expansion of a given time interval. (On the other hand, it appears that film makers draw more readily on slow-motion than on the reverse technique— perhaps simply because it does not require so lengthy preparations.)

As contrived reality pictures, the deviant images gained by both techniques, especially slow-motion, may well figure in nonrealistic experimental films. Yet they live up to the cinematic approach only if they are made to fulfill a revealing function within contexts focusing on physical existence. The late Jean Epstein, who felt so immensely attracted by "reality of another dimension," considered this their true destination. Referring to waves in slow-motion and clouds in accelerated-motion, he declared that for all their "startling physics and strange mechanics" they "are but a portrait—seen in a certain perspective—of the world in which we live."

Blind Spots of the Mind

The third and last group of things normally unseen consists of phenomena which figure among the blind spots of the mind; habit and prejudice prevent us from noticing them. The role which cultural standards and traditions may play in these processes of elimination is drastically illustrated by a report on the reactions of African natives to a film made on the spot. After the screening the spectators, all of them still unacquainted with the medium, talked volubly about a chicken they allegedly had seen picking food in the mud. The film maker himself, entirely unaware of its presence, attended several performances without being able to detect it. Had it been dreamed up by the natives? Only by scanning his film foot by foot did he eventually succeed in tracing the chicken: it appeared for a fleeting moment somewhere in a corner of a picture and then vanished forever.

The following types of objects are cinematic because they stubbornly escape our attention in everyday life.

Unconventional complexes.   Film may bare real-life complexes which the conventional figure-ground patterns usually conceal from view. Imagine a man in a room: accustomed as we are to visualize the human figure as a whole, it would take us an enormous effort to perceive instead of the whole man a pictorial unit consisting, say, of his right shoulder and arm, fragments of furniture and a section of the wall. But this is exactly what photography and, more powerfully, film may make us see. The motion picture camera has a way of disintegrating familiar objects and bringing to the fore—often just in moving about—previously invisible interrelationships between parts of them. These newly arising complexes lurk behind the things known and cut across their easily identifiable contexts. *Jazz Dance*, for instance, abounds with shots of ensembles built from human torsos, clothes, scattered legs, and what not—shapes which are almost anonymous. In rendering physical existence, film tends to reveal configurations of semi-abstract phenomena. Sometimes these textures take on an ornamental character. In the Nazi propaganda film *Triumph of the Will* moving banners fuse into a very beautiful pattern at the moment when they begin to fill the screen.

The refuse.   Many objects remain unnoticed simply because it never occurs to us to look their way. Most people turn their backs on garbage cans, the dirt underfoot, the waste they leave behind. Films have no such inhibitions; on the contrary, what we ordinarily prefer to ignore proves attractive to them precisely because of this common neglect. Ruttmann's *Berlin* includes a wealth of sewer grates, gutters, and streets littered with rubbish; and Cavalcanti in his *Rien que les heures* is hardly less garbage-minded. To be sure, shots in this vein may be required by the action, but intrigues inspired by a sense of the medium are often so devised that they offer the camera ample opportunity to satisfy its inborn curiosity and function as a rag-picker; think of the old silent comedies— e.g. Chaplin's *A Dog's Life*— or pictures which involve crime, war, or misery. Since sights of refuse are particularly impressive after spectacles extolling the joy of living, film makers have repeatedly capitalized on the contrast between glamorous festivities and their dreary aftermath. You see a banquet on the screen and then, when everybody has gone, you are made to linger for a moment and stare at the crumpled tablecloth, the half-emptied glasses, and the unappetizing dishes. The classical American gangster films indulged in this effect. *Scarface* opens on a restaurant at dawn, with the remnants of the nocturnal orgy strewn over floors and tables; and after the gangsters' ball in Sternberg's *Underworld* Bancroft totters through a maze of confetti and streamers left over from the feast.

The familiar.   Nor do we perceive the familiar. It is not as if we shrank from it, as we do in the case of refuse; we just take it for granted without giving it a thought. Intimate faces, streets we walk day by day, the house we live in—all these things are part of us like our skin, and because we know them by heart we do not know them with the eye. Once integrated into our existence, they cease to be objects of perception, goals to be attained. In fact, we would be immobilized if we focused on them. This is confirmed by a common experience. A man entering his room will immediately feel disturbed if during his absence something has been changed in it. But in order to find out about the cause of his uneasiness he must discontinue his routine occupations; only in deliberately scrutinizing, and thus estranging, the room will he be able to discover what it actually is that has been changed. Proust's narrator is acutely aware of this very estrangement when he suddenly sees his grandmother not as he always believed her to be but as she really is or at least as she would appear to a stranger—a snapshot likeness severed from his dreams and memories.

Films make us undergo similar experiences a thousand times. They alienate our environment in exposing it. One ever-recurrent film scene runs as follows: Two or more people are conversing with each other. In the middle of their talk the camera, as if entirely indifferent to it, slowly pans through the room, inviting us to watch the faces of the listeners and various furniture pieces in a detached spirit. Whatever this may mean within the given context, it invariably dissolves a well-known total situation and thereby confronts the spectator with isolated phenomena which he previously neglected or overlooked as matter-of-course components of that situation. As the camera pans, curtains become eloquent and eyes tell a story of their own. The way leads toward the unfamiliar in the familiar. How often do we not come across shots of street corners, buildings, and landscapes with which we were acquainted all our life; we naturally recognize them and yet it is as if they were virgin impressions emerging from the abyss of nearness. The opening sequence of Vigo's *Zéro de conduite* shows two boys traveling back to school by train. Is it just an ordinary night trip? Vigo manages to transform a familiar railway compartment into a magic wigwam in which the two, drunk from their boasts and pranks, are floating through the air.

This transformation is partly achieved with the aid of a device, both photographic and cinematic, which deserves some attention — the use of uncommon camera angles. Vigo occasionally represents the railway compartment slantwise and from below so that the whole room seems to drift along in the haze from the cigars which the high-strung schoolboys are smoking, while little toy balloons hover to and fro before their pale faces. Proust knew about the alienating effect of this device. After having mentioned that certain photographs of scenery and towns are called "admirable," he continues: "If we press for a definition of what their admirers mean by that epithet, we shall find that it is generally applied to some unusual picture of a familar object, a picture different from those that we are accustomed to see, unusual and yet true to nature, and for that reason doubly impressive because it startles us, makes us emerge from our habits, and at the same time brings us back to ourselves by recalling to us an earlier impression." And to concretize this definition, he refers to the picture of a cathedral which does not render it as it is normally seen — namely, in the middle of the town — but is taken from a point of view from which the building "will appear thirty times the height of the houses." . . .

Phenomena Overwhelming Consciousness

Elemental catastrophes, the atrocities of war, acts of violence and terror, sexual debauchery, and death are events which tend to overwhelm consciousness. In any case, they call forth excitements and agonies bound to thwart detached observation. No one witnessing such an event, let alone playing an active part in it, should therefore be expected accurately to account for what he has seen. Since these manifestations of crude nature, human or otherwise, fall into the area of physical reality, they range all the more among the cinematic subjects. Only the camera is able to represent them without distortion.

Actually the medium has always shown a predilection for events of this type. There is practically no newsreel that would not indulge in the ravages of an inundation, a hurricane, an airplane crash, or whatever catastrophe happens to be at hand. The same applies to feature films. One of the first film strips ever made was *The Execution of Mary Queen of Scots* (1895); the executioner cuts off her head and then holds it in his uplifted hand so that no spectator can possibly avoid looking at the frightful exhibit. Pornographic motifs also emerged at a very early date. The path of the cinema is beset with films reveling in disasters and nightmarish incidents. Suffice it to pick out, at random, the war horrors in Dovzhenko's *Arsenal* and Pabst's *Westfront 1918;* the terrible execution sequence at the end of *Thunder over Mexico,* a film based on Eisenstein's Mexican material; the earthquake in *San Francisco;* the torture episode in Rossellini's *Open City;* the depiction of a Polish Nazi concentration camp in *The Last Stop;* the scene with the young hoodlums wantonly mistreating a blind man in Buñuel's *Los Olvidados.*

Because of its sustained concern with all that is dreadful and off limits, the medium has frequently been accused of a penchant for cheap sensationalism. What lends support to this verdict is the indisputable fact that films have a habit of dwelling on the sensational much longer than any moral purpose would seem to justify; it often is as if that purpose served merely as a pretext for rendering a savage murder or the like.

In defense of the medium one might argue that it would not be the mass medium it is if it failed to provide stunning sensations; and that, in offering them, it only follows a venerable tradition. Since time immemorial, people have craved spectacles permitting them vicariously to experience the fury of conflagrations, the excesses of cruelty and suffering, and unspeakable lusts—spectacles which shock the shuddering and delighted onlooker into unseeing participation.

Yet this argument misses the point. The point is, rather, that the cinema does not simply imitate and continue the ancient gladiator fights or the *Grand Guignol* but adds something new and momentous: it insists on rendering visible what is commonly drowned in inner agitation. Of course, such revelations conform all the more to the cinematic approach if they bear on actual catastrophes and horrors. In deliberately detailing feats of sadism in their films, Rossellini and Buñuel force the spectator to take in these appalling sights and at the same time impress them on him as real-life events recorded by the imperturbable camera. Similarly, besides trying to put across their propaganda messages, the Russian films of the 'twenties convey to us the paroxysmal upheavals of real masses which, because of their emotional *and* spatial enormity, depend doubly upon cinematic treatment to be perceptible.

The cinema, then, aims at transforming the agitated witness into a conscious observer. Nothing could be more legitimate than its lack of inhibitions in picturing spectacles which upset the mind. Thus it keeps us from shutting our eyes to the "blind drive of things."

Special Modes of Reality

Finally films may expose physical reality as it appears to individuals in extreme states of mind generated by such events as we have mentioned, mental disturbances, or any other external or internal causes. Supposing such a state of mind is provoked by an act of violence, then the camera often aspires to render the images which an emotionally upset witness or participant will form of it. These images also belong among the cinematic subjects. They are distorted from the viewpoint of a detached observer; and they differ from each other according to the varying states of mind in which they originate.

In his *Ten Days That Shook the World*, for instance, Eisenstein composes a physical universe reflecting exultation. This episode runs as follows: At the beginning of the October Revolution, worker delegates succeed in bringing a contingent of Cossacks over to their side; the Cossacks put their half-drawn swords with the ornamented pommels back into their sheaths, and then the two groups boisterously fraternize in a state of euphoria. The ensuing dance scene is represented in the form of an accelerated montage sequence which pictures the world as experienced by the overjoyed. In their great joy, dancers and onlookers who constantly mingle cannot help perceiving incoherent pieces of their immediate environment in motion. It is a whirling agglomerate of fragments that surrounds them. And Eisenstein captures this jumble to perfection by having follow each other—in a succession which becomes ever faster with the growing ecstasy—shots of Cossack boots executing the *krakoviak*, worker legs dancing through a puddle, clapping hands, and faces inordinately broadened by laughter.

In the world of a panic-stricken individual laughter yields to grimacing and dazzling confusion to fearful rigidity. At any rate, this is how Ernö Metzner conceived of that world in his *Ueberfall*. Its "hero" is a wretched little fellow who gets a lucky break thanks to a coin he furtively picks up in the street and then stakes in a crap game. As he walks away with his wallet stuffed, a thug follows him at a steadily diminishing distance. The man is scared. No sooner does he take to his heels than all the objects about him make common cause with his pursuer. The dark railway underpass turns into a sinister trap; frozen threats, the dilapidated slum houses close ranks and stare at him. (It is noteworthy that these effects are largely due to accomplished photography.) Temporarily saved by a streetwalker, who puts him up in her room, the man knows that the thug continues to lie in wait for him down in the street. The curtain moves, and he feels that the room itself harbors dangers. There is no escape wherever he looks. He looks into the mirror: what shines out of it are distorted reflections of his mask-like features.

1960

RUDOLF ARNHEIM
FROM FILM AS ART

FILM AND REALITY

Film resembles painting, music, literature, and the dance in this respect—it is a medium that may, but need not, be used to produce artistic results. Colored picture post cards, for instance, are not art and are not intended to be. Neither are a military march, a true confessions story, or a strip tease. And the movies are not necessarily film art.

There are still many educated people who stoutly deny the possibility that film might be art. They say, in effect: "Film cannot be art, for it does nothing but reproduce reality mechanically." Those who defend this point of view are reasoning from the analogy of painting. In painting, the way from reality to the picture lies via the artist's eye and nervous system, his hand and, finally, the brush that puts strokes on canvas. The process is not mechanical as that of photography, in which the light rays reflected from the object are collected by a system of lenses and are then directed onto a sensitive plate where they produce chemical changes. Does this state of affairs justify our denying photography and film a place in the temple of the Muses?

It is worth while to refute thoroughly and systematically the charge that photography and film are only mechanical reproductions and that they therefore have no connection with art—for this is an excellent method of getting to understand the nature of film art.

With this end in view, the basic elements of the film medium will be examined separately and compared with the corresponding

characteristics of what we perceive "in reality." It will be seen how
fundamentally different the two kinds of image are; and that it is
just these differences that provide film with its artistic resources.
We shall thus come at the same time to understand the working
principles of film art.

THE PROJECTION OF SOLIDS
UPON A PLANE SURFACE

Let us consider the visual reality of some definite object such as
a cube. If this cube is standing on a table in front of me, its position
determines whether I can realize its shape properly. If I see, for
example, merely the four sides of a square, I have no means of
knowing that a cube is before me, I see only a square surface. The
human eye, and equally the photographic lens, acts from a particular position and from there can take in only such portions of the
field of vision as are not hidden by things in front. As the cube is
now placed, five of its faces are screened by the sixth, and therefore this last only is visible. But since this face might equally well
conceal something quite different—since it might be the base of a
pyramid or one side of a sheet of paper, for instance—our view of
the cube has not been selected characteristically.

We have, therefore, already established one important principle:
If I wish to photograph a cube, it is not enough for me to bring the
object within range of my camera. It is rather a question of my position relative to the object, or of where I place it. The aspect chosen
above gives very little information as to the shape of the cube. One,
however, that reveals three surfaces of the cube and their relation
to one another, shows enough to make it fairly unmistakable what
the object is supposed to be. Since our field of vision is full of solid
objects, but our eye (like the camera) sees this field from only one
station point at any given moment, and since the eye can perceive
the rays of light that are reflected from the object only by projecting
them onto a plane surface—the retina—the reproduction of even a
perfectly simple object is not a mechanical process but can be set
about well or badly.

The second aspect gives a much truer picture of the cube than the
first. The reason for this is that the second shows more than the
first—three faces instead of only one. As a rule, however, truth
does not depend on quantity. If it were merely a matter of finding
which aspect shows the greatest amount of surface, the best point
of view could be arrived at by purely mechanical calculation. There
is no formula to help one choose the most characteristic aspect:
it is a question of feeling. Whether a particular person is "more
himself" in profile than full face, whether the palm or the outside
of the hand is more expressive, whether a particular mountain is

better taken from the north or the west cannot be ascertained math-
ematically—they are matters of delicate sensibility.

Thus, as a preliminary, people who contemptuously refer to the
camera as an automatic recording machine must be made to realize
that even in the simplest photographic reproduction of a perfectly
simple object, a feeling for its nature is required which is quite
beyond any mechanical operation. We shall see later, by the way,
that in artistic photography and film, those aspects that best show
the characteristics of a particular object are not by any means always chosen; others are often selected deliberately for the sake of
achieving specific effects.

REDUCTION OF DEPTH

How do our eyes succeed in giving us three-dimensional impressions even though the flat retinae can receive only two-dimensional
images? Depth perception relies mainly on the distance between
the two eyes, which makes for two slightly different images. The
fusion of these two pictures into one image gives the three-dimensional impression. As is well known, the same principle is used in
the stereoscope, for which two photographs are taken at once,
about the same distance apart as the human eyes. This process
cannot be used for film without recourse to awkward devices, such
as colored spectacles, when more than one person is to watch the
projection. For a single spectator it would be easy to make a stereoscopic film. It would only mean taking two simultaneous shots of
the same incident a couple of inches apart and then showing one
of them to each eye. For display to a larger number of spectators,
however, the problem of stereoscopic film has not yet been solved
satisfactorily—and hence the sense of depth in film pictures is extraordinarily small. The movement of people or objects from front
to back makes a certain depth evident—but it is only necessary to
glance into a stereoscope, which makes everything stand out most
realistically, to recognize how flat the film picture is. This is another
example of the fundamental difference between visual reality and
film.

The effect of film is neither absolutely two-dimensional nor absolutely three-dimensional, but something between. Film pictures
are at once plane and solid. In Ruttmann's film *Berlin* there is a
scene of two subway trains passing each other in opposite directions. The shot is taken looking down from above onto the two
trains. Anyone watching this scene realizes, first of all, that one
train is coming toward him and the other going away from him
(three-dimensional image). He will then also see that one is moving
from the lower margin of the screen toward the upper and the other
from the upper toward the lower (plane image). This second im-

pression results from the projection of the three-dimensional movement onto the screen surface, which, of course, gives different
directions of motion.

The obliteration of the three-dimensional impression has as a
second result a stronger accentuation of perspective overlapping.
In real life or in a stereoscope, overlapping is accepted as due merely to the accidental arrangement of objects, but very marked cuts
result from superimpositions in a plane image. If a man is holding
up a newspaper so that one corner comes across his face, this corner
seems almost to have been cut out of his face, so sharp are the
edges. Moreover, when the three-dimensional impression is lost,
other phenomena, known to psychologists as the constancies of
size and shape, disappear. Physically, the image thrown onto the
retina of the eye by any object in the field of vision diminishes in
proportion to the square of the distance. If an object a yard distant
is moved away another yard, the area of the image on the retina is
diminished to one-quarter of that of the first image. Every photographic plate reacts similarly. Hence in a photograph of someone
sitting with his feet stretched out far in front of him the subject
comes out with enormous feet and much too small a head. Curiously enough, however, we do not in real life get impressions to
accord with the images on the retina. If a man is standing three
feet away and another equally tall six feet away, the area of the
image of the second does not appear to be only a quarter of that of
the first. Nor if a man stretches out his hand toward one does it
look disproportionately large. One sees the two men as equal in
size and the hand as normal. This phenomenon is known as the constancy of size. It is impossible for most people—excepting those
accustomed to drawing and painting, that is, artificially trained—
to see according to the image on the retina. This fact, incidentally,
is one of the reasons the average person has trouble copying things
"correctly." Now an essential for the functioning of the constancy
of size is a clear three-dimensional impression; it works excellently
in a stereoscope with an ordinary photograph, but hardly at all in
a film picture. Thus, in a film picture, if one man is twice as far
from the camera as another, the one in front looks very considerably the taller and broader.

It is the same with the constancy of shape. The retinal image of
a table top is like the photograph of it; the front edge, being nearer
to the spectator, appears much wider than the back; the rectangular
surface becomes a trapezoid in the image. As far as the average
person is concerned, however, this again does not hold good in
practice: he *sees* the surface as rectangular and draws it that way
too. Thus the perspective changes taking place in any object that
extends in depth are not observed but are compensated unconsciously. That is what is meant by the constancy of form. In a film

picture it is hardly operative at all—a table top, especially if it is near the camera, looks very wide in front and very narrow at the back.

These phenomena, as a matter of fact, are due not only to the reduction of three-dimensionality but also to the unreality of the film picture altogether—an unreality due just as much to the absence of color, the delimitation of the screen, and so forth. The result of all this is that sizes and shapes do not appear on the screen in their true proportions but distorted in perspective. . . .

THE MAKING OF A FILM

It has been shown above that the images we receive of the physical world differ from those on the movie screen. This was done in order to refute the assertion that film is nothing but the feeble mechanical reproduction of real life. The analysis has furnished us with the data from which we can hope to derive now the principles of film art.

By its very nature, of course, the motion picture tends to satisfy the desire for faithful reports about curious, characteristic, exciting things going on in this world of ours. The first sensation provided by film in its early music-hall days was to depict everyday things in a lifelike fashion on the screen. People were greatly thrilled by the sight of a locomotive approaching at top speed or the emperor in person riding down *Unter den Linden*. In those days, the pleasure given by film derived almost entirely from the subject matter. A film art developed only gradually when the movie makers began consciously or unconsciously to cultivate the peculiar possibilities of cinematographic technique and to apply them toward the creation of artistic productions. To what extent the use of these means of expression affects the large audiences remains a moot question. Certainly box-office success depends even now much more on what is shown than on whether it is shown artistically.

The film producer himself is influenced by the strong resemblance of his photographic material to reality. As distinguished from the tools of the sculptor and the painter, which by themselves produce nothing resembling nature, the camera starts to turn and a likeness of the real world results mechanically. There is serious danger that the film maker will rest content with such shapeless reproduction. In order that the film artist may create a work of art it is important that he consciously stress the peculiarities of his medium. This, however, should be done in such a manner that the character of the objects represented should not thereby be destroyed but rather strengthened, concentrated, and interpreted. . . .

People who did not understand anything of the art of film used to cite silence as one of its most serious drawbacks. These people regard the introduction of sound as an improvement or completion of silent film. This opinion is just as senseless as if the invention of three-dimensional oil painting were hailed as an advance on the hitherto known principles of painting.

From its very silence film received the impetus as well as the power to achieve excellent artistic effects. Charles Chaplin wrote somewhere that in all his films there was not a single scene where he "spoke," that is, moved his lips. Hundreds of the most various situations in human relationships are shown in his films, and yet he did not feel the need to make use of such an ordinary faculty as speech. And nobody has missed it. The spoken word in Chaplin's films is as a rule replaced by pantomime. He does not *say* that he is pleased that some pretty girls are coming to see him, but performs the silent dance, in which two bread rolls stuck on forks act as dancing feet on the table *(The Gold Rush)*. He does not argue, he fights. He avows his love by smiling, swaying his shoulders, and moving his hat. When he is in the pulpit he does not preach in words, but acts the story of David and Goliath *(The Pilgrim)*. When he is sorry for a poor girl, he stuffs money into her handbag. He shows renunciation by simply walking away (finale of *The Circus*). The incredible visual concreteness of every one of his scenes makes for a great part of Chaplin's art; and this should not be forgotten when it is said—as is often done and of course not without foundation—that his films are not really "filmic" (because his camera serves mainly as a recording machine).

Mention has already been made of the scene from Sternberg's *The Docks of New York* in which a revolver shot is illustrated by the rising of a flock of birds. Such an effect is not just a contrivance on the part of a director to deal with the evil of silence by using an indirect visual method of explaining to the audience that there has been a bang. On the contrary, a positive artistic effect results from the paraphrase. Such indirect representation of an event in a material that is strange to it, or giving not the action itself but only its consequences, is a favorite method in all art. To take an example at random: when Francesca da Rimini tells how she fell in love with the man with whom she was in the habit of reading, and only says "We read no more that day," Dante thereby indicates indirectly, simply by giving the consequences, that on this day they kissed each other. And this indirectness is shockingly impressive.

In the same way, the rising of the birds is particularly effective, and probably more so than if the actual sound of the pistol shot were heard. And then another factor comes in: the spectator does not simply *infer* that a shot has been fired, but he actually *sees* something of the quality of the noise—the suddenness, the abruptness of the rising birds, give visually the exact quality that the shot possesses acoustically. In Jacques Feyder's *Les Nouveaux Messieurs* a political meeting becomes very uproarious, and in order to calm the rising emotions Suzanne puts a coin into a mechanical piano. Immediately the hall is lit up by hundreds of electric bulbs, and now the music chimes in with the agitative speech. The music is not heard: it is a silent film. But Feyder shows the audience excitedly listening to the speaker; and suddenly the faces soften and relax; all the heads begin quite gently to sway in time to the music. The rhythm grows more pronounced until at last the spirit of the dance has seized them all; and they swing their bodies gaily from side to side as if to an unheard word of command. The speaker has to give way to the music. Much more clearly than if the music were actually heard, this shows the power that suddenly unites all these discontented people, puts them into the same merry mood; and indicates as well the character of the music itself, its sway and rhythm. What is particularly noteworthy in such a scene is not merely how easily and cleverly the director makes visible something that is not visual, but by so doing, actually strengthens its effect. If the music were really heard, the spectator might simply realize that music was sounding, but by this indirect method, the particular point, the important part of this music—its rhythm, its power to unite and "move" men—is conspicuously brought out. Only these special attributes of the music are given, and appear as the music itself. Similarly the fact that a pistol shot is sudden, explosive, startling, becomes doubly impressive by transposition into the visible, because only these particular attributes and not the shot itself are given. Thus silent film derives definite artistic potentialities from its silence. What it wishes particularly to emphasize in an audible occurrence is transposed into something visual; and thus instead of giving the occurrence "itself," it gives only some of its telling characteristics, and thereby shapes and interprets it.

Owing to its insubstantiality silent film does not in any way give the effect of being dumb pantomime. Its silence is not noticed, unless the action happens to culminate in something acoustic for which nothing can be substituted, and which is therefore felt as missing—or unless one is accustomed to sound film. Because of sound film, in the future it will be possible only with great difficulty to show speech in a silent way. Yet this is a most effective artistic device. For if a man is heard speaking, his gestures and facial expression only appear as an accompaniment to underline the sense of what is said. But if one does not hear what is said, the meaning becomes indirectly clear and is artistically interpreted by muscles of the face, of the limbs, of the body. The emotional quality of the conversation is made obvious with a clarity and definiteness which are hardly possible in the medium of actual speech. Moreover, the divergence between reality and dumb show gives the actor and his director plenty of leeway for artistic invention. (The creative power of the artist can only come into play where reality and the medium of representation do not coincide.)

Dialogue in silent film is not simply the visible part of a real spoken dialogue. If a real dialogue is shown without the sound, the spectator will often fail to grasp what it is all about; he will find the facial expression and the gestures unintelligible. In silent film, the lips are no longer word-forming physical organs but a means of visual expression—the distortion of an excited mouth or the fast chatter of lips are not mere by-products of talking; they are communications in their own right. Silent laughter is often more effective than if the sound is actually heard. The gaping of the open mouth gives a vivid, highly artistic interpretation of the phenomenon "laughter." If, however, the sound is also heard, the opening of the mouth appears obvious and its value as a means of expression is almost entirely lost. This opportunity of the silent film was once used by the Russians in a most unusual and effective manner. A shot of a soldier who had gone mad in the course of a battle and was laughing hideously with his mouth wide open was joined with a shot of the body of a soldier who had died of poison gas, and whose mouth was fixed in death in a ghastly, rigid grin.

The absence of the spoken word concentrates the spectator's attention more closely on the visible aspect of behavior, and thus the whole event draws particular interest to itself. Hence it is that very ordinary shots are often so impressive in silent films—such as a documentary shot of an itinerant hawker crying his wares with grandiose gestures. If his words could be heard the effect of the gestures would not be half as great, and the whole episode might attract very little attention. If, however, the words are omitted, the spectator surrenders entirely to the expressive power of the gestures. Thus by merely robbing the real event of something—the sound—the appeal of such an episode is greatly heightened. . . .

1933

BÉLA BALÁZS
FROM THEORY OF THE FILM

THE CLOSE-UP

THE FACE OF THINGS

The first new world discovered by the film camera in the days of the silent film was the world of very small things visible only from very short distances, the hidden life of little things. By this the camera showed us not only hitherto unknown objects and events: the adventures of beetles in a wilderness of blades of grass, the tragedies of day-old chicks in a corner of the poultry-run, the erotic battles of flowers and the poetry of miniature landscapes. It brought us not only new themes. By means of the close-up the camera in the days of the silent film revealed also the hidden mainsprings of a life which we had thought we already knew so well. Blurred outlines are mostly the result of our insensitive shortsightedness and superficiality. We skim over the teeming substance of life. The camera has uncovered that cell-life of the vital issues in which all great events are ultimately conceived; for the greatest landslide is only the aggregate of the movements of single particles. A multitude of close-ups can show us the very instant in which the general is transformed into the particular. The close-up has not only widened our vision of life, it has also deepened it. In the days of the silent film it not only revealed new things, but showed us the meaning of the old.

VISUAL LIFE

The close-up can show us a quality in a gesture of the hand we never noticed before when we saw that hand stroke or strike something, a quality which is often more expressive than any play of the features. The close-up shows your shadow on the wall with which you have lived all your life and which you scarcely knew; it shows the speechless face and fate of the dumb objects that live with you in your room and whose fate is bound up with your own. Before this you looked at your life as a concert-goer ignorant of music listens to an orchestra playing a symphony. All he hears is the leading melody, all the rest is blurred into a general murmur. Only those can really understand and enjoy the music who can hear the contrapuntal architecture of each part in the score. This is how we see life: only its leading melody meets the eye. But a good film with its close-ups reveals the most hidden parts in our polyphonous life, and teaches us to see the intricate visual details of life as one reads an orchestral score.

LYRICAL CHARM OF THE CLOSE-UP

The close-up may sometimes give the impression of a mere naturalist preoccupation with detail. But good close-ups radiate a tender human attitude in the contemplation of hidden things, a delicate solicitude, a gentle bending over the intimacies of life-in-the-miniature, a warm sensibility. Good close-ups are lyrical; it is the heart, not the eye, that has perceived them.

Close-ups are often dramatic revelations of what is really happening under the surface of appearances. You may see a medium shot of someone sitting and conducting a conversation with icy calm. The close-up will show trembling fingers nervously fumbling a small object — sign of an internal storm. Among pictures of a comfortable house breathing a sunny security, we suddenly see the evil grin of a vicious head on the carved mantelpiece or the menacing grimace of a door opening into darkness. Like the *leitmotif* of impending fate in an opera, the shadow of some impending disaster falls across the cheerful scene.

Close-ups are the pictures expressing the poetic sensibility of the director. They show the faces of things and those expressions on them which are significant because they are reflected expressions of our own subconscious feeling. Herein lies the art of the true cameraman.

In a very old American film I saw this dramatic scene: the bride at the altar suddenly runs away from the bridegroom whom she detests, who is rich and who has been forced on her. As she rushes away she must pass through a large room full of wedding presents. Beautiful things, good things, useful things, things radiating plenty and security smile at her and lean towards her with expressive faces. And there are the presents given by the bridegroom: faces of things radiating touching attention, consideration, tenderness, love —

and they all seem to be looking at the fleeing bride, because she looks at them; all seem to stretch out hands towards her, because she feels they do so. There are ever more of them—they crowd the room and block her path—her flight slows down more and more, then she stops and finally turns back. . . .

Having discovered the soul of things in the close-up, the silent film undeniably overrated their importance and sometimes succumbed to the temptation of showing "the hidden little life" as an end in itself, divorced from human destinies; it strayed away from the dramatic plot and presented the "poetry of things" instead of human beings. But what Lessing said in his *Laokoon* about Homer—that he never depicted anything but human actions and always described objects only inasmuch as they took part in the action—should to this day serve as a model for all epic and dramatic art as long as it centres around the presentation of man.

THE FACE OF MAN

Every art always deals with human beings, it is a human manifestation and presents human beings. To paraphrase Marx: "The root of all art is man." When the film close-up strips the veil of our imperceptiveness and insensitivity from the hidden little things and shows us the face of objects, it still shows us man, for what makes objects expressive are the human expressions projected on to them. The objects only reflect our own selves, and this is what distinguished art from scientific knowledge (although even the latter is to a great extent subjectively determined). When we see the face of things, we do what the ancients did in creating *gods* in man's image and breathing a human soul into them. The close-ups of the film are the creative instruments of this mighty visual anthropomorphism.

What was more important, however, than the discovery of the physiognomy of things, was the discovery of the human face. Facial expression is the most subjective manifestation of man, more subjective even than speech, for vocabulary and grammar are subject to more or less universally valid rules and conventions, while the play of features, as has already been said, is a manifestation not governed by objective canons, even though it is largely a matter of imitation. This most subjective and individual of human manifestations is rendered objective in the close-up.

A NEW DIMENSION

If the close-up lifts some object or some part of an object out of its surroundings, we nevertheless perceive it as existing in space;

we do not for an instant forget that the hand, say, which is shown by the close-up, belongs to some human being. It is precisely this connection which lends meaning to its every movement. But when Griffith's genius and daring first projected gigantic "severed heads" on to the cinema screen, he not only brought the human face closer to us in space, he also transposed it from space into another dimension. We do not mean, of course, the cinema screen and the patches of light and shadow moving across it, which being visible things, can be conceived only in space; we mean the expression on the face as revealed by the close-up. We have said that the isolated hand would lose its meaning, its expression, if we did not know and imagine its connection with some human being. The facial expression on a face is complete and comprehensible in itself and therefore we need not think of it as existing in space and time. Even if we had just seen the same face in the middle of a crowd and the close-up merely separated it from the others, we would still feel that we have suddenly been left alone with this one face to the exclusion of the rest of the world. Even if we have just seen the owner of the face in a long shot, when we look into the eyes in a close-up, we no longer think of that wide space, because the expression and significance of the face has no relation to space and no connection with it. Facing an isolated face takes us out of space, our consciousness of space is cut out and we find ourselves in another dimension: that of physiognomy. The fact that the features of the face can be seen side by side, i.e. in space—that the eyes are at the top, the ears at the sides and the mouth lower down—loses all reference to space when we see, not a figure of flesh and bone, but an expression, or in other words when we see emotions, moods, intentions and thoughts, things which although our eyes can see them, are not in space. For feelings, emotions, moods, intentions, thoughts are not themselves things pertaining to space, even if they are rendered visible by means which are.

MELODY AND PHYSIOGNOMY

We will be helped in understanding this peculiar dimension by Henri Bergson's analysis of time and duration. A melody, said Bergson, is composed of single notes which follow each other in sequence, i.e. in time. Nevertheless a melody has no dimension in time, because the first note is made an element of the melody only because it refers to the next note and because it stands in a definite relation to all other notes down to the last. Hence the last note, which may not be played for some time, is yet already present in the first note as a melody-creating element. And the last note completes the melody only because we hear the first note along with it. The notes sound one after the other in a time-sequence, hence they have a real duration, but the coherent line of melody has no dimension in time; the relation of the notes to each other is not a phenomenon occurring in time. The melody is not born gradually in the course of time but is already in existence as a complete entity as soon as the first note is played. How else would we know that a melody is begun? The single notes have duration in time, but their relation to each other, which gives meaning to the individual sounds, is outside time. A logical deduction also has its sequence, but premise and conclusion do not follow one another in time. The process of thinking as a psychological process may have duration; but the logical forms, like melodies, do not belong to the dimension of time.

Now facial expression, physiognomy, has a relation to space similar to the relation of melody to time. The single features, of course, appear in space; but the significance of their relation to one another is not a phenomenon pertaining to space, no more than are the emotions, thoughts and ideas which are manifested in the facial expressions we see. They are picture-like and yet they seem outside space; such is the psychological effect of facial expression.

SILENT SOLILOQUY

The modern stage no longer uses the spoken soliloquy, although without it the characters are silenced just when they are the most sincere, the least hampered by convention: when they are alone. The public of today will not tolerate the spoken soliloquy, allegedly because it is "unnatural." Now the film has brought us the silent soliloquy, in which a face can speak with the subtlest shades of meaning without appearing unnatural and arousing the distaste of the spectators. In this silent monologue the solitary human soul can find a tongue more candid and uninhibited than in any spoken soliloquy, for it speaks instinctively, subconsciously. The language of the face cannot be suppressed or controlled. However disciplined and practisedly hypocritical a face may be, in the enlarging close-up we see even that it is concealing something, that it is looking a lie. For such things have their own specific expressions superposed on the feigned one. It is much easier to lie in words than with the face and the film has proved it beyond doubt.

In the film the mute soliloquy of the face speaks even when the hero is not alone, and herein lies a new great opportunity for depicting man. The poetic significance of the soliloquy is that it is a manifestation of mental, not physical, loneliness. Nevertheless, on the stage a character can speak a monologue only when there is no one else there, even though a character might feel a thousand times more lonely if alone among a large crowd. The monologue of loneliness may raise its voice within him a hundred times even while he is audibly talking to someone. Hence the most deep-felt human soliloquies could not find expression on the stage. Only the film can offer the possibility of such expression, for the close-up can lift a character out of the heart of the greatest crowd and show how solitary it is in reality and what it feels in this crowded solitude.

The film, especially the sound film, can separate the words of a character talking to others from the mute play of features by means of which, in the middle of such a conversation, we are made to overhear a mute soliloquy and realize the difference between this soliloquy and the audible conversation. What a flesh-and-blood actor can show on the real stage is at most that his words are insincere and it is a mere convention that the partner in such a conversation is blind to what every spectator can see. But in the isolated close-up of the film we can see to the bottom of a soul by means of such tiny movements of facial muscles which even the most observant partner would never perceive.

A novelist can, of course, write a dialogue so as to weave into it what the speakers think to themselves while they are talking. But by so doing he splits up the sometimes comic, sometimes tragic, but always awe-inspiring, unity between spoken word and hidden thought with which this contradiction is rendered manifest in the human face and which the film was the first to show us in all its dazzling variety.

"POLYPHONIC" PLAY OF FEATURES

The film first made possible what, for lack of a better description, I call the "polyphonic" play of features. By it I mean the appearance on the same face of contradictory expressions. In a sort of physiognomic chord a variety of feelings, passions and thoughts are synthesized in the play of the features as an adequate expression of the multiplicity of the human soul.

Asta Nielsen once played a woman hired to seduce a rich young man. The man who hired her is watching the results from behind a curtain. Knowing that she is under observation, Asta Nielsen feigns love. She does it convincingly: the whole gamut of appropriate emotion is displayed in her face. Nevertheless we are aware that it is only play-acting, that it is a sham, a mask. But in the course of the scene Asta Nielsen really falls in love with the young man. Her facial expression shows little change; she had been "registering" love all the time and done it well. How else could she now show that this time she was really in love? Her expression changes only by a scarcely perceptible and yet immediately obvious nuance— and what a few minutes before was a sham is now the sincere expression of a deep emotion. Then Asta Nielsen suddenly remembers that she is under observation. The man behind the curtain must not be allowed to read her face and learn that she is now no longer feigning, but really feeling love. So Asta now pretends to be pretending. Her face shows a new, by this time threefold, change. First she feigns love, then she genuinely shows love, and as she is not permitted to be in love in good earnest, her face again registers a sham, a pretence of love. But now it is this pretence that is a lie. Now she is lying that she is lying. And we can see all this clearly in her face, over which she has drawn two different masks. At such times an invisible face appears in front of the real one, just as spoken words can by association of ideas conjure up things unspoken and unseen, perceived only by those to whom they are addressed.

In the early days of the silent film Griffith showed a scene of this character. The hero of the film is a Chinese merchant. Lillian Gish, playing a beggar-girl who is being pursued by enemies, collapses at his door. The Chinese merchant finds her, carries her into his house and looks after the sick girl. The girl slowly recovers, but her face remains stone-like in its sorrow. "Can't you smile?" the Chinese asks the frightened child who is only just beginning to trust him. "I'll try," says Lillian Gish, picks up a mirror and goes through the motions of a smile, aiding her face muscles with her fingers. The result is a painful, even horrible mask which the girl now turns towards the Chinese merchant. But his kindly friendly eyes bring a real smile to her face. The face itself does not change; but a warm emotion lights it up from inside and an intangible nuance turns the grimace into a real expression.

In the days of the silent film such a close-up provided an entire scene. A good idea of the director and a fine performance on the part of the actor gave as a result an interesting, moving, new experience for the audience.

MICROPHYSIOGNOMY

In the silent film facial expression, isolated from its surroundings, seemed to penetrate to a strange new dimension of the soul. It revealed to us a new world—the world of microphysiognomy which could not otherwise be seen with the naked eye or in everyday life. In the sound film the part played by this 'microphysiognomy' has greatly diminished because it is now apparently possible to express in words much of what facial expression apparently showed. But it is never the same—many profound emotional experiences can never be expressed in words at all.

Not even the greatest writer, the most consummate artist of the pen, could tell in words what Asta Nielsen tells with her face in close-up as she sits down to her mirror and tries to make up for the last time her aged, wrinkled face, raddled with poverty, misery, disease and prostitution, when she is expecting her lover, released after ten years in jail; a lover who has retained his youth in captivity because life could not touch him there.

ASTA AT THE MIRROR

She looks into the mirror, her face pale and deadly earnest. It expresses anxiety and unspeakable horror. She is like a general who, hopelessly encircled with his whole army, bends once more, for the last time, over his maps to search for a way out and finds there is no escape. Then she begins to work feverishly, attacking that disgustingly raddled face with a trembling hand. She holds her lipstick as Michelangelo might have held his chisel on the last night of his life. It is a life-and-death struggle. The spectator watches with bated breath as this woman paints her face in front of her mirror. The mirror is cracked and dull, and from it the last convulsions of a tortured soul look out on you. She tries to save her life with a little rouge! No good! She wipes it off with a dirty rag. She tries again. And again. Then she shrugs her shoulders and wipes it all off with a movement which clearly shows that she has now wiped off her life. She throws the rag away. A close-up shows the dirty rag falling on the floor and after it has fallen, sinking down a little more. This movement of the rag is also quite easy to understand— it is the last convulsion of a death agony.

In this close-up "microphysiognomy" showed a deeply moving human tragedy with the greatest economy of expression. It was a great new form of art. The sound film offers much fewer opportunities for this kind of thing, but by no means excludes it and it would be a pity if such opportunities were to be neglected, unnecessarily making us all the poorer. . . .

MUTE DIALOGUES

In the last years of the silent film the human face had grown more and more visible, that is, more and more expressive. Not only had "microphysiognomy" developed but together with it the faculty of understanding its meaning. In the last years of the silent film we saw not only masterpieces of silent monologue but of mute dialogue as well. We saw conversations between the facial expressions of two human beings who understood the movements of each others' faces better than each others' words and could perceive shades of meaning too subtle to be conveyed in words.

A necessary result of this was . . . that the more space and time in the film was taken up by the inner drama revealed in the "microphysiognomic" close-up, the less was left of the predetermined

The accusers and Joan (Falconetti) in *The Passion of Joan of Arc* (1928).
In "Dreyer's film . . . we move in the spiritual dimension of facial
expression alone" (BALÁZS, page 264). "It is a documentary of faces"
(BAZIN, page 367).

8,000 feet of film for all the external happenings. The silent film could thus dive into the depths—it was given the possibility of presenting a passionate life-and-death struggle almost exclusively by close-ups of faces.

Dreyer's film *Jeanne d'Arc* provided a convincing example of this in the powerful, lengthy, moving scene of the Maid's examination. Fifty men are sitting in the same place all the time in this scene. Several hundred feet of film show nothing but big close-ups of heads, of faces. We move in the spiritual dimension of facial expression alone. We neither see nor feel the space in which the scene is in reality enacted. Here no riders gallop, no boxers exchange blows. Fierce passions, thoughts, emotions, convictions battle here, but their struggle is not in space. Nevertheless this series of duels between looks and frowns, duels in which eyes clash instead of swords, can hold the attention of an audience for ninety minutes without flagging. We can follow every attack and riposte of these duels on the faces of the combatants; the play of their features indicates every stratagem, every sudden onslaught. The silent film has here brought an attempt to present a drama of the spirit closer to realization than any stage play has ever been able to do. . . .

1945

GERALD MAST
FROM FILM/CINEMA/MOVIE

PROJECTION

An obvious assumption of the preceding chapter is that the *aesthetic event* of cinema is the projection of the finished work—analogous to the reading of the type that is a novel, the attending to the motion and conversation that are a play, the listening to the sound that is a piece of music, or the looking at the color on canvas that is a painting. The creative process of shooting and assembling film is certainly a worthy subject of study—as are the notebooks of Henry James or the Georges Seurat sketches for *A Sunday Afternoon on the Island of La Grande Jatte*. To study this process reveals both the artist's specific choices and the general way he viewed his art and his craft. But it nonetheless studies the means to the end, and that end is experiencing the work of art itself, which remains its own testament and as solid a piece of evidence as any. With the cinema art it is perhaps an even solider piece of evidence than its maker's recollections of the creative process, since the memories of moviemakers are at least as prone to error as any, since the movie business encourages self-congratulation, and since the creative process of moviemaking is such an admittedly collective one.*

---

*Movie directors are notoriously unreliable. Frank Capra claims he watched Leo McCarey direct Laurel and Hardy at the Hal Roach studio in 1924 (L & H never worked together until 1927); Mack Sennett went to his grave claiming Buster Keaton was one of his Keystone Cops (never); Groucho Marx is under the impression that there are no musical numbers in *A Night at the Opera*

This emphasis on projection necessarily excludes certain interesting kinds of questions, among them some of the classic problems of film, cinema, and movie theory. It denies the notion of "the cinematic" altogether, since it assumes that any finished piece of cinema is indisputably a piece of cinema. The precise meaning of "cinematic" is "of or pertaining to the cinema," and its essence is merely that a succession of frames moves forward through the projector. You can, of course, then discuss whether that succession of frames is interesting or boring, beautiful or ugly, good or bad. True, the primitive film strips of Edison, Lumière, and most of their pre-Griffith contemporaries might properly be called "uncinematic," simply because they had no notion at all of one of the three principles of temporal succession (imagistic succession) and a very clumsy and undeveloped notion of another (structural succession). One of today's experimental, minimal films is certainly not uncinematic in the same way, for its maker was aware of all the possible principles of succession, but deliberately tried to extend or eliminate the use of some of them.

The insistence on projection has certain theoretical advantages. First, it clearly distinguishes cinema from a live theatrical performance, on the one hand, and from television on the other. The fact that film is projected alters its tense (it must necessarily *have been* photographed and processed in the past), whereas the tense of a live theatrical performance (dance, drama, opera) is the now. The fact that film is projected also means that it will be perceived and received differently from a live performance, particularly since projections are perceived and received as a series of different kinds of successions. In a live performance, although plot might parallel structural succession, there are no equivalents to the literal and imagistic successions of cinema; the stage movement is continuous, not successive. The visual power and concentration of cinema's successiveness (coupled with the kinetic power of the individual images) give the force of the spoken word a different (and lighter) "weight" in the cinema than in the drama (as noted and developed by Bazin). Television transmission is not a projection at all; nor is its literal succession identical to cinema's. These differences produce the re-

---

(poor Kitty Carlisle and Allan Jones; or rather, poor us — because Groucho is unfortunately wrong). One of the consistent mistakes of film historians is to quote the recollections of moviemakers as gospel; the American Film Institute has invested both time and money in the recording of some four-hundred "oral histories" of their recollections. To preserve these thoughts and voices for posterity is undeniably valuable, but gospel it isn't.

duced clarity, subtlety, luminosity, density, and (for the present anyway) size of the television image. This reduction also guarantees a different emotional response and reaction to our perception of the weakened kinesis of the television image.

Indeed, the emphasis on projection as the aesthetic event consistently forces our attention on how a work of cinema is received and perceived rather than on what cinema is. Arnheim gets into all kinds of trouble with this problem since he constantly explores the ways in which the cinema image differs physically from natural vision. What he never unscrambles, however, is whether the cinema makes us perceive its differences from nature or whether it fools us by erasing those physical differences so that we perceive the image as apparently quite natural. For example, Arnheim's first principle is that photography converts three-dimensional space into a two-dimensional plane. He then develops the ways that this "fact" can be exploited artistically, some of those exploitations based on the way that the focal lengths of various lenses can alter the way we perceive relative distances between objects. One of his examples is that a newspaper appears to be "cut out" of the face of the person reading it; the converse effect would be the way that a wide-angle lens can make a hand holding a gun in the foreground appear ten times larger than the assailant's face, only an arm's length away.

But do we perceive the projected image as two-dimensional at all? The very fact that we call one object in the projected image apparently close to or far away from another implies that there is some kind of mental translation of the two-dimensional image into three-dimensional terms. In the cinema, when we see large and small, we translate our perception either into close and far (based on our awareness of relative distances and the sizes of objects in life) or into not so close or far but deliberately distorted for some effect by the lens (as in that hand-face example, which we know is based on an impossible relationship of size and distance in nature). We perceive the projected image as a kind of three-dimensional system, once we have learned to translate it (which means that we must learn to watch cinema, just as we must learn any system of translation—and just as we learn to translate sizes into distances in life).

The occasional 3-D movie (or the re-release of one from the Great Flurry of '52) proves that our perception of the projected three-dimensional image is nothing like that of the natural three-dimensional one either. The whole tendency of the 3-D image is to push the action and motion at us; not simply the deliberately hurled objects that sail toward our heads, but even the horizontal movement of walking from left to right feels as if it were thrusting toward us. Even the stationary walls seem to loom out at us, in a way that I do not usually perceive walls to do in life.

The projected cinema image does not appear to be flat; light on a screen is not perceived the same way as paint on canvas. Why not? First, paint is itself a hard, physical material that refracts light. That refraction is the physical stimulus that produces the effect of the painting (since light produces our perception of color by refraction); but it also reminds us of the flatness of the canvas and the material on it (because light bounces off the paint material itself, and that bouncing is perceived as a kind of surface refraction). Those painters who became self-conscious about the flatness of paint on canvas (for example, the evolving rough-textured brush strokes of Van Gogh) simply called attention to the essential flatness of the art by trying to avoid or exploit it. And what else was the development of perspective but a response to the flatness of canvas and paint? It was not the modernist response, however, as was Van Gogh's.

But the "material" of projected images is the immaterial operation of light itself; the images of cinema are produced by light's bouncing off the beaded surfaced of a screen, a refraction that is not, however, perceived as a refractive bouncing of light off a surface, but as the images themselves. The screen seems more to absorb the images (like a sponge) than to refract and bounce them, although such a refraction is literally what we see (but not perceive). The immateriality of light itself and the perception that the screen is a kind of translucent sponge (yet another cinema illusion) militate against the flatness of the projected image, convincing us that the image has a kind of depth (which it obviously does not).

Second, paintings are still and projected images are not. The two physical forms of cinema succession work upon the eye by keeping the photographed subjects constantly in motion. Not only is this motion a further diversion from any consciousness of the screen's flatness, but it is also a way of defining distance and dimensionality. The enlarging or shrinking of an object over a period of time or the length of time required to travel between two points are two familiar ways of defining terms like "close" and "far." One of the striking effects of halting the cinema's motion—of the "freeze frame"—is the sudden reduction of the screen's apparent depth. Only by freezing the movement that is the essence of cinema's succession does one convert the photographed image into a truly two-dimensional plane.

The projection of successive images does not convert three-dimensional nature into a two-dimensional pattern, but changes three-dimensional nature into a different three-dimensional system using two-dimensional symbols. As always, there are exceptional films that attempt to make the projected image appear as flat as possible (the Zagreb animation films, any experimental films that deliberately use the static flatness of lettering and title cards, the films of Len Lye, Norman McLaren, Robert Breer, or anyone else who uses drawn figures of any kind). Walt Disney's entire career in animation can be chronicled as a progressive war against the flatness of cinema cartooning, as a struggle to make the drawn image as apparently three-dimensional as the photographed one. Like so many valuable cinema experiments, these uses or denials of two-dimensionality are ironic reversals or revelations of traits that seem inherent to cinema.

This insistence on projection also addresses whether cinema is or is not an "automatic" art (is for Bazin, Kracauer, Cavell, and their followers; is not for Arnheim, Eisenstein, and theirs). Projection is obviously "automatic," but is the shooting of a film equally "automatic"? And these theories of film as "automatic" art are all based on the recording, not the projection, process. There is *something* about the shooting of a film that is certainly automatic—the precise moment of etching the light on the film material itself. Other than that moment of recording, however, almost nothing about the shooting of a film is automatic. The creators control the intensity and quality of the light; even outdoor sequences use key lights, floodlights, reflectors, and scrims, as well as selecting the precise type and time of day for shooting—as Antonioni did in *Red Desert* or Mizoguchi did in all his films). They control the action within the shot, the setting, the colors, the objects, the details of décor. They control the specific lens that will be used, and the filters for it (if any), and the speed and type of film itself. To reduce the question to the absurd, could you call the shooting of an animated film automatic? Yes, the film captures the light automatically when the single frame is exposed. But no, the entire world that is so captured is the project of a human imagination.

The primacy of projection also solves the nature-nurture controversy in the cinema, since that controversy is a corollary of considering the shooting process as automatic (i.e., cinema automatically records the integrity of nature) or not (i.e., cinema is the artificial project of human choices, not a mechanical recording of nature). Obviously, the projection of a reel of film has nothing to do with nature—no more than does the reading of a novel or the looking at a painting. There may be a good deal of nature (or human life, or natural experience) in the work's succession of frames, images, and events, but there may also be a good deal of this same kind of nature in the content of a novel or the subject of a painting. To emphasize projection is to reiterate that the work of cinema is necessarily as artificial as any work of any art.

To emphasize projection is also to reiterate that an essential condition of the cinema experience is viewing flickering light in an enveloping darkness. This piercing of darkness by projected light is the source of cinema's hypnotic power, paralleling the way that the professional hypnotist entrances a subject by focusing attention on a bright and rhythmically flickering source of light. This light-in-darkness also generates several paradoxes that infuse and influence our experiencing of cinema: we both sit in darkness and are bathed in light; the experience is both private and public at the same time; the projected images both speak to our personal dreams and fantasies and seem to depict the most public and familiar realities. Projection gives us both the concreteness of visual images and the abstract play of light itself.

1977

STANLEY CAVELL
FROM THE WORLD VIEWED

PHOTOGRAPH AND SCREEN

Let us notice the specific sense in which photographs are of the world, of reality as a whole. You can always ask, pointing to an object in a photograph—a building, say—what lies behind it, totally obscured by it. This only accidentally makes sense when asked of an object in a painting. You can always ask, of an area photographed, what lies adjacent to that area, beyond the frame. This generally makes no sense asked of a painting. You can ask these questions of objects in photographs because they have answers in reality. The world of a painting is not continuous with the world of its frame; at its frame, a world finds its limits. We might say: A painting *is* a world; a photograph is *of* the world. What happens in a photograph is that *it* comes to an end. A photograph is cropped, not necessarily by a paper cutter or by masking but by the camera itself. The camera crops it by predetermining the amount of view it will accept; cutting, masking, enlarging, predetermine the amount after the fact. (Something like this phenomenon shows up in recent painting. In this respect, these paintings have found, at the extremest negation of the photographic, media that achieve the condition of photographs.) The camera, being finite, crops a portion from an indefinitely larger field; continuous portions of that field could be included in the photograph in fact taken; in principle, it could all be taken. Hence objects in photographs that run past the edge do not feel cut; they are aimed at, shot, stopped live. When a photograph is cropped, the rest of the world is cut *out*. The implied presence of the rest of the world, and its explicit rejection, are as essential in the experience of a photograph as what it explicitly presents. A camera is an opening in a box: that is the best emblem of the fact that a camera holding on an object is holding the rest of the world away. The camera has been praised for extending the senses; it may, as the world goes, deserve more praise for confining them, leaving room for thought.

The world of a moving picture is screened. The screen is not a support, not like a canvas; there is nothing to support, that way. It holds a projection, as light as light. A screen is a barrier. What does the silver screen screen? It screens me from the world it holds—that is, makes me invisible. And it screens that world from me—that is, screens its existence from me. That the projected world does not exist (now) is its only difference from reality. (There is no feature, or set of features, in which it differs. Existence is not a predicate.) Because it is the field of a photograph, the screen has no frame; that is to say, no border. Its limits are not so much the edges of a given shape as they are the limitations, or capacity, of a container. The screen *is* a frame; the frame is the whole field of the screen—as a frame of film is the whole field of a photograph, like the frame of a loom or a house. In this sense, the screen-frame is a mold, or form.

The fact that in a moving picture successive film frames are fit flush into the fixed screen frame results in a phenomenological frame that is indefinitely extendible and contractible, limited in the smallness of the object it can grasp only by the state of its technology, and in largeness only by the span of the world. Drawing the camera back, and panning it, are two ways of extending the frame; a close-up is of a part of the body, or of one object or small set of objects, supported by and reverberating the whole frame of nature. The altering frame is the image of perfect attention. Early in its history the cinema discovered the possibility of *calling* attention to persons and parts of persons and objects; but it is equally a possibility of the medium not to call attention to them but, rather, to let the world happen, to let its parts draw attention to themselves according to their natural weight. This possibility is less explored than its opposite. Dreyer, Flaherty, Vigo, Renoir, and Antonioni are masters of it.

AUDIENCE, ACTOR, AND STAR

The depth of the automatism of photography is to be read not alone in its mechanical production of an image of reality, but in its mechanical defeat of our presence to that reality. The audience in a theater can be defined as those to whom the actors are present while they are not present to the actors. But movies allow the audience to be mechanically absent. The fact that I am invisible and inaudible to the actors, and fixed in position, no longer needs accounting for; it is not part of a convention I have to comply with; the proceedings do not have to make good the fact that I do nothing in the face of tragedy, or that I laugh at the follies of others. In viewing a movie my helplessness is mechanically assured: I am present not at something happening, which I must confirm, but at something that has happened, which I absorb (like a memory). In this, movies resemble novels, a fact mirrored in the sound of narration itself, whose tense is the past.

It might be said: "But surely there is the obvious difference between a movie house and a theater that is not recorded by what has so far been said and that outweighs all this fiddle of differences. The obvious difference is that in a theater we are in the presence of an actor, in a movie house we are not. You have said that in both places the actor is in our presence and in neither are we in his, the difference lying in the mode of our absence. But there is also the plain fact that in a theater a real man is *there,* and in a movie no real man is there. That is obviously essential to the differences between our responses to a play and to a film." What that means must not be denied; but the fact remains to be understood. Bazin meets it head on by simply denying that "the screen is incapable of putting us 'in the presence of' the actor"; it, so to speak, relays his presence to us, as by mirrors. Bazin's idea here really fits the facts of live television, in which the thing we are presented with is happening simultaneously with its presentation. But in live television, what is present to us while it is happening is not the world, but an event standing out from the world. Its point is not to reveal, but to cover (as with a gun), to keep something on view.

It is an incontestable fact that in a motion picture no live human being is up there. But a human *something* is, and something unlike anything else we know. We can stick to our plain description of that human something as "in our presence while we are not in his" (present *at* him, because looking at him, but not present *to* him) and still account for the difference between his live presence and his photographed presence to us. We need to consider what is present or, rather, since the topic is the human being, *who* is present.

One's first impulse may be to say that in a play the character is present, whereas in a film the actor is. That sounds phony or false: one wants to say that both are present in both. But there is more to it, ontologically more. Here I think of a fine passage of Panofsky's:

> Othello or Nora are definite, substantial figures created by the playwright. They can be played well or badly, and they can be "interpreted" in one way or another; but they most definitely exist, no matter who plays them or even whether they are played at all. The character in a film, however, lives and dies with the actor. It is not the entity "Othello" interpreted by Robeson or the entity "Nora" interpreted by Duse, it is the entity "Greta Garbo" incarnate in a figure called Anna Christie or the entity "Robert Montgomery" incarnate in a murderer who, for all we know or care to know, may forever remain anonymous but will never cease to haunt our memories.

If the character lives and dies with the actor, that ought to mean that the actor lives and dies with the character. I think that is correct, but it needs clarification. Let us develop it slightly.

For the stage, an actor works himself into a role; for the screen, a performer takes the role onto himself. The stage actor explores his potentialities and the possibilities of his role simultaneously; in performance these meet at a point in spiritual space—the better the performance, the deeper the point. In this respect, a role in a play is like a position in a game, say, third base: various people can play it, but the great third baseman is a man who has accepted and trained his skills and instincts most perfectly and matches them most intimately with his discoveries of the possibilities and necessities of third base. The screen performer explores his role like an attic and takes stock of his physical and temperamental endowment; he lends his being to the role and accepts only what fits; the rest is nonexistent. On the stage there are two beings, and the being of the character assaults the being of the actor; the actor survives only by yielding. A screen performance requires not so much training as planning. Of course, both the actor and the performer require, or can make use of, experience. The actor's role is his subject for study, and there is no end to it. But the screen performer is essentially not an actor at all: he *is* the subject of study, and a study not his own. (That is what the content of a photograph is—its subject.) On a screen the study is projected; on a stage the actor is the projector. An exemplary stage performance is one which, for a time, most fully creates a character. After Paul Scofield's performance in *King Lear*, we know who King Lear is, we have seen him in flesh. An exemplary screen performance is one in which, at a time, a star is born. After *The Maltese Falcon* we know a new star, only distantly a person. "Bogart" *means* "the figure created in a given set of films." His presence in those films is who he is, not merely in the sense in which a photograph of an event is that event; but in the sense that if those films did not exist, Bogart would not exist, the name "Bogart" would not mean what it does. The figure it names is not only in our presence, we are in his, in the only sense we could ever be. That is all the "presence" he has.

But it is complicated. A full development of all this would require us to place such facts as these: Humphrey Bogart was a man, and he appeared in movies both before and after the ones that created "Bogart." Some of them did not create a new star (say, the stable groom in *Dark Victory*), some of them defined stars—anyway meteors—that may be incompatible with Bogart (e.g., Duke Mantee and Fred C. Dobbs) but that are related to that figure and may enter into our later experience of it. And Humphrey Bogart was both an accomplished actor and a vivid subject for a camera. Some people are, just as some people are both good pitchers and good hitters; but there are so few that it is surprising that the word "actor" keeps on being used in place of the more beautiful and more accurate word "star"; the stars are only to gaze at, after the fact, and their actions divine our projects. Finally, we must note the sense in which the creation of a (screen) performer is also the creation of a character—not the kind of character an author creates, but the kind that certain real people are: a type.

TYPES; CYCLES AS GENRES

Our attention turns from the physical medium of cinema in general to the specific forms or genres the medium has taken in the course of its history.

Both Panofsky and Bazin begin at the beginning, noting and approving that early movies adapt popular or folk arts and themes and performers and characters: farce, melodrama, circus, music hall, romance, etc. And both are gratifyingly contemptuous of intellectuals who could not come to terms with those facts of life. (Such intellectuals are the alter egos of the film promoters they so heartily despise. Roxy once advertised a movie as "Art, in every sense of the word"; his better half declaims, "This is not art, in any sense of the word.") Our question is, why did such forms and themes and characters lend themselves to film? Bazin, in what I have read of him, is silent on the subject, except to express gratitude to film for revivifying these ancient forms, and to justify in general the legitimacy of adaptation from one art to another. Arnold Hauser, if I understand him, suggests wrong answers, in a

passage that includes the remark "Only a young art can be popular," a remark that not only is in itself baffling (did Verdi and
Dickens and Shakespeare and Chaplin and Frank Loesser work
in young arts?) but suggests that it was only natural for the movies
to pick up the forms they did. It *was* natural—anyway it happened
fast enough—but not because movies were destined to popularity
(they were at first no more popular than other forms of entertainment). In any case, popular arts are likely to pick up the forms
and themes of high art for their material—popular theater naturally *burlesques*. And it means next to nothing to say that movies
are young, because we do not know what the normal life span of
an art is supposed to be, nor what would count as a unit of measure.
Panofsky raises the question of the appropriateness of these original forms, but his answer is misleading.

> The legitimate paths of evolution [for the film] were opened, not
> by running away from the folk art character of the primitive film
> but by developing it within the limits of its own possibilities. Those
> primordial archetypes of film productions on the folk art level—
> success or retribution, sentiment, sensation, pornography, and crude
> humor—could blossom forth into genuine history, tragedy and
> romance, crime and adventure, and comedy, as soon as it was re-
> alized that they could be transfigured—not by an artificial injection
> of literary values but by the exploitation of the unique and specific
> possibilities of the new medium.

The instinct here is sound, but the region is full of traps. What
are "the unique and specific possibilities of the new medium"?
Panofsky defines them as dynamization of space and spatialization
of time—that is, in a movie things move, and you can be moved
instantaneously from anywhere to anywhere, and you can witness
successively events happening at the same time. He speaks of these
properties as "self-evident to the point of triviality" and, because
of that, "easily forgotten or neglected." One hardly disputes this,
or its importance. But we still do not understand what makes these
properties "the possibilities of the medium." I am not now asking
how one would know that these are *the* unique and specific possibilities (though I will soon get back to that); I am asking what
it means to call them possibilities at all.

Why, for example, didn't the medium begin and remain in the
condition of home movies, one shot just physically tacked on to
another, cut and edited simply according to subject? (Newsreels
essentially did, and they are nevertheless valuable, enough so to
have justified the invention of moving pictures.) The answer seems
obvious: narrative movies emerged because someone "saw the
possibilities" of the medium—cutting and editing and taking shots
at different distances from the subject. But again, these are mere

actualities of film mechanics: every home movie and newsreel contains them. We could say: to make them "possibilities of the medium" is to realize what will give them *significance*—for example, the narrative and physical rhythms of melodrama, farce, American comedy of the 1930s. It is not as if film-makers saw these possibilities and then looked for something to apply them to. It is truer to say that someone with the wish to make a movie saw that certain established forms would give point to certain properties of film.

This perhaps sounds like quibbling, but what it means is that the aesthetic possibilities of a medium are not givens. You can no more tell what will give significance to the unique and specific aesthetic possibilities of projecting photographic images by thinking about them or seeing some, than you can tell what will give significance to the possibilities of paint by thinking about paint or by looking some over. You have to think about painting, and paintings; you have to think about motion pictures. What does this "thinking about them" consist in? Whatever the useful criticism of an art consists in. (Painters before Jackson Pollock had dripped paint, even deliberately. Pollock made dripping into a medium of painting.) I feel like saying: The first successful movies—i.e., the first moving pictures accepted as motion pictures—were not applications of a medium that was defined by given possibilities, but the *creation of a medium* by their giving significance to specific possibilities. Only the art itself can discover its possibilities, and the discovery of a new possibility is the discovery of a new medium. A medium is something through which or by means of which something specific gets done or said in particular ways. It provides, one might say, particular ways to get through to someone, to make sense; in art, they are forms, like forms of speech. To discover ways of making sense is always a matter of the relation of an artist to his art, each discovering the other.

Panofsky uncharacteristically skips a step when he describes the early silent films as an "unknown language . . . forced upon a public not yet capable of reading it." His notion is (with good reason, writing when he did) of a few industrialists forcing their productions upon an addicted multitude. But from the beginning the language was not "unknown"; it was known to its creators, those who found themselves speaking it; and in the beginning there was no "public" in question; there were just some curious people. There soon was a public, but that just proves how easy the thing was to know. If we are to say that there was an "unknown" something, it was less like a language than like a fact—in particular, the fact that something is intelligible. So while it may be true, as Panofsky says, that "for a Saxon peasant of around 800 it was not easy to understand the meaning of a picture showing a man as he pours water over the head of another man," this has nothing special to do with the problems of a moviegoer. The meaning of that act of pouring in certain communities is still not easy to understand; it was and is impossible to understand for anyone to whom the practice of baptism is unknown. Why did Panofsky suppose that comparable understanding is essential, or uniquely important, to the reading of movies? Apparently he needed an explanation for the persistence in movies of "fixed iconography"—"the well-remembered types of the Vamp and the Straight Girl . . . the Family Man, and the Villain," characters whose conduct was "predetermined accordingly"—an explanation for the persistence of an obviously primitive or folkloristic element in a rapidly developing medium. For he goes on, otherwise inexplicably, to say that "devices like these became gradually less necessary as the public grew accustomed to interpret the action by itself and were virtually abolished by the invention of the talking film." In fact such devices persist as long as there are still Westerns and gangster films and comedies and musicals and romances. *Which* specific iconography the Villain is given will alter with the times, but that his iconography remains specific (i.e., operates according to a "fixed attitude and attribute" principle) seems undeniable: if Jack Palance in *Shane* is not a Villain, no honest home was ever in danger. Films have changed, but that is not because we don't need such explanations any longer; it is because we can't *accept* them.

These facts are accounted for by the actualities of the film medium itself: types are exactly what carry the forms movies have relied upon. These media created new types, or combinations and ironic reversals of types; but there they were, and stayed. Does this mean that movies can never create individuals, only types? What it means is that this is the movies' way of creating individuals: they create *individualities*. For what makes someone a type is not his similarity with other members of that type but his striking separateness from other people.

Until recently, types of black human beings were not created in film: black people were stereotypes—mammies, shiftless servants, loyal retainers, entertainers. We were not given, and were not in a position to be given, individualities that projected particular *ways* of inhabiting a social role; we recognized only the role. Occasionally the humanity behind the role would manifest itself; and the result was a revelation not of a human individuality, but of an entire realm of humanity becoming visible. When in *Gone With the Wind* Vivien Leigh, having counted on Butterfly McQueen's professed knowledge of midwifery, and finding her as ignorant as herself, slaps her in rage and terror, the moment can stun us with a question: What was the white girl assuming about blackness when she believed the casual claim of a black girl, younger and duller and more ignorant than herself, to know all about the mysteries of childbirth? The assumption, though apparently complimentary, is dehumanizing—with such creatures knowledge of the body comes from nowhere, and in general they are to be trusted absolutely or not at all, like lions in a cage, with whom you either do or do not know how to deal. After the slap, we are left with two young girls equally frightened in a humanly desperate situation, one limited by a distraction which expects and forgets that it is to be bullied, the other by an energetic resourcefulness which knows only how to bully. At the end of Michael Curtiz' *Breaking Point*, as the wounded John Garfield is carried from his boat to the dock, awaited by his wife and children and, just outside the circle, by the other woman in his life (Patricia Neal), the camera pulls away, holding on the still waiting child of his black partner, who only the unconscious Garfield knows has been killed. The poignance of the silent and unnoticed black child overwhelms the yarn we had been shown. Is he supposed to symbolize the fact of general human isolation and abandonment? Or the fact that every action has consequences for innocent bystanders? Or that children are the real sufferers from the entangled efforts of adults to straighten out their lives? The effect here is to rebuke Garfield for attaching so much importance to the loss of his arm, and generally to blot out attention to individual suffering by invoking a massive social evil about which this film has nothing to say.

The general difference between a film type and a stage type is that the individuality captured on film naturally takes precedence over the social role in which that individuality gets expressed. Because on film social role appears arbitrary or incidental, movies have an inherent tendency toward the democratic, or anyway the idea of human equality. (But because of film's equally natural attraction to crowds, it has opposite tendencies toward the fascistic or populistic.) This depends upon recognizing film types as inhabited by figures we have met or may well meet in other circumstances. The recognized recurrence of film performers will become a central idea as we proceed. At the moment I am emphasizing only that in the case of black performers there was until recently no other place for them to recur in, except just the role within which we have already met them. For example, we would not have expected to see them as parents or siblings. I cannot at the moment remember a black person in a film making an ordinary purchase— say of a newspaper, or a ticket to a movie or for a train, let alone writing a check. (*Pinky* and *A Raisin in the Sun* prove the rule: in the former, the making of a purchase is a climactic scene in the film; in the latter, it provides the whole subject and structure.)

One recalls the list of stars of every magnitude who have pro-

vided the movie camera with human subjects—individuals capable
of filling its need for individualities, whose individualities in turn,
whose inflections of demeanor and disposition were given full
play in its projection. They provided, and still provide, staples
for impersonators: one gesture or syllable of mood, two strides,
or a passing mannerism was enough to single them out from all
other creatures. They realized the myth of singularity—that we
can still be found, behind our disguises of bravado and cowardice,
by someone, perhaps a god, capable of defeating our self-defeats.
This was always more important than their distinction by beauty.
Their singularity made them more like us—anyway, made their
difference from us less a matter of metaphysics, to which we must
accede, than a matter of responsibility, to which we must bend.
But then that made them even more glamorous. That they should
be able to stand upon their singularity! If one did that, one might
be found, and called out, too soon, or at an inconvenient moment.

What was wrong with type-casting in films was not that it displaced some other, better principle of casting, but that factors
irrelevant to film-making often influenced the particular figures
chosen. Similarly, the familiar historical fact that there are movie
cycles, taken by certain movie theorists as in itself a mark of un-
scrupulous commercialism, is a possibility internal to the medium;
one could even say, it is the best emblem of the fact that a medium
had been created. For a cycle is a genre (prison movies, Civil War
movies, horror movies, etc.); and a genre is a medium.

As Hollywood developed, the original types ramified into individualities as various and subtle, as far-reaching in their capacities to inflect mood and release fantasy, as any set of characters
who inhabited the great theaters of our world. We do not know
them by such names as Pulcinella, Crispin, Harlequin, Pantaloon,
the Doctor, the Captain, Columbine; we call them the Public Enemy, the Priest, James Cagney, Pat O'Brien, the Confederate Spy,
the Army Scout, Randolph Scott, Gary Cooper, Gable, Paul Muni,
the Reporter, the Sergeant, the Sheriff, the Deputy, the D.A., the
Quack, the Shyster, the Other Woman, the Fallen Woman, the
Moll, the Dance Hall Hostess. Hollywood was the theater in which
they appeared, because the films of Hollywood constituted a world,
with recurrent faces more familiar to me than the faces of the neighbors of all the places I have lived.

The great movie comedians—Chaplin, Keaton, W. C. Fields—
form a set of types that could not have been adapted from any
other medium. Its creation depended upon two conditions of the
film medium mentioned earlier. These conditions seem to be necessities, not merely possibilities, so I will say that two necessities
of the medium were discovered or expanded in the creation of
these types. First, movie performers cannot project, but are pro-

jected. Second, photographs are of the world, in which human beings are not ontologically favored over the rest of nature, in which objects are not props but natural allies (or enemies) of the human character. The first necessity—projected visibility—permits the sublime comprehensibility of Chaplin's natural choreography; the second—ontological equality—permits his Proustian or James-ian relationships with Murphy beds and flights of stairs and with vases on runners on tables on rollers: the heroism of momentary survival, Nietzsche's man as a tightrope across an abyss. These necessities permit not merely the locales of Keaton's extrications, but the philosophical mood of his countenance and the Olympic resourcefulness of his body; permit him to be perhaps the only constantly beautiful and continuously hilarious man ever seen, as though the ugliness in laughter should be redeemed. They permit Fields to mutter and suffer and curse obsessively, but heard and seen only by us; because his attributes are those of the gentleman (confident swagger and elegant manners, gloves, cane, outer hearti-ness), he can manifest continuously with the remorselessness of nature, the psychic brutalities of bourgeois civilization.

IDEAS OF ORIGIN

It is inevitable that in theorizing about film one at some point speculate about its origins, because despite its recentness, its origin remains obscure. The facts are well enough known about the invention and the inventors of the camera, and about improve-ments in fixing and then moving the image it captures. The problem is that the invention of the photographic picture is not the same thing as the creation of photography as a medium for making sense. The historical problem is like any other: a chronicle of the facts preceding the appearance of this technology does not explain why it happened when and as it did. Panofsky opens his study of film by remarking, "It was not an artistic urge that gave rise to the discovery and gradual perfection of a new technique; it was a technical invention that gave rise to the discovery and gradual perfection of a new art." We seem to understand this, but do we understand it? Panofsky assumes we know what it is that at any time has "given rise" to a "new art." He mentions an "artistic urge," but that is hardly a candidate to serve as an explanation; it would be about as useful as explaining the rise of modern science by appealing to "a scientific urge." There may be such urges, but they are themselves rather badly in need of explanation. Panofsky cites an artistic urge explicitly as the occasion for a new "tech-nique." But the motion picture is not a new *technique*, any more than the airplane is. (What did we use to do that such a thing enables us to do better?) Yet some idea of flying, and an urge to do it, preceded the mechanical invention of the airplane. What is "given rise to" by such inventions as movable type or the microscope or the steam engine or the pianoforte?

It would be surprising if the history of the establishment of an artistic medium were less complex a problem for the historical understanding than (say) the rise of modern science. I take Bazin to be suggesting this when he reverses the apparent relation between the relevant technology and the idea of cinema, emphasizing that the idea preceded the technology, parts of it by centuries, and that parts of the technology preceded the invention of movies, some of it by centuries. So what has to be explained is not merely how the feat was technically accomplished but, for example, what stood in the way of its happening earlier. Surprisingly, Bazin, in the selection of essays I have read, does not include the contemporary condition of the related arts as a part of the ideological superstructure that elicited the new material basis of film. But it is certainly relevant that the burning issue during the latter half of the nineteenth century, in painting and in the novel and in the theater, was realism. And unless film captured possibilities opened up by the arts themselves, it is hard to imagine that its possibilities as an artistic medium would have shown up as, and as suddenly as, they did.

The idea of and wish for the world re-created in its own image was satisfied *at last* by cinema. Bazin calls this the myth of total cinema. But it had always been one of the myths of art; each of the arts had satisfied it in its own way. The mirror was in various hands held up to nature. In some ways it was more fully satisfied in theater. (Since theater is on the whole not now a major art for us, it on the whole no longer makes contact with its historical and psychological sources; so we are rarely gripped by the trauma we must once have suffered when the leader of the chorus stopped contributing to a narrative or song and turned to face the others, suffering incarnation.)

What is cinema's way of satisfying the myth? Automatically, we said. But what does that mean—mean mythically, as it were? It means satisfying it without *my* having to do anything, satisfying it *by* wishing. In a word, *magically*. I have found myself asking: How could film be art, since all the major arts arise in some way out of religion? Now I can answer: Because movies arise out of magic; from *below* the world.

The better a film, the more it makes contact with this source of its inspiration; it never wholly loses touch with the magic lantern behind it. This suggests why movies of the fantastic (*The Cabinet of Dr. Caligari, Blood of a Poet*) and filmed scenes of magic (say, materialization and dematerialization), while they have provided moods and devices, have never established themselves as cine-matic media, however strongly this "possibility" is suggested by the physical medium of film: they are technically and psycho-logically trivial compared with the medium of magic itself. It is otherwise if the presented magic is itself made technically or physically interesting *(The Invisible Man, Dr. Jekyll and Mr. Hyde, Frankenstein, 2001: A Space Odyssey)*, but then that be-comes another way of confirming the physicality of our world. Science presents itself, in movies, as magic, which was indeed one source of science. In particular, projected science retains magic's mystery and forbiddenness. Science-fiction films exploit not merely certain obvious aspects of adventure, and of a physicality that special effects specialize in, but also the terrific mumbo-jumbo of hearsay science: "My God, the thing is impervious to the negative beta ray! We must reverse the atom recalcitration spatter, before it's too late!" The dialogue has the surface of those tinbox-and-lever contraptions that were sufficiently convincing in prime *Flash Gordon*. These films are carried by the immediacy of the fantasy that motivates them (say, destruction by lower or higher forms of life, as though the precariousness of human life is due to its biological stage of development); together with the myth of the one way and last chance in which the (external) danger can be averted. And certainly the beauty of forms and motions in Frank-enstein's laboratory is essential to the success of *Frankenstein;* computers seem primitive in comparison. It always made more sense to steal from God than to try to outwit him.

How do movies reproduce the world magically? Not by liter-ally presenting us with the world, but by permitting us to view it unseen. This is not a wish for power over creation (as Pygma-lion's was), but a wish not to need power, not to have to bear its burdens. It is, in this sense, the reverse of the myth of Faust. And the wish for invisibility is old enough. Gods have profited from it, and Plato tells it at the end of the *Republic* as the Myth of the Ring of Gyges. In viewing films, the sense of invisibility is an expression of modern privacy or anonymity. It is as though the world's projection explains our forms of unknownness and of our ability to know. The explanation is not so much that the world is passing us by, as that we are displaced from our natural habita-tion within it, placed at a distance from it. The screen overcomes our fixed distance; it makes displacement appear as our natural condition.

1971

F. E. SPARSHOTT
BASIC FILM AESTHETICS

The basic aesthetics of film as of any other art must be descriptive and analytic, giving an account of the relevant variables and their means of variation. And any such account must be rooted in some notion, however imprecise, of what a work of the art in question is. What, then, is a film? It seems to be characteristic of the art that acceptable definitions need to specify not only the nature of the work itself but also the means essential to its production and its characteristic effects. A sample definition might go like this: "A film is a series of motionless images projected onto a screen so fast as to create in the mind of anyone watching the screen an impression of continuous motion, such images being projected by a light shining through a corresponding series of images arranged on a continuous band of flexible material." Much variation in detail and in emphasis is possible, but no definition can dispense with two important features: a succinct description of at least the basic features of the *mechanism* employed, and an allusion to the creation of an *illusion* of motion. Let us consider these necessary features in turn.

MECHANISM

More than any other art, film is technologically determined. Music, dance, drawing, painting, sculpture, poetry, even architecture need for their original and rudimentary forms either no materials or materials lying everywhere at hand, but cinematography cannot begin without laboriously invented and precisely constructed equipment. The history of film is the history of the in-

vention of its means. Aestheticians of the cinema may often be differentiated by how they react to various aspects of its technology:
the properties of lenses and emulsions, the conditions of production and display. Thus the most notorious dogmas about how films
ought to be made are demands for truth to the supposed tendencies
of some aspect of the medium: to the clarity and convincingness
of photographic images, or to the impartial receptivity of a film
camera to whatever may be put before it, or to the camera's way of
reducing whatever is put before it to a homogeneous image, or to
the ease with which assorted scraps of film may be so cemented
as to suggest a common provenance, and so on. It is characteristic
of such dogmas that they fasten on one such aspect and tendency
and ignore the rest. All of them ignore one very important factor:
just because the means of cinema are so complex, anyone who has
mastered them (and, equally rare and difficult, who has regular access to them) will naturally use them to convey whatever message
or vision he may wish to convey, whether or not it is "cinematic"
by any plausible definition. People use their languages to say what
they wish to say, not what the language makes it easy to say. Most
theorists of cinema insist that the outcome of this natural tendency
is bound to be a bad film, but one hardly sees why. Whatever can
be done with a medium is among its possibilities and hence "true to"
it in a sense that has yet to be shown to be illegitimate. A person
may become (or may train himself to be) sensitive to the degree in
which films exploit or ignore some possibility of the medium, and
then may govern his taste or regulate his critical judgment accordingly, but one does not see why such arbitrary selective systems should be imposed on those who would reject them. It is one
thing to show that it is almost impossible to make a good film
by photographing a stage performance of a play, by enumerating
the probable sources of boredom and irritation; it is quite another
to declare that all filmed plays are necessarily nonfilmic and on
that account bad films.

ILLUSION

The second necessary feature of our sample definition was its
reference to an illusion. Perhaps alone among the arts, and certainly in a way quite different from any of the other major arts,
film is necessarily an art of illusion from the very beginning; and
illusion, like technology, serves as a focal point around which
aesthetic disputes arrange themselves. On the one hand, it may be
taken as an opportunity to be exploited. Both by fabricating the
images to be projected and by manipulating the speed and sequence
of their projection, films can and do revel in the creation of the
most elaborate illusions. On the other hand, illusion may be seen
as the temptation to be resisted. The motion on the screen has to

be unreal, but can and should faithfully portray a motion that really took place just so in the real world. Both tendencies go back to the earliest days of cinema, in the work of the realist Lumière and the fantasist Méliès. But that does not mean that film-makers have to choose between embracing and eschewing illusion: quite usually, and in the films of at least some acknowledged masters, fantasy is put at the service of realism (e.g. the stone lions in *Potemkin*) or realism at the service of fantasy (e.g. the homecoming in *Ugetsu*).

To speak broadly of "illusion" as we have done is misleading. While the basic illusion of motion is an automatic and unavoidable function of the mechanism of human vision, what I shall call the "secondary illusions" constructed upon it, to the effect that an event or movement of a certain sort is taking place, are not automatic but depend on the filmgoer's knowledge and his ability or willingness to acquiesce in a pretense. Writers on film often mention a scene in which an Indian villager is pursued by a tiger. The pursuit is shown entirely by intercut shots of scared man and slavering beast until, at the very end, pursuer and pursued at last appear together in a single shot. For Bazin, this saves the scene: previously one had assumed that the propinquity of man and beast was an illusion created by cutting, now one suddenly sees that it was not. For Montagu, it is stupid: the effect was created by the cutting, the concluding two-shot is a banal assertion. And of course on reflection one realizes that either it was a tame tiger or we are being served another trick shot. It seems obvious that different audiences will differ in their susceptibilities to such effects; trying to decide the proprieties (as both writers do) by invoking ultimate principles is surely a waste of time.

THE BIAS OF EXPOSITION

As the example we have just given shows, the secondary illusions of film relate not to what is projected on the screen but to the supposed provenance of the image. No more than when attending a stage play does anyone at the movies feel as if an event were really taking place before his eyes. But why should there be illusions of provenance? The answer seems to lie in the complex relations between cinematography and photography, and the peculiar nature of photographic images themselves. A clue to these relations may be found in the fact that all but one of the demands of "truth to the medium" that we used as examples mentioned some aspect of photography, although our sample definition of a film made no allusion to photography at all.

The images whose successive projection makes a film are most easily produced by photography; but they can be drawn directly on the film stock. A photograph to represent an object is most easily made by aiming a camera at an object of the appropriate kind; but what is photographed may also be a model or a drawing or even another photograph made for the purpose. A photograph of an event or happening is most easily made by finding one and photographing it; but scenes may be enacted and scenery constructed for the purpose. The required succession of images is most easily produced by using a device that will take a lot of photographs in rapid succession and fix them in the right order; but it can be (and in animated cartoons is) drawn or photographed frame by frame. And the obvious way to work the film camera (though not necessarily the easiest; rather it is synchronization that requires care) is to run it at the same speed as you will run your projector; but it can be run faster or slower. Film thus has a bias, quite strong though readily resistible, towards its simplest form, that in which the projector repeats a camera event; and one tends if not on one's guard to assume, wherever nothing in the film suggests the contrary, that what is shown on the screen represents such a repetition, as if the projector copied a camera that enacted the spectator's eye.

An eye is not a camera, and a photographic image does not show what eyes see. As you look around you, your eye constantly adjusts its iris as brightness changes and alters its focus as depth changes. The parallax effect of the use of two eyes gives everything you see a shifting and unstable character, since everything not focused on at the moment yields a vague doubled image. The eye in nature is therefore restless; in looking at a photograph, all in one plane and with a relatively small range of luminosity, the eye is spared much of its labor. However, though a photographic image is not at all like the visible world, it does have precisely the quality that old theorists used to ascribe to that venerable phantom of optics, the retinal image. A photographic image represents a sort of ideal projection, the way we normalize in imagination what we see. What the invention of photography did was not to reproduce vision but to achieve a dream of ideal vision. A photographic image is not so much a true one as a convincing one. Photographs tend to carry an irresistible sense of authenticity. Looking at a good photograph is not like looking at the photographed thing (this is so far from being the case that Peter Ustinov's famous remark, that he made *Billy Budd* in black-and-white because it was more realistic than color, hardly seems paradoxical); it is like looking at a faithful record.

The basic illusion of movement by itself gives an impression not of reality but of a sort of unattributable vivacity. This becomes evident when one watches an animated cartoon. Verisimilitude adds nothing to the lifelikeness of such films, and the elaborate devices used by Disney in his later years to suggest a third dimension have been abandoned as futile (as well as expensive). The sense of reality elicited by such films is akin to that of painting: we attribute the actions we see neither to the real world nor to the screen image, but to Donald Duck and the cartoon world created for him. It is not the illusion of movement, then, that moves us to attribute what we see to the world of experience; rather it is the photographic character of the image that lends films their characteristic bias of exposition, and to the extent that it is present and uncontradicted by the nature of what is presented encourages us to take what we see as the record of something that took place as we see it taking place. The viewer tends to normalize in this sense his perception of films made in the most diverse ways.

Many theories about how films ought to be made represent attitudes to the bias of exposition just described. The Soviet filmmakers of the twenties claimed that the whole art of film lay in exploiting its tendency by the use of montage or associative cutting, joining strips of photographed film in such a way as to synthesize in the spectator's mind an experiential reality that went beyond the images shown. Siegfried Kracauer urged on the contrary that the best use of film is an honest reliance on its capacity to convey authenticity, to preserve and celebrate the sense of reality. His argument was not that a film should actually be a record or chronicle, but that it should celebrate and "redeem," as no other medium can, the radiant actuality of the physical world, eschewing alike fantasies and superimposed formal arrangements. Other critics, noting that film bestows verisimilitude on the deserving and the undeserving alike, urge that film includes among its unique capacities that of making "dreams come true." Only film can *show* the impossible happening and thus make fantasy convincing. In the opposite direction, some exponents of contemporary "underground" film go beyond Kracauer (and beyond Rossellini and the Italian neorealists) in urging that to cut film at all is to falsify: the finished film should consist of all that the camera took in the order it was taken in, and if this means that some shots are out-of-focus, illexposed or irrelevant, they will thereby only be truer to the film experience. On this view, a film records not what happened in front of the camera but what happened to the film *in* the camera. And finally, some extremists might urge that the only honest way to make a film is to set a camera up somewhere and let it just run, taking in whatever may happen along. But at that point the urge to honesty would surely defeat itself by suggesting a standard it cannot fulfill. Films are not natural events, and it is pointless to prevaricate about the selective intervention of the film-maker.

FILM SPACE

That the realism of film is that of a graphic record and not that of an illusive actuality is apparent in the peculiar nature of film

space, the actual and suggested spatial relations between elements
of the film and between film and spectator. Many writers imply
that a film-goer ordinarily feels himself to be in the same relation
to the filmed scene as the camera was (or purports to have been).
On this basis such trick shots as those showing a room through the
flames of a fire in the fireplace are condemned on the ground that
the audience know that nobody would be in that position. But this
seems to be mistaken. Spectators seem to identify themselves with
the camera viewpoint only when some such process as Cinerama
is used which makes the screen approximate to the total visual
environment. Otherwise, shots taken looking straight downward
do not give one a sense of vertigo (though they may do to persons
extremely susceptible in this regard), and even the most rapid
changes in camera position do not produce in an experienced filmgoer any sense of nausea or disorientation. If one really accepted
a change in camera position as a change in one's personal viewpoint, rapid intercutting between different viewpoints would obviously be intolerable. There is certainly a sense in which one has
a feeling of spatial presence at the filmed scene (which is not to be
confused with psychological involvement in the action), construing
the scene as a three-dimensional space in which one is involved
and has a viewpoint. This depth and inclusiveness of cinema space
owes much to parallax, the differential motion and occlusion of distant objects as the viewpoint changes. It follows that when, as often
happens nowadays, action is interrupted by stop-motion, the whole
nature of the space in which the action takes place is instantly
transformed (a striking instance is the concluding scene of *The
Strawberry Statement*). This little-noted factor is important. Without such a change in spatiality, stop-motion might give the impression that the world had suddenly come to a halt; as it is, it confronts
us rather with a transition to a different mode of representation,
and hence perhaps a different mode of being.

The more one reflects on one's sense of cinema space, the more
it seems to be one peculiar to cinema. The use of a zoom lens increasing the (objective) size of the image does have the effect of
bringing the action nearer; but walking towards the screen, though
it produces a (subjectively) larger image and does bring the screen
nearer, does not bring the action nearer at all. One's sense of spatial
involvement in a scene does not depend on one's occupying any
particular seat, but only on one's being neither too close nor too far
to see the screen properly. Similar considerations apply to all the
distortions of space that result from the use of various lenses. The
resulting plasticity of space relations is accepted as a narrative
device or as an invitation to an imaginary viewpoint, it does not
disorient the audience. The use of a deep-focus lens for Miss Havi-
sham's room in *Great Expectations* certainly has a "magnifying"

effect, but a curious one: we do not feel that we are in a big room, but that "this is how it must have seemed to Pip." Again, in the scene where the girl runs toward the airplane in *Zabriskie Point* the scale-relations between girl and low horizon are such that for a second or two we accept what we see as an ordinary medium-shot; then we notice that for all her running the girl is not receding much, and realize that it is a typical telephoto shot. But the effect of this realization on me was not to alter my feeling of where I was in relation to the scene, but to change my interpretation of that relation. In fact, a telephoto shot answers to no possible real spatial relationship between spectator and event: there is a viewing angle, but no possible viewpoint. Yet this never disturbs anyone.

Phenomena of the sort we have been mentioning suggest that one's sense of space in film is somehow bracketed or held in suspense: one is aware of one's implied position and accepts it, but is not existentially committed to it. A simple explanation of this is that most of the time one is simultaneously aware of a film (as one is of a painting) both as a two-dimensional arrangement on the screen and as a three-dimensional scene, so that neither aspect dominates the mind except in moments of excitement or disaffection. A subtler explanation is that cinema vision is alienated vision. A man's sense of where he is depends largely on his sense of balance and his muscular senses, and all a filmgoer's sensory cues other than those of vision and hearing relate firmly to the theater and seat in which he sits. In the scene with the epileptic doctor in *Carnet du Bal*, which is taken with a consistently tilted camera, what one sees on the screen insists that one is off balance, but one's body insists that it is not; and the effect on me is the one Duvivier surely intended, a feeling of malaise accompanied by a sense of *vicarious* disorientation on behalf of the protagonist.

Some of the spatial ambiguity of film is shared with still photography. No matter how one moves a photograph around in relation to oneself, it continues to function as a faithful record implying a viewpoint from which it was taken: and there is a sense in which one continues to be "at" this viewpoint no matter what angle the photograph is inspected from. What differentiates film from still photography is not only the sense of vivacity and hence spatial reality that motion imparts, but also the great size and contrasting illumination of the film image in the darkened theater, whereby it comes much closer to dominating the visual sense, and the relatively invariant relation between screen and spectator.* The director determines the audience's spatial relation to his films, but

---

*Note that in being transferred to the domestic television screen a film loses all three characteristics: size, luminosity, and audience immobility. It becomes an object rather than an experience.

what he determines remains an imaginary space; we are within the film's space but not part of its world; we observe from a viewpoint at which we are not situated.

It is the alienation of the visual sense in cinema space that makes possible many of the uses and special effects of film that work against its function as record. Being deprived of so many sensory cues, the spectator loses all sense of absolute scale, so that back-projections and painted backgrounds may wear a convincing air of reality, and the apparent size of any object may be varied by placing it in a magnified or diminished setting, or simply (as when storms and wrecks are shot using models in tanks) by trading on the spectator's narrative assumptions.

FILM AND DREAM

Unique as it is, the alienated spatiality of film, in which the spectator participates without contact, and which he observes from a viewpoint that contrives to be both definite and equivocal or impossible, presents striking analogies to the space of dreams. Or perhaps, since different people seem to have widely varying dream perceptions, I should limit myself to saying that my own spatial relation to my dream worlds is like nothing in waking reality so much as it is like my relation to film worlds. In my dreams, too, I see from where I am not, and move helplessly in a space whose very nature is inconstant, and may see beside me the being whose perceptions I share. There are indeed many ways in which film-going is like dreaming; but the likeness is always qualified. Films are like dreams in involving one in a world whose course one cannot control, but unlike them in that their world does not incorporate the dream of effort and participation. Filmed reality shares with dreamed reality (as nothing else does) its tolerance of limitlessly inconsequent transitions and transformations; but it lacks that curious conceptual continuity of dreams in which what is a raven may become a writing-desk or may simultaneously *be* a writing-desk, and in which one *knows* that what looks like one person is really a quite different person. The conceptual equivalences essayed by film-makers (e.g. Eisenstein's equation of Kerensky with a peacock in *October*), which usually proceed by intercutting shots of the two entities to be equated, seem rather to be the visual equivalent of similes or metaphors than equivalents of the dream carryover, which depends on a dream-interpretation imposed on the dream-percept and not (as must be the case in film) on an interpretation suggested by the percept itself.

The dreamlikeness of film has often been noted. Usually the recognition takes the form of a loose analogy with daydreaming (which is quite different), but Susanne Langer for one has made the formal analogy with dreaming the basis of her account of the nature of film. The analogy must not be pushed too far. A quite fundamental difference between a filmgoer and a dreamer is that the former remains in control of his faculties, capable of sustained and critical attention. A dream-like inconsequentiality is thus far from typical of film, though it remains among filmic possibilities and the filmgoing public at large acquiesces in a degree of cheerful incoherence (as in *Casino Royale*) that in other arts is acceptable only to the sophisticate.

To the extent that the analogy between film and dream is taken seriously, it seems to invite Freudians to apply their methods of symbolic interpretation with even more confidence than they do to other arts. But they seem not to have accepted the invitation (except in so far as Freudian methodology lies behind the auteur theory of criticism), perhaps because not enough film-makers are safely dead yet. In any case, before we reach that level of interpretation we have to complete our survey of the basic attributes of the film world.

FILM TIME AND FILM REALITY

The same confusion between an actual event and a convincing record that has made critics write of the camera as a surrogate for the spectator's eye leads them to say that film time is present time, that in watching a film one seems to see things happening *now*, as though one were present not at the film but at the filmed event. But this contention is vulnerable to the same sort of objection that refutes the doctrine of the camera eye. In one sense it is true but trivial: of course what one sees is always here and now, because "here" and "now" are defined by one's presence. In any other sense it is false, or we should not be able to take in our stride the flashbacks and flash-forwards, the accelerations and decelerations, that are part of film's stock in trade. Rather, it is as though we were spectators of the temporality of the films we see. Film time has a quality analogous to that dreamlike floating between participation and observation, between definite and indeterminate relationships, that gives film space its pervasive character. Granted, the fundamental illusion of motion combines with the convincingness of a photographic record to ensure that we ordinarily do read the presented motion as continuous and as taking just as much time to happen as it takes us to observe it; but this supposition is readily defeated by any counterindication. D. W. Griffith, challenged on his early use of spatiotemporal discontinuities, justified himself by appealing to the example of Dickens, and surely he was right to do so. The time of a novel is filmic, as its space is not. Events can be filmed, as they can be narrated, with equal facility in any order, at any speed, with any degree of minuteness. Unlike the novelist, however, the film-maker has no language proper to his medium in which to specify temporal relations. He may use titles, trick dissolves, a narrator's voice, or datable visual clues to establish his temporal relations; but some directors seem to feel that such devices are clumsy or vulgar, and prefer to trust the public's acumen or simply to leave the relations indeterminate.

The dream-relationships of film space and the narrative nature of film time combine to encourage an ambiguity that may be fruitful or merely irritating. One often does not know whether one is seeing what in the film's terms is real, or only what is passing through the mind of one of the film's characters. This ambiguity becomes acute whenever there is a temporal jump, for time (as Kant observed) is the form of subjectivity. A flash-back may represent a character's memory, or may simply be a narrative device; a flash-forward may stand for a character's premonition, or simply an anticipation by the film-maker,* and, where the temporally displaced scene is recalled or foreseen, it may stand either for the event as it was or would be, or for the way it is (perhaps falsely) conjured up. The status of film events thus becomes equivocal, and such uncertainty may pervade an entire film. Thus in 8½ some scenes are remembered, some dreamed, some imagined, and some belong to the reality of the film's story. There are many scenes whose status is unclear at the time, and some whose status never becomes clear. Does the opening scene of the closed car in the traffic jam show a seizure which makes the cure necessary (as Arnheim seems to think), or is it a dream of a patient already undergoing treatment (as most critics suppose)? Nothing in the version of the film I saw determined either answer. A more striking equivocation occurs in *Easy Rider*, when a brief glimpse of an unexplained roadside fire is identified at the end of the film as the burning of the hero's motorcycle. Was that first glimpse a premonition of the hero's (and if so, just what did he foresee?), or a *memento mori* by the director, or just a pointless interjection to which no meaning can be assigned? In such a self-indulgent piece of hokum, who can say? In general, the tolerability of such unresolved ambiguities is likely to depend partly on the handling of "reality" in the film as a whole, partly on one's confidence in the director's control over his medium, and partly on one's own tolerance of ambiguity. In any case, one must not suppose that such questions as we have just posed need have a single "right"

---

*The terms "flash-back" and "flash-forward" are often used in such a way as to suggest that every film has a normal time from which all sequences assignable to other times are to be regarded as deviations. But why should this be so? The terms are better taken as marking temporal discontinuities rather than displacements.

answer (perhaps what the director "meant"). All the director has done is to splice celluloid, and if he has not provided enough clues to determine a reading then no meaning is determined. What the director may have had in mind is not the same as what he put on film, and directors sometimes have nothing at all in mind. The flexibility of film technique is a standing invitation to meaningless trickery, and the complexities of production involve endless risks of inadvertent nonsense.

As the apparent time of the action changes, then, so changes the subjectivity/objectivity rating of what we see; and so too may vary our degree of confidence in our ability to assign a rating. Nor are such ambiguities the prerogative of highbrow excursions like *Last Year at Marienbad*. They occur quite naturally in unsophisticated films. For example, in Jerry Lewis's Jekyll-and-Hyde fantasy *The Nutty Professor* the transformation scene in the laboratory slips onto a plane of witty extravagance quite removed from the surface naturalism of the rest of the film. Are we witnessing the event or a metaphor for the event? Who knows? One could spend a long time figuring out possible meanings for it, but in fact it comes across as just a happy episode and the popcorn-grinding jaws do not miss a beat.

FILM MOTION

The ambiguities of space and time combine to give film motion an endless complexity that we have no space to explore here. Let us confine our attention to some additional complications. In the earliest movies, each scene was taken with a fixed camera, so that the motion shown took place within a fixed frame and against an unchanging background. A scene in a modern film is likely to be enriched or muddled with three different kinds of camera motion. The camera may be shifted from place to place, turned horizontally or vertically to alter its field of reception, or modified by changing the focal length of its lens so as to take in a greater or smaller area. This third kind of camera shot is often dismissed as the equivalent of a tracking shot, moving the camera viewpoint toward or away from the scene, but it is not; it retains much of the sense of getting a different view from the same position. A camera can also be rotated on its focal axis, or joggled and steadied, but these can be set aside for now as occasional effects.

Even a shot of immobile objects taken with an immobile camera need not be devoid of movement, for there is also movement of light: illumination may change in direction, in intensity, in color, in sharpness. And even when the light remains unchanged, the much-used prints that most audiences see have a sort of constant surface shimmer, a vibrant presence derived from the random stains and lesions hard use imparts, that has a good deal to do with the "film experience" and is exploited by some film-makers in much the same spirit that furniture-makers fake a "distressed finish." The free combinations of all the kinds of film motion can impart to a single scene a plastic, balletic quality, a unique kind of formal beauty that is at once abstract and realistic and has no parallel in any other medium.

The mobility of the frame combines with the camera's typical neglect of natural boundaries to produce a marked contrast between the actions of theater and cinema. The stage world is a closed world; an actor who goes offstage loses all determinate existence for the audience; but the edge of a cinema screen functions like a window frame through which we glimpse part of a world to which we attribute infinite continuity. This sense of infinity adds an implicit freedom of movement to the actual freedom that the camera's mobility affords.

Because film space and time are observed rather than lived, film motion can be speeded up or slowed down within scenes in a way denied to theater, in which events take their proper time. (Conversely, theater has a way of achieving temporal plasticity denied to film, by exploiting the stage-unreality of the offstage world: in theater, but not in film, offstage actions are often performed in the course of a scene in an incongruously short time.) The effects of such variations in time depend on context, in a way that becomes easier to understand when we reflect that motion photography was invented to serve not one realistic purpose but two: not only to observe and record movements, but also to study and examine them. And of course very fast movements are best studied by slowing down their representation, very slow ones by speeding it up. Nature films are quite regularly made at unnatural speeds, accelerating plant growth and decelerating bird flight, and replays of crucial movements in sport are usually in slow motion. In this context of study the spectator has no sense of unreality at all: he feels simply that he is getting a better look. But in narrative contexts things are different. Acceleration was early discovered to have a reliably comic effect. But deceleration is more variable, for it may produce an impression of joy, or unreality, or obsessiveness, or solemnity, or inevitability. Its effects often evade description, but directors find them reliable enough for regular use, and they have hardened into more than one cliché. One such is the flash-back reverie, where the slow motion seems to work by suggesting weightlessness and hence ethereality (as in *The Pawnbroker*). Another is the use of weightlessness as a metaphor for lightheartedness (as in many TV commercials). A third is the slow-motion death by shooting (as in *Bonnie and Clyde*), partly an appeal to voyeurism but partly a symbolization of death through the transposition of the action into another key of reality.

One can think of acceleration and deceleration as a sort of pre-editing, the equivalent of adding or subtracting frames in a film taken at projector speed. It is basic to film that editing can produce an impression of motion by intercutting suitably spaced shots of the same object in different positions (as by successive still photographs). The impression does not depend on the basic illusion of continuity: provided that the mind can supply a possible trajectory, all that is needed is that the object should appear to be the same and that its position in successive shots should appear to be different. But beyond this, the effect of *any* sustainedly rapid cutting is to produce an impression of rapid motion, even if the intercut shots have no common content and one cannot say what (apart from "things") is moving. An intermediate sort of effect produced by editing is a two-dimensional movement of light, where the continuity of light and dark areas in successive shots is enough to entice the mind to complete a *Gestalt;* but this effect is of limited application, in that it draws attention away from the filmed world to the screen surface.

Cinema's repertory of motions both presented and psychologically suggested is so extensive and so essential that one might think that what film shares with still photography is unimportant, and specifically that two-dimensional composition within the frame can play no significant part in film at all. But that would be going too far. Not only does the awareness of the screen and its flat pattern play an essential part in grounding the ambiguous nature of film space, but directors in practice often do envisage their scenes statically. They make sketches for their key scenes beforehand, and use viewfinders to compose a scene before shooting it. A film no less than a play may proceed from tableau to tableau. Nonetheless, the tableau is insidiously misleading in more than one way. The more one reads about films the more clearly one sees how each film is invariably illustrated by a handful of constantly recurring still shots: *Potemkin* comes to be represented by half a dozen stills, *Caligari* by two, *Nosferatu* by one. Most of these are not even frames taken from the actual film, but photographs taken on a still camera before or after shooting. And they are chosen for their pictorial qualities. What I most vividly recall from *Bicycle Thieves* is the mountain of bundled clothing in the pawnshop, but that image would be nothing without the camera's movement and the action of adding one's own bundle to the mountain; and what the stills show me is a pretty, pathetic picture of the hero and his son sitting on the sidewalk. Thus in time one's recollection of what a film was like becomes distorted.

SOUND

We have been discussing film in visual terms. But for rather more than half its history film has been fully an art of sound as well as sight in the sense that the associated sound has been determined by the same celluloid strip that carries the image. The justification of our procedure is that sight remains primary. It is the requirements of the visual image that call for the elaboration of equipment and the circumstances of display that are fundamental to cinema. Film sound has no distinctive qualities in itself, and can be meaningfully discussed only as an adjunct to the visual.

Though a sound track for a film can be made directly at the time of shooting simply by hanging microphones near the action and recording on the film whatever they pick up, this is neither necessary nor usual. The sound track is usually made separately and combined with the visual film later. The resulting complexities for sound film are theoretically immense, though in practice the technology is not intimidating. The use of magnetic tape has made the recording, inventing, blending, splicing and modification of sounds easy and inexpensive as the analogous procedures for visual film can never be.

The fundamental classification of film sounds is that enunciated by Kracauer. A sound may belong to the world of the film (e.g. the dialogue of its characters) or it may be extraneous (e.g. background music or a commentary). In the former case, it may belong to the very scene being shown on the screen or it may not (you may hear what is happening elsewhere from what you see, or be reminded by the sound track of a previous scene, as a marginal case, what you hear may be a sound remembered by one of the characters). If the sound does belong to the scene being shown, its provenance may be on or off camera (as you hear someone talk, you may see him, or the person he is addressing, or someone who overhears him, or an opening door that he fails to notice). Thus sound may (and in a slackly made film often does) merely duplicate or reinforce what is visible, but it may play an independent structural or narrative role, and may affect the interpretation or emotional tone of what is seen. For example, distortions, fadings, and swellings of voices can be used to overcome one of the difficulties of film narrative, that of economically revealing to the audience a state of mind that someone is successfully hiding from those around him. Background music may supply an ironic comment, as when the refueling of aircraft in *Dr. Strangelove* is accompanied by a love song—a Russian film of the silent days would have made the point by intercutting shots of animals mating, and what a bore it would have been. One can even try to use a musical score to supplement narrative deficiencies, or even to contradict the apparent tendency of what is seen to be happening, though such techniques have some notorious fiascos to their credit.

When determinate sound was first introduced, many film-lovers were opposed to it. In principle, the objection was invalid, for films had never been shown without accompanying (and would-be relevant) sound (a "silent" film shown in silence is a curiosity rather than a significant experience), and in principle the change only guaranteed that from now on the sound would indeed be relevant. But in practice what was feared was the "talking film," in which the sound track merely enabled the audience to hear what they could already see. And the use of sound does indeed make sloppy and mindless film-making easier. But sound can be and properly is used not merely to add another dimension to the film experience but to add an extra perspective to the visual experience itself.

As an alternative to the mindless use of attached sound that they dreaded, the Russian theorists of the late twenties proposed that their favorite device of associative or metaphorical montage should be extended to sound: intercut images should form a counterpoint against intercut sounds. This did not happen. For one thing, auditory comprehension has a much slower tempo than visual; for another, sounds tend to blend whereas images contrast. The proposed contrapuntal montage would have been impossibly over-loaded, if not unintelligible. What montage requires from sound, it turns out, is not a contrapuntal pattern but a chordal backing for its visual melody, a continuous equivalent for or commentary on the character of the whole episode. In any case, the possibility of using sound effects as commentary on the visual images has made elaborate visual montage an obsolete device. This can be thought of as a catastrophic and uncompensated loss to the art of film, but the matter is open to question. Although Eisenstein and others made the use of associative intercutting into a Marxist aesthetic dogma (inasmuch as the conflict of contrasting shots forms a "dialectic" from which the realist truth is synthesized), others have pointed out that the device endears itself to totalitarian regimes by lending itself to lying propaganda: the associations it creates are entirely irrational. Partly, too, the reliance on cutting was enforced by the use of heavy and inflexible camera equipment. Conversely, the decreasing reliance on editing in scene construction is partly due to the introduction of ever more mobile and flexible equipment, partly to the familiarity of multicamera television procedures, partly to difficulties in synchronizing dialogue, but partly also to the fact that commercial directors tend not to do their own cutting anyway, losing effective control over their films as soon as shooting stops.

STRUCTURE

We have been dealing with the materials of film. To make a movie, the materials must somehow be organized. A film can be made simply by linking images and sounds in abstract rhythmic concatenation (as in McLaren's films), or by loosely arranging them around a theme (as in travelogues). But these straightforward methods, though in some ways they represent an ideal of pure cinema, seem to work well only for quite short films, and (especially since the decline of vaudeville) the staple of film production is the "feature," long enough to give the cash customers their money's worth. There are no theoretical limits to the length of a clearly articulated pattern of imagery, but most abstract films are short. The closest actual approximation to an abstract or purely formal method of organizing images is to associate them with extended musical forms, since the latter constitute long formal sequences of a kind that audiences already know and accept; but Disney's Fantasia, though often and lucratively revived, has not aroused emulation and in any case supplemented the musical structure with at least an illusion of parallel narrative form. More usually, coherence is sought through the organization of the subject matter of the imagery: by exploring a problem, or an object, or a place, or a situation, or an event (documentary), or, commonest of all, by constructing a fictitious or historical story. The contrast between documentary and the regular "feature" is not so much that between fact and fiction, for features may be factual and most documentaries have fictional aspects, as between exploratory and narrative methods of organization. The reason for the dominance of the narrative feature lies partly in the flexibility of the film medium, which makes it especially suitable for a free-running narrative whose closest affinities are with novels and biographies, but partly in the assumption that the "mass audience" will associate exploration with instruction and hence with tedium. Now that the mass audience is safely shut away with its TV set things may change: *Woodstock* is a portent. Meanwhile, writers on cinema are bound to assume that the narrative feature remains the norm.

It is from the normal narrative form that the customary description of the articulation of film is derived. In a sense, and from the editor's viewpoint, the unit is the frame, but this does not exist for perception. Aesthetically, a film consists of shots organized into scenes which are themselves articulated into sequences. This structure corresponds, very roughly, to an analysis of activity into movements (shots), actions (scenes), and episodes (sequences). Accordingly, shots cohere into scenes through relevance, each shot being experienced as relevant to expectations aroused earlier in the scene (ideally, I suppose, by the preceding shot). Scenes are divided by jump-cuts or dissolves marking a change of subject; sequences are divided by such more emphatic punctuation as fade-out and fade-in. But (as with novel and theater) no rules or firm conventions demand such articulation: the determining changes are discontinuities of place, time, participants or activities (in abstract films, changes in the kind of image or movement; in documentaries, changes of aspect or style). The film-maker's use of punctuating devices is merely incidental to these. Actually, the very concept of a "shot" becomes nebulous and archaic as cameras become more mobile: the distinction between scene and shot takes on a vagueness such as infects the distinction between an action and its constituent movements.

The plasticity of camera viewpoint is such that films, like novels and unlike plays, can focus one's attention precisely. Only what is irreducibly relevant to the story need to be shown. A raised eyebrow can fill the screen. In theater, perception follows attention: one looks at the relevant part of what is visible on stage and ignores the rest. In film, attention follows perception: whatever is not relevant is either not screened or thrown into shadow or out of focus. Hence, film storytelling can and sometimes does achieve great elegance and economy. Styles change, however. The introduction of the wide screen has made the use of close-ups to isolate relevant detail seem rather blatant, and encourages a more fluid and relaxed style of presentation in which more use is made of the simultaneous presence on the screen of more than one focus for attention.

The focusing habit of the camera and the necessary priority of the visual might make one think that the most filmic and hence the best film story was one in which the *precise* content of each shot set up the story through its dynamic connection with the next. One might further infer from this that tragedy with its overriding architectonic goes against the grain of film, which has a special affinity for such episodic forms as picaresque comedy. There is something in that, but we warned at the start against the facile assumption that the best works in any medium are those which take its most obvious opportunities as procedural rules, and an overly filmic film might have the mechanized aggressiveness of a "well-made play." One could more reasonably infer that the least filmic and hence dullest films would be those in which the dialogue carried the story and the camera just coasted along. And yet that is how most films seem to be made. One can see why. Many films are adapted from literary works in which the dialogue alone can be borrowed without alteration. But in any case the logistics of making a full-scale film are such that it more or less has to be constructed from a detailed shooting-script. Films are largely *written* before they are shot. But writers are bound to be word-oriented. Besides, dialogue is the only part of the script that contributes directly to determining the actual quality of the finished film: specifications of visual images cannot include what will differentiate the effective from the flat, the fine from the clumsy. Perhaps most important, to throw responsibility for the story onto the dialogue is to play safe and easy. So long as the actors mouth the lines the story will somehow come through, and the director can content himself with the most perfunctory and generalized camera work. If the story depends on what can be seen, much greater care must be taken over exactly what is shown, and that will add to the shooting time which is the variable on which the cost of a film chiefly depends.

ART, COMMERCE, AND CRITICISM

Now the cat is out of the bag. Films are traditionally about money, and film as most people know it is commercial film. Film did not begin as high art or as folk art, but as the offspring of technological curiosity and showmanship. It got into the public eye by way of peep-show and vaudeville, and its first exponents did not think of themselves as artists. The structural analogies between film and novel, and the superficial likenesses between film and drama, suggest affiliations that took some time to develop. A glance at the advertisements in your local newspaper should convince you that film has yet to free itself from the hectic world and accent of the fairground.

Though cheap and flexible sound and camera equipment has done much to effect what Andrew Sarris has called "demystifying the medium," the financial structure of the film industry has still some claim to be considered as part of the technological conditions that we have recognized to be paramount in cinema. The decisive factors here are that the initial costs of making even a cheap film are high, but the printing, distribution, and exhibition costs are low. So the costs can be recovered if enough people are willing to see the film—which they will be able to do only if enough people are willing to show it. Nor is this a consequence of the sickness of western bourgeois society. No one, socialist or capitalist, is going to be allowed to tie up so much of other people's labor and equipment unless there is some reasonable assurance that there will be something to show for it: if not money, then prestige or the approved performance of some supposed social function. By the same token, the complexities of the arrangements for distributing or showing films are almost certain to deprive the director of control over the final condition and destiny of his work. A film critic is seldom commenting on the work of an individual or a cohesive group so much as on the upshot of a loosely connected series of independent decisions. He may thus succumb to feelings of irrelevance.

There are three plausible lines a critic can take here. One is to confine his attention to noncommercial films. Of course, these are atypical, but the critic can say (as Parker Tyler says) that it is not typical for a film to be a work of art. Most drawings, to take a parallel case, are not works of art but advertisements or sources of technical information or doodles, and no one expects a critic to waste his time on such objects.

A second critical line is to accept that most films, both commercial and "underground," are junk, to be greeted with silence or a dismissive gesture, but that any kind of interest or excellence may turn up in any sort of film. Such a rejection of all commitments to styles and cultural traditions is in the line of twentieth-century critical orthodoxy, but may find it hard to steer between the Scylla of an empty formalistic aestheticism and the Charybdis of a relativism that accepts everything equally because everything succeeds in being what it is.

A third critical line is to accept cinema as a demotic art and devise a critical system appropriate to such an art. George Orwell has shown the way. His exemplary study of Frank Richards devoted itself to describing the "world" depicted or implied by the ensemble of Richard's work, and exploring the repertory of mannerisms which gave that world a facile coherence. Students of Jung and Frye have enlarged this critical armory by showing how to expose the underlying mythical archetypes and patterns in popular fiction. These methods have been applied to Hollywood films in what is misnamed the "auteur theory" of criticism (which is a policy rather than a theory). Whatever a studio does to a film, a strong-minded director can impregnate it indelibly with his own basic textures, his view of human relationships, his favorite narrative devices, and obsessive images. In fact, the measure of a director's stature may be the extent to which he can retain these elements of his own style when working on an uncongenial assignment from his studio. And by comparing a director's different films, which taken in isolation had been thought undistinguished if no worse, one can educe a complex world full of ironies and unexpected insights.

Some auteur critics seem to assume that any director whose work is susceptible to their methods is thereby proved to be an artist, and his films shown to be good films. This is a strange assumption. Critics of other arts are far from supposing that to show that a work is recognizable and typical of its author has any tendency to show that it is a good work. In fact, the analogue in other arts is a form of criticism specifically devised for handling material incapable of yielding anything of interest to a more searching critique. Auteur criticism may work best as a heuristic device: armed with his comparisons and with his trained eye for manners and genres, a critic can show us meaning where we saw none; but when we have been shown we must be able to see for ourselves. In other arts we accept that one may not understand any work by an innovating artist until one has familiarized oneself with his style; but it is strange to have a similar esoteric status claimed for the output of a studio work-horse. The paradox of auteur criticism is that while its methods are devised to handle cinema as a demotic art, it relies on a view of that art which is inaccessible to most of its normal public. How many people are going to get to see a Raoul Walsh festival?

In so far as the normal film is about human affairs, it is susceptible to criticism on the same basis as literary or dramatic works or figurative paintings, in terms of its verisimilitude, psychological richness, moral maturity, social significance, political viability, relations to the divine and the unconscious and so on. The fact that such topics are not specific to film does not make them trivial or irrelevant*: on the contrary, most actual serious discussion of films centers on this human side, and so it should. But we need say nothing about such criticism here. In practice we all know what we want to say; in theory the basic moves are familiar from discussions of criticism in the older arts. From this point of view, the art of film criticism would lie in knowledge of and sensitivity to the ways in which such human qualities can be conveyed by such cinematic means as we have been discussing.

The salient feature of film is the enormous range of its specific effects. Film is unique in its capacity for visual recording and analysis, in its ability to convey the unique present reality of things, in its ability to reveal the qualities of lives; but also in its formal freedom, its capacity for realizing fantasy and developing abstract forms. In view of this inexhaustible flexibility of the medium, it is ludicrous to lay down general principles as to what is a good film. Those critics who do so are in most cases obviously fixated on the kind of film that was around when they were first moved by movies. A judicious critic will equip himself with the most exhaustive possible grasp of the variables and variations accessible to filmmakers, and note just which of these the director is exploiting and how he is doing it. So much can be done in a film that it requires close attention and knowledge to discern what is actually being

---

*It has become fashionable among practitioners of the visual arts to apply the term "literary" to all humanistic or nonformal aspects of works of art, thus suggesting that in being a picture of something a work is somehow untrue of the visual. This implies that seeing or hearing something happen is an indirect way of reading about it. In fact, of course, scenes convey meaning as naturally and directly as words.

done. Technical assessment and appreciation can almost be read off from the roll of specific opportunities opened up by the director's initial options and then seized or missed: take care of the facts and the values will take care of themselves. Beyond that, the moral and cultural side of a critique must depend on the maturity and sensitivity of the critic's social and moral awareness. If you could teach someone to be a critic, you could teach him to be a man.

1971

DAVID ANTIN
VIDEO: THE DISTINCTIVE
FEATURES OF THE
MEDIUM

Video Art. The name is equivocal. A good name. It leaves open all the questions and asks them anyway. Is this an art form, a new genre? An anthology of valued activity conducted in a particular arena defined by display on a cathode ray tube? The kind of video made by a special class of people—artists— whose works are exhibited primarily in what is calld "the art world"—ARTISTS' VIDEO? An inspection of the names in the catalogue* gives the easy and not quite sufficient answer that it is this last we are considering, ARTISTS' VIDEO. But is this a class apart? Artists have been making video pieces for scarcely ten years—if we disregard one or two flimsy studio jobs and Nam June Paik's 1963 kamikaze TV modifications—and video has been a fact of gallery life for barely five years. Yet we've already had group exhibitions, panels, symposia, magazine issues devoted to this phenomen, for the very good reasons that more and more artists are using video and some of the best work being done in the art world is being done with video. Which is why a discourse has already arisen to greet it. Actually two discourses: one, a kind of enthusiastic welcoming prose peppered with fragments of communication theory and

---

*This essay was originally written in connection with the exhibition *Video Art* organized by the Institute of Contemporary Art, University of Pennsylvania, in Philadelphia and published in its original form in the catalogue for that exhibition in 1975.

McLuhanesque media talk; the other, a rather nervous attempt to locate the "unique properties of the medium." Discourse 1 could be called "cyberscat" and Discourse 2, because it engages the issues that pass for "formalism" in the art world, could be called "the formalist rap." Though there is no necessary relation between them, the two discourses occasionally occur together as they do in the words of Frank Gillette, which offers a convenient sample:

D1   The emergence of relationships between the culture you're in and the parameters that allow you expression are fed back through a technology. It's the state of the art technology within a particular culture that gives shape to ideas.

D2   What I'm consciously involved in is devising a way that is structurally intrinsic to television. For example, what makes it *not* film? Part of it is that you look *into* the source of light, with film you look *with* the source of light. In television, the source of light and the source of information are one.[1]

Though it is not entirely clear what "high class" technology has to do with the rather pleasantly shabby technical state of contemporary video art, or what the significance is to human beings of the light source in two adjacent representational media, statements of this type are characteristic, and similar quotes could be multiplied endlessly. And if these concerns seem somewhat gratuitous or insufficient with respect to the work at hand, they often share a kind of aptness of detail, even though it is rarely clear what the detail explains of the larger pattern of activity in which these artists are involved. In fact, what seems most typical of both types of discourse is a certain anxiety, which may be seen most clearly in a recent piece by Hollis Frampton:

Moreover it is doubly important that we try to say what video art is at present because we posit for it a privileged future. Since the birth of video art from the Jovian backside (I dare not say brow) of the Other Thing called television, I for one have felt a more and more pressing need for precise definitions of what film art is, since I extend to film, as well, the hope of a privileged future.[2]

[1] Judson Rosenbush, ed., *Frank Gillette Video: Process and Metaprocess.* Essay by Frank Gillette, interview by Willoughby Sharp (Syracuse, N.Y.: Everson Museum of Art, 1973), p. 21.

[2] Hollis Frampton, "The Withering Away of the State of Art," *Artforum* (December 1974): 50.

It would be so much more convenient to develop the refined discussion of the possible differences between film and video, if we could only forget the Other Thing—television. Yet television haunts all exhibitions of video art, though when actually present it is only minimally represented, with perhaps a few commercials or "the golden performances" of Ernie Kovacs (a television "artist"); otherwise its presence is manifest mainly in quotes, allusion, parody, and protest, as in Telethon's *TV History*, Douglas Davis's installation piece with the TV set forced to face the wall, or Richard Serra's *Television Delivers People*. No doubt, in time there will be an *auteur* theory of television, which will do for Milton Berle and Sid Caesar what Sarris and Farber and *Cahiers du cinéma* have done for John Ford and Nicholas Ray and Howard Hawks. But the politics of the art world is, for good reasons, rather hostile to Pop, and that kind of admiring discussion will have to wait; even *Cahiers du cinéma* has abandoned Hitchcock and Nicholas Ray for Dziga Vertov and the European avant-garde on sociopolitical, aesthetic grounds. But it's unwise to despise an enemy, especially a more powerful, older enemy, who happens also to be your frightful parent. So it is with television that we have to begin to consider video, because if anything has defined the formal and technical properties of the video medium, it is the television industry.

The history of television in the United States is well known. Commercial television is essentially a post-World War phenomenon, and its use was, logically enough, patterned on commercial radio, since control of the new medium was in the hands of the powerful radio networks, which constitute essentially a government-protected, private monopoly. This situation determined many of the fundamental communication characteristics of the new medium. The most basic of these is the social relation between "sending" and "receiving," which is profoundly unequal and asymmetrical. Since the main potential broadcasters, the powerful radio networks, were already deeply involved with the electronics industry through complex ownership affiliation, and since they also constituted the single largest potential customer for the electronic components of television, the components were developed entirely for their convenience and profit. While this may not seem surprising, the result was that the acts of "picture-taking" and "transmission" were made enormously expensive: Cameras and transmission systems were designed and priced out of the reach of anything but corporate ownership. Moreover, government regulations set standards on "picture quality" and the transmission signal, which effectively ensured that "taking" and "transmission" control would remain in the hands of the industry into which the federal government had already assigned the airwaves channel by channel. The receivers alone were priced within the range of individual ownership. This fundamental ordering establishing the relations between the taker-sender and the receiver—had, of course, been worked out for commercial radio.

Only ham transmission—also hemmed in severely by government regulation—and special uses like ship-to-shore, pilot-to-control tower, and police band radio deal in the otherwise merely potential equalities of wireless telephony. That this was not technically inevitable, but merely an outcome of the social situation and the marketing strategies of the industry, is obvious. There is nothing necessarily more complex or expensive in the camera than there is in the receiver. It is merely that the great expense of receiver technology was defrayed by the mass production of the sets, whose multiplication multiplied the dollar exchange value of transmission time sold by the transmitter to his advertisers. So the broadcasters underwrote receiver development, because every set brought delivers its viewers as salable goods in an exchange that pays for the "expensive" technology.

For television also there is a special-use domain—educational, industrial, and now artistic—where the relation between the camera and receiver may be more or less equalized, but this is because transmission is not an issue and the distribution of the images is severely restricted. The economic fact remains—transmission is more expensive than reception. This ensures a power hierarchy—transmission dominates reception. And it follows from this asymmetry of power relations that the taker-transmitter dominates whatever communication takes place.

This is clearer when you consider the manners of telephony. A would-be transmitter asks for permission to transmit, rings the home of a potential receiver. It's like ringing a doorbell. Or a would-be receiver rings the home of a possible transmitter, asks him/her to transmit. This formal set of relations has become even more refined with the introduction of the *Answerphone* and the answering service, which mediates between the ring—an anonymous invitation to communicate—and the response, requiring the caller to identify himself and leaving the receiver with a choice of whether or not to respond. In telephony manners are everything. While in commercial television manners are nothing. If you have a receiver you merely plug in to the possibility of a signal, which may or may not be there and which you cannot modify except in the trivial manner of switching to a nearly identical transmission or in a decisive but final manner by switching off. Choice is in the hands of the sender.

Now while this asymmetry is not inherent in the technology, it has become so normative for the medium that it forms the all-pervasive and invisible background of all video. This may not be so dramatically manifested in most artwork video, but that's because most artworks have very equivocal relations to the notion of communication and are, like industry, producer-dominated. Yet it has a formidable effect on all attempts at interactive video, which operates primarily in reaction to this norm. In this sense the social structure of the medium is a matrix that defines the formal properties of the medium — since it limits the possibilities of a video communication genre — and these limits then become the target against which any number of artists have aimed their works. What else could Ira Schneider have had in mind about the 1969 piece, *Wipe Cycle*, he devised with Frank Gillette:

> The most important thing was the notion of information presentation, and the notion of the integration of the audience into the information. One sees oneself exiting from the elevator. If one stands there for 8 seconds, one sees oneself entering the gallery from the elevator again. Now at the same time one is apt to be seeing oneself standing there watching *Wipe Cycle*. You can watch yourself live watching yourself 8 seconds ago, watching yourself 16 seconds ago, *eventually feeling free enough to interact with this matrix, realizing one's own potential as an actor*[3] [my italics].

What is attempted is the conversion (liberation) of an audience (receiver) into an actor (transmitter), which Schneider and Gillette must have hoped to accomplish by neutralizing as much as possible the acts of "taking" and electronic transmission. If they failed to accomplish this, they were hardly alone in their failure, which seems to have been the fate of just about every interactive artwork employing significantly technological means. Apparently, the social and economic distribution of technological resources in this culture has a nearly determining effect on the semiotics of technological resources.

More concretely, an expensive video camera and transmission system switched on and ready for use don't lose their peculiar prestigious properties just because an artist may make them available under special circumstances for casual use to

[3]Jud Yalkut, "TV As a Creative Medium at the Howard Wise Gallery," *Arts Magazine* (September 1961): 21.

an otherwise passive public. In fact, this kind of interactive video situation almost invariably begins by intimidating an unprepared audience, which has already been indoctrinated about the amount of preparedness (professionalism) the video camera deserved, regardless of the trivial nature of television professionalism, which is not measured by competence (as in the elegant relation of ends to means) but by the amount of money notably expended on this preparation. Yet while the most fundamental property of television is its social organization, this is manifested most clearly in its money metric which applies to every aspect of the medium, determining the tempo of its representations and the style of the performances, as well as the visual syntax of its editing. The money metric has also played a determining role in neutralizing what is usually considered the most markedly distinctive feature of the medium: the capacity for instantaneous transmission.

In principle, television seemed to combine the photographic reproduction capacities of the camera, the motion capabilities of film, and the instantaneous transmission properties of the telephone. But just as the photographic reproduction capacity of the camera is essentially equivocal and significant as mythology, so is the fabled instantaneity of television essentially a rumor that combines with photographic duplicity to produce a quasi-recording medium, the main feature of which is unlikeliness in relation to any notion of reality. The history of the industry is very instructive with respect to this remarkable outcome.

In the beginning television made widespread use of live broadcasting both for transmitting instant news of events that were elapsing in real time and for more or less well-rehearsed studio performances; and some of the most interesting events recorded by media were the result of the unpredictability of instantaneous transmission. Spokesmen for the industry never failed to call attention to this feature on instantaneity, and as late as 1968 a standard handbook for television direction and production by Stasheff and Bretz asserted:

> Perhaps the most distinctive function of television is its ability to show distant events at the moment when they are taking place. The Kefauver hearings, with a close-up of the hands of gangster Frank Costello; the Army-McCarthy hearings; the complete coverage of the orbital shots; the presidential nominating conventions; the Great Debates of 1960; the live transmissions from Europe and Japan via satellite—this is television doing what no other medium can do.[4]

---

[4] Edward Stasheff and Rudy Bretz, *The Television Program: Its Writing, Direction, and Production* (New York: A. A. Wyn, 1951), p. 3.

Yet the same handbook casually points out a few pages later that between 1947 and 1957, kine-recordings, films taken directly from the TV screen, were in constant and heavy use, especially for delayed broadcast of East Coast programs on the West Coast, in spite of the much poorer image quality of the kines, and that by 1961 virtually all television dramatic programs were being produced on film. There were, apparently, from the industry's standpoint, great inconveniences in instantaneous transmission. The most obvious of these was that at the same instant of time the life cycles of New York and Los Angeles are separated by three full hours, and since the day for the industry is metrically divided into prime and non-prime viewing time, in accordance with whether more or fewer viewers may be sold to the advertisers, the money value of instantaneous transmission is inversely related in a complicated way to the temporal distance of transmission. But this is only the most obvious manner in which the money metric worked to eliminate instantaneity. A more basic conflict exists between the structure of the industry and the possibility of instantaneity and unpredictability.

Any series of events that is unfolding for the first time, or in a new way, or with unanticipated intensity or duration threatens to overrun or elude the framing conventions of the recording artists (the cameramen and directors). This element of surprise is always in conflict with the image of smoothness, which has the semiotic function of marking the producer's competence by emphasizing his mastery and control, his grasp of events. The signs of unpredictability and surprise are discontinuities and ragged edges that mark the boundaries of that competence by puncturing or lacerating that grasp. The image of smoothness depends always upon the appearance of the unimpeded forward course of the producer's intention, of facility, which means that there must be no doubt in the viewer's mind that what is transmitted is what the transmitter wants to transmit. And the only ways to achieve this were through (a) repeated preparation of the events, (b) very careful selection of highly predictable events, or (c) deletion of unexpected and undesirable aspects of events, which meant editing a recorded version of these events. Videotape came in 1956, and at the beginning Ampex was taping the Douglas Edwards newscasts and, not much later, the stage presentations of *Playhouse 90*. Once again, according to Stasheff and Bretz:

> By 1957 a new TV revolution was under way. Undistinguishable from live TV on the home receiver, video tape quickly replaced the kine-recording done by the TV networks. Not only did the stations put out a better picture, but the savings were

tremendous. . . . Live production, video-tape recording of live production, kine-recording, and film began to assume complementary roles in the pattern of TV production. Videotape recording by 1961 became so commonplace that the true live production—reaching the home at the moment of its origination—was a rarity limited largely to sports and special events. *The live production on video tape, though delayed in reaching the home by a few hours or a few days, was generally accepted as actual live television by the average viewer* [5] [my italics].

Yet this did not place television in the same position as film, which from its origins appeared to be situated squarely in the domain of illusion. Film, after all, has made very few and very insubstantial claims to facticity. Amet's bathtub battle of Santiago Bay may have convinced Spanish military historians of its authenticity, but that was back in 1897 before the movie palaces together with the moviemakers dispelled any illusion of potential facticity. Flaherty looks as clearly fictional as Méliès now. But a genre that is marked "fictional" doesn't raise issues of truth and falsehood, and television never ceases to raise these issues. The social uses of television continually force the issue of "truth" to the center of attention. A President goes on television to declare his "honesty," a minister announces his "intentions," the evening news reports "what is being done to curb inflation." The medium maintains a continual assertion that it can and does provide an adequate representation of reality, while everyone's experience continually denies it. Moreover, the industry exhibits a persistent positive tropism toward the appearance of the spontaneous and unrehearsed event in its perpetually recurring panel shows and quiz programs and in the apparently casual format of its late-evening news shows. According to Stasheff and Bretz:

> The television audience will not only accept, but even enjoy, a production error or even a comedian who blows his lines and admits it or who asks his straight man to feed him a cue once again so that he can make another try at getting the gag to come out right. This leniency on the part of the audience is caused by the increased feeling of spontaneity and immediacy which minor crises create. The audience loves to admire the adroitness with which the performer "pulls himself out of a jam."[6]

The industry wishes, or feels obligated, to maintain the illusion of immediacy, which it defines rather precisely as "the *feeling* that what one sees on the TV screen is living and actual

[5] Ibid., p. 6.
[6] Ibid., p. 8.

reality, at that very moment taking place."[7] The perfection of videotape made possible the careful manipulation and selective presentation of desirable "errors" and "minor crises" as marks of spontaneity, which became as equivocal in their implications as the drips and blots of third-generation Abstract Expressionists. It's not that you couldn't see the Los Angeles police department's tactical assault squad in real time, in full living color, in your own living room, leveling a small section of the city in search of three or four suspected criminals, but that what you would see couldn't be certainly discriminated from a carefully edited videotape screened three hours later. So what television provides video with is a tradition not of falseness, which would be a kind of guarantee of at least a certain negative reliability, but of a profoundly menacing equivocation and mannerism, determining a species of unlikeness.

At first glance artists' video seems to be defined by the total absence of any of the features that define television. But this apparent lack of relation is in fact a very definite and predictable inverse relation. If we temporarily ignore the subfamily of installation pieces, which are actually quite diverse among themselves but nevertheless constitute a single genre, the most striking contrast between video pieces and television is in relation to time. It may not be quite hip to say so without qualification, but it is a commonplace to describe artists' videotapes as "boring" or "long," even when one feels that this in no way invalidates or dishonors the tapes in question (viz. Bruce Boice's comment that Lynda Benglis's video is "boring, interesting and funny";[8] or Richard Serra's own videotape, *Prisoners' Dilemma*, where one character advises another that he may have to spend two hours in the basement of the Castelli Gallery, which is "twice as long as the average boring videotape"). This perceived quality of being boring or long has little to do with the actual length of the tapes. It has much more to do with the attitude of just about all the artists using video to the task at hand. John Baldessari has a tape called *Some Words I Mispronounce*. He turns to a blackboard and writes:

1. poor	4. Beelzebub
2. cask	5. bough
3. bade	6. sword

[7] Ibid., p. 8.
[8] Bruce Boice, "Lynda Benglis at Paula Cooper Gallery," *Artforum* (May 1973): 83.

As soon as he completes the "d" of "sword" the tape is over. Running time is under a minute. It feels amazingly short. But it is longer than most commercials.

Robert Morris's *Exchange*, a series of verbal meditations on exchanges of information, collaborations, and interferences with a woman, accompanied by a variety of images taped and re-taped from other tapes and photographs for the most part as indefinite and suggestive as the discourse, goes on till it arrives at a single distinct and comic story of not getting to see the Gattamelata, after which the tape trails off in a more or less leisurely fashion. Running time is forty-three minutes. Television has many programs that are much longer. The two artists' tapes are very different. Baldessari's is a routine, explicitly defined from the outset and carried out deadpan to its swift conclusion. *Exchange* is a typical member of what is by now a well-defined genre of artist narrative, essentially an extended voiceover in a carefully framed literary style that seeks its end intuitively in the exhaustion of its mild narrative energy. But they both have the same attitude toward time: The work ends whenever its intention is accomplished. The time is inherent time, the time required for the task at hand. The work is "boring," as Les Levine remarked, "if you demand that it be something else. If you demand that it be itself then it is not boring."[9] Which is not to say that the videotapes may not be uninteresting. Whether they are interesting or not is largely a matter of judging the value of the task at hand, and this could hardly be the issue for people who can look with equanimity at what hangs on the wall in the most distinguished galleries. For whatever we think of the videotapes of Morris, or Sonnier, or Serra, these are certainly not inferior to whatever else they put in the gallery. Levine is right. Videotapes are boring if you demand that they be something else. But they're not judged boring by comparison with paintings or sculpture, they're judged boring in comparison with television, which for the last twenty years has set the standard of video time.

But the time standard of television is based firmly on the social and economic nature of the industry itself, and has nothing whatever to do with the absolute technical and phenomenological possibilities of visual representation by cathode ray tube. For television, time has an absolute existence independent of any imagery that may or may not be transmitted over its well-defined airwaves and cables. It is television's only solid, a tangible commodity that is precisely divisible into

[9] Les Levine, "Excerpts from a Tape: 'Artistic,' " *Art-Rite* (Autumn 1974):27.

further and further subdivisible homogeneous units, the smallest quantum of which is measured by the smallest segment that could be purchased by a potential advertiser, which is itself defined by the minimum particle required to isolate a salable product from among a variable number of equivalent alternatives. The smallest salable piece turns out to be the ten-second spot, and all television is assembled from it.

But the social conventions of television dictate a code of behavior according to which the transmitter must assume two apparently different roles in transmission. In one he must appear to address the viewer on the station's behalf as entertainer; in the other on the sponsor's behalf as salesman. The rules of the game, which are legally codified, prescribe a sharp demarcation between the roles, and the industry makes a great show of marking off the boundaries between its two types of performances—the programs and the commercials. At their extremes of hard-sell and soft-show, one might suppose that the stylistic features of the two roles would be sufficient to distinguish them; but the extremes are rare, the social function of the roles are not so distinct, and the stylistic features seldom provide sufficient separation. Since the industry's most tangible presentation is metrically divisible time, the industry seems to mark the separation emphatically by assigning the two roles different time signatures. The commercial is built on a scale of the minute out of multiple ten-second units. It comes in four common sizes—30, 60 and 120 seconds—of which the thirty-second slot is by far the commonest. The program is built on the scale of the hour out of truncated and hinged fifteen minute units that are also commonly assembled in four sizes—15, 30, and 60 and 120 minutes—of which the half-hour program is the commonest, though the hour length is usual for important programs, two hours quite frequent for specials and feature films, and fifteen minutes not entirely a rarity for commentary. Television inherited the split roles and the two time signatures from radio, as well as the habit of alternating them in regularly recurrent intervals, which creates the arbitrary-appearing, mechanical segmentation of both media's presentations. But television carried this mechanical segmentation to a new extreme and presented it in such a novel way—through a special combination of its own peculiar technology and production conventions—that television time, in spite of structural similarity with radio time, has an entirely different appearance from it, bearing the relationship to it of an electronically driven, digital counter to a spring-driven, handwound alarm clock.

Television achieved its extreme segmentation of transmission time mainly through the intense development of multiple sponsorship. Old radio programs from the 1930s and 1940s tended to have a single sponsor. *The Lone Ranger* was sponsored for years by Silvercup Bread, *Ma Perkins* by Oxydol, *Uncle Don* by Ovaltine, and these sponsors would reappear regularly at the beginning, middle, and end of each program with pretty much the same pitch. This pattern continued by and large into the early days of television with *Hallmark Theater, The Kraft Playhouse,* and so on. But current television practice is generally quite different. A half-hour program might have something like six minutes of commercial fitted to it in three two-minute blocks at the beginning, middle, and end of the program. But these six minutes of commercial time might promote the commodities of twelve different sponsors, or twelve different commodities of some smaller number of sponsoring agencies. The commodities could be nearly anything—a car, a cruise, a furniture polish, a breakfast food, a funeral service, a scent for men, a cure for smoking, an ice show, an X-rated movie, or a politician. In principle they could apply to nearly any aspect of human life and be presented in any order, with strategies of advocacy more various than the commodities themselves. In practice the range of commodity and styles of advocacy are somewhat more limited, but the fact remains that in half an hour you might see a succession of four complete, distinct, and unrelated thirty-second presentations, followed by a twelve-minute half of a presentation, followed by a one minute presentation, one thirty-second presentation, and two ten-second presentations, followed by the second and concluding half presentation (twelve minutes long), followed by yet another four unrelated thirty-second presentations. But since this would lead to bunching of two two-minute commercials into a four-minute package of commercial at the end of every hour, and since viewers are supposed to want mainly to look at the programs—or because program-makers are rather possessive about their own commercials and want complete credit for them—the program-makers have recently developed the habit of presenting a small segment of their own program as a kind of prologue before the opening commercial, to separate it from the tail end of the preceding program, while the program-makers of the preceding program may attempt to tag onto the end of their own program a small epilogue at the end of their last commercial, to affix it more securely to their own program. Meanwhile the station may itself interject a small commercial promoting itself or its future presentations. All of these additional segments—prologues, epilogues, station promotions, and coming attractions—usually last no more than two minutes, are scaled to commercial time, and are in their functional nature promotions for either immediately succeeding or eventually succeeding transmissions. This means that you may see upward of fourteen distinct segments of presentation in any half-hour, all but two of which will be scaled to commercial time. Since commercial time is the most common signature, we could expect it to dominate the tempo of television, especially since the commercial segments constitute the only example of integral (complete and uninterrupted) presentation in the medium. And it does, but not in the way one would generally suppose.

It is very easy to exaggerate the apparent differences between commercial time and program time by concentrating on the dramatic program. Television has many programs that share a mechanically segmented structure with the packet of commercials. The most extreme cases are the news programs, contests, and the so-called talk shows. What is called news on television is a chain of successive, distinct, and structurally unrelated narrations called stories. These average from thirty seconds to two minutes in length, are usually presented in successions of three or four in a row, and are bracketed between packets of commercials from one to two minutes long. The "full" story is built very much like a common commercial. It will usually have a ten- to thirty-second introduction narrated by an actor seen in a chest shot, followed by a segment of film footage about one minute in length. There are alternate forms, but all of them are built on exactly the same type of segmentation. The narrating actor may merely narrate (read off) the event from the same chest shot seen against a background of one or two slides plausibly related to the event. The only continuity for the six- or seven-minute packet of programming called news consists of an abstract categorical designation (e.g., national) and the recurrent shots of the newsmen, actors who project some well-defined character considered appropriate for this part of the show, such as informed concern, alert aggressiveness, world-weary moralism, or genial confidence. This tends to be more obvious in the packets designated as sports and weather, where what passes for information consists of bits so small, numerous, and unrelated that they come down to mere lists. These may be held together respectively by more obvious character actors like a suave ex-jock and a soft-touch comic.

Similarly, contests shows consist of structurally identical, separate events joined edge to edge and connected mainly by the continuous presence of the leading actor (the host). Television has also—through selection of the events themselves and manner of representation—managed to present most of its sports programs as sequences of nearly identical unrelated events. Baseball gets reduced to a succession of pitches, hits, and catches, football to a succession of runs, passes, and tackles, while the ensemble of events that may be unfolding lies outside the system of representation. If we count together all the programs that are constructed out of these linearly successive, distinct segments of commercial scale, the contrast between commercial and program becomes much less sharp. Moreover, a closer inspection of both will show that there are really no clear stylistic distinctions between commercials and programs, because just about every genre of program appears also as a commercial. Dramas, comedies, documentaries, science talks, lists, all show up in thirty- and sixty-second forms. Even their distinctive integralness can be exaggerated, because often there is a clean partition between the programmatic parts of the commercial—its dramatic or imagistic material—and the details of the pitch that specify the name of the product and where you can get it. This separation is so common that it is possible to watch three thirty-second commercials in succession with some pleasure and find it difficult to remember the name or even the nature of the commodity promoted. This is not a functional defect in the commercial, the main function of which is to produce a kind of praise poetry that will elevate to a mild prominence one member out of the general family of commodities that television promotes as a whole tribe all of its transmitting day. Poems in praise of particular princes are addressed to an audience already familiar with the tribe, and commercials are constructed to particularize an already existing interest. Nobody unconcerned with body odors will care which deodorant checks them best. It takes the whole television day to encode the positive images of smoothness, cleanliness, or blandness upon which the massive marketing of deodorants and soaps depends. There is no fundamental distinction between commercial and program, there is only a difference in focus and conciseness, which gives the thirty-second commercial its appearance of much greater elegance and style. Both commercials and programs are assembled out of the same syntax: the linear succession of logically independent units of nearly equal duration. But this mechanically divisible, metrical presentation had none of the percussive or disjunctive properties of radio presentation. This is because of the conventions of camerawork and editing that television has developed to soften the shock of its basically mechanical procedures.

It is probably fair to say that the entire technology, from the shape of the monitor screen to the design of camera mounts, was worked out to soften the tick of its metronome. Almost every instrument of television technique and technology seems to have the effect of a shock absorber. As in film, the television presentation is assembled out of separate shots. But these shots are very limited in type and duration. Because of the poor resolution of the television image (525 bits of information presented on photosensitive phosphors) and the normal screen size, the bread-and-butter shots of television are almost all subforms of what film would consider a close-up. Common shot names illustrate this—knee shot, thigh shot, waist shot, bust shot, head shot, tight head shot. Or else they count the number of people in the frame—two shot, four shot, etc. Probably primarily for this reason shot durations are very limited in range—usually from two to ten seconds—and very predictable in function and type. The two- to three-second shot is almost always a reaction shot or a transition detail of some activity. Distant shots of moving cars, or whatever, will usually run seven to ten seconds, like action in general. Shots of a second and under are very rare and only used for special occasions, but distinct shots over twenty seconds are practically nonexistent. "Distinct" because television's camera conventions include a cameraman who is trained to act like an antiaircraft gunner, constantly making minute adjustments of the camera—loosening up a bit here, tightening up there, gently panning and trucking in a nearly imperceptible manner to keep the target on some imaginary pair of cross hairs. These endless, silken adjustments, encouraged and sometimes specifically called for by the director and usually built into the cameraman's training, tend to blur the edges of what the film director would normally consider a shot. To this we can add the widespread use of fade-ins and fade-outs and dissolves to effect temporal and spatial transitions, and the director's regular habit of cutting on movement to cushion the switch from one camera to another. This whole arsenal of techniques has a single function—to soften all shocks of transition. Naturally the different apparent functions of various genres of program or commercial will alter the degree of softening, so a news program will maintain a sense of urgency through its use of cuts, soft though they may be, while the soap opera constantly melts together its various close shots with liquid adjustment and blends scene to scene in recurrent dissolves and fades. This ceaseless softening combines with the regular segmentation to transform the metronomic tick-tock of the transmission into the silent succession of numbers on a digital clock.

Because of the television industry's special aesthetic of time and the electronics industry's primary adaptation of the technology to the needs and desires of television, the appearance of an art-world video had to wait for the electronics industry to attempt to expand the market for its technology into special institutional and consumer domains. The basic tool kit of artists' video is the portapak with its small, mobile camera and one-half inch black-and-white videotape recorder that can accommodate nothing larger than thirty-minute tapes. Combined with a small monitor and perhaps an additional microphone, the whole operation costs something in the vicinity of $2000—a bit less than a cheap car and a bit more than a good stereo system. This is the fundamental unit, but it allows no editing whatever. The most minimal editing—edge-to-edge assembling of tapes into units larger than thirty minutes—requires access to at least another videotape recorder with a built-in editing facility, which means the investment of at least another $1200. This is a primitive editing capacity, but increases the unit cost by 50 percent to about $3000. Yet precision editing and smoothness are still out of the question. Unlike film, where editing is a scissors-and-paste job anyone can do with very little equipment, and where you can sit in a small room and shave pieces of film down to the half-frame with no great difficulty, video pictures have to be edited electronically by assembling image sequences from some source or sources in the desired order on the tape of a second machine. The images are electronically marked off from each other by an electronic signal recurring (in the U.S.) thirty times a second. If you want to place one sequence of images right after another that you've already recorded onto the second tape, you have to join the front edge of the first new frame to the final edge of the other, which means that motors of both machines have to be synchronized to the thirtieth of a second and that there must be a way of reading off each frame edge to assure that the two recorded sequences are in phase with each other. Half-inch equipment is not designed to do this, and the alignment of frame edge with frame edge is a matter of accident.

Alignment of a particular frame edge with a particular frame edge is out of the question. If the frame edges don't come together, the tape is marked by a characteristic momentary breakup or instability of the image. You may or may not mind this, but it's the distinctive mark of this type of editing. Since this is absolutely unlike television editing, it carries its special mark of homemade or cheap or unfinicky or direct or honest. But the dominance of television aesthetics over anything seen on a TV screen makes this rather casual punctuation mark very emphatic and loaded with either positive or negative value. An installation with synchronized, multiple cameras, with ca-

pabilities for switching through cutting, fading, and dissolving, and some few special effects like black-and-white reversal, will cost somewhere in the $10,000 range, provided you
stick to black-and-white and half-inch equipment. This is only
a minor increase in editing control and a cost increase of one
order of magnitude. If you want reliably smooth edits that will
allow you to join predictably an edge to an edge, without
specifying which edge, you will need access to an installation
whose cost begins at around $100,000. One major art gallery
has a reduced form of such a facility that permits this sort of
editing, which costs about half that. Again we have an increase of control that is nearly minimal and a cost increase of
another order of magnitude. Some artists have solved this
problem by obtaining occasional access to institutions possessing this kind of installation, but usually this takes complete editing control out of the hands of most artists. There are
also ways of adapting the one-inch system to precisionist
frame-for-frame capacity, but that requires the investment of
several thousand dollars more. A rule of thumb might specify
that each increase in editing capacity represents an order of
magnitude increase in cost. Color is still another special problem. Though it is hardly necessary, and possibly a great drawback in the sensible use of video for most artists' purposes
(viz., Sonnier's pointless color work), it is by now television's
common form and has certain normative marks associated with
it. To use black-and-white is a marked move, regardless of what
the mark may be construed to mean. So, many artists will seek
color for mere neutrality. But it comes at a price. There are
bargain-basement color systems, wonderfully cheesey in appearance, but the most common system is the three-quarter-
inch cassette ensemble, which together with camera, videotape recorder, and monitor goes at about $10,000. If the por-
tapak is the Volkswagen, this is the Porsche of individual artists' video. For editing control the system of escalation in color
runs parallel to black and white. The model of ultimate refinement and control is the television industry's two-inch system,
and since that's what you see in action in any motel over the
TV set, interesting or not, everyone takes it for the state of the
art.

   These conditions may not seem promising, but artists are as
good at surviving as cockroaches, and they're developed three
basic strategies for action. They can take the lack of technical
refinements as a given and explore the theater of poverty. They
can beg, borrow, or steal access to technical wealth and explore the ambiguous role of the poor relation, the unwelcome
guest, the court jester, the sycophant, or the spy. This isn't a

common solution; the studios don't make their facilities available so readily. But it includes works done by Allan Kaprow, Peter Campus, Les Levine, Nam June Paik, and numerous others. Artists can also raid the technology as a set of found objects or instruments with phenomenological implications in installation pieces. There are numerous examples from the work of Peter Campus, Dan Graham, Nam June Paik, Frank Gillette, etc. To a graat extent the significance of all types of video art derives from its stance with respect to some aspect of television, which is itself profoundly related to the present state of our culture. In this way video art embarks on a curiously mediated but serious critique of the culture. And this reference to television, and through it to the culture, is not dependent on whether or not the artist sees the work in relation to television. The relation between television and video is created by the shared technologies and conditions of viewing, in the same way the relation of movies to underground film is created by the shared conditions of cinema. Nevertheless, an artist may exploit the relation very knowingly and may choose any aspect of the relation for attack.

If Nancy Holt's *Underscan* is an innocent masterpiece that narrates in its toneless voice a terrifying, improverished story over a sequence of simple photographic images ruined twice over by the television raster, the correlated Benglis *Collage* and Morris *Exchange* are cunning parodies that use the cheesey video image to depreciate a filmic genre that would sensuously exploit the personal glamour of stars like Elizabeth Taylor and Richard Burton, replaced here by the mock glamour of two pseudocelebrities in a visual soup. Holt calls into question anything that the medium has ever represented as documentary with her sheer simplicity of means, while Morris and Benglis produce a total burlesque of the public figure through the manifest absurdity of their claims.

Acconci's *Undertone* is an even more precise example of this type of burlesque. In a visual style of address exactly equivalent to the Presidential address, the face-to-face camera regards The Insignificant Man making The Outrageous Confession that is as likely as not to be an Incredible Lie. Who can escape the television image of Nixon?

In Baldessari's wonderful *Inventory,* the artist presents to the camera for thirty minutes an accumulation of indiscriminate and not easily legible objects arranged in order of increasing size and accompanied by a deadpan description—only to have the sense of their relative size destroyed by the continual readjustment of the camera's focal length that is required to keep them within the frame. Who can forget Adlai Stevenson's solemn television demonstration of the "conclusive photographic evidence" of the Cuban missile sites, discernible over the TV screen as only gray blurs?

What the artists constantly re-evoke and engage with is television's fundamental equivocation and mannerism, which may really be the distinctive feature of the medium. But they may do this from two diametrically opposed angles, either by parodying the television system and providing some amazing bubble or by offering to demonstrate how, with virtually no resources, they can do all the worthwhile things that television should do or could do in principle and has never yet done and never will do.

Terry Fox's *Children's Tapes* exhibit nothing more nor less than the simple laws of the physical world in terms of small common objects—a spoon, a cup, an ice cube, a piece of cloth. They make use of a single camera, adjusted only enough to get the objects and events into the frame, and no edits. The hands crumple a spoon handle, place an ice cube in it over a small piece of cloth, balance it at the neck over the rim of a cup. You watch. It takes how long for you to figure out that the ice cube will melt? That the cloth will absorb the water. That the balance will be upset. But which way? Will the water absorbed into the cloth be drawn further from the fulcrum and increase the downward movement on the ice cube side? Or will the water dripping from the spoon reduce the downward movement and send the spoon toppling into the cup? You watch as though waiting for an explosion. It takes minutes to come and you feel relieved. It has the form of drama. You'll never see anything like it on educational television or any other television. It takes too much time, intelligence, and intensity of attention to watch—except on video. There are, I believe, twenty-two of them. They have the brilliance of still life and the intelligence of a powerful didactic art. But it is also a critique of means. Other works similar in this respect of means are Richard Serra's *Prisoners' Dilemma* and Eleanor Antin's *The Ballerina and the Bum*.

The Serra piece shamelessly adapts a casual stage skit and a contest show format to illustrate hilariously and with absolute simplicity a moral-logical dilemma with grave implications for human action. The problem is apparently simple. There are two prisoners, A and B. Each is offered a chance to betray the other and go free—but here is the first catch—provided the other refuses to betray him. In the event that this happens the prisoner who refuses to betray will receive the maximum sentence—this is the second catch. The other alternatives are that both prisoners will refuse to betray each other—this will get both prisoners the second lightest penalty; or that both prisoners will attempt to betray each other, which will get each prisoner the second gravest penalty. On the face of it we have a straightforward 2 × 4 matrix with four outcomes for each player, but all the outcomes are linked pairs: You go free only if he gets life imprisonment and he goes free only if you get life imprisonment; you both get away with two years' imprisonment if you both hold out against betrayal; you both get ten years' imprisonment if you both try betrayal. If each player plays the game as a zero-sum game for his own advantage, he will inspect the reward columns and come to the single conclusion that the worst possible outcome is life imprisonment, which can only happen if he refuses to betray. This prevents the other player from screwing him and leaves the original player the chance of screwing his opponent. Since both players—regarded as unrelated individuals who will consider their own individual advantage—will both play to minimize their loss, they will each play to cut their losses and inevitably come out with the next-to-worse payoff, ten years in prison. There is no way to win and no way to play for mutual nonbetrayal, because failure to betray always risks total loss. But the video piece is more brilliant than that. It sets up two precise illustrations—comic, yes; casual, yes—but elegant in the way it demonstrates that any two unrelated prisoners—say a pair of suspected criminals picked up in the street—will inevitably betray each other and take the consequences. But any two prisoners who have a real community bond between them have no choice but to play for nonbetrayal, because they must consider the value of the outcome in terms of its value for both players. Obviously, the differences in negative weights assigned to the penalties will work differently in deciding the outcome. Still, nothing in the world of this low-budget game could make Leo Castelli betray Bruce Boice in public. This low-budget marker calls up beautiful improvisational acting from all of the players and loose styles from all of the collaborators in this group piece. The logical structuring of the piece owes a great deal to Robert Bell, who occupies a role somewhere between scriptwriter and director, and to all of the actors, whose imprivisatory performances contribute markedly to the final outcome of the piece, which must be considered a community venture, with Richard Serra assuming the producer's role. This piece is also of a sort that will never appear on television and has the force of a parable.

Antin's *Ballerina and the Bum,* another low-budget job, with single Portapak camera and two improvising actors, declares itself, from its five-minute opening shot, against television, time, and money. The camera changes position only if it has to, to keep something in view, pans once along three cars of a freight train to count them, moves inside the car. The mike has no windscreen. The sounds of the world of 1974—cars, airplanes, children, and chickens—intermittently penetrate the film-style illusion of the image of a Sylphides-costumed, New York-accented ballerina "from the sticks" and a twenty-five-year-old grizzled bum on the way to the big city. Nothing happens but what they say and do. She practices ballet, sets up light housekeeping in the boxcar, they daydream of success, he cooks some beans, she eats them, the train goes nowhere. Everything else is moving—cars, planes, and other trains. A whole Chaplin movie for the price of a good dub.

Other successful examples of this low-budget strategy are Andy Mann's *One-Eyed Bum* and Ira Schneider and Beryl Korot's *4th of July in Saugerties*, which bring to bear the video of limited means upon documentary as a kind of artist's reminder of the ambiguities of "honesty" and "simplicity." It is no accident that the best of these works have, at least in part, a didactic and moral element behind them and are "exemplary." And even the tapes that are not specifically presented in an exemplary mode become exemplary in their fundamental disdain for television time.

But the theater of poverty isn't the only way. Peter Campus somehow infiltrated WGBH-TV, Boston, to produce a single deadly piece precisely aimed through their expensive equipment. A man holds a photograph, seemingly of himself. You see him set fire to it and watch it burn from all four sides. Gradually you notice that the photograph is breathing, its eyes are blinking. This is the image of television.

1976

IV

Film, Theater, and Literature

Theorists have often attempted to discover the characteristics of the film medium by comparing it with other media. Panofsky, for example, contrasts the theater's static use of space and its independence of the principle of co expressibility with cinema's more dynamic use of space and its rigorous subjection to that principle. For Panofsky, this difference explains why film adaptations of plays are so unlikely to succeed. Any attempt to transfer theater's essentially verbal resources to the cinema violates the principle that no more should be expressed verbally than can be expressed visually. The cinema's business is not the photographing of theatrical decor, a prestylized reality, but the photographing of actual physical reality so that it has style. Panofsky finds cinema the only medium that does justice to the materialistic interpretation of the universe which pervades contemporary civilization.

Like Panofsky, Hugo Munsterberg, the Harvard psychologist and philosopher who was a colleague of both William James and George Santayana, attempted in 1916 to delineate the features of the silent "photoplay" by contrasting it with the theater. For Munsterberg, the representation of physical reality is the concern not of cinema, but of theater. In true cinema, "the massive outer world has lost its weight, it has been freed from space, time and causality, and it has been clothed in the forms of our consciousness." Theater is bound by the same laws that govern nature, but the cinema is free to be shaped by the inner movements of the mind. Theater therefore trespasses on the realm of cinema when it employs any analogue of the close-up or the flash-back, and Munsterberg is as

harsh a critic of "cinematified" theater as Panofsky is of "theatrical-
ized" film.

For Munsterberg the true function of the close-up is not to provide a closer view of nature but to reproduce the mental act of attention. Similarly, the cut-back provides a cinematic equivalent of
human memory and is alien to theater, which is bound by the laws
of nature and the necessities of temporal succession. In the theater,
"men of flesh and blood with really plastic bodies stand before us.
They move like any moving body in our surroundings. Moreover,
those happenings on the stage, just like events in life, are independent of our subjective attention and memory and imagination.
They go their objective course." If it were the object of cinema,
then, to "imitate" nature, film could hardly compete with theater.
"The color of the world has disappeared, the persons are dumb, no
sound reaches our ears. The depth of the scene appears unreal, the
motion has lost its natural character. Worst of all, the objective
course of events is falsified . . ." The genius of cinema is not, then,
to "imitate" nature; rather it is to display the triumph of mind over
matter.

The essay by Susan Sontag, the influential American writer and
director, may be read as a critique of both Panofsky and Munsterberg. Despite their many and important differences, both "insist on
a single model for film" and for theater, too. Their conception of
the stage derives from notions of realism based on Ibsen and the
French well-made play more than it does on the epic use of the stage
by Shakespeare, the Russian constructivists, or Brecht. Similarly,
their views of film display a strong prejudice in favor of the methods of the silent film. They are all too ready to confine cinema
within rigid boundaries and to insist on maintaining artistic "purity," a separation of the various arts. Although Sontag understands
the impulse to purity, she also understands a contrasting artistic
ideal, one descending from Wagner rather than Lessing, which takes
as its ideal a comprehensive "mixed-media" art form in the tradition
of Greek theater and the Wagnerian music-drama. She does not
choose between puristic and anti-puristic conceptions of the cinema
or of the theater, but suggests awaiting future developments without prejudice.

Sontag accepts both the fact that many successful films have
been "adapted" from plays and the fact that cinematic effects have
been employed successfully in the theater. Andre Bazin, too, insists
on the value of adaptations. He thinks that Cocteau's *Les Parents
Terrible* and Olivier's *Henry V* are superb films. But he does not feel
that one should "cinematify," simply "open up" the original play by
moving around outdoors, in order to make a successful adaptation.
Rather, "a good adaptation should result in a restoration of the essence
and spirit" of the original play. Indeed, in films like Cocteau's and

Olivier's, one is "no longer adapting, one is staging a play by means of cinema."

Bazin realizes that if the living actor's presence were essential to the effects of theater, the successful staging of a play by means of cinema would be impossible. He therefore argues that there is a sense in which the actor is present on the screen just as a person is "present" in a mirror. Although Bazin's refutation of the importance of presence is not very convincing (Stanley Cavell treats the issue much more systematically in *The World Viewed*), it allows him to assert that the primary difference between stage and screen is not one of living beings but of architecture. Bazin thinks that theatrical speech often fails in a film not because it was written for living speakers but because it was written to be uttered in a particular kind of world. The problem of filming a play is to find a decor that preserves the closed, microcosmic qualities of theatrical architecture for which the dialogue was written and which at the same time preserves the natural realism of the screen. The screen is not a world in itself but a window on the world which consistently dwarfs and dissipates theatrical speech. Bazin believes this problem is worth solving, for even if original film scripts are preferable to adaptations, truly distinguished ones are rare. The cinema cannot afford to ignore its theatrical heritage, any more than the drama can afford the loss of the audiences that film can bring it.

Eisenstein too insists on the cultural heritage of cinema. He argues that Griffith even learned montage, which Eisenstein considers the essence of film, from the pages of Dickens. Eisenstein plainly sees no theoretical bar to adapting novels successfully to the screen, as proved by his own attempt to adapt Dreiser's *An American Tragedy*. Indeed, it is not implausible to argue, as Bazin and Sontag have, that the film's deepest affinities are with the novel, not with the play. The novel is "cinematic" in its fluid handling of time and space, in its "focused" narrative control, in its ability to alternate description with dialogue, and even in the privacy and isolation of its audiences. The film has adapted more fiction than drama.

In contrast, George Bluestone, a contemporary American scholar, argues that film and novel are fundamentally different. The novel (like the stage in Panofsky's view) is fundamentally a linguistic medium, while the film is primarily visual. Although both D. W. Griffith and Joseph Conrad state that their purpose is to make us "see," Bluestone contends that while we literally "see" films (we perceive the images themselves), we do not literally see anything in a sentence except the words (which we apprehend conceptually). The film, therefore, "necessarily leaves behind those characteristic contents of thought which only language can approximate: tropes, dreams, memories, conceptual consciousness." The adapter must treat the novel merely as raw material and create for the film its own form and content, which will be sensual and perceptual, rather than conceptual and discursive as was the original novel.

Like Eisenstein and Bazin, Robert Scholes, the contemporary American literary scholar, believes that story-telling in film is comparable to story-telling in any medium. And, like Bluestone, Scholes differentiates between the perceptual apprehension of film stories and the conceptual apprehension of written narrative texts. But Scholes locates the primary difference between written and filmed stories not in the texts themselves but in the way that "readers read" those texts. His central term, "narrativity," borrowed from recent French narrative theory, refers to the way that the "reader" reconstructs the story in his or her own mind, in effect puts the events and description of the story together into a coherent pattern of expectations and gratifications, based on a recognition of temporality and causality. The word "narrativity" refers to "the process by which a perceiver actively constructs a story from the fictional data provided by any narrative medium."

For Scholes, the written narrative, conveyed by the more abstract sign-system of words, requires and rewards a narrativity that concretizes and pictorializes the verbal images into more specific mental pictures of persons, places, actions, and things. But the concrete pictorialization of the filmed image requires and rewards precisely the opposite kind of narrativity—the abstracting of highly specific stimuli into more general patterns of structure and theme. "The cinematic world invites—even requires—conceptualization." By implication, any film that attempted to adapt a written narrative (or, conversely, any "novelization" of a film, making a novel from an original screenplay, —an increasingly common practice in the 1970s) would need to take account of the different kinds of narrativity the two media generate.

HUGO MUNSTERBERG
FROM THE FILM:
A PSYCHOLOGICAL STUDY
THE MEANS OF THE PHOTOPLAY

We have now reached the point at which we can knot together all our threads, the psychological and the esthetic ones. If we do so, we come to the true thesis of this whole book. Our esthetic discussion showed us that it is the aim of art to isolate a significant part of our experience in such a way that it is separate from our practical life and is in complete agreement within itself. Our esthetic satisfaction results from this inner agreement and harmony, but in order that we may feel such agreement of the parts we must enter with our own impulses into the will of every element, into the meaning of every line and color and form, every word and tone and note Only if everything is full of such inner movement can we really enjoy the harmonious coöperation of the parts. The means of the various arts, we saw, are the forms and methods by which this aim is fulfilled. They must be different for every material. Moreover the same material may allow very different methods of isolation and elimination of the insignificant and reënforcement of that which contributes to the harmony. If we ask now what are the characteristic means by which the photoplay succeeds in overcoming reality, in isolating a significant dramatic story and in presenting it so that we enter into it and yet keep it away from our practical life and enjoy the harmony of the parts, we must remember all the results to which our psychological discussion in the first part of the book has led us.

We recognized there that the photoplay, incomparable in this respect with the drama, gave us a view of dramatic events which was completely shaped by the inner movements of the mind. To be sure, the events in the photoplay happen in the real space with its depth. But the spectator feels that they are not presented in the three dimensions of the outer world, that they are flat pictures which only the mind molds into plastic things. Again the events are seen in continuous movement; and yet the pictures break up the movement into a rapid succession of instantaneous impressions. We do not see the objective reality, but a product of our own mind which binds the pictures together. But much stronger differences came to light when we turned to the processes of attention, of memory, of imagination, of suggestion, of division of interest and of emotion. The attention turns to detailed points in the outer world and ignores everything else: the photoplay is doing exactly this when in the close-up a detail is enlarged and everything else disappears. Memory breaks into present events by bringing up pictures of the past: the photoplay is doing this by its frequent cutbacks, when pictures of events long past flit between those of the present. The imagination anticipates the future or overcomes reality by fancies and dreams; the photoplay is doing all this more richly than any chance imagination would succeed in doing. But chiefly, through our division of interest our mind is drawn hither and thither. We think of events which run parallel in different places. The photoplay can show in intertwined scenes everything which our mind embraces. Events in three or four or five regions of the world can be woven together into one complex action. Finally, we saw that every shade of feeling and emotion which fills the spectator's mind can mold the scenes in the photoplay until they appear the embodiment of our feelings. In every one of these aspects the photoplay succeeds in doing what the drama of the theater does not attempt.

If this is the outcome of esthetic analysis on the one side, of psychological research on the other, we need only combine the results of both into a unified principle: *the photoplay tells us the human story by overcoming the forms of the outer world, namely, space, time, and causality, and by adjusting the events to the forms of the inner world, namely, attention, memory, imagination, and emotion.*

We shall gain our orientation most directly if once more, under this point of view, we compare the photoplay with the performance on the theater stage. We shall not enter into a discussion of the character of the regular theater and its drama. We take this for granted. Everybody knows that highest art form which the Greeks created and which from Greece has spread over Asia, Europe, and America. In tragedy and in comedy from ancient times to Ibsen, Rostand, Hauptmann, and Shaw we recognize one common purpose and one common form for which no further commentary is needed. How does the photoplay differ from a theater performance? We insisted that every work of art must be somehow separated from our sphere of practical interests. The theater is no exception. The structure of the theater itself, the framelike form of the stage, the difference of light between stage and house, the stage setting and costuming, all inhibit in the audience the possibility of taking the action on the stage to be real life. Stage managers have some-times tried the experiment of reducing those differences, for in-stance, keeping the audience also in a fully lighted hall, and they always had to discover how much the dramatic effect was reduced because the feeling of distance from reality was weakened. The photoplay and the theater in this respect are evidently alike. The screen too suggests from the very start the complete unreality of the events.

But each further step leads us to remarkable differences between the stage play and the film play. In every respect the film play is further away from the physical reality than the drama and in every respect this greater distance from the physical world brings it nearer to the mental world. The stage shows us living men. It is not the real Romeo and not the real Juliet; and yet the actor and the actress have the ringing voices of true people, breathe like them, have living colors like them, and fill physical space like them. What is left in the photoplay? The voice has been stilled: the photoplay is a dumb show. Yet we must not forget that this alone is a step away from reality which has often been taken in the midst of the dramatic world. Whoever knows the history of the theater is aware of the tremendous rôle which the pantomime has played in the de-velopment of mankind. From the old half-religious pantomimic and suggestive dances out of which the beginnings of the real drama grew to the fully religious pantomimes of medieval ages and, fur ther on, to many silent mimic elements in modern performances, we find a continuity of conventions which make the pantomime almost the real background of all dramatic development. We know how popular the pantomimes were among the Greeks, and how they stood in the foreground in the imperial period of Rome. Old Rome cherished the mimic clowns, but still more the tragic panto-mimics. "Their very nod speaks, their hands talk and their fingers have a voice." After the fall of the Roman empire the church used the pantomime for the portrayal of sacred history, and later cen-turies enjoyed very unsacred histories in the pantomimes of their ballets. Even complex artistic tragedies without words have tri-umphed on our present-day stage. *L'Enfant Prodigue* which came from Paris, *Sumurun* which came from Berlin, *Petroushka* which came from Petrograd, conquered the American stage; and surely the loss of speech, while it increased the remoteness from reality, by no means destroyed the continuous consciousness of the bodily existence of the actors.

Moreover the student of a modern pantomime cannot overlook a characteristic difference between the speechless performance on the stage and that of the actors of a photoplay. The expression of the inner states, the whole system of gestures, is decidedly different: and here we might say that the photoplay stands nearer to life than the pantomime. Of course, the photoplayer must somewhat exaggerate the natural expression. The whole rhythm and intensity of his gestures must be more marked than it would be with actors who accompany their movements by spoken words and who express the meaning of their thoughts and feelings by the content of what they say. Nevertheless the photoplayer uses the regular channels of mental discharge. He acts simply as a very emotional person might act. But the actor who plays in a pantomime cannot be satisfied with that. He is expected to add something which is entirely unnatural, namely a kind of artificial demonstration of his emotions. He must not only behave like an angry man, but he must behave like a man who is consciously interested in his anger and wants to demonstrate it to others. He exhibits his emotions for the spectators. He really acts theatrically for the benefit of the bystanders. If he did not try to do so, his means of conveying a rich story and a real conflict of human passions would be too meager. The photoplayer, with the rapid changes of scenes, has other possibilities of conveying his intentions. He must not yield to the temptation to play a pantomime on the screen, or he will seriously injure the artistic quality of the reel.

The really decisive distance from bodily reality, however, is created by the substitution of the actor's picture for the actor himself. Lights and shades replace the manifoldness of color effects and mere perspective must furnish the suggestion of depth. We traced it when we discussed the psychology of kinematoscopic perception. But we must not put the emphasis on the wrong point. The natural tendency might be to lay the chief stress on the fact that those people in the photoplay do not stand before us in flesh and blood. The essential point is rather that we are conscious of the flatness of the picture. If we were to see the actors of the stage in a mirror, it would also be a reflected image which we perceive. We should not really have the actors themselves in our straight line of vision; and yet this image would appear to us equivalent to the actors themselves, because it would contain all the depth of the real stage. The process which leads from the living men to the screen is more complex than a mere reflection in a mirror, but in spite of the complexity in the transmission we do, after all, see the real actor in the picture. The photograph is absolutely different from those pictures which a clever draughtsman has sketched. In the photoplay we see the actors themselves and the decisive factor which makes the impression different from seeing real men is not that we see the living persons through the medium of photographic reproduction but that this reproduction shows them in a flat form. The bodily space has been eliminated. We said once before that stereoscopic arrangements could reproduce somewhat this plastic form also. Yet this would seriously interfere with the character of the photoplay. We need there this overcoming of the depth, we want to have it as a picture only and yet as a picture which strongly suggests to us the actual depth of the real world. We want to keep the interest in the plastic world and want to be aware of the depth in which the persons move, but our direct object of perception must be without the depth. That idea of space which forces on us most strongly the idea of heaviness, solidity and substantiality must be replaced by the light flitting immateriality.

But the photoplay sacrifices not only the space values of the real theater; it disregards no less its order of time. The theater presents its plot in the time order of reality. It may interrupt the continuous flow of time without neglecting the conditions of the dramatic art. There may be twenty years between the third and the fourth act, inasmuch as the dramatic writer must select those elements spread over space and time which are significant for the development of his story. But he is bound by the fundamental principle of real time, that it can move only forward and not backward. Whatever the theater shows us now must come later in the story than that which it showed us in any previous moment. The strict classical demand for complete unity of time does not fit every drama, but a drama would give up its mission if it told us in the third act something which happened before the second act. Of course, there may be a play within a play, and the players on the stage which is set on the stage may play events of old Roman history before the king of France. But this is an enclosure of the past in the present, which corresponds exactly to the actual order of events. The photoplay, on the other hand, does not and must not respect this temporal structure of the physical universe. At any point the photoplay interrupts the series and brings us back to the past. We studied this unique feature of the film art when we spoke of the psychology of memory and imagination. With the full freedom of our fancy, with the whole mobility of our association of ideas, pictures of the past flit through the scenes of the present. Time is left behind. Man becomes boy; today is interwoven with the day before yesterday. The freedom of the mind has triumphed over the unalterable law of the outer world.

It is interesting to watch how playwrights nowadays try to steal the thunder of the photoplay and experiment with time reversals on the legitimate stage. We are esthetically on the borderland when a grandfather tells his grandchild the story of his own youth as a warning, and instead of the spoken words the events of his early years come before our eyes. This is, after all, quite similar to a play within a play. A very different experiment is tried in *Under Cover.* The third act, which plays on the second floor of the house, ends with an explosion. The fourth act, which plays downstairs, begins a quarter of an hour before the explosion. Here we have a real denial of a fundamental condition of the theater. Or if we stick to recent products of the American stage, we may think of *On Trial,* a play which perhaps comes nearest to a dramatic usurpation of the rights of the photoplay. We see the court scene and as one witness after another begins to give his testimony the courtroom is replaced by the scenes of the actions about which the witness is to report. Another clever play, *Between the Lines,* ends the first act with a postman bringing three letters from the three children of the house. The second, third, and fourth acts lead us to the three different homes from which the letters came and the action in the three places not only precedes the writing of the letters, but goes on at the same time. The last act, finally, begins with the arrival of the letters which tell the ending of those events in the three homes. Such experiments are very suggestive but they are not any longer pure dramatic art. It is always possible to mix arts. An Italian painter produces very striking effects by putting pieces of glass and stone and rope into his paintings, but they are no longer pure paintings. The drama in which the later event comes before the earlier is an esthetic barbarism which is entertaining as a clever trick in a graceful superficial play, but intolerable in ambitious dramatic art. It is not only tolerable but perfectly natural in any photoplay. The pictorial reflection of the world is not bound by the rigid mechanism of time. Our mind is here and there, our mind turns to the present and then to the past: the photoplay can equal it in its freedom from the bondage of the material world.

But the theater is bound not only by space and time. Whatever it shows is controlled by the same laws of causality which govern nature. This involves a complete continuity of the physical events: no cause without following effect, no effect without preceding cause. This whole natural course is left behind in the play on the screen. The deviation from reality begins with that resolution of the continuous movement which we studied in our psychological discussions. We saw that the impression of movement results from an activity of the mind which binds the separate pictures together. What we actually see is a composite; it is like the movement of a fountain in which every jet is resolved into numberless drops. We feel the play of those drops in their sparkling haste as one continuous stream of water, and yet are conscious of the myriads of drops, each one separate from the others. This fountainlike spray of pictures has completely overcome the causal world.

In an entirely different form this triumph over causality appears in the interruption of the events by pictures which belong to another series. We find this whenever the scene suddenly changes. The processes are not carried to their natural consequences. A movement is started, but before the cause brings its results another scene has taken its place. What this new scene brings may be an effect for which we saw no causes. But not only the processes are interrupted. The intertwining of the scenes which we have traced in detail is itself such a contrast to causality. It is as if different objects could fill the same space at the same time. It is as if the resistance of the material world had disappeared and the substances could penetrate one another. In the interlacing of our ideas we experience this superiority to all physical laws. The theater would not have even the technical means to give us such impressions, but if it had, it would have no right to make use of them, as it would destroy the basis on which the drama is built. We have only another case of the same type in those series of pictures which aim to force a suggestion on our mind. We have spoken of them. A certain effect is prepared by a chain of causes and yet when the causal result is to appear the film is cut off. We have the causes without the effect. The villain thrusts with his dagger—but a miracle has snatched away his victim.

While the moving pictures are lifted above the world of space and time and causality and are freed from its bounds, they are certainly not without law. We said before that the freedom with which the pictures replace one another is to a large degree comparable to the sparkling and streaming of the musical tones. The yielding to the play of the mental energies, to the attention and emotion, which is felt in the film pictures, is still more complete in the musical melodies and harmonies in which the tones themselves are merely the expressions of the ideas and feelings and will impulses of the mind. Their harmonies and disharmonies, their fusing and blending, is not controlled by any outer necessity, but by the inner agreement and disagreement of our free impulses. And yet in this world of musical freedom, everything is completely controlled by esthetic necessities. No sphere of practical life stands under such rigid rules as the realm of the composer. However bold the musical genius may be he cannot emancipate himself from the iron rule that his work must show complete unity in itself. All the separate prescriptions which the musical student has to learn are ultimately only the consequences of this central demand which music, the freest of the arts, shares with all the others. In the case of the film, too, the freedom from the physical forms of space, time, and causality does not mean any liberation from this esthetic bondage either. On the contrary, just as music is surrounded by more technical rules than literature, the photoplay must be held together by the esthetic demands still more firmly than is the drama. The arts which are subordinated to the conditions of space, time, and causality find a certain firmness of structure in these material forms which contain an element of outer connectedness. But where these forms are given up and where the freedom of mental play replaces their outer necessity, everything would fall asunder if the esthetic unity were disregarded.

This unity is, first of all, the unity of action. The demand for it is the same which we know from the drama. The temptation to neglect it is nowhere greater than in the photoplay where outside matter can so easily be introduced or independent interests developed. It is certainly true for the photoplay, as for every work of art, that nothing has the right to existence in its midst which is not internally needed for the unfolding of the unified action. Wherever two plots are given to us, we receive less by far than if we had only one plot. We leave the sphere of valuable art entirely when a unified action is ruined by mixing it with declamation, and propaganda which is not organically interwoven with the action itself. It may be still fresh in memory what an esthetically intolerable helter-skelter performance was offered to the public in *The Battlecry of Peace*. Nothing can be more injurious to the esthetic cultivation of the people than such performances which hold the attention of the spectators by ambitious detail and yet destroy their esthetic sensibility by a complete disregard of the fundamental principle of art, the demand for unity. But we recognized also that this unity involves complete isolation. We annihilate beauty when we link the artistic creation with practical interests and transform the spectator into a selfishly interested bystander. The scenic background of the play is not presented in order that we decide whether we want to spend our next vacation there. The interior decoration of the rooms is not exhibited as a display for a department store. The men and women who carry out the action of the plot must not be people whom we may meet tomorrow on the street. All the threads of the play must be knotted together in the play itself and none should be connected with our outside interests. A good photoplay must be isolated and complete in itself like a beautiful melody. It is not an advertisement for the newest fashions.

This unity of action involves unity of characters. It has too often been maintained by those who theorize on the photoplay that the development of character is the special task of the drama, while the photoplay, which lacks words, must be satisfied with types. Probably this is only a reflection of the crude state which most photoplays of today have not outgrown. Internally, there is no reason why the means of the photoplay should not allow a rather subtle depicting of complex character. But the chief demand is that the characters remain consistent, that the action be developed according to inner necessity and that the characters themselves be in harmony with the central idea of the plot. However, as soon as we insist on unity we have no right to think only of the action which gives the content of the play. We cannot make light of the form. As in music the melody and rhythms belong together, as in painting not every color combination suits every subject, and as in poetry not every stanza would agree with every idea, so the photoplay must bring action and pictorial expression into perfect harmony. But this demand repeats itself in every single picture. We take it for granted that the painter balances perfectly the forms in his painting, groups them so that an internal symmetry can be felt and that the lines and curves and colors blend into a unity. Every single picture of the sixteen thousand which are shown to us in one reel ought to be treated with this respect of the pictorial artist for the unity of the forms.

The photoplay shows us a significant conflict of human actions in moving pictures which, freed from the physical forms of space, time, and causality, are adjusted to the free play of our mental experiences and which reach complete isolation from the practical world through the perfect unity of plot and pictorial appearance.

1916

SUSAN SONTAG
FILM AND THEATRE

The big question is whether there is an unbridgeable division, even opposition, between the two arts. Is there something genuinely "cinematic"?

Almost all opinion holds that there is. A commonplace of discussion has it that film and theatre are distinct and even antithetical arts, each giving rise to its own standards of judgment and canons of form. Thus Erwin Panofsky argues, in his celebrated essay "Style and Medium in the Motion Pictures" (1934, rewritten in 1946), that one of the criteria for evaluating a movie is its freedom from the impurities of theatricality. To talk about film, one must first define "the basic nature of the medium." Those who think prescriptively about the nature of live drama, less confident in the future of their art than the *cinéphiles* in theirs, rarely take a comparably exclusivist line.

The history of cinema is often treated as the history of its emancipation from theatrical models. First of all from theatrical "frontality" (the unmoving camera reproducing the situation of the spectator of a play fixed in his seat), then from theatrical acting (gestures needlessly stylized, exaggerated—needlessly, because now the actor could be seen "close up"), then from theatrical furnishings (unnecessary "distancing" of the audience's emotions, disregarding the opportunity to immerse the audience in reality). Movies are regarded as advancing from theatrical stasis to cinematic fluidity, from theatrical artificiality to cinematic naturalness and immediacy. But this view is far too simple.

Such over-simplification testifies to the ambiguous scope of the camera eye. Because the camera *can* be used to project a relatively passive, unselective kind of vision—as well as the highly selective ("edited") vision generally associated with movies—cinema is a "medium" as well as an art, in the sense that it can encapsulate any of the performing arts and render it in a film transcription. (This "medium" or non-art aspect of film attained its routine incarnation with the advent of television. There, movies themselves became another performing art to be transcribed, miniaturized on film.) One *can* film a play or ballet or opera or sporting event in such a way that film becomes, relatively speaking, a transparency, and it seems correct to say that one is seeing the event filmed. But theatre is never a "medium." Thus, because one can make a movie "of" a play but not a play "of" a movie, cinema had an early but, I should argue, fortuitous connection with the stage. Some of the earliest films were filmed plays. Duse and Bernhardt and Barrymore are on film—marooned in time, absurd, touching; there is a 1913 British film of Forbes-Robertson playing Hamlet, a 1923 German film of *Othello* starring Emil Jannings. More recently, the camera has "preserved" Helene Weigel's performance of *Mother Courage* with the Berliner Ensemble, the Living Theatre production of *The Brig* (filmed by the Mekas brothers), and Peter Brook's staging of Weiss's *Marat/Sade*.

But from the beginning, even within the confines of the notion of film as a "medium" and the camera as a "recording" instrument, a great deal other than what occurred in theatres was taken down. As with still photography, some of the events captured on moving photographs were staged but others were valued precisely because they were *not* staged—the camera being the witness, the invisible spectator, the invulnerable voyeuristic eye. (Perhaps public happenings, "news," constitute an intermediate case between staged and unstaged events; but film as "newsreel" generally amounts to using film as a "medium.") To create on film a *document* of a transient reality is a conception quite unrelated to the purposes of theatre. It only appears related when the "real event" being recorded is a theatrical performance. And the first use of the motion picture camera was to make a documentary record of unstaged, casual reality: Louis Lumière's films of crowd-scenes in Paris and New York made in the 1890's antedate any use of film in the service of plays.

The other paradigmatic non-theatrical use of film, which dates from the earliest activity of the motion-picture camera, is for the creation of *illusion*, the construction of fantasy. The pioneer figure here is, of course, Georges Méliès. To be sure, Méliès (like many directors after him) conceived of the rectangle of the screen on analogy with the proscenium stage. And not only were the events staged; they were the very stuff of invention: imaginary journeys, imaginary objects, physical metamorphoses. But this, even adding the fact that Méliès situated his camera "in front of" the action and hardly moved it, does not make his films theatrical in an invidious sense. In their treatment of persons as things (physical objects) and in their disjunctive presentation of time and space, Méliès' films are quintessentially "cinematic" — so far as there is such a thing.

The contrast between theatre and films is usually taken to lie in the materials represented or depicted. But exactly where does the difference lie? It's tempting to draw a crude boundary. Theatre deploys artifice while cinema is committed to reality, indeed to an ultimately physical reality which is "redeemed," to use Siegfried Kracauer's striking word, by the camera. The aesthetic judgment that follows this bit of intellectual map-making is that films shot in real-life settings are better (i.e., more cinematic) than those shot in a studio (where one can detect the difference). Obviously, if Flaherty and Italian neo-realism and the cinema verité of Vertov, Rouch, Marker, and Ruspoli are the preferred models, one would judge rather harshly the period of 100% studio-made films inaugurated around 1920 by The Cabinet of Dr. Caligari, films with ostentatiously artificial landscapes and decor, and deem the right direction to be that taken at the same period in Sweden, where many films with strenuous natural settings were being shot "on location." Thus, Panofsky attacks Dr. Caligari for "prestylizing reality," and urges upon cinema "the problem of manipulating and shooting unstylized reality in such a way that the result has style."

But there is no reason to insist on a single model for film. And it is helpful to notice that, for the most part, the apotheosis of realism, the prestige of "unstylized reality," in cinema is actually a covert political-moral position. Films have been rather too often acclaimed as the democratic art, the art of mass society. Once one takes this description very seriously, one tends (like Panofsky and Kracauer) to want movies to continue to reflect their origins in a vulgar level of the arts, to remain loyal to their vast uneducated audience. Thus, a vaguely Marxist orientation jibes with a fundamental tenet of romanticism. Cinema, at once high art and popular art, is cast as the art of the authentic. Theatre, by contrast, means dressing up, pretense, lies. It smacks of aristocratic taste and the class society. Behind the objection of critics to the stagy sets of Dr. Caligari, the improbable costumes and florid acting of Renoir's Nana, the talkiness of Dreyer's Gertrud, as "theatrical," lay the feeling that such films were false, that they exhibited a sensibility both pretentious and reactionary which was out-of-step with the democratic and more mundane sensibility of modern life.

Anyway, whether aesthetic defect or not in the particular case, the synthetic look in films is not necessarily a misplaced theatrical-ism. From the beginning of film history, there were painters and sculptors who claimed that cinema's true future resided in artifice, construction. It lay not in figurative narration or story-telling of any kind (either in a relatively realistic or in a "surrealistic" vein), but in abstraction. Thus, Theo van Doesburg in his essay of 1929, "Film as Pure Form," envisages film as the vehicle of "optical poetry," "dynamic light architecture," "the creation of a moving ornament." Films will realize "Bach's dream of finding an optical equivalent for the temporal structure of a musical composition." Today, a few film-makers—for example, Robert Breer—continue to pursue this conception of film, and who is to say it is not cinematic?

Could anything be farther from the scope of theatre than such a degree of abstraction? It's important not to answer that question too quickly.

Some locate the division between theatre and film as the differ-ence between the play and the filmscript. Panofsky derives this difference from what he takes to be the most profound one: the difference between the *formal* conditions of seeing a play and those of seeing a movie. In the theatre, says Panofsky, "space is static, that is, the space represented on the stage, as well as the spatial relation of the beholder to the spectacle, is unalterably fixed," while in the cinema "the spectator occupies a fixed seat, but only physical-ly, not as the subject of an aesthetic experience." In the cinema, the spectator is "aesthetically . . . in permanent motion as his eye identifies with the lens of the camera, which permanently shifts in distance and direction."

True enough. But the observation does not warrant a radical dissociation of theatre from film. Like many critics, Panofsky is assuming a "literary" conception of theatre. To a theatre which is conceived of basically as dramatized literature, texts, words, he contrasts cinema which is, according to the received phrase, primar-ily "a visual experience." In effect, we are being asked to acknowl-edge tacitly the period of silent films as definitive of cinematic art and to identify theatre with "plays," from Shakespeare to Tennessee Williams. But many of the most interesting movies today are not adequately described as images with sound added. And what if theatre is conceived of as more than, or something different from, plays?

Panofsky may be over-simplifying when he decries the theatrical taint in movies, but he is sound when he argues that, historically, theatre is only one of the arts that feeds into cinema. As he remarks, it is apt that films came to be known popularly as moving *pictures* rather than as "photoplays" or "screen plays." Movies derive less from the theatre, from a performance art, an art that already moves, than they do from works of art which were stationary. Bad nineteenth-century paintings and postcards, wax-works à la Madame Tussaud, and comic strips are the sources Panofsky cites. What is surprising is that he doesn't connect movies with earlier narrative uses of still photography—like the family photo-album. The narrative techniques developed by certain nineteenth-century novelists, as Eisenstein pointed out in his brilliant essay on Dickens, supplied still another prototype for cinema.

Movies are images (usually photographs) that move, to be sure. But the distinctive unit of films is not the image but the principle of connection between the images, the relation of a "shot" to the one that preceded it and the one that comes after. There is no peculiarly "cinematic" as opposed to "theatrical" mode of linking images.

Panofsky tries to hold the line against the infiltration of theatre by cinema, as well as vice versa. In the theatre, not only can the spectator not change his angle of vision but, unlike movies, "the settings of the stage cannot change during one act (except for such incidentals as rising moons or gathering clouds and such illegitimate reborrowings from film as turning wings or gliding backdrops)." Were we to assent to this, the ideal play would be *No Exit*, the ideal set a realistic living room or a blank stage.

No less dogmatic is the complementary dictum about what is illegitimate in films—according to which, since films are "a visual experience," all components must be demonstrably subordinate to the image. Thus, Panofsky asserts: "Wherever a poetic emotion, a musical outburst, or a literary conceit (even, I am grieved to say, some of the wisecracks of Groucho Marx) entirely lose contact with visible movement, they strike the sensitive spectator as, literally, out of place." What, then, of the films of Bresson and Godard, with their allusive, densely thoughtful texts and their characteristic refusal to be visually beautiful? How could one explain the extraordinary rightness of Ozu's relatively immobilized camera?

The decline in average quality of films in the early sound period (compared with the level reached by films in the 1920's) is undeniable. Although it would be facile to call the sheer uninterestingness of most films of this period simply a regression to theatre, it is a fact that film-makers did turn more frequently to plays in the 1930's than they had in the preceding decade. Countless stage successes like *Outward Bound, Dinner at Eight, Blithe Spirit, Faisons un Rêve, Twentieth Century, Boudu Sauvé des Eaux, She Done Him Wrong, Anna Christie, Marius, Animal Crackers, The Petrified Forest*, were filmed. The success of movie versions of plays is measured by the extent to which the script rearranges and displaces the action and deals less than respectfully with the spoken text—as do certain films of plays by Wilde and Shaw, the Olivier Shakespeare films (at least *Henry V*), and Sjöberg's *Miss Julie*. But the basic disapproval of films which betray their origins in plays remains. A recent example: the outright hostility which greeted Dreyer's latest film, *Gertrud*. Not only does *Gertrud*, which I believe to be a minor masterpiece, follow a turn-of-the-century play that has characters conversing at length and quite formally, but it is filmed almost entirely in middle-shot.

Some of the films I have just mentioned are negligible as art; several are first-rate. (The same for the plays, though no correlation between the merits of the movies and those of the "original" plays can be established.) However, their virtues and faults cannot be sorted out as a cinematic versus a theatrical element. Whether derived from plays or not, films with complex or formal dialogue, films in which the camera is static or in which the action stays indoors, are not necessarily theatrical. *Per contra*, it is no more part of the putative "essence" of movies that the camera must rove over a large physical area, than it is that movies ought to be silent. Though most of the action of Kurosawa's *The Lower Depths*, a fairly faithful transcription of Gorki's play, is confined to one large room, it is as cinematic as the same director's *Throne of Blood*, a very free and laconic adaptation of *Macbeth*. The quality of Melville's claustrophobic *Les Enfants Terribles* is as peculiar to the movies as Ford's *The Searchers* or a train journey in Cinerama.

What does make a film theatrical in an invidious sense is when the narration becomes coy or self-conscious: compare Autant-Lara's *Occupe-Toi d'Amélie*, a brilliant cinematic use of the conventions and materials of theatricality, with Ophuls' clumsy use of similar conventions and materials in *La Ronde*.

Allardyce Nicoll, in his book *Film and Theatre* (1936), argues that the difference may be understood as a difference in kinds of characters. "Practically all effectively drawn stage characters are types [while] in the cinema we demand individualization and impute greater power of independent life to the figures on the screen." (Panofsky, it might be mentioned, makes exactly the opposite point: that the nature of films, in contrast to plays, requires flat or stock characters.)

Nicoll's thesis is not as arbitrary as it may at first appear. I would relate it to the fact that often the indelible moments of a film, and the most potent elements of characterization, are precisely the "irrelevant" or unfunctional details. (A random example: the ping-pong ball the schoolmaster toys with in Ivory's *Shakespeare Wallah*.) Movies thrive on the narrative equivalent of a technique familiar from painting and photography, off-centering. It is this that creates the pleasing disunity of fragmentariness (what Nicoll means by "individualization"?) of the characters of many of the greatest films. In contrast, linear "coherence" of detail (the gun on the wall in the first act that must go off by the end of the third) is the rule in Occidental narrative theatre, and gives rise to the sense of the unity of the characters (a unity that may appear like the statement of a "type").

But even with these adjustments, Nicoll's thesis seems less than appealing when one perceives that it rests on the idea that "When we go to the theatre, we expect theatre and nothing else." What is this theatre-and-nothing-else? It is the old notion of artifice. (As if art were ever anything else. As if some arts were artificial but others not.) According to Nicoll, when we are in a theatre "in every way the 'falsity' of a theatrical production is borne in upon us, so that we are prepared to demand nothing save a theatrical truth." In the cinema, however, every member of the audience, no matter how sophisticated, is on essentially the same level; we all believe that the camera cannot lie. As the film actor and his role are identical, so the image cannot be dissociated from what is imaged. Cinema, therefore, gives us what is experienced as the truth of life.

Couldn't theatre dissolve the distinction between the truth of artifice and the truth of life? Isn't that just what the theatre as ritual seeks to do? Isn't that what is being sought when theatre is conceived as an *exchange* with an audience?—something that films can never be.

If an irreducible distinction between theatre and cinema does exist, it may be this. Theatre is confined to a logical or *continuous* use of space. Cinema (through editing, that is, through the change of shot—which is the basic unit of film construction) has access to an alogical or *discontinuous* use of space. In the theatre, people are either in the stage space or "off." When "on," they are always visible or visualizable in contiguity with each other. In the cinema, no such relation is necessarily visible or even visualizable. (Example: the last shot of Paradjanov's *In the Shadows of Our Ancestors.*) Some films considered objectionably theatrical are those which seem to emphasize spatial continuities, like Hitchcock's virtuoso *Rope* or the daringly anachronistic *Gertrud.* But closer analysis of both these films would show how complex their treatment of space is. The longer and longer "takes" toward which sound films have been moving are, in themselves, neither more nor less cinematic than the short "takes" characteristic of silents.

Thus, cinematic virtue does not reside in the fluidity of the positioning of the camera nor in the mere frequency of the change of shot. It consists in the arrangement of screen images and (now) of sounds. Méliès, for example, though he didn't get beyond the static positioning of his camera, had a very striking conception of how to link screen images. He grasped that editing offered an equivalent to the magician's sleight of hand—thereby suggesting that one of the features of film (as distinct from theatre) is that *anything* can happen, that there is nothing that can't be represented convincingly. Through editing, Méliès presents discontinuities of physical substance and behavior. In his films, the discontinuities are, so to speak, practical, functional; they accomplish a transformation of ordinary reality. But the continuous *re*invention of space (as well as the option of temporal indeterminacy) peculiar to film narration does not pertain only to the cinema's ability to fabricate "visions," to show us a radically altered world. The most "realistic" use of the motion-picture camera also involves a discontinuous account of space.

Film narration has a "syntax," composed of the rhythm of associations and disjunctions. As Cocteau has written, "My primary concern in a film is to prevent the images from flowing, to oppose them to each other, to anchor them and join them without destroying their relief." (But does such a conception of film syntax entail, as Cocteau thinks, our disavowal of movies as "mere entertainment instead of a vehicle for thought"?)

In drawing a line of demarcation between theatre and films, the issue of the continuity of space seems to me more fundamental than the difference that might be pointed out between theatre as an organization of movement in three-dimensional space (like dance) versus cinema as an organization of plane space (like painting). The theatre's capacities for manipulating space and time are, simply, much cruder and more labored than film's. Theatre cannot equal the cinema's facilities for the strictly-controlled repetition of images, for the duplication or matching of word and image, and for the juxtaposition and over-lapping of images. (Through advanced lighting techniques, one can now "dissolve" on the stage. But as yet there is no equivalent, not even through the most adept use of scrim, of the "lap dissolve.")

Theatre has been described as a mediated art, presumably because it usually consists of a pre-existent play mediated by a particular performance which offers one of many possible interpretations of the play. Film, in contrast, is regarded as unmediated—because of its larger-than-life scale and more unrefusable impact on the eye, and because (in Panofsky's words) "the medium of the movies is physical reality as such" and the characters in a movie "have no aesthetic existence outside the actors." But there is an equally valid sense which shows movies to be the mediated art and theatre the unmediated one. We see what happens on the stage with our own eyes. We see on the screen what the camera sees. In the cinema, narration proceeds by ellipsis (the "cut" or change of shot); the camera eye is a unified point of view that continually displaces itself. But the change of shot can provoke questions, the simplest of which is: from *whose* point of view is the shot seen? And the ambiguity of point of view latent in all cinematic narration has no equivalent in the theatre.

Indeed, one should not neglect to emphasize the aesthetically positive role of disorientation in the cinema. Examples: Busby Berkeley dollying back from an ordinary-looking stage already established as some thirty feet deep to disclose a stage area three hundred feet square. Resnais panning from character X's point of view a full 360°, to come to rest upon X's face.

Much may be made of the fact that, in its concrete existence, cinema is an *object* (a *product*, even) while theatre is a *performance*. Is this so important? In a way, no. Whether objects (like films or paintings) or performances (like music or theatre), all art is first a mental act, a fact of consciousness. The object aspect of film, the performance aspect of theatre are merely means—means to the experience, which is not only "of" but "through" the film and the theatre-event. Each subject of an aesthetic experience shapes it to his own measure. With respect to any *single* experience, it hardly matters that a film is usually identical from one projection of it to another while theatre performances are highly mutable.

The difference between object-art and performance-art lies behind Panofsky's observation that "the screenplay, in contrast to the theatre play, has no aesthetic existence independent of its performance," and characters in movies *are* the stars who enact them. It is because the film is an object, a totality that is set, that movie roles are identical with the actors' performances; while in the theatre (in the West, an additive rather than an organic art?) only the written play is "fixed," an object and therefore existing apart from any staging of it. Yet this dichotomy is not beyond dispute. Just as movies needn't necessarily be designed to be shown in theatres at all (they can be intended for more continuous and casual looking), a movie *may* be altered from one projection to the next. Harry Smith, when he runs off his own films, makes each projection an unrepeatable performance. And, again, it is not true that all theatre is only about written plays which may be given a good or a bad production. In Happenings and other recent theatre-events, we are precisely being offered "plays" identical with their productions in the same sense as the screenplay is identical with the film.

Yet, a difference remains. Because the film is an object, it is totally manipulable, totally calculable. A film is like a book, another portable art-object; making a film, like writing a book, means constructing an inanimate thing, every element of which is determinate. Indeed, in films, this determinacy has or can have a quasi-mathematical form, like music. (A shot lasts a certain number of seconds, a change of angle of so many degrees is required to "match" two shots.) Given the total determinacy of the result on celluloid (whatever the extent of the director's conscious intervention), it was inevitable that some film directors would want to devise schemas to make their intentions more exact. Thus, it was neither perverse nor primitive of Busby Berkeley to have used only one camera to shoot the whole of each of his mammoth dance numbers. Every "set-up" was designed to be shot from only one exactly calculated angle. Bresson, working on a far more self-conscious level of artistry, has declared that, for him, the director's task is to find the single correct way of doing each shot. An image cannot be justified in itself, according to Bresson; it has an exactly specifiable relation to the temporally adjacent images, which relation constitutes its "meaning."

But the theatre allows only the loosest approximation to this sort of formal concern. (And responsibility. Justly, French critics speak of the director of a film as its "author.") Because they are performances, something always "live," theatre-events are not subject to a comparable degree of control, do not admit a comparably exact integration of effects.

It would be foolish to conclude that the best films are those which arise from the greatest amount of conscious planning; the plan may be faulty; and with some directors, instinct works better than any plan. Besides, there is an impressive body of "improvised" cinema. (To be distinguished from the work of some film-makers, notably Godard, who have become fascinated with the "look" of improvised cinema.) Nevertheless, it seems indisputable that cinema, not only potentially but by its nature, is a more rigorous art than theatre.

Thus, not merely a failure of nerve accounts for the fact that theatre, this seasoned art, occupied since antiquity with all sorts of local offices—enacting sacred rites, reinforcing communal loyalty, guiding morals, provoking the therapeutic discharge of violent emotions, conferring social status, giving practical instruction, affording entertainment, dignifying celebrations, subverting established authority—is now on the defensive before movies, this brash art with its huge, amorphous, passive audience. Meanwhile, movies continue to maintain their astonishing pace of formal articulation. (Take the commercial cinema of Europe, Japan, and the United States simply since 1960, and consider what audiences have become habituated to in the way of increasingly elliptical story-telling and visualization.)

But note: this youngest of the arts is also the one most heavily burdened with memory. Cinema is a time machine. Movies preserve the past, while theatres—no matter how devoted to the classics, to old plays—can only "modernize." Movies resurrect the beautiful dead; present intact vanished or ruined environments; employ, without irony, styles and fashions that seem funny today; solemnly ponder irrelevant or naïve problems. The historical flavor of anything registered on celluloid is so vivid that practically all films older than two years or so are saturated with a kind of pathos. (The pathos I am describing, which overtakes animated cartoons and drawn, abstract films as well as ordinary movies, is not simply that of old photographs.) Films age (being objects) as no theatre-event does (being always new). There is no pathos of mortality in theatre's "reality" as such, nothing in our response to a good performance of a Mayakovsky play comparable to the aesthetic role the emotion of nostalgia has when we see a film by Pudovkin.

Also worth noting: compared with the theatre, innovations in cinema seem to be assimilated more efficiently, seem altogether to be more shareable—and not only because new films are quickly and widely circulated. Also, partly because virtually the entire body of accomplishment in film can be consulted in the present, most film-makers are more knowledgeable about the history of their art than most theatre directors are about the recent past of theirs.

The key word in many discussions of cinema is "possibility." A merely classifying use of the word occurs, as in Panofsky's engaging judgment that, "within their self-imposed limitations the earlier Disney films . . . represent, as it were, a chemically pure distillation of cinematic possibilities." But behind this relatively neutral sense lurks a more polemical sense of cinema's "possibility." What is regularly intimated is the obsolescence of theatre, its supercession by films.

Thus, Panofsky describes the mediation of the camera eye as opening "up a world of possibility of which the stage can never dream." Artaud, earlier, thought that motion pictures may have made the theatre obsolete. Movies "possess a sort of virtual power which probes into the mind and uncovers undreamt of possibilities. . . . When this art's exhilaration has been blended in the right proportions with the psychic ingredient it commands, it will leave the theatre far behind and we will relegate the latter to the attic of our memories."

Meyerhold, facing the challenge head on, thought the only hope for theatre lay in a wholesale emulation of the cinema. "Let us 'cinematify' the theatre," he urged. The staging of plays must be "industrialized," theatres must accommodate audiences in the tens of thousands rather than in the hundreds, etc. Meyerhold also seemed to find some relief in the idea that the coming of sound signalled the downfall of movies. Believing that their international appeal depended entirely on the fact that screen actors didn't speak any particular language, he couldn't imagine in 1930 that, even if that were so, technology (dubbing, sub-titling) could solve the problem.

Is cinema the successor, the rival, or the revivifier of the theatre?

Art forms *have* been abandoned. (Whether because they became obsolete is another question.) One can't be sure that theatre is not in a state of irremediable decline, spurts of local vitality notwithstanding. But why should it be rendered obsolete by movies? It's worth remembering that predictions of obsolescence amount to declaring that a something has one peculiar task (which another something may do as well or better). Has theatre one peculiar task or aptitude?

Those who predict the demise of the theatre, assuming that cinema has engulfed its function, tend to impute a relation between films and theatre reminiscent of what was once said about photography and painting. If the painter's job had been no more than fabricating likenesses, the invention of the camera might indeed have made painting obsolete. But painting is hardly just "pictures," any more than cinema is just theatre for the masses, available in portable standard units.

In the naïve tale of photography and painting, painting was reprieved when it claimed a new task, abstraction. As the superior realism of photography was supposed to have liberated painting, allowing it to go abstract, cinema's superior power to represent (not merely to stimulate) the imagination may appear to have emboldened the theatre in a similar fashion, inviting the gradual obliteration of the conventional "plot."

Actually, painting and photography evidence parallel developments rather than a rivalry or a supercession. And, at least in principle, so have theatre and film. The possibilities for theatre that lie in going beyond psychological realism, in seeking greater abstractness, are not less germane to the future of narrative films. Conversely, the notion of movies as witness to real life, testimony rather than invention, the treatment of collective situations rather than the depiction of personal "dramas," is equally relevant to the stage. Not surprisingly, what follows some years after the rise of *cinema verité*, the sophisticated heir of documentary films, is a documentary theatre, the "theatre of fact." (Cf. Hochhuth, Weiss's *The Investigation*, recent projects of the Royal Shakespeare Company in London.)

The influence of the theatre upon films in the early years is well known. According to Kracauer, the distinctive lighting of *Dr. Caligari* (and of many subsequent German silents) can be traced to an experiment with lighting Max Reinhardt made shortly before, in his production of Sorge's play, *The Beggar*. Even in this period, however, the impact was reciprocal. The accomplishments of the "Expressionist film" were immediately absorbed by the Expressionist theatre. Stimulated by the cinematic technique of the "iris-in," stage lighting took to singling out a lone player, or some segment of the scene, masking out the rest of the stage. Rotating sets tried to approximate the instantaneous displacement of the camera eye. (More recently, reports have come of ingenious lighting techniques used by the Gorki Theatre in Leningrad, directed since 1956 by Georgi Tovstonogov, which allow for incredibly rapid scene changes taking place behind a horizontal curtain of light.)

Today traffic seems, with few exceptions, entirely one way: film to theatre. Particularly in France and in Central and Eastern Europe, the staging of many plays is inspired by the movies. The aim of adapting neo-cinematic devices for the stage (I exclude the outright use of films within the theatre production) seems mainly to tighten up the theatrical experience, to approximate the cinema's absolute control of the flow and location of the audience's attention. But the conception can be even more directly cinematic. Example: Josef Svoboda's production of The Insect Play by the Capek brothers at the Czech National Theatre in Prague (recently seen in London) which frankly attempted to install a mediated vision upon the stage, equivalent to the discontinuous intensifications of the camera eye. According to a London critic's account, "the set consisted of two huge, faceted mirrors slung at an angle to the stage, so that they reflect whatever happens there defracted as if through a decanter stopper or the colossally magnified eye of a fly. Any figure placed at the base of their angle becomes multiplied from floor to proscenium; farther out, and you find yourself viewing it not only face to face but from overhead, the vantage point of a camera slung to a bird or a helicopter."

Perhaps the first to propose the use of film itself as *one* element in a theatre experience was Marinetti. Writing between 1910 and 1914, he envisaged the theatre as a final synthesis of all the arts; and as such it had to use the newest art form movies. No doubt the cinema also recommended itself for inclusion because of the priority Marinetti gave to the use of existing forms of popular entertainment, such as the variety theatre and the *café-chantant*. (He called his projected art form "the Futurist Variety Theatre.") And cinema, at that time, was not considered as anything other than a vulgar art.

Soon after, the idea begins to occur frequently. In the total-theatre projects of the Bauhaus group in the 1920's (Gropius, Piscator, etc.), film had a regular place. Meyerhold insisted on its use in the theatre. (He described his program as fulfilling Wagner's once "wholly utopian" proposals to "use all means available from the other arts.") Film's actual employment has by now a fairly long history, which includes "the living newspaper," "epic theatre," and "happenings." This year marked the introduction of a film sequence into Broadway-type theatre. In two highly successful musicals, London's *Come Spy with Me* and New York's *Superman*, both parodic in tone, the action is interrupted to lower a screen and run off a movie showing the pop-art hero's exploits.

Thus far, the use of film within live theatre-events has tended to be stereotyped. Film is employed as *document*, supportive of or redundant to the live stage events (as in Brecht's productions in East Berlin). Or else it is employed as *hallucinant*; recent examples are Bob Whitman's Happenings, and a new kind of nightclub situation, the mixed-media discothèque (Andy Warhol's The Plastic Inevitable, Murray the K's World). The interpolation of film into the theatre-experience may be enlarging from the point of view of theatre. But in terms of what film is capable of, it seems a reductive, monotonous use of film.

Every interesting aesthetic tendency now is a species of radicalism. The question each artist must ask is: What is *my* radicalism, the one dictated by *my* gifts and temperament? This doesn't mean all contemporary artists believe that art progresses. A radical position isn't necessarily a forward-looking position.

Consider the two principal radical positions in the arts today. One recommends the breaking down of distinctions between genres: the arts would eventuate in one art, consisting of many different kinds of behavior going on at the same time, a vast behavioral magma or synaesthesis. The other position recommends the maintaining and clarifying of barriers between the arts, by the intensification of what each art distinctively is; painting must use only those means which pertain to painting, music only those which are musical, novels those which pertain to the novel and to no other literary form, etc.

The two positions are, in a sense, irreconcilable. Except that both are invoked to support a perennial modern quest—the quest for the definitive art form. An art may be proposed as definitive because it is considered the most rigorous, or most fundamental. For these reasons, Schopenhauer suggested and Pater asserted that all art aspires to the condition of music. More recently, the thesis that all the arts are leading toward one art has been advanced by enthusiasts of the cinema. The candidacy of film is founded on its being so exact and, potentially, so complex—a rigorous combination of music, literature, and the image.

Or, an art may be proposed as definitive because it is the most inclusive. This is the basis of the destiny for theatre held out by

Wagner, Marinetti, Artaud, John Cage—all of whom envisage theatre as nothing less than a total art, potentially conscripting all the
arts into its service. And as the ideas of synaesthesia continue to
proliferate among painters, sculptors, architects, and composers,
theatre remains the favored candidate for the role of summative
art. So conceived, of course, theatre's claims do contradict those of
cinema. Partisans of theatre would argue that while music, painting, dance, cinema, the speaking of words, etc. can all converge on
a "stage," the film-object can only become bigger (multiple screens,
360° projection, etc.) or longer in duration or more internally
articulated and complex. Theatre can be anything, everything; in
the end, films can only be more of what they specifically (that is to
say, cinematically) are.

Underlying the competing apocalyptic expectations for both arts,
one detects a common animus. In 1923 Béla Balázs, anticipating in
great detail the thesis of Marshall McLuhan, described movies as
the herald of a new "visual culture" that will give us back our
bodies, and particularly our faces, which have been rendered illeg-
ible, soulless, unexpressive by the centuries-old ascendancy of
"print." An animus against literature, against "the printing press"
and its "culture of concepts," also informs most of the interesting
thinking about the theatre in our time.

What's important is that no definition or characterization of
theatre and cinema, even the most self-evident, be taken for
granted.

For instance: both cinema and theatre are temporal arts. Like
music (and unlike painting), everything is *not* present all at once.

Could this be modified? The allure of mixed-media forms in theatre suggests not only a more elongated and more complex "drama"
(like Wagnerian opera) but also a more compact theatre-experience
which approaches the condition of painting. This prospect of increased compactness is broached by Marinetti; he calls it simultaneity, a leading idea of Futurist aesthetics. In becoming a final synthesis of all the arts, says Marinetti, theatre "would use the new
twentieth-century devices of electricity and the cinema; this would
enable plays to be extremely short, since all these technical means
would enable the theatrical synthesis to be achieved in the shortest
possible space of time, as all the elements could be presented
simultaneously."

A pervasive notion in both advanced cinema and theatre is the
idea of art as an act of violence. Its source is to be found in the
aesthetics of Futurism and of Surrealism; its principal "texts" are,
for theatre, the writings of Artaud and, for cinema, the two classic

films of Luis Buñuel, *L'Age d'Or* and *Un Chien Andalou*. (More recent examples: the early plays of Ionesco, at least as conceived; the "cinema of cruelty" of Hitchcock, Clouzot, Franju, Robert Aldrich, Polanski; work by the Living Theatre; some of the neo-cinematic lighting techniques used in experimental theatres; the sound of late Cage and LaMonte Young.) The relation of art to an audience understood to be passive, inert, surfeited, can only be assault. Art becomes identical with aggression.

This theory of art as assault on the audience—like the complementary notion of art as ritual—is understandable, and precious. Still, one must not neglect to question it, particularly in the theatre. For it can become as much a convention as anything else; and end, like all theatrical conventions, by reinforcing the deadness of the audience. (As Wagner's ideology of a total theatre played its role in confirming the stupidity and bestiality of German culture.)

Moreover, the depth of the assault must be assessed honestly. In the theatre, this entails not "diluting" Artaud. Artaud's writings represent the demand for a totally open (therefore, flayed, self-cruel) consciousness of which theatre would be *one* adjunct or instrument. No work in the theatre has yet amounted to this. Thus, Peter Brook has astutely and forthrightly disclaimed that his company's work in London in the "Theatre of Cruelty," which culminated in his celebrated production of Weiss's *Marat/Sade*, is genuinely Artaudian. It is Artaudian, he says, in a trivial sense only. (Trivial from Artaud's point of view, not from ours.)

For some time, all useful ideas in art have been extremely sophisticated. Like the idea that everything is what it is, and not another thing. A painting is a painting. Sculpture is sculpture. A poem is a poem, not prose. Etcetera. And the complementary idea: a painting can be "literary" or sculptural, a poem can be prose, theatre can emulate and incorporate cinema, cinema can be theatrical.

We need a new idea. It will probably be a very simple one. Will we be able to recognize it?

1966

ANDRÉ BAZIN
FROM WHAT IS CINEMA?

THEATRE AND CINEMA

The leitmotiv of those who despise filmed theater, their final and apparently insuperable argument, continues to be the unparalleled pleasure that accompanies the presence of the actor. "What is specific to theater," writes Henri Gouhier, in *The Essence of Theater*, "is the impossibility of separating off action and actor." Elsewhere he says "the stage welcomes every illusion except that of presence; the actor is there in disguise, with the soul and voice of another, but he is nevertheless there and by the same token space calls out for him and for the solidity of his presence. On the other hand and inversely, the cinema accommodates every form of reality save one — the physical presence of the actor." If it is here that the essence of theater lies then undoubtedly the cinema can in no way pretend to any parallel with it. If the writing, the style, and the dramatic structure are, as they should be, rigorously conceived as the receptacle for the soul and being of the flesh-and-blood actor, any attempt to substitute the shadow and reflection of a man on the screen for the man himself is a completely vain enterprise. There is no answer to this argument. The successes of Laurence Olivier, of Welles, or of Cocteau can only be challenged—here you need to be in bad faith—or considered inexplicable. They are a challenge both to critics and philosophers. Alternatively one can only explain them by casting doubts on that commonplace of theatrical criticism "the irreplacable presence of the actor."

THE CONCEPT OF PRESENCE

At this point certain comments seem called for concerning the concept of "presence," since it would appear that it is this concept, as understood prior to the appearance of photography, that the cinema challenges.

Can the photographic image, especially the cinematographic image, be likened to other images and in common with them be regarded as having an existence distinct from the object? Presence, naturally, is defined in terms of time and space. "To be in the presence of someone" is to recognize him as existing contemporaneously with us and to note that he comes within the actual range of our senses—in the case of cinema of our sight and in radio of our hearing. Before the arrival of photography and later of cinema, the plastic arts (especially portraiture) were the only intermediaries between actual physical presence and absence. Their justification was their resemblance which stirs the imagination and helps the memory. But photography is something else again. In no sense is it the image of an object or person, more correctly it is its tracing. Its automatic genesis distinguishes it radically from the other techniques of reproduction. The photograph proceeds by means of the lens to the taking of a veritable luminous impression in light—to a mold. As such it carries with it more than mere resemblance, namely a kind of identity—the card we call by that name being only conceivable in an age of photography. But photography is a feeble technique in the sense that its instantaneity compels it to capture time only piecemeal. The cinema does something strangely paradoxical. It makes a molding of the object as it exists in time and, furthermore, makes an imprint of the duration of the object.

The nineteenth century with its objective techniques of visual and sound reproduction gave birth to a new category of images, the relation of which to the reality from which they proceed requires very strict definition. Even apart from the fact that the resulting aesthetic problems cannot be satisfactorily raised without this introductory philosophical inquiry, it would not be sound to treat the old aesthetic questions as if the categories with which they deal had in no way been modified by the appearance of completely new phenomena. Common sense—perhaps the best philosophical guide in this case—has clearly understood this and has invented an expression for the presence of an actor, by adding to the placards announcing his appearance the phrase "in flesh and blood." This means that for the man in the street the word "presence," today, can be ambiguous, and thus an apparent redundancy is not out of place in this age of cinema. Hence it is no longer as certain as it was that there is no middle stage between presence and absence. It is likewise at the ontological level that the effectiveness of the cinema has its source. It is false to say that the screen is incapable of putting us "in the presence of" the actor. It does so in the same way as a mirror—one must agree that the mirror relays the presence of the person reflected in it—but it is a mirror with a delayed reflection, the tin foil of which retains the image.* It is true that in the theater Molière can die on the stage and that we have the privilege of living in the biographical time of the actor. In the film about Manolete however we are present at the actual death of the famous matador and while our emotion may not be as deep as if we were actually present in the arena at that historic moment, its nature is the same. What we lose by way of direct witness do we not recapture thanks to the artificial proximity provided by photographic enlargement? Everything takes place as if in the time-space perimeter which is the definition of presence. The cinema offers us effectively only a measure of duration, reduced but not to zero, while the increase in the space factor reestablishes the equilibrium of the psychological equation.

OPPOSITION AND IDENTIFICATION

An honest appraisal of the respective pleasures derived from theater and cinema, at least as to what is less intellectual and more direct about them, forces us to admit that the delight we experience at the end of a play has a more uplifting, a nobler, one might perhaps say a more moral, effect than the satisfaction which follows a good film. We seem to come away with a better conscience. In a certain sense it is as if for the man in the audience all theater is "Corneillian." From this point of view one could say that in the best films something is missing. It is as if a certain inevitable lowering of the voltage, some mysterious aesthetic short circuit, deprived us in the cinema of a certain tension which is a definite part of theater. No matter how slight this difference it undoubtedly exists, even between the worst charity production in the theater and the most brilliant of Olivier's film adaptations. There is nothing banal about this observation and the survival of the theater after fifty years of cinema, and the prophecies of Marcel Pagnol, is practical

---

*Television naturally adds a new variant to the "pseudopresences" resulting from the scientific techniques for reproduction created by photography. On the little screen during live television the actor is actually present in space and time. But the reciprocal actor-spectator relationship is incomplete in one direction. The spectator sees without being seen. There is no return flow. Televised theater, therefore, seems to share something both of theater and of cinema: of theater because the actor is present to the viewer, of cinema because the spectator is not present to the actor. Nevertheless, this state of not being present is not truly an absence. The television actor has a sense of the millions of ears and eyes virtually present and represented by the electronic camera. This abstract presence is most noticeable when the actor fluffs his lines. Painful enough in the theater, it is intolerable on television since the spectator who can do nothing to help him is aware of the unnatural solitude of the actor. In the theater in similar circumstances a sort of understanding exists with the audience, which is a help to an actor in trouble. This kind of reciprocal relationship is impossible on television.

proof enough. At the source of the disenchantment which follows the film one could doubtless detect a process of depersonalization of the spectator. As Rosenkrantz wrote in 1937, in *Esprit*, in an article profoundly original for its period, "The characters on the screen are quite naturally objects of identification, while those on the stage are, rather, objects of mental opposition because their real presence gives them an objective reality and to transpose them into beings in an imaginary world the will of the spectator has to intervene actively, that is to say, to will to transform their physical reality into an abstraction. This abstraction being the result of a process of the intelligence that we can only ask of a person who is fully conscious." A member of a film audience tends to identify himself with the film's hero by a psychological process, the result of which is to turn the audience into a "mass" and to render emotion uniform. Just as in algebra if two numbers equal a third, then they are equal to one another, so here we can say, if two individuals identify themselves with a third, they identify themselves with one another. Let us compare chorus girls on the stage and on the screen. On the screen they satisfy an unconscious sexual desire and when the hero joins them he satisfies the desire of the spectator in the proportion to which the latter has identified himself with the hero. On the stage the girls excite the onlooker as they would in real life. The result is that there is no identification with the hero. He becomes instead an object of jealousy and envy. In other words, Tarzan is only possible on the screen. The cinema calms the spectator, the theater excites him. Even when it appeals to the lowest instincts, the theater up to a certain point stands in the way of the creation of a mass mentality.* It stands in the way of any collective representation in the psychological sense, since theater calls for an active individual consciousness while the film requires only a passive adhesion.

These views shed a new light on the problem of the actor. They transfer him from the ontological to the psychological level. It is to the extent to which the cinema encourages identification with the hero that it conflicts with the theater. Put this way the problem is no longer basically insoluble, for it is a fact that the cinema has at its disposal means which favor a passive position or on the other hand, means which to a greater or lesser degree stimulate the consciousness of the spectator. Inversely the theater can find ways of lessening the psychological tension between spectator and actor. Thus theater and cinema will no longer be separated off by an unbridgeable aesthetic moat, they would simply tend to give rise to

---

*Crowd and solitude are not antinomies: the audience in a movie house is made up of solitary individuals. Crowd should be taken here to mean the opposite of an organic community freely assembled.

two attitudes of mind over which the director maintains a wide control.

Examined at close quarters, the pleasure derived from the theater not only differs from that of the cinema but also from that of the novel. The reader of a novel, physically alone like the man in the dark movie house, identifies himself with the character. That is why after reading for a long while he also feels the same intoxication of an illusory intimacy with the hero. Incontestably, there is in the pleasure derived from cinema and novel a self-satisfaction, a concession to solitude, a sort of betrayal of action by a refusal of social responsibility.

The analysis of this phenomenon might indeed be undertaken from a psychoanalytic point of view. Is it not significant that the psychiatrists took the term catharsis from Aristotle? Modern pedagogic research on psychodrama seems to have provided fruitful insights into the cathartic process of theater. The ambiguity existing in the child's mind between play and reality is used to get him to free himself by way of improvised theater from the repressions from which he suffers. This technique amounts to creating a kind of vague theater in which the play is of a serious nature and the actor is his own audience. The action that develops on these occasions is not one that is divided off by footlights, which are undoubtedly the architectural symbol of the censor that separates us from the stage. We delegate Oedipus to act in our guise and place him on the other side of a wall of fire—that fiery frontier between fantasy and reality which gives rein to Dionysiac monsters while protecting us from them. These sacred beasts will not cross this barrier of light beyond which they seem out of place and even sacrilegious—witness the disturbing atmosphere of awe which surrounds an actor still made up, like a phosphorescent light, when we visit him in his dressing room. There is no point to the argument that the theater did not always have footlights. These are only a symbol and there were others before them from the cothurnus and mask onwards. In the seventeenth century the fact that young nobles sat up on the stage is no denial of the role of the footlights, on the contrary, it confirms it, by way of a privileged violation so to speak, just as when today Orson Welles scatters actors around the auditorium to fire on the audience with revolvers. He does not do away with the footlights, he just crosses them. The rules of the game are also made to be broken. One expects some players to cheat.* With regard to the objection based on presence and on that

---

*Here is a final example proving that presence does not constitute theater except in so far as it is a matter of a performance. Everyone either at his own or someone else's expense has known the embarrassment of being watched without knowing it or in spite of knowing it. Lovers who kiss on public benches offer a spectacle to the

alone, the theater and the cinema are not basically in conflict. What is really in dispute are two psychological modalities of a performance. The theater is indeed based on the reciprocal awareness of the presence of audience and actor, but only as related to a performance. The theater acts on us by virtue of our participation in a theatrical action across the footlights and as it were under the protection of their censorship. The opposite is true in the cinema. Alone, hidden in a dark room, we watch through half-open blinds a spectacle that is unaware of our existence and which is part of the universe. There is nothing to prevent us from identifying ourselves in imagination with the moving world before us, which becomes *the* world. It is no longer on the phenomenon of the actor as a person physically present that we should concentrate our analysis, but rather on the ensemble of conditions that constitute the theatrical play and deprive the spectator of active participation. We shall see that it is much less a question of actor and presence than of man and his relation to the decor.

BEHIND THE DECOR

The human being is all-important in the theater. The drama on the screen can exist without actors. A banging door, a leaf in the wind, waves beating on the shore can heighten the dramatic effect. Some film masterpieces use man only as an accessory, like an extra, or in counterpoint to nature which is the true leading character. Even when, as in *Nanook* and *Man of Aran*, the subject is man's struggle with nature, it cannot be compared to a theatrical action. The mainspring of the action is not in man but nature. As Jean-Paul Sartre, I think it was, said, in the theater the drama proceeds from the actor, in the cinema it goes from the decor to man. This reversal of the dramatic flow is of decisive importance. It is bound up with the very essence of the *mise-en-scène*. One must see here one of the consequences of photographic realism. Obviously, if the cinema makes use of nature it is because it is able to. The camera puts at the disposal of the director all the resources of the telescope and the microscope. The last strand of a rope about to snap or an entire army making an assault on a hill are within our reach. Dramatic

passerby, but they do not care. My concierge who has a feeling for the *mot juste* says, when she sees them, that it is like being at the movies. Each of us has sometimes found himself forced to his annoyance to do something absurd before other people. On those occasions we experience a sense of angry shame which is the very opposite of theatrical exhibitionism. Someone who looks through a keyhole is not at the theater; Cocteau has rightly demonstrated in *Le sang d'un poète* that he was already at the cinema. And nevertheless there are such things as "shows," when the protagonists are present to us in flesh and blood but one of the two parties is ignorant of the fact or goes through with it reluctantly. This is not "play" in the theatrical sense.

causes and effects have no longer any material limits to the eye of the camera. Drama is freed by the camera from all contingencies of time and space. But this freeing of tangible dramatic powers is still only a secondary aesthetic cause, and does not basically explain the reversal of value between the actor and the decor. For sometimes it actually happens that the cinema deliberately deprives itself of the use of setting and of exterior nature—we have already seen a perfect instance of this in *Les Parents terribles*—while the theater in contrast uses a complex machinery to give a feeling of ubiquity to the audience. Is *La Passion de Jeanne d'Arc* by Carl Dreyer, shot entirely in close-up, in the virtually invisible and in fact theatrical settings by Jean Hugo, less cinematic than *Stagecoach*? It seems to me that quantity has nothing to do with it, nor the resemblance to certain theater techniques. The ideas of an art director for a room in *Les Dames aux camélias* would not noticeably differ whether for a film or a play. It's true that on the screen you would doubtless have some close-ups of the blood-stained handkerchief, but a skill-ful stage production would also know how to make some play with the cough and the handkerchief. All the close-ups in *Les Parents terribles* are taken directly from the theater where our attention would spontaneously isolate them. If film direction only differed from theater direction because it allows us a closer view of the scenery and makes a more reasonable use of it, there would really be no reason to continue with the theater and Pagnol would be a true prophet. For it is obvious that the few square yards of the decor of Vilar's *La Danse de la mort* contributed as much to the drama as the island on which Marcel Cravene shot his excellent film. The fact is that the problem lies not in the decor itself but in its nature and function. We must therefore throw some light on an essentially theatrical notion, that of the dramatic place.

There can be no theater without architecture, whether it be the cathedral square, the arena of Nîmes, the palace of the Popes, the trestle stage on a fairground, the semicircle of the theater of Vicenza that looks as if it were decorated by Bérard in a delirium, or the rococo amphitheaters of the boulevard houses. Whether as a performance or a celebration, theater of its very essence must not be confused with nature under penalty of being absorbed by her and ceasing to be. Founded on the reciprocal awareness of those taking part and present to one another, it must be in contrast to the rest of the world in the same way that play and reality are opposed, or concern and indifference, or liturgy and the common use of things. Costume, mask, or make-up, the style of the language, the footlights, all contribute to this distinction, but the clearest sign of all is the stage, the architecture of which has varied from time to time without ever ceasing to mark out a privileged spot actually or virtually distinct from nature. It is precisely in virtue of this *locus*

Theater in Cinema. Jean Marais, Yvonne de Bray, Gabrielle Dorziat,
Marcel André, and Josette Day in *Les Parents Terribles* (1948). It "deliberately deprives itself of the use of setting and of exterior nature"
(BAZIN, page 362). Anna Magnani onstage in the *commedia dell'arte* of
The Golden Coach (1952). Renoir incorporates the artifice of the theater
into the cinema without destroying "that realism of space without
which moving pictures do not constitute cinema" (BAZIN, page 369).

dramaticus that decor exists. It serves in greater or less degree to set the place apart, to specify. Whatever it is, the decor constitutes the walls of this three-sided box opening onto the auditorium, which we call the stage. These false perspectives, these façades, these arbors, have another side which is cloth and nails and wood. Everyone knows that when the actor "retires to his apartment" from the yard or from the garden, he is actually going to his dressing room to take off his make-up. These few square feet of light and illusion are surrounded by machinery and flanked by wings, the hidden labyrinths of which do not interfere one bit with the pleasure of the spectator who is playing the game of theater. Because it is only part of the architecture of the stage, the decor of the theater is thus an area materially enclosed, limited, circumscribed, the only discoveries of which are those of our collusive imagination.

Its appearances are turned inward facing the public and the footlights. It exists by virtue of its reverse side and of anything beyond, as the painting exists by virtue of its frame. Just as the picture is not to be confounded with the scene it represents and is not a window in a wall. The stage and the decor where the action unfolds constitute an aesthetic microcosm inserted perforce into the universe but essentially distinct from the Nature which surrounds it.

It is not the same with cinema, the basic principle of which is a denial of any frontiers to action.

The idea of a *locus dramaticus* is not only alien to, it is essentially a contradiction of the concept of the screen. The screen is not a frame like that of a picture but a mask which allows only a part of the action to be seen. When a character moves off screen, we accept the fact that he is out of sight, but he continues to exist in his own capacity at some other place in the decor which is hidden from us. There are no wings to the screen. There could not be without destroying its specific illusion, which is to make of a revolver or of a face the very center of the universe. In contrast to the stage the space of the screen is centrifugal. It is because that infinity which the theater demands cannot be spatial that its area can be none other than the human soul. Enclosed in this space the actor is at the focus of a two-fold concave mirror. From the auditorium and from the decor there converge on him the dim lights of conscious human beings and of the footlights themselves. But the fire with which he burns is at once that of his inner passion and of that focal point at which he stands. He lights up in each member of his audience an accomplice flame. Like the ocean in a sea shell the dramatic infinities of the human heart moan and beat between the enclosing walls of the theatrical sphere. This is why this dramaturgy is in its essence human. Man is at once its cause and its subject.

On the screen man is no longer the focus of the drama, but will become eventually the center of the universe. The impact of his action may there set in motion an infinitude of waves. The decor that surrounds him is part of the solidity of the world. For this reason the actor as such can be absent from it, because man in the world enjoys no a priori privilege over animals and things. However there is no reason why he should not be the mainspring of the drama, as in Dreyer's *Jeanne d'Arc*, and in this respect the cinema may very well impose itself upon the theater. As actions *Phèdre* or *King Lear* are no less cinematographic than theatrical, and the visible death of a rabbit in *La Règle du jeu* affects us just as deeply as that of Agnès' little cat about which we are merely told.

But if Racine, Shakespeare, or Molière cannot be brought to the cinema by just placing them before the camera and the microphone, it is because the handling of the action and the style of the dialogue were conceived as echoing through the architecture of the auditorium. What is specifically theatrical about these tragedies is not their action so much as the human, that is to say the verbal, priority given to their dramatic structure. The problem of filmed theater at least where the classics are concerned does not consist so much in transposing an action from the stage to the screen as in transposing a text written for one dramaturgical system into another while at the same time retaining its effectiveness. It is not therefore essentially the action of a play which resists film adaptation, but above and beyond the phases of the intrigue (which it would be easy enough to adapt to the realism of the screen) it is the verbal form which aesthetic contingencies or cultural prejudices oblige us to respect. It is this which refuses to let itself be captured in the window of the screen. "The theater," says Baudelaire, "is a crystal chandelier." If one were called upon to offer in comparison a symbol other than this artificial crystal-like object, brilliant, intricate, and circular, which refracts the light which plays around its center and holds us prisoners of its aureole, we might say of the cinema that it is the little flashlight of the usher, moving like an uncertain comet across the night of our waking dream, the diffuse space without shape or frontiers that surrounds the screen.

The story of the failures and recent successes of theater on film will be found to be that of the ability of directors to retain the dramatic force of the play in a medium that reflects it or, at least, the ability to give this dramatic force enough resonance to permit a film audience to perceive it. In other words, it is a matter of an aesthetic that is not concerned with the actor but with decor and editing. Henceforth it is clear that filmed theater is basically destined to fail whenever it tends in any manner to become simply the photographing of scenic representation even and perhaps most of all when the camera is used to try and make us forget the footlights and the backstage area. The dramatic force of the text, instead of being gathered up in the actor, dissolves without echo into the cinematic ether. This is why a filmed play can show due respect to the text, be well acted in likely settings, and yet be completely worthless. This is what happened, to take a convenient example, to *Le Voyageur sans baggages*. The play lies there before us apparently true to itself yet drained of every ounce of energy, like a battery dead from an unknown short. But over and beyond the aesthetic of the decor we see clearly both on the screen and on the stage that in the last analysis the problem before us is that of realism. This is the problem we always end up with when we are dealing with cinema.

THE SCREEN AND THE REALISM OF SPACE

The realism of the cinema follows directly from its photographic nature. Not only does some marvel or some fantastic thing on the screen not undermine the reality of the image, on the contrary it is its most valid justification. Illusion in the cinema is not based as it is in the theater on convention tacitly accepted by the general public; rather, contrariwise, it is based on the inalienable realism of that which is shown. All trick work must be perfect in all material respects on the screen. The "invisible man" must wear pyjamas and smoke a cigarette.

Must we conclude from this that the cinema is dedicated entirely to the representation if not of natural reality at least of a plausible reality of which the spectator admits the identity with nature as he knows it? The comparative failure of German expressionism would seem to confirm this hypothesis, since it is evident that *Caligari* attempted to depart from realistic decor under the influence of the theater and painting. But this would be to offer an oversimplified explanation for a problem that calls for more subtle answers. We are prepared to admit that the screen opens upon an artificial world provided there exists a common denominator between the cinematographic image and the world we live in. Our experience of space is the structural basis for our concept of the universe. We may say in fact, adapting Henri Gouhier's formula, "The stage welcomes every illusion except the illusion of presence," that "the cinematographic image can be emptied of all reality save one—the reality of space."

It is perhaps an overstatement to say "all reality" because it is difficult to imagine a reconstruction of space devoid of all reference to nature. The world of the screen and our world cannot be juxtaposed. The screen of necessity substitutes for it since the very concept of universe is spatially exclusive. For a time, a film is the Universe, the world, or if you like, Nature. We will see how the films that have attempted to substitute a fabricated nature and an artificial world for the world of experience have not all equally succeeded. Admitting the failure of *Caligari* and *Die Nibelungen* we then ask ourselves how we explain the undoubted success of *Nosferatu* and *La Passion de Jeanne d'Arc*, the criterion of success being that these films have never aged. Yet it would seem at first sight that the methods of direction belong to the same aesthetic family, and that viewing the varieties of temperament and period, one could group these four films together as expressionist as distinct from realist. However, if we examine them more closely we see that there are certain basic differences between them. It is clear in the case of R. Wiene and Murnau. *Nosferatu* plays, for the greater part of the time, against natural settings whereas the fantastic qualities of *Caligari* are derived from deformities of lighting and decor. The case of Dreyer's *Jeanne d'Arc* is a little more subtle since at first sight nature plays a nonexistent role. To put it more directly, the decor by Jean Hugo is no whit less artificial and theatrical than the settings of *Caligari;* the systematic use of close-ups and unusual angles is well calculated to destroy any sense of space. Regular cinéclub goers know that the film is unfailingly introduced with the famous story of how the hair of Falconetti was actually cut in the interest of the film and likewise, the actors, we are told, wore no make-up. These references to history ordinarily have no more than gossip value. In this case, they seem to me to hold the aesthetic secret of the film; the very thing to which it owes its continued survival. It is precisely because of them that the work of Dreyer ceases to have anything in common with the theater, and indeed one might say, with man. The greater recourse Dreyer has exclusively to the human "expression," the more he has to reconvert it again into Nature. Let there be no mistake, that prodigious fresco of heads is the very opposite of an actor's film. It is a documentary of faces. It is not important how well the actors play, whereas the pockmarks on Bishop Cauchon's face and the red patches of Jean d'Yd are an integral part of the action. In this drama-through-the-microscope the whole of nature palpitates beneath every pore. The movement of a wrinkle, the pursing of a lip are seismic shocks and the flow of tides, the flux and reflux of this human epidermis. But for me Dreyer's brilliant sense of cinema is evidenced in the exterior scene which every other director would assuredly have shot in the studio. The decor as built evoked a Middle Ages of the theater and of miniatures. In one sense, nothing is less realistic than this tribunal in the cemetery or this drawbridge, but the whole is lit by the light of the sun and the gravedigger throws a spadeful of real earth into the hole.*

---

*This is why I consider the graveyard scene in *Hamlet* and the death of Ophelia bad mistakes on Olivier's part. He had here a chance to introduce sun and soil by

It is these "secondary" details, apparently aesthetically at odds with the rest of the work, which give it its truly cinematic quality.

If the paradox of the cinema is rooted in the dialectic of concrete and abstract, if cinema is committed to communicate only by way of what is real, it becomes all the more important to discern those elements in filming which confirm our sense of natural reality and those which destroy that feeling. On the other hand, it certainly argues a lack of perception to derive one's sense of reality from these accumulations of factual detail. It is possible to argue that *Les Dames du Bois de Boulogne* is an eminently realistic film, though everything about it is stylized. Everything, except for the rarely noticeable sound of a windshield-wiper, the murmur of a waterfall, or the rushing sound of soil escaping from a broken vase. These are the noises, chosen precisely for their "indifference" to the action, that guarantee its reality.

The cinema being of its essence a dramaturgy of Nature, there can be no cinema without the setting up of an open space in place of the universe rather than as part of it. The screen cannot give us the illusion of this feeling of space without calling on certain natural guarantees. But it is less a question of set construction or of architecture or of immensity than of isolating the aesthetic catalyst, which it is sufficient to introduce in an infinitesimal dose, to have it immediately take on the reality of nature.

The concrete forest of *Die Nibelungen* may well pretend to be an infinite expanse. We do not believe it to be so, whereas the trembling of just one branch in the wind, and the sunlight, would be enough to conjure up all the forests of the world.

If this analysis be well founded, then we see that the basic aesthetic problem of filmed theater is indeed that of the decor. The trump card that the director must hold is the reconversion into a window onto the world of a space oriented toward an interior dimension only, namely the closed and conventional area of the theatrical play.

It is not in Laurence Olivier's *Hamlet* that the text seems to be rendered superfluous or its strength diminished by directorial interpretations, still less in Welles' *Macbeth*, but paradoxically in the stage productions of Gaston Baty, to the precise extent that they go out of their way to create a cinematographic space on the stage; to deny that the settings have a reverse side, thus reducing the sonority of the text simply to the vibration of the voice of the actor who is left without his "resonance box" like a violin that is nothing else but strings. One would never deny that the essential thing in the

way of counterpoint to the setting of Elsinore. Does the actual shot of the sea during the soliloquy of Hamlet show that he had sensed the need for this? The idea, excellent in itself, is not well handled technically.

theater is the text. The latter conceived for the anthropocentric expression proper to the stage and having as its function to bring nature to it cannot, without losing its raison d'être, be used in a space transparent as glass. The problem then that faces the film-maker is to give his decor a dramatic opaqueness while at the same time reflecting its natural realism. Once this paradox of space has been dealt with, the director, so far from hesitating to bring theatrical conventions and faithfulness to the text to the screen will find himself now, on the contrary, completely free to rely on them. From that point on it is no longer a matter of running away from those things which "make theater" but in the long run to acknowledge their existence by rejecting the resources of the cinema, as Cocteau did in *Les Parents terribles* and Welles in *Macbeth*, or by putting them in quotation marks as Laurence Olivier did in *Henry V.* The evidence of a return to filmed theater that we have had during the last ten years belongs essentially to the history of decor and editing. It is a conquest of realism—not, certainly, the realism of subject matter or realism of expression but that realism of space without which moving pictures do not constitute cinema.

1951

SERGEI EISENSTEIN
FROM DICKENS, GRIFFITH, AND THE FILM TODAY

The most thrilling figure was Griffith, for it was in his works that the cinema made itself felt as more than an entertainment or pastime. The brilliant new methods of the American cinema were united in him with a profound emotion of story, with human acting, with laughter and tears, and all this was done with an astonishing ability to preserve all that gleam of a filmically dynamic holiday, which had been captured in *The Gray Shadow* and *The Mark of Zorro* and *The House of Hate*. That the cinema could be incomparably greater, and that this was to be the basic task of the budding Soviet cinema—these were sketched for us in Griffith's creative work, and found ever new confirmation in his films.

Our heightened curiosity of those years in *construction and method* swiftly discerned wherein lay the most powerful affective factors in this great American's films. This was in a hitherto unfamiliar province, bearing a name that was familiar to us, not in the field of art, but in that of engineering and electrical apparatus, first touching art in its most advanced section—in cinematography. This province, this method, this principle of building and construction was *montage*.

This was the montage whose foundations had been laid by American film-culture, but whose full, completed, conscious use and world recognition was established by our films. Montage, the rise of which will be forever linked with the name of Griffith. Montage, which played a most vital rôle in the creative work of Griffith and brought him his most glorious successes.

Griffith arrived at it through the method of parallel action. And, essentially, it was on this that he came to a standstill. But we mustn't run ahead. Let us examine the question of how montage came to Griffith or—how Griffith came to montage.

Griffith arrived at montage through the method of parallel action, and he was led to the idea of parallel action by—Dickens! . . .

What were the novels of Dickens for his contemporaries, for his readers? There is one answer: they bore the same relation to them that the film bears to the same strata in our time. They compelled the reader to live with the same passions. They appealed to the same good and sentimental elements as does the film (at least on the surface); they alike shudder before vice, they alike mill the extraordinary, the unusual, the fantastic, from boring, prosaic and everyday existence. And they clothe this common and prosaic existence in their special vision.

Illumined by this light, refracted from the land of fiction back to life, this commonness took on a romantic air, and bored people were grateful to the author for giving them the countenances of potentially romantic figures.

This partially accounts for the close attachment to the novels of Dickens and, similarly, to films. . . .

Perhaps the secret lies in Dickens's (as well as cinema's) creation of an extraordinary plasticity. The observation in the novels is extraordinary—as is their optical quality. The characters of Dickens are rounded with means as plastic and slightly exaggerated as are the screen heroes of today. The screen's heroes are engraved on the senses of the spectator with clearly visible traits, its villains are remembered by certain facial expressions, and all are saturated in the peculiar, slightly unnatural radiant gleam thrown over them by the screen.

It is absolutely thus that Dickens draws his characters—this is the faultlessly plastically grasped and pitilessly sharply sketched gallery of immortal Pickwicks, Dombeys, Fagins, Tackletons, and others. . . .

Analogies and resemblances cannot be pursued too far—they lose conviction and charm. They begin to take on the air of machination or card-tricks. I should be very sorry to lose the conviction of the affinity between Dickens and Griffith, allowing this abundance of common traits to slide into a game of anecdotal semblance of tokens.

All the more that such a gleaning from Dickens goes beyond the limits of interest in Griffith's individual cinematic craftsmanship and widens into a concern with film-craftsmanship in general. This is why I dig more and more deeply into the film-indications of Dickens, revealing them through Griffith—for the use of future film-exponents. So I must be excused, in leafing through Dickens, for having found in him even—a "dissolve." . . .

However, let us turn to the basic montage structure, whose rudiment in Dickens's work was developed into the elements of film composition in Griffith's work. Lifting a corner of the veil over these riches, these hitherto unused experiences, let us look into *Oliver Twist*. Open it at the twenty-first chapter. Let's read its beginning:

CHAPTER XXI*

1. It was a cheerless morning when they got into the street; blowing and raining hard; and the clouds looking dull and stormy.

The night had been very wet: for large pools of water had collected in the road: and the kennels were overflowing.

There was a faint glimmering of the coming day in the sky; but it rather aggravated than relieved the gloom of the scene: the sombre light only serving to pale that which the street lamps afforded, without shedding any warmer or brighter tints upon the wet housetops, and dreary streets.

There appeared to be nobody stirring in that quarter of the town; for the windows of the houses were all closely shut; and the streets through which they passed, were noiseless and empty.

2. By the time they had turned into the Bethnal Green Road, the day had fairly begun to break. Many of the lamps were already extinguished;

a few country waggons were slowly toiling on, towards London;

and now and then, a stage-coach, covered with mud, rattled briskly by:

the driver bestowing, as he passed, an admonitory lash upon the heavy waggoner who, by keeping on the wrong side of the road, had endangered his arriving at the office, a quarter of a minute after his time.

The public-houses, with gas-lights burning inside, were already open.

By degrees, other shops began to be unclosed; and a few scattered people were met with.

Then, came straggling groups of labourers going to their work; then, men and women with fish-baskets on their heads:

donkey-carts laden with vegetables;

chaise-carts filled with live-stock or whole carcasses of meat;

milk-women with pails;

and an unbroken concourse of people, trudging out with various supplies to the eastern suburbs of the town.

3. As they approached the City, the noise and traffic gradually increased;

---

*For demonstration purposes I have broken this beginning of the chapter into smaller pieces than did its author; the numbering is, of course, also mine.

and when they threaded the streets between Shoreditch and Smith-field, it had swelled into a roar of sound and bustle.

It was as light as it was likely to be, till night came on again; and the busy morning of half the London population had begun. . . .

4. It was market-morning.

The ground was covered, nearly ankle-deep, with filth and mire;

and a thick steam, perpetually rising from the reeking bodies of the cattle,

and mingling with the fog,

which seemed to rest upon the chimney-tops, hung heavily above.
. . .

Countrymen,
butchers,
drovers,
hawkers,
boys,
thieves,
idlers,
and vagabonds of every low grade,
were mingled together in a dense mass;

5. the whistling of drovers,
the barking of dogs,
the bellowing and plunging of oxen,
the bleating of sheep,
the grunting and squeaking of pigs;
the cries of hawkers,
the shouts, oaths and quarrelling on all sides;
the ringing of bells
and roar of voices, that issued from every public-house;
the crowding, pushing, driving, beating,
whooping and yelling;
the hideous and discordant din that resounded from every corner of the market;

and the unwashed, unshaven, squalid, and dirty figures constantly running to and fro, and bursting in and out of the throng; rendered it a stunning and bewildering scene, which quite confounded the senses.

How often have we encountered just such a structure in the work of Griffith? This austere accumulation and quickening tempo, this gradual play of light: from burning street-lamps, to their being extinguished; from night, to dawn; from dawn, to the full radiance of day (It was as light as it was likely to be, till night came on again); this calculated transition from purely visual elements to an interweaving of them with aural elements: at first as an indefinite rumble, coming from afar at the second stage of increasing light, so that the rumble may grow into a roar, transferring us to a purely aural structure, now concrete and objective (section 5 of our breakdown); with such scenes, picked up *en passant*, and intercut into the whole—like the driver, hastening towards his office; and, finally, these magnificently typical details, the reeking bodies of the cattle, from which the steam rises and mingles with the over-all cloud of morning fog, or the close-up of the legs in the almost ankle-deep filth and mire, all this gives the fullest cinematic sensation of the panorama of a market. . . .

If in the above-cited examples we have encountered prototypes of characteristics for Griffith's *montage exposition*, then it would pay us to read further in *Oliver Twist*, where we can find another montage method typical for Griffith—the method of a *montage progression of parallel scenes, intercut into each other.*

For this let us turn to that group of scenes in which is set forth the familiar episode of how Mr. Brownlow, to show faith in Oliver in spite of his pick-pocket reputation, sends him to return books to the book-seller, and of how Oliver again falls into the clutches of the thief Sikes, his sweetheart Nancy, and old Fagin.

These scenes are unrolled absolutely à la Griffith: both in their inner emotional line, as well as in the unusual sculptural relief and delineation of the characters; in the uncommon full-bloodedness of the dramatic as well as the humorous traits in them; finally, also in the typical Griffith-esque montage of parallel interlocking of all the links of the separate episodes. Let us give particular attention to this last peculiarity, just as unexpected, one would think, in Dickens, as it is characteristic for Griffith!

CHAPTER XIV

COMPRISING FURTHER PARTICULARS OF OLIVER'S STAY AT MR. BROWNLOW'S, WITH THE REMARKABLE PREDICTION WHICH ONE MR. GRIMWIG UTTERED CONCERNING HIM, WHEN HE WENT OUT ON AN ERRAND.

. . . "Dear me, I am very sorry for that," exclaimed Mr. Brownlow; "I particularly wished those books to be returned tonight."

"Send Oliver with them," said Mr. Grimwig, with an ironical smile; "he will be sure to deliver them safely, you know."

"Yes; do let me take them, if you please, Sir," said Oliver. "I'll run all the way, Sir."

The old gentleman was just going to say that Oliver should not go out on any account; when a most malicious cough from Mr. Grimwig determined him that he should; and that, by his prompt discharge of the commission, he should prove to him the injustice of his suspicions: on this head at least: at once.

[Oliver is prepared for the errand to the bookstall-keeper.]

"I won't be ten minutes, Sir," replied Oliver, eagerly.

[Mrs. Bedwin, Mr. Brownlow's housekeeper, gives Oliver the directions, and sends him off.]

"Bless his sweet face!" said the old lady, looking after him. "I can't bear, somehow, to let him go out of my sight."

At this moment, Oliver looked gaily round, and nodded before he turned the corner. The old lady smilingly returned his salutation, and, closing the door, went back to her own room.

"Let me see; he'll be back in twenty minutes, at the longest," said Mr. Brownlow, pulling out his watch, and placing it on the table. "It will be dark by that time."

"Oh! you really expect him to come back, do you?" inquired Mr. Grimwig.

"Don't you?" asked Mr. Brownlow, smiling.

The spirit of contradiction was strong in Mr. Grimwig's breast, at the moment; and it was rendered stronger by his friend's confident smile.

"No," he said, smiting the table with his fist, "I do not. The boy has a new suit of clothes on his back; a set of valuable books under his arm; and a five-pound note in his pocket. He'll join his old friends the thieves, and laugh at you. If ever that boy returns to this house, Sir, I'll eat my head."

With these words he drew his chair closer to the table; and there the two friends sat, in silent expectation, with the watch between them.

This is followed by a short "interruption" in the form of a digres sion:

It is worthy of remark, as illustrating the importance we attach to our own judgments, and the pride with which we put forth our most rash and hasty conclusions, that, although Mr. Grimwig was not by any means a bad-hearted man, and though he would have been unfeignedly sorry to see his respected friend duped and deceived, he really did most earnestly and strongly hope, at that moment, that Oliver Twist might not come back.

And again a return to the two old gentlemen:

It grew so dark, that the figures on the dial-plate were scarcely discernible; but there the two old gentlemen continued to sit, in silence: with the watch between them.

Twilight shows that only a little time has passed, but the *close-up* of the watch, *already twice* shown lying between the old gentlemen, says that a great deal of time has passed already. But just then, as in the game of "will he come? won't he come?", involving not only the two old men, but also the kind-hearted reader, the worst fears and vague forebodings of the old housekeeper are justified by the cut to the new scene—Chapter XV. This begins with a short scene in the public-house, with the bandit Sikes and his dog, old Fagin and Miss Nancy, who has been obliged to discover the whereabouts of Oliver.

> "You are on the scent, are you, Nancy?" inquired Sikes, proffering the glass.
> "Yes, I am, Bill," replied the young lady, disposing of its contents; "and tired enough of it I am, too. . . ."

Then, one of the best scenes in the whole novel—at least one that since childhood has been perfectly preserved, along with the evil figure of Fagin—the scene in which Oliver, marching along with the books, is suddenly

> startled by a young woman screaming out very loud, "Oh, my dear brother!" And he had hardly looked up, to see what the matter was, when he was stopped by having a pair of arms thrown tight round his neck.

With this cunning maneuver Nancy, with the sympathies of the whole street, takes the desperately pulling Oliver, as her "prodigal brother," back into the bosom of Fagin's gang of thieves. This fifteenth chapter closes on the now familiar montage phrase:

> The gas-lamps were lighted; Mrs. Bedwin was waiting anxiously at the open door; the servant had run up the street twenty times to see if there were any traces of Oliver; and still the two old gentlemen sat, perseveringly, in the dark parlour: with the watch between them.

In Chapter XVI Oliver, once again in the clutches of the gang, is subjected to mockery. Nancy rescues him from a beating:

> "I won't stand by and see it done, Fagin," cried the girl. "You've got the boy, and what more would you have? Let him be—let him be, or I shall put that mark on some of you, that will bring me to the gallows before my time."

By the way, it is characteristic for both Dickens and Griffith to have these sudden flashes of goodness in "morally degraded" characters and, though these sentimental images verge on hokum, they are so faultlessly done that they work on the most skeptical readers and spectators!

At the end of this chapter, Oliver, sick and weary, falls "sound asleep." Here the physical time unity is interrupted—an evening and night, crowded with events; but the montage unity of the episode is not interrupted, tying Oliver to Mr. Brownlow on one side, and to Fagin's gang on the other.

Following, in Chapter XVIII, is the arrival of the parish beadle, Mr. Bumble, in response to an inquiry about the lost boy, and the appearance of Bumble at Mr. Brownlow's, again in Grimwig's company. The content and reason for their conversation is revealed by the very title of the chapter: OLIVER'S DESTINY CON-TINUING UNPROPITIOUS, BRINGS A GREAT MAN TO LONDON TO IN-JURE HIS REPUTATION . . .

> "I fear it is all too true," said the old gentleman sorrowfully, after looking over the papers. "This is not much for your intelligence; but I would gladly have given you treble the money, if it had been favourable to the boy."
> It is not at all improbable that if Mr. Bumble had been possessed of this information at an earlier period of the interview, he might have imparted a very different coloring to his little history. It was too late to do it now, however; so he shook his head gravely; and, pocketing the five guineas, withdrew. . . .
> "Mrs. Bedwin," said Mr. Brownlow, when the housekeeper appeared; "that boy, Oliver, is an impostor."
> "It can't be, Sir. It cannot be," said the old lady energetically. . . . "I never will believe it, Sir. . . . Never!"
> "You old women never believe anything but quack-doctors, and lying story-books," growled Mr. Grimwig. "I knew it all along. . . ."
> "He was a dear, grateful, gentle child, Sir," retorted Mrs. Bedwin, indignantly. "I know what children are, Sir; and have done these forty years; and people who can't say the same, shouldn't say anything about them. That's my opinion!"
> This was a hard hit at Mr. Grimwig, who was a bachelor. As it extorted nothing from that gentleman but a smile, the old lady tossed her head, and smoothed down her apron preparatory to another speech, when she was stopped by Mr. Brownlow.
> "Silence!" said the old gentleman, feigning an anger he was far from feeling. "Never let me hear the boy's name again. I rang to tell you that. Never. Never, on any pretence, mind! You may leave the room, Mrs. Bedwin. Remember! I am in earnest."

And the entire intricate montage complex of this episode is concluded with the sentence:

There were sad hearts in Mr. Brownlow's that night.

It was not by accident that I have allowed myself such full extracts, in regard not only to the composition of the scenes, but also to the delineation of the characters, for in their very modeling, in their characteristics, in their behavior, there is much typical of Griffith's manner. This equally concerns also his "Dickens-esque" distressed, defenseless creatures (recalling Lillian Gish and Richard Barthelmess in *Broken Blossoms* or the Gish sisters in *Orphans of the Storm*), and is no less typical for his characters like the two old gentlemen and Mrs. Bedwin; and finally, it is entirely characteristic of him to have such figures as are in the gang of "the merry old Jew" Fagin.

In regard to the immediate task of our example of Dickens's montage progression of the story composition, we can present the results of it in the following table:

1. *The old gentlemen.*
2. Departure of Oliver.
3. *The old gentlemen and the watch. It is still light.*
4. Digression on the character of Mr. Grimwig.
5. *The old gentlemen and the watch. Gathering twilight.*
6. Fagin, Sikes and Nancy in the public-house.
7. Scene on the street.
8. *The old gentlemen and the watch. The gas-lamps have been lit.*
9. Oliver is dragged back to Fagin.
10. Digression at the beginning of Chapter XVII.
11. The journey of Mr. Bumble.
12. *The old gentlemen* and Mr. Brownlow's command to forget Oliver forever.

As we can see, we have before us a typical and, for Griffith, a model of parallel montage of two story lines, where one (the waiting gentlemen) emotionally heightens the tension and drama of the other (the capture of Oliver). It is in "rescuers" rushing along to save the "suffering heroine" that Griffith has, with the aid of parallel montage, earned his most glorious laurels!

Most curious of all is that in the *very center* of our breakdown of the episode, is wedged another "interruption"—a whole digression at the beginning of Chapter XVII, on which we have been purposely silent. What is remarkable about this digression? It is Dickens's own "treatise" on the principles of this montage construction of the story which he carries out so fascinatingly, and which passed into the style of Griffith. Here it is:

> It is the custom on the stage, in all good murderous melodramas, to present the tragic and the comic scenes, in as regular alternation, as the layers of red and white in a side of streaky well-cured bacon. The hero sinks upon his straw bed, weighed down by fetters and misfortunes; and, in the next scene, his faithful but unconscious squire regales the audience with a comic song. We behold, with throbbing bosoms, the heroine in the grasp of a proud and ruthless baron: her virtue and her life alike in danger; drawing forth her dagger to preserve the one at the cost of the other; and just as our expectations are wrought up to the highest pitch, a whistle is heard: and we are

straightway transported to the great hall of the castle: where a grey-headed seneschal sings a funny chorus with a funnier body of vassals, who are free of all sorts of places from church vaults to palaces, and roam about in company, carolling perpetually.

Such changes appear absurd; but they are not so unnatural as they would seem at first sight. The transitions in real life from well-spread boards to death-beds, and from mourning-weeds to holiday garments, are not a whit less startling; only, there, we are busy actors, instead of passive lookers-on; which makes a vast difference. The actors in the mimic life of the theatre, are blind to violent transitions and abrupt impulses of passion of feeling, which, presented before the eyes of mere spectators, are at once condemned as outrageous and preposterous.

As sudden shiftings of the scene, and rapid changes of time and place, are not only sanctioned in books by long usage, but are by many considered as the great art of authorship; an author's skill in his craft being, by such critics, chiefly estimated with relation to the dilemmas in which he leaves his characters at the end of every chapter: this brief introduction to the present one may perhaps be deemed unnecessary. . . .

There is another interesting thing in this treatise: in his own words, Dickens (a life-long amateur actor) defines his direct relation to the theater melodrama. This is as if Dickens had placed himself in the position of a connecting link between the future, unforeseen art of the cinema, and the not so distant (for Dickens) past—the traditions of "good murderous melodramas."

This "treatise," of course, could not have escaped the eye of the patriarch of the American film, and very often his structure seems to follow the wise advice, handed down to the great film-maker of the twentieth century by the great novelist of the nineteenth. And Griffith, hiding nothing, has more than once acknowledged his debt to Dickens's memory. . . .

I don't know how my readers feel about this, but for me personally it is always pleasing to recognize again and again the fact that our cinema is not altogether without parents and without pedigree, without a past, without the traditions and rich cultural heritage of the past epochs. It is only very thoughtless and presumptous people who can erect laws and an esthetic for cinema, proceeding from premises of some incredible virgin-birth of this art!

Let Dickens and the whole ancestral array, going back as far as the Greeks and Shakespeare, be superfluous reminders that both Griffith and our cinema prove our origins to be not solely as of Edison and his fellow inventors, but as based on an enormous cultured past; each part of this past in its own moment of world history has moved forward the great art of cinematography. Let this past be a reproach to those thoughtless people who have

380 FILM, THEATER, AND LITERATURE

displayed arrogance in reference to literature, which has contributed so much to this apparently unprecedented art and is, in the
first and most important place: the art of viewing—not only the
eye, but *viewing*—both meanings being embraced in this term. . . .

1944

GEORGE BLUESTONE
FROM NOVELS INTO FILM
LIMITS OF THE NOVEL AND THE
FILM

THE MODES OF CONSCIOUSNESS

It is a commonplace by now that the novel has tended to retreat more and more from external action to internal thought, from plot to character, from social to psychological realities. Although these conflicting tendencies were already present in the polarity of Fielding and Sterne, it was only recently that the tradition of *Tristram Shandy* superseded the tradition of *Tom Jones*. It is this reduction of the novel to experiences which can be verified in the immediate consciousness of the novelist that Mendilow has called modern "inwardness" and E. M. Forster the "hidden life." Forster suggests the difference when he says that "The hidden life is, by definition, hidden. The hidden life that appears in external signs is hidden no longer, has entered the realm of action. And it is the function of the novelist to reveal the hidden life at its source." But if the hidden life has become the domain of the novel, it has introduced unusual problems.

In a recent review of Leon Edel's *The Psychological Novel: 1900–1950*, Howard Mumford Jones sums up the central problems which have plagued the modern novelist: the verbal limitations of nonverbal experience; the dilemma of autobiographical fiction in which the novelist must at once evoke a unique consciousness and yet communicate it to others; the difficulty of catching the flux of time in static language. The summary is acutely concise in picking out the nerve centers of an increasingly subjective novel where "after images fished out of the stream of past time . . . substitute a kind of smoldering dialectic for the clean impact of drama."

Béla Balázs has shown us how seriously we tend to underestimate the power of the human face to convey subjective emotions and to suggest thoughts. But the film, being a presentational medium (except for its use of dialogue), cannot have direct access to the power of discursive forms. Where the novel discourses, the film must picture. From this we ought not to conclude like J. P. Mayer that "our eye is weaker than our mind" because it does not *"hold* sight impressions as our imagination does." For sense impressions, like word symbols, may be appropriated into the common fund of memory. Perceptual knowledge is not necessarily different in strength; it *is* necessarily different in kind.

The rendition of mental states—memory, dream, imagination—cannot be as adequately represented by film as by language. If the film has difficulty presenting streams of consciousness, it has even more difficulty presenting states of mind which are defined precisely by the absence in them of the visible world. Conceptual imaging, by definition, has no existence in space. However, once I cognize the signs of a sentence through the conceptual screen, my consciousness is indistinguishable from nonverbal thought. Assuming here a difference between *kinds* of images—between images of things, feelings, concepts, words—we may observe that conceptual images evoked by verbal stimuli can scarcely be distinguished in the end from those evoked by nonverbal stimuli. The stimuli, whether they be the signs of language or the sense data of the physical world, lose their spatial characteristics and become components of the total ensemble which is consciousness.

On the other hand, the film image, being externalized in space, cannot be similarly converted through the conceptual screen. We have already seen how alien to the screen is the compacted luxuriance of the trope. For the same reasons, dreams and memories, which exist nowhere but in the individual consciousness, cannot be adequately represented in spatial terms. Or rather, the film having only arrangements of space to work with, cannot rende thought, for the moment thought is externalized it is no longer thought. The film, by arranging external signs for our visual perception, or by presenting us with dialogue, can lead us to *infer* thought. But it cannot show us thought directly. It can show us characters thinking, feeling, and speaking, but it cannot show us their thoughts and feelings. A film is not thought; it is perceived.

That is why pictorial representations of dreams or memory on the screen are almost always disappointing. The dreams and memories of *Holiday for Henrietta* and *Rashomon* are spatial referents to dreams and memories, not precise renditions. To show a memory or dream, one must balloon a separate image into the frame (Gypo remembering good times with Frankie in *The Informer*); or super-impose an image (Gypo daydreaming about an ocean voyage with Katie); or clear the frame entirely for the visual equivalent (in *Wuthering Heights*, Ellen's face dissolving to the house as it was years ago). Such spatial devices are always to some degree dis-satisfying. Acting upon us perceptually, they cannot render the conceptual feel of dreams and memories. The realistic tug of the film is too strong. If, in an effort to bridge the gap between spatial representation and nonspatial experience, we accept such devices at all, we accept them as cinematic conventions, not as renditions of conceptual consciousness.

Given the contrasting abilities of film and novel to render con-ceptual consciousness, we may explore further the media's handling of time. . . .

PSYCHOLOGICAL TIME: THE TIME-FLUX

As soon as we enter the realm of time-in-flux, we not only broach all but insoluble problems for the novel but we also find a sharp divergence between prose and cinema. The transient, sequential, and irreversible character of language is no longer adequate for this type of time experience. For in the flux, past and present lose their identity as discrete sections of time. The present becomes "specious" because on second glance it is seen as fused with the past, obliterat-ing the line between them.

Discussing its essential modernity, Mendilow lends support to the idea that the whole of experience is implicit in every moment of the present by drawing from Sturt's *Psychology of Time*. For Sturt tries to work out the sense in which we are caught by a per-petual present permeated by the past:

> One of the reasons for the feeling of pastness is that we are familiar with the things or events that we recognize as past. But it remains true that this feeling of familiarity is a *present* experience, and there-fore logically should not arouse a concept of the past. On the other hand, a present impression (or memory) of something which is past is different from a present impression of something which is present but familiar from the past.

How this seeming contradiction operates in practice may be seen when we attempt to determine precisely which of two past events is prior, and in what manner the distinction between the memory of a past thing and the impression of a present thing is to be made. At first glance, we seem perfectly able to deduce which of two re-membered events is prior. For example, on the way to the store this morning, I met a group of children going to school. I also mailed my letter just as the postman came by. I know that ordinarily the children go to school at nine o'clock and the postman comes by at eleven. Therefore, I deduce that I went to the store *before* I mailed my letter. Although I have not been able to give the act of my going to the store an exact location in the past, I have been able to establish its priority.

On second thought, however, it seems as if (apart from the deductions one makes by deliberate attention to relationships) the memory of a past event comes to me with its pastness already intended. The image I have of my friend *includes* the information that this is the way he looked the year before he died. Similarly, if I have a mental image of myself on a train to Kabul, then summon up an image of myself eating chestnuts, I know that the first is an image of a past thing and the second an image of a present thing because the image of myself on the train includes the information that the event took place last year. At the same time, I know that I am eating chestnuts right now. Here the perceptual witnessing of my present action checks and defines my mental images, confirming both the priority of the train ride and the presentness of the eating.

But suppose I bring my attention to bear on an object which is present now and which was also present yesterday at the same time, in the same place, in the same light. If, for example, I look at the lamp in my room, which fulfills all these requirements, then close my eyes and behold the mental image, how am I to know if that image refers to the lamp which was there yesterday or to the lamp which is there today? In this instance, which is tantamount to fusing a thing's past with its present, my present image, for all practical purposes, no longer respects the distinction between past and present. It offers me no way of knowing the exact location of its temporal existence.

This obliteration between past and present is precisely the problem which faces the novelist who wishes to catch the flux in language. If he is faced with the presentness of consciousness on the one hand, and the obliteration of the discrete character of past and present on the other, how is he to express these phenomena in a language which relies on tenses?

Whether we look at William James' "stream of consciousness," Ford Madox Ford's "chronological looping," or Bergson's *"durée,"* we find the theorists pondering the same problem: language, consisting as it does of bounded, discrete units cannot satisfactorily represent the unbounded and continuous. We have a sign to cover the concept of a thing's "becoming"; and one to cover the concept of a thing's "having become." But "becoming" is a *present* participle, "become" a *past* participle, and our language has thus far offered no way of showing the continuity between them.

So elusive has been the *durée* that the novelist has submitted to the steady temptation of trying to escape time entirely. But here, too, the failure has served to dramatize the medium's limitations. Speaking of Gertrude Stein's attempt to emancipate fiction from the tyranny of time, E. M. Forster notes the impasse: "She fails, because as soon as fiction is completely delivered from time it cannot express anything at all."

To be sure, there seem to be intuitive moments of illumination in Proust and Wolfe during which a forgotten incident floats up from oblivion in its pristine form and seems thereby to become free of time. Proust's involuntary memory fuses the experience of his mother's madeleine cake with the former experience of Aunt Léonie's, and the intervening time seems, for the moment, obliterated. But it is the precise point of Proust's agonizing effort that— despite our ability, through involuntary memory, to experience simultaneously events "with countless intervening days between" —there is always a sense in which these events remain "widely separated from one another in Time." The recognition of this conflict helps us understand why every formulation which attempts to define a "timeless" quality in a novel seems unsatisfactory, why Mendilow's attempt to find an "ideal time" in Kafka seems to say little more than that Kafka was not plagued by the problem. In the end, the phrase "timeless moment" poses an insuperable contradiction in terms.

We can see the problem exemplified concretely in a passage from Thomas Wolfe's *The Hills Beyond*. The passage describes Eugene Gant's visit to the house in St. Louis where his family had lived thirty years before. Eugene can remember the sights, shapes, sounds, and smells of thirty years ago, but something is missing a sense of absence, the absence of his brother Grover, of his family away at the fair·

> And he felt that if he could sit there on the stairs once more, in solitude and absence in the afternoon, he would be able to get it back again. Then would he be able to remember all that he had seen and been—that brief sum of himself, the universe of his four years, with all the light of Time upon it—that universe which was so short to measure, and yet so far, so endless, to remember. Then would he be able to see his own small face again, pooled in the dark mirror of the hall, and discover there in his quiet three years' self the lone integrity of "I," knowing: "Here is the House, and here House listening; here is Absence, Absence in the afternoon; and here in this House, this Absence, is my core, my kernel—here am I!"

The passage shows the characteristic, almost obsessive longing of the modern novel to escape the passage of time by memory; the recognition that the jump, the obliteration, cannot be made;

the appropriation of non-space as a reality in the novel—not the feeling of absence alone, but the absence of absence.

We arrive here at the novel's farthest and most logical remove from the film. For it is hard to see how any satisfactory film equivalents can be found for such a paragraph. We can show Eugene waiting in the house, then superimpose an image of the boy as he might have looked thirty years before, catch him watching a door as if waiting for Grover to return. But as in all cinematic attempts to render thought, such projection would inevitably fail. How are we to capture that combination of past absence and present longing, if both are conditions contrary to spatial fact?

The film-maker, in his own and perhaps more acute way, also faces the problem of how to render the flux of time. "Pictures have no tenses," says Balázs. Unfolding in a perpetual present, like visual perception itself, they cannot express either a past or a future. One may argue that the use of dialogue and music provides a door through which a sense of past and future may enter. Dialogue, after all, is language, and language does have referential tenses. A character whose face appears before us may *talk* about his past and thereby permeate his presence with a kind of pastness. Similarly, as we saw in our discussion of sound in editing, music may be used to counterpoint a present image (as in *High Noon* and *Alexander Nevsky*) and suggest a future event. In this way, apparently, a succession of present images may be suffused with a quality of past or future.

At best, however, sound is a secondary advantage which does not seriously threaten the primacy of the spatial image. When Ellen, the housekeeper, her withered face illumined by the fire, begins telling her story to Lockwood in *Wuthering Heights*, we do sense a certain tension between story-teller and story. But in the film we can never fully shake our attention loose from the teller. The image of her face has priority over the sound of her voice. When Terry Malone tells Edie about his childhood in *On the Waterfront*, the present image of his face so floods our consciousness that his words have the thinnest substance only. The scars around his eyes tell us more about his past than any halting explanation. This phenomenon is essentially what Panofsky calls the "principle of coexpressibility," according to which a moving picture—even when it has learned to talk—remains a picture that moves, and does not convert itself into a piece of writing that is enacted. That is why Shakesperian films which fail to adapt the fixed space of the stage to cinematic space so often seem static and talky.

In the novel, the line of dialogue stands naked and alone; in the film, the spoken word is attached to its spatial image. If we try to convert Marlon Brando's words into our own thought, we leave for a moment the visual drama of his face, much as we turn away from a book. The difference is that, whereas in the book we miss nothing, in the film Brando's face has continued to act, and the moment we miss may be crucial. In a film, according to Panofsky, "that which we hear remains, for good or worse, inextricably fused with that which we see." In that fusion, our seeing (and therefore our sense of the present) remains primary.

If, however, dialogue and music are inadequate to the task of capturing the flux, the spatial image itself reveals two characteristics which at least permit the film to make a tentative approach. The first is the quality of familiarity which attaches itself to the perceptual image of a thing after our first acquaintance. When I first see Gelsomina in *La Strada*, I see her as a stranger, as a girl with a certain physical disposition, but without a name or a known history. However, once I identify her as a character with a particular relationship to other characters, I am able to include information about her past in the familiar figure which now appears before me. I do not have to renew my acquaintance at every moment. Familiarity, then, becomes a means of referring to the past, and this past reference fuses into the ensemble which is the present Gelsomina. The spatial image of Gelsomina which I see toward the end of the film includes, in its total structure, the knowledge that she has talked to the Fool and returned to Zampano. In a referential sense, the pastness is built in.

That the film is in constant motion suggests the second qualification of film for approximating the time-flux. At first glance, the film seems bound by discrete sections, much as the novel is bound by discrete words. At the film's outer limit stands the frame; and within the frame appear the distinct outlines of projected objects, each one cut as by a razor's edge. But the effect of running off the frames is startlingly different from the effect of running off the sentence. For whether the words in a novel come to me as nonverbal images or as verbal meanings, I can still detect the discrete units of subject and predicate. If I say, "The top spins on the table," my mind assembles first the top, then the spinning, then the table. (Unless, of course, I am capable of absorbing the sentence all at once, in which case the process may be extended to a paragraph composed of discrete sentences.) But on the screen, I simply perceive a shot of a top spinning on a table, in which subject and predicate appear to me as *fused*. Not only is the top indistinguishable from its spinning, but at every moment the motion of the top seems to contain the history of its past motion. It is true that the top-image stimulated in my mind by the sentence resembles the top-image stimulated by the film in the sense that both contain the illusion of continuous motion. Yet this resemblance does not appear in the *process* of cognition. It appears only after the fact, as it were, only after the component words have been assembled. Although the mental and filmic images do meet in rendering the top's continuity of motion, it is in the mode of apprehending them that we find the qualitative difference.

In the cinema, for better or worse, we are bound by the forward looping of the celluloid through the projector. In that relentless unfolding, each frame is blurred in a total progression. Keeping in mind Sturt's analysis of the presentness of our conceptions, a presentness permeated by a past and therefore hardly ruled by tense at all, we note that the motion in the film's *present* is unique. Montage depends for its effects on instantaneous successions of different spatial entities which are constantly exploding against each other. But a succession of such variables would quickly become incomprehensible without a constant to stabilize them. In the film, that constant is motion. No matter how diverse the moving spaces which explode against each other, movement itself pours over from shot to shot, binding as it blurs them, reinforcing the relentless unrolling of the celluloid.

Lindgren advances Abercrombie's contention that completeness in art has no counterpart in real life, since natural events are never complete: "In nature nothing at any assignable point begins and nothing at any assignable point comes to an end: all is perfect continuity." But Abercrombie overlooks both our ability to perceive spatial discreteness in natural events and the film's ability to achieve "perfect continuity." So powerful is this continuity, regardless of the *direction* of the motion, that at times we tend to forget the boundaries of both frame and projected object. We attend to the motion only. In those moments when motion alone floods our attention and spatial attributes seem forgotten, we suddenly come as close as the film is able to fulfilling one essential requirement of the time-flux—the boundaries are no longer perceptible. The transience of the shot falls away before the sweeping permanence of its motion. Past and present seem fused, and we have accomplished before us a kind of spatial analogue for the flux of time.

If the film is incapable of maintaining the illusion for very long, if its spatial attributes, being primary, presently assert themselves, if the film's spatial appeal to the eye overwhelms its temporal appeal to the mind, it is still true that the film, above all other nonverbal arts, comes closest to rendering the time-flux. The combination of familiarity, the film's linear progression, and what Panofsky calls the "Dynamization of Space" permits us to intuit the *durée* insofar as it can, in spatial art, be intuited at all.

The film, then, cannot render the attributes of thought (metaphor, dream, memory); but it can find adequate equivalents for the kind of psychological time which is characterized by variations in rate (distension, compression; speed-up, *ralenti*); and it approaches, but ultimately fails, like the novel, to render what Bergson means by the time-flux. The failure of both media ultimately reverts to root differences between the structures of art and consciousness.

Our analysis, however, permits a usable distinction between the two media. Both novel and film are time arts, but whereas the formative principle in the novel is time, the formative principle in the film is space. Where the novel takes its space for granted and forms its narrative in a complex of time values, the film takes its time for granted and forms its narrative in arrangements of space. Both film and novel create the illusion of psychologically distorted time and space, but neither destroys time or space. The novel renders the illusion of space by going from point to point in time; the film renders time by going from point to point in space. The novel tends to abide by, yet explore, the possibilities of psychological law; the film tends to abide by, yet explore, the possibilities of physical law.

Where the twentieth-century novel has achieved the shock of novelty by explosions of words, the twentieth-century film has achieved a comparable shock by explosions of visual images. And it is a phenomenon which invites detailed investigation that the rise of the film, which preempted the picturing of bodies in nature, coincides almost exactly with the rise of the modern novel which preempted the rendition of human consciousness.

Finally, to discover distinct formative principles in our two media is not to forget that time and space are, for artistic purposes, ultimately inseparable. To say that an element is contingent is not to say that it is irrelevant. Clearly, spatial effects in the film would be impossible without concepts of time, just as temporal effects in the novel would be impossible without concepts of space. We are merely trying to state the case for a system of priority and emphasis. And our central claim—namely that time is prior in the novel, and space prior in the film—is supported rather than challenged by our reservations.

1957

ROBERT SCHOLES
NARRATION AND
NARRATIVITY IN FILM

Let us assume that there is something called narrative that can exist apart from any particular method of narration or any particular narrative utterance, as we assume that there is something called the English language that exists apart from any particular form of discourse or any individual speech act in English. Narration is, first of all, a kind of human behavior. It is specifically a mimetic or representative behavior, through which human beings communicate certain kinds of messages. The modes of narration may vary extraordinarily. (In passing, I should say that I am aware of our customary distinction between what is told and what is enacted, which leads us to oppose narrative representation to dramatic enactment. In this case, however, I am using the word narration in its broadest sense to include both plays and stories, along with other forms of imitation.) A narrative, then, may be recounted orally, committed to writing, acted out by a group of actors or a single actor, presented in wordless pantomime, represented as a sequence of visual images, with or without words, or as a cinematic flow of moving pictures, with or without sounds, speech, music, and written language.

All of these mimetic kinds of behavior have certain features in common, which enable us to consider them together as narrative. First of all, they belong to a special class of symbolic activity which forces the interpreter to make a distinction between his own immediate situation and some other situation

which is being presented to him through the medium of narration. In narrative there is always a spectator or interpreter
who is situated in a space/time reference different from that of
the events narrated. The *process* of narration culminates in the
interpreter's immediate frame of reference, but it *refers* to
events outside of that immediate situation. This is as true for
my dinner-time recital of the little events of my day as it is for
a performance of *King Lear* or *Swan Lake*, or a reading of *War
and Peace*. Narration, then, rests upon the presence of a narrator or narrative medium (actors, book, film, etc.) and the absence of the events narrated. These events are present as fictions but absent as realities. Given this situation, it is possible
to distinguish different kinds and qualities of narration by the
varying extents to which they emphasize either that immediate process of narration (as an actor may draw attention to
himself as performer or a writer to himself as stylist) or, on the
other hand, emphasize those mediated events themselves.
Using our common critical terminology, it is possible to say
that a narration is more fictional as it emphasizes the events
narrated, and more lyrical as it emphasizes its own language,
and more rhetorical as it uses either language or events for
some persuasive end.

Before looking more closely at the processes of narration, it
may be useful to pause here and consider the relationship of
narrative to theories of literature and literary value. The Russian formalists and the Prague school of structuralists, and in
particular Roman Jakobson, have attempted to isolate the quality of "literariness" as a feature added to ordinary language.
They have defined literariness as language calling attention to
itself, or as a kind of message in which emphasis is placed on
the form of the utterance rather than on its referential capacity.
For the student of narrative, however, it is clear that this notion is applicable only to the lyrical dimension of an utterance.
If narratives may be considered to be literary, they must be literary also in a way which is more purely narrative. Let me try
to put this problem in a more concrete fashion.

We can begin by considering a question: what distinguishes
a literary narrative from my recital of the events of my day? Is
it a matter of the style of my performance—my language,
voice, gesture, as opposed to those of a literary raconteur—or
is it a matter of the events themselves—the trivial, loosely ordered events of my day, as opposed to events of greater consequence shaped to a more aesthetically satisfying pattern? The
question—which need not be answered—reinforces the notion that there are two distinct formal dimensions to narrative
utterances: a presentational form which is immediate (lan-

guage, gesture, etc.), and a represented form which is at one remove from the level of performance itself. In a novel, for instance, there is the language of the author at one level, and the representation of character, situation, and event at another. In a play, there is the language of the author, the performance of the actor, and the deeds of the character to consider: three easily discerned levels at which form is perceptible. And film adds at least one level to these, just through the processes of photography itself: camera-angle, lighting, focus, etc.

In a sense, each of these formal levels adds a certain amount of literariness to the process simply by existing. Take, for instance, a text which can be read as a book, enacted on a stage, or filmed and projected on a screen—like Shakespeare's *Henry V*. Each of the added levels of presentational style intensifies the literariness of the experience by its own artifice: language plus enactment plus photography. And the achieved fiction is *there* with a specificity which the printed text alone can never hope to match. The price for this intensity is a reduction in the interpretive richness of the written text—and this happens as every level is added. When the play is staged, each performance makes interpretive choices for the reader—but no two performances make all the same choices. When the story is filmed, all choices are final. Which suggests that one ought to be very careful about confusing interpretive richness with the quality of literariness in any given work. Life itself, with all its quotidian contingency, provides the richest possible field for interpretation. Art reduces this field drastically. And that is why we value it—not the only reason why, but perhaps the main one. My example, of course, being a film based on an enactment of a particularly rich verbal text, is oversimple and may even be misleading in certain respects. Certainly I do not wish to suggest that verbal texts are rich and cinematic ones impoverished with respect to interpretability. Rather, it is my ultimate intention to indicate the different kinds of interpretation that verbal and cinematic texts entail, and to illustrate this with some brief examples drawn from recent American films. But first it will be necessary to return to some consideration of the general aspects of narrative behavior.

Any telling or recounting of a string of events may be called narration. But not every narration yields a narrative, and not every narrative makes a story. By becoming a story, or pretending to be a story, a narration arrives at literariness of the fictive kind. A story is a narration that attains a certain degree of completeness, and even a fragment of a story or an unfinished story will imply that completeness as an aspect of its informing principle—the intentionality that governs its con-

struction. Given its linear, consecutive character, it is not surprising that film has come to be a predominantly narrative medium. That it should be dominated by stories, however, is
somewhat more surprising, but dominated by stories it is, to a
much greater extent than printed books are dominated by
novels.

At this point it may be useful to review some terminology.
A *narration* is a process of enactment or recounting which is a
common feature of our cultural experience. We all do some of
it every day. When this process is sufficiently coherent and developed to detach itself from the flux of cultural interchange,
we perceive it as a *narrative*. As a perceived narrative begins
to imply a special kind of pointedness or teleology, we recognize that it is a *story*, and we regard it with a certain set of expectations about its expressive patterning and its semantic
content. We have a continuum here, like the color spectrum,
which our perceptual mechanism breaks into discrete levels.
And the level we recognize as "story" is distinguished by certain structural features in presentation which in turn require
of the perceiver an active participation which I should like to
call "narrativity." This word is presently used, by French
critics primarily, to refer to a property of films themselves—their narrative quality. But the word seems a trifle
misleading in English, in that it implies a more sentient character than we generally allow to an artifact. For this reason and
some others, I should like to suggest that we employ the word
"narrativity" to refer to the process by which a perceiver actively constructs a story from the fictional data provided by
any narrative medium. A fiction is presented to us in the form
of a narration which guides us as our own active narrativity
seeks to complete the process that will achieve a story.

The nature of narrativity is, to some extent, culture-bound.
It is a matter of learned or acquired behavior, like the acquisition of a particular language, but it is based on a predisposi-
tion or potential of the human species to acquire this particular kind of behavior. In the contemporary Western world, the
culture of narrativity appears to be sufficiently homogeneous
so that it may be considered in the way that a single language
may be—as a systematic whole. We are only beginning to
study "readers reading," as opposed to the texts that they
read, so my remarks on narrativity will have to be rough and
ready, based, to a certain extent, on intuitive extrapolations
from my own experience as a reader and a teacher of reading.
But it is also possible to base a study of narrativity at least partially upon texts, if we consider texts in various media. That
is, things that are left to the reader's narrativity in some media

are presented directly in others. The arrival of film on the narrative scene has enabled us to perceive certain features of fiction more clearly because they are part of the narration in film while they have only been part of the reader's narrativity in fiction. To take the most obvious instance, the visual quality of film reminds us forcibly of how much of fictional narrativity involves the supplying of physical details or the translating of verbal signs into images. Readers who are feeble at such visualizing often fail to realize important aspects of fictional texts. Film, of course, does not raise such problems of visualization. It raises other problems, however, which I shall consider later on. For the moment, it may be useful to break down a bit further the processes of aesthetic interpretation.

The activities of readers and spectators in the face of artistic or recreational texts involve both a passive or automatic translation of semiotic conventions into intelligible elements and an active or interpretive rearrangement of textual signs into significant structures. The automatic part of these operations is a matter of linguistic or semiotic competence and not of special interest to us upon this occasion. The interpretive part concerns us here. The interpreter of lyric poetry, for example, must of course know the language and the verbal conventions in which a poem is cast. But he must go beyond this level of competence to understand the poem. In particular, he must construct a situational structure from clues in the poem—who speaks, to whom, under what circumstances, etc.—and he must also decompose the special linguistic features of the poetic lexicon, grammar, and syntax in order to comprehend them. He must measure poetic structures against the prosaic structures he needs to understand the deviant features of poetic utterance. He must supply missing parts of metaphors; he must acknowledge the ordinary words replaced by unusual ones in order to grasp the functions of the usual ones; he must discover the fundamental syntactic structures in sentences that conceal aspects of those structures. In order to understand, he must explicate or unfold what is implicated or folded into the poem. And the poetic text must be designed to reward such interpretive activity. This activity is a matter of supplying semiotic features that the text requires for interpretation, a matter of building a hermeneutic structure around the text itself. The poem is not the text alone but the text used to construct a complete and intelligible interpretation of it. A poem is a text which requires and rewards poetic procedures (or "poeticity") in its interpretation.

Similarly, a narrative is a text which requires and rewards narrativity. Narrativity involves a number of procedures of in-

terpretive constructing, but one of these may be singled out as
the most characteristic feature of this activity. Just as the lyric
is characterized by the need to simplify its verbal construc-
tions for interpretation, the narrative is characterized by a
need to simplify certain elements in narration. We "make
sense" of a poem by perceiving familiar sentence patterns
within its unique verbal structure. We make sense of narration
in a similar fashion, but at a different level of the text. In a
story it is the order of events that concerns us, more than the
order of words. And our primary effort in attending to a narration is to construct a satisfying order of events. To do this we
must locate or provide two features: temporality and causality.

Narrativity is based upon a mental operation similar to a
logical fallacy: *post hoc ergo propter hoc.* What is a fallacy in
logic is a principle of fiction: that a cause and effect relationship links the temporal elements in any narrative
sequence. I am not suggesting that fiction itself is fallacious in
some way, but rather that it is constructed so as to make this
fallacy a feature of the fictional world. When we say that a
work is "episodic," for instance, we mean that the work frus-
trates the narrativitous urge for causal connection and we consider this a fictional deficiency (though obviously there may be
other non-fictional compensations in any given work). Above
all, when we recognize a work as a story, we regard it as having a temporal sequentiality based on cause and effect. This
means that if the events in a story are presented in their temporal sequence, much of our narrativity is devoted to establishing the causal connections between one event and the
next. It means further that if the events themselves are presented out of temporal sequence, we seek first to arrive at an
understanding of the true temporal sequence in order then to
grasp the causal sequence informing the temporal. In the
course of following even a simple fiction, the processes of narrativity can be quite complex, as we separate the causal from
the merely descriptive or contingent, as we seek to anticipate
the future events in the causal patterns we discern, and we re-
consider past events based on present understandings. The extraordinary popularity of detective fiction since its invention
by Poe is based upon the way in which this fictional form incorporates the principles of narrativity within the narration itself. We follow the detective moving through time from crime
to solution, while he, in turn, is in the process of constructing
a narration of the crime itself from a set of clues encountered
without their temporal and causal situations having been clari-
fied. From discrete clues, he constructs a criminal narrative,
which finally provides a verification or correction for our own

narrativity. Something like this pattern is as old as *Oedipus*, and is at least adumbrated in much drama and in melodramatic fiction. In the theater, the chronology of on stage events tends toward brevity and direct temporal flow, but frequently generates revelations that belong to the time before the play began. There is often a story in a play which includes important events that precede the plot enacted on stage.

The strength of the human disposition toward simple narrativity can be measured in part through the mounting assaults upon that disposition in various modern and post-modern media. Pirandello and Brecht represent in theater two ways of trying to work against the spectator's impulse towards narrativity. Pirandello breaks illusion for aesthetic reasons, to demonstrate the power of illusion, and finally to urge upon us the view that life itself is a matter of enactment and illusion. Brecht seeks to subvert narrativity to allow his theater ideological scope for the realization of ethical ends. And in film, Resnais and Godard represent positions similar to Pirandello and Brecht in theater. We could find fictional analogues for these figures as well, in the labyrinths of Robbe-Grillet, or the novelistic journalism of Norman Mailer. Yet all these assaults on narrativity—and their ancestors in Cervantes, Calderon, Diderot, Sterne, etc.—depend upon narrativity and could not function without it. It may even be that no long form of discourse can be received by a reader, spectator, or auditor unless it allows and encourages a certain amount of narrativity in its audience.

The nature of narrativity can be seen in another way. It is not only based upon what is a fallacy in logic, but upon behavior that in psychology must be seen as neurotic or psychotic. Narrativity is a form of licensed and benign paranoia. (How many school children refer to the author of a book as "they" or "them"?) The interpreter of a narrative process assumes a purposefulness in the activities of narration which, if it existed in the world would be truly destructive of individuality and personality as we know them. (I leave aside the question of whether this would be an improvement.) The spectator or reader of a narrative assumes that he is in the grip of a process controlled outside himself, designed to do things to him which he will be powerless to resist, and that all his struggles will only enmesh him further in the author's toils. Much of our impatience with inferior fiction comes from our loss of faith in the author's power. When he fails to anticipate our reactions and to lay traps for us into which we delightedly stumble, we begin to wonder if he is in control at all and to fear that we may have to move out of narrativity and into narration itself—or else simply return to entirely non-narrative behavior.

A feature of narrativity is our desire to abandon certain dimensions of existence, certain quotidian responsibilities, and place ourselves under the illusionary guidance of a maker of narratives, upon whom we rely because we respect his powers. There is something very undemocratic about all this, and uncritical as well. Criticism begins when narrativity ceases. Life resumes when narrativity ceases. Call it escape or call it transcendence, narrativity is a pleasurable state of consciousness which is as different from other states as the dreaming part of sleep is from the other parts. This element of narrativity, which is perhaps its most fundamental and most primitive dimension, is a source of dissatisfaction to many contemporary writers and filmmakers. This quality of submission and abandon, which is so characteristic of narrativitous activity, has led some creators of narrative artifacts to try forcing the reader out of his familiar patterns of narrativity and into some more dynamic and tendentious attitude toward the text. The search for a "zero degree" of writing, in which the writer simply provides materials out of which a reader constructs a text, is, in the terms I have been using, an attempt to turn narrativity into narration itself. The ultimate form of this tendency would be a book with blank pages, or a silent concert (which John Cage has given us), an empty picture frame, a motion-picture screen lit by the lamp of the projector but showing only its own texture and perhaps the motes in the middle distance or the specks on the lens. These anti-forms all have been or will be tried, but they are capable of little development. Even an encore to a silent concert presents a problem. And the zero degree of life is death.

I should like to suggest that the proper way for narrative artists to provide for their audiences an experience richer than submissive stupefaction is not to deny them the satisfactions of story, but to generate for them stories which reward the most energetic and rigorous kinds of narrativity. It is possible, as Shakespeare knew, to provide some plain satisfactions for the simple or the weary while also rewarding those who are ready to give a narrative the fullest attention of their mental and emotional powers. In the remaining portion of this paper, I wish to turn my attention to the way film, in particular, can achieve this and is achieving this at present, even in works of what might be called the middle range, that do not aspire to the summits of aesthetic approbation. In order to do this—

and at the risk of covering over-familiar ground for some of my audience—I shall begin with a brief review of the nature of cinematic signs.

As Christian Metz has made abundantly clear, film and narrative have such a powerful affinity that their relationship assumes a supreme naturalness. When, in the eighteenth century, Lessing sought so elaborately to contrast the mimetic possibilities of verbal narration and pictorial representation, he neatly (too neatly, doubtless) divided the world between them—assigning to the sequential, arbitrary signs of fiction the narration of actions, and to the simultaneous, motivated signs of painting, the description of objects and persons. If he were brought back to life today he would recognize in cinema the reconciliation of the parts of his divided world. For the motion-picture film gives us objects and persons moving and enacting in a visual system of narration which combines the powers of poetry and painting in an extraordinary synthesis.

The product of this synthesis, however, is a very different thing from verbal narration, more different than we sometimes realize, and it is different in a way that Lessing would understand—different because the signs in cinema function differently from the signs of verbal fiction. In the language of verbal narration, each sign is first interpreted as a concept or category, and then, where this is relevant and possible, connected to a referent of some sort. Thus, if I say to you, "There's a dog on the lawn," you translate the sound-image "dog" into some canine category of your own, and if you are moved to look out the window and see for yourself, you may finally perceive a specific referent which will supplant the conceptual category in your interpretive operation. If I provide you with a fictional dog, however, your concretization of the empty category will depend on an interaction between my narration and your narrativity. If I say, "He's lifting his leg," your image must lift a leg, preferably a hind leg, but the choice of leg is left up to you, unless and until I provide you with new verbal data which forces you to correct your image.

If, on the other hand, I present you with a cinematic dog—the signifying process is entirely different. You are confronted with a sign tightly tied to a specific referent, which you then may relate to a categorial concept or a set of such concepts by a process which may be partly conscious and partly not. I may misdirect you, if I can use words in my film, calling a male dog "Lassie," and if the dog is sufficiently wooly or the camera work and editing sufficiently adroit, you may never detect the imposture, and thus assign the referent to a category which is fictionally correct but factually false—a problem which can hardly come up in verbal narration, where if I call a dog Lassie you are obliged to provide her with all the proper equipment or to leave parts of her blank until I direct your attention to them.

The point of this excursion into sign language is to suggest that though the "same narrative" may be presented in both verbal and cinematic form, the narration and the narrativity will be extremely different. This is why my earlier example of *Henry V* was misleading to a certain extent. Since the verbal part of a play is entirely oral, it may be completely reproduced in a film. In a novel, however, much of the language is busy with description and reflection, which must be eliminated in cinematic translation. Even voice-over narration in films made from novels, which is used very effectively in a good film like *Farewell My Lovely* or a great one like *Jules et Jim*, is highly selective when compared to the total verbiage of the book. These differences in narration correspond to important differences in narrativity. The reader's narrative processes in dealing with printed fiction are mainly oriented toward visualization. This is what the reader must supply for a printed text. But in cinematic narrative, the spectator must supply a more categorial and abstract narrativity. This is one reason why film criticism is frequently more interesting than literary criticism. A well-made film requires interpretation while a well-made novel may only need understanding. There is a redundancy in providing a verbal gloss for a verbal object which does not apply when the object is significantly visual.

Some movements in contemporary fiction can be seen as attempts to acquire a cinematic opacity and freedom from conceptual thinking. Alain Robbe-Grillet has tried very hard to be a camera and produced some interesting verbal *tours de force*. But these experiments in writing against the grain of verbal narration are limited in their developmental possibilities. A writer who wants to be a camera should probably make a movie. Makers of narrative films can also work against the grain, and films have been made which try to conceptualize so much that they founder in seas of rhetoric. These two different narrative media require and must encourage two different kinds of narrativity—though both admit of great intensity and great complexity. Before concluding, I should like to explore some aspects of narrativity in recent American films—as an illustration of the processes I have been discussing perhaps too abstractly. These processes involve the conceptualization of images and the construction of frameworks of causality and value around such concepts.

In the past year I found myself moved in very different ways to different kinds of narrativity by the images of America presented in three films: *The Great Waldo Pepper, Godfather II,* and *The Parallax View.* Having seen each film only once, I am in no position to argue their merits vigorously or to analyze them with any pretensions to depth and rigor. But each of them proved striking to me, and left me with residues of narrativity that have become a part of my cognitive apparatus. *Waldo Pepper* is a charming film, perhaps too conscious of its charm. It summons up an America already coded for us by Norman Rockwell—but it transcends this quality on several occasions. In the crowd scenes around the fatal plane crash we find Rockwell's world metamorphosed into something like Nathaniel West's—with an economy and power far beyond the ponderous Westian fidelities of the cinematic *Day of the Locust.* Suddenly, the blood lust, the brutality behind the placid surface of mid-America bursts through the Rockwellian facade, and it is all the more convincing because of the sincerity with which that facade has been established in the film. In the processes of my own narrativity, continuing long after the viewing itself was completed, still continuing, joining the images of the great meta-film I am constructing in my mind, other images have come to dominate my recollection of that film. Not the Rockwellian faces, not even the marvellous aerial acrobatics, but features of landscape and humanity which are closer to Grant Wood than to Rockwell. In particular, I see a frame house, a tree, a person or two at home in these surroundings, and beyond them the fields and the sky. The camera is stationary or moving slowly, and the sense of peace, of man's harmony with nature, is overwhelming. These images generate in me the same feeling I experience when I go back to Iowa, where you can smell the fertility of the land and understand how people can love it, and how that farmer's love for the earth must transcend national boundaries and go back for centuries to beyond the beginning of history. That this sense of land should be so strong in a film about the sky, about restlessness, about people who find no resting place on the ground, is important. It is a measure of a kind of complexity in a film which is in many respects simple, and it is a complexity that comes from a loving attention to images which invite us to go through them to the meanings behind them.

Our narrativity with respect to a film like *Waldo Pepper* begins with a simple attempt to register the images, to categorize them and assign them value according to whatever cultural codes we have available. Where I use Norman Rockwell and Grant Wood, someone else might operate with different paradigms, which might not carry any labels at all. But in any case, as we proceed along the narrative track of the film, we construct the story of Waldo himself from the incidents presented to us, and we charge that story with value and emotion in very complex ways. What I wish to suggest here is that a part of that vital and complex process by which we accomplish this energizing of the narration depends upon such things as our codifying and assigning value to particular images. In this case, Waldo's fate is as it is because his life is torn between the placidity of that prairie landscape, tamed by man, and the pettiness and cruelty of man as a social being. Waldo cannot accept the placidity of the one side of his culture and he despises the mundane cupidity and sensationalism of the other. His lies and his flights are both attempts to transcend these realities, to construct a mythic world which he can comfortably inhabit. But one way or another, planes must come down. Myths may be created but they cannot be lived.

Some devotees of film may object to my discussion as moving too far from the reality of dissolves and jump cuts to some airy realm of thematic speculation. But my point is that this is precisely what we must do in the realization of a narrative film. The cinematic world invites—even requires—conceptualization. The images presented to us, their arrangement and juxtapositioning, are narrational blueprints for a fiction that must be constructed by the viewer's narrativity.

The images of America in *Godfather II* are different from those of *Waldo Pepper*, of course, as different as Little Italy from Nebraska or Las Vegas from Keokuk. But the images evoke similar processes of narrativity in our minds. For me, the scenes of Ellis Island were worth a stack of history books. One long shot in particular, the camera tracking slowly past the immigrant hordes, labeled and herded like cattle, brought the dream and reality of America into vertiginous proximity. Some of my ancestors stood in those lines, and I felt closer to them as I watched than I had ever felt before. The slow camera, the warm lighting, the hopeful patience of the crowds provided an image closer to the heart of this country than any Mayflower or Plymouth Rock. The film, of course, is about the betrayal of this dream: the mafioso in his fortress, the senator in his whorehouse, the conference of thugs and politicians in Batista's Cuba. These images must be set next to those patient lines of immigrants for the film's full irony to be achieved. But once we grasp them they remain with us for a long time.

The final film I wish to mention is less highly regarded than the other two and was, I believe, less successful commercially. But for me it is a film of extraordinary interest, despite its weaknesses—and to a certain extent because of them. *The*

Parallax View attempted two remarkable narrative feats. It took the paranoia that lies benevolently at the heart of the narrative process itself and the other paranoia that threatens to overwhelm our national life, and tried to make them congruent. And it undertook a single scene requiring the most intense narrativity I can recall encountering in a film. The picture provides a story that postulates a conspiracy behind the assassinations of various liberal political figures and satirizes the complacency or complicity of the inquiries into those assassinations. All the characters in the film who begin to perceive this plot against America die violently, and the last heroic defender is trapped into a situation where he is himself taken to be an assassin and is finally killed by those truly guilty who are pretending to aid in his arrest. It is a chilling film, pointedly and scandalously close to actual contemporary events. It shares a view of America with the frighteningly irrational readers of scandal magazines and the uncritical devotees of paranoid conspiracy theories. As a film, its lack of popular success probably stems from the fact that its audience could not accept the slaughter of their protagonist. In the formulas of popular fiction, this film called for a victorious hero who saved the country from a wicked gang of conspirators. By accepting the paranoia latent in a part of the mass audience while rejecting the power fantasy and wish fulfillment that regularly accompany it, the film alienated its most likely audience. And, of course, those who consider themselves above such things were disqualified from the beginning.

The film had other problems—in pacing and in the logic of its story-telling, leaning too heavily on the invisible masters of conspiracy to tie together the loose ends of its plot, encouraging a sloppy and careless narrativity in the viewer. But it did give us one extraordinary scene. In this episode, the intrepid protagonist, who is trying to infiltrate the conspiracy, faces a futuristic personality test. To qualify as an apprentice assassin, he must demonstrate that he has the emotional profile of an extremely psychotic individual. The test consists of his being strapped into an electronic chair which monitors his reactions while he is shown slides calculated to produce strong emotional effects upon him: authority figures, sex objects, flags, scenes of violence and brutality, mom-type ladies, homosexuals, apple pie, Captain America—all in a rapid sequence of repetitions and juxtapositions. Our protagonist, to pass the test, must try to generate the appropriate involuntary reactions for a paranoid psychopath, and we, in our own chairs watching the same slides, are inevitably drawn to assist him empathetically by trying to force the appropriate reactions out of our own nervous systems. The result is a kind of mind-blowing sensory overload, a short-circuiting of a narrativity asked to accomplish too much too fast. The vagueness of the monitoring itself, the absence of rules for this game, indicates that the makers of the film were not in imaginative control of their own conception. Thus, the film repeatedly attempts to allow a real and malevolent paranoia to substitute for the benign paranoia at the heart of narrative activity. The film tries to hide its own imaginative inadequacies behind one of its inadequately conceived fictions. This is truly an instructive failure, for we see ideas that might have functioned powerfully reduced to the level of sensational gimmicks before our eyes.

In these three glances into the processes of cinematic narrativity, I have been trying to suggest the power and importance of conceptualization by the viewer in the realization of narrative films. There is, of course, much more to cinematic narrative than this. And there is much less too. Some aspects of narrative film are simply matters of stimulus and response, in which conceptualization is held to a minimum. This, I take it, is a useful definition of pornography, whether it is the pornography of pleasure or of pain. We need no very elaborate concepts of erotic or brutal acts to be "moved" by enactments of them—and even more "moved" by photographs of the actuality. But such motion, however violent, is not derived from any narrative process. Presumably, to see someone tortured or gratified sexually before our eyes would be even more "moving," and to play the principal role in such a situation ourselves would be the most "moving" condition of all. And this would not be a narrative experience any more. It would be life, not fiction.

Film, because it excells all other narrative media in its rendition of material objects and the actions of creatures, is the closest to actuality, to undifferentiated thoughtless experience. Literature, beginning in language, must exert extraordinary pains to achieve some impression of the real. For this reason, written fiction has almost always used some notion of realism or verisimilitude as an evaluative standard. For film, the problem is different. It must achieve some level of reflection, or conceptualization, in order to reach its optimum condition as narrative. The best narrative films have always accomplished this, and they have done so cinematically, through scenes and images that induce an appropriate narrativity in their audiences.

1975

V

Film Genres

The study of artistic genres is as old as Aristotle, and at least one of his generic terms, "comedy," has been regularly applied to films. (Significantly, tragedy has not established itself as a film genre.) The generic approach to art has frequently been attacked, however, for its terms are often imprecise and its methods of categorization unclear. What, precisely, is a documentary film or a screwball comedy? Are films to be classified by their physical properties (silent, color), by their subject matter (gangster, western), or by their purpose or effect (comic, educational)? Further, are these categories legitimate? Of what interest is a category like the "educational" film? In any case, is it even proper to arrange works of art in classes, viewing them as instances of types? Benedetto Croce, the influential Italian philosopher and critic, argued that generic criticism was necessarily incompatible with an aesthetic point of view, which always treats works of art as individual and unique. Croce's views have not prevailed, however, and the concept of genre continues to be employed in film theory and criticism, as it is in all art theory and criticism, and with important results.

The most familiar system by which films are generically classified distinguishes between the different kinds of fictional narrative (almost inevitably American) feature films: westerns, gangster films, newspaper pictures, detective dramas, screwball comedies, courtroom dramas, *films noirs*, musicals, war films, spy films, prison films, horror films, science fictions, fantasies, thrillers. An obvious difficulty with such commonly used categories is that they overlap; a film might combine gangsters, detectives, newspapermen, a courtroom, a prison, suspense, and a bleak, *"noir"* atmosphere; a film might combine screwball comedy, newspapermen, and prisons (as *His Girl Friday* does), or screwball comedy, the western, and the musical (as *Calamity Jane* and *Annie Get Your Gun* do). In classifying such a film one would have to rely on a judgment about what is important. Or one might decide to employ a compound category. But this sort of adjustment does not present genre criticism with an insoluble difficulty, for to be able to speak of a compound genre at all implies that elemental genres existed in order to be compounded.

Another problem of classifying fictional narrative films in this way arises when we ask if such categories have any impact on the making of films or our responses to films. Are they critical and commercial conveniences, designed merely to help market a film or to describe a film for those who have not seen it? How conscious are filmmakers of their use of generic conventions? How conscious are audiences of these conventions? How do we recognize that a film does indeed represent a particular genre? How do the conventions of a genre evolve over the history of film? Are such evolutions the result of changing artistic conventions in films, of developing cultural standards in society, or both? Despite these questions, there can be no doubt that treating a film as a representative of a familiar and perceptively formulated genre is often essential to a proper understanding of it.

For Leo Braudy, the contemporary American film and literary critic, the concept of genre must first be rescued from the presumption that it can only describe a debased and degraded kind of art. "Genre films offend our most common definition of artistic excellence: the uniqueness of the art object, whose value can in part be defined by its desire to be uncaused and unfamiliar, as much as possible unindebted to any tradition, popular or otherwise." After tracing this critical prejudice to its roots in the aesthetic and literary theories of the Romantic Era, Braudy posits the two kinds of connection which genre films achieve. First, genre films forge a deliberate connection between each new instance of the genre and its past tradition and manifestations. Second, genre films, because of their popularity and familiarity, have a more powerful impact on their audience—and a highly democratic one—converting that audience into a unified cultural force: "Genre films strike beneath our intellectual appreciation of high art and make us one with a large mass audience, often despite our more articulate and elitist views." His specific look at musicals of the 1930s and 1940s demonstrates the way that the genre, especially as embodied in the contrast between Fred Astaire and Gene Kelly, sought to interject energy and spontaneity into the repetitiveness of everyday social reality, either by Astaire's escape into the perfect world of dance or by Kelly's making the imperfect world more perfect by making it dance.

Robert Warshow, the influential American analyst of the popular arts in the era just after World War II, would agree with Braudy's observation that the popular genre film makes connections both with its filmic past and with the temperaments of its contemporary viewers. Although he would be less willing to grant the general artistic excellence and importance to genre films that Braudy does, he does consider the gangster and the western as the two most important creations of American movies. The power of both genres derives from their concern with the problem of violence. The hero of the Western asserts his honor and demonstrates the possibility of "style" in the face of inevitable defeat. He asserts that even in killing and being killed we are not freed from the necessity of establishing an admirable mode of behavior. Because the pattern of the classical Western is so firmly fixed, our pleasure is that of the connoisseur. We must appreciate minor variations in the characteristics of the actors who play the hero's role, and it is only in virtue of the film's ability to record such variations that these films can remain interesting to us. Any attempt to break the set pattern (to violate the "rules" of the genre), either by turning the Western into a "social drama" (as in *The Ox-Bow Incident*) or by aestheticizing it (as in *Shane*), destroys its power. According to Warshow, part of our pleasure in this kind of complete and self-contained art derives precisely from its contrast with the more complex, uncertain, and self-conscious creations of modernism. The art of the Western is not an art that precedes modernism (as it is for Stanley Cavell), but one that is contemporary with it and draws strength from the contrast.

Susan Sontag also sees the relationship of a genre, the science fiction fantasy that emerged in the 1950s, to the most important issues of modernist works. She shows how, because of the differences in the media, the science fiction film differs from the science fiction novel, and her account of the genre indicates the relationship, recognized by Braudy and Warshow as well, between the rise and fall of genres and the social realities they reflect. Like the Western, the science fiction film has a typical hero and a recurrent structure. It too is concerned with the anxieties of contemporary life. But its fear of "deper-sonalization" is ambivalent and its attitude toward destruction is aesthetic; it fails to make the kind of authentic response to the contemporary situation that can be found in the best mod-ernist works.

Bruce Kawin, the contemporary film and literary critic, would disagree with Sontag about there being anything at all inade-quate in the horror or science fiction film's response to prob-lems of contemporary life. Kawin's essay, which reflects the most recent thinking about film genres, implicitly disagrees with Sontag on two key points. First, he sees the basis of au-dience experience with science fiction and horror films in myth and dreams, grounding his assumptions in the influential studies of Frazer and Freud: "One goes to the horror film in order to have a nightmare . . . a dream whose undercurrent of anxiety both presents and masks the desire to fulfill and be punished for certain conventionally unacceptable impulses." A horror film like *The Wolf Man*, for example, is a "transpar-ently Oedipal . . . playing out of castration anxiety." Second, Kawin draws a careful distinction between science fiction films and horror films (as opposed to Sontag's refusal to distinguish between the two types), arguing that these appeal to different mental activities: "Science fiction appeals to consciousness, horror to the unconscious." In his Freudian exploration of the subconscious appeal to horror films, Kawin's work leads di-rectly to the kinds of psychoanalytic criticism that have be-come so important to film theory in the last decade (see Sec-tion VII).

As we have seen, Braudy regards Fred Astaire and Gene Kelly as significant figures, and their musicals as among Holly-wood's greatest successes, while Warshow grants such places of honor to the gangster and the westerner. Others, however, would reserve that honor for the comedies of the silent period, a genre to which James Agee, the most celebrated film critic of the last generation, calls attention in his affectionate tribute. For Agee, however, sound comedy reveals a radical deteriora-tion, which he is inclined to attribute to an incompatibility between comic style and speech. No doubt there is such an incompatibility between some comic styles (particularly the most physical ones) and speech, but the Hollywood dialogue comedies of the 1930s and early 1940s have themselves come to be considered a genre, the screwball comedy, that look as good in retrospect as many of the silent classics (partially be-cause they also sound so good).

John Cawelti, the contemporary academic analyst of Ameri-can popular culture, treats the issue of genre in a much broader context. On the one hand, he traces a familiar film genre—the private-eye, detective film—back to its roots as a popular genre of American mass-market fiction. For Cawelti, the generic categories of American studio films have their analogues and ancestors in American popular fictions. On the other, he notes a new attitude toward genre that has dominated many American films of the past decade, particularly the most interesting and important ones—the generic transformation. This deliberately self-conscious transforming of familiar film genres might be seen as an American compromise between the modernist art-films of post-war Europe and the traditional American tendency toward generic plots and characters. Cawelti sees these contemporary generic transformations, though a manifestations of a single spirit, as having four emphases. The film can parody a familiar genre (as Mel Brooks's films do), can nostalgically evoke a familiar genre (as a film like *Farewell, My Lovely* does), can demythologize the familiar genre (as *Chinatown* and Arthur Penn's films do), or can recognize its artificiality but deliberately choose to sustain the myth of the familiar genre (as Sam Peckinpah's films do). Of these four transformations, Cawelti finds the demythologizing film the richest, most complex, and most challenging to its audience's values and responses, approaching the complexity of response required for European art-films. Like Braudy, Warshow, Sontag and Kawin, Cawelti sees this contemporary attitude toward genre as not merely a manifestation of evolving aesthetic tastes but of underlying social attitudes as well.

LEO BRAUDY
FROM
THE WORLD IN A FRAME

GENRE:
THE CONVENTIONS
OF CONNECTION

Actually I do not think that there are any wrong reasons for liking a statue or a picture . . . There are wrong reasons for disliking a work of art.

E. H. GOMBRICH,
The Story of Art

No part of the film experience has been more consistently cited as a barrier to serious critical interest than the existence of forms and conventions, whether in such details as the stereotyped character, the familiar setting, and the happy ending, or in those films that share common characteristics—westerns, musicals, detective films, horror films, escape films, spy films—in short, what have been called *genre* films. Films in general have been criticized for their popular and commercial appeal, seemingly designed primarily for entertainment and escape rather than enlightenment. Genre films especially are criticized because they seem to appeal to a pre-existing audience, while the film "classic" creates its own special audience through the unique power of the filmmaking artist's personal creative sensibility. Too often in genre films the creator seems gone and only the audience is present, to be attacked for its bad taste and worse politics for even appreciating this debased art.

The critical understanding of genre films therefore becomes

a special case of the problem of understanding films in general. Genre films offend our most common definition of artistic excellence: the uniqueness of the art object, whose value can in part be defined by its desire to be uncaused and unfamiliar, as much as possible unindebted to any tradition, popular or otherwise. The pure image, the clear personal style, the intellectually respectable content are contrasted with the impurities of convention, the repetitions of character and plot. We undervalue their attractions and inner dynamics because there seems to be no critical vocabulary with which to talk about them without condescending, and therefore no aesthetic criteria by which to judge them, no way of understanding why one horror film scares us and another leaves us cold, why one musical is a symphony of style and another a clashing disarray.

Critics have ignored genre films because of their prejudice for the unique. But why should art be restricted only to works of self-contained intensity, while many other kinds of artistic experience are relegated to the closet of aesthetic pleasure, unfit for the daylight? Genre films, in fact, arouse and complicate feelings about the self and society that more serious films, because of their bias toward the unique, may rarely touch. Within film the pleasures of originality and the pleasures of familiarity are at least equally important. Following Marcel Duchamp and Antonin Artaud, Andy Warhol in the early 1960s announced "no more classics." In painting and sculpture this meant an attack on the canonization of museum art and the acceptance of previously unacceptable, often popular, forms. For films, the problem has usually been the other way around. "No more classics" for film might mean no more films defined as separate from the popular forms that are the great energy of film, artistically as well as thematically.

The modern prejudice against genre in art can be traced to the aesthetic theories of the Romantic period. In the later eighteenth century the older idea of poetic inspiration began to be expanded into a major literary theory by works like Edward Young's *Conjectures on Original Composition* (1759). Poetic "imitation," the building of creativity on the achievements of the past, began to fade as the standard of personal vision became more important. Only conventions that could be understood literally survived, and the eighteenth-century unwillingness to accord imaginative sympathy to convention received its most famous expression in Samuel Johnson's attack on John Milton's *Lycidas*, a poem in the form of a pastoral elegy, which drew upon a tradition of lament that went back to Theocritus and Vergil. The English and German Romantic writers consoli-

dated this trend by establishing originality not only as a criterion of art, but, in their crudest statements, the *only* criterion
of art. Art could owe nothing to tradition or the past because
that debt qualified the power and originality of the individual
creator. The poet was inspired by what he saw and experienced, and the intervention of any prior categories for that experience doomed the work to secondary value unless the forms
that intervened were primitive forms — the folktale or the ballad — that had none of the hated sophistication of the art of the
previous age. Any use of genre and convention as such necessarily debarred a work and its author from the status of true
art. If poetry were defined as the spontaneous outpouring of
strong feelings, how could a work that employed stock characters and stock situations, stock images and stock resolutions,
have any art or originality in it? Folk art or popular art could
be used because it was generally assumed that serious art was
the purity of which popular art was the degeneracy, and that
purity necessarily precedes degeneracy.* Poetic inspiration
and self-sufficiency occupied the higher peaks of art, while
hack work and despised formulas inhabited the more populated and bourgeois valleys. Genre and convention were the
fare of the multitudes, while originality and storming self-as-
sertion, without a past, without any controls, was the caviar of
the truly aware audience.

Until the eighteenth century, artists had generally been distinguished by their class, their education, and their patrons.
But, with the growth of a mass society and a mass culture, the
hierarchy shifted from distinctions in genealogy to distinctions in sensibility. Almost all of the great eighteenth-century
English novelists and essayists had spent some time in Grub
Street, that world created to serve the new hunger for the
printed word. But the Romantic sensibility turned Grub Street
into a synonym for the convention-ridden enemies of art. The
true artist was noncommercial, struggling on the fringes of
human existence, with neither society nor companions (and
hardly any publishers), alone with his indomitable self. Only
Byron, the most eighteenth-century of the Romantics, could

---

*Ballad-collectors like Bishop Percy or Sir Walter Scott could therefore argue
that their rewritings were an effort to restore the ballads to the form in which
the "Bard" originally created them, before they were passed on to the fumbling brains of the folk. Pop Art has revived this theory in a somewhat different form. Ostensibly making us look at the common objects of the world
with new intensity, Pop Art also conveys the idea that serious art and artists
make popular themes and motifs worthy (read "self-conscious") by putting
them into museum settings and charging high prices. Warhol may have first
done this to satirize the whole elitist-popular division, but the joke seems to
have run thin.

have said, "I awoke to find myself famous" (on the publication of *Childe Harold*); such an obvious interest in the approval of a book-buying public was disdained in the Romantics' image of their calling. And Byron himself preoccupied much of his writing with the depiction of solitary heroes, striding mountainsides to challenge gloomy fates. The Romantic artist tried to make his work unique to escape from the dead hand of traditional form. The only serious use of the past was the contemplation of vanished greatness, to raise the artist out of what he believed to be an uncultured present and establish for himself a continuity with what has been best before the triumph of modern degeneracy. Like T. S. Eliot in *The Wasteland*, the serious, unpopular artist was the only one in a corrupt age who could summon up the artistic Eden of the past and collect its fragments into some coherence.

Such absolute creativity is finally a fraud because all art must exist in some relation to the forms of the past, whether in contrast or continuation. Both the generic work and the more self-contained work expand our sense of the possibilities of art. But the nineteenth-century stress on literary originality and freedom has inhibited our responses, both intellectual and emotional, to works that try to complicate our appreciation of tradition and form, works that may in fact embody a more radical critique of the past than those which ignore it. More people dislike westerns or musicals because such film genres outrage their inherited and unexamined sense of what art *should* be than because the films are offensive in theme, characterization, style, or other artistic quality. Every lover of musicals, for example, has heard the complaint that musicals are unrealistic and the viewer gets embarrassed when people start singing or dancing. But the relationship between realism and stylization is a central issue in musicals, not an absurd convention. When auteur critics applaud the studio director for triumphing over his material and point to the glimmers of original style shining through the genre assignment, they may awaken us to the merits of an individual artist. But they also fall into the Romantic trap of searching for only what is obviously original and personal in a work. In auteur theory, genre directors with large popular audiences become transformed into embattled Romantic artists trying to establish their personal visions in the face of an assembly-line commercialism. Frank Capra has pointed out the opposite possibility: in the days of big studio monopoly, there was a great deal of freedom to experiment because every film had guaranteed distribution, whereas now, with increased independent production, films have become more uniform and compromised, because each has to justify itself financially. Underground and avant-garde films with their emphasis on the individual creative sensibility above all, are naturally enough the most hostile to genre. But the bulk of films fall between pure personal expression and pure studio exploitation, mingling the demands of art and culture, creativity and talent. By their involvement in collective creativity, film directors have, at least practically, moved away from the image of the isolated Romantic artist, no matter how they may indulge that image in their public statements.

Instead of dismissing genre films from the realm of art, we should therefore examine what they accomplish. Genre in films can be the equivalent of conscious reference to tradition in the other arts—the invocation of past works that has been so important a part of the history of literature, drama, and painting. Miró's use of Vermeer, Picasso's use of Delacroix are efforts to distinguish their view of the proper ends of painting. Eliot's use of Spenser or Pynchon's of Joyce make similar assertions of continuity and difference. The methods of the western, the musical, the detective film, or the science-fiction film are also reminiscent of the way Shakespeare infuses old stories with new characters to express the tension between past and present. All pay homage to past works even while they vary their elements and comment on their meaning.

Perhaps the main difference between genre films and classic films is the way that genre films invoke past forms while classic films spend time denying them. The joy in genre is to see what can be dared in the creation of a new form or the creative destruction and complication of an old one. The ongoing genre subject therefore always involves a complex relation between the compulsions of the past and the freedoms of the present, an essential part of the film experience. The single, unique work tries to be unforgettable by solving the whole world at once. The genre work, because of its commitment to pre-existing forms, explores the world more slowly. Its hallmark is less the flash of inspiration than the deep exploration of craft. Like Ford's *Stagecoach* or Aldrich's *Ulzana's Raid* (1972) it can exist both in itself and as the latest in a line of works like it, picking and choosing among possible conventions, refusing one story or motif to indulge another, avoiding one "cliché" in order to show a self-conscious mastery of the cliché that has not been avoided. After all, the reason that an artistic element becomes a cliché is that it answers so well to the experience, intelligence, and feelings of the audience. Subsequent artists, perceiving the same aptness, want to exercise its power themselves, even in a potentially hostile new context, to discover if all the possibilities of the form have thoroughly been explored. The only test is its continuing relevance, and a genre will remain vital, as the western has, and the musical has not, so long as its conventions still express themes and conflicts that preoccupy its audience. When either minority or majority art loses contact with its audience, it becomes a mere signpost in history, an aesthetic rather than an art.

Genre films affect their audience especially by their ability to express the warring traditions in society and the social importance of understanding convention. When Irene Dunne, in *The Awful Truth* (Leo McCarey, 1937), disguises herself as Cary Grant's (fictitious) sister and arrives drunk and raucous at a society gathering where Grant is trying to establish himself, we can open a critical trapdoor and say that the other people at the party, who already know her, don't recognize her in her flimsy disguise because of the necessities of plot and comic form. But we must go on to say that this particular convention, used with all its force, allows McCarey, without dropping the general humorous tone, to point out that she is unrecognized because the upper classes base their estimates and knowledge of character on dress, voice, and manners—a theme supported by the rest of the film as well. The conflict between desire and etiquette can define both a social comedy like *The Awful Truth* and even a more obviously stylized genre work like *Dr. Jekyll and Mr. Hyde* (Rouben Mamoulian, 1932); it parallels in the plot the aesthetic contrast between the individual film and the conventions to which it plays a complex homage.

Genre demands that we know the dynamics of proper audience response and may often require a special audience because of the need to refer the latest instance to previous versions. But response is never invariable. Convention isn't only whatever we don't have to pay attention to. Explaining Shakespeare's use of soliloquies by observing that the practice was an Elizabethan dramatic convention tells us as little as saying that Picasso used blue because it was cheap or that Edward Everett Horton appeared in so many Fred Astaire-Ginger Rogers films because comic relief was needed. Why a soliloquy *now?* What does Horton's presence mean *here?* The possibility exists in all art that convention and comment coexist, that overlapping and even contradictory assumptions and conventions may be brought into play to test their power and make the audience reflect on why they were assumed. The genre film lures its audience into a seemingly familiar world, filled with reassuring stereotypes of character, action, and plot. But the world may actually be not so lulling, and, in some cases, acquiescence in convention will turn out to be bad judgment or even a moral flaw—the basic theme of such Hitchcock films as *Blackmail* (1929), *Rear Window* (1954), and *Psycho*. While avant-garde and original works congratulate the audience by implying it has the capacity to understand them, genre films can exploit the automatic conventions of response for the purposes of pulling the rug out from under their viewers. The very relaxing of the critical intelligence of the audience, the relief that we need not make decisions—aesthetic, moral, metaphysical—about the film, allows the genre film to use our expectations against themselves, and, in the process, reveal to us expectations and assumptions that we may never have thought we had. They can potentially criticize the present, because it too automatically *accepts* the standards of the past, to build subversion within received forms and thereby to criticize the forms instead of only setting up an alternate vision.*

Through a constant interplay between the latest instance and the history of a particular form, genre films can call upon a potential of aesthetic complexity that would be denied if the art defined itself only in terms of its greatest and most inimitable works. Because of the existence of generic expectations—how a plot "should" work, what a stereotyped character "should" do, what a gesture, a location, an allusion, a line of dialogue "should" mean—the genre film can step beyond the moment of its existence and play against its own aesthetic history. Through genre, movies have drawn upon their own tradition and been able to reflect a rich heritage unavailable to the "high" arts of the twentieth century which are so often intent upon denying the past and creating themselves totally anew each time out. Within the world of genre films one finds battles, equivalent to those in the history of literature, drama, and painting, between artists who are willing to reproduce a tradition through their own vision because they believe it still has the ability to evoke the emotional response that made it a satisfying artistic form to begin with, and those who believe the form has dried up and needs an injection, usually of "real-

---

*The three main American critics who appreciated such films before the New Wave popularized them critically—Otis Ferguson, James Agee, and Manny Farber—were less interested in them for their formal qualities than for their action and unpretentiousness, aspects of energy related to their formal self-consciousness. But both Agee and Farber (and Pauline Kael is their true heir in this) wanted to protect at all costs their beloved movies from any charge of art. As far as the definition of art they were attacking goes, they were right. But to continue such attacks now confuses where it once illuminated. One virtue of the French New Wave critics was that they didn't have to defend themselves simultaneously against pompous ideas of high art, the myth of the American tough guy artist, and the specter of Hollywood commercialism.

ism." Poets, for example, may contrast the city and the country because that opposition answers to some real beliefs in their audience and because the choice of the rural virtues of the country satisfactorily resolves the conflict. Others might question the authenticity of the traditional materials: did shepherds really play their pipes in singing contests? isn't the elaborate language untrue to rural idioms? or, to extend the analogy, did cowboys really respect law and justice so much? do people really break into dances on the street when they're happy, and does the neighborhood automatically join in? The later generations may feel an emotional pull in the form, but they might want to destylize it and make it more real. The directors of the "adult" western of the 1950s accepted the vitality of the western but thought that a more realistic treatment would strengthen its inherent virtues. If controversy were part of film tradition, we might have an argument between John Ford and Fred Zinnemann on the essence of the western like that between Alexander Pope and Ambrose Phillips on the pastoral, Ford and Pope arguing for the value of form and style, while Zinnemann and Phillips press the need to make the characters of art as close as possible to the real persons who live or lived in that place.

Genre films share many of the characteristics of the closed films I have described in the previous chapter. But, instead of being framed visually, genre films are primarily *closed by convention*. Of course, they may be visually enclosed as well, as, for example, are horror films and 1930s musicals; but the more important enclosure is the frame of pre-existing motifs, plot turns, actors, and situations—in short everything that makes the film a special place with its own rules, a respite from the more confusing and complicated worlds outside. The frame of genre, the existence of expectations to be used in whatever way the intelligence of the filmmaker is capable, allows freedoms within the form that more original films cannot have because they are so committed to a parallel between form and content. The typical genre situation is a contrast between form and content. With the expectations of stock characters, situations, or narrative rhythms, the director can choose areas of free aesthetic play within. In genre films the most obvious focus of interest is neither complex characterization nor intricate visual style, but pure story. Think about the novel we can't put down. That rare experience in literature is the common experience in film, where we stay only because we want to, where we often must be intrigued by the first five minutes or not at all, and where we know that once we leave the spell is broken. Like fairy tales or classical myths, genre films concentrate on large contrasts and juxtapositions. Genre plots are usually dismissed with a snide synopsis (a process that is never very kind to drama that employs conventions, like Shakespeare's plays). But, amid the conventions and expectations of plot, other kinds of emphasis can flourish. To the unsympathetic eye, the pleasures of variation are usually invisible, whether they appear in the medieval morality play, the Renaissance sonnet, the Restoration comedy, the eighteenth-century portrait, the Chopinesque etude, the horror film, the romantic comedy, the musical, or the western. When we can perceive the function of vampire-film conventions in *Persona* or boxing-film conventions in *On the Waterfront* as clearly as we note the debt of Kurosawa's samurai films to American westerns, or that of the New Wave films to American crime films of the 1950s, then we will be able to appreciate more fully the way in which films can break down the old visions between elite and popular art to establish, almost unbeknown to aesthetics and criticism, a vital interplay between them. . . .*

The epic sweep of the early westerns could be conveyed by the silent screen, but musicals necessarily begin their real film career with sound (and sound films begin, appropriate enough, with *The Jazz Singer*). The Charleston sequences of the silent *Our Dancing Daughters* (Harry Beaumont, 1928) look oddly impersonal and detached today, hardly more real than the bunny-costumed Rockettes. Sound not only individualizes the performer, but also provides a bridge of music between otherwise separate visual moments, a continuity against which the image can play, potentially freeing the film from a strict adherence to a one-to-one relation between sight and sound. Once sound frees image from the necessity to appear logical and casual, the director can experiment with different kinds of nonlogical, noncausal narrative. But, after the first years of sound and such experiments with the new form as René Clair's *Under the Roofs of Paris* (1929), Lang's *M* (1931), Renoir's *Boudu Saved from Drowning* (1932), and Ernst Lu-

---

*The way in which television "cannibalizes" material therefore has less to do with its constant demand than with the speed with which such material becomes outdated. When the audience accepts material as generic and ritualistic—situation comedy, talk shows, sports, news, weather—the form can include an infinite variety of nuance. But when the paradigms are no longer emotionally appealing, formal variety will do no good and there arises a desperate, cannibalizing, attempt to discover the new form of audience solace, whether the subject matter is Dick Cavett or the Vietnam War. Thus the whole process of cultural history is speeded up through successive purgations of used-up subject matter and style.

bitsch's *Trouble in Paradise* (1932), primarily musicals explored its possibilities. The western may be self-conscious about its myths, but the musical is self-conscious about its stylization, the heightened reality that is its norm. The games with continuous narrative that Busby Berkeley plays in the musical numbers of *Footlight Parade* (1933), *42nd Street* (1933), or *Gold Diggers of 1935* are hardly attempted by nonmusical directors until the jumpcutting achronicity of the New Wave.

Berkeley's films show how the stylistic self-consciousness of musicals directly concerns the relation of their art to the everyday world outside the confines of the film. His camera presses relentlessly forward, through impossible stages that open up endlessly, expanding the inner space of film and affirming the capacity of the world of style to mock the narrowness of the "real" world outside the theater walls, populated by bland tenors, greedy producers, and harried directors. Ford uses theater in *Liberty Valance* to purify his genre vision. But Berkeley uses theater, the impossible theater available to film artifice, to give a sense of exuberance and potential. Playing with space, Berkeley in *Footlight Parade* creates an incredible extravaganza supposedly taking place in miniature within a waterfall, with pyramids of swimming girls, diving cameras, and fifty-foot fountains.

Berkeley's real problem, however, is his concentration on the production number and the spectacle. The sense of play and opulence he brought to the musical, his effort to make its stage artifice a source of strength, was, if we look back upon the direction the musical took, a minor stream in its history. His influence appears in the show business biography (*A Star Is Born*, 1937; *The Jolson Story*, 1946; *Funny Girl*, 1968), the production story (*Summer Stock*, 1950; *The Band Wagon*, 1953), and that great amalgam of realized style and stylized realism, *Singin' in the Rain* (1952). There is also a darker side apparent in a film like *All About Eve* (1950), in which the urge to theater is considered to be manipulative, a reduction of the self rather than an expansion. The dark side may be the truer side of Berkeley's inheritance, because his musicals lack any sense of the individual. The strange melancholy of the "Lullaby of Broadway" number from *Gold Diggers of 1935*, in which, after some elaborately uplifting production numbers, an unsuccessful showgirl commits suicide, combines comedy and the tragedy of sentimental realism in a way that only penetrated serious films in the late 1940s. It presages the urbane tragedies of fatality in a theatrical setting that mark the late films of Julien Duvivier (*Flesh and Fantasy*, 1943) and Max Ophuls (*La Ronde*, 1950; *Lola Montès*, 1955). The showgirl commits suicide in "Lullaby of Broadway" in part because the Berkeley ensemble of faceless dancers holds no place for her at all, perhaps because of her lack of talent, but more clearly because her individuality is contrary to the demands of the uniform musical group. Like Eisenstein or the Lang of *Metropolis*, Berkeley magisterially juxtaposes sequences and articulates crowds with ritual symmetry. Berkeley's atttitude toward individuals is that of a silent film director, iconographic and symmetric. The community of the Berkeley girls is cold and anonymous, like Lang's workers, a community created by a nonparticipating choreographer-director. But the kind of musical that had the greatest popular strength, spawned the largest number of descendants, and historically defined the American musical film, is the musical in which the dancer-choreographer himself was a participant, in which an individual man danced with an individual woman, and in which the theme of the individual energy of the dance, the relation of the dancer to his own body, became the main theme of the film. Obviously I am referring to the films of Fred Astaire and Ginger Rogers.*

Shall We Dance (1937, songs by George and Ira Gershwin), the last film of the basic Astaire-Rogers series, is a model of their films, perhaps not least because it contains a final sequence that seems to be an implicit attack against the Berkeley emphasis on anonymous spectacle. Astaire plays the Great Petrov, star of the Russian ballet, who is in reality Peter P. Peters, from Philadelphia. The basic conflict of the film is established in the first scene, when Petrov's manager Jeff (Edward Everett Horton) comes into his rehearsal room to find Petrov improvising a dance to a jazz record. "The Great Petrov doesn't dance for fun," he tells him, emphasizing that ballet is a serious business to which the artist must devote his full time. "But I do," responds Astaire. "Remember me? Pete Peters from Philadelphia, P.A.?" Horton points to the taps on Astaire's ballet shoes and continues his insistence that whatever Astaire is doing, it's not art. "Maybe it's just the Philadelphia in me," says Astaire, and begins dancing again. The forces have been set in motion: the dancing that Astaire likes to do when he is alone directly expresses his personal emotions as well as his real identity— the American tap dancer under the high-culture disguise of the Russian ballet dancer.

---

*Rouben Mamoulian in *Love Me Tonight* (1932, songs by Rodgers and Hart) focuses on individuals (Jeanette MacDonald and Maurice Chevalier), but the style of the film is still one of directional control rather than a performer's energy. The most impressive song settings are those in which parts of the song are sung and played by people in isolated places, visually linked by the director's wit and style (for example, "Isn't It Romantic?").

Horton, as he usually does in these films, comically combines a commitment to high culture (and high society) with a definite antagonism to emotion and feeling. When Astaire falls in love with Linda Keene (Ginger Rogers), a nightclub dancer, after seeing a series of movie-like flip cards of her dancing, Horton speaks darkly of the danger to Astaire's "serious" career and the need to be personally pure (i.e., nonsexual and nonemotional) for art. Like so many musicals, *Shall We Dance* contrasts the emotionally detached and formal patterns of high art with the involved and spontaneous forms of popular art. (Vincente Minnelli's *Meet Me in St. Louis*, 1944, for example, establishes the same relationship between serious music and popular music, and many musicals include parodies of serious theater by vaudevillians.) The 1930s musical may have its historical roots in the silent-film urge to the respectability of theater, the importation of theatrical performers both to give the young industry tone and to banish the generally lower-class associations that film had from its vaudeville beginnings. But the sound musical—like so many genres of the 1930s, comedies and horror films included—begins to mock this respect for older forms just as it parodies the upper class in general. Tap dancing is superior to ballet as movies are superior to drama, not merely because they are more popular, but because they contain more life and possibility. The flip-card stills that turn into a sequence of Rogers dancing present her as a creature of the film, not the stage. Like Astaire in the film, Rogers is also an American, but more proudly: she doesn't like the "hand-kissing heel-clickers of Paris" and rejects Peters when he attempts to impress her by coming on as the formal Petrov. Berkeley attacks theater in favor of film and dance by destroying the limits of theatrical space. But Astaire and Rogers (and their directors, especially Mark Sandrich and choreographer Hermes Pan) attack all high art in favor of the new dancing forms of spontaneity, American style. The Berkeleyan world spawns the myth of show-business biography that success on stage buys only unhappiness in one's personal life. But the silvery world of Astaire and Rogers celebrates the ability of individual energy to break away from the dead hand of society, class and art as well. The open space of the western that offers a chance to build becomes in the musical the endless inner energy released in dance.

Shall We Dance is defined by the collision between the forces of inertia and stasis and the forces of vitality, between Astaire as Petrov—the commitment to high art and personal repression—and Astaire as Peters—the commitment to an art that attempts to structure individual energy instead of excluding it.

Musical comedy therefore also attacks any theories of acting in which character comes from the past. Character in musical comedy is physiological and external: the ability to dance and the way dancing functions in specific situations becomes a direct expression of the tensions within the self. In the first scene Astaire dances along at the proper speed; and then, when the machine needs to be wound up again, he slows down as the record itself slows down. On the ship that takes him and Rogers back to America, he descends into the engine room and dances there in time to the pistons while black members of the crew who are taking a musical break play for him. In both sequences the energy of the dance—the personal emphasis in the first, the relation to jazz and black music in the second ("Slap That Bass")—draws upon the analogy between body and machine. But here, unlike literary attacks against the machine, the film, true to its mechanical and technological origins, celebrates the machine as a possible element in the liberation of the individual rather than in his enslavement (similar to the ambivalence about machines that characterizes *Metropolis*). Machines are outside class, purifiers of movement. The real threat to individual energy and exuberance is not the machine, but the forces of society and respectability—the impresario Jeff, the rich suitor Jim with the weak chin (William Brisbane), who wants to take Rogers away from show business, and the punctilious hotel manager Cecil Flintridge (Eric Blore). Here they are comic, but they nevertheless play the same repressive roles as they would in the more melodramatic world of the western.*

At the end of *Shall We Dance*, the comically hostile forces (including an outside world of publicity and gossip) are reconciled by Astaire's typical process of self-realization—the search for the perfect partner. The perfect partner is always a dancing partner, since it is within the world of dance that true communication and complementarity can be achieved: the male-female dance duo is a model of male-female relationship in general. Dancing isn't a euphemism for sex; in Astaire-Rogers films at least, dancing is much better. Two sequences in *Shall We Dance* constitute the dance of courtship and they appear after the first dancing sequences, which establish the separate personalities of Astaire and Rogers. In the first, "They All Laughed," Astaire begins with ballet-like steps while

---

*The positive interpretation of the machine analogy to the body is a constant theme in musicals, most recently expressed in the Ken Russell film of *Tommy* (1975, words and music by Peter Townshend and The Who), in which the deaf, dumb, and blind boy first discovers his real nature through his symbiotic relation with pinball machines.

Rogers stands still. Then she begins to tap, and he responds, first with a ballet version of the tapping, then a straight tap. In the second such number, "Let's Call the Whole Thing Off," the importance of the dancing situation to their relationship is further underlined. They are taking a walk in a stage-set Central Park and decide to go skating, even though neither of them has skated in a long time. They begin very haltingly, with frequent stumbles. But, as soon as the music starts, they skate perfectly together. Then, at the end of the song, as the music ends, they hit the grass outside the skating rink and fall down. Once the magic world of dance and its ability to idealize personal energy into a model of relationship has vanished, Astaire and Rogers again become separate and even bickering individuals. "Let's Call the Whole Thing Off" memorializes their differences, even while it provides a context for their relationship. The next musical number, "They Can't Take That Away from Me," contains no dancing. It takes place at night on a ferry between New Jersey and New York and emphasizes the problems of their relationship, especially the seeming conflict between their real feelings, which can be expressed at night, and the public and social demands on them that the daylight world of the rest of the film exerts. Like Astaire and Rogers themselves, who feel the pressure to continue their successful film partnership despite their own wishes, Peter Peters and Linda Keene have been forced into marriage primarily so they can get divorced. The publicity generated by their managers is meant to connect them, but it succeeds only in driving them apart, as aesthetic as well as emotional partners.

Astaire solves the conflict and rejoins Rogers in the remarkable final sequence. In a theatrical setting reminiscent of the roof of the Winter Garden, an open space within the city, Astaire stages a show that summarizes the main elements of the film. In the early sequences Astaire plays a Russian ballet dancer; Rogers appears; he loses her. Meanwhile, the real Rogers, the comic Claudius in this mousetrap, sits in a box, part of the audience, but separate from it. Astaire reprises "You Can't Take That Away from Me" to lead into a sequence in which a whole group of dancing partners appear—all wearing a mask with Rogers' face on it. The song then becomes ironic, since the memory of her uniqueness that it celebrates has been confused in the many Rogers of the present. Ruby Keeler is obviously pleased to be multiplied into many images for the adoration of Dick Powell in Berkeley's *Dames* (1934), but the Ginger Rogers in the audience of *Shall We Dance* cannot take this anonymous crowd of Busby Berkeley chorus girls all wearing her face. Astaire's message makes the same plea: deliver me from the life of a single man amid innumerable faceless girls by asserting the perfection of our relationship. Rogers goes backstage and puts on one of the masks. She comes onstage, briefly reveals herself to Astaire, and then glides back into the anonymity of the many Rogers. Which is the real Rogers among the false, the reality and energy of the individual beneath the generalized artifice of the image? Astaire finds her and together they sing and dance the final song, "Shall We Dance," an invitation to let the dancing, emotional energetic self out, to reject depression and the forms of society, and to accept the frame of theater that allows one, through the exuberance of dance, to be free.

The figure of Fred Astaire implies that dance is the perfect form, the articulation of motion that allows the self the most freedom at the same time that it includes the most energy. The figure of Gene Kelly implies that the true end of dance is to destroy excess and attack the pretensions of all forms in order to achieve some new synthesis. Kelly the sailor teaching Jerry the Mouse to dance in *Anchors Aweigh* (George Sidney, 1945) stands next to Bill Robinson teaching Shirley Temple to dance in *The Little Colonel* (David Butler, 1935). Astaire may move dance away from the more formal orders of the ballet, but Kelly emphasizes its appeal to the somewhat recalcitrant, not quite socialized part of the self, where the emotions are hidden. Astaire and Kelly are part of the same continuum of themes and motifs in musicals (an interesting study could be done of the interaction of their images in the 1940s and 1950s). There are many contrasts that can be made between the way they use dance and the way they appear in their films, but the basic fact of their continuity should be remembered. The question of personal energy, which I have characterized as the musical's basic theme, once again appears centrally. The social world against which Astaire defined himself in the 1930s no longer had the same attraction to movie audiences in the 1940s; it was a hangover from the early days of film and their simultaneous fascination with 1920s high life and the higher seriousness of theater, in a double effort both to imitate and to mock. Astaire is the consummate theatrical dancer, while Kelly is more interested in the life outside the proscenium. The energy that Astaire defines within a theatrical and socially formal framework Kelly takes outside, into a world somewhat more "real" (that is, similar to the world of the audience) and therefore more recalcitrant. Kelly's whole presence is therefore more rugged and less ethereal than Astaire's. Both Astaire and Kelly resemble Buster Keaton, their prime ancestor in dancing's

Fred Astaire among the many masks of Ginger Rogers in *Shall We
Dance* (1937). "Which is the real Rogers among the false, the reality
and energy of the individual beneath the generalized artifice of the
image? Astaire finds her and together they sing and dance, 'Shall We
Dance', an invitation to let the dancing, emotional energetic self out
. . .'' (BRAUDY), page 425). Gene Kelly in *Singin' in the Rain* (1952) at
the climax of "the great set piece of 'Gotta Dance', another statement
of Kelly's belief that dancing is a compulsion from within, more authentic than the forms imposed from without" (BRAUDY, page 432).

paean to the freedom and confinement of the body. But Astaire is the spiritual Keaton while Kelly is the combative, energetic Keaton, compounded with the glee of Douglas Fairbanks. Kelly has more obvious physical presence than Astaire, who hides his well-trained body in clothes that give the impression he has nothing so disruptive as muscles, so that the form of his dancing is even more an ideal and a mystery. Astaire often wears suits and tuxedos, while Kelly generally wears open-collared shirts, slacks, white socks, and loafers—a studied picture of informality as opposed to Astaire's generally more formal dress. Astaire wears the purified Art Deco makeup of the 1930s, but Kelly keeps the scar on his cheek visible—an emblem of the interplay between formal style and disruptive realism in his definition of the movie musical.*

Astaire may mock social forms for their rigidity, but Kelly tries to explode them. Astaire purifies the relation between individual energy and stylized form, whereas Kelly tries to find a new form that will give his energy more play. Astaire dances onstage or in a room, expanding but still maintaining the idea of enclosure and theater; Kelly dances on streets, on the roofs of cars, on tables, in general bringing the power of dance to bear on a world that would ordinarily seem to exclude it. (Astaire absorbs this ability of Kelly's to reorganize normal space and integrates it with his own lighter-than-air quality in the dancing on the walls sequence in *Royal Wedding*, 1951, directed by Kelly's favorite collaborator Stanley Donen.) Astaire usually plays a professional dancer; Kelly sometimes does and sometimes does not, although he is usually an artist of some kind, often, as in *The Pirate*, a popular artist, or, as in *Summer Stock*, a director, associated with the stage but not totally inside it. Kelly therefore merges the director emphasis of Berkeley with the performer emphasis of Astaire. To complement the distance from theatrical form Kelly maintains, his whole style of acting is self-mocking, while Astaire's is almost always serious and heartfelt, as far as comedy will allow. Because the film attitude toward serious art is less defensive in the 1940s than in the 1930s, Kelly can include ballet and modern dance in his films, although always in a specifically theat-

---

*I have been using Astaire and Kelly to represent the change in the movie musical as much as I have been describing what they do themselves. A full account would also have to include a close consideration of Eleanor Powell, whose fantastic exuberance and bodily freedom often threatened to destroy the generally theatrical plots in which she was encased. The most important film for these purposes might be *Broadway Melody of 1940* (Norman Taurog), in which she and Astaire dance together with an equality of feeling and ability that presages the teaming of Kelly and Judy Garland.

rical setting (the pirate dream ballet in *The Pirate*, the gangster ballet in *Les Girls*). Theater and style in Astaire's films reconcile the conflict between personal life and social pressures, and allow the self to repair and renovate its energy. Many of his films have more or less autobiographical elements in them, not the autobiography of Astaire's private life, but the autobiography of Astaire's professional life: the effect to get a new partner after Ginger Rogers decided to do dramatic films instead (*Easter Parade*, Charles Walters, 1948, with Judy Garland), the celebration of Rogers' return to dance after several "serious" films (*The Barkleys of Broadway*, Charles Walters, 1949). Kelly, however, far from taking refuge in theater, wants to make theater take over daily life. His films are hardly ever autobiographical; unlike Astaire's, they have stories in which Kelly plays a role. Astaire may dance by himself, with a partner, or with a company of dancers. Kelly wants to galvanize a community of nondancers as well. Astaire and his partner are professionals; Kelly and his partner are often amateurs, but everyone they meet knows the steps to their dances and the words to their songs.*

A Kelly film that highlights the differences and similarities between the two great definers of the American musical comedy is Vincent Minnelli's *The Pirate* (1948, songs by Cole Porter, story by Frances Goodrich and Albert Hackett). In the beginning of *The Pirate*, Manuela (Judy Garland), the poor niece of a wealthy family on an eighteenth-century Caribbean island, is leafing through a book detailing the highly romanticized adventures of the pirate Macoco. She dreamily desires the embraces of Macoco but is realistically resigned to marrying the unromantic, fat town mayor (Walter Slezak), who courts her with propriety and respect. One of her companions tells her that the life of Macoco is pure fantasy and she responds by expressing the sense of separate worlds she feels within her: "I realize there's a practical world and a dream world. I won't mix them"‡ Enter Serafin (Gene Kelly), the head of a traveling company of players. He flirts with Manuela, and falls in love with her. By accidental hypnosis the reserved Manuela changes into a manic performer, and she

---

*It is worth mentioning that Astaire and Kelly are appropriately enough the two supreme examples of Hollywood stars who never really gave their private lives in any way over to the fan magazines or the mechanism of offscreen publicity, since their screen presences are personal enough.

‡Observers of Vincente Minnelli have often pointed out the constant interest in the clash of reality and dream in his films. Here, of course, I am considering these themes in terms of the larger issue of the history of musicals as a genre. The way specific directors, with their own thematic and stylistic

and Serafin dance and sing together in a funny scene in which Serafin thinks he's tricked this pretty girl into dancing with him, while the exuberance released in Manuela by the hypnosis threatens to knock him off the stage. Horrified at what she's done, Manuela leaves for her hometown away from the big city to prepare for her marriage to the mayor. Serafin follows her and recognizes the mayor as the real Macoco. He threatens to expose him unless the mayor allows Serafin to pretend that he is Macoco, since Serafin knows of Manuela's hero-worship. The mayor agrees, until he sees that Manuela's attraction to Serafin is increased by the impersonation. The mayor then arrests Serafin and is about to hang him when Serafin, asking for the opportunity to do a last act on stage, plays a scene with Manuela that reveals to the mayor her actual love for Macoco the Pirate. Unaware of the game, the mayor announces that he is the real Macoco and therefore Manuela should love him. He is arrested, and the united Kelly and Garland appear in the last scene as stage partners singing "Be a Clown" to the audience.

Through the personalities of Garland and Kelly, *The Pirate* explores the theme of identity I have discussed in Astaire's films in a very different way. Serafin's courtship of Manuela reveals that her desire for Macoco is a desire for a romantic individualism outside society— a theme made especially strong by setting the film in an eighteenth-century Spanish Roman Catholic country with all its elaborate social forms and ceremonies. Kelly hypnotizes her with a spinning mirror—an image of the many possible selves. The Manuela that is released, the self below the social surface, is a singing, dancing self. Her exuberance indicates that Serafin has in fact released more than he expects or may want. He is a professional artist. But she gets her art directly from her inner life, untamed by society or by learned craft. Garland is perfect for this kind of role because she projects so clearly the image of a restrained, almost mouse-like person until she begins to sing and dance. (Her first important film, *The Wizard of Oz*, Victor Fleming, 1939, solidified this tension in Garland between the acceptance of daily life in a world of drabness and moral boredom, and the possibility of escape to an exuberant singing, dancing world of dream. It appeared as well in *Meet Me in St. Louis*, 1944, another Minnelli film, where the pattern of stability and release is more parallel to that of *The Pirate*.)

preoccupations, interact with pre-existing conventions to change those conventions and clarify their own interests at the same time is a topic that requires much more minute examination that I can give it here.

Serafin is the alternative to Macoco in more ways than one. The real pirate has changed from an antisocial adventurer to a socially dictatorial mayor, thus rejecting the Macoco side of himself to become almost the opposite. But Kelly instead tries to mediate individuality and community. His first song in the film is "Niña," a typical Kelly dance in a street fair, where he sings and dances with half the surprised people there to weave together a kind of community of otherwise isolated individuals and objects through the catalyst of his own personality and artistic ability. The song relates how he calls every girl he meets "niña," that is, little girl. At the end of the song Garland appears and the amazed Kelly asks her what her name is. Like Rogers at the end of *Shall We Dance,* she stands apart from communal anonymity. Serafin is the articulate adventurer, the popular artist, who sees his art to be part of a creation of community; she is the individual artist, whose art is less craft than a swelling sense of herself from within. We admire and feel friendly to him because he includes us in his dance. But we identify with her, for she, like us, is not professional, even in the loose sense in which Serafin is professional. Serafin realizes this and therefore pretends to be Macoco to win her. In the climactic moment, when he is plotting to get the real Macoco to reveal himself and brings out the mirror to rehypnotize Garland, Slezak breaks the mirror. But it doesn't matter. Manuela is willing to go along with Serafin's plot, as Garland accepts Kelly's choreography and control. Her energy, once released, can be controlled, especially within the context of love and theater. *The Pirate* is therefore a next step from the themes of the Astaire-Rogers films. Kelly makes the perfect couple the center of an ideal community created by dance, a world of harmony where everyone on the street not only sympathizes with the exuberance you feel because you're in love, but also knows all the words and dance steps that express your feelings.

The context of the ideal, the place where the true self can be revealed, is still theatrical space. The final song, "Be a Clown," emphasizes the responsible escape of art, especially popular art, in a way very reminiscent of the title song at the end of *Shall We Dance.* But the inclusion of the Garland figure—the nonprofessional dancer from the heart—indicates the direction that Kelly has taken the musical, as does the fact that Kelly and Garland are not elegant in their world of theater, but clownish and self-mocking, more willing than Astaire and Rogers to include the potential disruptiveness of the world outside them and the world within. Astaire and Rogers dance for us, looking at each other primarily to integrate their dancing. Kelly and Garland convey a much friendlier and more personal relationship. We may watch Astaire and Rogers. But we empathize with Kelly and Garland.*

Kelly in *The Pirate* is an entertainer. But the emphasis of the film is less on his dancing and singing than on the world that dance and theater can create together. The stylization and historical setting of *The Pirate* emphasize the release from the stultifying social self dance allows; the contemporary setting of most other Kelly films further highlights Kelly's effort to bring his dancing out of the enclosed world of theater and make the whole world a theater, responsive to and changed by his energy. Astaire's dances define a world of perfect form, while Kelly's often reach out to include improvisation, spontaneity, and happenstance. The scene that contrasts best with Astaire's imitation of the record player and the machines in *Shall We Dance* is Kelly's marvelous interweaving of a creaky board and a piece of paper left on the stage in *Summer Stock* (1950). Kelly's self-mocking smile reflects the way most of his films continue the attack of Astaire's films against artistic pretension. Embodying the catalytic possibilities of dance to create a new coherence for the nontheatrical world, Kelly journeys through parody and realism, attacking formal excesses on the one hand and transforming everyday reality on the other.

Singin' in the Rain (Kelly and Stanley Donen, 1952), is one aspect of his effort and *On the Town* (Kelly and Stanley Donen, 1949) is the other. The frame of *Singin' in the Rain* is a full-scale parody of the early days of sound film (an appropriate subject for the musical), complete with an attack on artistic "high seriousness in favor of the comic exuberance of popular art. The essential scene is Donald O'Connor's incredible acrobatic dance "Make 'Em Laugh" (unfortunately often cut for television), like "Be a Clown" a description of the popular artist's relation to his audience. But this time, instead of being on a stage, the number is done amid a welter of different film sets depicting different worlds, with stagehands moving through the scene. O'Connor's partner for a while is a featureless, uncostumed dummy that he makes seem alive (a reminiscence of

---

*The strength of Minnelli's own vision obviously has its place in understanding *The Pirate* (1948), although the comparative visual stasis and the commitment to the values of stability that characterize *Meet Me in St. Louis* (1944) indicate the importance of Kelly in changing his style and his ideas. Minnelli's musicals may try to celebrate the triumph of the individual through art, but just as often (for example, in *The Band Wagon*, 1953) they catch a tint of gloom from his more melancholic nonmusical films, which often deal with artistic compromise and disintegration, either in the context of the world of film (*The Bad and the Beautiful*, 1952; *Two Weeks in Another Town*, 1962) or the other arts (*Lust for Life*, 1956; *Some Came Running*, 1958). Only in the pure world of the musical can art and individuality succeed without compromise.

the Ginger Rogers dummy in *Shall We Dance*), and for a finale he starts walking up the set walls and finally jumps right through them. In the early scenes of the film, Kelly, the phony silent-screen lover, needs to set up a sound stage and props before he can tell Debbie Reynolds he loves her and sings "You Were Meant for Me." But the declaration becomes acceptable as real emotion only when, in the next scene, he and Donald O'Connor parody the demands of their diction coach in "Moses Supposes." By this time, to parallel his change from form to substance, Kelly has left his suits and tuxedoes behind and dresses in the more familiar open-collared shirt and loafers. Once again, the scar on his cheek is an emblem of the reality that will emerge. In *Singin' in the Rain* silent films are artificial in their stylized actions and hoked-up emotions; only sound is real. The discovery of communication with an audience changes clearly from "Shall We Dance" to "Be a Clown" to "Make 'Em Laugh," with an increasing emphasis on the place of informality and personal style. The solution of the plot of *Singin' in the Rain* is to make the bad serious film into the parodic musical; almost all the dances in the film contain parodies of earlier dances and dancers, in the same somewhat mocking homage that characterizes the attitude to Impressionism in *An American in Paris* (Minnelli, 1951). This is the essence of the kind of energy Kelly's film embodies: theater, like the ability to dance, is a manner of inner perspective on the world outside. The reality of sound film that Kelly discovers follows his own curve of increased dancing in the film until the great set piece of "Gotta Dance," another statement of Kelly's belief that dancing is a compulsion from within more authentic than the forms imposed from without. The final scene, in which Debbie Reynolds is revealed as the voice of Jean Hagen from behind the curtain, repeats on still another level the basic theme of outer form and inner reality. Music and dance are the real spirit of film in the same way they are the real soul and energy of New York in *On the Town*, or Paris in *An American in Paris*.

Kelly's dancing tries not to be the aesthetic escape of Astaire's. It is more utopian because it aims to bring the world together. Astaire's films often imply that dance and therefore energy itself can be a refuge from a stuffy world of social forms; Kelly's films imply that dance and the individual can change the world. The three sailors on leave in *On the Town* — Kelly, Frank Sinatra, and Jules Munshin — are searching for the perfect partner and all find their girls, not in a purified world of dance, but in a real New York (the first musical made on location) that embraces both their dancing and their search.

The women—Vera-Ellen, Ann Miller, and Betty Garrett—are all at least the equals of the men in exuberance, energy, and wit. They make their own space in a public world, like Kelly in the "Singin' in the Rain" sequence, splashing through puddles of chance and nature. The great pretenders in *On the Town* are Kelly and Vera-Ellen, the small-town kids who come on to each other as sophisticates. The moral is that of almost all Kelly films: don't worry about the true self; it will turn out to be better than the one you're pretending to be. Kelly's kind of musical doesn't retreat from reality. It tries to subvert reality through its new energy, an energy available to everyone in the audience through Kelly's insistence on the nonprofessional character, the musical self that wells from inside instead of being imposed from without, whether by training, tradition, or society. . . .

1976

ROBERT WARSHOW
MOVIE CHRONICLE:
THE WESTERNER

They that have power to hurt and will do none,
That do not do the thing they most do show,
Who, moving others, are themselves as stone,
Unmoved, cold, and to temptation slow;
They rightly do inherit heaven's graces,
And husband nature's riches from expense;
They are the lords and owners of their faces,
Others but stewards of their excellence.

The two most successful creations of American movies are the gangster and the Westerner: men with guns. Guns as physical objects, and the postures associated with their use, form the visual and emotional center of both types of films. I suppose this reflects the importance of guns in the fantasy life of Americans; but that is a less illuminating point than it appears to be.

The gangster movie, which no longer exists in its "classical" form, is a story of enterprise and success ending in precipitate failure. Success is conceived as an increasing power to work injury, it belongs to the city, and it is of course a form of evil (though the gangster's death, presented usually as "punishment," is perceived simply as defeat). The peculiarity of the gangster is his unceasing, nervous activity. The exact nature of his enterprises may remain vague, but his commitment to enterprise is always clear, and all the more clear because he operates outside the field of utility. He is without culture, without manners, without leisure, or at any rate his leisure is likely to be spent in debauchery so compulsively aggressive as to seem only another aspect of his "work." But he is graceful, moving like a dancer among the crowded dangers of the city.

Like other tycoons, the gangster is crude in conceiving his ends but by no means inarticulate; on the contrary, he is usually expansive and noisy (the introspective gangster is a fairly recent development), and can state definitely what he wants: to take over the North Side, to own a hundred suits, to be Number One. But new "frontiers" will present themselves infinitely, and by a rigid convention it is understood that as soon as he wishes to rest on his gains, he is on the way to destruction.

The gangster is lonely and melancholy, and can give the impression of a profound worldly wisdom. He appeals most to adolescents with their impatience and their feeling of being outsiders, but more generally he appeals to that side of all of us which refuses to believe in the "normal" possibilities of happiness and achievement; the gangster is the "no" to that great American "yes" which is stamped so big over our official culture and yet has so little to do with the way we really feel about our lives. But the gangster's loneliness and melancholy are not "authentic"; like everything else that belongs to him, they are not honestly come by: he is lonely and melancholy not because life ultimately demands such feelings but because he has put himself in a position where everybody wants to kill him and eventually somebody will. He is wide open and defenseless, incomplete because unable to accept any limits or come to terms with his own nature, fearful, loveless. And the story of his career is a nightmare inversion of the values of ambition and opportunity. From the window of Scarface's bulletproof apartment can be seen an electric sign proclaiming: "The World Is Yours," and, if I remember, this sign is the last thing we see after Scarface lies dead in the street. In the end it is the gangster's weakness as much as his power and freedom that appeals to us; the world is not ours, but it is not his either, and in his death he "pays" for our fantasies, releasing us momentarily both from the concept of success, which he denies by caricaturing it, and from the need to succeed, which he shows to be dangerous.

The Western hero, by contrast, is a figure of repose. He resembles the gangster in being lonely and to some degree melancholy. But his melancholy comes from the "simple" recognition that life is unavoidably serious, not from the disproportions of his own temperament. And his loneliness is organic, not imposed on him by his situation but belonging to him intimately and testifying to his completeness. The gangster must reject others violently or draw them violently to him. The Westerner is not thus compelled to seek love; he is prepared to accept it, perhaps, but he never asks of it more than it can give, and we see him constantly in situations where love is at best an irrelevance. If there is a woman he loves, she is usually unable to understand his motives; she is against killing and being killed, and he finds it impossible to explain to her that there is no point in being "against" these things: they belong to his world.

Very often this woman is from the East and her failure to understand represents a clash of cultures. In the American mind, refinement, virtue, civilization, Christianity itself, are seen as feminine, and therefore women are often portrayed as possessing some kind of deeper wisdom, while the men, for all their apparent self-assurance, are fundamentally childish. But the West, lacking the graces of civilization, is the place "where men are men"; in Western movies, men have the deeper wisdom and the women are children. Those women in the Western movies who share the hero's understanding of life are prostitutes (or, as they are usually presented, barroom entertainers)—women, that is, who have come to understand in the most practical way how love can be an irrelevance, and therefore "fallen" women. The gangster, too, associates with prostitutes, but for him the important things about a prostitute are her passive availability and her costliness: she is part of his winnings. In Western movies, the important thing about a prostitute is her quasi-masculine independence: nobody owns her, nothing has to be explained to her, and she is not, like a virtuous woman, a "value" that demands to be protected. When the Westerner leaves the prostitute for a virtuous woman—for love—he is in fact forsaking a way of life, though the point of the choice is often obscured by having the prostitute killed by getting into the line of fire.

The Westerner is *par excellence* a man of leisure. Even when he wears the badge of a marshal or, more rarely, owns a ranch, he appears to be unemployed. We see him standing at a bar, or playing poker—a game which expresses perfectly his talent for remaining relaxed in the midst of tension—or perhaps camping out on the plains on some extraordinary errand. If he does own a ranch, it is in the background; we are not actually aware that he owns anything except his horse, his guns, and the one worn suit of clothing which is likely to remain unchanged all through the movie. It comes as a surprise to see him take money from his pocket or an extra shirt from his saddlebags. As a rule we do not even know where he sleeps at night and don't think of asking. Yet it never occurs to us that he is a poor man; there is no poverty in Western movies, and really no wealth either: those great cattle domains and shipments of gold which figure so largely in the plots are moral and not material quantities, not the objects of contention but only its occasion. Possessions too are irrelevant.

Employment of some kind—usually unproductive—is always

Easterners and Westerners. Paul Muni in *Scarface* (1932); John Carradine, Andy Devine, Chris Martin, George Bancroft, Louise Platt, Donald Meek, Claire Trevor, and John Wayne in *Stagecoach* (1939). "The two most successful creations of American movies are the gangster and the Westerner: men with guns. . . . The land and the horses have . . . a moral significance: the physical freedom they represent belongs to the moral 'openness' of the West—corresponding to the fact that guns are carried where they can be seen. . . . The gangster's world is less open . . ." (WARSHOW, pages 434, 438).

open to the Westerner, but when he accepts it, it is not because he needs to make a living, much less from any idea of "getting ahead." Where could he want to "get ahead" to? By the time we see him, he is already "there": he can ride a horse faultlessly, keep his countenance in the face of death, and draw his gun a little faster and shoot it a little straighter than anyone he is likely to meet. These are sharply defined acquirements, giving to the figure of the Westerner an apparent moral clarity which corresponds to the clarity of his physical image against his bare landscape; initially, at any rate, the Western movie presents itself as being without mystery, its whole universe comprehended in what we see on the screen.

Much of this apparent simplicity arises directly from those "cinematic" elements which have long been understood to give the Western theme its special appropriateness for the movies: the wide expanses of land, the free movement of men on horses. As guns constitute the visible moral center of the Western movie, suggesting continually the possibility of violence, so land and horses represent the movie's material basis, its sphere of action. But the land and the horses have also a moral significance: the physical freedom they represent belongs to the moral "openness" of the West—corresponding to the fact that guns are carried where they can be seen. (And, as we shall see, the character of land and horses changes as the Western film becomes more complex.)

The gangster's world is less open, and his arts not so easily identifiable as the Westerner's. Perhaps he too can keep his countenance, but the mask he wears is really no mask: its purpose is precisely to make evident the fact that he desperately wants to "get ahead" and will stop at nothing. Where the Westerner imposes himself by the appearance of unshakable control, the gangster's pre-eminence lies in the suggestion that he may at any moment lose control; his strength is not in being able to shoot faster or straighter than others, but in being more willing to shoot. "Do it first," says Scarface expounding his mode of operation, "and keep on doing it!" With the Westerner, it is a crucial point of honor *not* to "do it first"; his gun remains in its holster until the moment of combat.

There is no suggestion, however, that he draws the gun reluctantly. The Westerner could not fulfill himself if the moment did not finally come when he can shoot his enemy down. But because that moment is so thoroughly the expression of his being, it must be kept pure. He will not violate the accepted forms of combat though by doing so he could save a city. And he can wait. "When you call me that—smile!"—the villain smiles weakly, soon he is laughing with horrible joviality, and the crisis is past. But it is allowed to pass because it must come again: sooner or later Trampas will "make his play," and the Virginian will be ready for him.

What does the Westerner fight for? We know he is on the side of justice and order, and of course it can be said he fights for these things. But such broad aims never correspond exactly to his real motives; they only offer him his opportunity. The Westerner himself, when an explanation is asked of him (usually by a woman), is likely to say that he does what he "has to do." If justice and order did not continually demand his protection, he would be without a calling. Indeed, we come upon him often in just that situation, as the reign of law settles over the West and he is forced to see that his day is over; those are the pictures which end with his death or with his departure for some more remote frontier. What he defends, at bottom, is the purity of his own image—in fact his honor. This is what makes him invulnerable. When the gangster is killed, his whole life is shown to have been a mistake, but the image the Westerner seeks to maintain can be presented as clearly in defeat as in victory: he fights not for advantage and not for the right, but to state what he is, and he must live in a world which permits that statement. The Westerner is the last gentleman, and the movies which over and over again tell his story are probably the last art form in which the concept of honor retains its strength.

Of course I do not mean to say that ideas of virtue and justice and courage have gone out of culture. Honor is more than these things: it is a style, concerned with harmonious appearances as much as with desirable consequences, and tending therefore toward the denial of life in favor of art. "Who hath it? he that died o' Wednesday." On the whole, a world that leans to Falstaff's view is a more civilized and even, finally, a more graceful world. It is just the march of civilization that forces the Westerner to move on; and if we actually had to confront the question it might turn out that the woman who refuses to understand him is right as often as she is wrong. But we do not confront the question. Where the Westerner lives it is always about 1870—not the real 1870, either, or the real West—and he is killed or goes away when his position becomes problematical. The fact that he continues to hold our attention is evidence enough that, in his proper frame, he presents an image of personal nobility that is still real for us.

Clearly, this image easily becomes ridiculous: we need only look at William S. Hart or Tom Mix, who in the wooden absoluteness of their virtue represented little that an adult could take seriously; and doubtless such figures as Gene Autry or Roy Rogers are no better, though I confess I have seen none of their movies. Some film enthusiasts claim to find in the early, unsophisticated Westerns a "cinematic purity" that has since been lost; this idea is as valid, and finally as misleading, as T. S. Eliot's statement that *Everyman* is the only play in English that stays within the limitations of art. The truth is that the Westerner comes into the field of serious art only when his moral code, without ceasing to be compelling, is seen also to be imperfect. The Westerner at his best exhibits a moral ambiguity which darkens his image and saves him from absurdity; this ambiguity arises from the fact that, whatever his justifications, he is a killer of men.

In *The Virginian*, which is an archetypal Western movie as *Scarface* or *Little Caesar* are archetypal gangster movies, there is a lynching in which the hero (Gary Cooper), as leader of a posse, must supervise the hanging of his best friend for stealing cattle. With the growth of American "social consciousness," it is no longer possible to present a lynching in the movies unless the point is the illegality and injustice of the lynching itself; *The Ox-Bow Incident*, made in 1943, explicitly puts forward the newer point of view and can be regarded as a kind of "anti-Western." But in 1929, when *The Virginian* was made, the present inhibition about lynching was not yet in force; the justice, and therefore the necessity, of the hanging is never questioned—except by the school-teacher from the East, whose refusal to understand serves as usual to° set forth more sharply the deeper seriousness of the West. The Virginian is thus in a tragic dilemma where one moral absolute conflicts with another and the choice of either must leave a moral stain. If he had chosen to save his friend, he would have violated the image of himself that he had made essential to his existence, and the movie would have had to end with his death, for only by his death could the image have been restored. Having chosen instead to sacrifice his friend to the higher demands of the "code"—the only choice worthy of him, as even the friend understands—he is none the less stained by the killing, but what is needed now to set accounts straight is not his death but the death of the villain Trampas, the leader of the cattle thieves, who had escaped the posse and abandoned the Virginian's friend to his fate. Again the woman intervenes: Why must there be *more* killing? If the hero really loved her, he would leave town, refusing Trampas's challenge. What good will it be if Trampas should kill him? But the Virginian does once more what he "has to do," and in avenging his friend's death wipes out the stain on his own honor. Yet his victory cannot be complete: no death can be paid for and no stain truly wiped out; the movie is still a tragedy, for though the hero escapes with his life, he has been forced to confront the ultimate limits of his moral ideas.

This mature sense of limitation and unavoidable guilt is what gives the Westerner a "right" to his melancholy. It is true that the gangster's story is also a tragedy—in certain formal ways more clearly a tragedy than the Westerner's—but it is a romantic tragedy, based on a hero whose defeat springs with almost mechanical inevitability from the outrageous presumption of his demands: the gangster is *bound* to go on until he is killed. The Westerner is a more classical figure, self-contained and limited to begin with, seeking not to extend his dominion but only to assert his personal value, and his tragedy lies in the fact that even this circumscribed demand cannot be fully realized. Since the Westerner is not a murderer but (most of the time) a man of virtue, and since he is always prepared for defeat, he retains his inner invulnerability and his story need not end with his death (and usually does not); but what we finally respond to is not his victory but his defeat.

Up to a point, it is plain that the deeper seriousness of the good Western films comes from the introduction of a realism, both physical and psychological, that was missing with Tom Mix and William S. Hart. As lines of age have come into Gary Cooper's face since *The Virginian*, so the outlines of the Western movie in general have become less smooth, its background more drab. The sun still beats upon the town, but the camera is likely now to take advantage of this illumination to seek out more closely the shabbiness of buildings and furniture, the loose, worn hang of clothing, the wrinkles and dirt of the faces. Once it has been discovered that the true theme of the Western movie is not the freedom and expansiveness of frontier life, but its limitations, its material bareness, the pressures of obligation, then even the landscape itself ceases to be quite the arena of free movement it once was, but becomes instead a great empty waste, cutting down more often than it exaggerates the stature of the horseman who rides across it. We are more likely now to see the Westerner struggling against the obstacles of the physical world (as in the wonderful scenes on the desert and among the rocks in *The Last Posse*) than carelessly surmounting them. Even the horses, no longer the "friends" of man or the inspired chargers of knight-errantry, have lost much of the moral significance that once seemed to belong to them in their careering across the screen. It seems to me the horses grow tired and stumble more often than they did, and that we see them less frequently at the gallop.

In *The Gunfighter*, a remarkable film of a couple of years ago, the landscape has virtually disappeared. Most of the action takes place indoors, in a cheerless saloon where a tired "bad man" (Gregory Peck) contemplates the waste of his life, to be senselessly killed at the end by a vicious youngster setting off on the same futile path. The movie is done in cold, quiet tones of gray, and every object in it—faces, clothing, a table, the hero's heavy mustache—is given an air of uncompromising authenticity, suggesting those dim photographs of the nineteenth-century West in which Wyatt Earp, say, turns out to be a blank untidy figure posing awkwardly before some uninteresting building. This "authenticity," to be sure, is only aesthetic; the chief fact about nineteenth-century photographs, to my eyes at any rate, is how stonily they refuse to yield up the truth.

But that limitation is just what is needed: by preserving some hint of the rigidity of archaic photography (only in tone and décor, never in composition), *The Gunfighter* can permit us to feel that we are looking at a more "real" West than the one the movies have accustomed us to—harder, duller, less "romantic"—and yet without forcing us outside the boundaries which give the Western movie its validity.

We come upon the hero of *The Gunfighter* at the end of a career in which he has never upheld justice and order, and has been at times, apparently, an actual criminal; in this case, it is clear that the hero has been wrong and the woman who has rejected his way of life has been right. He is thus without any of the larger justifications, and knows himself a ruined man. There can be no question of his "redeeming" himself in any socially constructive way. He is too much the victim of his own reputation to turn marshal as one of his old friends has done, and he is not offered the sentimental solution of a chance to give up his life for some good end; the whole point is that he exists outside the field of social value. Indeed, if we were once allowed to see him in the days of his "success," he might become a figure like the gangster, for his career has been aggressively "anti-social" and the practical problem he faces is the gangster's problem: there will always be somebody trying to kill him. Yet it is obviously absurd to speak of him as "anti-social," not only because we do not see him acting as a criminal, but more fundamentally because we do not see his milieu as a society. Of course it has its "social problems" and a kind of static history: civilization is always just at the point of driving out the old freedom; there are women and children to represent the possibility of a settled life; and there is the marshal, a bad man turned good, determined to keep at least his area of jurisdiction at peace. But these elements are not, in fact, a part of the film's "realism," even though they come out of the real history of the West; they belong to the conventions of the form, to that accepted framework which makes the film possible in the first place, and they exist not to provide a standard by which the gunfighter can be judged, but only to set him off. The true "civilization" of the Western movie is always embodied in an individual, good or bad is more a matter of personal bearing than of social consequences, and the conflict of good and bad is a duel between two men. Deeply troubled and obviously doomed, the gunfighter is the Western hero still, perhaps all the more because his value must express itself entirely in his own being—in his presence, the way he holds our eyes—and in contradiction to the facts. No matter what he has done, he *looks* right, and he remains invulnerable because, without acknowledging anyone else's right to judge him, he has judged his own failure and has already assimilated it, understanding—as no one else understands except the

The aging Westerner—Gary Cooper (with Mary Brian) in *The Virginian* (1929) and (with Grace Kelly) in *High Noon* (1952). "As lines of age have come into Gary Cooper's face since *The Virginian*, so the outlines of the Western movie in general have become less smooth, its background more drab. . . . In *High Noon* we find Gary Cooper still the upholder of order that he was in *The Virginian*, but twenty-four years older, stooped, slower moving . . . the flesh sagging . . ." (WAR-SHOW, pages 441, 444).

marshal and the barroom girl—that he can do nothing but play out the drama of the gun fight again and again until the time comes when it will be he who gets killed. What "redeems" him is that he no longer believes in this drama and nevertheless will continue to play his role perfectly: the pattern is all.

The proper function of realism in the Western movie can only be to deepen the lines of that pattern. It is an art form for connoisseurs, where the spectator derives his pleasure from the appreciation of minor variations within the working out of a pre-established order. One does not want too much novelty: it comes as a shock, for instance, when the hero is made to operate without a gun, as has been done in several pictures (e.g., *Destry Rides Again*), and our uneasiness is allayed only when he is finally compelled to put his "pacifism" aside. If the hero can be shown to be troubled, complex, fallible, even eccentric, or the villain given some psychological taint or, better, some evocative physical mannerism, to shade the colors of his villainy, that is all to the good. Indeed, that kind of variation is absolutely necessary to keep the type from becoming sterile; we do not want to see the same movie over and over again, only the same form. But when the impulse toward realism is extended into a "reinterpretation" of the West as a developed society, drawing our eyes away from the hero if only to the extent of showing him as the one dominant figure in a complex social order, then the pattern is broken and the West itself begins to be uninteresting. If the "social problems" of the frontier are to be the movie's chief concern, there is no longer any point in reexamining these problems twenty times a year; they have been solved, and the people for whom they once were real are dead. Moreover, the hero himself, still the film's central figure, now tends to become its one unassimilable element, since he is the most "unreal."

The Ox-Bow Incident, by denying the convention of the lynching, presents us with a modern "social drama" and evokes a corresponding response, but in doing so it almost makes the Western setting irrelevant, a mere backdrop of beautiful scenery. (It is significant that *The Ox-Bow Incident* has no hero; a hero would have to stop the lynching or be killed in trying to stop it, and then the "problem" of lynching would no longer be central.) Even in *The Gunfighter* the women and children are a little too much in evidence, threatening constantly to become a real focus of concern instead of simply part of the given framework; and the young tough who kills the hero has too much the air of juvenile criminality: the hero himself could never have been like that, and the idea of a cycle being repeated therefore loses its sharpness. But the most striking example of the confusion created by a too conscientious "social" realism is in the celebrated *High Noon*.

In *High Noon* we find Gary Cooper still the upholder of order that he was in *The Virginian*, but twenty-four years older, stooped, slower moving, awkward, his face lined, the flesh sagging, a less beautiful and weaker figure, but with the suggestion of greater depth that belongs almost automatically to age. Like the hero of *The Gunfighter*, he no longer has to assert his character and is no longer interested in the drama of combat; it is hard to imagine that he might once have been so youthful as to say, "When you call me that—smile!" In fact, when we come upon him he is hanging up his guns and his marshal's badge in order to begin a new, peaceful life with his bride, who is a Quaker. But then the news comes that a man he had sent to prison has been pardoned and will get to town on the noon train; three friends of this man have come to wait for him at the station, and when the freed convict arrives the four of them will come to kill the marshal. He is thus trapped; the bride will object, the hero himself will waver much more than he would have done twenty-four years ago, but in the end he will play out the drama because it is what he "has to do." All this belongs to the established form (there is even the "fallen woman" who understands the marshal's position as his wife does not). Leaving aside the crudity of building up suspense by means of the clock, the actual Western drama of *High Noon* is well handled and forms a good companion piece to *The Virginian*, showing in both conception and technique the ways in which the Western movie has naturally developed.

But there is a second drama along with the first. As the marshal sets out to find deputies to help him deal with the four gunmen, we are taken through the various social strata of the town, each group in turn refusing its assistance out of cowardice, malice, irresponsibility, or venality. With this we are in the field of "social drama"—of a very low order, incidentally, altogether unconvincing and displaying a vulgar anti-populism that has marred some other movies of Stanley Kramer's. But the falsity of the "social drama" is less important than the fact that it does not belong in the movie to begin with. The technical problem was to make it necessary for the marshal to face his enemies alone; to explain *why* the other townspeople are not at his side is to raise a question which does not exist in the proper frame of the Western movie, where the hero is "naturally" alone and it is only necessary to contrive the physical absence of those who might be his allies, if any contrivance is needed at all. In addition, though the hero of *High Noon* proves himself a better man than all around him, the actual effect of this contrast is to lessen his stature: he becomes only a rejected man of virtue. In our final glimpse of him, as he rides away through the town where he has spent most of his life without really imposing himself on it, he is a pathetic rather than a tragic figure. And his departure has another meaning as well; the "social drama" has no place for him.

But there is also a different way of violating the Western form.

This is to yield entirely to its static quality as legend and to the "cinematic" temptations of its landscape, the horses, the quiet men. John Ford's famous *Stagecoach* (1938) had much of this unhappy preoccupation with style, and the same director's *My Darling Clementine* (1946), a soft and beautiful movie about Wyatt Earp, goes further along the same path, offering indeed a superficial accuracy of historical reconstruction, but so loving in execution as to destroy the outlines of the Western legend, assimilating it to the more sentimental legend of rural America and making the hero a more dangerous Mr. Deeds. (*Powder River*, a recent "routine" Western shamelessly copied from *My Darling Clementine*, is in most ways a better film; lacking the benefit of a serious director, it is necessarily more concerned with drama than with style.)

The highest expression of this aestheticizing tendency is in George Stevens' *Shane*, where the legend of the West is virtually reduced to its essentials and then fixed in the dreamy clarity of a fairly tale. There never was so broad and bare and lovely a landscape as Stevens puts before us, or so unimaginably comfortless a "town" as the little group of buildings on the prairie to which the settlers must come for their supplies and to buy a drink. The mere physical progress of the film, following the style of *A Place in the Sun*, is so deliberately graceful that everything seems to be happening at the bottom of a clear lake. The hero (Alan Ladd) is hardly a man at all, but something like the Spirit of the West, beautiful in fringed buckskins. He emerges mysteriously from the plains, breathing sweetness and a melancholy which is no longer simply the Westerner's natural response to experience but has taken on spirituality; and when he has accomplished his mission, meeting and destroying in the black figure of Jack Palance a Spirit of Evil just as metaphysical as his own embodiment of virtue, he fades away again into the more distant West, a man whose "day is over," leaving behind the wondering little boy who might have imagined the whole story. The choice of Alan Ladd to play the leading role is alone an indication of this film's tendency. Actors like Gary Cooper or Gregory Peck are in themselves, as material objects, "realistic," seeming to bear in their bodies and their faces mortality, limitation, the knowledge of good and evil. Ladd is a more "aesthetic" object, with some of the "universality" of a piece of sculpture; his special quality is in his physical smoothness and serenity, unworldly and yet not innocent, but suggesting that no experience can really touch him. Stevens has tried to freeze the Western myth once and for all in the immobility of Alan Ladd's countenance. If *Shane* were "right," and fully successful, it might be possible to say there was no point in making any more Western movies; once the hero is apotheosized, variation and development are closed off.

The lawyer from the East learns the law of the West: John Wayne and James Stewart in John Ford's *The Man Who Shot Liberty Valance* (1962). "Ford's . . . preoccupation with style" has the tendency "to destroy the outlines of the Western legend, assimilating it to the more sentimental legend of rural America and making the hero a more dangerous Mr. Deeds . . ." (WARSHOW, page 446).

Shane is not "right," but it is still true that the possibilities of fruitful variation in the Western movie are limited. The form can keep its freshness through endless repetitions only because of the special character of the film medium, where the physical difference between one object and another—above all, between one actor and another—is of such enormous importance, serving the function that is served by the variety of language in the perpetuation of literary types. In this sense, the "vocabulary" of films is much larger than that of literature and falls more readily into pleasing and significant arrangements. (That may explain why the middle levels of excellence are more easily reached in the movies than in literary forms, and perhaps also why the status of the movies as art is constantly being called into question.) But the advantage of this almost automatic particularity belongs to all films alike. Why does the Western movie especially have such a hold on our imagination?

Chiefly, I think, because it offers a serious orientation to the problem of violence such as can be found almost nowhere else in our culture. One of the well-known peculiarities of modern civilized opinion is its refusal to acknowledge the value of violence. This refusal is a virtue, but like many virtues it involves a certain willful blindness and it encourages hypocrisy. We train ourselves to be shocked or bored by cultural images of violence, and our very concept of heroism tends to be a passive one: we are less drawn to the brave young men who kill large numbers of our enemies than to the heroic prisoners who endure torture without capitulating. In art, though we may still be able to understand and participate in the values of the Iliad, a modern writer like Ernest Hemingway we find somewhat embarrassing: there is no doubt that he stirs us, but we cannot help recognizing also that he is a little childish. And in the criticism of popular culture, where the educated observer is usually under the illusion that he has nothing at stake, the presence of images of violence is often assumed to be in itself a sufficient ground for condemnation.

These attitudes, however, have not reduced the element of violence in our culture but, if anything, have helped to free it from moral control by letting it take on the aura of "emancipation." The celebration of acts of violence is left more and more to the irresponsible: on the higher cultural levels to writers like Céline, and lower down to Mickey Spillane or Horace McCoy, or to the comic books, television, and the movies. The gangster movie, with its numerous variations, belongs to this cultural "underground" which sets forth the attractions of violence in the face of all our higher social attitudes. It is a more "modern" genre than the Western, perhaps even more profound, because it confronts industrial society on its own ground—the city—and because, like much of our advanced art, it gains its effects by a gross insistence on its own narrow logic. But it is anti-social, resting on fantasies of irresponsible freedom. If we are brought finally to acquiesce in the denial of these fantasies, it is only because they have been shown to be dangerous, not because they have given way to a better vision of behavior.*

In war movies, to be sure, it is possible to present the uses of violence within a framework of responsibility. But there is the disadvantage that modern war is a co-operative enterprise; its violence is largely impersonal, and heroism belongs to the group more than to the individual. The hero of a war movie is most often simply a leader, and his superiority is likely to be expressed in a denial of the heroic: you are not supposed to be brave, you are supposed to get the job done and stay alive (this too, of course, is a kind of heroic posture, but a new—and "practical"—one). At its best, the war movie may represent a more civilized point of view than the Western, and if it were not continually marred by ideological sentimentality we might hope to find it developing into a higher form of drama. But it cannot supply the values we seek in the Western.

Those values are in the image of a single man who wears a gun on his thigh. The gun tells us that he lives in a world of violence, and even that he "believes in violence." But the drama is one of self-restraint: the moment of violence must come in its own time and according to its special laws, or else it is valueless. There is little cruelty in Western movies, and little sentimentality; our eyes are not focused on the sufferings of the defeated but on the deportment of the hero. Really, it is not violence at all which is the "point" of the Western movie, but a certain image of man, a style, which expresses itself most clearly in violence. Watch a child with his toy guns and you will see: what most interests him is not (as we so much fear) the fantasy of hurting others, but to work out how a man might look when he shoots or is shot. A hero is one who looks like a hero.

Whatever the limitations of such an idea in experience, it has always been valid in art, and has a special validity in an art where appearances are everything. The Western hero is necessarily an archaic figure; we do not really believe in him and would not have him step out of his rigidly conventionalized background. But his archaicism does not take away from his power; on the contrary, it adds to it by keeping him just a little beyond the reach both of com-

---

* I am not concerned here with the actual social consequences of gangster movies, though I suspect they could not have been so pernicious as they were thought to be. Some of the compromises introduced to avoid the supposed bad effects of the old gangster movies may be, if anything, more dangerous, for the sadistic violence that once belonged only to the gangster is now commonly enlisted on the side of the law and thus goes undefeated, allowing us (if we wish) to find in the movies a sort of "confirmation" of our fantasies.

mon sense and of absolutized emotion, the two usual impulses of our art. And he has, after all, his own kind of relevance. He is there to remind us of the possibility of style in an age which has put on itself the burden of pretending that style has no meaning, and, in the midst of our anxieties over the problem of violence, to suggest that even in killing or being killed we are not freed from the necessity of establishing satisfactory modes of behavior. Above all, the movies in which the Westerner plays out his role preserve for us the pleasures of a complete and self-contained drama—and one which still effortlessly crosses the boundaries which divide our culture—in a time when other, more consciously serious art forms are increasingly complex, uncertain, and ill-defined.

1954

SUSAN SONTAG
THE IMAGINATION
OF DISASTER

The typical science fiction film has a form as predictable as a Western, and is made up of elements which, to a practiced eye, are as classic as the saloon brawl, the blonde schoolteacher from the East, and the gun duel on the deserted main street.

One model scenario proceeds through five phases.

(1) The arrival of the thing. (Emergence of the monsters, landing of the alien spaceship, etc.) This is usually witnessed or suspected by just one person, a young scientist on a field trip. Nobody, neither his neighbors nor his colleagues, will believe him for some time. The hero is not married, but has a sympathetic though also incredulous girl friend.

(2) Confirmation of the hero's report by a host of witnesses to a great act of destruction. (If the invaders are beings from another planet, a fruitless attempt to parley with them and get them to leave peacefully.) The local police are summoned to deal with the situation and massacred.

(3) In the capital of the country, conferences between scientists and the military take place, with the hero lecturing before a chart, map, or blackboard. A national emergency is declared. Reports of further destruction. Authorities from other countries arrive in black limousines. All international tensions are suspended in view of the planetary emergency. This stage often includes a rapid montage of news broadcasts in various languages, a meeting at the UN, and more conferences between the military and the scientists. Plans are made for destroying the enemy.

(4) Further atrocities. At some point the hero's girl friend is in

grave danger. Massive counter-attacks by international forces, with brilliant displays of rocketry, rays, and other advanced weapons, are all unsuccessful. Enormous military casualties, usually by incineration. Cities are destroyed and/or evacuated. There is an obligatory scene here of panicked crowds stampeding along a highway or a big bridge, being waved on by numerous policemen who, if the film is Japanese, are immaculately white-gloved, preternaturally calm, and call out in dubbed English, "Keep moving. There is no need to be alarmed."

(5) More conferences, whose motif is: "They must be vulnerable to something." Throughout the hero has been working in his lab to this end. The final strategy, upon which all hopes depend, is drawn up; the ultimate weapon—often a super-powerful, as yet untested, nuclear device—is mounted. Countdown. Final repulse of the monster or invaders. Mutual congratulations, while the hero and girl friend embrace cheek to cheek and scan the skies sturdily. "But have we seen the last of them?"

The film I have just described should be in color and on a wide screen. Another typical scenario, which follows, is simpler and suited to black-and-white films with a lower budget. It has four phases.

(1) The hero (usually, but not always, a scientist) and his girl friend, or his wife and two children, are disporting themselves in some innocent ultra-normal middle-class surroundings—their house in a small town, or on vacation (camping, boating). Suddenly, someone starts behaving strangely; or some innocent form of vegetation becomes monstrously enlarged and ambulatory. If a character is pictured driving an automobile, something gruesome looms up in the middle of the road. If it is night, strange lights hurtle across the sky.

(2) After following the thing's tracks, or determining that It is radioactive, or poking around a huge crater—in short, conducting some sort of crude investigation—the hero tries to warn the local authorities, without effect; nobody believes anything is amiss. The hero knows better. If the thing is tangible, the house is elaborately barricaded. If the invading alien is an invisible parasite, a doctor or friend is called in, who is himself rather quickly killed or "taken possession of" by the thing.

(3) The advice of whoever further is consulted proves useless. Meanwhile, It continues to claim other victims in the town, which remains implausibly isolated from the rest of the world. General helplessness.

(4) One of two possibilities. Either the hero prepares to do battle alone, accidentally discovers the thing's one vulnerable point, and destroys it. Or, he somehow manages to get out of town and suc-

ceeds in laying his case before competent authorities. They, along the lines of the first script but abridged, deploy a complex technology which (after initial setbacks) finally prevails against the invaders.

Another version of the second script opens with the scientist-hero in his laboratory, which is located in the basement or on the grounds of his tasteful, prosperous house. Through his experiments, he unwittingly causes a frightful metamorphosis in some class of plants or animals which turn carnivorous and go on a rampage. Or else, his experiments have caused him to be injured (sometimes irrevocably) or "invaded" himself. Perhaps he has been experimenting with radiation, or has built a machine to communicate with beings from other planets or transport him to other places or times.

Another version of the first script involves the discovery of some fundamental alteration in the conditions of existence of our planet, brought about by nuclear testing, which will lead to the extinction in a few months of all human life. For example: the temperature of the earth is becoming too high or too low to support life, or the earth is cracking in two, or it is gradually being blanketed by lethal fallout.

A third script, somewhat but not altogether different from the first two, concerns a journey through space—to the moon, or some other planet. What the space-voyagers discover commonly is that the alien terrain is in a state of dire emergency, itself threatened by extra-planetary invaders or nearing extinction through the practice of nuclear warfare. The terminal dramas of the first and second scripts are played out there, to which is added the problem of getting away from the doomed and/or hostile planet and back to Earth.

I am aware, of course, that there are thousands of science fiction novels (their heyday was the late 1940s), not to mention the transcriptions of science fiction themes which, more and more, provide the principal subject-matter of comic books. But I propose to discuss science fiction films (the present period began in 1950 and continues, considerably abated, to this day) as an independent sub-genre, without reference to other media—and, most particularly, without reference to the novels from which, in many cases, they were adapted. For, while novel and film may share the same plot, the fundamental difference between the resources of the novel and the film makes them quite dissimilar.

Certainly, compared with the science fiction novels, their film counterparts have unique strengths, one of which is the immediate representation of the extraordinary: physical deformity and mutation, missile and rocket combat, toppling skyscrapers. The movies are, naturally, weak just where the science fiction novels (some of them) are strong—on science. But in place of an intellectual work-out, they can supply something the novels can never provide—sensuous elaboration. In the films it is by means of images and sounds, not words that have to be translated by the imagination, that one can participate in the fantasy of living through one's own death and more, the death of cities, the destruction of humanity itself.

Science fiction films are not about science. They are about disaster, which is one of the oldest subjects of art. In science fiction films disaster is rarely viewed intensively; it is always extensive. It is a matter of quantity and ingenuity. If you will, it is a question of scale. But the scale, particularly in the wide-screen color films (of which the ones by the Japanese director Inoshiro Honda and the American director George Pal are technically the most convincing and visually the most exciting), does raise the matter to another level.

Thus, the science fiction film (like that of a very different con-temporary genre, the Happening) is concerned with the aesthetics of destruction, with the peculiar beauties to be found in wreaking havoc, making a mess. And it is in the imagery of destruction that the core of a good science fiction film lies. Hence, the disadvantage of the cheap film—in which the monster appears or the rocket lands in a small dull-looking town. (Hollywood budget needs usually dictate that the town be in the Arizona or California desert. In *The Thing From Another World* [1951] the rather sleazy and con-fined set is supposed to be an encampment near the North Pole.) Still, good black-and-white science fiction films have been made. But a bigger budget, which usually means color, allows a much greater play back and forth among several model environments. There is the populous city. There is the lavish but ascetic interior of the spaceship—either the invaders' or ours—replete with stream-lined chromium fixtures and dials and machines whose complexity is indicated by the number of colored lights they flash and strange noises they emit. There is the laboratory crowded with formidable boxes and scientific apparatus. There is a comparatively old-fashioned-looking conference room, where the scientists unfurl charts to explain the desperate state of things to the military. And each of these standard locales or backgrounds is subject to two modalities—intact and destroyed. We may, if we are lucky, be treated to a panorama of melting tanks, flying bodies, crashing walls, awesome craters and fissures in the earth, plummeting spacecraft, colorful deadly rays; and to a symphony of screams, weird electronic signals, the noisiest military hardware going, and the leaden tones of the laconic denizens of alien planets and their subjugated earthlings.

Certain of the primitive gratifications of science fiction films—for instance, the depiction of urban disaster on a colossally magnified scale—are shared with other types of films. Visually there is little difference between mass havoc as represented in the old horror and monster films and what we find in science fiction films, except (again) scale. In the old monster films, the monster always headed for the great city, where he had to do a fair bit of rampaging, hurling busses off bridges, crumpling trains in his bare hands, toppling buildings, and so forth. The archetype is King Kong, in Schoedsack and Cooper's great film of 1933, running amok, first in the native village (trampling babies, a bit of footage excised from most prints), then in New York. This is really no different in spirit from the scene in Inoshiro Honda's *Rodan* (1957) in which two giant reptiles—with a wingspan of 500 feet and supersonic speeds—by flapping their wings whip up a cyclone that blows most of Tokyo to smithereens. Or the destruction of half of Japan by the gigantic robot with the great incinerating ray that shoots forth from his eyes, at the beginning of Honda's *The Mysterians* (1959). Or, the devastation by the rays from a fleet of flying saucers of New York, Paris, and Tokyo, in *Battle in Outer Space* (1960). Or, the inundation of New York in *When Worlds Collide* (1951). Or, the end of London in 1966 depicted in George Pal's *The Time Machine* (1960). Neither do these sequences differ in aesthetic intention from the destruction scenes in the big sword, sandal, and orgy color spectaculars set in Biblical and Roman times—the end of Sodom in Aldrich's *Sodom and Gomorrah*, of Gaza in De Mille's *Samson and Delilah*, of Rhodes in *The Colossus of Rhodes*, and of Rome in a dozen Nero movies. Griffith began it with the Babylon sequence in *Intolerance*, and to this day there is nothing like the thrill of watching all those expensive sets come tumbling down.

In other respects as well, the science fiction films of the 1950s take up familiar themes. The famous 1930s movie serials and comics of the adventures of Flash Gordon and Buck Rogers, as well as the more recent spate of comic book super-heroes with extraterrestrial origins (the most famous is Superman, a foundling from the planet Krypton, currently described as having been exploded by a nuclear blast), share motifs with more recent science fiction movies. But there is an important difference. The old science fiction films, and most of the comics, still have an essentially innocent relation to disaster. Mainly they offer new versions of the oldest romance of all—of the strong invulnerable hero with a mysterious lineage come to do battle on behalf of good and against evil. Recent science fiction films have a decided grimness, bolstered by their much greater degree of visual credibility, which contrasts strongly with the older films. Modern historical reality has greatly enlarged the imagination of disaster, and the protagonists—perhaps by the very nature of what is visited upon them—no longer seem wholly innocent.

The lure of such generalized disaster as a fantasy is that it releases one from normal obligations. The trump card of the end-of-the-world movies—like *The Day the Earth Caught Fire* (1962)—is that great scene with New York or London or Tokyo discovered empty, its entire population annihilated. Or, as in *The World, The Flesh, and The Devil* (1957), the whole movie can be devoted to the fantasy of occupying the deserted metropolis and starting all over again, a world Robinson Crusoe.

Another kind of satisfaction these films supply is extreme moral simplification—that is to say, a morally acceptable fantasy where one can give outlet to cruel or at least amoral feelings. In this respect, science fiction films partly overlap with horror films. This is the undeniable pleasure we derive from looking at freaks, beings excluded from the category of the human. The sense of superiority over the freak conjoined in varying proportions with the titillation of fear and aversion makes it possible for moral scruples to be lifted, for cruelty to be enjoyed. The same thing happens in science fiction films. In the figure of the monster from outer space, the freakish, the ugly, and the predatory all converge—and provide a fantasy target for righteous bellicosity to discharge itself, and for the aesthetic enjoyment of suffering and disaster. Science fiction films are one of the purest forms of spectacle; that is, we are rarely inside anyone's feelings. (An exception is Jack Arnold's *The Incredible Shrinking Man* [1957].) We are merely spectators; we watch.

But in science fiction films, unlike horror films, there is not much horror. Suspense, shocks, surprises are mostly abjured in favor of a steady, inexorable plot. Science fiction films invite a dispassionate, aesthetic view of destruction and violence—a *technological* view. Things, objects, machinery play a major role in these films. A greater range of ethical values is embodied in the décor of these films than in the people. Things, rather than the helpless humans, are the locus of values because we experience them, rather than people, as the sources of power. According to science fiction films, man is naked without his artifacts. *They* stand for different values, they are potent, they are what get destroyed, and they are the indispensable tools for the repulse of the alien invaders or the repair of the damaged environment.

The science fiction films are strongly moralistic. The standard message is the one about the proper, or humane, use of science, versus the mad, obsessional use of science. This message the science fiction films share in common with the classic horror films of the 1930s, like *Frankenstein, The Mummy, Island of Lost Souls,*

Dr. Jekyll and Mr. Hyde. (George Franju's brilliant *Les Yeux Sans Visage* [1959], called here *The Horror Chamber of Doctor Faustus*, is a more recent example.) In the horror films, we have the mad or obsessed or misguided scientist who pursues his experiments against good advice to the contrary, creates a monster or monsters, and is himself destroyed—often recognizing his folly himself, and dying in the successful effort to destroy his own creation. One science fiction equivalent of this is the scientist, usually a member of a team, who defects to the planetary invaders because "their" science is more advanced than "ours."

This is the case in *The Mysterians*, and, true to form, the renegade sees his error in the end, and from within the Mysterian spaceship destroys it and himself. In *This Island Earth* (1955), the inhabitants of the beleaguered planet Metaluna propose to conquer earth, but their project is foiled by a Metalunan scientist named Exeter who, having lived on earth a while and learned to love Mozart, cannot abide such viciousness. Exeter plunges his spaceship into the ocean after returning a glamorous pair (male and female) of American physicists to earth. Metaluna dies. In *The Fly* (1958), the hero, engrossed in his basement-laboratory experiments on a matter-transmitting machine, uses himself as a subject, exchanges head and one arm with a housefly which had accidentally gotten into the machine, becomes a monster, and with his last shred of human will destroys his laboratory and orders his wife to kill him. His discovery, for the good of mankind, is lost.

Being a clearly labeled species of intellectual, scientists in science fiction films are always liable to crack up or go off the deep end. In *Conquest of Space* (1955), the scientist-commander of an international expedition to Mars suddenly acquires scruples about the blasphemy involved in the undertaking, and begins reading the Bible mid-journey instead of attending to his duties. The commander's son, who is his junior officer and always addresses his father as "General," is forced to kill the old man when he tries to prevent the ship from landing on Mars. In this film, both sides of the ambivalence toward scientists are given voice. Generally, for a scientific enterprise to be treated entirely sympathetically in these films, it needs the certificate of utility. Science, viewed without ambivalence, means an efficacious response to danger. Disinterested intellectual curiosity rarely appears in any form other than caricature, as a maniacal dementia that cuts one off from normal human relations. But this suspicion is usually directed at the scientist rather than his work. The creative scientist may become a martyr to his own discovery, through an accident or by pushing things too far. But the implication remains that other men, less imaginative—in short, technicians—could have administered the same discovery better and more safely. The most ingrained contemporary mistrust of the intellect is visited, in these movies, upon the scientist-as-intellectual.

The message that the scientist is one who releases forces which, if not controlled for good, could destroy man himself seems innocuous enough. One of the oldest images of the scientist is Shakespeare's Prospero, the overdetached scholar forcibly retired from society to a desert island, only partly in control of the magic forces in which he dabbles. Equally classic is the figure of the scientist as satanist (*Doctor Faustus*, and stories of Poe and Hawthorne). Science is magic, and man has always known that there is black magic as well as white. But it is not enough to remark that contemporary attitudes — as reflected in science fiction films — remain ambivalent, that the scientist is treated as both satanist and savior. The proportions have changed, because of the new context in which the old admiration and fear of the scientist are located. For his sphere of influence is no longer local, himself or his immediate community. It is planetary, cosmic.

One gets the feeling, particularly in the Japanese films but not only there, that a mass trauma exists over the use of nuclear weapons and the possibility of future nuclear wars. Most of the science fiction films bear witness to this trauma, and, in a way, attempt to exorcise it.

The accidental awakening of the super-destructive monster who has slept in the earth since prehistory is, often, an obvious metaphor for the Bomb. But there are many explicit references as well. In *The Mysterians*, a probe ship from the planet Mysteroid has landed on earth, near Tokyo. Nuclear warfare having been practiced on Mysteroid for centuries (their civilization is "more advanced than ours"), ninety percent of those now born on the planet have to be destroyed at birth, because of defects caused by the huge amounts of Strontium 90 in their diet. The Mysterians have come to earth to marry earth women, and possibly to take over our relatively uncontaminated planet. . . . In *The Incredible Shrinking Man*, the John Doe hero is the victim of a gust of radiation which blows over the water, while he is out boating with his wife; the radiation causes him to grow smaller and smaller, until at the end of the movie he steps through the fine mesh of a window screen to become "the infinitely small." . . . In *Rodan*, a horde of monstrous carnivorous prehistoric insects, and finally a pair of giant flying reptiles (the prehistoric Archeopteryx), are hatched from dormant eggs in the depths of a mine shaft by the impact of nuclear test explosions, and go on to destroy a good part of the world before they are felled by the molten lava of a volcanic eruption. . . . In the English film, *The Day the Earth Caught Fire*, two simultaneous hydrogen bomb tests by the United States and Russia change by

11 degrees the tilt of the earth on its axis and alter the earth's orbit so that it begins to approach the sun.

Radiation casualties—ultimately, the conception of the whole world as a casualty of nuclear testing and nuclear warfare—is the most ominous of all the notions with which science fiction films deal. Universes become expendable. Worlds become contaminated, burnt out, exhausted, obsolete. In *Rocketship X-M* (1950) explorers from the earth land on Mars, where they learn that atomic warfare has destroyed Martian civilization. In George Pal's *The War of the Worlds* (1953), reddish spindly alligator-skinned creatures from Mars invade the earth because their planet is becoming too cold to be inhabitable. In *This Island Earth*, also American, the planet Metaluna, whose population has long ago been driven underground by warfare, is dying under the missile attacks of an enemy planet. Stocks of uranium, which power the force field shielding Metaluna, have been used up; and an unsuccessful expedition is sent to earth to enlist earth scientists to devise new sources for nuclear power. In Joseph Losey's *The Damned* (1961), nine icy-cold radioactive children are being reared by a fanatical scientist in a dark cave on the English coast to be the only survivors of the inevitable nuclear Armageddon.

There is a vast amount of wishful thinking in science fiction films, some of it touching, some of it depressing. Again and again, one detects the hunger for a "good war," which poses no moral problems, admits of no moral qualifications. The imagery of science fiction films will satisfy the most bellicose addict of war films, for a lot of the satisfactions of war films pass, untransformed, into science fiction films. Examples: the dogfights between earth "fighter rockets" and alien spacecraft in the *Battle in Outer Space* (1960); the escalating firepower in the successive assaults upon the invaders in *The Mysterians*, which Dan Talbot correctly described as a nonstop holocaust; the spectacular bombardment of the underground fortress of Metaluna in *This Island Earth*.

Yet at the same time the bellicosity of science fiction films is neatly channeled into the yearning for peace, or for at least peaceful coexistence. Some scientist generally takes sententious note of the fact that it took the planetary invasion to make the warring nations of the earth come to their senses and suspend their own conflicts. One of the main themes of many science fiction films— the color ones usually, because they have the budget and resources to develop the military spectacle—is this UN fantasy, a fantasy of united warfare. (The same wishful UN theme cropped up in a recent spectacular which is not science fiction, *Fifty-Five Days in Peking* [1963]. There, topically enough, the Chinese, the Boxers, play the role of Martian invaders who unite the earthmen, in this case the

United States, England, Russia, France, Germany, Italy, and Japan.) A great enough disaster cancels all enmities and calls upon the utmost concentration of earth resources.

Science—technology—is conceived of as the great unifier. Thus the science fiction films also project a Utopian fantasy. In the classic models of Utopian thinking—Plato's Republic, Campanella's City of the Sun, More's Utopia, Swift's land of the Houyhnhnms, Voltaire's Eldorado—society had worked out a perfect consensus. In these societies reasonableness had achieved an unbreakable supremacy over the emotions. Since no disagreement or social conflict was intellectually plausible, none was possible. As in Melville's *Typee*, "they all think the same." The universal rule of reason meant universal agreement. It is interesting, too, that societies in which reason was pictured as totally ascendant were also traditionally pictured as having an ascetic or materially frugal and economically simple mode of life. But in the Utopian world community projected by science fiction films, totally pacified and ruled by scientific consensus, the demand for simplicity of material existence would be absurd.

Yet alongside the hopeful fantasy of moral simplification and international unity embodied in the science fiction films lurk the deepest anxieties about contemporary existence. I don't mean only the very real trauma of the Bomb—that it has been used, that there are enough now to kill everyone on earth many times over, that those new bombs may very well be used. Besides these new anxieties about physical disaster, the prospect of universal mutilation and even annihilation, the science fiction films reflect powerful anxieties about the condition of the individual psyche.

For science fiction films may also be described as a popular mythology for the contemporary *negative* imagination about the impersonal. The other-world creatures that seek to take "us" over are an "it," not a "they." The planetary invaders are usually zombie-like. Their movements are either cool, mechanical, or lumbering, blobby. But it amounts to the same thing. If they are non-human in form, they proceed with an absolutely regular, unalterable movement (unalterable save by destruction). If they are human in form—dressed in space suits, etc.—then they obey the most rigid military discipline, and display no personal characteristics whatsoever. And it is this regime of emotionlessness, of impersonality, of regimentation, which they will impose on the earth if they are successful. "No more love, no more beauty, no more pain," boasts a converted earthling in *The Invasion of the Body Snatchers* (1956). The half-earthling, half-alien children in *The Children of the Damned* (1960) are absolutely emotionless, move as a group and understand each others' thoughts, and are all prodigious intellects.

They are the wave of the future, man in his next stage of development.

These alien invaders practice a crime which is worse than murder. They do not simply kill the person. They obliterate him. In *The War of the Worlds*, the ray which issues from the rocket ship disintegrates all persons and objects in its path, leaving no trace of them but a light ash. In Honda's *The H-Man* (1959), the creeping blob melts all flesh with which it comes in contact. If the blob, which looks like a huge hunk of red Jello and can crawl across floors and up and down walls, so much as touches your bare foot, all that is left of you is a heap of clothes on the floor. (A more articulated, size-multiplying blob is the villain in the English film *The Creeping Unknown* [1956].) In another version of this fantasy, the body is preserved but the person is entirely reconstituted as the automatized servant or agent of the alien powers. This is, of course, the vampire fantasy in new dress. The person is really dead, but he doesn't know it. He is "undead," he has become an "unperson." It happens to a whole California town in *The Invasion of the Body Snatchers*, to several earth scientists in *This Island Earth*, and to assorted innocents in *It Came From Outer Space, Attack of the Puppet People* (1958), and *The Brain Eaters* (1958). As the victim always backs away from the vampire's horrifying embrace, so in science fiction films the person always fights being "taken over"; he wants to retain his humanity. But once the deed has been done, the victim is eminently satisfied with his condition. He has not been converted from human amiability to monstrous "animal" bloodlust (a metaphoric exaggeration of sexual desire), as in the old vampire fantasy. No, he has simply become far more efficient—the very model of technocratic man, purged of emotions, volitionless, tranquil, obedient to all orders. (The dark secret behind human nature used to be the upsurge of the animal—as in *King Kong*. The threat to man, his availability to dehumanization, lay in his own animality. Now the danger is understood as residing in man's ability to be turned into a machine.)

The rule, of course, is that this horrible and irremediable form of murder can strike anyone in the film except the hero. The hero and his family, while greatly threatened, always escape this fate and by the end of the film the invaders have been repulsed or destroyed. I know of only one exception, *The Day That Mars Invaded Earth* (1963), in which after all the standard struggles the scientist-hero, his wife, and their two children are "taken over" by the alien invaders—and that's that. (The last minutes of the film show them being incinerated by the Martians' rays and their ash silhouettes flushed down their empty swimming pool, while their simulacra drive off in the family car.) Another variant but upbeat switch on the rule occurs in *The Creation of the Humanoids* (1964), where

Attack of the Space Ship Invaders in *The War of the Worlds* (1953). "In *The War of the Worlds*, the ray which issues from the rocket ship disintegrates all persons and objects in its path, leaving no trace of them but a light ash" (SONTAG, page 461).

the hero discovers at the end of the film that he, too, has been turned into a metal robot, complete with highly efficient and virtually indestructible mechanical insides, although he didn't know it and detected no difference in himself. He learns, however, that he will shortly be upgraded into a "humanoid" having all the properties of a real man.

Of all the standard motifs of science fiction films, this theme of dehumanization is perhaps the most fascinating. For, as I have indicated, it is scarcely a black-and-white situation, as in the old vampire films. The attitude of the science fiction films toward depersonalization is mixed. On the one hand, they deplore it as the ultimate horror. On the other hand, certain characteristics of the dehumanized invaders, modulated and disguised—such as the ascendancy of reason over feelings, the idealization of teamwork and the consensus-creating activities of science, a marked degree of moral simplification—are precisely traits of the savior-scientist. It is interesting that when the scientist in these films is treated negatively, it is usually done through the portrayal of an individual scientist who holes up in his laboratory and neglects his fiancée or his loving wife and children, obsessed by his daring and dangerous experiments. The scientist as a loyal member of a team, and therefore considerably less individualized, is treated quite respectfully.

There is absolutely no social criticism, of even the most implicit kind, in science fiction films. No criticism, for example, of the conditions of our society which create the impersonality and dehumanization which science fiction fantasies displace onto the influence of an alien It. Also, the notion of science as a social activity, interlocking with social and political interests, is unacknowledged. Science is simply either adventure (for good or evil) or a technical response to danger. And, typically, when the fear of science is paramount—when science is conceived of as black magic rather than white—the evil has no attribution beyond that of the perverse will of an individual scientist. In science fiction films the antithesis of black magic and white is drawn as a split between technology, which is beneficent, and the errant individual will of a lone intellectual.

Thus, science fiction films can be looked at as thematically central allegory, replete with standard modern attitudes. The theme of depersonalization (being "taken over") which I have been talking about is a new allegory reflecting the age-old awareness of man that, sane, he is always perilously close to insanity and unreason. But there is something more here than just a recent, popular image which expresses man's perennial, but largely unconscious, anxiety about his sanity. The image derives most of its power from a supplementary and historical anxiety, also not experienced *consciously* by most people, about the depersonalizing conditions of modern urban life. Similarly, it is not enough to note that science fiction allegories are one of the new myths about—that is, one of the ways of accommodating to and negating—the perennial human anxiety about death. (Myths of heaven and hell, and of ghosts, had the same function.) For, again, there is a historically specifiable twist which intensifies the anxiety. I mean, the trauma suffered by everyone in the middle of the 20th century when it became clear that, from now on to the end of human history, every person would spend his individual life under the threat not only of individual death, which is certain, but of something almost insupportable psychologically—collective incineration and extinction which could come at any time, virtually without warning.

From a psychological point of view, the imagination of disaster does not greatly differ from one period in history to another. But from a political and moral point of view, it does. The expectation of the apocalypse may be the occasion for a radical disaffiliation from society, as when thousands of Eastern European Jews in the 17th century, hearing that Sabbatai Zevi had been proclaimed the Messiah and that the end of the world was imminent, gave up their homes and businesses and began the trek to Palestine. But people take the news of their doom in diverse ways. It is reported that in 1945 the populace of Berlin received without great agitation the news that Hitler had decided to kill them all, before the Allies arrived, because they had not been worthy enough to win the war. We are, alas, more in the position of the Berliners of 1945 than of the Jews of 17th century Eastern Europe; and our response is closer to theirs, too. What I am suggesting is that the imagery of disaster in science fiction is above all the emblem of an *inadequate response*. I don't mean to bear down on the films for this. They themselves are only a sampling, stripped of sophistication, of the inadequacy of most people's response to the unassimilable terrors that infect their consciousness. The interest of the films, aside from their considerable amount of cinematic charm, consists in this intersection between a naïve and largely debased commercial art product and the most profound dilemmas of the contemporary situation.

Ours is indeed an age of extremity. For we live under continual threat of two equally fearful, but seemingly opposed, destinies: unremitting banality and inconceivable terror. It is fantasy, served out in large rations by the popular arts, which allows most people to cope with these twin specters. For one job that fantasy can do is to lift us out of the unbearably humdrum and to distract us from terrors—real or anticipated—by an escape into exotic, dangerous situations which have last-minute happy endings. But another of the things that fantasy can do is to normalize what is psychologically unbearable, thereby inuring us to it. In one case, fantasy beautifies the world. In the other, it neutralizes it.

The fantasy in science fiction films does both jobs. The films reflect world-wide anxieties, and they serve to allay them. They inculcate a strange apathy concerning the processes of radiation, contamination, and destruction which I for one find haunting and depressing. The naïve level of the films neatly tempers the sense of otherness, of alien-ness, with the grossly familiar. In particular, the dialogue of most science fiction films, which is of a monumental but often touching banality, makes them wonderfully, unintentionally funny. Lines like "Come quickly, there's a monster in my bathtub," "We must do something about this," "Wait, Professor. There's someone on the telephone," "But that's incredible," and the old American stand-by, "I hope it works!" are hilarious in the context of picturesque and deafening holocaust. Yet the films also contain something that is painful and in deadly earnest.

There is a sense in which all these movies are in complicity with the abhorrent. They neutralize it, as I have said. It is no more, perhaps, than the way all art draws its audience into a circle of complicity with the thing represented. But in these films we have to do with things which are (quite literally) unthinkable. Here, "thinking about the unthinkable"—not in the way of Herman Kahn, as a subject for calculation, but as a subject for fantasy—becomes, however inadvertently, itself a somewhat questionable act from a moral point of view. The films perpetuate clichés about identity, volition, power, knowledge, happiness, social consensus, guilt, responsibility which are, to say the least, not serviceable in our present extremity. But collective nightmares cannot be banished by demonstrating that they are, intellectually and morally, fallacious. This nightmare—the one reflected, in various registers, in the science fiction films—is too close to our reality.

1965

BRUCE KAWIN
THE MUMMY'S POOL

Helen: Have I been asleep? I had—strange dreams. Dreams of ancient Egypt, I think. There was someone like you in them.
Ardeth Bey: My pool is sometimes troubled. One sees strange fantasies in the water. But they pass, like dreams.

                                                            The Mummy

Sir John Talbot: All astronomers are amateurs. When it comes to the heavens, there's only one professional.

                                                            The Wolf Man

Karl Freund's *The Mummy* (1932), George Waggner's *The Wolf Man* (1941), Reginald LeBorg's *The Mummy's Ghost* (1944), and Peter Weir's *The Last Wave* (1978) each point to some very interesting connections among horror films, nightmares, and prophetic dreams—connections that might help explain what horror films do and why they remain interesting to viewers who probably stopped believing in Dracula along with Santa Claus. To clarify some of these points—such as the relations between displacement and reflexivity, prophecy and the attractions of being the "first victim," catharsis and the Land of the Dead, reincarnation and repression—it is necessary to define the elementary ways in which films are like dreams and the broad characteristics of horror film as a genre.

Watching a film and having a dream are both passive and

active events. The dreamer/audience is physically cushioned in a darkened room, most of his movements restricted to slight shifts of position in a bed or chair, and mentally in various degrees of alertness, watching a visual process that often tells a story and often masks/presents some type of thought. In both cases the eyes move and the mind exercises creative attention. The dreamer might be considered more creative since the dream manifests his own thought processes, but the role of the film audience is also an active one since the viewer creates his own experience of the work: we all have different interpretations of *Persona* not because the film is difficult, but because we interact with the signs in the generation of meaning and because our attention is selective. Although the dreamer is completely responsible for the dream, he usually avoids this awareness and casts himself in the role of participant or spectator; although the filmmakers are responsible for the movie, the viewer decides which film to attend and so chooses the general content of his experience. Thus dreamer and filmgoer approach a middle ground of pseudo-responsibility for what is watched. Both dreams and films include verbal and visual information but are effectively dominated by the limits of pictorialization. Film is primarily a visual medium, and the stories and symbols in dreams are subject not only to condensation, displacement, and secondary revision, but also to translation into pictorial and concrete representability, according to Freud.[1] In *Mindscreen*[2] I have attempted to show how the visual fields of film and dream are analogous, particularly in the ways each field indicates the "offscreen" activity of a consciousness. In a film this "narrating" mind may be that of the artist, of a character within the fiction, or of the work's self-awareness; "mindscreen" generally refers to the visual and sometimes aural field of such a consciousness, as opposed for instance to "subjective camera," which imitates the visual field of the physical eye of a character. A dream is the mindscreen of its dreamer, as the color section of *The Wizard of Oz* is the mindscreen of Dorothy and as *Persona* is the mindscreen of its own systemic self-consciousness. A film like Wise's *The Curse of the Cat People* plays with the question of whether the ghost is "real" or an aspect of the mindscreen of the child.

One goes to a horror film in order to have a nightmare — not

[1] Sigmund Freud, *The Interpretation of Dreams*, in *The Basic Writings of Sigmund Freud*, ed. A. A. Brill (N.Y.: Random House/Modern Library, 1938), pp. 319–68.
[2] Bruce Kawin, *Mindscreen: Bergman, Godard, and First-Person Film* (Princeton: Princeton Univ. Press, 1978).

simply a frightening dream, but a dream whose undercurrent of anxiety both presents and masks the desire to fulfill and be punished for certain conventionally unacceptable impulses. This may be a matter of unconscious wish fulfillment, following Freud; of confronting a hidden evil in the culture, as in *Alien* or *The Stepford Wives;* or of voyaging through the Land of the Dead and indulging a nostalgia for ritual, as we shall see when we turn to Frazer. Horror films function as nightmares for the individual viewer, as diagnostic eruptions for repressive societies, and as exorcistic or transcendent pagan rituals for supposedly post-pagan cultures. They can be analyzed in all these ways because they represent a unique juncture of personal, social, and mythic structure and because each of these structures has a conscious/official and an unconscious/repressed dualism, whose dialectic finds expression in the act of masking.

The clearest way to define the horror film genre is to compare it with that of science fiction, since the two are regularly confused with each other and often draw on the same materials (*Alien,* for instance, is a monster movie set in outer space). In what may seem like an unnecessarily long digression. I would like to show how horror and science fiction tend to present radically opposite interpretations of what may look like comparable situations, because the closed-system world view of horror may be a key to its personal and societal dreamwork.

Genres are determined not by plot-elements so much as of attitudes toward plot-elements. Horror and science fiction are different because of their attitudes toward curiosity and the openness of systems, and comparable in that both tend to organize themselves around some confrontation between an unknown and a would-be knower. To lay to rest the usual assumption that a film is science fiction if it has scientists in it and horror if it has monsters, let us look quickly at a science fiction film, *The Day the earth Stood Still,* and a horror film, *The Thing,* both of which are 1951 Cold War American studio films about flying saucers with highly intelligent pilots.

The Day the Earth Stood Still (directed by Robert Wise) is the story of a spaceman, Klaatu (Michael Rennie), who sets down his flying saucer in Washington, D.C. with the intention of putting Earth on notice: anything resembling nuclear violence will be punished by the obliteration of the planet, courtesy of a race of interstellar robot police. The spaceman has three forces to contend with: the army, which wants to destroy him; the scientists, who are willing to listen to him; and a woman (Patricia Neal) who understands and helps him. The central scientist (Sam Jaffe) is a kooky but open-minded and serious figure. Although it is suggested that earthlings understand violence better than most kinds of communication, they do respond to a nonviolent demonstration of Klaatu's power, and he does manage to deliver his message—perhaps at the expense of his life. The film's bias is in favor of open-minded communication, personal integrity, nonviolence, science, and friendship. The major villain (Hugh Marlowe) is a man who values personal fame and power more than integrity and love; he is willing to turn Klaatu over to the army, which shoots first and asks questions later—even if it means losing Neal, his fiancee.

The Thing from Another World (directed by Christian Nyby with considerable assistance from the producer, Howard Hawks) is deliberately formulaic, and so it is particularly valuable as a key to the genre. It is the story of a team of military men sent to an Arctic station at the request of its scientists, to investigate what turns out to be the crash of a flying saucer. The saucer's pilot (James Arness) is a blood-sucking vegetable that is described as intelligent but spends most of its time yelling and killing and leaving evidence of plans for conquest. The minor villain is a scientist (Robert Corthwaite) who wants to communicate with the Thing rather than destroy it and who admires the alien race for its lack of sexual emotion. The Thing, however, has no interest in the scientist; and the human community (from which the scientist wishes to exclude himself), led by an efficient, hard-headed, and sexually active Captain (Kenneth Tobey), manages to electrocute the "super carrot." The film's bias is in favor of that friendly, witty, sexy, and professionally effective—Hawksian—human community, and opposed to the dark forces that lurk outside (the Thing as *Beowulf's* Grendel). The film also opposes the lack of a balanced professionalism (the scientist who becomes indifferent to the human community and whose professionalism approaches the fanatical, as opposed to the effective Captain and the klutzy but less seriously flawed reporter), and what was meant in that paranoid time by the term Communism (we are all one big vegetable or zombie with each cell equally conscious).

This is how the oppositions between these two movies stack up:

1. *Army vs. Scientists.* In both films the army and the scientists are in conflict with each other. The army sees the alien as a threatening invader to be defended against and, if necessary or possible, destroyed. The scientists see the alien as a visitor with superior knowledge, to be learned from and, if possible, joined. In *The Thing* the army is right and the scientist is an obsessive visionary who gets in the way of what obviously

needs to be done. In *The Day* the scientists are right and the army is an impulsive force that is almost responsible for the end of the world (hardly a far-fetched perspective).

2. *Violence vs. Intelligence.* The Thing is nonverbal and destructive; Klaatu is articulate and would prefer to be nonviolent. The army, which meets violence with violence, is correct in *The Thing* and wrong in *The Day* because of the nature of the alien; but what I am suggesting here is that the alien has its nature because of each genre's implicit attitude toward the unknown. The curious scientist is a positive force in *The Day* and a negative force in *The Thing*, for the same reasons.

3. *Closing vs. Opening.* Both horror and science fiction open our sense of the possible (mummies can live, men can turn into wolves, Martians can visit) especially in terms of community (the Creature walks among us). Most horror films are oriented toward the restoration of the status quo rather than toward any permanent opening. *The Day* is about man's opportunity to join an interstellar political system; it opens the community's boundaries and leaves them open. *The Thing* is about the expulsion of an intruder and ends with a warning to "watch the skies" in case more monsters show up; in other words, the community is opened against its will and attempts to reclose. What the horrified community has generally learned from the opening is to be on guard and that chaos can be repressed.

4. *Inhuman vs. Human,* Science fiction is open to the potential value of the inhuman; one can learn from it, take a trip with it (*Close Encounters*), include it in a larger sense of what is. Horror is fascinated by transmutations between human and inhuman (wolfmen, etc.), but the inhuman characteristics decisively mandate destruction. This can be rephrased as Uncivilized vs. Civilized or as Id vs. Superego, suggesting the way a horror film allows forbidden desire to find masked expression before it is destroyed by more decisive repression. The Id attempts to includes itself in the wholeness of the dream-picture but is perceived as a threat and expelled from the community of what is human.

It is not too heavy a borrowing from *The Republic* to observe that the Gestalts of an artwork, a person, and a society are comparable. *The Wolf Man* expresses and exorcises the Id-force of uncontrolled aggression in its own system (the werewolf), in Larry Talbot (his werewolf phases), and in the community (the destabilizing forces of rape, murder, gypsy liminality, and aristocratic privilege—Talbot often behaves as if he had *droit du seigneur* when courting the engaged Gwen) In *The Invasion of the Body Snatchers* the egoless emotionless attitude of the "pods" is as undesirable in Becky as it is in the culture.

5. *Communication vs. Silence.* This links most of the above. The Thing doesn't talk; Klaatu does. (Or: Romero's Living Dead are completely nonverbal, while the climax of *Close Encounters* is an exchange of languages.) What one can talk with, one can generally deal with. Communication is vital in *The Day,* absurd in *The Thing.* The opened community can be curious about and learn from the outsiders, while the closed community talks only among itself. Horror emphasizes the dread of knowing, the danger of curiosity, while science fiction emphasizes the danger and irresponsibility of the closed mind. Science fiction appeals to consciousness, horror to the unconscious.

In Gestalt terms, any dream (or fantasy or artwork) involves the projection of aspects of the self and the arrangement or interplay of those projections in a structure that corresponds to the whole self; the therapist's task is to help the dreamer re-own the projections. If I dream that I am walking in the desert and see a flower, a therapist might have me speak in the voice of the flower and then in the voice of the desert, to help me realize that they are as much myself as that image of the wandering observer and that the whole scene is a display of my wholeness. In this sense the science fiction Gestalt features a split-off creative hope that, once re-owned, can lead to an open, growthful, positive system. The horror Gestalt features a split-off destructive element that will be feared until it is re-owned, at which point the system can become stable. In most horror films, however, the negative projection is not re owned but rejected and repressed: the Blob is frozen but can never be killed, the Mummy is burned but reappears in sequel, and in *Alien* the monster is destroyed but the corporate evil survives. Repression solves nothing, but (coupled with the momentary wish-fulfillment) gives a temporary sense of relief. Henry Frankenstein (leaving the novel out of this) may attempt to reverse the Original Sin and re-enter the community by acquiescing to the horror cliché that "there are things we are not meant to know" — except that his initial hubristic motive was not just to figure out eternity but to create life without the help of any Eve (he wants to "be as God" in a double sense) and when in the sequel he manages to get married it is a sure bet that some Dr. Praetorius will "force" him into an all-male effort to create a bride for the monster, Henry's split-off rejected/rejecting child-self.

In the dreamworld of movies, horror films come under two headings: in the Freudian sense, they are anxiety dreams or nightmares; anthropologically they express a nostaligia for contact with the spirit world. In his *Introductory Lectures on Psycho-Analysis*, Freud observed that "the attitude of the dreamer towards his wishes is a peculiar one; he rejects them, censors them, in short, he will have none of them. Their fulfillment, then, can afford him no pleasure, rather the opposite, and here experience shows that this 'opposite,' which has still to be explained, takes the form of *anxiety*." [3]

In *The Wolf Man* this process is extremely clear. Larry Talbot (Lon Chaney Jr.) is a big Americanized engineer who is being groomed by his short and controlling father, Sir John (Claude Rains) to take over Talbot castle and the role of village Baron, Larry meets Gwen (Evelyn Ankers) and comes on like a "wolf," despite her being engaged to his father's gamekeeper (a model of controlled animal aggression, who is suited for the civilized institution of marriage). After he is bitten by a gypsy werewolf (Bela Lugosi) Larry splits into a wolf and a man. The man experiences pain and anxiety at the prospect of acting out his unconscious desires; at the climax the wolf begins to attack Gwen and then abandons her for more pressing game, Sir John. Larry insures he will be punished for this, for although he has given Gwen his own protective medallion, he has given his father the silver-headed wolf cane that can kill him. *The Wolf Man* is a transparently Oedipal nightmare, a full playing out of castration anxiety, and a clear example of how some horror films are analogous to one kind of dream. Although it can be said that *The Wolf Man* is the dream of the screenwriter (Curt Siodmak, who went on to dream the similar *Bride of the Gorilla*), it could also be analyzed as Larry's dramatized dream-world — or, taking a cue from *Beauty and the Beast*, as Gwen's projection of the two sides of her sexuality, werewolf andgamekeeper; but it is also obviously the dream of the audience, which has decided to let its own unconscious desires find as-if expression, with the scariness of the film carrying the dream's anxiety quotient and the killing of the beast appearing to vindicate repression.

There is yet another side to all this. Sir John (a prize-winning researcher) believes in God, the universal "professional"; his religious sense is conventionally patriarchal, and Larry's Oedipal rebellion includes his participation in an erupting/repressed religion, gypsy superstition. (Recall the scene where Larry is too upset to join his father in church.) Whereas Sir John believes that all this is in Larry's mind and that werewolfery can be explained as a split between "the good and

[3] *The Interpretation of Dreams*, p. 520n.

evil in a man's soul," with the evil finding expression in a
fantasy of animality, the film attempts to prove him wrong. Sir
John finds that all this is *not* a dream, that the wolf he has
killed is his son. In this sense the horror film asserts the survival of "paganism" (the gypsies are right) and the inadequacy
of science ("all astronomers are amateurs," a theme recognizable in *The Thing*)—a return to magic. Judaeo-Christianity represses, in this sense, the mystical unconscious that the hor-
ror-system allows to be expressed. (All this opens the
possibility of a Jungian reading as well.) We may recall Van
Helsing's pronouncement in *Dracula* that, "the strength of the
vampire is that people will *not* believe in him."

In *The Golden Bough* Frazer observed that dreams are often
considered instances of contact with the spirits of the dead
and that such dreams may serve as keys to the future and
(through the symbolism of mistletoe, placed under pillows to
induce prophetic dreams[4] and, as "the golden bough," an illuminating open-sesame) to the Underworld. Freud too mentions the ancient concept of "true and valuable dreams which
were sent to the dreamer as warnings, or to foretell future
events,"[5] and there is a considerable surviving literature of
dreaming as genuine out-of-body travel, usually on the astral
plane.[6] A medieval poem like *Pearl* (in which the poet mourns
the death of his daughter and then has a dream of her full-
grown in heaven) can be Electra-cuted by any number of
Freudian readings, but its appeal and point are clearly in the
way it presents itself as a genuine visionary experience.

Horror films appeal to this kind of dreaming through the
figures of seer and "first victim," and thus to the audience's
desire to glimpse the truth, no matter how horrible. (A Freudian might translate this into the desire to learn about sex and
be punished for it, which is often a legitimate reading.) In
science fiction the visionary is usually rewarded, in horror,
punished. Peter Weir's *The Last Wave* is the story of an Aus-
tralian lawyer named David (Richard Chamberlain) who defends a group of aborigines involved in a ritual murder, one
of whom (Gulpilil) begins to appear in his dreams. These
dreams put him in touch with a parellel world ("the other side,"
in Western terminology) and remind him of his childhood experiences of night travel and prophetic dreaming. Eventually

[4] Sir James George Frazer, *The Golden Bough* (N.Y.: Macmillan, 1963), pp. 818–19.
[5] *The Interpretation of Dreams*, p. 184.
[6] For an interesting and unusual approach to the question of night travel, see John-Roger, *Dreams* (N.Y.: Baraka Press, 1976).

David discovers that he is a member of a race of priests and that the aborigines expect and may even have summoned up a great wave to destroy the intruding white civilization. As soon as he accepts his true vocation, David sees the wave and becomes its first victim. The wish such a horror film fulfills is that of *seeing,* and the world view it confirms is that "the other side" is real. In other words, David is a surrogate for the audience's desire to have, through watching a horror film, a spiritual vision. The satisfaction of being "first victim" is that one knows the hidden truth.

In the greatest of all horror films, Dreyer's *Vampyr,* the world and "the other side" continuously overlap, a dream within this dreamworld reveals to the hero the identity of the vampire. It is within this dream—of nearly being burned in a coffin whose window is clearly a reference to the frame of the movie-screen, so that the audience is cast as the victim/dreamer of the film-as-horror-object—that the hero is most in danger. The survival of Dreyer's dreamer and the death of Weir's visionary show that the crucial issue is not the destruction of the seer, but the threat of victimization. They also show that, although the more common impulse in the horror film is to exorcise the demon and save the community (*Vampyr, Jaws, The Thing, Tarantula, The Blob, Frankenstein,* etc.), there is a parallel track in which the community is rightfully destroyed (*The Last Wave, Dawn of the Dead, Dr. Strangelove*).

"The other side" may be a parallel spirit-world or it may be the Underworld, the Land of the Dead; in horror films these are usually comparable. At the climax of *The Last Wave,* David finds that he is a reincarnated priest, in a sense his own ghost. In *Apocalypse Now* (which advertises its indebtedness to *The Golden Bough*) the possibility of the community's being restored by the exorcism of Kurtz is overwhelmingly ironic, since the truths of the Underworld have more integrity than the lies of the conscious Establishment and the transfigured seer can never rejoin "their fucking army." So although there are many horror films that play on the dangerous attractions of prophecy and spirit-contact, the cathartic journey into the Land of the Dead presents itself as the larger category and as the key to all the patterns observed so far, especially if one makes the link between death and the rigidity of unconscious fixations. Freud's work on the relations between compulsive repetition and the death instinct (*Beyond the Pleasure Principle*) is very useful here, but the more luminous juncture is that between the Mummy films and *The Golden Bough.*

The Mummy opens with the best "first victim" scene I know of. An expedition has discovered a mummy, Imhotep (Boris

Karloff), and with him a sealed casket bearing a formidable curse. While two senior Egyptologists (one a straight scientist, one superstititous) discuss whether to open the box, the junior researcher, left alone, opens it and finds the Scroll of Troth. Mouthing an impromptu translation under his breath, he inadvertently raises the Mummy from the dead. Imhotep takes the scroll and exits, leaving a terminal madman in his wake. Here the desire to discover what is forbidden is related to the thrills of danger and self-destruction that are part of the cathartic masochism of attending horror films and having nightmares; and the mechanism of releasing an unconscious deathless force is tied into the legend of Isis and Osiris.

According to Frazer, the spell of Thoth was first used by Isis to raise her son Horus from the dead. When her brother/husband Osiris was murdered and dismembered, Isis had the aid of several gods and relatives in reassembling the body-parts (except for his genitals) and raising him from the dead. Revived, Osiris became the King of the Underworld, Lord of Eternity, and Ruler of the Dead. The rituals Isis practiced were imitated in Egyptian burial ceremonies so that the decreased might be born again in the Underworld (although Osiris, the first mummy, was supposed to have been revived in this world too).[7] In Freund's film, this is condensed into Isis' using the Scroll of Thoth to revive Osiris from the dead. The story is that Imhotep had tried to read the scroll over the body of his beloved Anckesenamon, a priestess of Isis and daughter of the Pharoah; for this atempted sacrilege, Imhotep had been buried alive along with the scroll, which could thus never again be used. Revived and in possession of the scroll, however, Imhotep (now calling himself Ardeth Bey) sets out to find the reincarnation of Anckesenamon, who turns out to be Helen Grosvener (Zita Johann). He nearly convinces her to die and be reborn as a living mummy like himself, but at the last moment Helen decides to live rather than to let her ancient identity dominate her (i.e., she chooses health over neurosis) and appeals to Isis to teach her again the spells she has forgotten over the ages. The statue of Isis responds to the spells and kills the Mummy; this implies it was not enough for Helen simply to reject Imhotep, that she had to integrate her Helen and her Anckesenamon aspects in order to come into her full power. This is very similar to what Imhotep wanted her to do, except that he would have had her proceed from that integration to a fuller Anckesenamon rather than to a fuller Helen. What this shows is that there is no safety in ignoring the

[7] *The Golden Bough*, pp. 422–26.

Id/Underworld/monster (the attitude of the ineffectual patsy in most horror films, e.g., the mayor in *Jaws* and Helen's modern boyfriend [David Manners] in *The Mummy*) but that there is considerable strength in confronting the danger and surviving that deeply acknowledged contact—in other words, re-owning the projection. In this sense horror films are valuable and cathartic, for they may offer the possibility of participating in the acting-out of an unacknowledged wish or fear in a context of resolution rather than of repression. This is of course what happens to Helen and not to the Mummy. He is a walking repetition compulsion, determined to complete his frustrated sacrilege and consummate his romance (the sexist aspects of all this are quite blatant in the film). He would have her "go through moments of horror for an eternity of love," but what he means by love is the insatiability of unconscious drives (which are, to be fair, often involved in fantasies of eternal romance). There is value, then, not in being Imhotep but in, like Helen and like the audience, *almost* being Imhotep.

We are now back to Osiris and Frazer. One of the major points of *The Golden Bough* is that the agricultural year and the sacred year are closely related in a great many cultures, and that the myth of the death and resurrection of Osiris (like that of Jesus, whose death and resurrection occur in the spring) may have served the Egyptians as an explanation or prompter (through ritual re-enactment) of the land's return to life in the spring after its death in the winter. The parallel with horror films should be immediately obvious: one enters the Land of the Dead, gives death temporary dominion, in order to emerge reborn and refreshed. Horror films are the Land of the Dead, the visionary/ghost-world where shades and demons have power, one goes to the theatre as to the Underworld, becomes Imhotep or Helen on an as-if basis, undergoes a catharsis, and steps back into the light of day (if it happens to be a matinee, which is how most children see horror films and form lasting impressions of the paradigmatic content of the experience). For Osiris, this transit left him in a position of power over the Underworld, and it will be remembered that Jesus too harrowed Hell when he died; thus for the community, the benefits include an assured sense of the existence of divinity and a reborn economy, and for the god, the benefits include life and power. But not all dreams, not all winters, and not all horror films have such happy resolutions. The stories of Osiris and Jesus do not depend on repression. A Freudian dream solves little or nothing until it is understood in analysis, simply to allow the unconscious wish to find masked fulfillment does not remodel the psyche. Left to his own devices, the Mummy will simply repeat his compulsive and insatiable project in sequel after sequel, like an incarnation of neurosis itself. So it is valuable to have a character within the film who can, like Helen, acknowledge the unconscious drive and go on from there into an integrated life, or a dreamer who can re-own projections and live a free, healthy, flexible future.

This reduces itself to a question of audience intention, since even a film like *The Thing* or *The Wolf Man* in which the horror object is simply repressed/killed and the community reasserts its boundaries can serve its audience as a visit to the Land of the Dead. The overall structure of such a visit may be cathartic in the same way that to dream may promote psychic health regardless of dream content. One could, in any case, go to *The Wolf Man* because one would enjoy participating in a fantasy of uncontrolled aggression and victimization (which is why most people went to *Jaws* and *Alien* and *The Texas Chainsaw Massacre*). But once there, one has the option of feeling that one's private beast has been purged and will require no further playground, or of enjoying the punishment and anxiety that attend unconscious wish-fulfillment and planning to attend another horror film the next time one feels in conflict about such desires. The latter is clearly more in line with Freud's reading of dreamwork, and with my outline of closed-system behavior, and it is doubtless the more common experience of horror films. Yet the former response is possible and legitimate, and it strikes me as being encouraged in those films that call the viewer's attention to the fact that he is watching a horror film and pretending to believe it, much as the analyst may attempt to engage the patient's ego while interpreting a dream. This is the method of *Vampyr* and of the bizarre, neglected, wonderful *Mummy's Ghost*.

The intervening sequels—*The Mummy's Hand* (1940) and *The Mummy's Tomb* (1942)—changed many of the terms of the story. The Mummy, Kharis, is now presented as having tried to raise the Princess Ananka by giving her the fluid from nine tana leaves; his tongue is torn out (Kharis is silent, unlike Ardeth Bey), and he is buried with a box of the leaves and charged with guarding her tomb for eternity. The Banning expedition discovers Ananka and ships her mummy back to the Scripps Museum in America, despite considerable interference from Kharis, who has been revived by a cult of priests (led by George Zucco). Kharis' motives are to keep the dead Ananka with him (neurotic possessiveness) and to defend the integrity of the Ancient Gods (against whom he rebelled in the first place). Therefore in these two films he is fulfilling the curse made against himself and has no strategy for reviving Ananka. The climax of these films comes when the priest (George Zucco in *Hand*, Turhan Bey in *Tomb*) decides to administer tana fluid to himself and the nearest heroine (who is never Ananka), but is foiled or killed, after which the Mummy is burned and the community of Americans restored. So if Kharis represents anything here, it is the deathless persistence of compulsive fixation that may have begun in sexual desire but has become only an undead, rigid, destructive, rejecting anger.

The Mummy's Ghost may be a brilliant parody of the series, a self-deconstructing masterpiece, or simply what used to be called a really good bad movie. It exploits every formula it can, turning them against themselves, right up to the climax where the monster, for once, gets the girl. It begins in the tombs of Arkham (a reference to Lovecraft?), where Zucco explains his role to the new priest, Yusef Bey (John Carradine). When told of his mission, Yusef Bey says incredulously, "Kharis—still *lives?*" His "you've got to be putting me on" tone puts the film in sync with the audience immediately, as the sequel declares its awareness of being a formulaic sequel or its worldly equivalent. Next we see Professor Norman explaining to his college students the legend of Kharis, who was supposedly destroyed in their own town, Mapleton. A student argues that, "Maybe it was a man made up as a mummy, to keep the legend alive." The student is of course right in a way he could not guess but the audience can. The professor, however, insists that he saw the monster (i.e., this is a horror-film-like world and these dangers are real). This scientist is of course the first victim.

The romantic lead, Tom Harvey (Robert Lowery), has a crush on an Egyptian, Amina Monzouri (Ramsay Ames) who is working on the college staff; he also has a little dog named Peanuts. Whenever Amina thinks of Egypt, she gets a chill, but Tom insists that Egypt is just like any other modern country. Tom is the all-time ineffectual patsy of the formula, blindly confident in the status quo of modern America and uncomplicated marriage, while Amina is in conflict about her destiny, which is called Egypt but means sex and death—"forbidden love." When Kharis is on his way to kill Professor Norman, his shadow crosses her sleeping face and Amina walks in a trance to the site of the murder. When she is found in the morning, her wrist bears the birthmark of Ananka and her hair has a white streak. The next evening, Tom manages to convince Amina to neck with him in his car; while they kiss, Kharis' shadow crosses her face again.

By this time Yusef Bey has brought Kharis to the museum. Downstairs a guard prepares to relax, hanging his hat on a realistic statue of a woman (i.e., he doesn't believe art is real), opening a crime magazine, and turning on the radio ("This is *The Hour of Death*. The forces of evil stand at the threshold. A man shall die tonight . . . Did you ever meet a killer, my friend? You will tonight—"). The guard is a surrogate for the horror audience, who enjoys pretending that horrors exist, and a play on and against the suspension of disbelief—because the lies on the radio describe the truth of his situation. The reflexivity of this picture allows it to disarm the audience completely, since it continually calls attention to the fact that it is just a ghost story and just as continually presents its horrors as *real anyway*.

Upstairs Kharis finally touches the mummy of Ananka; there is a straight cut to Amina in bed, waking and screaming; straight cut back to a collapsed pile of wrappings. Ananka's soul has been reborn in Amina, again to seek its salvation. (This would frustrate the curse—for in this version of the story, Ananka and Kharis are equally culpable for their forbidden love, and the priests' motives include keeping either of them from working out their karma through reincarnation.) The site of Amina's joining her repressed Ananka is, as usual, implicitly sexual. A friend reassures her that she "must have been having a nightmare." Back at the museum, Kharis kills the guard ("gunshots—crash—" the radio had said; the guard shoots Kharis and then is smashed against a glass door before being strangled).

Kharis finds Amina in bed and takes her away, unconscious, to a shack where Yusef Bey waits. Yusef Bey soon tells her that she is Ananka, and points to Kharis as an example of eternal unfulfillment and restlessness; she faints, and in her sleep her hair turns completely white. Then Yusef Bey decides to give her and himself the tana fluid—the most blatant instance of formula (or compulsive role-playing) in the whole film, coming absolutely out of nowhere—and Kharis kills him. Peanuts has led Tom to the scene, and Kharis knocks him out; then he carries Amina into the swamp (in New England?— again, more formula than "reality"). Tom is joined by the sheriff's posse (which has been digging a pit for the Mummy and burning tana leaves—another fakeout, since the Mummy transcends his compulsive desire for the fluid and walks on with his romantic burden; i.e., the fixed pattern of his sexual desire is stronger than the fixed pattern of the movie's formula; this pit business would have served as a typical solution in many films of the period). A formulaic rush to the rescue ensues—reminiscent of the torchlight parades in *Frankenstein* and *The Mummy's Tomb*—with Peanuts and Tom and the posse all chasing the Mummy. Such crosscut chase scenes have signified climax and resolution since Griffith, and aside from the St. Bartholomew's Day Massacre sequence of *Intolerance* there are very few examples of failed climactic chases in the whole history of film. One of the most troubling closes *The Mummy's Ghost.*

Because the chase does fail, and in a masterful way. As Kharis carries her, Amina becomes entirely Ananka: her flesh dries, her frame contracts, but she is still alive. Imhotep's project has been fulfilled (Kharis too has returned to his origins): the two lovers are united as living mummies. This rare moment of absolute fulfillment of forbidden love, which Amina has been shrinking from and growing toward and which Kharis has been yearning after for 3000 years, is immediately succeeded by their deaths—they drown in the swamp. The posse stands there looking beaten; Tom (who has seen Ananka's face) is a wreck; Peanuts is alone on the swampbank cocking his puzzled head. There is a sudden feeling of "what happened!" Suddenly a real horror has asserted itself—Amina has given herself over to her unconscious drives; the Mummy has abducted her and gotten away with it; all the formulas have failed at once. And at this point a George Zucco voice-over intones the curse: "The fate of those who defy the will of the Ancient Gods will be a cruel and violent death." (This is what Derrida would recognize as a good place to begin deconstructing the film, except that the film has already done it for us.) Although it seems that Ananka has repeated her sin rather than sought her salvation, and therefore is properly punished (Freud again), there is no denying the satisfactions of romantic apotheoisis. Except if one views it from a feminist perspective, whereby Amina could be seen as surrendering to the deadly obsessions of her abductor, utterly identifying with her state of victimization; the horror of her no-win situation is that her only alternative to Kharis, in this culture, would be to play the role of Tom's wife. Whether Amina is seen as joining her demon lover or as the victim of a cosmic rape, it is still clear that the curse, as formulated, is not in control, and that horror has triumphed.

Behaving according to formula is one aspect of repetition compulsion and of neurosis. In this film the force of Kharis and Ananka's unconscious desires is so strong that they at least balance and perhaps make irrelevant the repressive curse. (To say that Amina has these "desires" is to say that she behaves like a Freudian construct of masochistic femininity; if one abandons the feminist reading, one is left with the less complex observation that she allows the aspects of her sexuality that frighten her to find complete expression.) Kharis is so compulsive that he wins, even if briefly, and the formulaic aspects of the genre are turned against themselves; the community is not restored. The audience is unable to take comfort from the expected formulaic resolution and has been made aware of the presence of formula all along: so the possibility exists that this film educates its audience (engages the ego in self-consciousness) rather than encouraging it only to participate in unconscious wish fulfillment (while, as usual, having it both ways and fulfilling the wish completely). As it reminds the audience that it is a formulaic film, *The Mummy's Ghost* is like a dream, one of whose major strategies has been undermined— since one of the basic functions of displacement and secondary revision is not just to mask the desire but to keep the dreamer asleep, to keep the dreamer from realizing what these masked desires are, and that they are his own. Like the most intense nightmares, *The Mummy's Ghost* awakens the audience in a moment of anxious clarity and fulfillment. It may be, to reverse the phrase, that the sleep of monsters breeds reason.

1981

JAMES AGEE
COMEDY'S GREATEST ERA

In the language of screen comedians four of the main grades of laugh are the titter, the yowl, the belly laugh and the boffo. The titter is just a titter. The yowl is a runaway titter. Anyone who has ever had the pleasure knows all about a belly laugh. The boffo is the laugh that kills. An ideally good gag, perfectly constructed and played, would bring the victim up this ladder of laughs by cruelly controlled degrees to the top rung, and would then proceed to wobble, shake, wave and brandish the ladder until he groaned for mercy. Then, after the shortest possible time out for recuperation, he would feel the first wicked tickling of the comedian's whip once more and start up *a new ladder*.

The reader can get a fair enough idea of the current state of screen comedy by asking himself how long it has been since he has had that treatment. The best of comedies these days hand out plenty of titters and once in a while it is possible to achieve a yowl without overstraining. Even those who have never seen anything better must occasionally have the feeling, as they watch the current run or, rather, trickle of screen comedy, that they are having to make a little cause for laughter go an awfully long way. And anyone who has watched screen comedy over the past ten or fifteen years is bound to realize that it has quietly but steadily deteriorated. As for those happy atavists who remember silent comedy in its heyday and the belly laughs and boffos that went with it, they have something close to an absolute standard by which to measure the deterioration.

When a modern comedian gets hit on the head, for example, the

most he is apt to do is look sleepy. When a silent comedian got
hit on the head he seldom let it go so flatly. He realized a broad
license, and a ruthless discipline within that license. It was his business to be as funny as possible physically, without the help or hindrance of words. So he gave us a figure of speech, or rather of
vision, for loss of consciousness. In other words he gave us a poem,
a kind of poem, moreover, that everybody understands. The least
he might do was to straighten up stiff as a plank and fall over backward with such skill that his whole length seemed to slap the floor
at the same instant. Or he might make a cadenza of it—look vague,
smile like an angel, roll up his eyes, lace his fingers, thrust his hands
palms downward as far as they would go, hunch his shoulders,
rise on tiptoe, prance ecstatically in narrowing circles until, with
tallow knees, he sank down the vortex of his dizziness to the floor
and there signified nirvana by kicking his heels twice, like a swimming frog.

Startled by a cop, this same comedian might grab his hatbrim
with both hands and yank it down over his ears, jump high in the
air, come to earth in a split violent enough to telescope his spine,
spring thence into a coattail-flattening sprint and dwindle at rocket
speed to the size of a gnat along the grand, forlorn perspective of
some lazy back boulevard.

Those are fine clichés from the language of silent comedy in its
infancy. The man who could handle them properly combined
several of the more difficult accomplishments of the *acrobat*, the
dancer, the *clown* and the *mime*. Some very gifted comedians,
unforgettably Ben Turpin, had an immense vocabulary of these
clichés and were in part so lovable because they were deep conservative classicists and never tried to break away from them.
The still more gifted men, of course, simplified and invented, finding out new and much deeper uses for the idiom. They learned to
show emotion through it, and comic psychology, more eloquently
than most language has ever managed to, and they discovered
beauties of comic motion which are hopelessly beyond reach of
words.

It is hard to find a theater these days where a comedy is playing;
in the days of the silents it was equally hard to find a theater which
was not showing one. The laughs today are pitifully few, far between, shallow, quiet and short. They almost never build, as they
used to, into something combining the jabbering frequency of a
machine gun with the delirious momentum of a roller coaster.
Saddest of all, there are few comedians now below middle age
and there are none who seem to learn much from picture to picture,
or to try anything new.

To put it unkindly, the only thing wrong with screen comedy
today is that it takes place on a screen which talks. Because it talks,

the only comedians who ever mastered the screen cannot work, for they cannot combine their comic style with talk. Because there is a screen, talking comedians are trapped into a continual exhibition of their inadequacy as screen comedians on a surface as big as the side of a barn.

At the moment, as for many years, the chances to see silent comedy are rare. There is a smattering of it on television—too often treated as something quaintly archaic, to be laughed at, not with. Some two hundred comedies—long and short—can be rented for home projection. And a lucky minority has access to the comedies in the collection of New York's Museum of Modern Art, which is still incomplete but which is probably the best in the world. In the near future, however, something of this lost art will return to regular theaters. A thick straw in the wind is the big business now being done by a series of revivals of W. C. Field's memorable movies, a kind of comedy more akin to the old silent variety than anything which is being made today. Mack Sennett now is preparing a sort of potpourri variety show called *Down Memory Lane* made up out of his old movies, featuring people like Fields and Bing Crosby when they were movie beginners, but including also interludes from silents. Harold Lloyd has re-released *Movie Crazy*, a talkie, and plans to revive four of his best silent comedies, *Grandma's Boy*, *Safety Last*, *Speedy* and *The Freshman*. Buster Keaton hopes to remake at feature length, with a minimum of dialogue, two of the funniest short comedies ever made, one about a porous homemade boat and one about a prefabricated house.

Awaiting these happy events, we will discuss here what has gone wrong with screen comedy and what, if anything, can be done about it. But mainly we will try to suggest what it was like in its glory in the years from 1912 to 1930, as practiced by the employees of Mack Sennett, the father of American screen comedy, and by the four most eminent masters: Charlie Chaplin, Harold Lloyd, the late Harry Langdon and Buster Keaton.

Mack Sennett made two kinds of comedy: parody laced with slapstick, and plain slapstick. The parodies were the unceremonious burial of a century of hamming, including the new hamming in serious movies, and nobody who has missed Ben Turpin in *A Small Town Idol*, or kidding Erich von Stroheim in *Three Foolish Weeks* or as *The Shriek of Araby*, can imagine how rough parody can get and still remain subtle and roaringly funny. The plain slapstick, at its best, was even better: a profusion of hearty young women in disconcerting bathing suits, frisking around with a gaggle of insanely incompetent policemen and of equally certifiable male civilians sporting museum-piece mustaches. All these people zipped and caromed about the pristine world of the screen as jazzily as a convention of water bugs. Words can hardly suggest how energetically they collided and bounced apart, meeting in full gallop around the corner of a house; how hard and how often they fell on their backsides; or with what fantastically adroit clumsiness they got themselves fouled up in folding ladders, garden hoses, tethered animals and each other's headlong cross-purposes. The gestures were ferociously emphatic; not a line or motion of the body was wasted or inarticulate. The reader may remember how splendidly upright wandlike old Ben Turpin could stand for a Renunciation Scene, with his lampshade mustache twittering and his sparrowy chest stuck out and his head flung back like Paderewski assaulting a climax and the long babyish back hair trying to look lionlike, while his Adam's apple, an orange in a Christmas stocking, pumped with noble emotion. Or huge Mack Swain, who looked like a hairy mushroom, rolling his eyes in a manner patented by French romantics and gasping in some dubious ectasy. Or Louise Fazenda, the perennial farmer's daughter and the perfect low-comedy housemaid, primping her spit curl; and how her hair tightened a good-looking face into the incarnation of rampant gullibility. Or snouty James Finlayson, gleefully foreclosing a mortgage, with his look of eternally tasting a spoiled pickle. Or Chester Conklin, a myopic and inebriated little walrus stumbling around in outsize pants. Or Fatty Arbuckle, with his cold eye and his loose, serene smile, his silky manipulation of his bulk and his satanic marksmanship with pies (he was ambidextrous and could simultaneously blind two people in opposite directions).

The intimate tastes and secret hopes of these poor ineligible dunces were ruthlessly exposed whenever a hot stove, an electric fan or a bulldog took a dislike to their outer garments: agonizingly elaborate drawers, worked up on some lonely evening out of some Godforsaken lace curtain; or men's underpants with big round black spots on them. The Sennett sets—delirious wallpaper, megalomaniacally scrolled iron beds, Grand Rapids in extremis— outdid even the underwear. It was their business, after all, to kid the squalid braggadocio which infested the domestic interiors of the period, and that was almost beyond parody. These comedies told their stores to the unaided eye, and by every means possible they screamed to it. That is one reason for the India ink silhouettes of the cops, and for convicts and prison bars and their shadows in hard sunlight, and for bare-footed husbands, in tigerish pajamas, reacting like dervishes to stepped-on tacks.

The early silent comedians never strove for or consciously thought of anything which could be called artistic "form," but they achieved it. For Sennett's rival, Hal Roach, Leo McCarey once devoted almost the whole of a Laurel and Hardy two-reeler to pie throwing. The first pies were thrown thoughtfully, almost philosophically. Then innocent bystanders began to get caught into the vortex. At full pitch it was Armageddon. But everything was calculated so nicely that until late in the picture, when havoc took over, every pie made its special kind of point and piled on its special kind of laugh.

Sennett's comedies were just a shade faster and fizzier than life. According to legend (and according to Sennett) he discovered the tempo proper to screen comedy when a green cameraman, trying to save money, cranked too slow. Realizing the tremendous drumlike power of mere motion to exhilarate, he gave inanimate objects a mischievous life of their own, broke every law of nature the tricked camera would serve him for and made the screen dance like a witches' Sabbath. The thing one is surest of all to remember is how toward the end of nearly every Sennett comedy, a chase (usually called the "rally") built up such a majestic trajectory of pure anarchic motion that bathing girls, cops, comics, dogs, cats, babies, automobiles, locomotives, innocent bystanders, sometimes what seemed like a whole city, an entire civilization, were hauled along head over heels in the wake of that energy like dry leaves following an express train.

"Nice" people, who shunned all movies in the early days, condemned the Sennett comedies as vulgar and naive. But millions of less pretentious people loved their sincerity and sweetness, their wild-animal innocence and glorious vitality. They could not put these feelings into words, but they flocked to the silents. The reader who gets back deep enough into that world will probably even remember the theater: the barefaced honky-tonk and the waltzes by Waldteufel, slammed out on a mechanical piano; the searing redolence of peanuts and demirep perfumery, tobacco and feet and sweat; the laughter of unrespectable people having a hell of a fine time, laughter as violent and steady and deafening as standing under a waterfall.

Sennett wheedled his first financing out of a couple of ex-bookies to whom he was already in debt. He took his comics out of music halls, burlesque, vaudeville, circuses and limbo, and through them he tapped in on that great pipeline of horsing and miming which runs back unbroken through the fairs of the Middle Ages at least to ancient Greece. He added all that he himself had learned about the large and spurious gesture, the late decadence of the Grand Manner, as a stage-struck boy in East Berlin, Connecticut, and as a frustrated opera singer and actor. The only thing he claims to have invented is the pie in the face, and he insists, "Anyone who tells you he has discovered something new is a fool or a liar or both."

The silent-comedy studio was about the best training school the movies have ever known, and the Sennett studio was about as free and easy and as fecund of talent as they came. All the major comedians we will mention worked there, at least briefly. So did some of the major stars of the '20s and since—notably Gloria Swanson, Phyllis Haver, Wallace Beery, Marie Dressler and Carole Lombard. Directors Frank Capra, Leo McCarey and George Stevens also got their start in silent comedy; much that remains most flexible, spontaneous and visually alive in sound movies can be traced, through them and others, to this silent apprenticeship. Everybody did pretty much as he pleased on the Sennett lot, and everybody's ideas were welcome. Sennett posted no rules, and the only thing he strictly forbade was liquor. A Sennett story conference was a most informal affair. During the early years, at least, only the most important scenario might be jotted on the back of an envelope. Mainly Sennett's men thrashed out a few primary ideas and carried them in their heads, sure that better stuff would turn up while they were shooting, in the heat of physical action. This put quite a load on the prop man; he had to have the most improbable apparatus on hand—bombs, trick telephones, what not—to implement whatever idea might suddenly turn up. All kinds of things did—and were recklessly used. Once a low-comedy auto got out of control and killed the cameraman, but he was not visible in the shot, which was thrilling and undamaged; the audience never knew the difference.

Sennett used to hire a "wild man" to sit in on his gag conferences, whose whole job was to think up "wildies." Usually he was an all but brainless, speechless man, scarcely able to communicate his idea; but he had a totally uninhibited imagination. He might say nothing for an hour; then he'd mutter, "You take . . ." and all the relatively rational others would shut up and wait. "You take this cloud . . ." he would get out, sketching vague shapes in the air. Often he could get no further; but thanks to some kind of thought transference, saner men would take this cloud and make something of it. The wild man seems in fact to have functioned as the group's subconscious mind, the source of all creative energy. His ideas were so weird and amorphous that Sennett can no longer remember a one of them, or even how it turned out after rational processing. But a fair equivalent might be one of the best comic sequences in a Laurel and Hardy picture. It is simple enough—simple and real, in fact, as a nightmare. Laurel and Hardy are trying to move a piano across a narrow suspension bridge. The bridge is slung over a sickening chasm, between a couple of Alps. Midway they meet a gorilla.

Had he done nothing else, Sennett would be remembered for giving a start to three of the four comedians who now began to apply their sharp individual talents to this newborn language. The one whom he did not train (he was on the lot briefly but Sennett barely remembers seeing him around) wore glasses, smiled a great deal and looked like the sort of eager young man who might have quit divinity school to hustle brushes. That was Harold Lloyd. The others were grotesque and poetic in their screen characters in degrees which appear to be impossible when the magic of silence is broken. One, who never smiled, carried a face as still and sad as a daguerreotype through some of the most preposterously ingenious and visually satisfying physical comedy ever invented. That was Buster Keaton. One looked like an elderly baby and, at times, a baby dope fiend; he could do more with less than any other comedian. That was Harry Langdon. One looked like Charlie Chaplin, and he was the first man to give the silent language a soul.

When Charlie Chaplin started to work for Sennett he had chiefly to reckon with Ford Sterling, the reigning comedian. Their first picture together amounted to a duel before the assembled professionals. Sterling, by no means untalented, was a big man with a florid Teutonic style which, under this special pressure, he turned on full blast. Chaplin defeated him within a few minutes with a wink of the mustache, a hitch of the trousers, a quirk of the little finger.

With *Tillie's Punctured Romance*, in 1914, he became a major star. Soon after, he left Sennett when Sennett refused to start a landslide among the other comedians by meeting the raise Chaplin demanded. Sennett is understandably wry about it in retrospect, but he still says, "I was right at the time." Of Chaplin he says simply, "Oh well, he's just the greatest artist that ever lived." None of Chaplin's former rivals rates him much lower than that; they speak of him no more jealously than they might of God. We will try here only to suggest the essence of his supremacy. Of all comedians he worked most deeply and most shrewdly within a realization of what a human being is, and is up against. The Tramp is as centrally representative of humanity, as many-sided and as mysterious, as Hamlet, and it seems unlikely that any dancer or actor can ever have excelled him in eloquence, variety or poignancy of motion. As for pure motion, even if he had never gone on to make his magnificent feature-length comedies, Chaplin would have made his period in movies a great one singlehanded even if he had made nothing except *The Cure*, or *One A.M.* In the latter, barring one immobile taxi driver, Chaplin plays alone, as a drunk trying to get upstairs and into bed. It is a sort of inspired elaboration on a soft-shoe dance, involving an angry stuffed wildcat, small rugs on slippery floors, a Lazy Susan table, exquisite footwork on a flight of stairs, a contretemps with a huge, ferocious pendulum and the funniest and most perverse Murphy bed in movie history—

A shivering Tramp in *The Gold Rush* (1925). "Of all comedians he worked most deeply and most shrewdly within a realization of what a human being is, and is up against. . . . The finest pantomime, the deepest emotion, the richest and most poignant poetry were in Chaplin's work" (AGEE, pages 488, 490).

and, always made physically lucid, the delicately weird mental processes of a man ethereally sozzled.

Before Chaplin came to pictures people were content with a couple of gags per comedy; he got some kind of laugh every second. The minute he began to work he set standards—and continually forced them higher. Anyone who saw Chaplin eating a boiled shoe like brook trout in *The Gold Rush*, or embarrassed by a swallowed whistle in *City Lights*, has seen perfection. Most of the time, however, Chaplin got his laughter less from the gags, or from milking them in any ordinary sense, than through his genius for what may be called *inflection*—the perfect, changeful shading of his physical and emotional attitudes toward the gag. Funny as his bout with the Murphy bed is, the glances of awe, expostulation and helpless, almost whimpering desire for vengeance which he darts at this infernal machine are even better.

A painful and frequent error among tyros is breaking the comic line with a too-big laugh, then a letdown; or with a laugh which is out of key or irrelevant. The masters could ornament the main line beautifully; they never addled it. In *A Night Out* Chaplin, passed out, is hauled along the sidewalk by the scruff of his coat by staggering Ben Turpin. His toes trail; he is as supine as a sled. Turpin himself is so drunk he can hardly drag him. Chaplin comes quietly to, realizes how well he is being served by his struggling pal, and with a royally delicate gesture plucks and savors a flower.

The finest pantomime, the deepest emotion, the richest and most poignant poetry were in Chaplin's work. He could probably pantomime Bryce's *The American Commonwealth* without ever blurring a syllable and make it paralyzingly funny into the bargain. At the end of *City Lights* the blind girl who has regained her sight, thanks to the Tramp, sees him for the first time. She has imagined and anticipated him as princely, to say the least; and it has never seriously occurred to him that he is inadequate. She recognizes who he must be by his shy, confident, shining joy as he comes silently toward her. And he recognizes himself, for the first time, through the terrible changes in her face. The camera just exchanges a few quiet close-ups of the emotions which shift and intensify in each face. It is enough to shrivel the heart to see, and it is the greatest piece of acting and the highest moment in movies.

Harold Lloyd worked only a little while with Sennett. During most of his career he acted for another major comedy producer, Hal Roach. He tried at first to offset Chaplin's influence and establish his own individuality by playing Chaplin's exact opposite, a character named Lonesome Luke who wore clothes much too small for him and whose gestures were likewise as un-Chaplinesque as possible. But he soon realized that an opposite in itself was a kind of slavishness. He discovered his own comic identify when he saw a movie about a fighting parson: a hero who wore glasses. He began to think about those glasses day and night. He decided on horn rims because they were youthful, ultravisible on the screen and on the verge of becoming fashionable (he was to make them so). Around these large lensless horn rims he began to develop a new character, nothing grotesque or eccentric, but a fresh, believable young man who could fit into a wide variety of stories.

Lloyd depended more on story and situation than any of the other major comedians (he kept the best stable of gagmen in Hollywood, at one time hiring six); but unlike most "story" comedians he was also a very funny man from inside. He had, as he has written, "an unusually large comic vocabulary." More particularly he had an expertly expressive body and even more expressive teeth, and out of this thesaurus of smiles he could at a moment's notice blend prissiness, breeziness and asininity, and still remain tremendously likable. His movies were more extroverted and closer to ordinary life than any others of the best comedies: the vicissitudes of a New York taxi driver; the unaccepted college boy who, by desperate courage and inspired ineptitude, wins the Big Game. He was especially good at putting a very timid, spoiled or brassy young fellow through devastating embarrassments. He went through one of his most uproarious Gethsemanes as a shy country youth courting the nicest girl in town in *Grandma's Boy*. He arrived dressed "strictly up to date for the Spring of 1862," as a subtitle observed, and found that the ancient colored butler wore a similar flowered waistcoat and moldering cut-away. He got one wandering, nervous forefinger dreadfully stuck in a fancy little vase. The girl began cheerfully to try to identify that queer smell which dilated from him, Grandpa's best suit was rife with mothballs. A tenacious litter of kittens feasted off the goose grease on his home-shined shoes.

Lloyd was even better at the comedy of thrills. In *Safety Last*, as a rank amateur, he is forced to substitute for a human fly and to climb a medium-sized skyscraper. Dozens of awful things happen to him. He gets fouled up in a tennis net. Popcorn falls on him from a window above, and the local pigeons treat him like a cross between a lunch wagon and St. Francis of Assisi. A mouse runs up his britches leg, and the crowd below salutes his desperate dance on the window ledge with wild applause of the daredevil. A good deal of this full-length picture hangs thus by its eyelashes along the face of a building. Each new floor is like a new stanza in a poem; and the higher and more horrifying it gets, the funnier it gets.

In this movie Lloyd demonstrates beautifully his ability to do more than merely milk a gag, but to top it. (In an old, simple example of topping, an incredible number of tall men get, one by one, out of a small closed auto. After as many have clambered out as the joke will bear, one more steps out: a midget. That tops the gag. Then the auto collapses. That tops the topper.) In *Safety Last* Lloyd is driven out to the dirty end of a flagpole by a furious dog; the pole breaks and he falls, just managing to grab the minute hand of a huge clock. His weight promptly pulls the hand down from IX to VI. That would be more than enough for any ordinary comedian, but there is further logic in the situation. Now, hideously, the whole clockface pulls loose and slants from its trembling springs above the street. Getting out of difficulty with the clock, he makes still further use of the instrument by getting one foot caught in one of these obstinate springs.

A proper delaying of the ultrapredictable can of course be just as funny as a properly timed explosion of the unexpected. As Lloyd approaches the end of his horrible hegira up the side of the building in *Safety Last*, it becomes clear to the audience, but not to him, that if he raises his head another couple of inches he is going to get murderously conked by one of the four arms of a revolving wind gauge. He delays the evil moment almost interminably, with one distraction and another, and every delay is a suspense-tightening laugh; he also gets his foot nicely entangled in a rope, so that when he does get hit, the payoff of one gag sends him careening head downward through the abyss into another. Lloyd was outstanding even among the master craftsmen at setting up a gag clearly, culminating and getting out of it deftly, and linking it smoothly to the next. Harsh experience also taught him a deep and fundamental rule: Never try to get "above" the audience.

Lloyd tried it in *The Freshman*. He was to wear an unfinished, basted-together tuxedo to a college party, which would gradually fall apart as he danced. Lloyd decided to skip the pants, a low-comedy cliché, and lose just the coat. His gag men warned him. A preview proved how right they were. Lloyd had to reshoot the whole expensive sequence, build it around defective pants and climax it with the inevitable. It was one of the funniest things he ever did.

When Lloyd was still a very young man he lost about half his right hand (and nearly lost his sight) when a comedy bomb exploded prematurely. But in spite of his artificially built-out hand he continued to do his own dirty work, like all of the best comedians. The side of the building he climbed in *Safety Last* did not overhang the street, as it appears to. But the nearest landing place was a roof three floors below him, as he approached the top, and he did everything, of course, the hard way, i.e., the comic way, keeping his bottom stuck well out, his shoulders hunched, his hands and feet skidding over perdition.

If great comedy must involve something beyond laughter, Lloyd

Harold Lloyd in trouble in *Safety Last* (1923). "Lloyd was outstanding
. . . at setting up a gag clearly, culminating and getting out of it
deftly, and linking it smoothly to the next" (AGEE, page 492).

was not a great comedian. If plain laughter is any criterion—and it is a healthy counterbalance to the other—few people have equaled him, and nobody has ever beaten him.

Chaplin and Keaton and Lloyd were all more like each other, in one important way, than Harry Langdon was like any of them. Whatever else the others might be doing, they all used more or less elaborate physical comedy; Langdon showed how little of that one might use and still be a great silent-screen comedian. In his screen character he symbolized something as deeply and centrally human, though by no means as rangily so, as the Tramp. There was, of course, an immense difference in inventiveness and range of virtuosity. It seemed as if Chaplin could do literally anything, on any instrument in the orchestra. Langdon had one queerly toned, unique little reed. But out of it he could get incredible melodies.

Like Chaplin, Langdon wore a coat which buttoned on his wishbone and swung out wide below, but the effect was very different: he seemed like an outsized baby who had begun to outgrow his clothes. The crown of his hat was rounded and the brim was turned up all around, like a little boy's hat, and he looked as if he wore diapers under his pants. His walk was that of a child which has just got sure on its feet, and his body and hands fitted that age. His face was kept pale to show off, with the simplicity of a nursery school drawing, the bright, ignorant, gentle eyes and the little twirling mouth. He had big moon cheeks, with dimples, and a Napoleonic forelock of mousy hair; the round, docile head seemed large in ratio to the cream-puff body. Twitchings of his face were signals of tiny discomforts too slowly registered by a tinier brain; quick, squirty little smiles showed his almost prehuman pleasures, his incurably premature trustfulness. He was a virtuoso of hesitations and of delicately indecisive motions, and he was particularly fine in a high wind, rounding a corner with a kind of skittering toddle, both hands nursing his hatbrim.

He was as remarkable a master as Chaplin of subtle emotional and mental process and operated much more at leisure. He once got a good three hundred feet of continuously bigger laughs out of rubbing his chest, in a crowded vehicle, with Limburger cheese, under the misapprehension that it was a cold salve. In another long scene, watching a brazen show girl change her clothes, he sat motionless, back to the camera, and registered the whole lexicon of lost innocence, shock, disapproval and disgust, with the back of his neck. His scenes with women were nearly always something special. Once a lady spy did everything in her power (under the Hays Office) to seduce him. Harry was polite, willing, even flir-

A childish Harry Langdon (complete with bicycle) tips his hat to a gun moll in *Long Pants* (1927). "Langdon's magic was in his innocence . . . [he] looked like an elderly baby and, at times, a baby dope fiend . . ." (AGEE, pages 496, 488).

tatious in his little way. The only trouble was that he couldn't imagine what in the world she was leering and pawing at him for, and that he was terribly ticklish. The Mata Hari wound up foaming at the mouth.

There was also a sinister flicker of depravity about the Langdon character, all the more disturbing because babies are premoral. He had an instinct for bringing his actual adulthood and figurative babyishness into frictions as crawly as a fingernail on a slate blackboard, and he wandered into areas of strangeness which were beyond the other comedians. In a nightmare in one movie he was forced to fight a large, muscular young man; the girl Harry loved was the prize. The young man was a good boxer; Harry could scarcely lift his gloves. The contest took place in a fiercely lighted prize ring, in a prodigious pitch-dark arena. The only spectator was the girl, and she was rooting against Harry. As the fight went on, her eyes glittered ever more brightly with blood lust and, with glittering teeth, she tore her big straw hat to shreds.

Langdon came to Sennett from a vaudeville act in which he had fought a losing battle with a recalcitrant automobile. The minute Frank Capra saw him he begged Sennett to let him work with him. Langdon was almost as childlike as the character he played. He had only a vague idea of his story or even of each scene as he played it; each time he went before the camera Capra would brief him on the general situation and then, as this finest of intuitive improvisers once tried to explain his work, "I'd go into my routine." The whole tragedy of the coming of dialogue as far as these comedians were concerned—and one reason for the increasing rigidity of comedy ever since—can be epitomized in the mere thought of Harry Langdon confronted with a script.

Langdon's magic was in his innocence, and Capra took beautiful care not to meddle with it. The key to the proper use of Langdon, Capra always knew, was "the principle of the brick." "If there was a rule for writing Langdon material," he explains, "it was this: His only ally was God. Langdon might be saved by the brick falling on the cop, but it was *verboten* that he in any way motivate the brick's fall." Langdon became quickly and fantastically popular with three pictures, *Tramp, Tramp, Tramp, The Strong Man* and *Long Pants*; from then on he went downhill even faster. "The trouble was," Capra says, "that high-brow critics came around to explain his art to him. Also he developed an interest in dames. It was a pretty high life for such a little fellow." Langdon made two more pictures with highbrow writers, one of which *(Three's a Crowd)* had some wonderful passages in it, including the prizering nightmare; then First National canceled his contract. He was reduced to mediocre roles and two-reelers which were more rehashes of his old gags; this time around they no longer seemed funny. "He never did really understand what hit him," says Capra. "He died broke [in 1944]. And he died of a broken heart. He was the most tragic figure I ever came across in show business."

Buster Keaton started work at the age of three and a half with his parents in one of the roughest acts in vaudeville ("The Three Keatons"); Harry Houdini gave the child the name Buster in admiration for a fall he took down a flight of stairs. In his first movies Keaton teamed with Fatty Arbuckle under Sennett. He went on to become one of Metro's biggest stars and earners; a Keaton feature cost about $200,000 to make and reliably grossed $2 million. Very early in his movie career friends asked him why he never smiled on the screen. He didn't realize he didn't. He had got the deadpan habit in variety; on the screen he had merely been so hard at work it had never occurred to him there was anything to smile about. Now he tried it just once and never again. He was by his whole style and nature so much the most deeply "silent" of the silent comedians that even a smile was as deafeningly out of key as a yell. In a way his pictures are like a transcendent juggling act in which it seems that the whole universe is in exquisite flying motion and the one point of repose is the juggler's effortless, uninterested face.

Keaton's face ranked almost with Lincoln's as an early American archetype; it was haunting, handsome, almost beautiful, yet it was irreducibly funny; he improved matters by topping it off with a deadly horizontal hat, as flat and thin as a phonograph record. One can never forget Keaton wearing it, standing erect at the prow as his little boat is being launched. The boat goes grandly down the skids and, just as grandly, straight on to the bottom. Keaton never budges. The last you see of him, the water lifts the hat off the stoic head and it floats away.

No other comedian could do as much with the deadpan. He used this great, sad, motionless face to suggest various related things: a one-track mind near the track's end of pure insanity; mulish imperturbability under the wildest of circumstances; how dead a human being can get and still be alive; an awe-inspiring sort of patience and power to endure, proper to granite but uncanny in flesh and blood. Everything that he was and did bore out this rigid face and played laughs against it. When he moved his eyes, it was like seeing them move in a statue. His short-legged body was all sudden, machinelike angles, governed by a daft aplomb. When he swept a semaphorelike arm to point, you could almost hear the electrical impulse in the signal block. When he ran from a cop his transitions from accelerating walk to easy jog trot to brisk canter to headlong gallop to flogged-piston sprint— always floating, above this frenzy, the untroubled, untouchable

Buster Keaton surveying the situation in *The General* (1926). "He was by his whole style and nature so much the most deeply 'silent' of the silent comedians that even a smile was as deafeningly out of key as a yell" (AGEE, page 497).

face—were as distinct and as soberly in order as an automatic gearshift.

Keaton was a wonderfully resourceful inventor of mechanistic gags (he still spends much of his time fooling with Erector sets); as he ran afoul of locomotives, steamships, prefabricated and over-electrified houses, he put himself through some of the hardest and cleverest punishment ever designed for laughs. In *Sherlock Jr.*, boiling along on the handlebars of a motorcycle quite unaware that he has lost his driver, Keaton whips through city traffic, breaks up a tug-of-war, gets a shovelful of dirt in the face from each of a long line of Rockette-timed ditchdiggers, approaches at high speed a log which is hinged open by dynamite precisely soon enough to let him through and, hitting an obstruction, leaves the handle-bars like an arrow leaving a bow, whams through the window of a shack in which the heroine is about to be violated, and hits the heavy feet first, knocking him through the opposite wall. The whole sequence is as clean in motion as the trajectory of a bullet.

Much of the charm and edge of Keaton's comedy, however, lay in the subtle leverages of expression he could work against his nominal deadpan. Trapped in the side wheel of a ferryboat, saving himself from drowning only by walking, then desperately running, inside the accelerating wheel like a squirrel in a cage, his only real concern was, obviously, to keep his hat on. Confronted by Love, he was not as deadpan as he was cracked up to be, either; there was an odd, abrupt motion of his head which suggested a horse nipping after a sugar lump.

Keaton worked strictly for laughs, but his work came from so far inside a curious and original spirit that he achieved a great deal besides, especially in his feature-length comedies. (For plain hard laughter his nineteen short comedies—the negatives of which have been lost—were even better.) He was the only major comedian who kept sentiment almost entirely out of his work, and he brought pure physical comedy to its greatest heights. Beneath his lack of emotion he was also uninsistently sardonic; deep below that, giving a disturbing tension and grandeur to the foolishness, for those who sensed it, there was in his comedy a freezing whisper not of pathos but of melancholia. With the humor, the craftsmanship and the action there was often, besides, a fine, still and sometimes dreamlike beauty. Much of his Civil War picture *The General* is within hailing distance of Mathew Brady. And there is a ghostly, unforgettable moment in *The Navigator* when, on a deserted, soft-ly, rolling ship, all the pale doors along a deck swing open as one behind Keaton and, as one, slam shut, in a hair-raising illusion of noise.

Perhaps because "dry" comedy is so much more rare and odd

than "dry" wit, there are people who never much cared for Keaton. Those who do cannot care mildly.

As soon as the screen began to talk, silent comedy was pretty well finished. The hardy and prolific Mack Sennett made the transfer; he was the first man to put Bing Crosby and W. C. Fields on the screen. But he was essentially a silent-picture man, and by the time the Academy awarded him a special Oscar for his "lasting contribution to the comedy technique of the screen" (in 1938), he was no longer active. As for the comedians we have spoken of in particular, they were as badly off as fine dancers suddenly required to appear in plays.

Harold Lloyd, whose work was most nearly realistic, naturally coped least unhappily with the added realism of speech; he made several talking comedies. But good as the best were, they were not so good as his silent work, and by the late '30s he quit acting. A few years ago he returned to play the lead (and play it beautifully) in Preston Sturges' *The Sin of Harold Diddlebock*, but this exceptional picture—which opened, brilliantly, with the closing reel of Lloyd's *The Freshman*—has not yet been generally released.

Like Chaplin, Lloyd was careful of his money; he is still rich and active. Last June, in the presence of President Truman, he became Imperial Potentate of the A.A.O.N.M.S. (Shriners). Harry Langdon, as we have said, was a broken man when sound came in.

Up to the middle '30s Buster Keaton made several feature-length pictures (with such players as Jimmy Durante, Wallace Beery and Robert Montgomery); he also made a couple of dozen talking shorts. Now and again he managed to get loose into motion, without having to talk, and for a moment or so the screen would start singing again. But his dark, dead voice, though it was in keeping with the visual character, tore his intensely silent style to bits and destroyed the illusion within which he worked. He gallantly and correctly refuses to regard himself as "retired." Besides occasional bits, spots and minor roles in Hollywood pictures, he has worked on summer stages, made talking comedies in France and Mexico and clowned in a French circus. This summer he has played the straw hats in *Three Men on a Horse*. He is planning a television program. He also has a working agreement with Metro. One of his jobs there is to construct comedy sequences for Red Skelton.

The only man who really survived the flood was Chaplin, the only one who was rich, proud and popular enough to afford to stay silent. He brought out two of his greatest nontalking comedies, *City Lights* and *Modern Times*, in the middle of an avalanche of talk, spoke gibberish and, in the closing moments, plain English in *The Great Dictator*, and at last made an all-talking picture, *Monsieur Verdoux*, creating for that purpose an entirely new char-

acter who might properly talk a blue streak. *Verdoux* is the greatest
of talking comedies though so cold and savage that it had to find
its public in grimly experienced Europe.

Good comedy, and some that was better than good, outlived
silence, but there has been less and less of it. The talkies brought
one great comedian, the late, majestically lethargic W. C. Fields,
who could not possibly have worked as well in silence; he was
the toughest and the most warmly human of all screen comedians,
and *It's a Gift* and *The Bank Dick*, fiendishly funny and incisive
white-collar comedies, rank high among the best comedies (and
best movies) ever made. Laurel and Hardy, the only comedians
who managed to preserve much of the large, low style of silence
and who began to explore the comedy of sound, have made nothing since 1945. Walt Disney, at his best an inspired comic inventor
and teller of fairy stories, lost his stride during the war and has
since regained it only at moments. Preston Sturges has made brilliant, satirical comedies, but his pictures are smart, nervous com-
edy-dramas merely italicized with slapstick. The Marx Brothers
were sidesplitters but they made their best comedies years ago.
Jimmy Durante is mainly a night-club genius; Abbott and Costello
are semiskilled laborers, at best; Bob Hope is a good radio comedian with a pleasing presence, but not much more, on the screen.

There is no hope that screen comedy will get much better than
it is without new, gifted young comedians who really belong in
movies, and without freedom for their experiments. For everyone
who may appear we have one last, invidious comparison to offer
as a guidepost.

One of the most popular recent comedies is Bob Hope's *The
Paleface*. We take no pleasure in blackening *The Paleface*; we
single it out, rather, because it is as good as we've got. Anything
that is said of it here could be said, with interest, of other comedies
of our time. Most of the laughs in *The Paleface* are verbal. Bob
Hope is very adroit with his lines and now and then, when the
words don't get in the way, he makes a good beginning as a visual
comedian. But only the beginning, never the middle or the end.
He is funny, for instance, reacting to a shot of violent whisky.
But he does not know how to get still funnier (i.e., how to build
and milk) or how to be funniest last (i.e., how to top or cap his
gag). The camera has to fade out on the same old face he started
with.

One sequence is promisingly set up for visual comedy. In it,
Hope and a lethal local boy stalk each other all over a cow town
through streets which have been emptied in fear of their duel. The
gag here is that through accident and stupidity they keep just failing to find each other. Some of it is quite funny. But the fun slack-
ens between laughs like a weak clothesline, and by all the logic

of humor (which is ruthlessly logical) the biggest laugh should come at the moment, and through the way, they finally spot each other. The sequence is so weakly thought out that at that crucial moment the camera can't afford to watch them; it switches to Jane Russell.

Now we turn to a masterpiece. In *The Navigator* Buster Keaton works with practically the same gag as Hope's duel. Adrift on a ship which he believes is otherwise empty, he drops a lighted cigarette. A girl finds it. She calls out and he hears her; each then tries to find the other. First each walks purposefully down the long, vacant starboard deck, the girl, then Keaton, turning the corner just in time not to see each other. Next time around each of them is trotting briskly, very much in earnest; going at the same pace, they miss each other just the same. Next time around each of them is going like a bat out of hell. Again they miss. Then the camera withdraws to a point of vantage at the stern, leans its chin in its hand and just watches the whole intricate superstructure of the ship as the protagonists stroll, steal and scuttle from level to level, up, down and sidewise, always managing to miss each other by hairbreadths, in an enchantingly neat and elaborate piece of timing. There are no subsidiary gags to get laughs in this sequence and there is little loud laughter; merely a quiet and steadily increasing kind of delight. When Keaton has got all he can out of this fine modification of the movie chase he invents a fine device to bring the two together: the girl, thoroughly winded, sits down for a breather, indoors, on a plank which workmen have left across sawhorses. Keaton pauses on an upper deck, equally winded and puzzled. What follows happens in a couple of seconds at most: Air suction whips his silk topper backward down a ventilator; grabbing frantically for it, he backs against the lip of the ventilator, jackknifes and falls in backward. Instantly the camera cuts back to the girl. A topper falls through the ceiling and lands tidily, right side up, on the plank beside her. Before she can look more than startled, its owner follows, head between his knees, crushes the topper, breaks the plank with the point of his spine and proceeds to the floor. The breaking of the plank smacks Boy and Girl together.

It is only fair to remember that the silent comedians would have as hard a time playing a talking scene as Hope has playing his visual ones, and that writing and directing are as accountable for the failure as Hope himself. But not even the humblest journeyman of the silent years would have let themselves off so easily. Like the masters, they knew, and sweated to obey, the laws of their craft.

1949

JOHN G. CAWELTI
CHINATOWN AND GENERIC TRANSFORMATION IN RECENT AMERICAN FILMS

One of the fascinating things about Roman Polanski's *China-town* is that it invokes in so many ways the American popular genre of the hard-boiled detective story. Most of us, I suppose, associate this tradition particularly with two films, both of which starred Humphrey Bogart: John Huston's *The Maltese Falcon* (1941) and Howard Hawks' *The Big Sleep* (1946). But these are only the two most-remembered and perhaps the most memorable versions of a narrative formula which has been replicated in hundreds of novels, films, and television programs. Next to the western, the hard-boiled detective story is America's most distinctive contribution to the world's stock of action-adventure stories, our contemporaneous embodiment of the drama of heroic quest which has appeared in so many different cultures in so many different guises. Unlike the western—heroic quest on the frontier—which can perhaps be traced back as far as the Indian captivity narratives of the late seventeenth century, and certainly to Cooper's Leatherstocking saga of the early nineteenth century, the hard-boiled detective story is of quite recent origin. It developed in the twenties through the medium of short action stories in pulp magazines like the famous *Black Mask*. By 1929, Dashiell Hammett had produced in *Red Harvest*, the first hard-boiled detective novel. Before retiring into literary silence in the mid-thirties, Hammett had created a basic core of hard-boiled adventure in his Continental Op stories and his novels—*The*

Maltese Falcon (1930), *The Dain Curse* (1929), *The Glass Key* (1931) and *The Thin Man* (1934). In very short order, the hard-boiled detective made the transition from novel to film. *The Maltese Falcon* appeared in two film versions in the early 30s, before John Huston made the definitive version in 1941. *The Glass Key* was produced in the early 30s and in the 40s; *The Thin Man* became one of the great movie successes of the later 30s, so popular that it led to a number of invented sequels. And while the hard-boiled detective flourished in film, Hammett's example was followed in novels by writers whose literary approach ranged from the subtlety and depth of Raymond Chandler and Ross Macdonald to the sensational—and best-selling—crudity of Mickey Spillane. Radio and television, too, made many series based on the figure of the hard-boiled detective and his quest for justice through the ambiguous landscape of the modern American city. If a myth can be defined as a pattern of narrative known throughout the culture and presented in many different versions by many different tellers, then the hard-boiled detective story is in that sense an important American myth.

Chinatown invokes this myth in many different ways. Its setting in Los Angeles in the 1930s is very much the archetypal "hard-boiled" setting, the place and time of Hammett's and Chandler's novels. While it is true that many hard-boiled novels and films are set in different places and times—Mickey Spillane's Mike Hammer stories in New York City, John D. Macdonald's Travis McGee saga in Florida—the California city setting of Hammett and Chandler and the approximate time of their stories, memorialized in the period furnishings, visual icons, and style of the great hard-boiled films of the 1940s, have become for us the look and the temporal-spacial aura of the hard-boiled myth. It is this aura which Polanski generates, though there is something not quite right, something disturbingly off about it. In this case, it is the color. The world of the hard-boiled myth is preeminently a world of black and white. Its ambience is that compound of angular light and shadow enmeshed in webs of fog which grew out of the visual legacy of German expressionism in drama and film, transformed into what is now usually called *film noir* by its adjustment to American locales and stories. Polanski carefully controls his spectrum of hue and tone in order to give it the feel of *film noir*, but it is nonetheless color with occasional moments of rich golden light—as in the scene in the dry riverbed. These moments of warm color often relate to scenes that are outside the usual setting or thematic content—for example, scenes in the natural landscape outside the city—which are themselves generally

outside the world of the hard-boiled detective story. The invocation of many other traditional elements of the hard-boiled
myth, the *film noir* tone and the 1930s setting cue us to expect
the traditional mythical world of the private eye hero. But the
presence of color, along with increasing deviations from established patterns of plot, motive and character give us an
eerie feeling of one myth colliding with and beginning to give
way to others.

Let us begin by examining *Chinatown*'s relation to the traditional myth of the hard-boiled detective. The established narrative formula of the hard-boiled story has as its protaganist a
private investigator who occupies a marginal position with respect to the official social institutions of criminal justice. The
private eye is licensed by the state, but though he may be a
former member of a police force or district attorney's staff, he
is not now connected with such an organization. In the course
of the story, he is very likely to come into conflict with representatives of the official machinery, though he may also have
friends who are police officers. His position on the edge of the
law is very important, because one of the central themes of the
hard-boiled myth is the ambiguity between institutionalized
law enforcement and true justice. The story shows us that the
police and the courts are incapable of effectively protecting the
innocent and bringing the guilty to appropriate justice. Only
the individual of integrity who exists on the margins of society, can solve the crime and bring about a true justice.

The marginal character of the private eye hero is thus crucial
to his role in the myth. It is also central to his characterization.
We see him not only as a figure outside the institutionalized
process of law enforcement, but as the paradoxical combination of a man of character who is also a failure. The private eye
is a relatively poor man who operates out of a seedy office and
never seems to make very much money by his exploits; he is
the most marginal sort of lower-middle class quasi-profes-
sional. Yet unlike the usual stereotype of this social class, he is
a man of honor and integrity who cannot be made to give up
his quest for true justice. He is a compelling American hero
type, clearly related to the traditional western hero who manifests many of the same characteristics and conditions of
marginality.

The story begins when the hard-boiled hero is given a mission by a client. It is typical that this initial mission is a deceptive one. Either the client is lying, as Brigid O'Shaughnessy
lies to Sam Spade in *The Maltese Falcon*, or the client has himself been deceived and does not understand what is really at
stake when he gives the detective his case, as with General

Sternwood in *The Big Sleep*. Often the detective is being used as a pawn in some larger plot of the client's. Whatever his initial impetus to action, the detective soon finds himself enmeshed in a very complex conspiracy involving a number of people from different spheres of society. The ratiocinative English detective in authors like Dorothy Sayers, Agatha Christie, or Ngaio Marsh, investigates crimes by examining clues, questionning witnesses and then using his intellectual powers of insight and deduction to arrive at the solution. The hard-boiled detective investigates through movement and encounter; he collides with the web of conspiracy until he has exposed its outlines. The crime solved by the ratiocinative detective is usually that of a single individual. With this individual's means and motives for the criminal act rationally established he can be turned over to the law for prosecution. But the hard-boiled detective encounters a linked series of criminal acts and responsibilities; he discovers not a single guilty individual, but a corrupt society in which wealthy and respectable people are linked with gangsters and crooked politicians. Because it is society and not just a single individual which is corrupt, the official machinery of law enforcement is unable to bring the guilty to justice. The hard-boiled detective must decide for himself what kind of justice can be accomplished in the ambiguous urban world of modern America, and he must, in many instances, undertake to see this justice through, himself. There have always been two different tendencies within the hard-boiled myth. Some writers, like Mickey Spillane and his many current followers, place their emphasis on the hero as private vigilante avenger. Their stories climax with the hero playing the role of executioner as well as detective and judge. More complex and artistic writers, like Hammett, Chandler and Ross Macdonald, develop instead the theme of the hero's own relationship to the mythical role of lawman-outside-the-law. Their versions of the story rarely end with the detective's execution of the criminal; they prefer instead either to arrange for the criminal's self-destruction as in Chandler's *Farewell, My Lovely*, or simply to bring about the criminal's exposure and confession, as in *The Maltese Falcon*. But this latter trend, though it has produced greater literature, is perhaps best understood as a humane avoidance of the true thrust of the myth which is, I think, essentially toward the marginal hero becoming righteous judge and executioner, culture-hero for a society which has profoundly ambiguous conflicts in choosing between its commitment to legality and its belief that only individual actions are ultimately moral and just.

One further element of the hard-boiled myth needs to be particularly noted: the role of the feminine antagonist. In almost every case, the hard-boiled hero encounters a beautiful and dangerous woman in the course of his investigations and he finds himself very much drawn toward her, even to the point of falling in love. Sometimes the woman is his client, sometimes a figure in the conspiracy. In a surprising number of cases (*The Maltese Falcon, The Big Sleep, Farewell, My Lovely, I, The Jury,* and many others) the woman turns out to be the murderess, and, in Spillane at least, is killed by her detective-lover. This murky treatment of the "romance" between detective and dangerous female is occasionally resolved happily as in the Bogart-Bacall relationship at the end of the film version of *The Big Sleep* (in the novel this romantic culmination does not take place). However, such an outcome is rare. Even if the beautiful woman does not turn out to be a murderess, the detective usually separates from her at the end to return to his marginal situation, basically unchanged by what has happened to him and ready to perform more acts of justice when the occasion arises.

We can see from this brief resumé of the hard-boiled formula how close a resemblance *Chinatown* bears to it. But the film deviates increasingly from the myth until, by the end of the story, the film arrives at an ending almost contrary to that of the myth. Instead of bringing justice to a corrupt society, the detective's actions leave the basic source of corruption untouched. Instead of protecting the innocent, his investigation leads to the death of one victim and the deeper moral destruction of another. Instead of surmounting the web of conspiracy with honor and integrity intact, the detective is overwhelmed by what has happened to him.

True, the action of *Chinatown* increasingly departs from the traditional hard-boiled formula as the story progresses; however, there are, from the very beginning, a number of significant departures from the standard pattern. The choice of Jack Nicholson and Faye Dunaway as leading actors is a good instance of this. Nicholson and Dunaway have certain physical and stylistic resemblances to Bogart and Bacall and these are obviously played up through costume, makeup and gesture. Indeed, there is one early scene in a restaurant between them which is almost eerily reminiscent of the famous horse-racing interchange between Bogart and Bacall in *The Big Sleep.* But much as they echo the archetypal hard-boiled duo in a superficial way, Nicholson and Dunaway play characters which are very different. Dunaway has a neurotic fragility, an underlying quality of desperation which becomes even more apparent as her true situation is revealed. She never generates the sense of independence and courage that Bacall brought to her hard-boiled roles; her qualities of wit and sophistication—those characteristics which made Bacall such an appropriate romantic partner for the hard-boiled detective—are quickly seen to be a veneer covering depths of anguish and ambiguity. Nicholson also portrays, at least early on, a character who is not quite what he seems. His attempt to be the tough, cynical, and humorous private eye is undercut on all sides; he is terribly inept as a wit, as his attempt to tell his assistants the Chinese joke makes clear. Nor is he the tough, marginal man of professional honor he pretends to be at the beginning; actually, he is a successful small businessman who has made a good thing out of exploiting the more sordid needs of his fellowmen. One of the most deeply symbolic clichés of the traditional hard-boiled formula is the hero's refusal to do divorce business, in fact one of the primary functions of the private detective. By this choice the traditional private-eye of the myth established both his personal sense of honor and his transcendent vocation, distinguishing himself from the typical private investigator. However, from the beginning of *Chinatown*, it is clear that the accumulation of evidence of marital infidelity is Jake Gittes' primary business. He is, indeed, drawn into the affairs of Noah Cross, his daughter, and her husband by a commission to document a supposedly clandestine affair between the latter and a much younger woman. The name, J. J. Gittes, which Polanski and Robert Towne, the screenwriter, chose for their protagonist is a good indication of this aspect of his character. Think of the names of the traditional hard-boiled detectives: Sam Spade, with its implication of hardness and digging beneath the surface; Philip Marlowe with its aura of knightliness and chivalry; Lew Archer with its mythical overtones. Gittes, or "Gits" as Noah Cross ironically keeps pronouncing it, connotes selfishness and grasping and has, in addition, a kind of ethnic echo very different from the pure Anglo of Spade, Marlowe and Archer.

Yet, qualified and even "anti-heroic" as he is, Gittes is swept up into the traditional hard-boiled action. His initial and deceptive charge involves him in the investigation of a murder, which in turn leads him to evidence of a large-scale conspiracy involving big business, politics, crime and the whole underlying social and environmental structure of Los Angeles. Like the traditional hard-boiled detective, Gittes begins as a marginal individual, but gradually finds himself becoming a moral agent with a mission. At the same time he becomes romantically involved with a character deeply implicated in the web of conspiracy, the mysterious widow of the man who has been murdered. By the middle of the film Gittes is determined to expose the political conspiracy which he senses beneath the surface, and also to resolve the question of the guilt or innocence of the woman to whom he has been so strongly attracted. Thus far, the situation closely resembles that of *The Maltese Falcon* and *The Big Sleep*. It is at this point, however, that the action again takes a vast departure from that of the traditional hard-boiled story. Instead of demonstrating his ability to expose and punish the guilty, Gittes steadily finds himself confronting a depth of evil and chaos so great that he is unable to control it. In relation to the social and personal depravity represented by Noah Cross and the world in which he can so successfully operate, the toughness, moral concern, and professional skill of Gittes not only seem ineffectual, but lead to ends that are the very opposite of those intended. At the end of the film, Noah Cross is free to continue his rapacious depredations on the land, the city and the body of his own daughter-granddaughter; and the one person who might have effectively brought Cross to some form of justice— his daughter-mistress—has been destroyed. Gittes' confrontation with a depth of depravity beyond the capacity of the hard-boiled ethos of individualistic justice is, I think, the essential significance of the Chinatown motif in the film. Chinatown becomes a symbol of life's deeper moral enigmas, those unintended consequences of action that are past understanding and control. Gittes has been there before. In another case his attempts at individual moral action had led to the death of a woman he cared for. It is apparently this tragedy that motivated him to leave the police force and set up as a private investigator. Now he has been drawn back into moral action, and it is again, in Chinatown, that his attempt to live out the myth of individualistic justice collides with the power of evil and chance in the world. The result is not heroic confrontation and the triumph of justice, but tragic catastrophe and the destruction of the innocent.

Chinatown places the hard-boiled detective story within a view of the world that is deeper and more catastrophic, more enigmatic in its evil, more sudden and inexplicable in its outbreaks of violent chance. In the end, the image of heroic, moral action embedded in the traditional private-eye myth turns out to be totally inadequate to overcome the destructive realities revealed in the course of this story. This revelation of depths beneath depths is made increasingly evident in the film's relentless movement toward Chinatown, the symbolic locus of darkness, strangeness and catastrophe; but it also appears in the film's manipulation of action and image. The themes of water and drought, which weave through the action, not only reveal the scope of Noah Cross's conspiracy to dominate a city by manipulating its water supply, but create a texture of allusion which resonates with the mythical meanings traditionally associated with water and drought. Polanski's version of Los Angeles in the 1930s reveals the transcendent mythical world of the sterile kingdom, the dying king and the drowned man beneath it—the world, for example, of Eliot's *Wasteland* and before that of the cyclical myths of traditional cultures. Another of the film's motifs, its revelation of the rape-incest by which Noah Cross has fathered a daughter on his own daughter and is apparently intending to continue this method of establishing a progeny through the agency of his daughter-granddaughter, is another of the ways in which the hard-boiled myth is thrust into depths beyond itself. Though traditionally an erotically potent figure, the private eye's sexuality seems gentility itself when confronted with the potent perversity embodied in the figure of Noah Cross. Cross is reminiscent of the primal father imagined by Freud in *Totem and Taboo*, but against his overpowering sexual, political and economic power, our hero-Oedipus in the form of J. J. Gittes proves to be tragically impotent, an impotence symbolized earlier in the film by the slashing of his nose and the large comic bandage he wears throughout much of the action.

In its manipulation of a traditional American popular myth and the revelation of the tragic inadequacy of this myth when it collides with a universe that is deeper and more enigmatic in its evil and destructive force, *Chinatown* is one of the richest and most artistically powerful instances of a type of film of which we have seen many striking instances in the last decade. It is difficult to know just what to call this type of film. On one level, it relates to the traditional literary mode of burlesque or parody in which a well-established set of conventions or a style is subjected to some form of ironic or humorous exploitation. Indeed, many of the most striking and successful films of the period have been out and out burlesques of traditional popular genres such as Mel Brooks' *Blazing Saddles* (westerns), *Young Frankenstein* (the Frankenstein horror cycle), and *High Anxiety* (Hitchcock's psychological suspense films). However, burlesque and parody embody a basically humorous thrust, and many of the most powerful generic variations of the last decade or so—films like *Bonnie and Clyde, The Wild Bunch, The Godfather* and *Nashville*—tend more toward tragedy than comedy in their overall structures. It seems odd to speak of a tragic parody or a doomed burlesque. Therefore, one is at first tempted to conclude that the connection between *Blazing Saddles* and *The Wild Bunch,* or *The Black Bird* and *The Long Goodbye* is only superficial. Yet it is clear that in many of these films the line between comedy and tragedy is not so simply drawn. What, for example, of the extraordinary combination of Keystone Cops chase scenes and tragic carnage in *Bonnie and Clyde,* or the interweaving of sophomoric high jinks and terrible violence in Altman's *MASH*? This puzzling combination of humorous burlesque and high seriousness seems to be a mode of expression characteristic of our period, not only in film, but in other literary forms. It is at the root of much that is commonly described as the literature of the absurd, or of so-called "Black humor," and is, as well, characteristic of the style of major contemporary novelists like Thomas Pynchon. By adopting this mode, American movies have, in a sense, become a more integral part of the mainstream of postmodernist literature, just as, through their frequent allusion to the narrative conventions of American film, contemporary novelists and dramatists have created a new kind of relationship between themselves and the traditions of popular culture.

The linkage between these many different kinds of contemporary literary, dramatic and cinematic expression is their use of the conventions of traditional popular genres. Basically, they do in different ways what Polanski does in *Chinatown:* set the elements of a conventional popular genre in an altered context, thereby making us perceive these traditional forms and images in a new way. It appears to me that we can classify the various relationships between traditional generic elements and altered contexts into four major modes.

First, there is the burlesque proper. In this mode, elements of a conventional formula or style are situated in contexts so incongruous or exaggerated that the result is laughter. There are many different ways in which this can be done. The formulaic elements can be acted out in so extreme a fashion that they come into conflict with our sense of reality forcing us to see these aspects of plot and character as fantastic contrivances. A good example of this is the burlesque image of the gunfighter in *Cat Ballou.* In this film we are shown how, by putting on his gunfighter costume, a process that involves strapping himself into a corset within which he can barely move, an old drunk can become the terror of the bad guys. Or, in a closely related type of altered context, a situation that we are ordinarily accustomed to seeing in rather romanticized terms can be suddenly invested with a sense of reality. This is

Roy Jenson and John Huston threaten Jack Nicholson in a scene from *Chinatown* (1974) that is "outside the usual setting or thematic content— for example, scenes in the natural landscape outside the city— which are themselves outside the world of the hardboiled detective story." (CAWELTI, page 504). The Black Sheriff (Cleavon Little) encounters the Count Basie band on the prairie in *Blazing Saddles* (1972). "Many of the most striking and successful films of the period have been out and out burlesques of traditional popular genres such as Mel Brooks' *Blazing Saddles* . . ." (CAWELTI, page 510).

how the famous campfire scene in *Blazing Saddles* operates. The cowboys sit around a blazing campfire at night, a scene in which we are accustomed to hearing mournful and lyrical cowboy ballads performed by such groups as the Sons of the Pioneers. Instead we are treated to an escalating barrage of flatulence. Anyone who knows the usual effect of canned wilderness fare is likely to be delighted at this sudden exposure of the sham involved in the traditional western campfire scene. Sam Peckinpah's *Ride the High Country* offers another instance of the humorous effect of a sudden penetration of reality into a fantasy when one of his aging heroes attempts to spring gracefully into the saddle and is suddenly halted by a twinge of rheumatism.

In addition to these sudden confrontations with "reality" conventional patterns can be turned into laughter by inverting them. A good example of this is the device of turning a character who shows all the marks of a hero into a coward, or vice versa. A favorite manifestation of this in recent films and novels is what might be called the hard-boiled schlemiehl, the private detective who turns out to be totally unable to solve a crime or resist villains except by accident. This type of burlesque is even more effective when the inverted presentation actually seems to bring out some latent meanings which were lurking all the time in the original convention. Mel Brooks is a particular master of this kind of burlesque. In his *Young Frankenstein,* the monster attacks Frankenstein's fiancee Elizabeth a moment of tragic violence in the original novel—and the result is complete sexual satisfaction on both sides, something most of us had suspected all along.

These two primary techniques of burlesque, the breaking of convention by the intrusion of reality and the inversion of expected implications, have frequently appeared in the history of literature as a response to highly conventionalized genres. Just as the Greek tragedies gave rise to their burlesque counterparts in the plays of Aristophanes, the western, one of our most formally distinctive genres, has been the inspiration of parody and burlesque throughout its history from Twain and Harte's assaults on James Fenimore Cooper to Brooks' send-up of *Shane* and *High Noon.* Thus, there is nothing particularly new in the penchant toward humorous burlesque so evident in recent films. What is more striking in the films of the last decade is their use of these techniques of generic parody for ultimately serious purposes.

The second major mode of generic transformation is the cultivation of nostalgia. In this mode, traditional generic features of plot, character, setting and style are deployed to recreate the aura of a past time. The power of nostalgia lies especially in its capacity to evoke a sense of warm reassurance by bringing before our mind's eye images from a time when things seemed more secure and full of promise and possibility. Though one can, of course, evoke nostalgia simply by viewing films of the past, a contemporary nostalgia film cannot simply duplicate the past experience, but must make us aware in some fashion of the relationship between past and present. Attempts to evoke nostalgia merely by imitating past forms, as was the case with the television series *City of Angels,* do not generally work because they seem simply obsolescent. A truly successful nostalgia film—like Fred Zinneman's *True Grit,* one of the last highly popular westerns—succeeds because it set its highly traditional generic content in a slightly different context, thereby giving us both a sense of contemporaneity and of pastness. In *True Grit,* this was done in a number of ways. First of all, the central character played by Kim Darby represented an extremely contemporary image of adolescent girlhood. She was independent, aggressive and full of initiative, a shrewd horsetrader and a self-confident, insistent moralist, unlike the shy desert rose of the traditional western. John Wayne, aging and paunchy, did not attempt to cover up the ravages of the years and reaffirm without change the vigorous manhood of his earlier films. Instead, with eyepatch, unshaven face and sagging flesh, he fully enacted his aging. Similarly, the film's images of the western landscape were in many ways deromanticized. But out of this context of contemporaneity there sprang the same old story of adventure and heroism culminating in an exhuberant shootout which seemed to embody everybody's best dreams of Saturday matinees. The same quality of nostalgic reinvocation of the past played an even more powerful role in Peckinpah's *Ride the High Country* in which two tired, aging and obsolescent heroes ride again, and in Dick Richard's recent version of Raymond Chandler's *Farewell, My Lovely* where a sagging Robert Mitchum moves out of the malaise of modernity and reenacts once more the ambiguous heroic quest of the hard-boiled detective of the 1930s and 1940s.

The difference between nostalgic reincarnation of an earlier genre like *Farewell, My Lovely* and the more complex ironies of *Chinatown* and Robert Altman's *The Long Goodbye* is considerable. It is a difference similar to the one between *True Grit* and neo-westerns like Altman's *McCabe and Mrs. Miller* or Arthur Penn's *Little Big Man.* In the former case, nostalgia is the end result of the film. In the latter nostalgia is often powerfully evoked, but as a means of undercutting or ironically commenting upon the generic experience itself. This brings us to the third and, in many respects, the most powerful mode of generic transformation in recent films: the use of traditional generic structures as a means of demythologization. A film like *Chinatown* deliberately invokes the basic characteristics of a traditional genre in order to bring its audience to see that genre as the embodiment of an inadequate and destructive myth. We have seen how this process of demythologization operates in *Chinatown* by setting the traditional model of the hard-boiled detective's quest for justice and integrity over and against Polanski's sense of a universe so steeped in ambiguity, corruption and evil that such individualistic moral enterprises are doomed by their innocent naiveté to end in tragedy and self-destruction.

The work of Arthur Penn has also explored the ironic and tragic aspects of the myths implicit in traditional genres. His *Night Moves,* a transformation of the detective story, was, like *Chinatown,* the ambiguous enactment of a reluctant quest for the truth about a series of crimes. As the detective approaches a solution to the crimes, he becomes morally and emotionally involved in the quest, making it more and more difficult for him to integrate truth, feeling, and morality. In the end, like Polanski's Jake Gittes, he is more dazed than fulfilled by the catastrophe his investigation has brought about.

In other films, such as *The Left-Handed Gun, Bonnie and Clyde* and *Little Big Man,* Penn created a version of the western or the gangster film in which traditional meanings were inverted, but the effect was tragic rather than humorous. In *Little Big Man,* for example, the conventional western opposition between Indians and pioneers serves as the basis of the plot, which embodies two of the most powerful of our western myths, the Indian captivity and the massacre. However, the conventional renderings of these myths pit the humanely civilizing thrust of the pioneers against the savage ferocity and eroticism of the Indians and thereby justify the conquest of the West. Penn reverses these implications. In his film it is the Indians who are humane and civilized, while the pioneers are violent, corrupt, sexually repressed and madly ambitious. By the end, when Custer's cavalry rides forward to attack the Indian villages, our sympathies are all with the Indians. From this perspective, the conquest of the West is demythologized from the triumph of civilization into a historical tragedy of the destruction of a rich and vital human culture.

Despite its many virtues, the film version of *Little Big Man* was less artistically successful than Thomas Berger's novel on which it was based, primarily because as the film proceeds,

Penn loses the ironic detachment which Berger successfully maintains throughout the novel. Penn's portrayal of Custer as a lunatic symbol of aggressive American imperialism is overstated, and toward the end the cinematic *Little Big Man* tends to fall back from the serious exploration of mythical meanings into melodramatic burlesque. This is an artistic problem common to films in the mode of demythologization of traditional genres. Penn was far more successful in *Bonnie and Clyde*, which will remain one of the major masterpieces of recent American film. Taking off from the traditional gangster film with its opposition between the outlaw and society, *Bonnie and Clyde* establishes a dialectic between conventional and inverted meanings which is far richer and more powerfully sustained throughout the film. In the traditional gangster film, a powerful individual, frustrated by the limitations of his lower-class origin, is driven to a life of crime. Initially the audience is inclined to sympathize and identify with this character, but as he becomes involved in criminal actions, he overreaches himself and becomes a vicious killer who must be tracked down and destroyed by the representatives of society. The underlying myth of this genre affirms the limits of individual aggression in a society which tolerates and even encourages a high degree of personal enterprise and violence. The gangster becomes a tragic figure not because he is inherently evil, but because he fails to recognize these limits. The myth assures us that society is not repressive or violent; instead it shows how criminal violence evokes its own inevitable doom.

It is this comforting myth of proper and improper violence that Penn demythologizes in *Bonnie and Clyde*. As in *Little Big Man*, meanings become inverted. Instead of representing a limit to aggression and violence, society is portrayed as its fountainhead, while the outlaw protagonists are seen as victims of society's bloodlust. Throughout the film, we are shown a society of depression and chaos which yearns for action, and which projects this yearning into a vicarious excitement about the robberies and murders of the Barrow gang. Penn effectively develops this theme through his representation of the newspapers which so avidly report the gang's adventures and by the reactions of witnesses to the gang's attacks on banks. Finally, its lust for the hunt aroused, society itself takes up the pursuit in packs and posses and, in a final ambush which set a new level in explicit screen violence, the doomed Bonnie and Clyde are shot to pieces. But the inversion of generic meanings is still more complex, for Penn refuses to make the opposition between gangster and society a simple reversal of traditional generic meanings as he does in *Little Big Man*. The protagonists of *Bonnie and Clyde* are not simply victims of society. They are themselves very much a part of the society they are attacking. They share its basic aspirations and confusions and they yearn above all to be reintegrated with it. In many respects, their actions reflect a desperate and misconceived attempt to achieve some measure of the status, security and belongingness which ought to be among the basic gifts of a society to its members. Instead of simply reversing the meanings conventionally ascribed to the opposing forces of criminal and society in the gangster genre, *Bonnie and Clyde* expressed a more complex and dark awareness that this basic opposition was itself a mythical simplification, and showed us the deeper and more difficult irony of the twisted and inseparable fates of individuals and their society. This was in its way a recognition of that skein of ambiguous inevitability which Polanski summed up in the symbol of Chinatown, and which Francis Ford Coppola developed through the fateful intertwining of individuals, "families" and society in *The Godfather*.

Though the demythologization of traditional genres has been primarily evident in the work of younger directors, it has also had some influence on the later work of some of the classic filmmakers, most noticeably perhaps in the later westerns of John Ford, particularly *The Searchers, Cheyenne Autumn* and *The Man who Shot Liberty Valance*. Indeed, in the latter film, Ford symbolized the conquest of the West through a story in which the territory's last major outlaw was killed in a shootout by a man destined to lead the territory into the blessings of civilization. In fact, the legend of Senator Stoddard's heroic deed was a myth, the actual shooting of Liberty Valance having been done by another man. Toward the end of the film, the newspaper editor to whom Senator Stoddard confesses the truth about his past, makes the famous and ambiguous comment "when the legend becomes a fact, print the legend." But is this an ironic comment on the falsity of legends and newspapers alike, or is it some kind of affirmation of the significance of myth in spite of its unreality? Ford was apparently inclined to the latter interpretation, for he once told Peter Bogdanovich, "We've had a lot of people who were supposed to be great heroes and you know damn well they weren't. But it's good for the country to have heroes to look up to."*

This brings us to a fourth and final mode of generic transformation which might be described as the affirmation of myth for its own sake. In films in this mode, a traditional genre and

---

*Quoted in Jon Tuska, *The Filming of the West*. (Garden City, N.Y.: Doubleday and Co., 1976, p. 519.)

its myth are probed and shown to be unreal, but then the myth itself is at least partially affirmed as a reflection of authentic human aspirations and needs. This is the element which becomes dominant in Ford's later westerns in which he seems to see the heroic ethos of the West in critical terms and becomes more and more sympathetic with the Indian victims of the Westward movement. Yet, at the same time that he became more cynical about the reality of the West, he seemed to feel even more strongly the need to affirm its heroic ideals. Thus, in his powerful late film *The Searchers,* Ford turns to the old western theme of Indian captivity, portraying the mad obsessive hatred with which a White man pursues a band of Indians who have captured and adopted his niece. Yet Ford also accepted a change in the ending of the original novel, where this mad Indian hater was finally destroyed by his obsession, in order to reaffirm at the end the heroism and self-sacrifice of this obsessive quest. *The Searchers* is a powerful and beautiful film, yet one feels uncomfortable at the end, as if the gap between Ford's sense of historical reality and his feelings about genre and myth have come into collision.

Sam Peckinpah's *The Wild Bunch,* for all its ugliness and violence, is a more coherent example of the destruction and reaffirmation of myth. Throughout the film, Peckinpah points up the gap betwen the conventional western's heroic struggle between pioneers and outlaws. His pioneer lawmen are despicable bounty hunters in the employ of the railroad and they kill the guilty and the innocent indiscriminately. His outlaws are not much better; they are brutal, coarse, and quite capable of leaving a wounded comrade behind. Moreover, their type of criminal operation has become absurdly obsolescent in the early twentieth-century West of the film. In the end, Peckinpah's outlaw protagonists are drawn into a ridiculously destructive shootout with an entire Mexican village full of troops and are completely wiped out in the process. Yet the film also leaves us with a sense that through their hopeless action these coarse and vicious outlaws have somehow transcended themselves and become embodiments of a myth of heroism that men need in spite of the realities of their world.

While I have separated the four modes of generic transformation—humorous burlesque, evocation of nostalgia, demythologization of generic myth, and the affirmation of myth as myth—into separate categories in order to define them more clearly, it should be clear that most films which employ one of these modes are likely to use another at some point. Probably the best films based on generic transformation employ some combination of several of these modes in the service of one overriding artistic purpose; *Chinatown* uses both humorous burlesque and nostalgic evocation as a basis for its devastating exploration of the genre of the hard-boiled detective and his myth. Some directors seem to have a primary predilection for one of these modes; Brooks is primarily oriented toward burlesque, Bogdanovich toward nostalgia, Penn toward demythologization and Peckinpah toward reaffirmation. Some directors—Robert Altman springs particularly to mind—have, in their best films, worked out a rich and fascinating dialectic between different modes of generic transformation. In films like *McCabe and Mrs. Miller, The Long Goodbye, Thieves Like Us,* and *Nashville* it is quite difficult to decide at the end whether Altman is attacking or reaffirming the genre on which he has based each particular work. In fact, until the last two or three years, Altman's filmography looks almost as if he had planned a systematic voyage through the major traditional film genres. That generic transformation has been so important a source of artistic energy to the most vital younger directors suggests that it is a central key to the current state of the American film.

There are probably many reasons for the importance of these modes of filmmaking in the last decade, but in conclusion, I will comment briefly on what seem to me the most important factors involved in the proliferation of this kind of film. I think it is not primarily the competition of television. Though television has been somewhat more conservative in its use of generic transformation than film, the same modes seem to be turning up with increasing frequency in television series. Instead I would point to the tendency of genres to exhaust themselves, to our growing historical awareness of modern popular culture, and finally, to the decline of the underlying mythology on which traditional genres have been based since the late nineteenth century. Generic exhaustion is a common phenomenon in the history of culture. One can almost make out a life-cycle characteristic of genres as they move from an initial period of articulation and discovery, through a phase of conscious self-awareness on the part of both creators and audiences, to a time when the generic patterns have become so well-known that people become tired of their predictability. It is at this point that parodic and satiric treatments proliferate and new genres gradually arise. Our major traditional genres—the western, the detective story, the musical, the domestic comedy—have, after all, been around for a considerable period of time and it may be they have simply reached a point of creative exhaustion.

In our time, the awareness of the persistence of genres has been intensified by an increasing historical awareness of film. A younger generation of directors has a sense of film history quite different from many of their predecessors who, like Ford and Hawks, were involved with the art of film almost from its beginnings. Similarly, audiences have a kind of sophistication about the history of genres different from earlier film publics because of the tremendous number of past films now regularly shown on television and by college film societies.

But I am inclined to think that there is more to it than that. The present significance of generic transformation as a creative mode reflects the feeling that not only the traditional genres, but the cultural myths they once embodied, are no longer fully adequate to the imaginative needs of our time. It will require another essay to explain and justify this assertion, but if I may hazard a final prediction, I think we will begin to see emerging out of this period of generic transformation a new set of generic constructs more directly related to the imaginative landscape of the second half of the twentieth century. Thus, the present period of American filmmaking will seem in retrospect an important time of artistic and cultural transition. Like many transition periods, it may also turn out to be a time of the highest artistic accomplishment.

1978

VI

The Film Artist

The infant American film business grew into a multi-million-dollar industry in the first decade of the twentieth century. By the mid 1910s, in the years during and just after World War I, that industry organized itself according to what came to be called the Hollywood studio system (although, in fact, the real power of the system resided not in the Hollywood studios where the films were made but in the New York business offices where they were financed and distributed). A contemporary of Henry Ford's automobile assembly plant, the Hollywood studio was also very much a factory where goods — motion picture entertainments — were manufactured in mass for the masses. The film rolled down the assembly line, like one of Henry Ford's Model A's, through story departments, past departments of scenic and costume design, and onto the set where technicians (scenic and make-up craftsmen, camera and lighting crews) and actors united to forge the product. After that it rolled on down the line to the cutting and release departments, until it was shipped to the company's showrooms — whether the small-town Bijous or the big-city Movie Palaces.

From its beginnings, this industrialized studio system provoked a predictable question: how can a work of art result from such varied intentions and collective labors? For years, most American critics argued (or simply assumed) that art could not possibly result from such mechanized organization and collective chaos; they regarded the products of Hollywood as mere commercial entertainments that could not be compared to the "art films" of Europe or the "underground" films of the personal, experimental filmmaker.

One reply to this argument is to deny that a purely aesthetic intention or the vision of a single artist is necessary to create a work of art. Panofsky specifically compares the making of a film to the building of a cathedral, for the cathedral was built for the greater glory of God and was the result of the collective labor of as many specialists as a Hollywood film. François Truffaut, beginning in 1954 with his *Cahiers du cinéma* essay, "On Certain Tendencies in the French Cinema," developed an opposite response to the collective labor of filmmaking. His *"politique des auteurs"* defended the Hollywood studio film by maintaining that, although unappreciated or even unnoticed, the work of an author, an *auteur*, could be seen in many Hollywood films. This *auteur* was not the film's script writer, as many French film critics believed at the time, but the film's director, whose "signature" could be discerned by the sensitive critic who bothered to look for it. Truffaut's aim in this and succeeding articles was not to posit a general theory of film value; the pieces were polemics, specific reactions against contemporary French film critics and their valued style of French filmmaking, the "tradition of quality," which extolled the polished literary adaptations of such scenarists as Aurench and Bost (*La Symphonie Pastorale, The Red and the Black, The Idiot*) at the expense of the genuinely cinematic thinking of Jacques Tati, Jean Renoir, or Robert Bresson.

According to what has become known as the *"auteur* theory," the director's "style" or his "basic motifs," as the British critic Peter Wollen calls them, can be discerned by viewing his work as a whole—for these marks of directorial authorship will manifest themselves in all of a true *auteur*'s films, even as he works with different writers, cinematographers, and stars. Andrew Sarris, the primary American spokesman for the *auteur* theory, suggests that not only is the distinguishable personality of the director a criterion of value, but that the "meaning" which he is able to impose on the material with which he must work is the "ultimate" glory of the cinema. This observation raises a problem, however, concerning Wollen's two key terms—"style" and "basic motifs." Does Sarris mean that the "ultimate" glory is a director's imposition of "style" (e.g., the use of deep-focus photography) on a film's given "basic motifs" (e.g., domestic melodrama) or does he mean that the glory is the director's imposition of "style" that elicits new "basic motifs" (i.e., the meaning of love) from that melodrama? If the latter, does Sarris realize that the same can be said of any artist (say, Shakespeare in *King Lear* or *Othello*)? If the former, does Sarris mean that a director whose films deal with trash stylishly is an artist worthy of our attention?

Pauline Kael's reply to Sarris's "Notes on the Auteur Theory in 1962," is fiercely critical of Sarris's original version of the *auteur* theory—precisely because of the fuzziness about content and style. First, she finds it platitudinous to observe that one can discover an artistic "signature" or "basic motifs" in the work of an artist. Critics in all the arts assume that the artist has such a "signature," otherwise they would not bother to study him at all. Besides, as she observes, the sheer distinguishability of an artistic personality has no bearing on the value of that personality or his work. What an artist's works have in common may simply be signs of his ineptitude or his limitations. Finally, she thinks, there is something perverse about admiring an artist for managing to make an artistic silk purse out of the sow's ear of Hollywood trash. Isn't the true artist responsible for the choice of his materials and for finding an appropriate form for his chosen subject?

Although Kael's refutation of Sarris is largely correct, it is worth remarking that those who proposed the *auteur* theory were not simply arguing that an artist's personality will manifest itself in his works. They were seeking to establish that there was, indeed, an artist at work where many had never seen one. In doing so, they unquestionably helped to establish or re-establish the reputations of certain directors who worked within the Hollywood system, directors who did not exert much more control over the total project than many studio hacks, but who managed to make the kind of personal, significant statement that John Ford or (as Peter Wollen shows) Howard Hawks did. But Sarris's insistence on the sheer value of an artist's triumphing over his material seems a mistake, even from Sarris's own point of view. This is a useful strategy for rescuing some Hollywood reputations, but it lays the wrong groundwork for demonstrating the merits of the directors that Sarris (and almost everyone else) most admires. Directors such as Lubitsch, Renoir, Chaplin, Welles, and Keaton in fact enjoyed a large measure of individual control over scripts, shooting, and cutting. One does not, as Kael puts it, admire these directors for "shoving bits of style up the crevasses of the plots." In extending Truffaut's defense of the effective Hollywood studio director to cinema in general, Sarris has betrayed its limitations. His more recent writings on the theory have realized these very limitations and have softened or modified many of his original contentions.

Despite the limitations of Sarris's original formulation, critics and scholars have remained committed to directorial studies over the last decade. Gerald Mast's study of Howard Hawks addresses some of the difficulties that have affected the discussions of this particular *auteur* and, by implication, the *auteur* theory in general. By calling Hawks a storyteller, rather than an *auteur*, Mast removes the filmmaker from the specific confines of the Hollywood studio system to place him within a much broader and older narrative tradition, which includes novelists and dramatists as well. Mast avoids the conflict between emphasizing stylistic motifs or thematic commitments to the exclusion of the other that dominated earlier *auteur* discussions by arguing that the two are inseparable in Hawks's work, that style leads directly to meaning and vice versa. Perhaps this inseparability expresses what Sarris originally meant by his puzzling and provocative term (at least it provoked Kael's censure), "interior meaning." Mast also seeks to disentangle a confusion about what precisely a director does, particularly the differences between a director and a producer—especially the director who is, in name or in fact, his own producer rather than the employee of another. Mast has claimed that those American *auteurs* most admired by Sarris have indeed been the producers as well as the directors of their major films.

But the vast army of creative contributors to a film, such as those indicated by Donald Knox's collection of interviews with those responsible for the ballet of MGM's *An American in Paris*, suggests further problems with any director-centered *auteur* theory. The choreographer, musical arrangers, costume and scenic designers, and performers are not merely mechanics who execute someone else's idea. They contribute their own ideas to the final product, which becomes that much richer as a result of their own richly creative thinking. These major collaborators on a film are themselves *auteurs*, exercising not merely craft or artisanship but imagination and invention as well. Perhaps the *auteur* argument for directorial individuality might be modified in favor of another view—the directorial figure who is individual artist, efficient organizer, and catalytic stimulator of the talents of others.

If a director's signature can be recognized by a careful examination of all his works, this is equally true of certain screen writers, cinematographers, composers, and stars. Often the mark they leave on a film will be as great as or greater than that of its director. Richard Corliss, the current film critic for *Time* magazine, points out, for instance, that a film whose script is by a Norman Krasna or a Jules Furthman (who also wrote

frequently for Hawks) will more likely display their personalities than that of its director. The noted cinematographer, Nes-
tor Almendros, can observe the distinctive photographic style
of a Rudolph Maté in films as diverse as the French silent *The
Passion of Joan of Arc,* directed by Carl-Theodore Dreyer, and
the Hollywood studio production *Gilda,* directed by Charles
Vidor. Almendros, who has worked with some of the greatest
directors on both sides of the Atlantic (Truffaut, Rohmer, Ros-
selini, Pakula, Malick, Malle), calls particular attention to one
of the most easily overlooked elements of filmmaking—light
itself. He is able to characterize the style of the influential
French New Wave merely by referring to he problem of lighting real locations with available light. Almendros clearly sees
himself as the director's helper and assistant: he is conscious
of not working on " 'our' film but 'his' film"; he describes his
job as helping the director "express his artistic desires in practical and material terms." Nevertheless, one wonders how much
any *auteur* could accomplish without such a knowledgeable
master of lighting, framing, and the details of laboratory processing at his side.

Another frequently overlooked artist is the composer of the
film's score (an oversight resulting, perhaps, from the very tenacious prejudice that automatically considers film a visual art
rather than one both seen *and* heard). Royal Brown, a contemporary film and literary scholar, demonstrates that even one of
the most distinctive and respected cinema stylists, Alfred
Hitchcock, made some of his finest works in collaboration with
a single composer, Bernard Herrmann, who began his career
with Orson Welles, both on the radio and on *Citizen Kane.* Because music is "the least rational element in a film," the least
tied to concrete referents in reality, Herrmann could use his
scores to communicate the underlying irrationality of Hitchcock's stories (and Hitchcock's view of human interaction).
Herrmann's musical compositions work against "standards of
normalcy." Rather than writing lengthy melodies for the
Hitchcock films, Herrmann constructed very short, repetitive
motives of just one or two measures, for, according to Brown,
"melody is the most rational element of music." Despite
Hitchcock's indisputable importance as a true *auteur,* his works
cannot be fully understood and would not be fully felt without
the collaborative contribution of his composer.

Of course, the most serious difficulty for any theory of the
film *maker* as artist is the fact that many stars have made the
most decisive contributions to the Hollywood films in which
they have appeared, and that their unique "presence" can also
be determined by viewing the totality of their works. In *The*

World Viewed Stanley Cavell remarks how surprising he found the *auteur* theory, for it never previously occurred to him that anyone *made* a Hollywood film. For Cavell, the world of film revolved about, and was determined by, the star. When the European semiologist, Roland Barthes, writes of Garbo's "face," he implies that it is the main object of interest and the main conveyer of meaning in most of the films in which she appears. Kenneth Tynan, the British film and theatre critic, observes that "often during the decade in which [Garbo] talked to us, she gave signs that she was on the side of life against darkness: they seeped through a series of banal, barrel-scraping scripts like code-messages borne through enemy lines."

Even more complicated is the film star who does not merely perform in the scripts of others, like Garbo, but who writes her own scripts and whose characters on screen seek goals which very much resemble her own off screen. According to the feminist film critic Joan Mellen, Mae West was such a star, not merely a performer but an *auteur* who wrote her own films, wrote the plays on which many of them were based, wrote the songs she sang, and portrayed screen characters who, like West herself, were professional entertainers seeking self-sufficiency and independence in a world dominated by men. For Mellen, West herself is the most interesting thing about any of her films, not only for her artistry but for the social issues which the West persona both generated and avoided. Mellen sees West as a deeply paradoxical figure who simultaneously reduced herself to a sexual object, pandering to the prevailing sexist notions of her era, yet who simultaneously manipulated those notions as the only means to achieve self-sufficient control over her own life. For Mellen, West is free spirit and sexist—as well as racist. Such social issues indicate that the study of film art and the film artist cannot be isolated from the functions of that art and artist in the society as a whole—an issue which will become the concern of this volume's next section.

ANDREW SARRIS
NOTES ON
THE AUTEUR THEORY IN
1962

I call these sketches Shadowgraphs, partly by the designation to remind you at once that they derive from the darker side of life, partly because, like other shadowgraphs, they are not directly visible. When I take a shadowgraph in my hand, it makes no impression on me, and gives me no clear conception of it. Only when I hold it up opposite the wall, and now look not directly at it, but at that which appears on the wall, am I able to see it. So also with the picture I wish to show here, an inward picture that does not become perceptible until I see it through the external. This external is perhaps not quite unobtrusive, but, not until I look through it, do I discover that inner picture that I desire to show you, an inner picture too delicately drawn to be outwardly visible, woven as it is of the tenderest moods of the soul.

SØREN KIERKEGAARD, *in Either/Or*

An exhibitor once asked me if an old film I had recommended was *really* good or good only according to the *auteur* theory. I appreciate the distinction. Like the alchemists of old, *auteur* critics are notorious for rationalizing leaden clinkers into golden nuggets. Their judgments are seldom vindicated, because few spectators are conditioned to perceive in individual works the organic unity of a director's career. On a given evening, a film by John Ford must take its chances as if it were a film by Henry King. Am I implying that the weakest Ford is superior to the strongest King? Yes! This kind of unqualified affirmation seems to reduce the *auteur* theory to a game of aesthetic solitaire with all the cards turned face up. By *auteur* rules, the Fords will come up aces as invariably as the Kings will come up deuces. Presumably, we can all go home as soon as the directorial signature is flashed on the screen. To those who linger, *The Gunfighter* (King 1950) may appear worthier than *Flesh* (Ford 1932). (And how deeply one must burrow to undermine Ford!) No matter. The *auteur* theory is unyielding. If, by definition, Ford is invariably superior to King, any evidence to the contrary is merely an optical illusion. Now what could be sillier than this inflexible attitude? Let us abandon the absurdities of the *auteur* theory so that we may return to the chaos of common sense.

My labored performance as devil's advocate notwithstanding, I intend to praise the *auteur* theory, not to bury it. At the very least, I would like to grant the condemned system a hearing before its execution. The trial has dragged on for years, I know, and everyone is now bored by the abstract reasoning involved. I have little in the way of new evidence or new arguments, but I would like to change some of my previous testimony. What follows is, consequently, less a manifesto than a credo, a somewhat disorganized credo, to be sure, expressed in formless notes rather than in formal brief.

I. AIMEZ-VOUS BRAHMS?

Goethe? Shakespeare? Everything signed with their names is consid-ered good, and one wracks one's brains to find beauty in their stu-pidities and failures, thus distorting the general taste. All these great talents, the Goethes, the Shakespeares, the Beethovens, the Michel-angelos, created, side by side with their masterpieces, works not merely mediocre, but quite simply frightful.
                                        —LEO TOLSTOY, *Journal*, 1895–99

The preceding quotation prefaces the late André Bazin's famous critique of *"la politique des auteurs,"* which appeared in the *Cahiers du Cinéma* of April, 1957. Because no comparably lucid statement opposing the *politique* has appeared since that time, I would like to discuss some of Bazin's arguments with reference to the current situation. (I except, of course, Richard Roud's penetrating arti-cle "The French Line," which dealt mainly with the post-*Nou-velle Vague* situation when the *politique* had degenerated into McMahonism.)

As Tolstoy's observation indicates, *la politique des auteurs* ante-dates the cinema. For centuries, the Elizabethan *politique* has decreed the reading of every Shakespearean play before any en-counter with the Jonsonian repertory. At some point between *Timon of Athens* and *Volpone*, this procedure is patently unfair to

Jonson's reputation. But not really. On the most superficial level of artistic reputations, the *auteur* theory is merely a figure of speech. If the man in the street could not invoke Shakespeare's name as an identifiable cultural reference, he would probably have less contact with all things artistic. The Shakespearean scholar, by contrast, will always be driven to explore the surrounding terrain, with the result that all the Elizabethan dramatists gain more rather than less recognition through the pre-eminence of one of their number. Therefore, on balance, the *politique*, as a figure of speech, does more good than harm.

Occasionally, some iconoclast will attempt to demonstrate the fallacy of this figure of speech. We will be solemnly informed that *The Gambler* was a potboiler for Dostoyevsky in the most literal sense of the word. In Jacques Rivette's *Paris Nous Appartient*, Jean-Claude Brialy asks Betty Schneider if she would still admire *Pericles* if it were not signed by Shakespeare. Zealous musicologists have played *Wellington's Victory* so often as an example of inferior Beethoven that I have grown fond of the piece, atrocious as it is. The trouble with such iconoclasm is that it presupposes an ency-clopedic awareness of the *auteur* in question. If one is familiar with every Beethoven composition, *Wellington's Victory*, in itself, will hardly tip the scale toward Mozart, Bach, or Schubert. Yet that is the issue raised by the *auteur* theory. If not Beethoven, who? And why? Let us say that the *politique* for composers went Mozart, Beethoven, Bach, and Schubert. Each composer would represent a task force of compositions, arrayed by type and quality with the mighty battleships and aircraft carriers flanked by flotillas of cruisers, destroyers, and mine sweepers. When the Mozart task force collides with the Beethoven task force, symphonies roar against symphonies, quartets maneuver against quartets, and it is simply no contest with the operas. As a single force, Beethoven's nine symphonies, outgun any nine of Mozart's forty-one sympho-nies, both sets of quartets are almost on a par with Schubert's, but *The Magic Flute*, *The Marriage of Figaro*, and *Don Giovanni* will blow poor *Fidelio* out of the water. Then, of course, there is Bach with an entirely different deployment of composition and instru-mentation. The Haydn and Handel cultists are moored in their inlets ready to join the fray, and the moderns with their nuclear noises are still mobilizing their forces.

It can be argued that any exact ranking of artists is arbitrary and pointless. Arbitrary up to a point, perhaps, but pointless, no. Even Bazin concedes the polemical value of the *politique*. Many film critics would rather not commit themselves to specific rankings ostensibly because every film should be judged on its own merits. In many instances, this reticence masks the critic's condescension to the medium. Because it has not been firmly established that the

cinema is an art at all, it requires cultural audacity to establish
a pantheon for film directors. Without such audacity, I see little
point in being a film critic. Anyway, is it possible to honor a work
of art without honoring the artist involved? I think not. Of course,
any idiot can erect a pantheon out of hearsay and gossip. Without
specifying any work, the Saganesque seducer will ask quite cyni-
cally, "Aimez-vous Brahms?" The fact that Brahms is included in
the pantheon of high-brow pickups does not invalidate the industri-
ous criticism that justifies the composer as a figure of speech.

Unfortunately, some critics have embraced the *auteur* theory as a
short-cut to film scholarship. With a "you-see-it-or-you-don't"
attitude toward the reader, the particularly lazy *auteur* critic can
save himself the drudgery of communication and explanation. Indeed, at their worst, *auteur* critiques are less meaningful than the
straight-forward plot reviews that pass for criticism in America.
Without the necessary research and analysis, the *auteur* theory can
degenerate into the kind of snobbish racket that is associated with
the merchandising of paintings.

It was largely against the inadequate theoretical formulation of
la politique des auteurs that Bazin was reacting in his friendly
critique. (Henceforth, I will abbreviate *la politique des auteurs* as
the *auteur* theory to avoid confusion.) Bazin introduces his arguments within the context of a family quarrel over the editorial
policies of *Cahiers*. He fears that, by assigning reviews to admirers
of given directors, notably Alfred Hitchcock, Jean Renoir, Roberto
Rossellini, Fritz Lang, Howard Hawks, and Nicholas Ray, every
work, major and minor, of these exalted figures is made to radiate
the same beauties of style and meaning. Specifically, Bazin notes
a distortion when the kindly indulgence accorded the imperfect
work of a Minnelli is coldly withheld from the imperfect work of
Huston. The inherent bias of the *auteur* theory magnifies the gap
between the two films.

I would make two points here. First, Bazin's greatness as a critic,
(and I believe strongly that he was the greatest film critic who ever
lived) rested in his disinterested conception of the cinema as a universal entity. It follows that he would react against a theory that
cultivated what he felt were inaccurate judgments for the sake of
dramatic paradoxes. He was, if anything, generous to a fault, seeking in every film some vestige of the cinematic art. That he would
seek justice for Huston vis-à-vis Minnelli on even the secondary
levels of creation indicates the scrupulousness of his critical personality.

However, my second point would seem to contradict my first.
Bazin was wrong in this instance, insofar as any critic can be said
to be wrong in retrospect. We are dealing here with Minnelli in his
Lust for Life period and Huston in his *Moby Dick* period. Both

films can be considered failures on almost any level. The miscasting alone is disastrous. The snarling force of Kirk Douglas as the tormented Van Gogh, the brutish insensibility of Anthony Quinn as Gauguin, and the nervously scraping tension between these two absurdly limited actors, deface Minnelli's meticulously objective decor, itself inappropriate for the mood of its subject. The director's presentation of the paintings themselves is singularly unperceptive in the repeated failure to maintain the proper optical distance from canvases that arouse the spectator less by their detailed draughtsmanship than by the shock of a *gestalt* wholeness. As for *Moby Dick*, Gregory Peck's Ahab deliberates long enough to let all the demons flee the Pequod, taking Melville's Lear-like fantasies with them. Huston's epic technique with its casually shifting camera viewpoint then drifts on an intellectually becalmed sea toward a fitting rendezvous with a rubber whale. These two films are neither the best nor the worst of their time. The question is: Which deserves the harder review? And there's the rub. At the time, Huston's stock in America was higher than Minnelli's. Most critics expected Huston to do "big" things, and, if they thought about it at all, expected Minnelli to stick to "small" things like musicals. Although neither film was a critical failure, audiences stayed away in large enough numbers to make the cultural respectability of the projects suspect. On the whole, *Lust for Life* was more successful with the audiences it did reach than was *Moby Dick*.

In retrospect, *Moby Dick* represents the turning downward of Huston as a director to be taken seriously. By contrast, *Lust for Life* is simply an isolated episode in the erratic career of an interesting stylist. The exact size of Minnelli's talent may inspire controversy, but he does represent something in the cinema today. Huston is virtually a forgotten man with a few actors' classics behind him surviving as the ruins of a once-promising career. Both Eric Rohmer, who denigrated Huston in 1957, and Jean Domarchi, who was kind to Minnelli that same year, somehow saw the future more clearly on an *auteur* level than did Bazin. As Santayana has remarked: "It is a great advantage for a system of philosophy to be substantially true." If the *auteur* critics of the 1950's had not scored so many coups of clairvoyance, the *auteur* theory would not be worth discussing in the 1960's. I must add that, at the time, I would have agreed with Bazin on this and every other objection to the *auteur* theory, but subsequent history, that history about which Bazin was always so mystical, has substantially confirmed most of the principles of the *auteur* theory. Ironically, most of the original supporters of the *auteur* theory have now abandoned it. Some have discovered more useful *politiques* as directors and would-be directors. Others have succumbed to a European-oriented pragmatism where intention is now more nearly equal to talent in critical relevance. Luc Moullet's belated discovery that Samuel Fuller was, in fact, fifty years old, signaled a reorientation of *Cahiers* away from the American cinema. (The handwriting was already on the wall when Truffaut remarked recently that, whereas he and his colleagues had "discovered" *auteurs*, his successors have "invented" them.)

Bazin then explores the implications of Giraudoux's epigram: "There are no works; there are only authors." Truffaut has seized upon this paradox as the battle cry of *la politique des auteurs*. Bazin casually demonstrates how the contrary can be argued with equal probability of truth or error. He subsequently dredges up the equivalents of *Wellington's Victory* for Voltaire, Beaumarchais, Flaubert, and Gide to document his point. Bazin then yields some ground to Rohmer's argument that the history of art does not confirm the decline with age of authentic geniuses like Titian, Rembrandt, Beethoven, or nearer to us, Bonnard, Matisse, and Stravinsky. Bazin agrees with Rohmer that it is inconsistent to attribute senility only to aging film directors while, at the same time, honoring the gnarled austerity of Rembrandt's later style. This is one of the crucial propositions of the *auteur* theory, because it refutes the popular theory of decline for aging giants like Renoir and Chaplin and asserts, instead, that, as a director grows older, he is likely to become more profoundly personal than most audiences and critics can appreciate. However, Bazin immediately retrieves his lost ground by arguing that, whereas the senility of directors is no longer at issue, the evolution of an art form is. Where directors fail and fall is in the realm not of psychology but of history. If a director fails to keep pace with the development of his medium, his work will become obsolescent. What seems like senility is, in reality, a disharmony between the subjective inspiration of the director and the objective evolution of the medium. By making this distinction between the subjective capability of an *auteur* and the objective value of a work in film history, Bazin reinforces the popular impression that the Griffith of *Birth of a Nation* is superior to the Griffith of *Abraham Lincoln* in the perspective of timing, which similarly distinguishes the Eisenstein of *Potemkin* from the Eisenstein of *Ivan the Terrible*, the Renoir of *La Grande Illusion* from the Renoir of *Picnic in the Grass*, and the Welles of *Citizen Kane* from the Welles of *Mr. Arkadin*.

I have embroidered Bazin's actual examples for the sake of greater contact with the American scene. In fact, Bazin implicitly denies a decline in the later works of Chaplin and Renoir and never mentions Griffith. He suggests circuitously that Hawks's *Scarface* is clearly superior to Hawks's *Gentlemen Prefer Blondes*, although the *auteur* critics would argue the contrary. Bazin is particularly critical of Rivette's circular reasoning on *Monkey Business* as the proof of Hawks's genius. "One sees the danger," Bazin warns, "which is an aesthetic cult of personality."

Bazin's taste, it should be noted, was far more discriminating than that of American film historians. Films Bazin cites as unquestionable classics are still quite debatable here in America. After all, *Citizen Kane* was originally panned by James Agee, Richard Griffith, and Bosley Crowther, and *Scarface* has never been regarded as one of the landmarks of the American cinema by native critics. I would say that the American public has been ahead of its critics on both *Kane* and *Scarface*. Thus, to argue against the *auteur* theory in America is to assume that we have anyone of Bazin's sensibility and dedication to provide an alternative, and we simply don't.

Bazin, finally, concentrates on the American cinema, which invariably serves as the decisive battleground of the *auteur* theory, whether over *Monkey Business* or *Party Girl*. Unlike most "serious" American critics, Bazin likes Hollywood films, but not solely because of the talent of this or that director. For Bazin, the distinctively American comedy, western, and gangster genres have their own mystiques apart from the personalities of the directors concerned. How can one review an Anthony Mann western, Bazin asks, as if it were not an expression of the genre's conventions. Not that Bazin dislikes Anthony Mann's westerns. He is more concerned with otherwise admirable westerns that the *auteur* theory rejects because their directors happen to be unfashionable. Again, Bazin's critical generosity comes to the fore against the negative aspects of the *auteur* theory.

Some of Bazin's arguments tend to overlap each other as if to counter rebuttals from any direction. He argues, in turn, that the cinema is less individualistic an art than painting or literature, that Hollywood is less individualistic than other cinemas, and that, even so, the *auteur* theory never really applies anywhere. In upholding historical determinism, Bazin goes so far as to speculate that, if Racine had lived in Voltaire's century, it is unlikely that Racine's tragedies would have been any more inspired than Voltaire's. Presumably, the Age of Reason would have stifled Racine's neoclassical impulses. Perhaps. Perhaps not. Bazin's hypothesis can hardly be argued to a verifiable conclusion, but I suspect somewhat greater reciprocity between an artist and his *zeitgeist* than Bazin would allow. He mentions, more than once and in other contexts, capitalism's influence on the cinema. Without denying this influence, I still find it impossible to attribute X directors and Y films to any particular system or culture. Why should the Italian cinema be superior to the German cinema after one war, when the reverse was true after the previous one? As for artists conforming to the spirit of their age, that spirit is often expressed in contradictions, whether between Stravinsky and Sibelius, Fielding and Richardson, Picasso and Matisse, Chateaubriand and Stendhal. Even if the artist does not spring from the idealized head of Zeus, free of the embryonic stains of history, history itself is profoundly affected by his arrival. If we cannot imagine Griffith's *October* or Eisenstein's *Birth of a Nation* because we find it difficult to transpose one artist's unifying conceptions of Lee and Lincoln to the other's dialectical conceptions of Lenin and Kerensky, we are, nevertheless, compelled to recognize other differences in the personalities of these two pioneers beyond their respective cultural complexes. It is with these latter differences that the *auteur* theory is most deeply concerned. If directors and other artists cannot be wrenched from their historical environments, aesthetics is reduced to a subordinate branch of ethnography.

I have not done full justice to the subtlety of Bazin's reasoning and to the civilized skepticism with which he propounds his own arguments as slight probabilities rather than absolute certainties. Contemporary opponents of the *auteur* theory may feel that Bazin himself is suspect as a member of the *Cahiers* family. After all, Bazin does express qualified approval of the *auteur* theory as a relatively objective method of evaluating films apart from the subjective perils of impressionistic and ideological criticism. Better to analyze the director's personality than the critic's nerve centers or politics. Nevertheless, Bazin makes his stand clear by concluding: "This is not to deny the role of the author, but to restore to him the preposition without which the noun is only a limp concept. 'Author,' undoubtedly, but of what?"

Bazin's syntactical flourish raises an interesting problem in English usage. The French preposition "de" serves many functions, but among others, those of possession and authorship. In English, the preposition "by" once created a scandal in the American film industry when Otto Preminger had the temerity to advertise *The Man With the Golden Arm* as a film "by Otto Preminger." Novelist Nelson Algren and the Screenwriters' Guild raised such an outcry that the offending preposition was deleted. Even the noun "author" (which I cunningly mask as *"auteur"*) has a literary connotation in English. In general conversation, an "author" is invariably taken to be a writer. Since "by" is a preposition of authorship and not of ownership like the ambiguous "de," the fact that Preminger both produced and directed *The Man with the Golden Arm* did not entitle him in America to the preposition "by." No one would have objected to the possessive form: "Otto Preminger's *The Man with the Golden Arm.*" But, even in this case, a novelist of sufficient reputation is usually honored with the possessive designation. Now, this is hardly the case in France, where *The Red and the Black* is advertised as "un film de Claude Autant-Lara." In America, "directed by" is all the director can claim, when he is not also a well-known producer like Alfred Hitchcock or Cecil B. de Mille.

Since most American film critics are oriented toward literature or journalism, rather than toward future film-making, most American film criticism is directed toward the script instead of toward the screen. The writer-hero in *Sunset Boulevard* complains that people don't realize that someone "writes a picture; they think the actors make it up as they go along." It would never occur to this writer or most of his colleagues that people are even less aware of the director's function.

Of course, the much-abused man in the street has a good excuse not to be aware of the *auteur* theory even as a figure of speech. Even on the so-called classic level, he is not encouraged to ask "Aimez-vous Griffith?" or "Aimez-vous Eisenstein?" Instead, it is which Griffith or which Eisenstein? As for less acclaimed directors, he is lucky to find their names in the fourth paragraph of the typical review. I doubt that most American film critics really believe that an indifferently directed film is comparable to an indifferently written book. However, there is little point in wailing at the Philistines on this issue, particularly when some progress is being made in telling one director from another, at least when the film comes from abroad. The Fellini, Bergman, Kurosawa, and Antonioni promotions have helped push more directors up to the first paragraph of a review, even ahead of the plot synopsis. So, we mustn't complain.

Where I wish to redirect the argument is toward the relative position of the American cinema as opposed to the foreign cinema. Some critics have advised me that the *auteur* theory only applies to a small number of artists who make personal films, not to the run-of-the-mill Hollywood director who takes whatever assignment is available. Like most Americans who take films seriously, I have always felt a cultural inferiority complex about Hollywood. Just a few years ago, I would have thought it unthinkable to speak in the same breath of a "commercial" director like Hitchcock and a "pure" director like Bresson. Even today, *Sight and Sound* uses different type sizes for Bresson and Hitchcock films. After years of tortured revaluation, I am now prepared to stake my critical reputation, such as it is, on the proposition that Alfred Hitchcock is artistically superior to Robert Bresson by every criterion of excellence and, further, that, film for film, director for director, the American cinema has been consistently superior to that of the rest of the world from 1915 through 1962. Consequently, I now regard the *auteur* theory primarily as a critical device for recording the history of the American cinema, the only cinema in the world worth exploring in depth beneath the frosting of a few great directors at the top.

These propositions remain to be proven and, I hope, debated. The proof will be difficult because direction in the cinema is a nebulous force in literary terms. In addition to its own jargon, the director's craft often pulls in the related jargon of music, painting, sculpture, dance, literature, theatre, architecture, all in a generally futile attempt to describe the indescribable. What is it the old jazz man says of his art? If you gotta ask what it is, it ain't? Well, the cinema is like that. Criticism can only attempt an approximation, a reasonable preponderance of accuracy over inaccuracy. I know the exceptions to the *auteur* theory as well as anyone. I can feel the human attraction of an audience going one way when I am going the other. The temptations of cynicism, common sense, and facile culture-mongering are always very strong, but, somehow, I feel that the *auteur* theory is the only hope for extending the appreciation of personal qualities in the cinema. By grouping and evaluating films according to directors, the critic can rescue individual achievements from an unjustifiable anonymity. If medieval architects and African sculptors are anonymous today, it is not because they deserved to be. When Ingmar Bergman bemoans the alienation of the modern artist from the collective spirit that rebuilt the cathedral at Chartres, he is only dramatizing his own individuality for an age that has rewarded him handsomely for the travail of his alienation. There is no justification for penalizing Hollywood directors for the sake of collective mythology. So, invective aside, "Aimez-vous Cukor?"

II. WHAT IS THE *AUTEUR* THEORY?

As far as I know, there is no definition of the *auteur* theory in the English language, that is, by any American or British critic. Truffaut has recently gone to great pains to emphasize that the *auteur* theory was merely a polemical weapon for a given time and a given place, and I am willing to take him at his word. But, lest I be accused of misappropriating a theory no one wants anymore, I will give the *Cahiers* critics full credit for the original formulation of an idea that reshaped my thinking on the cinema. First of all, how does the *auteur* theory differ from a straightforward theory of directors. Ian Cameron's article "Films, Directors, and Critics," in *Movie* of September, 1962, makes an interesting comment on this issue: "The assumption that underlies all the writing in *Movie* is that the director is the author of a film, the person who gives it any distinctive quality. There are quite large exceptions, with which I shall deal later." So far, so good, at least for the *auteur* theory, which even allows for exceptions. However, Cameron continues: "On the whole, we accept the cinema of directors, although without going to the farthest-out extremes of the *la politique des auteurs*, which makes it difficult to think of a bad director making a good film and almost impossible to think of a good director making a bad one." We are back to Bazin again, although Cameron naturally uses different examples. That three otherwise divergent critics like Bazin, Roud, and Cameron make essentially the same point about the *auteur* theory suggests a common fear of its abuses. I believe there is a misunderstanding here about what the *auteur* theory actually claims, particularly since the theory itself is so vague at the present time.

First of all, the *auteur* theory, at least as I understand it and now intend to express it, claims neither the gift of prophecy nor the option of extracinematic perception. Directors, even *auteurs*, do not always run true to form, and the critic can never assume that a bad director will always make a bad film. No, not always, but almost always, and that is the point. What is a bad director, but a director who has made many bad films? What is the problem then? Simply this: The badness of a director is not necessarily considered the badness of a film. If Joseph Pevney directed Garbo, Cherkassov, Olivier, Belmondo, and Harriet Andersson in *The Cherry Orchard*, the resulting spectacle might not be entirely devoid of merit with so many subsidiary *auteurs* to cover up for Joe. In fact, with this cast and this literary property, a Lumet might be safer than a Welles. The realities of casting apply to directors as well as to actors, but the *auteur* theory would demand the gamble with Welles, if he were willing.

Marlon Brando has shown us that a film can be made without a director. Indeed, *One-Eyed Jacks* is more entertaining than many films with directors. A director-conscious critic would find it difficult to say anything good or bad about direction that is nonexistent. One can talk here about photography, editing, acting, but not direction. The film even has personality, but, like *The Longest Day* and *Mutiny on the Bounty*, it is a cipher directorially. Obviously, the *auteur* theory cannot possibly cover every vagrant charm of the cinema. Nevertheless, the first premise of the *auteur* theory is the technical competence of a director as a criterion of value. A badly directed or an undirected film has no importance in a critical scale of values, but one can make interesting conversation about the subject, the script, the acting, the color, the photography, the editing, the music, the costumes, the decor, and so forth. That is the nature of the medium. You always get more for your money than mere art. Now, by the *auteur* theory, if a director has no technical competence, no elementary flair for the cinema, he is automatically cast out from the pantheon of directors. A great director has to be at least a good director. This is true in any art. What constitutes directorial talent is more difficult to define abstractly. There is less disagreement, however, on this first level of the *auteur* theory than there will be later.

The second premise of the *auteur* theory is the distinguishable personality of the director as a criterion of value. Over a group of films, a director must exhibit certain recurring characteristics of style, which serve as his signature. The way a film looks and moves should have some relationship to the way a director thinks and feels. This is an area where American directors are generally superior to foreign directors. Because so much of the American cinema is commissioned, a director is forced to express his personality through the visual treatment of material rather than through the literary content of the material. A Cukor, who works with all sorts of projects, has a more developed abstract style than a Bergman, who is free to develop his own scripts. Not that Bergman lacks personality, but his work has declined with the depletion of his ideas largely because his technique never equaled his sensibility. Joseph L. Mankiewicz and Billy Wilder are other examples of writer-directors without adequate technical mastery. By contrast, Douglas Sirk and Otto Preminger have moved up the scale because their miscellaneous projects reveal a stylistic consistency.

The third and ultimate premise of the *auteur* theory is concerned with interior meaning, the ultimate glory of the cinema as an art. Interior meaning is extrapolated from the tension between a director's personality and his material. This conception of interior meaning comes close to what Astruc defines as *mise en scène*, but not quite. It is not quite the vision of the world a director projects nor quite his attitude toward life. It is ambiguous, in any literary sense, because part of it is imbedded in the stuff of the cinema and cannot be rendered in noncinematic terms. Truffaut has called it the temperature of the director on the set, and that is a close approximation of its professional aspect. Dare I come out and say what I think it to be is an *élan* of the soul?

Lest I seem unduly mystical, let me hasten to add that all I mean by "soul" is that intangible difference between one personality and another, all other things being equal. Sometimes, this difference is expressed by no more than a beat's hesitation in the rhythm of a film. In one sequence of *La Règle du Jeu*, Renoir gallops up the stairs, turns to his right with a lurching movement, stops in hoplike uncertainty when his name is called by a coquettish maid, and, then, with marvelous postreflex continuity, resumes his bearishly shambling journey to the heroine's boudoir. If I could describe the musical grace note of that momentary suspension, and I can't, I might be able to provide a more precise definition of the *auteur* theory. As it is, all I can do is point at the specific beauties of interior meaning on the screen and, later, catalogue the moments of recognition.

The three premises of the *auteur* theory may be visualized as three concentric circles: the outer circle as technique; the middle circle, personal style; and the inner circle, interior meaning. The corresponding roles of the director may be designated as those of a technician, a stylist, and an *auteur*. There is no prescribed course by which a director passes through the three circles. Godard once remarked that Visconti had evolved from a *metteur en scène* to an *auteur*, whereas Rossellini had evolved from an *auteur* to a *metteur en scène*. From opposite directions, they emerged with comparable status. Minnelli began and remained in the second circle as a stylist; Buñuel was an *auteur* even before he had assembled the technique of the first circle. Technique is simply the ability to put a film together with some clarity and coherence. Nowadays, it is possible to become a director without knowing too much about the technical side, even the crucial functions of photography and editing. An expert production crew could probably cover up for a chimpanzee in the director's chair. How do you tell the genuine director from the quasichimpanzee? After a given number of films, a pattern is established.

In fact, the *auteur* theory itself is a pattern theory in constant flux. I would never endorse a Ptolemaic constellation of directors in a fixed orbit. At the moment, my list of *auteurs* runs something like this through the first twenty: Ophuls, Renoir, Mizoguchi, Hitchcock, Chaplin, Ford, Welles, Dreyer, Rossellini, Murnau, Griffith, Sternberg, Eisenstein, von Stroheim, Buñuel, Bresson, Hawks, Lang, Flaherty, Vigo. This list is somewhat weighted toward seniority and established reputations. In time, some of these *auteurs* will rise, some will fall, and some will be displaced either by new directors or rediscovered ancients. Again, the exact order is less important than the specific definitions of these and as many as two hundred other potential *auteurs*. I would hardly expect any other critic in the world fully to endorse this list, especially on faith. Only after thousands of films have been revaluated, will any personal pantheon have a reasonably objective validity. The task of validating the *auteur* theory is an enormous one, and the end will never be in sight. Meanwhile, the *auteur* habit of collecting random films in directorial bundles will serve posterity with at least a tentative classification.

Although the *auteur* theory emphasizes the body of a director's work rather than isolated masterpieces, it is expected of great directors that they make great films every so often. The only possible exception to this rule I can think of is Abel Gance, whose greatness is largely a function of his aspiration. Even with Gance, *La Roue* is as close to being a great film as any single work of Flaherty's. Not that single works matter that much. As Renoir has observed, a director spends his life on variations of the same film.

Two recent films—*Boccaccio '70* and *The Seven Capital Sins*—unwittingly reinforced the *auteur* theory by confirming the relative standing of the many directors involved. If I had not seen either film, I would have anticipated that the order of merit in *Boccaccio*

'70 would be Visconti, Fellini, and De Sica, and in *The Seven Capital Sins* Godard, Chabrol, Demy, Vadim, De Broca, Molinaro. (Dhomme, Ionesco's stage director and an unknown quantity in advance, turned out to be the worst of the lot.) There might be some argument about the relative badness of De Broca and Molinaro, but, otherwise, the directors ran true to form by almost any objective criterion of value. However, the main point here is that even in these frothy, ultracommercial servings of entertainment, the contribution of each director had less in common stylistically with the work of other directors on the project than with his own previous work.

Sometimes, a great deal of corn must be husked to yield a few kernels of internal meaning. I recently saw *Every Night at Eight*, one of the many maddeningly routine films Raoul Walsh has directed in his long career. This 1935 effort featured George Raft, Alice Faye, Frances Langford, and Patsy Kelly in one of those familiar plots about radio shows of the period. The film keeps moving along in the pleasantly unpretentious manner one would expect of Walsh until one incongruously intense scene with George Raft thrashing about in his sleep, revealing his inner fears in mumbling dream-talk. The girl he loves comes into the room in the midst of his unconscious avowals of feeling and listens sympathetically. This unusual scene was later amplified in *High Sierra* with Humphrey Bogart and Ida Lupino. The point is that one of the screen's most virile directors employed an essentially feminine narrative device to dramatize the emotional vulnerability of his heroes. If I had not been aware of Walsh in *Every Night at Eight*, the crucial link to *High Sierra* would have passed unnoticed. Such are the joys of the *auteur* theory.

1962

PAULINE KAEL
CIRCLES AND SQUARES

> *. . . the first premise of the* auteur *theory is the technical competence of a director as a criterion of value . . . The second premise of the* auteur *theory is the distinguishable personality of the director as a criterion of value. . . . The third and ultimate premise of the* auteur *theory is concerned with interior meaning, the ultimate glory of the cinema as an art. Interior meaning is extrapolated from the tension between a director's personality and his material. . . .*

Sometimes a great deal of corn must be husked to yield a few kernels of internal meaning. I recently saw Every Night at Eight, *one of the many maddeningly routine films Raoul Walsh has directed in his long career. This 1935 effort featured George Raft, Alice Faye, Frances Langford and Patsy Kelly in one of those familiar plots about radio shows of the period. The film keeps moving along in the pleasantly unpretentious manner one would expect of Walsh until one incongruously intense scene with George Raft thrashing about in his sleep, revealing his inner fears in mumbling dream talk. The girl he loves comes into the room in the midst of his unconscious avowals of feeling, and listens sympathetically. This unusual scene was later amplified in* High Sierra *with Humphrey Bogart and Ida Lupino. The point is that one of the screen's most virile directors employed an essentially feminine narrative device to dramatize the emotional vulnerability of his heroes. If I had not been aware of Walsh in* Every Night at Eight, *the crucial link to*

High Sierra would have passed unnoticed. Such are the joys of the auteur *theory.*
        —Andrew Sarris, "Notes on the Auteur Theory in 1962,"
                                Film Culture, Winter 1962–1963.

Perhaps a little more corn should be husked; perhaps, for example, we can husk away the word "internal" (is "internal meaning" any different from "meaning"?). We might ask why the link is "crucial"? Is it because the device was "incongruously intense" in *Every Night at Eight* and so demonstrated a try for something *deeper* on Walsh's part? But if his merit is his "pleasantly unpretentious manner" (which is to say, I suppose, that, recognizing the limitations of the script, he wasn't trying to do much) then the incongruous device was probably a misconceived attempt that disturbed the manner—like a bad playwright interrupting a comedy scene because he cannot resist the opportunity to tug at your heartstrings. We might also ask why this narrative device is "essentially feminine": is it more feminine than masculine to be asleep, or to talk in one's sleep, or to reveal feelings? Or, possibly, does Sarris regard the device as feminine because the listening woman becomes a sympathetic figure and emotional understanding is, in this "virile" context, assumed to be essentially feminine? Perhaps only if one accepts the narrow notions of virility so common in our action films can this sequence be seen as "essentially feminine," and it is amusing that a critic can both support these clichés of the male world and be so happy when they are violated.

This is how we might quibble with a different *kind* of critic but we would never get anywhere with Sarris if we tried to examine what he is saying sentence by sentence.

So let us ask, what is the meaning of the passage? Sarris has noticed that in *High Sierra* (not a very good movie) Raoul Walsh repeated an uninteresting and obvious device that he had earlier used in a worse movie. And for some inexplicable reason, Sarris concludes that he would not have had this joy of discovery without the *auteur* theory.

But in every art form, critics traditionally notice and point out the way the artists borrow from themselves (as well as from others) and how the same devices, techniques, and themes reappear in their work. This is obvious in listening to music, seeing plays, reading novels, watching actors; we take it for granted that this is how we perceive the development or the decline of an artist (and it may be necessary to point out to *auteur* critics that repetition without development is decline). When you see Hitchcock's *Saboteur* there is no doubt that he drew heavily and clumsily from *The 39 Steps,* and when you see *North by Northwest* you can see that he is once again toying with the ingredients of *The 39 Steps*—and apparently having a good time with them. Would Sarris not notice the repetition in the Walsh films without the *auteur* theory? Or shall we take the more cynical view that without some commitment to Walsh as an *auteur*, he probably wouldn't be spending his time looking at these movies?

If we may be permitted a literary analogy, we can visualize Sarris researching in the archives of the *Saturday Evening Post*, tracing the development of Clarence Budington Kelland, who, by the application of something like the *auteur* theory, would emerge as a much more important writer than Dostoyevsky; for in Kelland's case Sarris's three circles, the three premises of the *auteur* theory, have been consistently congruent. Kelland is technically competent (even "pleasantly unpretentious"), no writer has a more "distinguishable personality," and if "interior meaning" is what can be extrapolated from, say, *Hatari!* or *Advise and Consent* or *What Ever Happened to Baby Jane?* then surely Kelland's stories with their attempts to force a bit of character and humor into the familiar plot outlines are loaded with it. Poor misguided Dostoyevsky, too full of what he has to say to bother with "technical competence," tackling important themes in each work (surely the worst crime in the *auteur* book) and with his almost incredible unity of personality and material leaving you nothing to extrapolate from, he'll never make it. If the editors of *Movie* ranked authors the way they do directors, Dostoyevsky would probably be in that almost untouchable category of the "ambitious."

It should be pointed out that Sarris's defense of the *auteur* theory is based not only on aesthetics but on a rather odd pragmatic statement: "Thus to argue against the *auteur* theory in America is to assume that we have anyone of Bazin's sensibility and dedication to provide an alternative, and we simply don't." Which I take to mean that the *auteur* theory is necessary in the absence of a critic who wouldn't need it. This is a new approach to aesthetics, and I hope Sarris's humility does not camouflage his double-edged argument. If his aesthetics is based on expediency, then it may be expedient to point out that it takes extraordinary intelligence and discrimination and taste to use any theory in the arts, and that without those qualities, a theory becomes a rigid formula (which is indeed what is happening among *auteur* critics). The greatness of critics like Bazin in France and Agee in America may have something to do with their using their full range of intelligence and intuition, rather than relying on formulas. Criticism is an art, not a science, and a critic who follows rules will fail in one of his most important functions: perceiving what is original and important in *new* work and helping others to see.

THE OUTER CIRCLE

. . . the first premise of the auteur *theory is the technical competence of a director as a criterion of value.*

This seems less the premise of a theory than a commonplace of judgment, as Sarris himself indicates when he paraphrases it as, "A great director has to be at least a good director." But this commonplace, though it *sounds* reasonable and basic, is a shaky premise: sometimes the greatest artists in a medium bypass or violate the simple technical competence that is so necessary for hacks. For example, it is doubtful if Antonioni could handle a routine directorial assignment of the type at which John Struges is so proficient *(Escape from Fort Bravo* or *Bad Day at Black Rock),* but surely Antonioni's *L'Avventura* is the work of a great director. And the greatness of a director like Cocteau has nothing to do with mere technical competence: his greatness is in being able to achieve his own personal expression and style. And just as there were writers like Melville or Dreiser who triumphed over various kinds of technical incompetence, and who were, as artists, incomparably greater than the facile technicians of their day, a new great film director may appear whose very greatness is in his struggling toward grandeur or in massive accumulation of detail. An artist who is not a good technician can indeed create new standards, because standards of technical competence are based on comparisons with work already done.

Just as new work in other arts is often attacked because it violates the accepted standards and thus seems crude and ugly and incoherent, great new directors are very likely to be condemned precisely on the grounds that they're not even good directors, that they don't know their "business." Which, in some cases, is true, but does it matter when that "business" has little to do with what they want to express in films? It may even be a hindrance, leading them to banal slickness, instead of discovery of their own methods. For some, at least, Cocteau may be right: "The only technique worth having is the technique you invent for yourself." The director must be judged on the basis of what he produces—his films—and if he can make great films without knowing the standard methods, without the usual craftsmanship of the "good director," then that is the way he works. I would amend Sarris's premise to, "In works of a lesser rank, technical competence can help to redeem the weaknesses of the material." In fact it seems to be precisely this category that the *auteur* critics are most interested in—the routine material that a good craftsman can make into a fast and enjoyable movie. What, however, makes the *auteur* critics so incomprehensible, is not their *preference* for works of this category (in this they merely follow the lead of children who also prefer simple action films and westerns and horror films to works that make demands on their understanding) but their truly astonishing inability to exercise taste and judgment *within* their area of preference. Moviegoing kids are, I think, much more reliable guides to this kind of movie than the *auteur* critics: every kid I've talked to knows that Henry Hathaway's *North to Alaska* was a surprisingly funny, entertaining movie and *Hatari!* (classified as a "masterpiece" by half the *Cahiers* Conseil des Dix, Peter Bogdanovich, and others) was a terrible bore.

THE MIDDLE CIRCLE

. . . the second premise of the auteur *theory is the distinguishable personality of the director as a criterion of value.*

Up to this point there has really been no theory, and now, when Sarris begins to work on his foundation, the entire edifice of civilized standards of taste collapses while he's tacking down his floorboards. Traditionally, in any art, the personalities of all those involved in a production have been a factor in judgment, but that the *distinguishability* of personality should in itself be a criterion of value completely confuses *normal* judgment. The smell of a skunk is more distinguishable than the perfume of a rose; does that make it better? Hitchcock's personality is certainly more distinguishable in *Dial M for Murder, Rear Window, Vertigo,* than Carol Reed's in *The Stars Look Down, Odd Man Out, The Fallen Idol, The Third Man, An Outcast of the Islands,* if for no other reason than because Hitchcock repeats while Reed tackles new subject matter. But how does this distinguishable personality function as a criterion for judging the works? We recognize the hands of Carné and Prévert in *Le Jour se Lève,* but that is not what makes it a beautiful film; we can just as easily recognize their hands in *Quai des Brumes* —which is not such a good film. We can recognize that *Le Plaisir* and *The Earrings of Madame de . . .* are both the work of Ophuls, but *Le Plaisir* is not a great film, and *Madame de . . .* is.

Often the works in which we are most aware of the personality of the director are his worst films—when he falls back on the devices he has already done to death. When a famous director makes a good movie, we look at the movie, we don't think about the director's personality; when he makes a stinker we notice his familiar touches because there's not much else to watch. When Preminger makes an expert, entertaining whodunit like *Laura,* we don't look for his personality (it has become part of the texture of the film); when he makes an atrocity like *Whirlpool,* there's plenty of time to look for his "personality"—if that's your idea of a good time.

It could even be argued, I think, that Hitchcock's uniformity, his mastery of tricks, and his cleverness at getting audiences to respond according to his calculations—the feedback he wants and gets from them—reveal not so much a personal style as a personal theory of audience psychology, that his methods and approach are not those of an artist but a prestidigitator. The *auteur* critics respond just as Hitchcock expects the gullible to respond. This is not so surprising —often the works *auteur* critics call masterpieces are ones that seem to reveal the contempt of the director for the audience.

It's hard to believe that Sarris seriously attempts to apply "the distinguishable personality of the director as a criterion of value" because when this premise becomes troublesome, he just tries to brazen his way out of difficulties. For example, now that John Huston's work has gone flat* Sarris casually dismisses him with: "Huston is virtually a forgotten man with a few actors' classics behind him . . ." If *The Maltese Falcon*, perhaps the most high-style thriller ever made in America, a film Huston both wrote and directed, is not a director's film, what is? And if the distinguishable personality of the director is a criterion of value, then how can Sarris dismiss the Huston who comes through so unmistakably in *The Treasure of Sierra Madre*, *The African Queen*, or *Beat the Devil*, or even in a muddled Huston film like *Key Largo*? If these are actors' movies, then what on earth is a director's movie?

Isn't the *auteur* theory a hindrance to clear judgment of Huston's movies and of his career? Disregarding the theory, we see some fine film achievements and we perceive a remarkably distinctive directorial talent; we also see intervals of weak, half-hearted assignments like *Across the Pacific* and *In This Our Life*. Then, after *Moulin Rouge*, except for the blessing of *Beat the Devil*, we see a career that splutters out in ambitious failures like *Moby Dick* and confused projects like *The Roots of Heaven* and *The Misfits*, and strictly commercial projects like *Heaven Knows, Mr. Allison*. And this kind of career seems more characteristic of film history, especially in the United States, than the ripening development and final mastery envisaged by the *auteur* theory—a theory that makes it almost de rigueur to regard Hitchcock's American films as superior to his early English films. Is Huston's career so different, say, from Fritz Lang's? How is it that Huston's early good—almost great— work, must be rejected along with his mediocre recent work, but Fritz Lang, being sanctified as an *auteur*, has his bad recent work

---

* And, by the way, the turning point came, I think, not with *Moby Dick*, as Sarris indicates, but much earlier, with *Moulin Rouge*. This may not be so apparent to *auteur* critics concerned primarily with style and individual touches, because what was shocking about *Moulin Rouge* was that the content was sentimental mush. But critics who accept even the worst of Minnelli probably wouldn't have been bothered by the fact that *Moulin Rouge* was soft in the center, it had so many fancy touches at the edges.

praised along with his good? Employing more usual norms, if you respect the Fritz Lang who made *M* and *You Only Live Once*, if you enjoy the excesses of style and the magnificent absurdities of a film like *Metropolis*, then it is only good sense to reject the ugly stupidity of *Journey to the Lost City*. It is an insult to an artist to praise his bad work along with his good; it indicates that you are incapable of judging either.

A few years ago, a friend who reviewed Jean Renoir's University of California production of his play *Carola*, hailed it as "a work of genius." When I asked my friend how he could so describe this very unfortunate play, he said, "Why, of course, it's a work of genius. Renoir's a genius, so anything he does is a work of genius." This could almost be a capsule version of the *auteur* theory (just substitute *Hatari!* for *Carola*) and in this reductio ad absurdum, viewing a work is superfluous, as the judgment is a priori. It's like buying clothes by the label: this is Dior, so it's good. (This is not so far from the way the *auteur* critics work, either.)

Sarris doesn't even play his own game with any decent attention to the rules: it is as absurd to praise Lang's recent bad work as to dismiss Huston's early good work; surely it would be more consistent if he also tried to make a case for Huston's bad pictures? That would be more consistent than devising a category called "actors' classics" to explain his good pictures away. If *The Maltese Falcon* and *The Treasure of Sierra Madre* are actors' classics, then what makes Hawks's *To Have and Have Not* and *The Big Sleep* (which were obviously tailored to the personalities of Bogart and Bacall) the work of an *auteur*?

Sarris believes that what makes an *auteur* is "an élan of the soul." (This critical language is barbarous. Where else should élan come from? It's like saying "a digestion of the stomach." A film critic need not be a theoretician, but it is necessary that he know how to use words. This might, indeed, be a first premise for a theory.) Those who have this élan presumably have it forever and their films reveal the "organic unity" of the directors' careers; and those who don't have it—well, they can only make "actors' classics." It's ironic that a critic trying to establish simple "objective" rules as a guide for critics who he thinks aren't gifted enough to use taste and intelligence, ends up—where, actually, he began—with a theory based on mystical insight. This might really make demands on the *auteur* critics if they did not simply take the easy way out by arbitrary decisions of who's got "it" and who hasn't. Their decisions are not merely not based on their theory; their decisions are *beyond* criticism. It's like a woman's telling us that she feels a certain dress *does* something for her: her feeling has about as much to do with critical judgment as the *auteur* critics' feeling that Minnelli *has* "it," but Huston never had "it."

Even if a girl had plenty of "it," she wasn't expected to keep it forever. But this "élan" is not supposed to be affected by the vicissitudes of fortune, the industrial conditions of moviemaking, the turmoil of a country, or the health of a director. Indeed, Sarris says, "If directors and other artists cannot be wrenched from their historical environments, aesthetics is reduced to a subordinate branch of ethnography." May I suggest that if, in order to judge movies, the *auteur* critics must wrench the directors from their historical environments (which is, to put it mildly, impossible) so that they can concentrate on the detection of that "élan," they are reducing aesthetics to a form of idiocy. Élan as the permanent attribute Sarris posits can only be explained in terms of a cult of personality. May I suggest that a more meaningful description of élan is what a man feels when he is working at the height of his powers—and what we respond to in works of art with the excited cry of "This time, he's really done it" or "This shows what he could do when he got the chance" or "He's found his style" or "I never realized he had it in him to do anything so good," a response to his joy in creativity.

Sarris experiences "joy" when he recognizes a pathetic little link between two Raoul Walsh pictures (he never does explain whether the discovery makes him think the pictures are any better) but he wants to see artists in a pristine state—their essences, perhaps?—separated from all the life that has formed them and to which they try to give expression.

THE INNER CIRCLE

The third and ultimate premise of the auteur *theory is concerned with interior meaning, the ultimate glory of the cinema as an art. Interior meaning is extrapolated from the tension between a director's personality and his material.*

This is a remarkable formulation: it is the opposite of what we have always taken for granted in the arts, that the artist expresses himself in the unity of form and content. What Sarris believes to be "the ultimate glory of the cinema as an art" is what has generally been considered the frustrations of a man working against the given material. Fantastic as this formulation is, it does something that the first two premises didn't do: it clarifies the interests of the *auteur* critics. If we have been puzzled because the *auteur* critics seemed so deeply involved, even dedicated, in becoming connoisseurs of trash, now we can see by this theoretical formulation that trash is indeed their chosen province of film.

Their ideal *auteur* is the man who signs a long-term contract, directs any script that's handed to him, and expresses himself by shoving bits of style up the crevasses of the plots. If his "style" is

in conflict with the story line or subject matter, so much the better
—more chance for tension. Now we can see why there has been so
much use of the term "personality" in this aesthetics (the term
which seems so inadequate when discussing the art of Griffith or
Renoir or Murnau or Dreyer)—a routine, commercial movie can
sure use a little "personality."

Now that we have reached the inner circle (the bull's eye turns
out to be an empty socket) we can see why the shoddiest films are
often praised the most. Subject matter is irrelevant (so long as it
isn't treated sensitively—which is bad) and will quickly be disposed
of by *auteur* critics who know that the smart director isn't responsible for that anyway; they'll get on to the important subject—his
mise-en-scène: The director who fights to do something he cares
about is a square. Now we can at least begin to understand why
there was such contempt toward Huston for what was, in its way,
a rather extraordinary effort—the *Moby Dick* that failed; why
Movie considers Roger Corman a better director than Fred Zinnemann and ranks Joseph Losey next to God, why Bogdanovich,
Mekas, and Sarris give their highest critical ratings to *What Ever
Happened to Baby Jane?* (mighty big crevasses there). If Carol Reed
had made only movies like *The Man Between*—in which he obviously worked to try to make something out of a ragbag of worn-out
bits of material—he might be considered "brilliant" too. (But this is
doubtful: although even the worst Reed is superior to Aldrich's
Baby Jane, Reed would probably be detected, and rejected, as a
man interested in substance rather than sensationalism.)

I am angry, but am I unjust? Here's Sarris:

> A Cukor who works with all sorts of projects has a more developed
> abstract style than a Bergman who is free to develop his own scripts.
> Not that Bergman lacks personality, but his work has declined with
> the depletion of his ideas largely because his technique never equaled
> his sensibility. Joseph L. Mankiewicz and Billy Wilder are other ex-
> amples of writer-directors without adequate technical mastery. By
> contrast, Douglas Sirk and Otto Preminger have moved up the scale
> because their miscellaneous projects reveal a stylistic consistency.

How neat it all is—Bergman's "work has declined with the depletion of his ideas largely because his technique never equaled his
sensibility." But what on earth does that mean? How did Sarris perceive Bergman's sensibility except through his technique? Is Sarris
saying what he seems to be saying, that if Bergman had developed
more "technique," his work wouldn't be dependent on his ideas?
I'm afraid this *is* what he means, and that when he refers to Cukor's
"more developed abstract style" he means by "abstract" something
unrelated to ideas, a technique not dependent on the content of the

films. This is curiously reminiscent of a view common enough in the business world, that it's better not to get too involved, too personally interested in business problems, or they take over your life; and besides, you don't function as well when you've lost your objectivity. But this is the *opposite* of how an artist works. His technique, his *style*, is determined by his range of involvements, and his preference for certain themes. Cukor's style is no more *abstract*(!) than Bergman's: Cukor has a range of subject matter that he can handle and when he gets a good script within his range (like *The Philadelphia Story* or *Pat and Mike*) he does a good job; but he is at an immense *artistic* disadvantage, compared with Bergman, because he is dependent on the ideas of so many (and often bad) scriptwriters and on material which is often alien to his talents. It's amusing (and/or depressing) to see the way *auteur* critics tend to downgrade writer-directors—who are in the *best* position to use the film medium for personal expression.

Sarris does some pretty fast shuffling with Huston and Bergman; why doesn't he just come out and admit that writer-directors are disqualified by his third premise? They can't arrive at that "interior meaning, the ultimate glory of the cinema" because a writer-director has no tension between his personality and his material, so there's nothing for the *auteur* critic to extrapolate from.

What is all this nonsense about extrapolating "interior" meaning from the tension between a director's personality and his material? A competent commercial director generally does the best he can with what he's got to work with. Where is the "tension"? And if you can locate some, what kind of meaning could you draw out of it except that the director's having a bad time with lousy material or material he doesn't like? Or maybe he's trying to speed up the damned production so he can do something else that he has some *hopes* for? Are these critics honestly (and futilely) looking for "interior meanings" or is this just some form of intellectual diddling that helps to sustain their pride while they're viewing silly movies? Where is the tension in Howard Hawks's films? When he has good material, he's capable of better than good direction, as he demonstrates in films like *Twentieth Century*, *Bringing Up Baby*, *His Girl Friday*; and in *To Have and Have Not* and *The Big Sleep* he demonstrates that with help from the actors, he can jazz up ridiculous scripts. But what "interior meaning" can be extrapolated from an enjoyable, harmless, piece of kitsch like *Only Angels Have Wings*; what can the *auteur* critics see in it beyond the sex and glamor and fantasies of the high-school boys' universe—exactly what the mass audience liked it for? And when Hawks's material and/or cast is dull and when his heart isn't in the production—when by the *auteur* theory he should show his "personality," the result is something soggy like *The Big Sky*.

George Cukor's modest statement, "Give me a good script and I'll be a hundred times better as a director"* provides some notion of how a director may experience the problem of the given material. What can Cukor do with a script like *The Chapman Report* but try to kid it, to dress it up a bit, to show off the talents of Jane Fonda and Claire Bloom and Glynis Johns, and to give the total production a little flair and craftsmanship. At best, he can make an entertaining bad movie. A director with something like magical gifts *can* make a silk purse out of a sow's ear. But if he has it in him to do more in life than make silk purses, the triumph is minor—even if the purse is lined with gold. Only by the use of the *auteur* theory does this little victory become "ultimate glory." For some unexplained reason those traveling in *auteur* circles believe that making that purse out of a sow's ear is an infinitely greater accomplishment than making a solid carrying case out of a good piece of leather (as, for example, a Zinnemann does with *From Here to Eternity* or *The Nun's Story*).

I suppose we should be happy for Sirk and Preminger elevated up the glory "scale," but I suspect that the "stylistic consistency" of say, Preminger, could be a matter of his *limitations*, and that the only way you could tell he made some of his movies was that he used the same players so often (Linda Darnell, Jeanne Crain, Gene Tierney, Dana Andrews, et al., gave his movies the Preminger look). But the argument is ludicrous anyway, because if Preminger shows stylistic consistency with subject matter as varied as *Carmen Jones, Anatomy of a Murder,* and *Advise and Consent,* then by any rational standards he should be attacked rather than elevated. I don't think these films are stylistically consistent, nor do I think Preminger is a great director—for the very simple reason that his films are consistently superficial and facile. (*Advise and Consent,* an *auteur* "masterpiece"—Ian Cameron, Paul Mayersberg, and Mark Shivas of *Movie* and Jean Douchet of *Cahiers du Cinéma* rate it first on their ten best lists of 1962 and Sarris gives it his top rating—seems not so much Preminger-directed as other-directed. That is to say, it seems calculated to provide what as many different groups as possible want to see: there's something for the liberals, something for the conservatives, something for the homosexuals,

---

* In another sense, it is perhaps immodest. I would say, give Cukor a clever script with light, witty dialogue, and he will know what to do with it. But I wouldn't expect more than glossy entertainment. (It seems almost too obvious to mention it, but can Sarris really discern the "distinguishable personality" of George Cukor and his "abstract" style in films like *Bhowani Junction, Les Girls, The Actress, A Life of Her Own, The Model and the Marriage Broker, Edward, My Son, A Woman's Face, Romeo and Juliet, A Double Life?* I wish I could put him to the test. I can only *suspect* that many *auteur* critics would have a hard time seeing those telltale traces of the beloved in their works.)

something for the family.) An editorial in *Movie* states: "In order to enjoy Preminger's films the spectator must apply an unprejudiced intelligence; he is constantly required to examine the quality not only of the characters' decisions but also of his own reactions," and "He presupposes an intelligence active enough to allow the spectator to make connections, comparisons and judgments." May I suggest that this spectator would have better things to do than the editors of *Movie* who put out Preminger issues? They may have, of course, the joys of discovering links between *Centennial Summer, Forever Amber, That Lady in Ermine,* and *The Thirteenth Letter,* but I refuse to believe in these ever-so-intellectual protestations. The *auteur* critics aren't a very *convincing* group.

I assume that Sarris's theory is not based on his premises (the necessary causal relationships are absent), but rather that the premises were devised in a clumsy attempt to prop up the "theory." (It's a good thing he stopped at three: a few more circles and we'd really be in hell, which might turn out to be the last refinement of film tastes—Abbott and Costello comedies, perhaps?) These critics work embarrassingly hard trying to give some semblance of intellectual respectability to a preoccupation with mindless, repetitious commercial products—the kind of action movies that the restless, rootless men who wander on Forty-Second Street and in the Tenderloin of all our big cities have always preferred just because they could respond to them without thought. These movies soak up your time. I would suggest that they don't serve a very different function for Sarris or Bogdanovich or the young men of *Movie*— even though they devise elaborate theories to justify soaking up their time. An educated man must have to work pretty hard to set his intellectual horizons at the level of *I Was a Male War Bride* (which, incidentally, wasn't even a good *commercial* movie).

"Interior meaning" seems to be what those in the know know. It's a mystique—and a mistake. The *auteur* critics never tell us by what divining rods they have discovered the élan of a Minnelli or a Nicholas Ray or a Leo McCarey. They're not critics; they're inside dopesters. There must be another circle that Sarris forgot to get to —the one where the secrets are kept. . . .

1963

PETER WOLLEN
FROM SIGNS AND MEANING IN THE CINEMA

THE AUTEUR THEORY

The *politique des auteurs*—the *auteur* theory, as Andrew Sarris calls it—was developed by the loosely knit group of critics who wrote for *Cahiers du Cinéma* and made it the leading film maga-zine in the world. It sprang from the conviction that the American cinema was worth studying in depth, that masterpieces were made not only by a small upper crust of directors, the cultured gilt on the commercial gingerbread, but by a whole range of authors, whose work had previously been dismissed and consigned to oblivion. There were special conditions in Paris which made this conviction possible. Firstly, there was the fact that American films were banned from France under the Vichy government and the German Occupation. Consequently, when they reappeared after the Libera-tion they came with a force—and an emotional impact—which was necessarily missing in the Anglo-Saxon countries themselves. And, secondly, there was a thriving ciné-club movement, due in part to the close connections there had always been in France between the cinema and the intelligentsia: witness the example of Jean Cocteau or André Malraux. Connected with this ciné-club movement was the magnificent Paris *Cinémathèque*, the work of Henri Langlois, a great *auteur*, as Jean-Luc Godard described him. The policy of the *Cinémathèque* was to show the maximum number of films, to plough back the production of the past in order to produce the culture in which the cinema of the future could thrive. It gave French *cinéphiles* an unmatched perception of the historical di-mensions of Hollywood and the careers of individual directors.

The *auteur* theory grew up rather haphazardly; it was never elaborated in programmatic terms, in a manifesto or collective statement. As a result, it could be interpreted and applied on rather broad lines; different critics developed somewhat different methods within a loose framework of common attitudes. This looseness and diffuseness of the theory has allowed flagrant misunderstandings to take root, particularly among critics in Britain and the United States. Ignorance has been compounded by a vein of hostility to foreign ideas and a taste for travesty and caricature. However, the fruitfulness of the *auteur* approach has been such that it has made headway even on the most unfavorable terrain. For instance, a recent straw poll of British critics, conducted in conjunction with a Don Siegel Retrospective at the National Film Theatre, revealed that, among American directors most admired, a group consisting of Budd Boetticher, Samuel Fuller and Howard Hawks ran immediately behind Ford, Hitchcock and Welles, who topped the poll, but ahead of Billy Wilder, Josef Von Sternberg and Preston Sturges.

Of course, some individual directors have always been recognised as outstanding: Charles Chaplin, John Ford, Orson Welles. The *auteur* theory does not limit itself to acclaiming the director as the main author of a film. It implies an operation of decipherment; it reveals authors where none had been seen before. For years, the model of an author in the cinema was that of the European director, with open artistic aspirations and full control over his films. This model still lingers on; it lies behind the existential distinction between art films and popular films. Directors who built their reputations in Europe were dismissed after they crossed the Atlantic, reduced to anonymity. American Hitchcock was contrasted unfavourably with English Hitchcock, American Renoir with French Renoir, American Fritz Lang with German Fritz Lang. The *auteur* theory has led to the revaluation of the second, Hollywood careers of these and other European directors; without it, masterpieces such as *Scarlet Street* or *Vertigo* would never have been perceived. Conversely, the *auteur* theory has been sceptical when offered an American director whose salvation has been exile to Europe. It is difficult now to argue that *Brute Force* has ever been excelled by Jules Dassin or that Joseph Losey's recent work is markedly superior to, say, *The Prowler*.

In time, owing to the diffuseness of the original theory, two main schools of *auteur* critics grew up: those who insisted on revealing a core of meanings, of thematic motifs, and those who stressed style and *mise en scène*. There is an important distinction here, which I shall return to later. The work of the *auteur* has a semantic dimension, it is not purely formal; the work of the *metteur en scène*, on the other hand, does not go beyond the realm of performance, of transposing into the special complex of cinematic codes and channels a pre-existing text: a scenario, a book or a play. As we shall see, the meaning of the films of an *auteur* is constructed *a posteriori;* the meaning—semantic, rather than stylistic or expressive—of the films of a *metteur en scène* exists *a priori.* In concrete cases, of course, this distinction is not always clear-cut. There is controversy over whether some directors should be seen as *auteurs* or *metteurs en scène.* For example, though it is possible to make intuitive ascriptions, there have been no really persuasive accounts as yet of Raoul Walsh or William Wyler as *auteurs,* to take two very different directors. Opinions might differ about Don Siegel or George Cukor. Because of the difficulty of fixing the distinction in these concrete cases, it has often become blurred; indeed, some French critics have tended to value the *metteur en scène* above the *auteur.* MacMahonism sprang up, with its cult of Walsh, Lang, Losey and Preminger, its fascination with violence and its notorious text: "Charlton Heston is an axiom of the cinema." What André Bazin called "aesthetic cults of personality" began to be formed. Minor directors were acclaimed before they had, in any real sense, been identified and defined.

Yet the *auteur* theory has survived despite all the hallucinating critical extravaganzas which it has fathered. It has survived because it is indispensable. Geoffrey Nowell-Smith has summed up the *auteur* theory as it is normally presented today:

> One essential corollary of the theory as it has been developed is the discovery that the defining characteristics of an author's work are not necessarily those which are most readily apparent. The purpose of criticism thus becomes to uncover behind the superficial contrasts of subject and treatment a hard core of basic and often recondite motifs. The pattern formed by these motifs . . . is what gives an author's work its particular structure, both defining it internally and distinguishing one body of work from another.

It is this "structural approach," as Nowell-Smith calls it, which is indispensable for the critic.

The test case for the *auteur* theory is provided by the work of Howard Hawks. Why Hawks, rather than, say, Frank Borzage or King Vidor? Firstly, Hawks is a director who has worked for years within the Hollywood system. His first film, *Road to Glory,* was made in 1926. Yet throughout his long career he has only once received general critical acclaim, for his wartime film, *Sergeant York,* which closer inspection reveals to be eccentric and atypical of the main *corpus* of Hawks's films. Secondly, Hawks has worked in almost every genre. He has made westerns *(Rio Bravo),* gangsters *(Scarface),* war films *(Air Force),* thrillers *(The Big Sleep),* science fiction *(The Thing from Another World)*, musicals *(Gentlemen Prefer Blondes)*, comedies *(Bringing up Baby)*, even a Biblical epic *(Land of the Pharaohs)*. Yet all of these films (except perhaps *Land of the Pharaohs*, which he himself was not happy about) exhibit the same thematic preoccupations, the same recurring motifs and incidents, the same visual style and tempo. In the same way that Roland Barthes constructed a species of *homo racinianus*, the critic can construct a *homo hawksianus*, the protagonist of Hawksian values in the problematic Hawksian world.

Hawks achieved this by reducing the genres to two basic types: the adventure drama and the crazy comedy. These two types express inverse views of the world, the positive and negative poles of the Hawksian vision. Hawks stands opposed, on the one hand, to John Ford and, on the other hand, to Budd Boetticher. All these directors are concerned with the problem of heroism. For the hero, as an individual, death is an absolute limit which cannot be transcended: it renders the life which preceded it meaningless, absurd. How then can there be any meaningful individual action during life? How can individual action have any value—be heroic— if it cannot have transcendent value, because of the absolutely devaluing limit of death? John Ford finds the answer to this question by placing and situating the individual within society and within history, specifically within American history. Ford finds transcendent values in the historic vocation of America as a nation, to bring civilisation to a savage land, the garden to the wilderness. At the same time, Ford also sees these values themselves as problematic; he begins to question the movement of American history itself. Boetticher, on the contrary, insists on a radical individualism. "I am not interested in making films about mass feelings. I am for the individual." He looks for values in the encounter with death itself: the underlying metaphor is always that of the bull-fighter in the arena. The hero enters a group of companions, but there is no possibility of group solidarity. Boetticher's hero acts by dissolving groups and collectives of any kind into their constituent individuals, so that he confronts each person face-to-face; the films develop, in Andrew Sarris's words, into "floating poker games, where every character takes turns at bluffing about his hand until the final showdown." Hawks, unlike Boetticher, seeks transcendent values beyond the individual, in solidarity with others. But, unlike Ford, he does not give his heroes any historical dimension, any destiny in time.

For Hawks the highest human emotion is the camaraderie of the exclusive, self-sufficient, all-male group. Hawk's heroes are cattlemen, marlin-fishermen, racing-drivers, pilots, big-game hunters, habituated to danger and living apart from society, actually cut off from it physically by dense forest, sea, snow or desert. Their aerodromes are fog-bound; the radio has cracked up; the next mail-coach or packet-boat does not leave for a week. The *élite* group strictly preserves its exclusivity. It is necessary to pass a test of ability and courage to win admittance. The group's only internal tensions come when one member lets the other down (the drunk deputy in *Rio Bravo*, the panicky pilot in *Only Angels Have Wings*) and must redeem himself by some act of exceptional bravery, or occasionally when too much 'individualism' threatens to disrupt the close-knit circle (the rivalry between drivers in *Red Line 7000*, the fighter pilot among the bomber crew in *Air Force*). The group's security is the first commandment: "You get a stunt team in acrobatics in the air—if one of them is no good, then they're all in trouble. If someone loses his nerve catching animals, then the whole bunch can be in trouble." The group members are bound together by rituals (in *Hatari!* blood is exchanged by transfusion) and express themselves univocally in communal sing-songs. There is a famous example of this in *Rio Bravo*. In *Dawn Patrol* the camaraderie of the pilots stretches even across the enemy lines: a captured German ace is immediately drafted into the group and joins in the sing-song; in *Hatari!* hunters of different nationality and in different places join together in a song over an intercom radio system.

Hawks's heroes pride themselves on their professionalism. They ask: "How good is he? He'd better be good." They expect no praise for doing their job well. Indeed, none is given except: 'The boys did all right.' When they die, they leave behind them only the most meagre personal belongings, perhaps a handful of medals. Hawks himself has summed up this desolate and barren view of life:

It's just a calm acceptance of a fact. In *Only Angels Have Wings*, after Joe dies, Cary Grant says: "He just wasn't good enough." Well, that's the only thing that keeps people going. They just have to say: "Joe wasn't good enough, and I'm better than Joe, so I go ahead and do it." And they find out they're not any better than Joe, but then it's too late, you see.

In Ford films, death is celebrated by funeral services, an impromptu prayer, a few staves of "Shall we gather at the river?"—it is inserted into an ongoing system of ritual institutions, along with the wedding, the dance, the parade. But for Hawks it is enough that the routine of the group's life goes on, a routine whose only relieving features are "danger" *(Hatari!)* and "fun." Danger gives existence pungency: "Every time you get real action, then you have danger. And the question, 'Are you living or not living?' is probably the biggest drama we have." This nihilism, in which 'living' means no more than being in danger of losing your life—a danger entered into quite gratuitously—is augmented by the Hawksian concept of having "fun." The word "fun" crops up constantly in Hawks's interviews and scripts. It masks his despair.

When one of Hawks's *élite* is asked, usually by a woman, why he risks his life, he replies: "No reason I can think of makes any sense. I guess we're just crazy." Or Feathers, sardonically, to Colorado in *Rio Bravo*: "You haven't even the excuse I have. We're all fools." By "crazy" Hawks does not mean psychopathic: none of his characters are like Turkey in Peckinpah's *The Deadly Companions* or Billy the Kid in Penn's *The Left-Handed Gun*. Nor is there the sense of the absurdity of life which we sometimes find in Boetticher's films: death, as we have seen, is for Hawks simply a routine occurrence, not a *grotesquerie*, as in *The Tall T* ('Pretty soon that well's going to be chock-a-block') or *The Rise and Fall of Legs Diamond*. For Hawks "craziness" implies difference, a sense of apartness from the ordinary, everyday, social world. At the same time, Hawks sees the ordinary world as being "crazy" in a much more fundamental sense, because devoid of any meaning or values. "I mean crazy reactions—I don't think they're crazy, I think they're normal—but according to bad habits we've fallen into they seemed crazy." Which is the normal, which the abnormal? Hawks recognises, inchoately, that to most people his heroes, far from embodying rational values, are only a dwindling band of eccentrics. Hawks's 'kind of men' have no place in the world.

The Hawksian heroes, who exclude others from their own *élite* group, are themselves excluded from society, exiled to the African bush or to the Arctic. Outsiders, other people in general, are perceived by the group as an undifferentiated crowd. Their role is to gape at the deeds of the heroes whom, at the same time, they hate. The crowd assembles to watch the showdown in *Rio Bravo*, to see the cars spin off the track in *The Crowd Roars*. The gulf between the outsider and the heroes transcends enmities among the *élite*: witness *Dawn Patrol* or Nelse in *El Dorado*. Most dehumanised of all is the crowd in *Land of the Pharaohs*, employed in building the Pyramids. Originally the film was to have been about Chinese labourers building a "magnificent airfield" for the American army, but the victory of the Chinese Revolution forced Hawks to change his plans. ("Then I thought of the building of the Pyramids; I thought it was the same kind of story.") But the presence of the crowd, of external society, is a constant covert threat to the Hawksian *élite*, who retaliate by having "fun." In the crazy comedies ordinary citizens are turned into comic butts, lampooned and tormented: the most obvious target is the insurance salesman in *His Girl Friday*. Often Hawks's revenge becomes grim and macabre. In *Sergeant York* it is "fun" to shoot Germans "like turkeys"; in *Air Force* it is "fun" to blow up the Japanese fleet. In *Rio Bravo* the geligniting of the badmen "was very funny." It is at these moments that the *élite* turns against the world outside and takes the opportunity to be brutal and destructive.

Besides the covert pressure of the crowd outside, there is also an overt force which threatens: woman. Man is woman's "prey." Women are admitted to the male group only after much disquiet and a long ritual courtship, phased round the offering, lighting and exchange of cigarettes, during which they prove themselves worthy of entry. Often they perform minor feats of valour. Even then though they are never really full members. A typical dialogue sums up their position:

Woman: You love him, don't you?

Man (embarrassed): Yes . . . I guess so. . . .

Woman: How can I love him like you?

Man: Just stick around.

The undercurrent of homosexuality in Hawks's films is never crystallised, though in *The Big Sky*, for example, it runs very close to the surface. And he himself described *A Girl in Every Port* as "really a love story between two men." For Hawks men are equals, within the group at least, whereas there is a clear identification between women and the animal world, most explicit in *Bringing Up Baby*, *Gentlemen Prefer Blondes* and *Hatari!* Man must strive to maintain his mastery. It is also worth noting that, in Hawks's adventure dramas and even in many of his comedies, there is no married life. Often the heroes were married or at least intimately committed, to a woman at some time in the distant past but have suffered an unspecified trauma, with the result that they have been suspicious of women ever since. Their attitude is "Once bitten, twice shy." This is in contrast to the films of Ford, which almost always include domestic scenes. Woman is not a threat to Ford's heroes; she falls into her allotted social place as wife and mother, bringing up the children, cooking, sewing, a life of service, drudgery and subordination. She is repaid for this by being sentimentalised. Boetticher, on the other hand, has no obvious place for women at all; they are phantoms, who provoke action, are pretexts for male modes of conduct, but have no authentic significance in themselves. "In herself, the woman has not the slightest importance."

Hawks sees the all-male community as an ultimate; obviously it is very retrograde. His Spartan heroes are, in fact, cruelly stunted. Hawks would be a lesser director if he was unaffected by this, if his adventure dramas were the sum total of his work. His real claim as an author lies in the presence, together with the dramas,

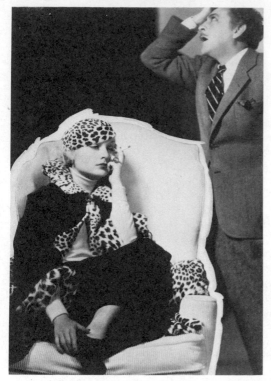

Howard Hawks's battle between the sexes. Carole Lombard and John Barrymore in *Twentieth Century* (1934), Cary Grant and Katharine Hepburn in *Bringing Up Baby* (1938). "Besides the covert pressure of the crowd outside, there is also an overt force which threatens: woman. Man is woman's 'prey'" (WOLLEN, page 559).

of their inverse, the crazy comedies. They are the agonised exposure of the underlying tensions of the heroic dramas. There are
two principal themes, zones of tension. The first is the theme of
regression: of regression to childhood, infantilism, as in *Monkey
Business*, or regression to savagery: witness the repeated scene of
the adult about to be scalped by painted children, in *Monkey
Business* and in *The Ransom of Red Chief*. With brilliant insight,
Robin Wood has shown how *Scarface* should be categorised among
the comedies rather than the dramas: Camonte is perceived as
savage, child-like, subhuman. The second principal comedy theme
is that of sex-reversal and role-reversal. *I Was A Male War Bride*
is the most extreme example. Many of Hawks's comedies are
centred round domineering women and timid, pliable men: *Bringing Up Baby* and *Man's Favourite Sport*, for example. There are
often scenes of male sexual humiliation, such as the trousers being
pulled off the hapless private eye in *Gentlemen Prefer Blondes*.
In the same film, the Olympic Team of athletes are reduced to
passive objects in an extraordinary Jane Russell song number; big-
game hunting is lampooned, like fishing in *Man's Favourite Sport*;
the theme of infantilism crops up again: "The child was the most
mature one on board the ship, and I think he was a lot of fun."

Whereas the dramas show the mastery of man over nature, over
woman, over the animal and childish; the comedies show his
humiliation, his regression. The heroes become victims; society,
instead of being excluded and despised, breaks in with irruptions
of monstrous farce. It could well be argued that Hawks's outlook,
the alternative world which he constructs in the cinema, the
Hawksian heterocosm, is not one imbued with particular intellectual subtlety or sophistication. This does not detract from its
force. Hawks first attracted attention because he was regarded
naïvely as an action director. Later, the thematic content which I
have outlined was detected and revealed. Beyond the stylemes,
semantemes were found to exist; the films were anchored in an
objective stratum of meaning, a plerematic stratum, as the Danish
linguist Hjelmslev would put it. Thus the stylistic expressiveness
of Hawks's films was shown to be not purely contingent, but
grounded in significance.

Something further needs to be said about the theoretical basis of
the kind of schematic exposition of Hawks's work which I have
outlined. The 'structural approach' which underlies it, the definition of a core of repeated motifs, has evident affinities with methods
which have been developed for the study of folklore and mythology. In the work of Olrik and others, it was noted that in different
folk-tales the same motifs reappeared time and time again. It
became possible to build up a lexicon of these motifs. Eventually
Propp showed how a whole cycle of Russian fairy-tales could be

analysed into variations of a very limited set of basic motifs (or moves, as he called them). Underlying the different, individual tales was an archi-tale, of which they were all variants. One important point needs to be made about this type of structural analysis. There is a danger, as Lévi-Strauss has pointed out, that by simply noting and mapping resemblances, all the texts which are studied (whether Russian fairy-tales or American movies) will be reduced to one, abstract and impoverished. There must be a moment of synthesis as well as a moment of analysis: otherwise, the method is formalist, rather than truly structuralist. Structuralist criticism cannot rest at the perception of resemblances or repetitions (redundancies, in fact), but must also comprehend a system of differences and oppositions. In this way, texts can be studied not only in their universality (what they all have in common) but also in their singularity (what differentiates them from each other). This means of course that the test of a structural analysis lies not in the orthodox canon of a director's work, where resemblances are clustered, but in films which at first sight may seem eccentricities.

In the films of Howard Hawks a systematic series of oppositions can be seen very near the surface, in the contrast between the adventure dramas and the crazy comedies. If we take the adventure dramas alone it would seem that Hawks's work is flaccid, lacking in dynamism; it is only when we consider the crazy comedies that it becomes rich, begins to ferment: alongside every dramatic hero we are aware of a phantom, stripped of mastery, humiliated, inverted. With other directors, the system of oppositions is much more complex: instead of there being two broad strata of films there are a whole series of shifting variations. In these cases, we need to analyse the roles of the protagonists themselves, rather than simply the worlds in which they operate. The protagonists of fairy-tales or myths, as Lévi-Strauss has pointed out, can be dissolved into bundles of differential elements, pairs of opposites. Thus the difference between the prince and the goose-girl can be reduced to two antinomic pairs: one natural, male versus female, and the other cultural, high versus low. We can proceed with the same kind of operation in the study of films, though, as we shall see, we shall find them more complex than fairy-tales. . . .

1969

GERALD MAST
FROM HOWARD HAWKS, STORYTELLER

AUTEUR OR STORYTELLER

All I'm trying to do is tell a story and I just imagine the way it should be if you tell it and so I do it. [1]

In America . . . . they're just beginning to appreciate the work of directors. They're beginning to find out that some directors put a stamp on their work and some don't. Some are good storytellers and some aren't. [2]

Above all in a motion picture is the story. [3]

He is one of those directors of whom it is said: I will go see everything he does because he is a good storyteller. [4]

One approach to film criticism has specifically set itself the task of articulating the unique artistic qualities of this uniquely American art: the *auteur* theory, first advocated in France by the young François Truffaut in 1953 (as the *politique des au-*

---

[1]DGA Interview, p. 3.

[2]Howard Hawks, "An Interview with Howard Hawks," by Naomi Goodwin and Michael Wise, *Take One* 3, no. 8 (Nov.–Dec. 1971): (hereafter referred to as Goodwin-Wise Interview).

[3]Howard Hawks, Interview by Jacques Rivette and François Truffaut originally published in *Cahiers du Cinéma*, translated and published in *Interviews with Film Directors*, edited by Andrew Sarris (New York, 1967), p. 189 (hereafter referred to as *Cahiers* Interview).

[4]Ibid., p. 195.

teurs), then developed in America a decade later by Andrew Sarris and others of his persuasion. The name of Howard Hawks has been inextricably linked to the *auteur* undertaking, and if there is a single concrete accomplishment that can justify that entire undertaking it is the resuscitation of the reputation of Howard Hawks and the rediscovery of his films. The original *auteur*ist aim (an aim which has been both broadened and softened with the passage of time)[5] was to identify an individual artistic personality in a Hollywood film's director, a personality which could be distinguished from both the film's script and its stars. The undertaking works particularly well with a director like Douglas Sirk, who made domestic melodramas (also called "women's pictures," "weepers," "'soapers," and several other derogatory synonyms) at Universal-International for producer Ross Hunter in the 1950s (among them, *All That Heaven Allows, Tarnished Angels, Written On the Wind, Imitations of Life*).

A careful look at Sirk's films reveals that the director built as many scenes as possible around hard, reflective visual materials (glass, mirrors, window panes, the shiny surfaces of furniture); that he used ordinary domestic objects (teapots, television sets, cups, saucers, clothing, sofas, pictures, tablecloths) as symbolic commentaries on the lives and values of the people who lived with those objects; and that he filled his motion picture frame with frames-within-the-frame (doorways, archways, window panes, mirrors) so that his films refer not only to life but also to imitations of life—in particular to the way life is imitated in movies themselves. Despite the tawdry, melodramatic scripts of these films, despite their saccharine musical soundtracks, and despite the leaden embodiments of the characters by those dim "stars" under contract to Universal who peopled Sirk's would (Jane Wyman, Rock Hudson, Sandra Dee, Lana Turner, John Gavin, John Saxon), the unique, personal devices of a creator named Douglas Sirk can be identified—devices which perform a devastatingly ironic critique of the very bourgeois world which is the film's milieu. For such films, the *auteur* theory's urging us to perceive the "tension" between the director's personality and the script's demands is the only way to come to know that such a creator named Douglas Sirk exists.

[5]The original and most extreme statement of *auteur* intentions can be found in Andrew Sarris's major essay, "Notes on the Auteur Theory in 1962," collected in Gerald Mast and Marshall Cohen, eds., *Films Theory and Criticism: Introductory Readings*, 2nd ed. (New York, 1979), pp. 650–65. Later Sarris writings, particularly the introductory essay to his *The American Cinema* (New York, 1968), have pulled back from many of his most provocative claims.

But Howard Hawks did not make such films. He spent his apprenticeship as a scriptwriter and producer. He developed (if not actually wrote) every script he shot (and he rewrote whole chunks of them himself on the set). He produced most of the films he directed (and he walked out on many he did not produce when some meddling Mayer or Goldwyn told him what and what not to do). As a producer Hawks controlled all those decisions about a film project that the director (in his job as director) does not: he hired the writers and approved their work; he hired the set designer, editor, musical director, cinematographer and approved their work; and, extremely important in film, he hired the actors who would embody the characters. While the director (in his job as director) is responsible only for what happens in front of the camera on the set, the producer (as the title implies) is responsible for the whole production and the production of the whole. In his work on a film, Howard Hawks was as much a creative producer, like David O. Selznick, as a creative director, like Douglas Sirk. This confusion between the director's and producer's responsibilities on a film leads to an *auteur*ist inconsistency with Hawks—the acceptance of *The Thing* as a Howard Hawks film when in fact Howard Hawks did not direct the film (not one scene) but produced it.[6] The contribution of Howard Hawks to a film cannot be illuminated (as can Sirk's) by his separation from or antagonism to his content or script or performers. His contribution *is* the whole film: "his acting style, his script, and his visual style are all one."[7]

A second problem the *auteur*ist encounters with Hawks can also be illustrated by the treatment of Sirk. Proving the existence of reflective surfaces, symbolic objects, and frames within frames in every Sirk film certainly establishes the existence of a presence named Sirk—but little more. It in no way proves that the films are of any value—or even that Sirk is of any

---

[6]Several Howard Hawks interviews contain his insistence that Christian Nyby directed *The Thing*. Hawks produced the film, helped shape the script, and advised Nyby repeatedly on how he might handle scenes (as any creative producer might). Christian Nyby, in a personal tape-recorded interview with the author in May 1980, makes the same claim: he discussed script and shots with Hawks but he himself directed every scene of the film. The relevance of such controversy to a discussion of Howard Hawks is not to attempt to determine exactly who directed what. The collaboration of Nyby and Hawks on *The Thing* reveals that the separation of script and film, directing and producing, cannot be maintained in evaluating Hawks's work. Hawks did not simply direct any of his major films. But if he had directed *The Thing*, the film might not only have shown traces of Hawks's structure and themes; it might also have been a lot more energetic and spontaneous than it turned out to be.

[7]John Belton, "Hawks and Co." in *Focus on Howard Hawks*, p. 108.

value. To prove the distinguishability of a director's personality (the heart of the original *auteur* undertaking) cannot demonstrate in itself the talent of a director or the excellence of his work. *Auteur* discussions of Hawks, insistent on demonstrating that there *is* a Howard Hawks beneath the genre conventions of his films, seize on the bits of themes and business that link the films: the exchange of cigarettes, the professionalism of his characters, the sexual role reversals and the use of animals in his comedies, male friendship and the rites of passage that allow a female entrance to the male group in the adventure films, and so forth. Picking through the Hawks films to reveal these consistent bits both fails to demonstrate the value of individual films and tends to collapse Hawks's career into one giant work, making little distinction between the concerns and quality of any one of them. This tendency to equate the identification of Hawks motifs with the artistic quality of a Hawks film perhaps led *auteur*ist critics to value Hawks films from *Rio Bravo* onward so highly, though Hawks himself found many of these films to be among his greatest failures.

What did Howard Hawks think made his best films best? If one reads the interviews he gave over the final fifteen years of his life, one encounters the term "story" repeatedly—"I'm just trying to tell a story," "that's the kind of story that interests me," "that makes a good story," "that's how I wanted to tell that story," and so forth. Many of Hawks's *auteur*ist admirers steer clear of this embarrassing term: story means script, story means characters, story means "literature" and not "cinema," plot, not camera angles, editing, composition, lighting, and decor. Stories are not unique to cinema but common to novels, plays, operas, ballets, poems, even paintings. In this view (which underlies almost every major theory of film as a medium), the story is merely the premise, the given of any cinema work, and the real stuff—the cinema—is what gets added on. This view works best with those directors who add the most on—and are easiest to discuss because of all that addition. But such a view will simply not work for Hawks, who does not add cinema to his stories but pours his stories into cinema. To demonstrate that Hawks is of any value is to demonstrate that he told good stories.

What is a good story? First, there is the construction of an action—not just enumerating a string of events but organizing those events into a coherent and powerful shape. The construction of a narrative action relies on a very interesting paradox, of which Hawks was well aware. On the one hand, the events in a narrative must seem to flow spontaneously, naturally, surprisingly; nothing must be expected, nothing foreseen. On the other hand, the events in a narrative must be prepared for, motivated, foreshadowed; nothing is unexpected, everything foreseen. On the one hand, everything that happens to King Lear is a surprise; on the other, everything in the play proceeds from Kent's command in the beginning to "See better, Lear." It is surprising that Emma Woodhouse discovers that it is Mr. Knightley whom she really must marry; yet everything in *Emma* points the way to this inevitable and inescapable discovery. The paradox of narrative construction is that it synthesizes the accidents of nature—which seem random—and the patterns of logic—which are fixed; the outcome of events is simultaneously inevitable yet surprising to the reader or viewer when the inevitable occurs. The narrative that is insufficiently spontaneous and surprising is familiarly condemned as contrived, overplotted, unnatural, and stilted; the narrative that is insufficiently patterned is familiarly condemned as random, wandering, arbitrary, and formless.

How does Hawks's story construction relate to this paradox of surprising inevitability? In over forty years of filmmaking, collaborating with over a dozen major writers, Howard Hawks builds every story in an identical four-part structure. The first part is a prologue that either (1) establishes the conflict in a past or present close relationship of the major characters (this is the usual pattern of Ben Hecht's scripts for Hawks) or (2) initiates a conflict by the collision of two apparently opposite characters upon their initial meeting (this is the usual Furthman–Faulkner pattern). The second and third parts develop the central conflict established in the first, either by letting one of the conflicting characters or life styles dominate in the second part, then the other in the third, or by letting one of the characters work alone in the second part, then both of them together in the third. And the fourth section resolves the central conflict, often by a return to the original physical setting of the prologue but in which setting the warring characters now see themselves and one another in a new light. Occasionally Hawks adds a very brief epilogue or "tag" to return the narrative full circle to its beginning. Whatever else one can say about this narrative structure, it gives a Hawks story the firmness of shape, the elegance, economy, and symmetry that allow surprising events to transpire within the firm logic and structure of a controlled pattern.

Then, of course, this narrative structure must be peopled (indeed propelled) by characters, human portraits that are consistent, credible, and motivated, either interesting and complex in themselves or viewed in an interesting and complex way by the storyteller. But as important as the vitality and

complexity of the individual human portraits themselves is the
necessity of creating those particular characters for that particular narrative structure in which they exist. The very structure
of a Howard Hawks narrative requires a central pair of characters who, at its beginning, seem to be warring opposites but
who, by its end, realize that they are somehow alike. The
clashing opposites discover they are spiritual partners, extensions of one another, complements not antagonists. This inter-
relation of narrative structure and character has several consequences.

The first is that, despite the apparent conflict of this pair on
the surface, beneath that surface the two really *do* belong together. An inevitable gap develops between what the characters seem to be and feel and what they really are and feel. Any
storyteller must communicate this kind of gap to the viewer-
reader from the beginning (for it is only by perceiving this gap
that the viewer-reader will find the ultimate resolution credible). This communication requires great psychological subtlety
and perception on the part of the storyteller—to convey from
the outset the feelings that lie beneath the surface to the viewer-
reader without the characters giving away these feelings at the
outset to each other. Such stories can succeed only by developing the complex and careful texture of internal human psychology—usually by a counterpoint between what the characters say and what the characters do (which casts suspicion
on whether they really mean what they say).

Second, this kind of story can be resolved only by the characters' discovery of the way each really feels about he other—
often accompanied and accomplished by the character's discovering how he or she feels about himself or herself. This
discovery closes the gap between appearance and feeling established early in the narrative and, in effect, allows the characters' knowledge of one another and themselves to coincide
with the viewer-reader's knowledge.

Third, this kind of narrative almost inevitably demands an
outside observer (or observers) emotionally attached to one (or
both) of the central antagonist-protagonists and who, like the
audience, has already discovered the genuine feelings beneath
the surfaces but must allow the central pair's discoveries to
happen for themselves, since people can only discover things
by discovering them for themselves. If the outsiders are closely
attached to one of the central characters initially, their acceptance of the other precedes and foreshadows the final reconciliation of the warring pair. In their sharing of the audience's
knowledge about what lies beneath the surface these outsiders
serve as a classic chorus and, in their providing the author's

attitude toward the merely apparent antagonism, they serve as the classic *raisonneur*. There is something logically and theoretically inevitable about the consequences of this particular interrelation of narrative action and character—and almost every Hawks film is woven from this identical pattern of events and human psychology.

The discovery which brings the narrative pattern to its completion is a moral discovery as well as an emotional one. The characters not only discover their feelings about themselves and one another but also the moral bases that make such feelings and responses meaningful. In making this personal, emotional discovery the character implicitly discovers the entire moral system on which the narrative has been constructed. What does this mean? In Jane Austen's *Emma,* when Emma discovers that she loves Mr. Knightley and he loves her (something that he has known all along but which she must discover for herself), she also discovers that she has been very foolish to believe that she can regulate every other character's personal and emotional experience while so neglecting her own. She in effect learns that no one can order anyone else's personal life and that everyone has the responsibility of setting his or her own life and feelings in order. Similarly, when Othello discovers that he has murdered an innocent wife, he not only feels personal anguish and pain at his terrible mistake but discovers his own inability to separate the apparent and the real—real innocence from seeming innocence, real honesty from seeming honesty. The innocent Othello learns that he has indeed been innocent of the world's potential duplicity.

Now everything in the narratives of both *Emma* and *Othello* —their events, their characters, their speeches—have been built around the moral issues that culminate in the discovery. The female characters in the Jane Austen novel—Emma, Harriet Smith, Jane Fairfax, Mrs. Elton—represent a spectrum of moral and emotional awareness, both of themselves and of the world in which they live. The male characters—Mr. Elton, Frank Churchill, Robert Martin, and Mr. Knightley—represent a spectrum of male partners, each of whom appropriately belongs with a particularly fitting, matching female. Part of Emma's moral blindness is her emotional blindness about which man belongs with which female partner—including, and especially, her own emotional partner. And in *Othello,* all of the characters represent different shades of real or seeming guilt or honesty—from the Moor, whose outside is black but his inside white, to Iago, whose outside is white but inside black, to Desdemona, whose outside and inside are white but appear black to Othello, to Cassio, who is similarly guiltless but made to seem tainted. Without understanding these moral issues it is impossible for us to follow the narrative at all. As Wayne Booth has shown in *The Rhetoric of Fiction*, the moral system that the author has built into the work is an essential element of a narrative's rhetoric, of our understanding the progress of both the events and the characters.[8] Fictional narrative cannot proceed at all without presumptions at the culture's moral beliefs. . . .

But if the author's creation of a moral system of characters and actions is essential to a story's rhetoric—without which there can be no story—the paradox of this moral system is that it then can be turned back upon itself and examined to assess the depth, complexity, and richness of that author's moral vision in general. The reason that certain stories seem morally superficial, hackneyed, and shallow is not that they lack a moral system (for no story could be told without one) but because the moral system on which the story depends is itself superficial, hackneyed, and shallow—an accumulation of the most banal, conventional, and formulaic moral clichés that pass for moral wisdom in the culture. Jane Austen's *Emma* is admired as a rich, important human work, not solely for its carefully structured action, deeply and subtly observed characters, and gracefully perceptive writing but for the very depth, ironies, and complexities of the moral system that permeates it. It is important for human beings to know what Emma discovers, for what she discovers is one of the essential principles that makes life meaningful, human, and livable. *Emma* was certainly not written to teach the reader a didactic lesson about manipulating other people's lives; the reader already knows what Emma discovers in the course of the story (if the reader did not, there could be no story of Emma's coming to know what the reader and the author already know). But part of Jane Austen's reputation as a writer can be traced to her ability to construct such a complex and insightful moral universe as her means to elaborate her story of one woman's discovery. The moral and philosophical seriousness of Shakespeare's *Othello* stems from the same source—the elaboration of a rich moral universe through action and character, based on human issues which are enormously complicated and important.

Yet there is probably no more ludicrous response to Shakespeare's play than Thomas Rymer's dismissing it on the moral grounds that the only lesson it teaches is that "women should be careful how they bestow their linen."[9] Rymer's response is

---

[8]Wayne C. Booth, *The Rhetoric of Fiction* (Chicago, 1960), pp. 3–20.

[9]As quoted in Elder Olson, *Tragedy and the Theory of Drama* (Detroit, 1961), p. 158.

ludicrous because it ignores the *implicit* moral system that underlies the entire narrative; instead, it looks only for some explicit, morally edifying homily. This point brings us back again to Howard Hawks after what might seem a very long digression. If Hawks is to be considered a great storyteller it is essential that he convey a view of human life and aspiration that is serious and complex. Since his stories are obviously neither explicitly didactic nor polemical, and since they appear to be merely escapist genre stories, if they display any moral or philosophical seriousness at all it can only be in the implicit moral system that underlies the films' characters and their actions. Since the narrative structures of Hawks's actions bring his characters to a discovery, the potential seriousness and intellectual richness of his stories can only reside in what it is they discover and why and how—if the moral system that allows Hawks's stories to proceed is a complex and stimulating one. And because Hawks has created so many stories,[10] each of them with its own action leading the central characters to a discovery, and therefore each of them with an underlying system of moral value to be discovered, the power of Hawks's moral vision becomes even more compelling if these underlying moral systems are consistently, carefully, and complexly related to one another. To demonstrate this consistency is to demonstrate the importance and value of Howard Hawks.

1982

[10]Hawks received screen credit for directing 39 whole films, co-directing 2 others. But he worked on scripts he did not direct (like Josef von Sternberg's *Underworld* and George Stevens's *Gunga Din*); he directed parts of films for which he received no credit, and he produced several films directed by others.

DONALD KNOX
FROM THE MAGIC FACTORY

THE *AMERICAN IN PARIS* BALLET

Vincente Minnelli (Director):

We had no definite plan for the ballet all the while we were shooting the book. We knew in a vague way that it had to incorporate parts of Paris that artists had paintd, but we had no time to figure this out until Nina Foch came down with chicken pox. There was nothing left to shoot whatever, so Irene Sharaff, who I had hired to design the costumes, and Gene Kelly and I locked ourselves in my office for hours and hours and hours on end. We worked out the entire ballet during those days. It was the luckiest chicken pox I've ever known.

We started out by racking our brains on all the material that we had. We knew we wanted to do certain things. Gene had this idea that he wanted to do Toulouse-Lautrec's *Chocolat*, so we tried to work that in some way. Well, you know, I had done several ballets in the shows I'd done in New York—the first surrealist ballet with Balanchine, in one of his shows, a thing called *Death in the Afternoon*, so they rather looked to me for a synopsis.

You had to have a central idea, because the ballet went on for a long time. Gene thought you had to have a story. I said, "You can't have a story, because, if it's a new story, that's bewildering. It wouldn't work at all. You're at an emotional crisis here, and, if you retell the story we've been telling, it becomes redundant." I said, "It has to be something to do with emotions, the time in his mind, the way he feels having just lost his girl, and a whole thing about Paris." Everything had to become a jumble in his mind, a kind of delirium because Leslie's leaving him hits him so hard. When she leaves, he has already drawn a black-and-white sketch, rather like a Dufy, and he's explained to her that Paris can not only be exciting, warm, and wonderful, but it can also be very cold, that the color would go out of everything if she left. It wouldn't be the same city. He loved Paris; he painted there; he loved the men who had painted Paris, greater than he would ever be— Rouault, Van Gogh, the Impressionists. Then you slide into the ballet, keeping in mind his delirium. This is, of course, easy to say, but the first problem we had was how to go from the black-and-white ball into the color of the ballet. We felt there was no sense of continuing into the ballet until we had solved the question of that transition.

Gene Kelly (*Actor and Choreographer*):

In effect, the problem was: Leslie has left and I'm very sad. I'm on a balcony looking out over Paris, and I'm thinking about what the city means to me, my life, what it's done for me, and what I am in respect to the city and to painting. Then, we had to somehow get into this ballet. Once we got into it, it was just fun, but it was torture trying to find a way to slide into the thing. Here's a case where we didn't have a song to get us into it. It's easy if you have something to sing, like "Here is a ballet about a painter who lives in Paris." If George Gershwin had still been around, we probably would have asked him to write it. It's always a little tougher without the song.

The solution to our problem was very much like a dance I did with a newspaper and a squeaky board in a picture called *Summer Stock*. One night, I was having drinks with a fellow who's dead now, Nick Castle, choreographer, and he asked me to listen to a sound that he was making with a newspaper. I said, "My God! It's perfect for a number. Would you mind if I used it?" But I needed another sound to complement it, something to give it dramatic contrast. For days I went around walking over sewer gratings and kicking things around the house, but I couldn't find the sound. Finally, I found what I needed, the sound of a squeaky board. So Nick found one thing and I found the other. Well, with the transition to the ballet I remembered a rose that Leslie had dropped as she left, and Vincente came up with the charcoal sketch that I tore up. The two together gave us something to invent with.

Vincente Minnelli:

It had to start off in black and white—that was the charcoal sketch—and then we had to introduce color into it, and the rose was perfect. Then it had to go to total color. I didn't want to do things that were done at the lab. Months later they turn up with something and show it to you and it's horrible.

Preston Ames (Art Director):

Vincente wanted to do the resolution of black and white to color in the studio. We were aware that we had a rose dropped by Leslie and a sketch made by Gene Kelly of the Place de la Concorde. Then there were to be splashes of color introduced, and we were to be aware of this same sketch in color and not in black and white. Again, that was, and I probably use the word ill-advisedly, thrown at us. All the things were challenges on this picture. How do we do it? Everybody had a different idea until the head of the Camera Department, John Arnold, was brought in, and he said, "I don't think this is too difficult if you have the right tools," and he introduced to us a photographic mirror, or black-glass mirror. This gave you an opportunity to either see through the mirror or to photograph a reflection. So what we did at first was to see this sketch reflected into our mirror in black and white. Now, the color was in an identical sketch on the other side of the glass, and that at the moment was not lit. As you took light off your black-and-white sketch and lit up the colored one on the other side of the mirror, it became a perfect match dissolve, until all you saw was the colored sketch. So we solved the transition by taking light from one image and putting it on another image.

Vincente Minnelli:

Gene picks up the rose, they turn on the spotlights, and the color splashes in. Once we solved that problem, we returned to the bigger problem of what to do with the ballet. The clue to the ballet was the emotions, and we knew we had to start high. You see, the music dictates a lot of it because you start with "yum de dum a yum ta ta," which is Paris and traffic and policeman, the people, the Orientals, and everybody. It's Paris that is gay; it's Paris and it's wonderful. Its traffic is frightening, and Gershwin actually uses auto horns in the music. Gene catches a glimpse of a girl, who is Leslie. By the time he crosses the square, she's gone. Then the lights fade and the scene turns into a flower market. The girl is still on his mind. He dances

The *American in Paris* Ballet: Gene Kelly and Leslie Caron combine tap and ballet in a Rousseau zoo. "I saw only two ways to make an American look *really* American amongst all those French Impressionist paintings: the first was to incorporate servicemen in it somehow, and the second, to find a place where we could do some tap dancing, as opposed to classic ballet" (KNOX, page 576).

"I made the sketch of the Place de la Concorde *à la* Raoul Dufy. . . . Then Henry Greutert, who was the modeler and the sculptor down in the plaster shop, modeled up a fountain that was as much Dufy as you could make a three-dimensional object" (KNOX, pages 580–581).

with her as if she is a ghost, and finally, as he is slowly turning with her, it becomes just the sorrowful flower market, and
he is alone. Then, for the next section, I had a clue from Deems
Taylor's original program notes for *An American in Paris*, which
was that section of the music where the American is wanting
his own roots, lonesome for his own rhythms. That's where
the servicemen come in. Then the American is happy, gay,
and goes to the zoological gardens. It's very gay, and they imitate Americans, and they are all very happy until . . . What
he can't forget is the passion that's under it. Then comes the
long, passionate dance on the fountain that turns into the Van
Gogh Place de l'Opéra. Now the dancers are part of Paris again.
They see the sign of the exhibition for Toulouse-Lautrec, and
Gene imagines himself as Chocolat. Then it erupts into the
whole city of Paris, the music reaches its climax, everything is
up, wonderful, gay, exciting, and, bang, everybody disappears. He's alone again.

So the ballet goes from highs to lows, as you do in deliriums
like that. You had to keep the story going, so you knew at the
end of the ballet that the girl had gone. So it had to be a thing
of emotions and vision—then a very quick ending to the story
and picture after that.

Gene Kelly:

Sharaff, Minnelli, and I met for several days in Vincente's
office to try to "lay out" the theme of the ballet As for myself,
I was only adamant about one thing: We must not use the
paintings of Degas. I had a strong feeling for Toulouse-Lautrec
because one section of the music cried out for him, especially
the character of Chocolat. Because it was postwar Paris, I saw
only two very clear ways to make an American look *really*
American amongst all those French Impressionist paintings:
The first was to incorporate servicemen in it somehow, and
the second, to find a place where we could do some tap dancing, as opposed to classic ballet. Now, tap dancing is almost
always done as a rhythm accompaniment like drum beats, but
here I put it right on the melody. It worked, and it looked as
American as a hot dog.

Two of the scenes in the ballet, the Dufy opening and the
Van Gogh colors of the Paris Opera, were done completely by
Irene Sharaff. I'm afraid Vincente and I just threw those at her
and said, "Flood us with costumes and we'll make it work."
The rest, of course, came out of the choreographic plan.

Irene Sharaff (Costume Designer):

There was nothing when I came out that had been written down on paper about *An American in Paris* except that it was to be a ballet about painters. There was nothing on paper for the ballet except Gershwin's score for *An American in Paris,* the concert piece, and the fact that Arthur Freed and, I suppose, Vincente and Gene, wanted it around the painters of that time.

One must give tremendous credit to Arthur Freed, who is a very peculiar man with a great love for painting as well as all the other creative arts. He is an inarticulate man and not one who is full of great knowledge, but his instinct is extraordinary. Arthur fell in love with the Impressionist painters, and, as *An American in Paris* was a story about Paris, I think he felt this was some way of showing his love for nineteenth century and early twentieth-century painters.

Vincente, Gene, and I first jotted down a whole series of sequences into which we could incorporate the different painters. I also did the scenery for the ballet. Now, that doesn't mean I sat down with a T-square and triangle, did the mechanical drawings for it, or constructed it, but I did do the basic springboard for the *décor* of the ballet.

It was extraordinary that a studio like Metro was so generous in allowing us this kind of freedom to do the ballet. There were no holds on what we did. The ballet was based on the painters Raoul Dufy, Toulouse-Lautrec, Utrillo, Henri Rousseau, van Gogh, and a bit of Monet. Of course, nobody can reproduce a scene exactly like a Raoul Dufy; this was to be an impression of something.

Keogh Gleason (Set Decorator):

Sharaff was something! Minnelli wouldn't do a picture without her, but she used to drive Freed right up the wall. She made lots of demands, like her own car with chauffeur at her disposal and "Stand by; I'll call you; don't call me, but be there." And don't call her a costumer; she is a designer. Someone called her a costumer once; well, that's like a wardrobe woman. Boy did she blow!

Saul Chaplin (Music Codirector):

At another studio, the sudden introduction at this point of Irene Sharaff into a team that had been working on *An American in Paris* for six months might have caused problems, but not at Metro. There you didn't have to worry about getting to know each other's personalities. We'd worked with each other before and so knew and respected each other. We didn't have to waste twelve meetings on trying not to offend somebody.

Irene Sharaff:

I chose certain things mainly because it had to become a continuity. I played the *An American in Paris* score constantly while I was designing it, and certain characters in Gershwin's scores came out. For example, a costume that I did for a black dancer came out through my subconscious as I listened to the music. It was a jazz thing that my ear caught that Gene utilized. I dressed the dancer as a spahi with a white turban and a blue burnoose. I was completely open in the characters I invented at my drawing board, and let my subconscious come out listening to the music. I don't say that I have that direct connection with my unconscious to let it work that way all the time. I would be silly to say that. I mean there was a plan. For example, the group of *pompiers*, the firemen, that run through it were obviously the leitmotiv for *An American in Paris*. I can't sing the tune for you, but it's a very marching, lilting kind of music. I thought it would be marvelous because at that time, certainly, the *gendarmes* were a little more romantic looking than they are today, and so were the *pompiers*. Everybody's uniform was a little more dramatic than the kind of utilitarian uniform that you see on servicemen today. So I made a dramatic form out of the uniforms. They wore brass helmets, and they had an awful lot of brass shining around. They never walked singly. They always walked in groups, like the *gendarmes*. So then it was up to Gene to decide how to use them. All I did was feed him certain characters that he would then utilize.

The Rousseau section I definitely based on *The Sleeping Gypsy*, and the carnival came from his *Notre Dame*. With Renoir I used the *Pont Neuf*. The Von Gogh section, which was placed in the place of Place de l'Opéra, found its style from the pattern of his *Cypresses*, painted at Arles—all the yellows and sunflowers. There I tried to get the Van Gogh palette. With Toulouse-Lautrec, I used Lucite figures of actual characters that he painted, like *Chocolat at the Achilles Bar*.

Gene Kelly:

Other times Irene would just feed me a background and I would stage the scene around it, as was the case for the Utrillo street scene in Montmartre, when the GIs jump out and dance with me. Irene decided that she would wash their GI uniforms as if Utrillo painted them. She took a brush and painted the marine, sailor, air-force, and army uniforms right on the dancers.

Preston Ames:

The ballet became a series of meetings with a number of people because, obviously, Gene had his choreography to do, Sharaff had her costumes to do, the music people had their things to do, and I had the sets to do. We went off into various groups to try and figure out how this would be done. After a few weeks, it was resolved that some Impressionist paintings, which we were going to create in a third dimension, were to be the background for Kelly to do his choreography in. Now, we did several things. We came up with a multitude of sketches and models to show Minnelli how we could photograph it. With the models, he was able to look at it through his little finder and see whether or not it gave him the kind of fluidity he required. When we got all through, we had a couple of dozen models and a multitude of sketches to help him decide whether this was the right thing or not. We were always interrupting his shooting of *Father's Little Dividend*. But he loved it. It gave him an audience of his crew there, and he was never so happy. He was really the king on his throne when this all took place. He had suggestions, but he was giving us our head. He wanted us to come up with something, and he wasn't going to destroy this creative quality.

We got to a preliminary point when we finally got to the great meeting with management and all of our people. We sat down with them and said, "Okay, here is our ballet—*x* number of dollars, *x* number of days to shoot, *x* number of people that we need." It was a monumental request. We were asking to do something that had never been done before, and for big money. There was only one little humorous moment, when it was decided who would emcee this meeting. Everybody had so much to say that if you loused it up by too many words or too much description you could have thrown the whole thing in the garbage pail. Dore Schary said, "Excuse me. I think I'll go out and come back in again because I can see somebody has to take the floor on this thing," so he made a little humorous moment. It was Vincente who finally said, "Okay I'll do the honors." After that, it was all seriousness. Vincente took the floor and described the whole thing the way it was, what we would do, and how it would work. Nobody knew really what we were doing, much less ourselves, but we had a pretty good idea of what we wanted to do. My God! It was so big that it was a little bit beyond all of us, and yet we weren't afraid. . . .

Alan Jay Lerner (*Author and Screenwriter*):

At that time, the idea of spending $500,000 on a ballet was a very adventurous decision, to say the least. In terms of this ballet, Mayer played a key role in making the decision to keep the ballet in no matter what the cost. As a matter of fact, that decision was probably one of the last major picturemaking decisions he was to make. I remember that Louis B. Mayer left the studio sometime before *An American in Paris* was previewed. All during the time of the making of the picture, there was a lot of animosity between Mr. Mayer and Dore Schary, a lot of in-fighting. It had to do with Dore working more closely with the New York office. I never really understood all of what was happening, nor did I care to get involved. Anyway, I remember very clearly the day that Arthur Freed went up and discussed the whole thing with Mr. Mayer. Freed then came right down and told me that it would be all right. Louis B. Mayer had okayed the money for the ballet.

Preston Ames:

Concretely, we needed first a set that would give us a big area, which would give Gene space to choreograph in. We also needed something that gave a color palette which was red, white, and blue. These, of course, are typical Dufy colors. Consequently, combining these two elements, we came up with a treatment of Place de la Concorde which, incidentally, Dufy had never painted. But that wasn't important. The fact was that he contributed a color palette which gave a whole pattern to this opening scene. Arthur Freed describes Dufy as a calligraphic painter, which means the background was a mass of color in which line drawings give you the details.

George Gibson (*Head of the Scenic Art Department*):

Raoul Dufy is essentially a water-color painter with a lot of calligraphic strokes and a lot of color. So Preston said, "I know that we can't get anybody in the other departments to do this, so could you make a sketch for the model of this thing?" I made the sketch of the Place de la Concorde à la Raoul Dufy. I'm a water-color painter myself, so it was no great problem for me. Then Henry Greutert, who was the modeler and the sculptor down in the plaster shop, modeled up a fountain that was as much Dufy as you could make a three-dimensional object. It was very difficult to do this kind of thing. He had to make it so it could be seen through—penetrable, you know. It was all disrupted by shapes and forms within it, while it still retained the feeling of the fountain that exists in the Place de la Concorde.

Preston Ames:

The third-dimensional thing, where Henry Greutert came in, was creating a Dufy-like fountain for the Place de la Concorde as if it were a calligraphic thing. That became a battle royal that lasted a month at least, to say "This looks like Dufy painted it."

Vincente Minnelli:

Greutert designed this marvelous fountain in miniature first. There was a bad time for a while about that design. Cedric Gibbons who was head of the Art Department, wanted to make it a different way. He said, "That's not in the style of Dufy. Dufy is with lines; therefore, make it solid and paint in these lines." He just got this idea in his head. "You have to do these kinds of figures, and then you make broken lines." I said, "But, Cedric, that isn't going to work with the light changes, because, when you silhouette it, it'll look just like a Henry Moore, you know those doughlike figures. It will just look like a blob, nothing." He was rather stubborn about it. All he saw was how it wouldn't be like Dufy. Finally, I convinced him this was the only possible way we could operate with the dancers and still get all these changes of mood in. . . .

Irene Sharaff:

Each one of the painters that I used had a palette that was very much his own. I mean, after all, painting is a very personal thing, isn't it? Certainly a painter with the stature of the painters we used in this picture had his own style, his own sense of color, and his own sense of light. In designing the colors for these balletic settings, I used my senses. There is no theory about this. This is the thing that only people sitting behind closed doors worry about, thinking that there are theories. There are many books that have been written about color theories, and it's a lot of nonsense. If you have a great passion for color, as I do, you do it with your instincts; you do it with your guts. You don't sit down and say, "Oh, red has a certain amount of white things compared to green, which has certain other things." That to me is sheer nonsense! I love color and I understand color. My whole springboard is color. I'm a visual person, and I use color from my guts, I don't use it because of theory, and I don't think one bloody painter, a great painter, uses color in any other way. I'm not interested in a technical class of why green and red do certain things. I know it instinctively; I don't have to know it technically. I feel certain colors to me have happiness; certain colors to me mean sadness. You can't have a theory about that. I don't say "I can't use that because it's against the rule." If there's anything in the world that's free, believe me, it's color. All you need is some tubes of paint.

An American in Paris was probably one of the largest ballets ever done. It was equivalent to a full-size Broadway show. I did something like five hundred costumes.

This is one of the strange, dreadful things about time and the fact that, at times, very few things are planned—planned in advance, the way when building a building an architect would have blueprints down to the finest detail. But, as time is of the essence in both the theater and the movies, you really improvise three-quarters of the time and feel lucky that you can get things done on time. Gene choreographed as quickly as I designed the costumes. Everybody was working on a terribly tight time schedule. Sometimes it's kind of marvelous when a movie works and when people get on the same beam. The real magic is how you can work quickly with the kind of collaborative forces that allow you to use that extra degree of energy that people always have stored away and can conjure forth when the occasion is needed. I worked around the clock, literally, because, when I wasn't at the costumer watching the costumes being made, I was at the drawing board designing them. I didn't sleep and I didn't eat and I would work at home on a board propped up on a desk, because I knew by a certain time I had to have certain costumes into the costumers to be made. It's fascinating. Sometimes, however, I would love to be given the great present of being able to design something not casually but leisurely.

Preston Ames:

Irene Sharaff came up with a presentation of costume sketches which incorporated a very interesting treatment for the background. She was saying, and rightly so, "I just cannot give you a sketch of a costume and not show you how it works and where it works." So there was a little professional jealousy on everybody's part. But it did no harm, because she has a way of doing things her way, and in this particular instance she made the whole thing possible. She felt that the various painters should come into the picture, and she tried to give her sketches that treatment. She gave a color key which was invaluable that ran through the whole ballet. Maybe they were only suggestive things, but they were there, and, when you got all through with it, there was a completeness to it.

The art director, me, has the right to say, "Look, you have a color thing, and I'll work with you colorwise, but my background is going to be my background." But, in this instance, it was a correlation between the color of the costume and where it was to work. Now, needless to say, this didn't take me off the hook at all, because, when we finally agreed that this was it, then I had to take all of this stuff and make it work, and that was not easy. It's one thing to have a pretty sketch—and in this case they *were* pretty sketches; they didn't intend to be anything else—and another thing to then take those sketches and put them into a three-dimensional set and have them painted to look like Dufys and Renoirs and Van Goghs.

George Gibson:

The first one we tackled was the Dufy Place de la Concorde. We thought we could do it, but we didn't know. There were all kinds of technical problems inherent in the techniques of the various painters that had been chosen. You see, when you do a water color it's essentially a washy thing, and much of a water color becomes a sort of accidental happening which you take advantage of and use in the development of your painting. Dufy, of course, is no different from anybody else in this respect. He likes to put on a big splash of a wash and drop color into it, a splash here and a splash there, before he starts all these calligraphic delineations of buildings or whatever. This is all right, doing it on a sketch which might run 40 inches long and about 20 inches high. But, when we got into painting the backing proper, you realize that we couldn't rely on these happy accidents. It all had to be done on this huge scale because, you see, this darn backing we painted on was 35 or 40 feet high, maybe 250 feet long. The happy accidents that existed in the original sketch had to be painted absolutely on our enormous canvas. All the accidents had to be literally drawn. The feeling of watery wash and all of these things had to be consciously done.

We were on Stage 27 with that. Then, of course, we asphalted the stage floor. They used to put paper over the wood and then lay asphalt and roll it, a thin inch-and-a-half-thick topping of asphalt, which they ran right up to the backing. Well, we picked up with little profile balustrades, painted à la Dufy, and carried the color off the backing right onto the floor so that the whole stage became a complete painting. Of course, this astounded everyone. I remember Preston saying, "Minnelli walked in and saw all this going on, and he was astonished." He'd never seen this type of thing before. Well, this was something that Ames and I had talked about: "We'll do it this way, carrying the color down on the floor, and we'll get it so that it has a vertical appearance, although it is a three-dimensional thing as far as the set and the backing are concerned."

Of course, once we proved it could be done, we had to go with the whole thing. All the sets had to be done on this gigantic scale. "We want a Toulouse-Lautrec, we want a Utrillo street, we want a Rousseau zoo, we want a Van Gogh opera house," and one enormous painting became another and another and another.

Meantime, along with the design of the Place de la Concorde, Preston would have people designing the Utrillo set. Then, that would be fed into us as it was finished in the design stage. There is no problem for us as far as construction is concerned. All we have to have is the sewing room put the muslin together and we can start in on the backing. We would maybe be working on the backing for the Utrillo set two weeks ahead of the time that we would get the flats for the Utrillo set from the mill. By the time it would be delivered, we would have everything pretty well keyed and anchored. That way there were no delays.

John Green (*Executive in Charge of Music and Music Codirector*):

Simultaneous to the design and construction of the sets, a similar process was happening to the original score that Gershwin wrote for *An American in Paris*. Namely, we were arranging and orchestrating the score to fit our dramatic needs. "Arrangement" meant for us the adaptation of *An American in Paris* to the needs of our ballet. For instance, there is a trombone theme that comes in early in *An American in Paris*. The next substantive motif that you hear in the picture George Gershwin never wrote. Saul Chaplin wrote it. Before this picture, it didn't exist.

Saul Chaplin (Music Codirector):

One reason why we had to do it was because we did one painter at a time. We did Dufy first, and we decided certain things fit with Dufy. Then another piece of music fit with Toulouse-Lautrec, like *Chocolat,* the jazz theme—that's perfect. Well, that comes early in the music, but we couldn't have Toulouse-Lautrec up early and then come back to him at the end, so that's one reason why the ballet music was changed to fit the needs of the separate dramatic sections.

John Green:

That's arrangement—now about orchestration: If you look at the printed score that you buy for $25 or $30 of *An American in Paris* you will see "edited by F. Campbell Watson." F. Campbell Watson was an English orchestrator, arranger, and music editor-type fellow. Gershwin, as you know, didn't get around to the larger and extended forms of music until comparatively late in his life. George started writing *An American in Paris* in the fall of 1924. The previous February was that famous first performance of *Rhapsody in Blue* on Lincoln's birthday in Aeolian Hall, with Paul Whiteman. The following year (1925), George was in Boston with a show called *Rosalie,* of which he was a collaborative composer. He and Ira wrote a song for this show called "Oh Gee, Oh Joy." You know who copied the parts? At night? Me! I was satellite number one hanging around Gershwin. If he would smile at me, this was already a joy. I copied the parts because the reading with the orchestra was the next morning and there was no other copyist available that night. Between the time of *Rosalie* and 1927, George wrote *An American in Paris.* At that time, he was not a master orchestrator; he literally wasn't even sure of the transpositions—B flat clarinet, B flat trumpet—and he was shaky about the viola clef, things of that nature. Consequently, he lacked orchestral courage. He was also a compulsive doubler because he didn't really know the orchestral sonorities. He ultimately began to learn them and would have, if he had lived. What I'm getting at is this: Something that would have been perfectly fine by itself in solo bassoon he'd double in the viola. That would be one double. Then, for safety's sake, he would put it also in the celli. Everything was all doubled up all through the orchestra, which made for great weight and often thickness.

We were using this music for a recorded medium, the microphone, in terms of our recording techniques as of 1950. Also,

money for us was a consideration—speed. What Connie Sal-
inger and I did was make that stuff foolproof for the recording
stage. If we had used Mr. F. Campbell Watson per se, the
printed thing, the recordist in there would have been frantic
with the dials and moving microphones. We made it foolproof
recordingwise. The sound as you hear it on the track, that's
what you've always heard, except that we wrote it more practically for recording. The same registration, the same color, but
effective for the microphones the first time down. That's why
we reorchestrated it. If George had been alive and on the picture, I can assure you that neither Solly nor Connie nor I would
have done any adaptation. George would have done it. But he
would have done exactly what we did; I know it.

Recording sessions are set up in three-hour units. As I recall, we recorded the ballet in three days, meaning that there
were six sessions and some overtime.

Saul Chaplin:

I remember one session was at night. I think one day we
had three sessions, so I think it took five sessions, or fifteen
hours, just to record the 17-minute score. . . .

Leslie Caron (Actress):

Arthur Freed would drift into the rehearsing studio quite
often. Always his hands in his pockets, always jangling coins,
always on a diet, always fat and completely inarticulate and
monosyllabic, but a genius for what was good and what wasn't.
He knew how to put talented people together, and he knew
when the combination was good and the result was good. He
also knew when it wasn't good. He couldn't tell you why. He
cannot articulate why it's not good enough or why it does work,
but he knows when it's on the right path. He was very shy,
too.

Saul Chaplin:

The interpolation in the ballet, where the five dancers do a
tap dance, was Gene's idea. Because he felt that the thing was
full of girl dancers and all kinds of costumes, he wanted to do
a section with five men.

Gene Kelly:

When we did the Rousseau, the zoo thing, I purposely had
the fellows do everything the way George M. Cohan would do

it, like an American would do it. In the middle of that Frenchy
scene, and that's as Frenchy looking as you can get, I wanted
to do something immediately identifiable as American. The
little girls came out with their hats and had their hands up in
little white gloves, which we tried to make look like white
doves, Frenchy as could be. But the American men were to be
as American as you can get. Don't forget, this is an American
looking at Paris, so we had the canes and the straw hats and
we walked like Cohan and we did a tap dance. Now, you could
go into the jungles of Africa and you'd know immediately that
those fellows were Americans. That's what I wanted.

Also, tap dancing fit the music exactly. You can tap dance to
practically anything in *An American in Paris*. Gershwin's beat
is perfect tap music. I don't necessarily like to tap, and if I
hadn't felt I needed it to portray the Americans I probably
wouldn't have done it. None of us ever like to tap that much
because you always have to synchronize those taps in a pos-
trecording session. Because of leakage on the sound track during the playback of the music, you have to wear earphones
and look at yourself on the screen and then somehow synchronize your taps. It's the worst chore in show business, and
everybody's who's had to do it hates it!

Preston Ames:

We went from the Dufy setting into a flower market in the
style of Renoir. We created the style of Renoir in what we
needed to tell our story. Then we went to the Montmartre street,
and we felt that nobody ever did Montmartre streets like Utrillo,
so that was painted and built as if by Utrillo. His palette
worked itself into the costumes of the men. They started in
military uniforms and then changed into their George M. Cohan costumes. The next transition took us into the Henri
Rousseau carnival square and zoo. This was the kind of thing
that Rousseau had painted. Van Gogh was next, and this was
the Place de l'Opéra. This probably, as far as George Gibson
and his Scenic Department was concerned, was the most difficult to do, not because of the painting but because of the
actual physical job of using paint that was 15 per cent plaster.
Those poor guys went home exhausted at night from just tot-
ing buckets of plaster. Then, from there we went to a frozen
frame of Gene Kelly in one of the little sketches of Toulouse-
Lautrec's called *Chocolat*. This was a monochromatic transition
which was very difficult to do because it was color without
color. This then dissolved to a wildly brilliant, colorful section
with mirrors, back in the Van Gogh Place de l'Opéra and ended
with a return to the Place de la Concorde and a huge finale.

Irene Sharaff:

The scale that these things were done in was staggering. Just to do a painting as a backdrop is a bore, but trying to catch the feel of these painters in this grand form was a very tricky thing.

Vincente Minnelli:

Preston and myself got Gibson very excited about this. He made the paintings of these backings almost like a game, a competition among all his men.

Preston Ames:

George Gibson was the unsung hero of this entire film, especially of the ballet. Without him there would have been no ballet as we did it. We would have had to settle for something a lot less. . . .

Vincente Minnelli:

As I have mentioned, I wasn't too well pleased with Gilks's work as a cameraman, because every single little thing was lit, and there were certain things that had to have mood. So when we got to the ballet, we laid off to rehearse, and I insisted on using another cameraman, someone who had never worked in color, John Alton. I'd made *Father of the Bride* with him. Before that, he'd only done melodramas and some very fine black-and-white things at Eagle-Lion. He was disliked, however, by the other cameramen because he had written a book called *Painting with Light.* They all thought he was egotistical. But he was so fast and used so few lights. I got along just wonderfully with him. I felt that the ballet needed someone who would live dangerously. We had to take chances because in the ballet there is nothing that was done afterwards in the lab; everything you see was done on the set. So I decided it needed John Alton.

Joe Cohn (MGM Vice-President):

I remember I saw something of Alton's which I was greatly impressed with. He used one light and threw it against a building with enormous economy, I think it might have been in *T Men.* I got him to the studio and I hired him. I had to pay him $800 a week, more money than I was paying any other cameraman. I gave him that salary because I wanted to hire him and he wouldn't work for less, and I wanted to shake up the other cameramen, I thought our cameramen had become too complacent, and I felt we needed a cameraman who would shake the hell out of the place, and I thought Alton could do that for me. In lighting, he saved a lot of time by lighting only from the floor. This made him very unpopular with the other cameramen.

Walter Strohm *(Head of the Production Department)*:

Most people hated him. They said, "How can Minnelli put Alton on the ballet?" I said, "Because he knows how to light." Believe me, he knew how to light! I'll tell you a director who's difficult to get along with but who was crazy about Alton: Richard Brooks. He thought Alton was just great. Alton had a technique for a production man—and now I'm talking about my side of it—that was very helpful. I know why they didn't like him, and that was the thing that we liked about him most: He had none of this old studio technique. Some cameramen used the same lighting technique every time to light a set, because, the more units they had up there to light with, the more electricians it gave jobs to. Alton didn't give a damn about any of that. He was interested in getting an effect, and he could get an effect like that. He was very fast. Of course, that killed them; he was too fast for them. They didn't like that. He was ready, and the director was left holding the set. He just said to the director, "I'm ready." The director wanted to take two hours while they rehearsed and fussed around, and Alton said, "No, I'm ready. Anytime you want to."

Ed Woehler *(Unit Production Manager)*:

Minnelli would suggest something, and Alton would "yes" him right away. Gilks wouldn't necessarily do that. I think Alton probably married some very rich woman; that's the type of guy he was—Wore spats and gloves and everything. He was a kind of go-getter, a society man.

Gene Kelly:

Vincente suggested a lot of the light effects. We'd say, "Wouldn't this be great?" but often they took a lot of time, because cameramen can get very stubborn. But we found Alton willing to try anything. We'd say, "Can you do this?" He'd say, "Yeah, that's easy. Yeah." And for the first few days we were sort of worried because we'd been used to a lot of cameramen saying, "You guys are nuts. You can't do that." It seemed that about every picture we'd try something new and the person with whom we'd be working would say, "No, you can't do that," because they had never done it before. . . .

Leslie Caron (Actress):

The ballet part of it was the hardest. It was very unsatisfactory from a dancer's point of view, coming straight from the stage. First of all, I was forever struggling with the floors. They were too hard, and they had a mania for painting them bright colors. Some very conscientious prop man would come and shine them with dust cloths, so that before we started rehearsing they were like mirrors. Now, everybody knows that you can't dance on a mirror. It's got to be rather unslippery; otherwise you just fall all the time. Gene would always take me to the set. We had this delicious pianist, Saul Chaplin, and Saul and Gene would troop along, and everybody would come and test the stage. It was terrifying because it was so flat! You see, the stages that I'd danced on were all raked, and this one-was was flat, endless, and completely slippery. Also, there was no give to the floor at all, which is terrible on your ankles, calves, and knees. So I would fall once or twice and mutter, "Well, it's so slippery, Gene." Then I would put resin on my shoes and leave great, big white marks. So Gene said, "Well, it's terribly simple. All we have to do is repaint the floor." So, every time we had a new set we had to repaint the floor. Then the painters just got into the habit of putting sand in the paint when I had to dance somewhere. But that didn't solve the problem, either. You see, on wood you don't slip; you can turn. The satin of your shoe just doesn't stay on the ground; it rotates. But, when you have sandy paint, it rips the satin, and your shoe sort of stays as your foot turns. I mean it was frightening! Anyway, we went through it, and on some of the dancing for my little numbers, which we started with, I was a great pain in the neck for everybody.

Also, I was feeding myself then, and I didn't know much about nutrition, and in order to keep slim I would just eat nothing. Consequently, I was very weak and very much anemic, but Gene was my defender. He'd say to me, "If you're too ill, just tell me and stand by me, and I'll say you're too ill, and we will collect insurance and go off one day, and you can lie in bed all day and rest up." But we finally did get it done, and I must say I was pleased with it.

Preston Ames:

Gene choreographed it, but Vincente was the one who was the director. We never lost the fact that he was the skipper. Gene also realized that you have to have one director. It's one thing to choreograph it and another thing to have the thing pulled together. After all, it wasn't just one ballet, one dance number, it was six or eight numbers, six or eight big sets, and you had to have a preconceived notion.

Gene Kelly:

I had already shot the insert numbers, but I did not want to shoot the ballet without Vincente, for two reasons — number one, we were not only colleagues but pals, which would have been reason enough, emotionally; but, number two, his eye, his experience, is just invaluable. Nobody does a musical alone. Nobody! Minnelli's eye for color is the great thing. I don't think you can find a better costume designer in the world than Irene Sharaff, but, when you get all the choreography done and get everybody down on the stage floor, you can always find that Minnelli will have some way to adjust the color so that we'll have a better composition, a better look. In the ballet, for example, when he came out of doing *Father's Little Dividend*, which just took him six weeks in all, the whole ballet was planned and staged. It was all ready. All we had to do was say, "Roll 'em." But Vincente was able to polish it even more.

One setting in the ballet, the Toulouse-Lautrec café scene, with various characters here and there, is a good indication of what he could do.

We both came out of the school of John Murray Anderson on Broadway; he was sort of our mentor. He knew what to do with color and light. He was a great man of the theater, and Minnelli and I had worked under him. He was just great! Anderson could put a blue light on a scene and make the scene work where it wouldn't work with an amber or pink light. Like Minnelli, he was not a dance director. He just had this kind of an eye. Anyway, I remember, in the Toulouse-Lautrec scene Minnelli said, "Let's switch these two people around," and he switched them. He put the chap who's in blue down front, I remember very well, moved him down front and moved somebody else about 5 feet in back, and it was suddenly much better than Irene and I had visualized it.

Arthur Freed (Producer):

Then we just did it. We shot the ballet in a couple of weeks, without a flaw. You've got to prepare; then it's easy.

Preston Ames:

Arthur Fred was purring like a Cheshire cat because now this thing which he had always wanted to do had come to life. It had happened.

1973

RICHARD CORLISS
THE HOLLYWOOD
SCREENWRITER

Eight years ago, when popular movie criticism consisted mainly
of plot summaries and star-gazing, and Bosley Crowther of *The
New York Times* was scorning Godard and ignoring Ford and
Hawks, *Film Culture* magazine published two articles by Andrew
Sarris that were to revolutionize film criticism in the United
States. In the first article, "Notes on the Auteur Theory in 1962,"
Sarris proposed an Americanization of the *politique des auteurs*,
which held that the director is the author of a film and that visual
style is the key to assessing a director's standing as an *auteur*. In
The American Cinema, he evaluated—indeed, he rated—106 Amer-
ican directors (and seven foreigners) in categories ranging from the
"Pantheon" to "Oddities and One Shots."

It took some time for the importance of Sarris' work to become
evident to the community of film scholars. Hadn't Pauline Kael
demolished his stratified silliness for good in a *Film Quarterly*
polemic read by far more people than Sarris' original articles?
Hadn't Dwight Macdonald resigned his regular column in *Film
Quarterly* because Sarris was invited to contribute, and hadn't
he done so with a venom that suggested an angry redneck burning
a cross on the lawn of his new Negro neighbor's house? Hadn't
Richard Dyer MacCann conspicuously omitted Sarris' writing
(or any *auteur* criticism) from his anthology, *Film: A Montage of
Theories*, which did include a piece by Kael the theory-baiter?

It's a pity that Academia didn't notice what Sarris had going for
him: an engaging prose style that ranged from entertainingly analytical to deliriously lyrical; a popular, hip publication *(The Village*

Voice) just right for reaching the young intellectuals for whom film was the most exciting art; a subject matter (the Hollywood sound film) that he knew almost viscerally, and whose product was bound to interest his readers more than the "serious" European films praised by his detractors; and a burgeoning group of articulate acolytes (like Roger Greenspun and James Stoller) who could spread the faith without his losing face.

Came the Revolution, which coincided with the growing number of film courses and monographs. Sarris' thoughtful and well-timed challenge to the near-monopoly of social-realist criticism was adopted by most of the younger critics, and even adapted by some of the less secure older ones. It was refreshing to examine films as the creations of artists rather than of social forces, and to be able to do so in a manner that was serious without being solemn. Americans could finally admit that their movies weren't sinful just because they were entertaining, and that the films deserved to be judged by the same artistic standards applicable to any film.

By 1969, when Sarris expanded *The American Cinema* to book length, the critical attitude that had begun as a reaction to the party line was in serious danger of hardening into the Gospel According to St. Andrew. *The New York Times* had been converted into a veritable *auteur* shrine; its first- and second-string critics adhered closely to Sarris' tastes and standards, and its Almanac welcomed the word *auteur* into the English language, along with *acid*, *activist* and *Afro*. Film societies mounted ambitious retrospectives of directors, from John Ford and Jean Renoir to Sam Fuller and Russ Meyer. Publishers commissioned extended studies of Fritz Lang (who has made forty-three films) and Roman Polanski (who has made five). The Revolution was victorious.

In some respects, however, the anarchists show tendencies of close-minded classicism. They put the spotlight on the once-despised Hollywood movie system and sprinkled a little cultural respectability on the industry's "hack" directors—fine. But in doing so they retarded investigation of other, equally vital film crafts, especially that of the screenwriter, who creates (or creatively adapts) a film's plot, characters, dialogue and theme.

The director *is* right in the middle of things. At the very least, he's on the sound stage while the director of photography is lighting the set that the art director has designed and, later, while the actors are speaking the lines that the screenwriter wrote. Quite often, he steers all these factors—story, actors, camera—in the right *direction*. So why not just say it's his film, that he is the author? Simply because the director is almost always an interpretive artist, not a creative one, and because the Hollywood film is a corporate art, not an individual one. This doesn't diminish the importance of the director, or the validity of the Hollywood film as an art. Both Chartres and *Charade* were the work of a number of individuals who contributed their unique talents to a corporate enterprise, but this fact doesn't necessarily make either work less appropriate for serious study than, say, the Mona Lisa or *Mothlight*. It just makes it more difficult for the critic to assign sole authorship to the work—and why should he waste time on a Name Game like this?

In the same way, both Stanley Donen and Stan Brakhage may be called film artists, but Donen is an interpretive artist while Brakhage is a creative one; Donen is a conductor and Brakhage is a composer. Donen is a film *director* who collaborates with his writers, actors and technicians in a completely different way than Brakhage, the film*maker*, collaborates with his film strips and viewer. The case can be made that Donen is a better film director than Brakhage is a filmmaker; they work in separate but equal film traditions, and it is possible that Donen succeeds in his genre, whereas Brakhage may fail in his. The theory used to be that the solitary, creative artist produced Art, and the corporate, interpretive craftsman produced Entertainment—a prejudice that kept people from examining the Hollywood movie. The *auteur* theory says, in effect, "What you thought was just Entertainment is really Art, because it is the work of an individual creator—an *auteur*. Therefore the Hollywood movie is worthy to be examined."

Many films are indeed dominated by the personality of the director, although not, perhaps, in the way the auteurists mean. The phrase "directorial personality" makes more sense if taken quite literally. The good director is usually a man with a strong, persuasive personality. He has to be a combination of tough guy, to make the technicians respond to his commands, and best friend, to coax a good performance out of a sensitive actress. Whether he directs with a riding crop (Stroheim), an icy stare (Sternberg), or a few soft-spoken words (Cukor), his personality is often crucial to the success of a film. The importance of a director's personal—or even visual—style is not questioned here, only the assumption that he creates a style out of thin air (with his collaborating craftsmen acting merely as paint, canvas, bowl of fruit, and patron), instead of adapting it to the equally important styles of the story and performers. The same literal meaning can apply to a director's "authority," which accurately describes his function on the set.

But the director need not be the only dominant force in a successful film. Often the actor is the *auteur*. Keaton and Chaplin may be fine directors, but it is their screen personalities that we especially cherish. Who would trade Keaton the actor for Keaton the director? And who would prefer analyzing the directorial styles of James W. Horne, Donald Crisp, Edward Sedgwick or Charles F. Reisner to savoring that sublime bodily mechanism that Buster controls so beautifully? The unique cinema personae of W. C. Fields, Mae West and Laurel and Hardy also flourished with little regard to the director of record, and can be defined without much reference to him — although, quite naturally, the combination of the comedians with different scripts and directors produced varying results. The same can be said of such incandescent performers as Greta Garbo, Katharine Hepburn and Cary Grant. Just as one can be drawn to an exercise in visual style like Blake Edwards' *Darling Lili* without finding it a completely successful film, so can one delight in the way Garbo dignifies and illuminates a rickety melodrama like *Mata Hari* with her beauty, her passion, and her ironic acceptance of an innate and tragic superiority.

It's instructive — indeed, it's often fun — to see a great actor transcend a ridiculous script and unfeeling direction; it's interesting to watch a fine director play around with an incredible story and poor performers. But the real joy in movies comes from seeing the fortuitous communion of forces (story, script, direction, acting, lighting, editing, design, scoring) that results in a great Hollywood film. *Frankenstein, Scarface, Love Me Tonight, Camille, Holiday, Mr. Smith Goes to Washington, His Girl Friday, Citizen Kane, Penny Serenade, Casablanca, Double Indemnity, Body and Soul, Rachel and the Stranger, Born Yesterday, Seven Brides for Seven Brothers, The Searchers, Invasion of the Body Snatchers, Psycho, The Manchurian Candidate, Charade* and *Planet of the Apes* are just a few examples of collaborative movie-making at its best. Intelligent appreciation of films like these, and not scholastic disputes over the validity of individual signatures, should be our first critical concern.

The cry *"cherchez l'auteur"* can lead unwary film scholars astray when the *auteur* happens to be the author — or rather, when the script is the basis for a film's success. More often than not, when a fine film is signed by a mediocre director, the film's distinctive qualities can be traced to the screenwriter. There's no need to rescue Mitchell Leisen, Garson Kanin, Sam Wood and William D. Russell from the underworld of neglected directors simply because they were each fortunate enough to direct a comedy written by Norman Krasna (*Hands Across the Table, Bachelor Mother, The Devil and Miss Jones,* and *Dear Ruth,* respectively). The direction of these films is usually adroit and sensitive, and the presence of charming comediennes enhances them even further; but the delightfully dominant personality behind the screen is undoubtedly Krasna's. Similarly, the team of Sydney Gilliatt and Frank Launder constructed the frame — and contributed most of the furnishings — for two witty thrillers of the Thirties, Alfred Hitchcock's *The Lady Vanishes* and Carol Reed's *Night Train.* With the credits and Hitchcock's cameo cut from the films (but with the Gilliatt and Launder

figures, in the puckish persons of Naunton Wayne and Basil Rad-
ford, left in), even an auteurist might have trouble determining
which director was responsible for which film. That is because
the authorship, and thus the responsibility, belonged to the two
writers.

Body and Soul, written by Abraham Polonsky and directed by
Robert Rossen, fits securely into Polonsky's very personal urban
Hellmouth, with its Breughelesque, subway-at-rush-hour density,
its stylized but fiercely realistic dialogue, and its cheeky characters
who seem to carry both a chip and an albatross on their shoulders.
His authorship of *Body and Soul* can be certified, if need be, by a
look at his next film, the malignant *Force of Evil*, which he also
directed, and which extends and enriches the penny-ante pessimism
of *Body and Soul*. Waldo Salt's adaptations of *Rachel and the
Stranger* (1948) and *Midnight Cowboy* (1969) are both graced by
intelligent empathy for some very unusual characters, and by the
gentle humor he evokes from the most improbable situations.
Ring Lardner Jr.'s penchant for bantering, overlapping dialogue
distinguishes *Woman of the Year* (1942) and *M*a*s*h* (1970),
although most of his other assignments during those three decades
offered him little chance to display his talent. Paul Mazursky and
Larry Tucker, not director Hy Averback, are surely the authors
of *I Love You, Alice B. Toklas*; its successor, *Bob & Carol & Ted
& Alice*, evinced the same social concerns and behavioral absurdities, while Averback has loped further into obscurity with each
new film. (Significantly, now that Mazursky is a director, he tends
to ignore the contribution of his writing partner.)

It's clear that some method of classification and evaluation is
necessary, both to identify and to assess the contributions of the
over-paid but underrated *genus* known as the screenwriter. But that
is a game that conceals even more perils than Sarris' Hit Parade
of Directors. Once the *auteur* scholar accepts the myth of the omnipotent director, his game is won: he can Pass Kael and Collect
$200. Indeed, even an adherent of the *politique des collaborateurs*
can be fairly sure that the director of record is the man who hol-
lered "Action!" and "Cut!"—though his importance in controlling
what went on between those two commands may be disputed.
But the size of a screenwriter's contribution to any given film is
often far more difficult to ascertain. A writer may have received
screen credit for work he didn't do (such as Sidney Buchman on
Holiday) or for a few minor suggestions (Orson Welles on *Citizen
Kane*). More likely, his name may not appear on the screen even if
he has written virtually the entire script. Ben Hecht was responsible
for far more of *Gone with the Wind*'s dialogue than Sidney
Howard, who had merely written a treatment of the Margaret
Mitchell novel for producer David O. Selznick. But it was Howard

who received sole screen credit, as well as a posthumous Oscar—for Hecht's work. Michael Wilson wrote the screenplay for *Friendly Persuasion* and co-scripted *The Bridge on the River Kwai*. But the Hollywood Blacklist kept his name off both films, and the writing Oscar for *Kwai* was awarded to Pierre Boulle, who had nothing to do with the film adapted from his novel.

A more subtle problem is appraising the work of a screenwriter who specializes in adaptations. Few screenwriters can boast a more impressive list of credits than Donald Ogden Stewart. As with George Cukor, the director for whom he produced his finest scripts, Stewart's "filmography is his most eloquent defense." Both Stewart and Cukor, however, had the good luck to be assigned adaptations of some of the wittiest and most actable theatre pieces of their time —*Holiday*, *The Women* (for which Stewart received no screen credit), *The Philadelphia Story*, and *Edward, My Son*, among others—and Stewart adhered closely to both in spirit and letter. Stewart's achievement should not be degraded; many screenwriters failed at the delicate craft he mastered. But, as with directors, one can distinguish several levels of screenwriting: the indifferent work of a mediocre writer, whether an original script or an adaptation (which we may call procrustean); the gem polishing of a gifted adaptor like Stewart (protean); and the creation of a superior original script, like Herman J. Mankiewicz's *Citizen Kane* or Polonsky's *Body and Soul* (promethean). When faced with the career of a Stewart, the critic who has discarded the convenience of the *auteur* theory must compare Stewart's adaptation with the source work, in hopes of detecting such changes as plot compression or expansion, bowdlerization, addition or deletion of dialogue, and differences in theme and tone. At worst, this research will exhaust and discourage the critic; at best, it will convince him that the creation of a Hollywood movie involves a complex weave of talents, properties, and personalities.

When a screenwriter, like Preston Sturges or George Axelrod, has a distinctive style, his contributions to films with multiple script credits can usually be discerned. But the hallmark of many of the best screenwriters is versatility, not consistency. Subject matter dictates style. Given the chameleon-like quality of these writers, how are we to know which part of the *Casablanca* script is the work of the sophisticated but self-effacing Howard Koch, and which part was written by Warners' prolific Epstein brothers? Luckily, Koch himself has told the *Casablanca* production story, and revealed that the Epsteins fabricated a plot around the name of a saloon—Rick's—they had found in an unproduced play, and that, when the brothers moved on to another assignment, Koch developed the strands of their story into a full-blooded screenplay that reads as well as it plays. We don't have many of these memoirs, though, and since most Hollywood egos are about as large as the Graf Zeppelin, the accounts of screenwriters may be taken with the same pillar of salt we keep handy for directors' interviews and actors' autobiographies.

Nevertheless, a screenwriter's work should, and can, be judged by considering his entire career, as is done with a director. If a writer has been associated with a number of favorite films, if we can distinguish a common style in films with different directors and actors, and if he has received sole writing credit on several films, an authorial personality begins to appear. The high polish and excitement of Koch's other work, for example (he wrote *Invasion from Mars*, better known as *War of the Worlds*, for the Orson Welles Mercury Theatre, and his film scripts include *The Letter, Sergeant York, Three Strangers, Letter from an Unknown Woman*, and *The Thirteenth Letter*), and his fulfillment of the three conditions mentioned above, give credence to his account of the writing of *Casablanca*. In fact, most of the best screenwriters were the sole authors of a substantial number of scripts.

The paucity of critical and historical literature makes all screenwriters "Subjects for Further Research." The cavalier group-headings on the following lists are meant only to emphasize the tentative nature of the classifications. As more films are seen from a screenwriter's point of view, names will be shuffled from one list to another. Ultimately, each of these fine screenwriters, and a hundred more, should have an artistic identity clear enough so that such capricious classifications will be unnecessary. Until that enlightened time comes to pass, we must make do with an Acropolis of Screenwriters something like the one which follows. (To make matters even more delphic, the screenwriter's work is defined simply by three of his finest films.)

The men and women so honored, by adapting their conspicuous talents to the byzantine demands of the trade, developed the most successful screenwriting techniques. Success usually begat power, and power begat authority. By authority is meant the right to complete your own script without being forced to surrender it to the next fellow on the assembly line, the right to consult with any actor or director who wants changes, and the right to fight for your film through the taffy pull of front-office politics, pressure groups, and publicists. The power of the most important screenwriters often resulted in superior films, in which the distinctive contributions of writer and director can be analyzed with greater assurance. Inevitably, some writers had literary pretensions, not only for themselves but for the cinemah, and when these men achieved some measure of autonomy, the cheerful cynicism of their earlier, more successful scripts was replaced by sesquipedalian platitudes on The Brotherhood of Man Through World Government. Thus, the most famous screenwriters, such as Dudley Nichols, Dalton Trumbo and, of late, Buck Henry, are not necessarily the best. Nichols' thoughtful articles on the need for sparse, realistic dialogue were not often matched by his actual scripts, which tend to talk the characters into the ground with palaver and pontification. Dalton Trumbo's private letters (now published in book form) reveal an easy-going but pungent wit that was concealed by his attempts to radicalize bourgeois movie melodrama. The pomp currently surrounding

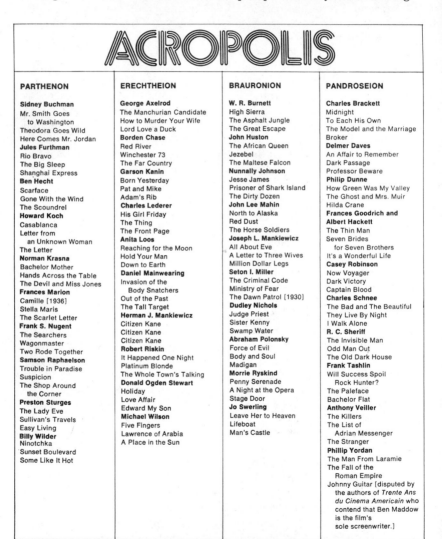

ACROPOLIS

PARTHENON	ERECHTHEION	BRAURONION	PANDROSEION
Sidney Buchman	**George Axelrod**	**W. R. Burnett**	**Charles Brackett**
Mr. Smith Goes	The Manchurian Candidate	High Sierra	Midnight
to Washington	How to Murder Your Wife	The Asphalt Jungle	To Each His Own
Theodora Goes Wild	Lord Love a Duck	The Great Escape	The Model and the Marriage
Here Comes Mr. Jordan	**Borden Chase**	**John Huston**	Broker
Jules Furthman	Red River	The African Queen	**Delmer Daves**
Rio Bravo	Winchester 73	Jezebel	An Affair to Remember
The Big Sleep	The Far Country	The Maltese Falcon	Dark Passage
Shanghai Express	**Garson Kanin**	**Nunnally Johnson**	Professor Beware
Ben Hecht	Born Yesterday	Jesse James	**Philip Dunne**
Scarface	Pat and Mike	Prisoner of Shark Island	How Green Was My Valley
Gone With the Wind	Adam's Rib	The Dirty Dozen	The Ghost and Mrs. Muir
The Scoundrel	**Charles Lederer**	**John Lee Mahin**	Hilda Crane
Howard Koch	His Girl Friday	North to Alaska	**Frances Goodrich and**
Casablanca	The Thing	Red Dust	**Albert Hackett**
Letter from	The Front Page	The Horse Soldiers	The Thin Man
an Unknown Woman	**Anita Loos**	**Joseph L. Mankiewicz**	Seven Brides
The Letter	Reaching for the Moon	All About Eve	for Seven Brothers
Norman Krasna	Hold Your Man	A Letter to Three Wives	It's a Wonderful Life
Bachelor Mother	Down to Earth	Million Dollar Legs	**Casey Robinson**
Hands Across the Table	**Daniel Mainwaring**	**Seton I. Miller**	Now Voyager
The Devil and Miss Jones	Invasion of the	The Criminal Code	Dark Victory
Frances Marion	Body Snatchers	Ministry of Fear	Captain Blood
Camille [1936]	Out of the Past	The Dawn Patrol [1930]	**Charles Schnee**
Stella Maris	The Tall Target	**Dudley Nichols**	The Bad and The Beautiful
The Scarlet Letter	**Herman J. Mankiewicz**	Judge Priest	They Live By Night
Frank S. Nugent	Citizen Kane	Sister Kenny	I Walk Alone
The Searchers	Citizen Kane	Swamp Water	**R. C. Sheriff**
Wagonmaster	Citizen Kane	**Abraham Polonsky**	The Invisible Man
Two Rode Together	**Robert Riskin**	Force of Evil	Odd Man Out
Samson Raphaelson	It Happened One Night	Body and Soul	The Old Dark House
Trouble in Paradise	Platinum Blonde	Madigan	**Frank Tashlin**
Suspicion	The Whole Town's Talking	**Morrie Ryskind**	Will Success Spoil
The Shop Around	**Donald Ogden Stewart**	Penny Serenade	Rock Hunter?
the Corner	Holiday	A Night at the Opera	The Paleface
Preston Sturges	Love Affair	Stage Door	Bachelor Flat
The Lady Eve	Edward My Son	**Jo Swerling**	**Anthony Veiller**
Sullivan's Travels	**Michael Wilson**	Leave Her to Heaven	The Killers
Easy Living	Five Fingers	Lifeboat	The List of
Billy Wilder	Lawrence of Arabia	Man's Castle	Adrian Messenger
Ninotchka	A Place in the Sun		The Stranger
Sunset Boulevard			**Phillip Yordan**
Some Like It Hot			The Man From Laramie
			The Fall of the
			Roman Empire
			Johnny Guitar [disputed by
			the authors of *Trente Ans*
			du Cinema Americain who
			contend that Ben Maddow
			is the film's
			sole screenwriter.]

Buck Henry derives largely from the fortuitous circumstance of his visible connection with Mike Nichols and *The Graduate*, a film whose dialogue was lifted, almost word for word, from Charles Webb's novel. When on his own (in *The Troublemaker* and *Candy*), Henry's humor is decidedly undergraduate, even sophomoric.

Unfortunately, the best screenwriters are likely to be ignored by film critics and historians. It's a minor scandal that film students are aware of Don Siegel's montages for *Casablanca* but not of Howard Koch's script; that Jules Furthman is trampled under foot in the mad rush to canonize Hawks and Sternberg; that film buffs, who can trace Gregg Toland's deep-focus work from *Wuthering Heights* through *Citizen Kane*, don't know, and probably don't care, that Herman Mankiewicz wrote *Citizen Kane* with only nominal assistance from Orson Welles. "In my opinion," Welles said twenty years ago, "the writer should have the first and last word in filmmaking, the only better alternative being the writer-director, but with the stress on the first word."

Perhaps the day of the hyphenate, the writer-director, has already dawned, and the screenwriter will become just another high-priced artifact in that great Hollywood auction in the sky. Perhaps not. Some of the most successful and popular films of the Right-Now Generation have been close adaptations of novels, with tight, efficient scripts (such as *The Graduate*, *Rosemary's Baby* and *Midnight Cowboy*). It's also encouraging to note the return to prominence of veteran screenwriters who have learned to meet the demands of a youth market while doing work that an adult can be proud of: Waldo Salt with *Midnight Cowboy*, Ring Lardner Jr. with *M*a*s*h*, Abraham Polonsky with *Tell Them Willie Boy is Here*, and Albert Maltz with *Two Mules for Sister Sara*. But whether these trends are heralding the screenwriter's second wind or portending his last gasp, the first forty years of the American commercial sound film cannot be evaluated without considering the crucial role he has played. The best screenwriters were talented and tenacious enough to assure that their visions and countless revisions would be realized on the screen. Now it is time for them to be remembered in film history.

1970

NESTOR ALMENDROS
FROM MAN WITH A CAMERA

"SOME THOUGHTS ON MY PROFESSION"

People outside the film world have often asked me, What is a director of photography? What does he do?

The answer is: almost everything and hardly anything. His function differs so much from one film to another that it is hard to define it exactly. My work may be simply to press the button on the camera, and sometimes not even that. There are films where the camera operator actually handles the camera while I sit nearby in a folding chair with my name on the back. In this case I am there to supervise the image, give advice, and . . . have my name on the credits. In the extreme case of the huge super-productions, with all their special effects, one hardly knows who is responsible for the photography, for it ends up absorbing everything and everybody. In a low budget movie, however, a director of photography collaborating with a director who is inexperienced or just beginning can not only choose the lens but decide on the framing of the shots, the movements of the camera, the choreography of the actors in relation to the shot, and, of course, the lighting—the visual atmosphere of each scene. I even get involved in the choice of the colors, materials, and shapes of the sets and wardrobe. And whenver I can, I like to operate the camera myself.

The director of photography must always intervene when the director's technical knowledge does not allow him to express his artistic desires in material and practical terms. He must remind him of the laws of optics when they are being disregarded. But first and foremost, he must never forget he is there to help the director. Though the cinematographer may pride himself on having his own style, he mustn't try to impose it. He must do his best to understand the director's style, see as many of the director's films as possible (if there are any), and immerse himself in the director's "manner." It is not "our" film but "his" film.

People have asked me why I gave up my ambition to be a director so early on and devoted myself entirely to photography. Actually, at the beginning I was trying to pursue both careers simultaneously. One unexpectedly took off like a rocket; the other—directing—stood still. So let's say life decided for me; I am convinced I have the best position on the crew. I have no intention of changing. I am the first to "see" the film through the viewfinder. If the film is a failure, the cinematographer is rarely blamed; if it is a success, on the other hand, his work invariably gets praised. Another advantage is that one gets many opportunities to travel; being able to change from crew to crew, from director to director, makes for a varied, adventurous life.

Though it is generally the director who suggests each shot, I always like to talk an idea over with him first and develop it, sometimes suggesting my own modifications; for example, what lens to use, or how much to move the camera toward or away from an actor. I like to discuss the scene, to propose photogenic ideas, even for the set. Of course, all this depends on the director. Some of them don't want any dialogue with their collaborators. Throughout my career I have noticed that the most arrogant directors are not necessarily the best.

When we were very young students in the Centro Sperimentale di Cinematografia in Rome, some of us made a practice of verbally tearing down almost everything our predecessors had done. Naturally we despised the "glamorous" photography of Hollywood films; also, we inveighed against neorealism, then in its death throes (1956). We couldn't understand how a supposedly radical change in theme, intentions, and directing could fail to produce a corresponding renovation of photographic techniques. Since this movement was attempting a "new" realism, we were especially irritated by its use of lighting, which depended on the arbitrary, pseudoaesthetic interplay of light and shade.

Among the neorealists, G. R. Aldo was the only director of photography whom we admired. His style seemed completely new, and he differed from everyone else. Aldo began as a still photographer. Visconti first used him for the staging of his theatrical spectaculars, and then brought him in on *La terra trema*. The normal way to become a director of photography at that time—and today, for that matter—was to begin by cleaning and loading cameras, moving on to the job of focus puller. Then, after several years as camera operator, one finally got to do the lighting. Probably because he was never anyone's assistant, so that he had no one to imitate and had to invent his own methods, Aldo's lighting was never conventional. His work was a source of inspiration for us all. Other neorealistic Italian films of the same period, like *Open City* or *Shoeshine*, made by other directors of photography, also had a crude, realistic texture, but not because their cinematographers had this in mind. These men were accustomed to working in studios, and suddenly, because of the postwar shortages, Rossellini and De Sica made them shoot in natural settings. With no access to the usual technical aids, they had to manage as best they could. I am sure that if they had been given a bigger budget and more technical support, they would have done something more "professional." However, in Aldo's case, his realistic style originated in a totally different conception. *La terra trema*, *Umberto D* (De Sica), *Cielo sulla palude* (Heaven over the Marshes) (Genina), and *Senso* (Visconti) are all completely modern. Aldo's last film *Senso* (he died suddenly during the shooting), was his first in color. Insofar as image is concerned, this film marks the origin of contemporary cinema.

But Aldo's influence was not immediately felt, although in Italy Rotunno and Di Venanzo can be considered his earliest followers. Throughout the world, however, the fashionable directors of photography were still wedded to conventional, academic techniques. By the late fifties, this style had reached a saturation point. The younger generation wanted to break with everything and start over.

And when our time arrived, this is what happened, or so we thought. The new wave marked the moment of change. In France, Raoul Coutard in particular began systematically using the new methods of lighting by reflection. Until then, filming had generally been done in studios, on sets constructed without ceilings. The luminous beams of the lights were projected onto the actors and sets from catwalks that ran along the walls. When the New Wave adopted the basic principle of Italian neorealism, which was shooting in natural sets (sets with ceilings), lighting techniques necessarily had to be modified. These were low-budget films but there were aesthetic reasons behind the decision to work with natural sets. The position of the lights was reversed. Instead of shining from the catwalks down onto the actors, the beams of the lights, which were placed out of the camera's angle of vision, shone the other way, that is, toward the ceiling, so the light reached the actors on the rebound, indirectly, and was therefore diffuse, with no pronounced shadows. Instead of making things look as if they had been outlined, flooded everything evenly and softly, as in an aquarium.

At first sight this looked like an antiaesthetic parti pris. All that filigree work, those laborious lights and shadows of earlier movies, seemed to have fallen by the wayside. At the same time, color film became the norm, replacing black and white. People thought that even with "flat" lighting, colors alone were enough to separate shapes and create the impression of relief. And another advantage was that the actors could move as they wished. With the earlier method they had had to keep to specific spots and positions where their faces looked most suggestive, depending upon the greater or lesser brightness of each area.

Since reflected light casts no pronounced shadows, the boom man could place his microphone more easily, without casting its indiscreet shape on the set. Last but not least, this kind of lighting needed fewer work hours, fewer technicians and electricians, and fewer salaries for producers to pay. All these changes gave the impression of a total revolution; at the same time, more sensitive negatives needing less light and smaller, more portable cameras had appeared. But it soon became clear that the adoption of simpler, more economical methods increased productivity but not quality. From the point of view of the image, we had moved from an aesthetic with shadows to an aesthetic without them. As the work process was simplified, it became accessible to anyone. After the first two or three years of experiments and surprises (1959–1961, the early films of Godard, Truffaut, Resnais, Demy . . .), for every creator of real talent there were a half dozen pretentious upstarts without any originality. That shadowless light always shining down from a strange sky (the ceiling), by day or by night, had eventually destroyed visual atmosphere in modern cinema. We had moved from old conventions to new ones, but unfortunately these new conventions were oversimplified, impoverished. The films of the so-called young cinema ended up all looking alike. What began as a healthy reaction against a certain photographic mannerism, a nonconformist attitude to traditional cinema, soon created its own breed of conformers who were even more uniform and monotonous. The result was that a decade later the aesthetic level of film photography was probably lower than it had been.

The present trend seems to synthesize the old and the new.

Those direct lights of the black-and-white days are unbearable now in color film. From the early experiments of the New Wave we kept the use of indirect or diffuse lighting, but instead of directing it only from the ceiling, we direct it from the sides, the windows or the lamps, from the real sources of light within a given setting. One must try to discover a different and original visual atmosphere for each film and even for each sequence, to obtain variety, wealth, and texture in one's use of lighting while still taking advantage of modern techniques.

Until quite recently the director of photography ruled the set like a tyrant. He devoted so many hours to setting up the lighting that there was no time left for the actors to rehearse or for the directors to direct. European cinema took this kind of complicated lighting to extremes. One has only to think of Carne's *Gates of the Night*. American cinema was able to maintain a certain naturalness (except in some types of film that demanded stylization, of course). The French films that came out just after the war, before the New Wave, were unbearable with their laborious interweaving of lights. The actors could barely move. The light hit them right between the eyes, an "artistic" gloom hid the rest of their faces, their bodies were illuminated separately, all of which made them move and act like robots. The lighting didn't exist for the actors; the actors existed for the lighting. Therefore, it is not surprising that the reaction began in Europe with the innovations of Italian neo-realism and the New Wave. Caught unawares for once, American cinema was slow to assimilate the new photography. Nevertheless, it made a rapid recovery and caught up with, then outstripped, its European counterpart. For example, it has been astonishingly quick in adapting and even developing light-weight filming equipment. Some of the new cinematographers I admire are Gordon Willis (*Interiors*), Michael Chapman (*Taxi Driver*), Haskell Wexler (*Bound for Glory*), Conrad Hall (*Fat City*), Vilmos Zsigmond (*The Deer Hunter*). It is also interesting to see how American cinema has gotten around union restrictions, and has imported certain talented Europeans, like the Swede Sven Nykvist (*Pretty Baby*) and the Italians Vittorio Storaro (*Apocalypse Now*) and Giuseppe Rotunno (*All That Jazz*).

More and more I tend to use only one light source, which is what usually happens in nature. I reject the typical lighting of the forties and fifties, which consisted of a main or "key" light, supplemented by a "fill" light, with another light behind to show off the stars' hairdos and make them stand out against the background, yet another for the background itslf, another to show off the wardrobe, and so on *ad infinitum*. The result had nothing to do with reality, where a window or a lamp, or at most both of them, normally provide the only sources of light. Since I lack imagination, I seek inspiration in nature, which offers me an infinite variety of forms. Once the key light has been decided, the space around it and the areas that might be left in total darkness are reinforced with a very soft shadowless light, until what is reproduced on film is just what the eye would really see.

I don't always use a backlight, which is the light that used to be placed behind the actors to set off their hair. Or rather, I use it only when it is justified. I use Fresnel lights only very rarely and for special effects, when I need an extremely precise, sharp light. In interiors my main light is often very soft, as it usually is in real life. When sunlight is needed and there is no sun, the best way to reproduce it is with arc lights, H.M.I.s, or minibrutes, though nothing can replace the real thing.

When it comes to lighting, one of my basic principles is that the light sources must be justified. I believe that what is functional is beautiful, that functional light is beautiful light. I try to make sure that my light is logical rather than aesthetic. In a natural set I use what light there is, reinforcing it when necessary. In a studio set I imagine that the sun is shining from a certain point outside, and I decide how the light would come through the windows. The rest is easy.

From the days of my first feature film, *La Collectionnneuse*, I realized that most technicians lie or exaggerate. They arrange things so that they use huge quantities of light (which means electricity). Even when it is unnecessary, they love to make themselves more important, to justify their salaries, whereas there is really little technique to know. To make their work seem more difficult than it actually is, they turn up with their famous briefcases full of filters, gauzes, diffusers, and sophisticated light meters, when the important thing is not what is inside the camera but what is in front of it. Then they surround themselves with an army of electricians and grips that makes them look like sea captains (though it is true that the presence of this large crew is sometimes due to union regulations). No doubt because of my individualistic temperament I have always tried to avoid the folklore of my profession.

I think of cinema as a generous art form. Through the lens, something like an automatic transfiguration is produced on the photographic emulsion. Everything seems more interesting on film than in life. The process is somewhat similar to the art of engraving. The artist takes a piece of wood, inscribes some sort of design on it with a tool, inks it, prints it on paper, and the result is usually interesting. The same design done directly on paper would have no value at all. Somehow the reproduction enhances the work. In the same way, there is a sort of magic in cinema; the camera heightens reality. Films are sometimes superior to their makers. This may explain why at times I like films made by people whom I find unpleasant or whose ideas are contrary to my own. It is possible to sit through a film made by someone who personally doesn't deserve five minutes of one's time. With a modicum of knowledge of composition and narrative, anyone can film something acceptable. This is not true of other art forms. In the case of cinema, the medium certainly helps; it is a grateful medium.

In fact, one of the dangers of cinema is precisely its ease. Everything tends to seem prettier through the lens, and one must often forget aesthetics. This is especially obvious when films dealing with poverty or ugliness make those things look lovely.

In my opinion, the main qualities a director of photography needs are plastic sensitivity and a solid cultural background. So-called cinematographic technique is only of secondary importance, and depends above all on one's assistants. Many cinematographers take refuge in technique. Once a few basic rules have been learned, the job is not very complicated, especially with an assistant to take care of focusing, measuring distances, and looking after the mechanics of the camera.

I make all my decisions about lighting by eye, without bothering at first about footcandles and all the other calculations. I size up contrasts directly, using the exposure meter only at the last minute to decide on the lens stop. Today's emulsions are so true to life that if something looks good at first sight, it will be equally good when it is printed on film.

At first I used Norwood light meters, which measure incidental light. However, for the past few years I have been using the old Weston Master V for reflected light, taking a reading on the palm of my hand or aiming it directly at the scene to be photographed. This system gives me a global reading, without considering contrasts. I do that myself, by eye, as I have explained.

For daylight exteriors, when I am using today's Kodak emulsion 5247, I usually give the emulsion a rating of 80 ASA and use an 85 filter. When I am shooting with artificial tungsten light, I set my light meter on 125 ASA, without a filter, of course. When I want to increase the sensitivity of the negative, I set the meter at 200 ASA, which gives me an extra stop when I have the negative pushed, or forced, in the laboratory. Nowadays this manipulation of the negative can be done perfectly, with no visible increase in the grain. However, in some of my latest films—*Kramer vs. Kramer, The Blue Lagoon*—I have rarely pushed the negative, no doubt because of my new classicist scruples. Both Fuji and Kodak (5293) recently have created even faster emulsions. I rated them at 400 ASA in *Sophie's Choice.*

Contrary to popular belief, it is my opinion that the more complex the movie, the more one needs to be at the viewfinder oneself. Whenever complicated movements of camera or scene are required, every slight displacement produces a new frame, and it is virtually impossible to be constantly telling the camera operator what composition is needed. People who believe that lighting should be separate from camera operating claim that if these two functions are carried out by the same person it takes longer to prepare the shots. Producers as well as many technicians recommend this duality. (They are not really concerned with aesthetics; they merely want to increase productivity.) I think the issue is debatable. Time can be lost explaining in detail to the camera operator just what he has to do and lining up the shot beforehand; the director has to deal with two people instead of one, with the complications and confusions that inevitably result.

But I think the most important thing is that the balance of lights in the frame can be evaluated perfectly only when the director of photography is constantly looking through the viewfinder while the shot is being prepared and rehearsed. The image seen through the viewfinder is what is going to be seen on the screen. The cameraman is not bothered by what is going on around him (microphones, lights, technical crew), sometimes on the very edge of the frame but outside the field of vision of the lens.

I need the frame with its four sides. I need its limits. In art, there is no artistic transposition without limits. I think the frame was a great discovery (long before cinema, naturally). (During the Stone Age, the men of Lascaux and Altamira did not frame their paintings.) And what counts in two-dimensional art is not only what is seen but what is not seen, what does not let itself be seen. Eisenstein hit upon a brilliant explanation of why we Westerners need the frame. We see our landscapes through windows, whereas the Japanese, who are used to architecture with sliding walls and no windows, did their painting on scrolls that could be unrolled and had only two edges.

In the cinema, the spectator can concentrate on the essential when everything marginal or tangential to the theme is eliminated. I am therefore aesthetically opposed to certain experiments like "total cinema" in a dome. Though people think a cinematographer has to take care of lighting first and foremost, I believe the frame is just as important. By means of the camera's viewfinder, the outside world goes through a process of selection and organization. Things become pertinent; thanks to the parameters of the frame, they take shape in relation to vertical and horizontal limits. We know at once what is good and what is bad. Like the microscope, the frame is an analyzing tool.

The word "frame" immediately suggests another term, "composition." To the layman the word sounds mysterious, and its rules difficult, whereas in fact to a greater or lesser extent everyone possesses an innate sense of composition. It is one of the distinctive characteristics of the human being, like the gift of speech or a feeling for rhythm. The capacity for composition could be defined simply as a sense of arrangement. A secretary who organizes objects on a desktop (pencils, papers, a telephone), a housewife who harmonizes the arrangement of furniture, carpets, curtains, are both displaying a sense of spatial composition.

Achieving good composition within a cinematographic frame is, after all, a matter of organizing the different visual elements so that the whole is intelligible, useful within the narrative, and therefore pleasing to look at. In the art of cinema, the director of photography's skill is measured by his capacity to keep an image clear, to "clean it," as Truffaut says, by separating each shape, be it a person or an object, in relation to a background or a set; in other words, by his ability to organize a scene visually in front of the lens and avoid confusion by emphasizing the various elements that are of interest.

Of course, the so-called natural laws of composition were discovered long before the days of film, as the art of antiquity proves. There are many bas-reliefs on the rectangular metopes in the Parthenon which are perfect compositions. But leaving aside the examples from Ancient Greece, we can still find an extraordinary sense of composition in the visual creations of primitive man. In *The Valley*, which I filmed for Barbet Schroeder among the Hagen tribes of New Guinea in the South Pacific, we were able to document this innate gift with scenes where these jungle dwellers paint their faces and bodies. Their technique adheres to strict rules of symmetry, with refined contrasts of colors and shapes. Children's artwork is another example. If children are given paper and crayons, they will start drawing at once. What do they produce? Without realizing it, a child will begin from the principle of *horror vacui*, dread of the void; if part of the paper is left blank, the child immediately fills it with another elements—for example, the sun, if the scene is a landscape—to restore the equilibrium.

From the Renaissance onward, many long treatises have been written on the rules of composition. A cinematographer should first know them and then forget them, or at least not consciously think about them all the time, for if he does, he risks eliminating all naturalness from his cinematographic narrative. Here I will just remind my readers of a few simple, classic principles:

Horizontal lines suggest repose, peace, serenity. Perhaps we unconsciously applied this idea in the opening scenes of the vast wheatfields in *Days of Heaven;* vertical lines denote strength, authority, dignity, as in the tall, three-stored mansion, alone in the middle of the prairie in the same film. Diagonal lines crossing the frame evoke action, movement, the power to overcome obstacles. This is why in the cinema many battle scenes or violent encounters are set on sloping ground as ascending or descending compositions, with cannons or swords at 45-degree angles. The forked flames of the fire that destroyed the wheatfields in *Days of Heaven* were our application—I hope a subtle one—of this principle. Curved lines transmit ideas of fluidity and sensuality. Curved compositions that move circularly communicate feelings of exaltation, euphoria, and joy. This principle is noticeable in most of the ride equipment in fun fairs. And it is no coincidence that so many folk dances are done in circles.

Slavko Vorkapich talks about the effect of the moving camera—tracking—on dynamic compositions. If the camera moves forward and enters a scene, it creates the impression of bringing the audience into the heart of the narrative, and therefore making it participate intimately in the story that is being told. The opposite movement, when the camera withdraws from the scene, is often used as a way of ending a film.

Basically, a cinema production of any value must be visually interesting, even for a person who comes in halfway through the screening, it must be visually exciting even for someone who has missed the beginning of the story. I am eclectic in that I like cinema in black and white or in color. I will return to this in more detail in the chapters on *My Night at Maud's, The Wild Child,* and *Vivement Dimanche,* but I admit now that I prefer black and white, especially in old films. However, such recent attempts at Woody Allen's *Manhattan* have less interest for me. For one thing, nowadays the laboratories have forgotten how to develop black-and-white film. They fail to bring out the richness and variety that the blacks, whites, and grays once had. Then again, today we directors of photography don't know anymore how to light properly for black and white. It is a lost art.

We learn about eras before the twentieth century through painting, that is, through colors. We know the first third of this century through black-and-white cinema more than anything else. I admit I have a conditioned reflex. As a spectator or director of photography, I "see" periods before our own in color. However, in the case of a film that reconstructs the decades of the twenties, thirties, or forties, I feel that color is an anachronism: *Bonnie and Clyde* (Penn), *Lacombe Lucien* (Malle), and my own work in *The Last Métro* (Truffaut) are good examples.

Generally, though, I prefer color. The image carries more information, it reveals more. I am nearsighted, and color helps me see, interpret, "read" an image. As it reached its apogee, black-and-white cinematography ended its cycle and exhausted its practical possibilities. In color photography there is still room for experimentation.

Nowadays people think that color has reached its ultimate perfection. This is true of the ease with which it can be used, but it is not true of faithfulness of reproduction and chromaticism. The fact is that the old Technicolor—which apparently had only 8 ASA—was an excellent process, faithful to reality and much more durable than what exists today. We remember it as a system of overbright, shrill colors because the art direction, sets, and wardrobes were all exaggerated on purpose, not because it was defective. When the first experiments in Technicolor began, the public was demanding color and producers had to please them. In *Becky Sharp* (Rouben Mamoulian, 1935), which I had the good luck to see in a flawless copy at the Milan cinémathèque, characters appear in the same shot dressed in different colors, red, green, pink, violet. Those early attempts at color film were remarkably charming.

The film industry is said to have made great technological progress. I would contest this claim. From the 1930s on, when sound was added and the first color films appeared, progress has really been minimal. One has only to think of the degree of perfection achieved by John Ford in *Drums Along the Mohawk* (1939) and by David O. Selznick, who produced the much better known *Gone With the Wind* (1939). The mechanism of cameras has not undergone any fundamental change in the last forty years. The most notable developments are that they have become smaller, lighter, and therefore more transportable, and now have gadgets like the reflex system, which eliminates parallax and allows direct focusing through the lens. Raw stock film has become more sensitive, the lens can register images at lower light readings, but ultimately all these advances only mean that film equipment has become simpler and cheaper and is now available to all countries and budgets. There has been a generalization of what once was the Hollywood exception. Only the new ultraluminous lenses and ultrasensitive film have contributed to a significant progress from the point of view of aesthetics.

Wide-aperture lenses and emulsions able to capture extremes of light have only recently appeared on the market. This has indeed been a revolution, one that is still happening and has much further to go. I like to compare this revolution in cinematography with the revolution of the Impressionists in painting. With the invention of tubes of oil paint, the artist could leave his studio carrying only a case of these tubes, go anywhere—Rouen's cathedral, for example, like Monet—and capture fleeting moments of light on the cathedral façade on different canvases. Earlier painters had been obliged to prepare and mix the colors themselves in their workshops. Nowadays, those of us who work in color film can also capture instantly difficult and extreme moments of light even at low exposures. The method of pushing the negative has given color film the sensitivity of 200 or 400 ASA, and the new emulsions go further still. But I will return to this theme later in connection with *Days of Heaven* and *Sophie's Choice*.

I am very fond of silent films. The magic of silence fascinates me. I know these early films were in fact not totally silent. There was always piano or orchestra music in the background. Yet I like them as they are now, without any music and in highly contrasted dupe negatives. They are a bit like the beautiful ruins of antiquity, like Greek statues of which only the torsos remain, with no arms or heads, and no polychromy. I am hypnotized by those characters who gesticulate and move their lips without uttering a sound; there is something oneiric and strange about them.

I also love sound in films. Like color, sound adds realism. When I say sound, I exclude background music added to the mixing later on; I mean noises, dialogue. Sound, especially direct sound, is a great help to the image, giving it density and relief. Therefore, I always try to work closely with the sound men.

I generally don't like images with out-of-focus backgrounds, the function of which is merely graphic and aesthetic, and which are sometimes quite unreal, especially in color films with a commercial look (TV spots). But I also don't think that the background and sets should be too precise. If there is too much depth of field, the audience's attention, which in the cinema should be centered most of the time on the actors, is dispersed to the whole frame. Therefore, I prefer backgrounds to be slightly out of focus—but only slightly. Of course, in the case of a shot that brings together several equally important characters, depth of field becomes indispensable because the spectator must be able to see different levels of the action at the same time.

There is a fairly widespread notion that the close-up is one of the specific elements of cinematographic art that distinguishes it from theater. But people forget that the theater also had close-ups. Theatergoers used to look through opera glasses to "create" their own close-ups when they wanted to. The difference in film is that it is the director who decides when they are necessary. I like close-ups a great deal, perhaps because I am nearsighted.

I take an equally eclectic position vis-à-vis the old polemic introduced by André Bazin as to the superiority of the unedited *plan-séquence*. For example, I admire continuous scenes, with no cuts, no fakery, where the whole truth of a moment of interpretation is presented to the audience just as it is. In this sense I am a fanatical admirer of George Cukor (*Adam's Rib*) and his school. But this does not prevent me from enjoying tremendously films that use editing. These have been our heritage from Griffith on, and such a legacy is not to be rejected. I love seeing a modern film like Wim Wenders's *The American Friend*, which goes back to the editing that so annoyed the New Wave. I thoroughly enjoy the mathematics, the geometry, the precision of the cutting that we see in silent films. But I appreciate it only when it emanates from pure inspiration and when an overriding sense of style unifies every shot. Like Truffaut or Malick, Wenders does not edit to make filming easier, multiplying the angles in order to decide later on what can be done at the Moviola. Ideally, each shot must be conceived in a certain way. The film will derive its form from this concept. If there is no concept to begin with, there is no style. In art I believe in discipline.

After my recent experiences with American filmmaking, I can state categorically that American directors shoot far too many hundreds of thousands of feet of negative. I don't think it is necessary, at least not to such an exaggerated extent. The producers are the ones who insist on this procedure, since they reason that raw stock is the cheapest item in the budget. However, they forget that this wastefulness bedevils the other stages of production, too. In each set shooting goes on forever. Then, when it comes to the editing, there is an enormous amount of film to be looked at, cut, synchronized, and selected; the problem is that when there are many options, there is a tendency to use them all. I have been very lucky in that most of the American directors with whom I have worked have known how to choose only the meaningful shots and get rid of the others. But some film directors look as if they cut without rhyme or reason, just to put in one more take—from yet another angle. Films made out of a super-abundance of material tend to resemble each other, because they have all been shot according to the same methods. A computer could make this sort of film equally well. It could easily decide which positions and angles of the camera are needed to cover a certain scene.

The function of the director of photography as depository or transmitter of progress or discoveries in what has been called "cinematographic language" is neither well known nor well researched. When he was just a beginner in 1941 Orson Welles astonished the world with *Citizen Kane*, a film that was to revolutionize cinematographic "writing." At that time Welles was twenty-five years old and had little experience, but Gregg Toland, his director of photography and a man of great dedication, had just finished *The Long Voyage Home* and *The Grapes of Wrath* for John Ford. These films already had wide-angled shots, sets with ceilings, depth of field. If these two films are compared with *Kane*, it is not hard to see the influence on Welles of Ford via Toland. Through Stanley Cortez, who had been his cinematographer on *The Magnificent Ambersons*, Welles in turn influenced another neophyte director, Charles Laughton in his film *The Night of the Hunter*. At the time when the big production companies reached their apogee (during the thirties and forties), each "house" developed its own style. Of course, the individual style was set by the producers and the directors on staff, but the importance of cinematographers has received little attention. The old Columbia comedies owe their characteristic look to Joseph Walker, who was Capra's photographer but who also made *Penny Serenade* for George Stevens, *The Awful Truth* for Leo McCarey, *Theodora Goes Wild* for Richard Boleslawsky, and *His Girl Friday* for Howard Hawks. All these films have curious stylistic similarities despite the different personalities of their directors.

Greta Garbo is another representative case. All her films resemble one another, so that they form an amazingly unified body of work, even though she acted under different directors: Clarence Brown (*Anna Christie*), Edmund Goulding (*Grand Hotel*), Rouben Mamoulian (*Queen Christina*), George Cukor

(*Camille*). Garbo knew what she was doing: she always asked for the same cinematographer—William Daniels.

I would even go so far as to compare two dissimilar films that I admire, both photographed by Rudolph Maé: *The Passion of Joan of Arc* by Dreyer and *Gilda* by Charles Vidor. If they are shown one after the other, and if the religious theme of the first and the Hollywood eroticism of the second are overlooked, it becomes clear that the lighting, frames, and camera movements are less different than might have been expected. Some sequences, like the one of the gamblers in *Gilda*, have an extraordinary, curious resemblance to those of the judgment scene in Dreyer's masterpiece. It is very likely that I have unconsciously transmitted to younger and less experienced directors certain mannerisms and figures of expression from Rohmer and Truffaut, the two masters with whom I have most often worked.

In recent years film criticism has devoted more space and attention to the men who handle the camera. Perhaps this is due to the current tendency to recognize the specific responsibility of each of the professionals taking part in shooting a film. I do believe, however, that this trend started in the States, not Europe. European experts veer toward the cult of the director, the so-called *politique des auteurs* or auteurs' theory. In my case, for example, it is the English and American critics who have commented more favorably on my work and rewarded it. European critics, particularly the French, do not usually mention the director of photography. The most eloquent proof that in Europe little importance is given to the cinematographer is that in the most important festivals like the Cannes Film Festival there are no prizes for the image. Yet from the start the Oscar has been awarded not only to the director but also to the other technicians who participate in a film. And the first international festival to organize a symposium for cinematographers took place in Los Angeles.

The interest our profession receives is cyclical. Right now we are on the crest of the wave. There was a similar moment during the last days of the silent films (*Sunrise* by Charles Rosher and Karl Struss). With the advent of sound, the image temporarily lost its powers of attraction, but it had regained its importance by 1940 and reached new heights of perfection and classicism (Gregg Toland's *Grapes of Wrath* and *Citizen Kane*). As color gradually took over during the fifties and sixties, its importance diminished, as it had with the arrival of sound, but for other reasons; the old cinematographers of black-and-white films were disoriented. Slowly new generations have come along, and cinematography in color is entering a new heyday. Once again the names of the directors of photography stand out in the credits. . . .

1984

ROYAL S. BROWN
HERMANN, HITCHCOCK, AND THE MUSIC OF THE IRRATIONAL

[Hitchcock] only finishes a picture 60%. I have to finish it for him.

BERNARD HERRMANN[1]

While it may very well be that Alfred Hitchcock was the "master of suspense," he was also, and perhaps even more strongly, a master of the irrational. When we think of Hitchcock's films, the images that immediately come to mind are those of a villain falling from the Statue of Liberty, a hero being attacked by an airplane in the middle of nowhere, and a nude woman being stabbed to death in a shower. In these and many other instances, the violence has the aura of a mythic predestination far removed from the causality of everyday existence, even though the latter, in Hitchcock, almost always serves as a point of departure. The things that happen to Hitchcock characters rarely occur for reasons these characters—and sometimes even the audiences—can understand. And the often grotesque settings for key events further remove everything from the domain of reason and understanding.

And yet, from the artistic and human points of view, Hitchcock was the most rational of beings. Even though the director

[1]Royal S. Brown, "An Interview with Bernard Herrmann (1911–1975)," *High Fidelity*, 26, no. 9 (September 1976), 65. Hereafter referred to as "Interview."

was fully aware of the "beneficial shocks" he provided to his public, most of his discussions on his film making center around the importance of style and the painstaking care he took putting his sequences together. As is well known, the physical act of actually shooting the film had less importance to him than the meticulous setting up of shots before a single frame of film was ever exposed. And to anyone who goes beyond narrative involvement, the results of this care are immediately evident in the finished product, whether in the composition of a single shot, such as the *Pietà* scene from *The Lodger*, or in the editing of an entire sequence, such as the famous 78-shot/45-second shower scene in *Psycho*. From this perspective, the relationship between the director's art and its subject matter bears a strong but perhaps not unexpected resemblance to Greek tragedy as defined, for instance, by Michael Grant:

> For it is in the myths, even the cruellest myths, that Sophocles sees the permanent human battleground, accepting their horrors with his dramatic (if not altogether with his moral) sense, and more than Aeschylus adhering to their traditional framework. Yet these stories would be nothing without the poetry, for there comes a point, and this is reached by Sophocles, where form is so nearly perfect as to achieve the autonomous originality of a new concept. This is also true of the contemporary Parthenon in which, likewise, the achievement depends not on lavish ornament but on a simplicity modified by subtle constructional and stylistic effects. These, like the effects of Sophocles, "triumphantly escape, but just escape, the prosaic."[2]

Grant's discussion of Euripides's *The Bacchae* provides another enlightening parallel with Hitchcock: "Its excitement is enhanced by the tension between the strange, savage myth and the classical severity of its presentation—by the contrast of a more than usual state of emotion, as Coleridge put it, with more than usual order" (p. 279).

One might think, then, that this tension between mythic irrationality and artisan rationality would suffice to create the desired artistic impression. Hitchcock obviously felt this way when he initially tried to avoid using music behind the *Psycho* shower scene.[3] Yet even the Greeks did not rely simply on the

[2]Michael Grant, *Myths of the Greeks and Romans* (Cleveland and New York: World Publishing Co., 1962), pp. 222–23.
[3]This fact has been documented by James Naremore in his *Filmguide to Psycho* (Bloomington: Indiana University Press, 1973), p. 22. It has also been brought up by John Russell Taylor in his *Hitch: The Life and Times of Alfred Hitchcock* (New York: Pantheon, 1978; rpt. New York: Berkeley, 1980), p. 264.

mythic narrative and its acting out to counterbalance the "more than usual order" of their plays' formal structures. In order to express those forces that escape the everyday and that cannot be communicated by means of normal or even poetic parlance, the Greeks turned to the art that has the fewest obvious ties with what we normally consider to be reality—music:

> The great dramatists were therefore composers as well as poets, actors, playwrights, and producers. . . . When we read a play such as the *Suppliants* of Aeschylus, it is as if we were seeing only the libretto of an opera to which all the music, dances, and stage directions are missing. It is so clearly a lyric drama that the music itself must have been the principal means by which the poet conveyed his meaning. Euripides' *The Bacchae,* on the other hand, has far greater intrinsic dramatic substance, but even here the emotional intensity of the individual scenes often rises to such a pitch that music had to take over where the words left off; just as when a person is so overcome with feeling that words fail, and he resorts to inarticulate sounds and gestures.[4]

As Hitchcock discovered, the existential distance and the emotional gap between a movie audience and what is transpiring on the screen are so great that even the sight of a knife repeatedly entering the body of a nude woman, and even the sounds of her screams and gasps, did not create sufficient visceral involvement in the scene. What was needed—and what Hitchcock got at the instigation of *Psycho's* composer, Bernard Herrmann—was music, and a very particular kind of music, as we shall soon see, to fully communicate the sequence's irrationality *on its own terms.*

It would seem that, even by his personality, Bernard Herrmann was destined to come together with Alfred Hitchcock because of the age-old principle, "opposites attract." Hitchcock, whether in his deliberately cultivated public persona, his radio and television interviews, or on the movie set, was forever the calm, rational being, the very prototype of British unflappability. At the opposite extreme, the American-born Herrmann was possessed of an almost legendary irascibility. Director Brain De Palma, for instance, has given a revealing and yet warm account of the composer's bursts of temper during his initial work on the film *Sisters.*[5] But Herrmann's emo-

[4]William Fleming, *Art and Ideas* (New York: Holt, Rinehart, and Winston, 1955), pp. 33–34.

[5]See Brian De Palma, "Murder by Moog: Scoring the Chill," *The Village Voice,* 11 October 1973, p. 85; rpt. as "Remembering Herrmann," *Take One,* 5, no. 2 (May 1976), 40–41; 39.

tionalism did not show only a negative side. He was a romantic in every sense of the word. I have a strong memory of the
composer breaking into tears and sobbing unashamedly following a screening, in the Summer of 1975, of De Palma's second Herrmann-scored film, *Obsession*. Not only was Herrmann
obviously moved by *Obsession*'s ending, he was also quite sorry
to see the conclusion of a project towards which he had felt
particularly close. Oliver Daniel, formerly of B.M.I., has provided the following overview of Herrmann's personality and
of the way it translated into his music:

> Oscar Levant has remarked on Herrmann's "apprenticeship in
> insolence," and well he might. Those who have worked with
> him know that he can be insulting, vehement, raucous, and
> even brutal. But those who know him better are aware that he
> can also be kind, sentimental, tender, and loving. He has withal
> a capacity to inspire devotion as well as anger. Having worked
> with him at CBS for over a decade, I can attest to that. And it
> is no surprise to find *Sturm und Drang*—Herrmann fashion—
> abruptly alternating with almost sentimental serenity in his
> works.[6]

And as Unicorn Records' Oliver Goldsmith, another long-
standing Herrmann acquaintance, wrote a little over a year after
the composer's death in December 1975, "As, of course, is well
known, Benny was not the easiest of men to get along with
and he could be extremely irrational and outspoken, often for
no particular reason. In this respect he naturally made himself
unpopular with many people; but underneath his gruff exterior he was a kind and generous man in whose company I
spent many happy hours and whose loss I very much regret."[7]
The affective depth of Hermann's music was precisely what
Hitchcock's cinema needed, what, in fact, it had sorely lacked
even in certain masterpieces of the early 1950s such as *Strangers
on a Train*. And so, in 1955, Alfred Hitchcock, the cool, Roman
Catholic, British classicist who became an American citizen,
and Bernard Herrmann, the fiery, Jewish, American romantic
who spent the last years of his life in London, came together
for the first of their seven collaborations, *The Trouble with
Harry*.

---

[6]Oliver Daniel, "A Perspective of Herrmann," *Saturday Review*, 51, no. 28
(13 July 1968), 49.
[7]Oliver Goldsmith, from a letter dated 16 March 1977 and sent to Dr. Harry
M. McCraw of the University of Southern Mississippi.

I

At first glance, *The Trouble with Harry*, with its picture-post-card settings shot in Technicolor and its extended but decidedly nonsuspenseful black humor, seems like atypical Hitchcock. Yet this strange amalgam of British humor and the American ethos was one of the director's personal favorites among his films, and, according to Taylor (pp. 234–35), he even screened it for James Alardyce, who scripted Hitchcock's television monologues, in order to give the writer an idea of the desired persona for "Alfred Hitchcock Presents," which began the same year as *The Trouble with Harry* was shot. Bernard Herrmann saw the film as the most personal of Hitchcock's efforts,[8] and he used the score as the basis for a musical sketch of the director entitled "A Portrait of 'Hitch.' " Just as *The Trouble with Harry* is atypical Hitchcock, Hermann's bantering and scherzo-like music does not immediately bring to mind the composer's better known scores, nor does it seem to pave the way for the great collaborations that began with *Vertigo* in 1958. And yet a rapid glance at several details in the music for the title sequence reveals devices, mostly harmonic in nature, that are already wholly characteristic of the Herrmann/ Hitchcock collaboration.

One thing Hermann obviously fathomed, consciously and/or unconsciously, in Hitchcock and his art was the perfect ambivalency: for every dose of the calm, the rational, and the everyday, there is a counterbalancing dose of the violent, the irrational, and the extraordinary. In *The Trouble with Harry's* Prelude, one way in which this ambivalency can be felt is in the contrast, as the music unfolds, between the more ghoulish passages and the jocular main theme. Perhaps even in choosing the keys of G-flat major and the related E-flat minor, Herrmann may have intended a musicological ambiguity, since these two keys, which have six flats, have exact, enharmonic mirror-images in the keys of F-sharp major and D-sharp minor, which have six sharps.[9] But the essence of Hermann's Hitchcock scoring lies in a kind of harmonic ambiguity

---

[8]See Hermann's brief comments on the album jacket for "Music from the Great Movie Thrillers" (see Discography).

[9]Since the score for *The Trouble with Harry* was unavailable to me, I can only assume from listening to the recording and the film soundtrack that the keys and the notation in general are as I have mentioned. In all cases, however, I have used accidentals rather than giving a key signature, as this corresponds to Hermann's practice. In this paper, examples 1–4; 6A, 6B, and 12 were all obtained by listening; other examples from Hermann's music come from the scores themselves or from quotations of these scores in various articles and books.

whereby the musical language familiar to Western listeners serves as a point of departure, only to be modified in such a way that norms are thrown off center and expectations are held in suspense for much longer periods of time than the listening ears and feeling viscera are accustomed to. The opening, four-note motive, played by the horns, establishes the key and mode of E-flat minor but ends on an unstable D, the seventh note in the harmonic minor scale on E-flat:

EXAMPLE 1

Following a downward, E-flat minor run, Herrmann establishes a characteristic accompaniment figure, played in the low strings, contrabassoon, and clarinets (both bass and regular), which is a typical instrumental sound for the composer:

EXAMPLE 2

Here, the music already hints at the kind of seventh-chord that will become the aural trademark for *Vertigo* and *Psycho*. Were, in fact, the root E-flat to be added beneath the D, B-flat, and G-flat of Example 2 that later form the chord of Example 4 below, the resultant chord would have a structure identical to the one in *Vertigo*'s Prelude. But *The Trouble with Harry*'s much less ominous nature does not allow that E-flat to creep in. Instead, Herrmann suddenly turns to a motive, played in the clarinet, that will soon blossom into the Prelude's main theme and that suddenly switches to the major mode in G-flat, the related major of E-flat minor:

EXAMPLE 3

But before allowing the main theme to take full shape from the above motive, Herrmann turns the notes from Example 2 into a bona fide chord in the horns. Always repeated five times, this figure will assert its obsessive presence throughout *The Trouble with Harry:*

EXAMPLE 4

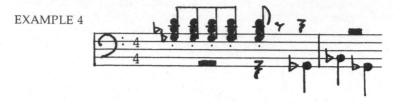

At this point, the chord has a double identity: following, as it does, the motive in Example 3, the chord can be considered as the augmented triad, in the root position, of G-flat major; or, considering its earlier context and the way it brusquely interrupts the motive in Example 3, the chord can be seen as a reaffirmation of the seventh chord built on the E-flat minor triad with the root missing.

In the same way, then, that Hitchcock's films have their point of departure in everyday reality, Herrmann's music begins in the traditional tonal system of Western music. In this sense, the music is no different from that of the composer's film-music contemporaries and predecessors. But just as Hitchcock moves into new territory by the way in which he calmly breaks down the normal orders, Herrmann, in *The Trouble with Harry*, already begins to set himself apart not only from his colleagues but also, to a certain extent, from the scores he had penned prior to this first Hitchcock collaboration by the way he makes musical standards work against their normalcy. The essence of Western tonality, and in particular of diatonic harmonies, is the resolution, the eventual return to "normalcy" in the music's various departures from the tonal center. One expects, for instance, a particular theme or motive to quickly break away from the clutches of the unstable seventh note rather than to solidly end on it, as *The Trouble with Harry*'s opening motive does. The obsessive presence of the D natural in *The Trouble with Harry*'s Prelude, whether as the last note of the opening motive, the prominent repeated note in the accompaniment figure of Example 2, or the top of the chord in Example 4, leaves the listener lost in seemingly known, aural settings which, like Hitchcock's Statue of Liberty or Mount Rushmore (or, for that matter, the little bourgeois town of Santa Rosa, California), had come to be taken for granted but where unexpected things begin to take place.

One also expects that an unstable chord such as the triad in Example 4 will *lead,* one way or the other, to some kind of resolution. Instead, it takes on an identity all of its own since, 1) its relationship to material both preceding and following it is almost entirely juxtapositional rather than musically logical, and, 2) it is repeated, in the same rhythmic pattern, throughout the Prelude so that it becomes, in fact, a motive—not one that is connected with any particular element of the movie but rather one that communicates, synchronically, a certain mood. The same effect occurs, but in an opposite sense, with the interval of the third, which abounds in Herrmann and in particular in the Hitchcock scores, in a manner that is disproportionate with its nonetheless frequent use in Western music. Defined as "the most characteristic interval of the Western harmonic system,"[10] the third normally acts as a pillar of stability, often signaling not only the key involved but also the mode (major or minor) as well. One might think, then, that the stability of the third would, in Herrmann, counterbalance the instability of the oft-used seventh. In fact, however, the third, when isolated from the major or minor triad, can be manipulated so that its identity becomes quite ambiguous. The classic example of this, perhaps, is the opening of the first movement of Beethoven's Fifth Symphony. Even though that initial, G-G-G-E-flat motive signals the beginning of one of the most solidly minor-mode movements ever penned, the interval itself is a *major* third! Our hearing of it as C minor rather than as E-flat major depends on our acquaintance with the movement as a whole and also, perhaps, on the motive's downward direction.

As can be seen, then, the true major-minor identity of a triad depends only on the positioning of its component thirds:

EXAMPLE 5

MAJOR TRIAD   minor third / major third   MINOR TRIAD   major third / minor third

What Herrmann began to do with great consistency in his Hitchcock scores was to isolate the characteristically Western interval of the third from the minor/major or major/minor equilibrium of the tonic triad. The augmented interval of Ex-

[10]Willi Apel, *Harvard Dictionary of Music,* 2nd ed. (Cambridge, Mass.: The Belknap Press, 1969), p. 848.

ample 4, for instance, contains *two* major thirds, which, as we have seen, can be considered as belonging either to G-flat major or to E-flat minor. Add the lower E-flat and you get what I will refer to as the "Hitchcock chord," a minor major-seventh in which there are two major thirds and one minor. Like the triad in Example 4 from *The Trouble with Harry*, then, and like the four-note seventh chords of the later films, the isolated, two-note interval of the third takes on a character, a color of its own, much as it does in Debussy's piano *Prélude* entitled *"Voiles,"* or, in a manner that foreshadows Herrmann even more closely, the Prelude to Act III of Wagner's *Tristan und Isolde*, where slowly rising, parallel thirds evoke the desolate settings of a run-down castle overlooking the sea.

Even as early as *The Trouble with Harry*, Herrmann broke with standard practices—and certainly with the Viennese traditions that had dominated much of film music—by making harmonic profile, which he added to his already developed sense of instrumental color, the most important element of his movie music. To an extent, it can be said that all the Hollywood composers of the first and second generations (Herrmann more or less belonged to the latter) fashioned their scores in a manner that follows quite closely American composer Roger Sessions's description of the Wagnerian *leitmotiv*:

> The "dissonances" in Bach or Mozart have a significance, both "musical" and "emotional" far different from that often lent them by hearers nurtured on nineteenth- and early twentieth-century music, in which dissonances are rather individual features than organic portions of a musical line. Here the influence of the Wagnerian leit-motif—more often than not extremely short and characterized by a single harmonic orrhythmic trait—is paramount. Its introduction is often motivated by dramatic, not musical necessities and once introduced it intentionally dominates the scene, to the obliteration of what surrounds it. The musical coherence is there, to be sure—but in a passive sense; the detail is more significant than the line, and the "theme" more important than its development. It is all too seldom noted to what an overwhelming extent the reverse is the case in the earlier music.[11]

But the direction followed by Herrmann's predecessors and contemporaries was towards the creation of themes which, if longer than the usual leitmotif, would nonetheless *immediately*

[11]Roger Sessions, "The New Musical Horizon," *Modern Music*, 14, no. 2 (January/February 1937), 59–66; rpt. in *Roger Sessions on Music, Collected Essays*, ed. Edward T. Cone (Princeton, New Jersey: Princeton University Press, 1979), p. 47.

arouse the audience; the bulk of the work in their film scores was given to such themes. In the death scene from William Wyler's 1939 *Wuthering Heights,* Alfred Newman's score repeats Cathy's theme, in various garbs, an incredible number of times. In many instances, in fact, it could be said that the purpose of the big Hollywood theme was not so much to involve audiences directly in the specifics of a given film but simply to put their emotions in gear on a more generalized level. Erich Korngold's main theme for the 1942 *King's Row,* for instance, owes its regal nature to nothing more than the film's title, which the composer misunderstood as indicating the kind of pomp and circumstance he had so skillfully handled in earlier endeavors.

From the outset, Bernard Herrmann never had a great deal of use for themes per se. In fact, what in Herrmann often strikes the listener as a particularly attractive melody actually owes most of its character to a striking harmonic progression or coloration, with instrumental hues also playing a considerable role. This can certainly be said of even one of the composer's most lyrical scores (and one of his personal favorites), the music for Joseph Mankiewicz's *The Ghost and Mrs. Muir* (1947). The core of most Herrmann themes generally consists of a motive a measure or two in length. The extension of such a motive into what resembles a theme more often than not is accomplished by the repetition of the motive, either literally or in harmonic sequence. *The Trouble with Harry*'s principal melody is formed almost entirely from the repetition of the half-measure, three-note figure bracketed in Example 3. The reasons for this technique can be seen as follows:

1) As Herrmann has stated, "I think a short phrase has certain advantages. Because I don't like the leitmotif system. The short phrase is easier to follow for audiences, who listen with only half an ear. Don't forget that the best they do is half an ear" ("Interview," p. 66).

2) The "short phrase" also serves as a more manipulable building block better suited than a developed "theme" to the rapidly changing nature of the cinema and its edited flows of images. It has always been obvious that the larger forms of musical composition and the cinema could not work together. No composer has ever sat down, for instance, and written a symphony intended to be used as a film score (certain works, of course, such as Herrmann's "*Hangover Square* Concerto," have been made a part of a film's narrative); and when, conversely, works such as symphonies, concertos, and/or sonatas have been raided for use in a movie, they have inevitably been chopped into small segments. Even such a convention-shatter-

ing director as Jean-Luc Godard discovered that he could not use the theme and eleven variations he had asked Michel Legrand to do for *Vivre sa vie,* itself intended as a theme and eleven variations; instead, Godard resorted to using one part of one variation throughout the film.[12] What is not generally considered, however, is that melody itself, as it is more often than not put together in Western music, implies certain structural formalities that can be adapted to such musical genres as the opera but that have much less in common with what is going on in the cinema. The basic unit of Western melody tends to be the so-called four-bar phrase (*vierhebigkeit*), implying certain principles of symmetry and parallelism so that the typical theme is made up of two four-bar (or -measure) phrases that must be answered by another pair of four-bar phrases, etc. As Herrmann has said, "the reason I don't like this tune business is that a tune has to have eight or sixteen bars, which limits a composer. Once you start, you've got to finish—eight or sixteen bars. Otherwise the audience doesn't know what the hell it's all about" ("Interview," p. 66). A composer such as David Raksin has gotten around the "tune" problem by composing asymmetrical melodies often formed from individual measures of different meters. Turning in the opposite direction, Herrmann all but eliminated melody per se from the film score.

3) Melody is the most rational element of music. Precisely because it organizes a certain number of notes into a reconizable pattern, conventional melody generally has little trouble finding a niche for itself in the conscious mind. This is not to say that melody cannot stir the emotions, or that the return of a particular theme cannot have a deeply moving effect on the listener. But even in these instances, the organization of the themes gives a coherency to the work as a whole; and the very nature of melody very often allows it to have specific associations. While somewhat the same effect can be obtained with the motive and/or the short phrase, as Wagner's operas certainly prove, its use permits a shift in emphasis from the horizontal movement forward of music to a more vertical immediacy that is particularly inherent in its harmonic and instrumental components. It can be seen, then, how much of early American cinema lent itself to melodic logic, but that Hitchcock's movies demanded something quite different.

The anti- "tune" tendency in Herrmann's music goes hand in hand with the composer's isolation of harmonic colors.

---

[12]See my "Music and *Vivre sa vie,*" *Quarterly Review of Film Studies,* 5, no. 3 (Summer 1980), 319–33.

Whereas, in normal musical practice, the identity of a particular chord generally depends on its position within the context of a melodic flow, the lack of such flow in a composer such as Hermann allows the chord or chords—and also the instrumental coloration—to speak more for themselves. The technique is not without its pitfalls, as one can hear in a number such as the Overture to *The Seventh Voyage of Sinbad* which, with its facile, sequential repetitions, often borders on the puerile and amateurish. But it would seem that Hitchcock provided Herrmann with the impetus to develop certain devices and to carry them further than he had previously done. One reason for this might be the *musical* nature of Hitchcock's cinematic style. Certainly, one of the keys to the Hitchcock touch would have to be considered the manner in which the entire body of shots of a given film follows a prearranged plan, so that any one particular shot, much like the "normal" musical chord discussed above, has meaning only when considered in the context of the shots surrounding it and, more broadly, within the temporal elaboration of the entire artistic conception. In this sense, one can set Hitchcock against a much more static, pictorially oriented director such as Jean Cocteau, who used the cinematic frame as a pretext for what often amounts to a succession of dazzling still shots. The Hitchcock technique can also be opposed to that of conventional directors whose use of "invisible editing" tends to create the illusion of a coincidence of cinematic and "normal" time. Like all great artists, Hitchcock managed to come up with forms that neither call excessive attention to themselves nor melt passively into the walls of the everyday. And with the director's particular genius being linked to the *temporal* unfurling of a given formal conception, the overall effect is very much like the one described by Claude Lévi-Strauss for music:

> Below the level of sounds and rhythms, music acts upon a primitive terrain, which is the physiological time of the listener; this time is irreversible and therefore irredeemably diachronic, yet music transmutes the segment devoted to listening to it into a synchronic totality, enclosed within itself. Because of the internal organization of the musical work, the act of listening to it immobilizes passing time; it catches and enfolds it as one catches and enfolds a cloth flapping in the wind.[13]

Although Herrmann, with his non-thematic devices, had already been heading towards a more nearly pure film-music

[13]Claude Lévi-Strauss, *The Raw and the Cooked, Introduction to a Science of Mythology: I*, trans. John and Doreen Weightman (New York: Harper Colophon Books, 1975), p. 16.

genre that would not cut across the grain of inherently cinematic procedures, the composer obviously sensed that he would
have to further stifle Western music's natural tendency to organize itself into temporally elaborated blocks, in order not to
gild the lily of Hitchcock's ingeniously organized, filmic total-
ities or to cut into their effectiveness by setting up conflicting
movements. Thus, for example, Herrmann began to rely even
less on the types of dramatic shifts from major to minor mode
that one can find in numerous romantic composers such as
Tchaikovsky; instead, he devised a chordal language that *simultaneously* has major and minor implications. With this, and
with the long stretches where no harmonic resolution takes
place, so that the harmonic colors stand even more strongly on
their own and so that the listener-viewer remains suspended,
Herrmann created a *vertical* synchronicity that sets up a strong
opposition to Hitchcock's *horizontally* created synchronicity.
And, of course, the immediacy of effect in Herrmann's music
fortifies and stresses the deepest emotional content of individual Hitchcock shots or sequences.

II

In his next two films for Hitchcock, the 1956 remake of *The
Man Who Knew Too Much* and *The Wrong Man* (1957), Herrmann did not exactly have the leeway he was later to acquire.
Perhaps the main reason for this is that both films have their
points of departure in music. In the true story of *The Wrong
Man*, the protagonist is a string-bass player in a band at New
York's Stork Club. The film opens with Hitchcock himself
speaking a few words, behind which Herrmann's music introduces a somber, two-note motive that will later be heard after
the plane crash in *North by Northwest*. There follows a night-
club scene in which a rather innocuous Latin ditty alternates
with a more characteristically Herrmannesque motive. Prominent in some of the soundtrack music further on is a string
bass played pizzicato, giving a mildly jazzy flavor to the music
and also reminding us of the protagonist's job. Both versions
of *The Man Who Knew Too Much* center around a composition
for soprano, mixed chorus, and orchestra, Australian-born
composer Arthur Benjamin's "Storm Cloud Cantata." For the
1956 remake, however, Herrmann not only re-orchestrated the
music, he is actually seen conducting the score in the twelve-
minute Albert Hall sequence, one of the true *tours de force* in
Hitchcock's cinema. Interestingly, since the non-stop music of
the cantata drowns out all dialogue once it starts, Hitchcock's
style changes noticeably, and in many ways the film at this

point takes on the appearance of a silent movie. The Benjamin[14] cantata, plus the song "Que sera sera" (by Jay Livingston and Ray Evans) performed twice by Doris Day in the film, left little room for *The Man Who Knew Too Much* to acquire a distinctively Herrmannesque musical profile.

Nonetheless, the second *Man Who Knew Too Much*, even more strongly than *The Trouble with Harry*, reveals in many of the diverse soundtrack music cues a solid Herrmann/Hitchcock "sound" beginning to take shape. In what is perhaps *The Man Who Knew Too Much's* key suspense scene, other than the Albert Hall sequence, Doris Day and James Stewart discover Ambrose Chapel, while Hitchcock's cross-cutting reveals to the audience that this is the spot where the couple's kidnapped son is being held. The descending, four-note motive of Example 6A, which is in D minor, is reused note-for-note in the nightmare sequence from *Vertigo* and during the final sequence in *North by Northwest:*

EXAMPLE 6A

pizz. violins (later bowed violas)

clarinet & bass clarinet (an octave lower)

The measures that follow, in which the high violins play parallel, major thirds over the same repeated D, strikingly foreshadow the habanera motive from *Vertigo:*

EXAMPLE 6B

The two above figures, which alternate regularly, with minor variations, throughout the beginning of the Ambrose Chapel sequence, form a musical cue that lasts close to a minute and forty seconds, arranged as follows:

[14]Whether by accident or design, the first name of the character played by James Stewart in this film that climaxes in the "Storm Cloud Cantata" is Benjamin.

```
                                              resolution
A    B    A         B       A    A    B    A ——→   on
    (violas)      (var.)   (violas)      (violas)   D
```

The "A" part of the cue offers an excellent example of a Herr-mann "short phrase," while "B" segment is essentially pure, harmonic color. In addition, the repeated D, while helping to establish the key of D minor, enhances the suspense quality of motive 6A above, since the expected D below the E (the last note of the motive) does not arrive until the end of the cue. The repeated D also refuses to allow the cue to modulate, thus creating a feeling of stasis that aids in the isolation of the parallel thirds in Example 6B. Given the two contrasting sections of the cue, one might expect that their alternation would follow the editing, which mixes shots of Doris Day waiting outside the chapel with shots inside revealing the place where the kidnapped boy is being kept. Yet, precisely because the more static nature of the music keeps its movement forward from interfering with that of the editing, the music is allowed to express in its own rhythms the opposition communicated at a different pace by the cross-cutting. Furthermore, with the repeated D linking the entire musical cue, Herrmann is able to stress that what appears to be an opposition is also the inside and outside of the same situation.

III

By the time he finished *The Wrong Man*, Bernard Herrmann had already done for Hitchcock what he had not previously been able to do and was to do only once again: he had scored more than two films for the same director.[15] As for Hitchcock, the director found himself in the happy position of having assembled

> his own little group, which included his cinematographer Robert Burks, his camera operator Leonard J. South, his television cameraman John L. Russel [who was also the cinematographer for [*Psycho*], his editor George Tomasini, his composer Bernard Herrmann, his personal assistant Peggy Robertson, his costume

[15]In 1962, Herrmann did the music for a third Henry King film, *Tender Is the Night*, eight years after his last King collaboration. François Truffaut later used the composer for two successive films, *Fahrenheit 451* and *The Bride Wore Black*. It is quite probable that Herrmann would have become the official suspense-film composer for Brian De Palma who, after *Sister* and *Obsession* (both Hitchcock tributes), would have involved the composer in *Carrie*; Herrmann's death in December 1975 cut short the fruition of that potential tandem.

designer Edith Head, and a number of actors with whom he
felt thoroughly at home. (Taylor, p. 266).

The presence of Saul Bass, who did the titles for *Vertigo, North
by Northwest,* and *Psycho,* did not hurt matters either. One has
to think that the establishment of a solid rapport with many
of the most important artists and artisans who can contribute
to the realization of a film helped bring Hitchcock to the peak
he reached in his next three films, *Vertigo* (1958), *North by
Northwest* (1959), and *Psycho* (1960). One also has to feel that
the opportunity to become immersed over a period of time in
the style and manner of a great artist such as Hitchcock helped
Herrmann produce not only what most would consider to be
his masterpieces as a film composer but also to pen music that
gives the impression of being a totally inseparable part not
only of the films for which it was composed but also an extension of Hitchcock's personal vision.

Not surprisingly, the music for *North by Northwest,* a comic-
thriss respite between the tragedy of *Vertigo* and the horror of
Psycho, does not immediately strike the listener as offering a
typical Herrmann/Hitchcock sound. Indeed, Herrmann designated as "Overture" the fandango (a quick, Spanish dance)
that opens *North by Northwest,* while the initial music for *Vertigo* and *Psycho* is entitled "Prelude." To the listener, *North by
Northwest*'s Overture appears to be a kind of set piece easily
separable from the body of the film, while *Vertigo* and *Psycho*'s
Preludes seem inextricably attached to the cine-musical action
that follows the title sequences. And yet the delicate balances
between film music and film obviously perceived by both
Hitchcock and Herrmann dictated an interesting reversal. Both
the *Vertigo* and *Psycho* Preludes, which segue into new musical cues heard behind the post-title sequences, reach a brief
point of resolution on D. Herrmann did write a snappy, two-
chord conclusion to bring the *North by Northwest* Overture to
a decisive conclusion in A major (the Overture opens in A minor). But it was obviously felt that the Overture as originally
scored separated the title sequence too much from the film, all
the more so since there is no musical segue from the title to
the ensuing New York City shots. Therefore, the Overture's
final two chords, although performed on both the phonograph
recordings made of the work, were cut from the film, so that
the music—and therefore the film—remains suspended on a
sustained seventh chord that never resolves, a device used fairly
frequently in the early days of film scoring.

One might also expect that the lighter nature of *North by
Northwest* would allow for more expansive themes in its Over-

ture, while the gloomier character of *Vertigo* and *Psycho* would justify a non-thematic stasis in their music. Yet the *North by Northwest* Overture contains not one example of anything that could be designated as a theme on the cue sheet.[16] Instead, it is made up of numerous, brief motives sewn together in sometimes audaciously chromatic harmonic progressions and presented in brilliant orchestral colors, with totally unhummable interval leaps being the order of the day. In fact, the rhythmic character of many of these figures has more importance than their fragmented melodic contours, so that their reprise in the Mount Rushmore finale is on occasion played only in the percussion. The use of these figures throughout *North by Northwest* often creates a balletic relationship between film and music considerably different from the more operatic relationship one finds in film scores from Hollywood's earlier generation.

Unlike *North by Northwest, Vertigo* and *Psycho* immediately establish the type of harmonic color, already discussed, through the pervasive use of the "Hitchcock chord." In *Vertigo*, this chord, formed by adding a major third above a root position, E-flat minor triad, is first heard as a repeated series of contrary-motion arpeggios played in the high strings, winds, and vibraphone; the figure is heard throughout much of the Prelude:

EXAMPLE 7

The identity of this chord is reinforced, twelve measures into the Prelude, by an unbroken, sustained presentation of it in mid-range brass:

---

[16]For purposes of royalties and copyright, the American Society of Composers, Authors, and Publishers (A.S.C.A.P.) keeps on file a complete breakdown, with precise timings, of every single musical cue heard in any manner in the final cut of a given film. Even Cary Grant's mumbled few seconds from the Lerner/Loewe "I've Grown Accustomed to Her Face" are listed on the *North by Northwest* cue sheet.

EXAMPLE 8

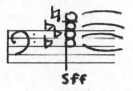

The strings-only *Psycho* music presents an identically struc-tured chord—this one built up by adding a major third above the root position B-flat minor triad—in the upper register, while the lower register configuration stresses more the augmented nature of the chord in a manner not unlike what we have al-ready seen in *The Trouble with Harry*. This chord, repeated five times in a characteristic rhythmic pattern, becomes a motive of sorts for the first third of the film (as do several other of the obsessively repeated figures from the Prelude):

EXAMPLE 9

Near the end of *Psycho*, just before Lila Crane (Vera Miles) touches Mrs. Bates's mummified body, the high violins sus-tain a chord on C-sharp-A-F that suggests the Hitchcock chord with the root missing and is identical in structure with the *Trouble with Harry* chord discussed earlier. The very nature of these chords, with their simultaneously minor/major aura, im-mediately throws the viewer/listener off the rationalized center of normal Western tonality into a more irrational, mythic do-main in which oppositions have no implications that will be resolved by the passing of time but exist only as two equal poles of the same unity. Both *Vertigo*'s and *Psycho*'s Preludes maintain this framework by having their respective "Hitch-cock chords" act as a focal point, continually repeated throughout the 1' 11" length of the former and 1' 50" length of the latter. The Preludes for both films conclude on a D unison. The dreamier *Vertigo* Prelude, marked "*Moderato assai*," ac-companies a dazzling succession of slowly turning, colored, geometrical whorls that appear against a black background and that have their point of departure in a woman's eye. In the music, the D on which the Prelude will conclude is almost constantly present, both as the top note of the "Hitchcock chord" and from time to time in the bass. In measures 3–5, for instance, unisions beneath the arpeggiated figure of Example 8 move from D to C, suggesting the harmonic relationship between the Prelude (in D Minor) and the ensuing "Rooftop" sequence (in C minor) and then, in measures 6–9, from a lower E/flat back to D. While *Vertigo*'s Prelude, then, suggests tonality, it generally lacks the sense of harmonic movement characteristic of Western music and instead creates a sense of stasis that seconds the feminine orientation of the title sequence and its imagery, not to mention the whole Orphic bent of *Vertigo*'s narrative and structure. Indeed, Herrmann will later use a similar technique, already noted for a segment from *The Man Who Knew Too Much*, to suggest not only the painting of Carlotta Valdez but also the apparent reincarnation of the Spanish woman in Madeleine: Carlotta's "theme" plays, initially in parallel, major thirds, over a repeated D, the characteristic habanera rhythm of which — ♩. ♪ ♪ ♪ — provides the audience with a musical point of reference for Carlotta's Hispanic origins. The repeated D in a habanera rhythm will likewise dominate the "Nightmare" sequence.

In *Psycho*'s Prelude, the Hitchcock chord is repeated so often and at such musically strong points that it seems to be not only a point of departure but a point of return as well. The Prelude also goes beyond any other Hitchcock music, Herrmann scored or otherwise, in its array of jarringly dissonant chords, the bitonality of which reflects on the film's ultimate narrative theme. But the lack of harmonic movement is counterbalanced by a frenetic rhythmic drive—the Prelude is marked "*Allegro (Molto agitato)*" —that goes beyond even *North by Northwest*'s opening fandango in intensity.[17] In fact, the *Psycho* Prelude moves along at such a headstrong pace that it can move in and out of almost conventional resolutions without the audience ever getting a chance to relax on them. Thus, the Prelude's first motive, which starts off as a simple breaking up of the Hitchcock chord, strongly suggests the key of D minor by transforming the D-flat of the Hitchcock chord into a leading-tone C-sharp:

---

[17]The tempo used in the film—quarter note = 160—is considerably faster than what one hears on the recording—quarter note = 132—although the composer conducts in all cases.

EXAMPLE 10

This potential of *Psycho*'s particular Hitchcock chord to be utilized as a rather kinky cadence chord is borne out by the end
of the Prelude, in which a differently voiced version of the
opening chord, repeated a number of times in groups of four
in the high violins, finally gives way to a single, pizzicato,
unison D, thus creating something not unlike a V → I cadence
with the fifth (A) as the top note and the D-flat/C-sharp leading tone prominent in the chordal construction. All of this
seems to second the much more linear movement of the black
and white, horizontal lines of Saul Bass's title sequence, not to
mention the more phallic orientation of *Psycho*'s particular
brand of violence.

But, although the Prelude, like any good prelude, in many
ways sums up the entire work to follow it, it at least comes to
a point of rest, which is more than can be said of *Psycho*'s
conclusion, as we shall see in a moment. Hitchcock immediately picks up on this by giving the audience, in the film's first
shot, an excessively precise orientation in time and space,
something he almost never does (*Notorious* is the only other
example that comes to mind): over an aerial shot of Phoenix,
Arizona, superimposed titles give us the name of that city,
along with the date (Friday, December the eleventh) and even
the time (2:43 p.m.). To accompany this, and the descent implied by the aerial shot, Herrmann segues from the Prelude to
a descending series of ninth chords, the openness of which
strongly contrasts with the Prelude's more claustrophobic
chordal language. Furthermore, the key that can be felt in the
chords of this "City" cue and that is suggested in their spelling in the score, which has no key signature, is that of A-flat
minor, a key which, in its number of flats (seven) and in the
tritone relationship of its tonic note to D, is about as far from
D minor as it is possible to get. Thus Herrmann, in his post-
title music, and Hitchcock, in his presentation of what seems

to be a very ordinary lovers' tryst, set up a marked polarity between the night world of the title sequence and the day world of "The City." The attempts to keep these two worlds separate will, of course, come to an end when Marion Crane (Janet Leigh) and Norman Bates (Anthony Perkins) come together in a seemingly accidental way that is actually set up to be felt as strongly fatalistic. Once this meeting occurs, the two worlds become inseparable, as Hitchcock suggests by the film's pen-ultimate shot, in which a few frames showing the face of Norman's mummified mother lead into the film's final shot of Marion's car being dragged up from the quicksand. Herr-mann, in turn, resorts to bitonality for the film's final chord: over a D unison in the bass (the last note of a motive that will be discussed further on) we hear a chord that brings together the A-flat minor of "The City" with the D of the Prelude:

EXAMPLE 11

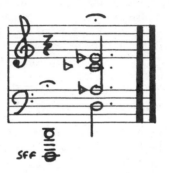

From this there is no escape!

Unlike the *North by Northwest* Overture, both the *Vertigo* and *Psycho* Preludes also contain passages that have themes of sorts. Indeed, in *Vertigo*'s Prelude, following a series of rising trills in the woodwinds and strings, the arpeggiated figure, while continuing, suddenly abandons the Hitchcock-chord config-uration and switches, in a manner recalling the transition from *Psycho*'s Prelude to the "City" cue, to a series of more open, broken ninth chords, the top notes of which—D-C-B-E—form the backbone of *Vertigo*'s principal "love music," which is, in fact, how this twice-heard segment is labeled on the cue sheet (these same four notes are also played, not always in sync with the above, in the orchestra beneath the arpeggiated figure). Furthermore, the harmonization of these notes in the broken chords of the arpeggiated figure is identical to the harmoniza-tion, in unbroken chords, of the principal love theme. Thus is

Herrmann able, with the two contrasting portions of *Vertigo*'s Prelude, to suggest the two sides of the hero's "vertigo."

Herrmann likewise breaks up the *Psycho* Prelude's obsessively repeated chords and motives with a theme repeated at three different points and labeled "*Psycho* Theme" on the cue sheet. *As a theme* (as opposed to separate motives expanded in harmonic sequences), it is paradoxically more developed and self-contained than anything to be found in *Vertigo* or *North by Northwest*. Working chromatically around the key of D minor, the twelve-bar theme starts off in E-flat minor, modulates to E minor, and finally ends up on an F beneath which a form of the Hitchcock chord can be heard alternating with another chord, thus acting, as I have already suggested, as a point of return as well as a point of departure. Unlike *Vertigo*'s love theme, which appears throughout the film and is linked to a very specific element of the narrative, the "*Psycho* Theme" remains an inseparable part of the Prelude music and is heard only within that context when it appears twice more during the first third of the film. In contrast, the Hitchcock chord and arpeggiated figure from *Vertigo*'s Prelude return only for a brief eleven seconds during the "Beauty Parlor" sequence towards the end of the film, where a close-up of Kim Novak's face suggests the opening shot of *Vertigo*'s abstract title sequence. As far as *Psycho*'s Prelude is concerned, one has the impression that the limiting of its reappearances, in various forms and with or without the "theme," to the first third of the picture — the last time it shows up is as a brief snippet starting with the figure in Example 10 as the detective Arbogast (Martin Balsam) begins his search — corresponds with the "red herring" nature of the film's initial action. For while the *Psycho* Prelude has a much more ominous cast to it than *North by Northwest*'s, like the latter its fast moving, frenetic pace also suggests the flight and pursuit that are what the opening of *Psycho* seems to be about. Once the shower scene abruptly changes that impression, the remaining music takes on a much more static quality and the Prelude is forgotten — save in the brief Arbogast cue — except in the subtlest of ways, including the occasional appearance of forms of the Hitchcock chord.

IV

The following additional observations, presented in no particular order, are to my mind among the more important of the many that can be made concerning the music in *Vertigo*, *North by Northwest*, and *Psycho*:

1) It has been remarked often enough that Herrmann's music for *Psycho* offers a rare example of a film score composed for strings alone.[18] As composer/musicologist Fred Steiner has noted, "such a device imposes strict limits on the available range of tone colors."[19] A quotation Steiner gives from a Herrmann interview shows that the composer obviously intended the restriction of tonal color as a musical equivalent of Hitchcock's exclusion of spectrum colors in favor of blacks, whites, and all the various greys in between: "I felt that I was able to complement the black and white photography of the film with a black and white sound."[20] If, as Steiner points out, the use of black-and-white photography and of strings-only music can actually be considered as enhancing the expressive potential rather than limiting it, the music and photography also have the effect of giving the audience even fewer than the usual number of links with "normal" reality onto which to grasp, since *Psycho* offers neither the usual array of colors associated with everyday objects (and it must be remembered that, by this point in film history, more and more Hollywood films were being shot in color—*Psycho* was Hitchcock's last black-and-white film, and only the second one since *I Confess* in 1952) nor the usual diversity of instruments of the symphony orchestra in general and the film-score orchestra in particular.

2) Another way in which *Psycho* cuts its audience off from normal reality is by its total avoidance of "source" music. The absence of any music coming over a radio, phonograph, or what have you, has the function of heightening the effect of the film-music convention whereby the appearance of soundtrack (as opposed to source) music generally "means" that something out of the ordinary is happening or is about to happen. Since *Psycho* has no source music, the appearance of *any* music tends to heighten expectations. This sets *Psycho* apart from the much more open *North by Northwest*, which not only makes spectacular use of large orchestral forces, it also contains a substantial amount of source music. Indeed, *North by Northwest*'s first, post-title musical cue is cocktail-lounge mu-

[18]Another interesting experiment in the limiting of instrumental color can be noted in the David Snell music for Robert Montgomery's 1942 mystery thriller, *Lady in the Lake*. Using a Christmas carol as a point of departure, Snell scored *Lady in the Lake* for a vocalizing, a cappella chorus, while Montgomery tried the unusual experiment of deploying an entirely subjective camera throughout the film.

[19]Fred Steiner, "Herrmann's 'Black and White' Music for Hitchcock's *Psycho*," *Filmmusic Notebook*, 1, no. 1 (Fall 1974), 28–36 (Part I), and 1, no. 2 (Winter 1974–75), 26–46 (Part II). The quotation is from Part I, p. 31.

[20]*Ibid.*, Part I, p. 32. The interview quoted is Leslie Zador, "Movie Music's Man of the Moment," *Coast FM and Fine Arts*, June 1971, p. 31.

sic played on violin and piano in the Plaza Hotel. As it happens, this particular song, the McHugh/Adamson "It's a Most Unusual Day," serves as an ironically light-hearted presage of things to come. More noteworthy, however, is the ambiguous way in which apparent source music slips into apparent soundtrack music at the very moment the love affair between Thornhill (Gary Grant) and Eve (Eva Marie Saint) begins to get steamy. As soon as Thornhill enters the dining car on the 20th Century Limited, we hear an innocuous piece of background music by Andre Previn entitled "Fashion Show," which MGM dug out of its own vaults from the 1957, Previn-scored *Designing Woman*, since it is the type of music Herrmann steadfastly refused to write. The audience's impression is undoubtedly that this is background music being piped into the dining car to create a relaxing ambience, and it is, in fact, allowed to run for three and a half minutes to its end as Eve and Thornhill talk. Coincidentally, however, the Previn music concludes shortly after Eve "unmasks" Thornhill and begins to openly suggest that they spend the night together. A five-second break occurs during the following dialogue:

> Eve: And I don't particularly like the book I've started.
> Thornhill: Ah.
> Eve: You know what I mean?

Then, as Thornhill begins his next line ("Oh, let me think."), we hear for the first time the love theme, composed by Herrmann. (Typical of the film/music industry is the fact that the love theme is indicated on the cue sheet as "Song from North by Northwest" and is even assigned a different publisher from the rest of the score.) In fact, both the Previn and the Herrmann cues are soundtrack music that *can* be considered as source music, given the manner in which they are presented. But both the musical quality of the Previn cue and its use in the sequence to back up preliminary small talk cause us to perceive it as source music linked with the prosaic realities of train travel. The more lyrical nature and the chromatic modulations of Herrmann's love theme, and the association of it in the sequence with the warming up of Eve and Thornhill's liaison, cause us to associate it with the calmer irrationalities of sexual love and therefore to *feel* the cue as soundtrack music that will undoubtedly reappear in subsequent love scenes, which in fact it will.

But it is *Vertigo* that has the farthest-reaching implications in the relationship established between source and soundtrack music. Unlike *North by Northwest* and *Psycho*, *Vertigo* opens with *three* segued musical cues: the Prelude, the Rooftop, and a work of "classical" music that Midge (Barbara Bel Geddes) has playing on her phonograph as she and Scottie (James Stewart) discuss the consequences of the rooftop incident. As can be seen, the final of these three cues is an obvious example of source music,[21] identified in at least one article as the Mozart symphony heard further on in the film, and indicated in the script as Vivaldi. In fact, the source music is the second movement of an obscure Sinfonia in E-flat, Op. 9, no. 2, composed around 1775 by Johann Christian Bach, the youngest of Johann Sebastian's many sons. Although the change in setting from the rooftop sequence to Midge's apartment carries the audience out of nightmarish irrationality—and a totally athematic musical accompaniment—into a world of order that includes the classical strains from J. C. Bach's Sinfonia, the C-minor key of that work's second movement provides at least one link with the preceding sequence. More important, however, is Scottie's rejection of that music: shortly after peevishly telling his ex-fiancée, "Midge, don't be so motherly. I'm not going to crack up," Scottie asks her to turn off the phonograph, which she does.

The gesture seems innocuous enough; yet it is symptomatic of Scottie's refusal to accept the normal world, or even one of the better examples of music it has to offer. Even this early in the film, Hitchcock and Herrmann are able to take advantage of the soundtrack-music-versus-source-music opposition as one of the delineating factors in the on-going give-and-take between the irrational and the rational. This delineation is stressed in an even more pointed—and poignant—fashion in the two sequences that open the second half of *Vertigo* (following the apparent death of Madeleine and the inquest scene). The first of these two sequences begins with a shot of Scottie at Madeleine's grave; this is followed by a dramatic, overhead shot of Scottie lying in bed. Playing behind these two shots, a soft version of the love theme communicates Scottie's obsession for the dead Madeleine. It is indicative of the *musical* nature of Hitchcock's cinematic style that the nightmare sequence that follows is foreshadowed more strongly by the camerawork than by the music per se: the overhead shot of Scottie lying in bed suggests the nightmare to follow by creating a quasi-musical sense of anticipation, not only because of

[21]The paradox here is that the J. C. Bach work was actually performed by the studio orchestra, conducted by Muir Mathieson, who takes it at a rather fast pace, and "laid in" on the soundtrack. It becomes source music only by association (with the phonograph) and not in fact.

the bizarre point of view it gives us of an ordinary scene but also because the looking-down-from-above perspective has already become an integral part, and therefore a visual theme of sorts, of the two previous sequences leading to death (the police officer's and Madeleine's). The ensuing nightmare sequence, which is accompanied on the soundtrack by Herrmann's grotesque reworking of the habanera (Carlotta) theme, thus acts as a darker parallel of the film's initial (rooftop) "nightmare."

Similarly, the post-nightmare sequence, which takes place in a sanatorium room with Midge trying to bring Scottie back from the depths of complete depression, gives a more somber parallel of the initial Scottie-Midge sequence discussed above. Here, however, there is a short break between the nightmare and the classical music, which has changed from J. C. Bach to the second movement (which is in the key of F major) from Mozart's Symphony No. 34 in C (1780). This piece is *deliberately* played on a phonograph, as of the first shot within the sanatorium room, by Midge in an effort to use it as therapy to bring Scottie back to rationality.[22] Unlike the first Scottie-Midge sequence, where the classical music remained a casual part of the overall ambience of everyday order (which Scottie nonetheless rejects), here it plays an active role, in a setting that suggests irrationality, in the attempts of the film's most normal character (Midge) to restore rationality. Scottie's rejection of her—he remains totally impassive and immobile throughout the sanatorium sequence—indicates an even deeper alienation because of the marked jump forward in musical quality from the J. C. Bach *Sinfonia* to the Mozart Symphony. Interestingly, the soundtrack music picks up again in the low strings with the final, long shot of Midge (the only point in *Vertigo* where the *soundtrack* score *begins* with her in frame, and only the second time in the film where it is heard with her at all) at the end of the sanatorium corridor, signaling the departure of this bastion of the everyday from the film, and then continues, after a brief interlude in strings and harp, with a wistful version of the love theme as Scottie seeks "Madeleine" in San Francisco. The whole way in which "present" source music is contrasted with off-screen soundtrack music in *Vertigo* seems almost to be a comment on the function of film music in general: this

---

[22]Like the J. C. Bach work in the initial Scottie-Midge sequence, the Mozart here is performed at rather too fast a tempo, leading one to wonder whether or not there was a deliberate intention on someone's part—Hitchcock's, Herrmann's, or perhaps even conductor Muir Mathieson's—to throw the audience slightly off center in this manner.

"invisible" music that film audiences have always accepted as an integral part of the movies is almost always associated with the invisible, the bigger-than-life side of what transpires within the filmic narrative. And when we have a character such as *Vertigo*'s Scottie Ferguson who is tragically attracted to what *is not*, then even Mozart and Johann Christian Bach are powerless to pull him out of the world, whether love or nightmare, that is reserved for the soundtrack score.

3) The love music in *Vertigo* certainly stands as one of the outstanding components of this remarkable score, which I would consider as the greatest film score ever composed. Donald Spoto even makes a comparison between Herrmann's love music and the *"Liebestod"* from Wagner's *Tristan und Isolde*.[23] Herrmann's outrageous statement that he would have cast Charles Boyer in the lead role and set the film in sultry New Orleans (see "Interview") shows the importance he attributed to *Vertigo*'s love element. Yet, with his feeling for nuance that particularly characterizes his Hitchcock collaborations, Herrmann does not immediately pull out all the stops. The first time Scottie sees "Madeleine" in the film, the score introduces a secondary theme (Madeleine's theme) which, while suggesting the love theme, remains much more restrained in its mid-range instrumentation and more closely knit melodic line. A similar use of a subordinate musical theme can be noted in *Spellbound:* the first time Gregory Peck sees Ingrid Bergman, it is not Miklós Rózsa's famous love theme from that picture that we hear on the soundtrack, but rather a much tamer, but nonetheless lyrical, theme. In *Vertigo,* it is Madeleine's theme that is heard, along with the habanera, throughout Scottie's first encounters with her, including her jump into San Francisco Bay. It is only as the couple is driving to the Sequoia forest that the love theme appears for the first time. Once the latter fully blooms later on, however, Madeleine's theme is ingeniously incorporated into it as a second phase of the melody.

One of the most striking uses of Madeleine's theme, however, does not occur in *Vertigo* but in *North by Northwest*. Following the famous cornfield sequence (for which there is no music, save at the very end), Thornhill traces Eve to her hotel room. As she opens the door and sees Thornhill, the soundtrack music starts with *North by Northwest*'s love theme. The motivic nature of this theme, however, allows Madeleine's theme, in the same, mid-range and low-string instrumentation and same key as when it is first heard in *Vertigo,* to suddenly take over. If this seems like little more than a simple tie-over from one film to the next, it should be remembered that *Vertigo* contains a very similar scene. When, after the sanitorium sequence, Scottie sees Judy Barton (also Kim Novak, who has played the role of Madeleine in the film's first half), he follows her back to her hotel room. Although the latter sequence has no music, Judy and Eve find themselves in the identical situation of having to conceal their surprise upon seeing, at their hotel-room door, the man they had helped set up. Herrmann's revival of the Madeleine theme in *North by Northwest* both stresses the parallel between the two scenes and the similarity between the two heroines. *North by Northwest*'s love theme, on the other hand, never takes on the intensity of *Vertigo*'s, since the Eve/Thornhill love never acquires the quality of the fatalistic obsession of the Scottie/Madeleine love.

4) There is, in *Psycho*, one particularly striking example where music and cinematic movement complement each other in a manner that in certain ways sums up the entire Herrmann/Hitchcock music/movie relationship. In the sequence where Lila climbs the hill towards the imposingly gothic house where she hopes to find Mrs. Bates, Hitchcock, using cross-cutting, alternates objective shots of Lila with subjective shots (her point of view) of the house. At the same time, the camera continues to track in towards the house, which becomes larger and larger in the frame (ultimately being replaced by the front door) and back from Lila in the objective shots (which might be said to represent the house's point of view!), thus bringing closer and closer together the house and the person the audience is certain will be the next victim there. On the music track, Herrmann starts with a sustained F in the violins over another sustained F four octaves lower in the cellos and basses. Just above the bass note, the cellos (later the violas) play a four-note motive that rises a semitone at the end. Herrmann then proceeds to slowly bring down the violin line in half steps while, in contrary motion, the bass line and the four-note motive rise in half-steps:

EXAMPLE 12

etc.

This sequence repeats a total of twenty-four times during the fifty-two-second "Hill" cue until the violins and the first notes of the motive both reach a common F-sharp as Lila and the house also come together. The music then "resolves" on—what else—a D–A-sharp–F-sharp chord—the Hitchcock chord minus the root. Once again, what Hitchcock accomplishes in the horizontal movement of the editing Herrmann suggests more vertically thanks to the simultaneity afforded by the textures of Example 12.

5) Finally, the three notes mentioned above as closing *Psycho* form an extremely important motive, which Herrmann has called the *real Psycho* theme, that not only plays an extremely important role in *Psycho* but that also has a strong importance in Herrmann's overall musical vision. First heard during the cue labeled "The Madhouse," during which Marion suggests to Norman that he should perhaps put his mother in a home, this slow-tempo motive is formed of a rising minor seventh and a falling minor ninth, the latter an especially dissonant interval to the Western ear (a rising, minor ninth that opens the last movement of Bruckner's 9th Symphony casts its somber shadow over the entire movement to follow):

EXAMPLE 13

It has been noted by Graham Bruce[24] that these three notes represent a distortion of a much calmer motive associated with Marion Crane. Repeated a number of times in a descending, chromatic sequence during the initial hotel-room sequence, this motive likewise contains three notes in a rising-falling pattern; in this case, however, the interval is a very consonant fifth in both directions, thus forming a calm and static figure that begins and ends on the same note. As Bruce indicates, the opposition of these two three-note motives seems to support the line, "We all go a little mad sometimes" and to delineate Norman's madness and Marion's sanity as two sides of the same

---

[24]Graham Bruce, who teaches at the College of Advanced Education in Queensland, Australia, is preparing a doctoral dissertation for New York University on the film music of Bernard Herrmann. The idea mentioned here is contained in a rough draft of his chapter on *Psycho*.

coin, a characteristic Hitchcock theme. It is also interesting to note, however, that the "madness" motive has its roots far back in Herrmann's musical career. Not only does the fourth-movement "Interlude" from Herrmann's 1936 *Sinfonietta* for strings begin with that motive, the entire movement was lifted by Herrmann, with only a few rhythmic and dynamic changes, and used as the "Swamp" cue in *Psycho*. Modified versions of the motive also turn up to close Herrmann's cantata "Moby Dick" (1936–38) and to introduce a description of the wild Heathcliff in the composer's 1950 opera, *Wuthering Heights*. After the fact, Herrmann, at the end of his career, brought back the motive one final time to suggest how he saw the psychotic "hero" of Martin Scorsese's 1975 *Taxi Driver*, which was released after the composer's death and is dedicated to his memory.

V

It is obvious that one thing that inspired Bernard Herrmann to produce his Hitchcock masterpieces was the director's obvious sensitivity to music in general and to the film-score/film relationship in particular, a fact that Herrmann himself has admitted. Even Hitchcock films that do not contain notable scores reveal such nice touches as the song-writer's tune that is not completed until the resolution of *Rear Window*'s mysteries. In the same way that the Hitchcock style carries his suspense thrillers well beyond the usual limitations of the genre, his use of music carried the film score past many of the established Hollywood conventions towards becoming, in many different respects, an integral part of his films. The rapport that the director came to establish with Bernard Herrmann showed that Hitchcock was not seeking the type of one-for-one relationship between music and filmic action that one finds in many movies. Instead of the more operatic relationships one finds within older cinema, in which film and music tend to move much more in sync with each other, Hitchcock sought a music that expressed in its own aesthetic terms what the filmic style was expressing in its particular manner. The general lack of direct interference between film and music in the Herrmann/Hitchcock collaborations allows the full communication of the deepest strata each art has to offer.

Ultimately, what makes the greatness of the Herrmann/Hitchcock scores is that the musical solutions Herrmann came up with for Hitchcock's particular brand of cinema seen in many ways to be the only ones possible. For a director primarily concerned with showing the eruptions of the irrational,

potential and otherwise, within the context of a solidly established ethos, perhaps the only thing to do was to take the tria-
dally oriented harmonic system familiar to listeners within that
ethos and, while using it as an ever-present base, turn it against
itself. In one of his supreme moments as a film composer,
Herrmann musically brought to the surface, in his famous music to accompany the *Psycho* shower scene, the subliminal pulse
of violence which, in 1960, still lay beneath the surface of
American society. With his violins first building up a jarring
chord in descending, major sevenths and then returning in
screeching, upward glissandi, Herrmann reminds us of Thomas
Mann's fictional Adrian Leverkühn using vocal glissandi in his
Apocalypse. Describing the latter work, the narrator of *Dr.
Faustus* reminds us that "ordering and normalizing the notes
was the condition and first self-manifestation of what we understand by music. Stuck there, so to speak, a naturalistic
atavism, a barbaric rudiment from pre-musical days, is the
gliding voice, the glissando . . . ; certainly, these images of
terror offer a most tempting and at the same time most legitimate occasion for the employing of that savage device."[25]

So perfect does Herrmann's solution seem that it has been
widely imitated in post-*Psycho* films that express the actual
upheaval of which Hitchcock's film was the presage. As Brian
De Palma, who brings in snippets of the *Psycho* score in his
1976 film *Carrie*, has put it, "we used a lot of the *Psycho* violins
when we were screening the film before it had a score. We
found it very effective, and we couldn't find anything better.
Consequently, when we recorded the score, we recorded
something very similar to that violin sound. It's a great sound,
probably one of the best in cinema. So, thank you, Benny
Herrmann."[26]

A DISCOGRAPHY OF
HERRMANN/HITCHCOCK SCORES

All scores are conducted by Herrmann unless otherwise
noted:
1. *Vertigo*. Muir Mathieson, cond. Mercury MG 20384 (out
of print). Reissued on Mercury Golden Imports SRI 75117.
2. "Music from the Great Movie Thrillers" (excerpts from *The*

[25]Thomas Mann, *Doctor Faustus, The Life of the German Composer Adrian Leverkühn as Told by a Friend*, trans. H. T. Lowe-Porter (New York: Vintage, 1971),
p. 374.
[26]Royal S. Brown, "Considering De Palma," *American Film*, 2, no. 9
(July/August 1977), 58.

Trouble with Harry, Vertigo, North by Northwest, Psycho, and *Marnie*). With the London Philharmonic Orchestra. London Phase 4 SP 44126.

   3. *Marnie*. Sound/Stage Recordings (pirate label) 2306.

   4. *Psycho*. With the National Philharmonic Orchestra. Unicorn RHS 336; reissued on Unicorn 75001 (out of print).

   5. *Torn Curtain*. Royal Philharmonic Orchestra, Elmer Bernstein, cond. Filmmusic Collection FMC-10; also issued on Warner Brothers BSK 3185 (out of print).

   6. *North by Northwest*. London Studio Symphony Orchestra, Laurie Johnson, cond. Starlog/Varese Sarabande SV-95001(D); also issued on Unicorn/Kanchana DKP 9000.

   Excerpts of No. 2 above have been reused on other London Phase 4 recordings devoted to Herrmann's music.[27]

1982; revised 1984

[27]I wish to express my deep gratitude to Donald Spoto, Graham Bruce, Harry M. McCraw, Sara Kerber (of A.S.C.A.P.), Douglas Gallez and Jeffrey Marcus for their help in the preparation of this study.

ROLAND BARTHES
THE FACE OF GARBO

Garbo still belongs to that moment in cinema when capturing the human face still plunged audiences into the deepest ecstasy, when one literally lost oneself in a human image as one would in a philtre, when the face represented a kind of absolute state of the flesh, which could be neither reached nor renounced. A few years earlier the face of Valentino was causing suicides; that of Garbo still partakes of the same rule of Courtly Love, where the flesh gives rise to mystical feelings of perdition.

It is indeed an admirable face-object. In *Queen Christina*, a film which has again been shown in Paris in the last few years, the make-up has the snowy thickness of a mask: it is not a painted face, but one set in plaster, protected by the surface of the colour, not by its lineaments. Amid all this snow at once fragile and compact, the eyes alone, black like strange soft flesh, but not in the least expressive, are two faintly tremulous wounds. In spite of its extreme beauty, this face, not drawn but sculpted in something smooth and friable, that is, at once perfect and ephemeral, comes to resemble the flour-white complexion of Charlie Chaplin, the dark vegetation of his eyes, his totem-like countenance.

Now the temptation of the absolute mask (the mask of antiquity, for instance) perhaps implies less the theme of the secret (as is the case with Italian half mask) than that of an archetype of the human face. Garbo offered to one's gaze a sort of Platonic Idea of the human creature, which explains why her face is almost sexually undefined, without however leaving one in doubt. It is true that this film (in which Queen Christina is by turns a woman and a young cavalier) lends itself to this lack of differentiation; but Garbo does not perform in it any feat of transvestism; she is always herself, and carries without pretence, under her crown or her wide-brimmed hats, the same snowy solitary face. The name given to her, *the Divine*, probably aimed to convey less a superlative state of beauty than the essence of her corporeal person, descended from a heaven where all things are formed and perfected in the clearest light. She herself knew this: how many actresses have consented to let the crowd see the ominous maturing of their beauty. Not she, however; the essence was not to be degraded, her face was not to have any reality except that of its perfection, which was intellectual even more than formal. The Essence became gradually obscured, progressively veiled with dark glasses, broad hats and exiles: but it never deteriorated.

And yet, in this deified face, something sharper than a mask is looming: a kind of voluntary and therefore human relation between the curve of the nostrils and the arch of the eyebrows; a rare, individual function relating two regions of the face. A mask is but a sum of lines; a face, on the contrary, is above all their thematic harmony. Garbo's face represents this fragile moment when the cinema is about to draw an existential from an essential beauty, when the archetype leans towards the fascination of mortal faces, when the clarity of the flesh as essence yields its place to a lyricism of Woman.

Viewed as a transition the face of Garbo reconciles two iconographic ages, it assures the passage from awe to charm. As is well known, we are today at the other pole of this evolution: the face of Audrey Hepburn, for instance, is individualized, not only because of its peculiar thematics (woman as child, woman as kitten) but also because of her person, of an almost unique specification of the face, which has nothing of the essence left in it, but is constituted by an infinite complexity of morphological functions. As a language, Garbo's singularity was of the order of the concept, that of Audrey Hepburn is of the order of the substance. The face of Garbo is an Idea, that of Hepburn, an Event.

1957

KENNETH TYNAN
GARBO

What, when drunk, one sees in other women, one sees in Garbo sober. She is woman apprehended with all the pulsating clarity of one of Aldous Huxley's mescalin jags. To watch her is to achieve direct, cleansed perception of something which, like a flower or a fold of silk, is raptly, unassertively, and beautifully itself. Nothing intrudes between her and the observer except the observer's neuroses: her contribution is calm and receptiveness, an absorbent repose which normally, in women, coexists only with the utmost vanity. Tranced by the ecstasy of existing, she gives to each onlooker what he needs: her largesse is intarissable. Most actresses in action live only to look at men, but Garbo looks at flowers, clouds, and furniture with the same admiring compassion, like Eve on the morning of creation, and better cast than Mr. Huxley as Adam. Fame, by insulating her against a multitude of experiences which we take for granted, has increased rather than diminished her capacity for wonder. In England two years ago she visited Westminster Abbey, early one morning when no one was about, and in this most public of places found a source of enormous private enchantment. A walk along a busy street is for her a semi-mystical adventure. Like a Martian guest, she questions you about your everyday life, infecting you with her eagerness, shaming you into a heightened sensitivity. Conversing with her, you feel like Ramon Novarro, blinded in *Mata Hari*, to whom she said: "Here are your eyes," and touched her own.

I half-believed, until I met her, the old hilarious slander which whispered that she was a brilliant Swedish female impersonator who had kept up the pretence too long; behind the dark glasses, it was hinted, beneath the wild brown hair, there lurked the features of a proud Scandinavian diplomat, now proclaiming their masculinity so stridently that exposure to cameras was out of the question. This idle fabrication was demolished within seconds of her entering the room; sidelong, a little tentative, like an animal thrust under a searchlight, she advanced, put out a hand in greeting, murmured something muted and sibilant to express her pleasure, and then, gashing her mouth into a grin, expunged all doubt. This was a girl, all right. It is an indication of the mystery which surrounds her that I felt pleased even to have ascertained her sex.

"Are you all things to all men?" someone asks her in *Two-Faced Woman;* to which the honest reply (I forget the scripted one) would be: "To all men, women, and children." Garbo, Hepburn, and Dietrich are perhaps the only screen personalities for whom such a claim could seriously be made. "She has sex, but no particular gender," I once wrote of Dietrich, "her masculinity appears to women, and her sexuality to men"; which is also true of Hepburn. Yet Garbo transcends both of them. Neither Hepburn nor Dietrich could have played Garbo's scenes with her son in *Anna Karenina;* something predatory in them would have forbidden such selfless maternal raptures. Garbo alone can be intoxicated by innocence. She turns her coevals into her children, taking them under her wing like a great, sailing swan. Her love is thus larger than Hepburn's or Dietrich's, which does not extend beyond the immediately desired object. It was Alistair Cooke who pointed out that in her films she seemed to see life in reverse and, because she was aware of the fate in store for them, offered the shelter of her sympathy to all around her. Through the cellophane *Kitsch* (how it dates!) of the Lubitsch touch she pierced, in *Ninotchka,* to affirm her pity for the human condition. The words were addressed to Melvyn Douglas, but we all knew for whom they were really intended, and glowed in the knowledge: "Bomps will fall, civilizations will crumble—but *not yet. . . . Give us our moment!"* She seemed to be pleading the world's cause, and to be winning, too. Often, during the decade in which she talked to us, she gave signs that she was on the side of life against darkness: they seeped through a series of banal, barrel-scraping scripts like code messages borne through enemy lines. Sometimes, uttering sentences that were plainly designed to speed the end of literature, she could convey her universal charity only in glimpses, such as, for instance, a half-mocking, half-despairing catch in the wine-dark voice. Round the militant bluster of M-G-M dialogue she wrapped a Red Cross bandage of humanity.

It is likely that too many volumes have been read into and written about her, and that every additional adulatory word reinforces the terror I am sure she feels at the thought of having to face us again and measure up to the legend. Possibly we exaggerated her intelligence from the beginning; perhaps she was perfectly happy with the velvet-lung, musk-scented tin lizzies that Salka Viertel and S. N. Behrman (among others) turned out as vehicles for her. Perhaps association with Lewis Stone and Reginald Owen, a stout pair of uncle-substitutes who crop up, variously bewigged, in many of her films, was vitally necessary to inspire her. Recall, too, that Carl Brisson and John Gilbert are known to have been high on her list of ideal men; and that we have no evidence that she has ever read a book. Except physically, we know little more about Garbo than we know about Shakespeare. She looks, in fact, about thirty-four, but her date of birth is disputable; the textbooks oscillate between 1905 and 1906, and one biography ungallantly plumps for 1903, which may, of course, be a wound left by an embittered typesetter. Stockholm cradled her, and like Anna Christie, she was the daughter of an impoverished sailor. She had a brother and two sisters, left school at fourteen, entered the newly expanding Swedish film industry, and was discovered by Mauritz Stiller. After the completion of *Gösta Berling* in 1924, her life is a list of movies, twelve silent, fourteen talking, and a file of newspaper pictures catching her aghast and rain-coated, grey-faced and weirdly hatted, on the gangplanks of ships or the stairways to planes. We often know where she is going, but never why. Occasionally a man is with her, a sort of Kafkaesque guard, employed to escort her to her next inscrutable rendezvous. Baffled, we consult the astrologers, who tell us that those born, as she was, between the end of August and the end of September are almost bound to be perfectionists; but what, we are left sighing, is she perfecting?

She changed her name from Gustaffson to Garbo, the Swedish word for a sprite. I used to think the Spanish "garbo" an insult to her, having heard it applied to matadors whose work seemed to me no more than pretty or neat. A Hispanophile friend has lately corrected me: "garbo," he writes, "is animal grace sublimated—the flaunting of an assured natural charm, poise infected by *joie de vivre*, innate, high-spirited, controlled, the essentially female attribute (even in bullfighters). . . ." In short, "garbo" is Garbo without the melancholy, with no intimations of mortality. The word describes the embryo, the capital letter invests it with a soul. It is the difference between *Gösta Berling* and *Anna Karenina*.

But here again I am acquiescing in the myth of gloom. Long before the fit of hoarse hysterics that convulsed her when Melvyn Douglas fell off his chair, Garbo had laughed, even if it was only "wild laughter in the throat of death," and made us laugh too. She was never wholly austere. Posing as a man in the tavern scene of *Queen Christina*, how blithely she made us smile at her awkwardness when asked to share a bedroom with the Spanish ambassador!

A secret half-smile, with the lips drawn back as if bobbing for apples, was always her least resistible weapon. Her gaiety coalesced, to the dismay of academic distinctions, with plangency. Her retirement is unforgivable if only because it means that now we shall never see her as Masha in *The Three Sisters*, a part Chekhov might have written for her. It takes lesser actresses to express a single emotion, mirth or mirthlessness. Garbo's most radiant grins were belied always by the anxiety in the antennae-like eyebrows; and by the angle of her head she could effect a transition, not alone of mood, but of age. When it was tilted back, with the mouth sagging open, she was a child joyously anticipating a sweet; when it was tipped forward, the mouth still agape, she became a parent wide-eyed at her child's newest exploit.

Some of her impact, certainly, was derived from the exoticism of her accent; hers was probably the first Swedish voice that many a million filmgoers had ever heard. Anglo-Saxons are notoriously prone to ascribe messianic characteristics to any stranger with a Slavic, Teutonic, or Nordic intonation; Bergner and Bergman are examples that come to mind, and the history of the London stage is punctuated with shrieks of exultation over long-forgotten soubrettes with names like Marta Kling, Svenda Stellmar, on Ljuba Van Strusi. Garbo was unquestionably assisted by the fact that she had to be cast, more often than not, as an exile: how often, to go about her business of home-wrecking, she arrives by train from afar! The smoke clears, revealing the emissary of fate, hungrily licking her lips. The displaced person always inspires curiosity: who displaced her, what forces drove her from her native land? If it was Garbo's luck to provoke these inquiries, it was her gift which answered them. The impulse behind her voyages was romantic passion. Bergner might have left home to collect Pekes, Bergman to go on a hiking tour: Garbo could only have journeyed to escape or to seek a lover. Which is, as a line in *Ninotchka* has it, "a netchul impulse common to all."

Superficially, she changed very little in the course of her career; a certain solidity in her aspect suggested, at the very end, a spiritualized reworking of Irene Dunne, but that was all. She could still (and often did) fling her head flexibly back at right-angles to her spine, and she kissed as thirstily as ever, cupping her man's head in both hands and seeming very nearly to drink from it. And her appeal never lost its ambiguity. The after-dinner cooch-dance which drives Lionel Barrymore to hit the bottle in *Mata Hari* reveals an oddly androgynous physique, with strong-kneed legs as "capable," in their way, as the spatulate fingers: nothing is here of Herrick's "fleshie Principalities." Pectorally, the eye notes a subsidence hardly distinguishable from concavity: the art that conceals art could scarcely go further. If this undenominational temple-dance is seduc-

Greta Garbo in *Love* (1927) and *Anna Christie* (1930). "Garbo still belongs to that moment in cinema when capturing the human face still plunged audiences into the deepest ecstasy . . ." (BARTHES, page 650). "*Anna Christie,* where she could ensconce herself, most of the time, in mute or monosyllabic sullenness . . ." (PANOFSKY, page 256).

tive (and, like the swimming-pool sequence in *Two-Faced Woman*, it is), the explanation lies in our awareness that we are watching a real, imperfectly shaped human being, and not a market-fattened glamour-symbol.

I dwell on Garbo's physical attributes because I think the sensual side of acting is too often under-rated: too much is written about how actors feel, too little about how they look. Garbo's looks, and especially her carriage, always set up a marvellous dissonance with what she was saying. The broad ivory yoke of her shoulders belonged to a javelin-thrower; she walked obliquely, seeming to sidle even when she strode, like a middle-weight boxer approaching an opponent: how could this athletic port enshrine so frail and suppliant a spirit? Queen Christina, reputedly her favourite character, is encased for several reels in masculine garb, and when besought by her counsellors to marry, she replies: "I shall die a bachelor!" And think of: "I am Mata Hari—I am my own master!" To lines like these Garbo could impart an enigmatic wit which nobody else could have carried off. Deficient in all the surface frills of femininity, she replaced them with a male directness. Her Marie Walewska was as lion-hearted as Napoleon himself, and I have heard her described as "Charlemagne's Aunt." Her independence (in the last analysis) of either sex is responsible for the cryptic amorality of her performances. In most of the characters she played the only discernible moral imperative is loyalty, an animal rather than a human virtue—that "natural sense of honour" which, as Shaw says, "is nowhere mentioned in the Bible."

"Animal grace sublimated": I return to my correspondent's phrase. If it is true (as I think it is) that none of Garbo's clothes ever appear to be meant for her, much less to fit her, that is because her real state is not in clothes at all. Her costumes hamper her, whether they are stoles or redingotes or (as on one occasion) moiré, sè-quinned, principal-boy tights. She implies a nakedness which is bodily as well as spiritual. It is foolish to complain that, basically, she gave but one performance throughout her life. She has only one body, and in this incarnation that is all we can expect.

Through what hoops, when all is said and done, she has been put by Seastrom, Cukor, Clarence Brown, and the rest of her mentors! She has gone blonde for them, danced "La Chica-Choca" for them, played a travesty of Sarah Bernhardt for them, stood straight-faced by for them as Lewis Stone warned her of "a new weapon called The Tank." Can we ask for more self-abnegation? A life of Duse was once mooted for her—what an *éducation senti-mentale*, one guesses, she would have supplied for D'Annunzio! Later she hovered over, but did not settle on, a mimed role in Lifar's ballet version of *Phèdre*. And at the last moment, when all seemed fixed, she sidestepped the leading part in Balzac's *La Duchesse de Langeais*. The most recent, least plausible rumour of all insisted that she would film *La Folle de Chaillot*, with Chaplin as the Rag-Picker. . . .

So it looks as if we were never to know whether or not she was a great actress. Do I not find the death scene of *Camille* or the bedroom-stroking scene of *Queen Christina* commensurate with the demands of great acting? On balance, no. The great actress, as G. H. Lewes declared, must show her greatness in the highest reaches of her art; and it must strictly be counted against Garbo that she never attempted Hedda, or Masha, or St Joan, or Medea. We must acclaim a glorious woman who exhibited herself more profoundly to the camera than any of her contemporaries; but the final accolade must, if we are honest, be withheld.

1953

JOAN MELLEN
FROM WOMEN AND THEIR SEXUALITY IN THE NEW FILM

THE MAE WEST NOBODY KNOWS

In my long and colorful career, one thing stands out; I have been misunderstood

MAE WEST

The Mae West of legend has long excited men and infuriated women. Her voluptuous image, exploited by the Hollywood dream machine, appears to women as a mockery. West as sex queen and manipulator of weak, drooling men represents a liberation in reverse. Aggressively flaunting herself, Mae West thinks she thereby transcends the sexual role of passive and fawning object set for women. In reality, she compounds the injury. While scorning passivity, the image of woman as bestower of sexual favors seems to be perpetuated by Mae West unrelentingly. Her belief that liberation and frankness about the risqué are synonymous is, of course, outdated, and sexuality in Mae West has been made a repository for abundant energies directed by more liberated women to activities providing satisfaction beyond the physical. The stereotyped image thus draws upon a partial truth.

But there are two sides to Mae West. In most of her films she reduces herself to a sexual object in quest of economic security while she is, simultaneously, defiant and self-sufficient, seeking mastery over her life. It is the latter aspect of the West personality that is revolutionary. It projects a uniquely free image of woman rare for Hollywood during the 1930's, or now.

Mae West understands the fact that in our culture women have obtained acceptance primarily by offering their bodies in contract, although the pattern has been surrounded by legitimacy to conceal its meaning. Hence, submissive coyness has been approved, excessive forwardness not. The exception is when the sexual aggressiveness of women is part of a condemned subculture, the prostitute or the burlesque queen solicited and stigmatized. In this sense Mae West fulfills the canons of our culture where women are concerned, but frequently for the purpose of subverting them. Often her license, bawdy humor, sexual explicitness and bravado are invested with a challenge to those who disapprove. It is true that Mae West, no social revolutionary, does not project new values. But within the existing structure of attitudes defining the appropriate responses of men and women, West turns the tables. It is she who is superior and achieved, she for whom sexual command affirms feminine strength.

This reversal often renders her men uncomfortable and off-balance, her first victory. They approach her expecting to enhance their masculine pride and sexual self-esteem—at her expense. West reverses the roles. It is true that men often become *her* sexual objects, leaving us with the old pattern of exploiter-exploited that has long distorted relations between men and women. But West also transforms sexual allure on the part of women into an item of pride, power and autonomy. She transcends the cultural meaning of sexual availability in women because she separates it from servility and servitude.

Despite her moments approaching the licentious, if West uses her sensuality to entice, she is also the polar opposite of the simpering coquette or the manipulative subordinate. West looks over the field, reduces and discards, takes lovers at will, but never surrenders freedom or control. Although her example is difficult to imitate successfully, she takes a first step toward challenge of the expected female role; she arrogates to herself all the insolent privilege, haughtiness and self-esteem which our culture had until her time in the film granted the male alone.

Mae West thus deploys her own brand of sexism to create an image of a liberated woman—and Hollywood is her vehicle. At her best moments, we forget the reversal of a repugnant sexual politics to relish the free spirit of the West *persona*. It is the common thread of *She Done Him Wrong* (based on West's own Broadway play, *Diamond Lil*), *I'm No Angel, Klondike Annie, Belle of The Nineties, My Little Chickadee, Go West Young Man, Goin' To Town* and *The Heat's On*. What has been cited as her narcissism was hardly a liberated response; but West's endless filing of her fingernails, bored by all, or examining herself in multiple mirrors, are also devices she employs as foils for shrewd observations into a petty, ambitious and hypocritical society where women have always had to conceal their intelligence and remain on guard. When West masks her intellectuality, it is of course a measure of continued enslavement. That she can act upon her own insights shows her on the path to liberation.

It could be said that the elaborate facade West presents of rejecting dominance in men is retrograde because it conceals her unconscious fear of them, or, her longing for that man against whom she would not pre-emptively have to defend so fiercely. But such a psychologism, although it may entail a prescient guess about West's interaction with her much admired, strong and brawling father, misses the point. It is precisely because our culture recreates for women the situation of the paternal male figure who would dominate as a price for approval and love that West's response is so liberating and true to the common experience. And West's *persona* actually merges with the real woman. Mae West married only once, as an adolescent to a husband as young as she. Regretting her decision, she refused to set up house with him and was separated so quickly that her indulgent parents were unaware that a marriage had occurred.

In her own life West's energy was directed as much toward the hard work of writing as toward romantic attachments. She wrote a series of successful Broadway plays followed by novels, and finally by the screenplays and the diaglogue for virtually all her films. (An exception like *The Heat's On* suffers accordingly in loss of verve and intelligence). "All my life," West writes in her autobiography, "I would not conform to the old-fashioned limits they had set on a woman's freedom of action. Or the myth of a woman's need of male wisdom and protection."

Mae West on screen always retains the decision about whether to commit herself to a man for an extended time; and she is wary about choosing one partner for life. "Ever meet a man that could make you happy?" she is asked. "Sure, lots of times," is her reply. In *I'm No Angel* a fortune teller promises West "a man in your life," to the swift retort, "what, only one?" It is no wonder that even Adolph Zukor, who would have insisted otherwise had she not enriched the coffers of Paramount Pictures, called her "the strong, confident woman, always in command."

She Done Him Wrong pictures West as a "gold digger" named

Lady Lou attached to a saloon whose owner is involved in the white slave trade, in which Lou takes no part. Lou prefers the poor Salvation Army "Captain" Cummings (Cary Grant), a poor detective in disguise. Accidentally murdering the slave trade proprietess, Lady Lou faces arrest. Yet when she is tempted by detective Grant to marry him and escape punishment, she refuses to submit. The last line of the film gives an impenitent West the sentiment usually implicit in the male's attitude to his conquest. "I always knew you could be had," she tells her leading man. Captain Cummings wants to be "her jailer for a long, long time." But Lady Lou's ironic view of marriage was conveyed when she said earlier of Cummings that "he'd be the kind a woman would have to marry to get rid of." Lou would remain free in the event she were to marry, even as some men do, rejecting the hint of a double standard.

The West character, despite her sexism, will neither acknowledge nor accede to the superior wisdom of any man. Interestingly, the charcterizations of males which she creates in her films are often of personalities rich in talents of their own, i.e. the inventor in *Go West Young Man* (Randolph Scott) and the successful executive in *I'm No Angel* (Cary Grant). It is in relation to men of talent and not merely the inadequate male that she makes it clear that their qualities could never oblige relinquishment of her judgment for theirs. In this sense the West character is far more liberated than the women of an overtly feminist writer like Doris Lessing, whose male characters are weak, whining and tiresome.

Contrary to popular belief, the image of West is only partially that of a woman soliciting by wiles the support of a man or his gifts. In all her films West earns her own way, making hard work appear easy. In most of the films West plays a professional entertainer, one of the few arenas for economic independence open to a woman of her limited resources and education, especially durng the depression era when her films were made. Thus even as Diamond Lil she is primarily supported by her work. This undercuts and renders ambivalent the image of the West character as reliant for luxuries upon her physical attributes, as indeed she also is.

Frequently she assumes professions normally available to men alone, and she is never unequal to them. *I'm No Angel* has West as a lion tamer who sues Grant for breach of promise. The circus owner, fearful of losing his star to marriage, had planted a "lover" in West's room, the discovery of whom causes Grant to break their engagement. West conducts her own defense at the trial, exposing with panache the lies of witness after witness, while simultaneously flirting with an unnerved, if spellbound, judge and jury. Again we are presented with the two sides of Mae West, attorney and coquette, the liberated woman and the tease, a character not yet strong enough to transcend the old values completely.

This theme is enlarged upon in other films. In *Goin' To Town* she is a rich "widow" whose "husband" dies before the wedding. She proceeds to manage his oil wells and a huge cattle ranch with skill and ease while at the same time searching for and pursuing her next husband! In *Klondike Annie* West as the "San Francisco Doll" (again the sex queen) escapes with great daring from an infamous saloon in San Francisco and proceeds by ship to Nome, Alaska. There she transforms an abandoned settlement house into a financially thriving center of activity. Disguised as "Sister Annie," a Salvation Army worker who dies aboard ship, West relates religious platitudes to the deeply felt needs of lonely miners. Underlying her toughness is a demonstrated sympathy for those who are disadvantaged. The miners are indeed enticed by her sexual allure, barely concealed in Salvation Army garb, but she uses it not for sexual encounters, but to win an audience for the meeting house.

West's independence and strength of will are epitomized in the lion taming sequence of *I'm No Angel*. The head trainer was absent from the set because he had been attacked by one of the lions that morning. West actually went in among the lions for the shooting. No trembling Hollywood ingenue, she enjoyed the experience which expresses again the two sides of her personality: independent woman and seeker of revenge and power over the male. She places her head in the lion's mouth and wisecracks, "remember my contract, baby, . . . speak up for yourself or you'll end up as a rug!" "Every man wants to protect me," says Mae West disingenuously in *My Little Chickadee*, "I can't figure out what from."

In *My Little Chickadee*, a Western with a female hero, Flower Belle (West) is run out of her home town for behavior unbecoming a proper young lady (she has been "kidnapped" by her lover, the "masked bandit"). On the train bound for a neighboring village, Flower Belle single-handedly routs an army of attacking Indians. Presented later with the opportunity to teach a class of wild and unruly boys, she wins and tames them (like the lions) through wit and bravado, despite spare knowledge. "Two and two are four, and five will get you ten if you know how to work it" becomes part of their arithmetic lesson. When she is jailed for collusion with the "masked bandit," Flower Belle escapes through cunning, if also through the use of her charms, in time to rescue W. C. Fields from imminent hanging as the "real" bandit. If her sexuality is always presented as an enticement, her boldness and self-possession present another focus to her film character.

Another side of West's rejection of passivity which goes beyond sexism is a refusal to wait for events to turn in her direction. She appears ever ready for the unexpected, and the quick response is her trademark. At the end of *My Little Chickadee*, when a departing Fields asks West to "come up and see me sometime," it is West who calls *him* "my little Chickadee," emphasizing that such an appellation, contrary to custom, may just as easily be attached to a male. During the film two attractive men, the masked bandit (the saloon owner in disguise) and the local newspaper editor pursue her, but Flower Belle will marry neither, keeping both at bay with "maybe tomorrow, maybe never." She can return to her home town only when she is "respectable and married." Rather than capitulate to the norms of a society that would not acknowledge her existence in terms other than marriage and family, West prefers to live elsewhere.

The hostile view of Mae West which notes, simplistically, only her vulgarity, also regards her as selfish and hard-boiled, but this too cannot survive close examination. There is self-irony in her portrayals and her characters display generosity and a sense of justice which are understated if omnipresent. When it appears that she may implicate the man she loves, Klondike Annie returns from Nome to San Francisco to face murder charges. Cleo Borden in *Goin' To Town* is generous toward a weak aristocrat, although, regressing, she married him in the first place for his name and social position. In *She Done Him Wrong*, Lady Lou warmly takes under her wing the "fallen" girl Sally and persuades her that "betrayal" by a man does not mean her life is over: "When women go wrong, men go right after them!" If the content of the advice does not free woman from her traditional role, its spirit redresses the balance. West shields the local Runyonesque characters from police bullies and befriends all whom she finds in need. Flower Belle (*Chickadee*), for example, saves the obnoxious Fields not because she has any feeling for him, but because he has been falsely accused. Free of the stereotype of woman as weak or in need of man as protector, West's values transcend her sexual role. A sense of fair play is the complement to her indefatigable spirit.

Sex itself for the West *persona* is always a matter of *her own* pleasure. The men she invites to "come up and see me sometime" are only those who appeal to her. If her aggressive personality attracted the label of "predatory," West was well aware that this would be the social response to any woman bold enough to take sexual initiatives. It should be rememberd as well that men were most often the predators of the kind of woman West portrayed in her films—and for whom she has sympathy—poor, uneducated women living on the margins of a hostile society by singing in saloons. And it is in response to such traatment that West advises these women to "take all you can, and give as little as possible." The context is one of unceasing struggle against potential and actual victimization, although this advice also replaces men with women as victimizers.

There is another facet to West's rebellion against sexual orthodoxy. She is relaxed about sex, not faintly hysterical, as Hollywood custom usually required. She treats her adventures with bountiful humor and her exaggerated "sexy" walk is at once a sexist bploy and a mockery of the sexual signals assumed to bind men to women. She is also ironic when men assume that her sexuality is an invitation to easy usage. Lady Lou, admiring a nude portrait of herself, wishes only that it were not "hung up over the free lunch!"

"When I was fourteen," Mae West said in a recent interview, "I resented men having all the freedom of sex and from then on I thought women should have it too." Such remarks about "free lunch," the lurid and mercenary side of this character, should not obscure the irony and rebellion which are continually present as well. And West's response to the very different virtues of each of her lovers, from Victor McLaughlin (*Klondike Annie*) to Gilbert Roland (*She Done Him Wrong*) to Cary Grant (*She Done Him Wrong, I'm No Angel*) belies the allegation that men are only faceless objects to her. "A man's kiss is his signature," she declares, stressing her respect for the uniqueness of her lovers, in contrast to the image of a woman who would turn men solely into objects. There is far more discrimination and less promiscuity in West's approach than that accorded, for example, to intellectual women by men on the Hollywood screen. "There's something about every man," says West. "A man may be short, dumpy and rapidly getting bald—but if he has *fire*, women will like him." West may celebrate promiscuity in her sexual encounters, but generosity and kindness are important to her as well. Klondike Annie is genuinely moved when the ship captain (McLaughlin) is prepared to risk his life and career for her. "Your love is terrific," Annie tells him. A good heart is matched by West in kind and there is considerable pride and self-esteem even in her prurience.

There are aspects of her films that pander to the most corrupt values of the Hollywood of her day: the black maids named Beulah or Pearl, invariably fat and childish, the racist portrayals of sinister Chinese, such as the infamous Chan Lo of *Klondike Annie's* San Francisco Chinatown, the "savage" Indian horde which Flower Belle overwhelms and such salty, questionable ballads as "I'm An Occidental Woman In An Oriental Mood For Love." And the Hollywood of the 1930's delighted in Mae West because her screen personality fit in so well with the American myth that with enough energy, drive and initative, any deprived person might achieve riches and status. The dream machine must especially have welcomed this theme in 1932 when Mae West first went to Hollywood. Made during the depression, most of West's films are set in an earlier period, usually the gay nineties, when the myth that fortunes could be made overnight seemed more credible.

West as free spirit constantly combines with West as sexist. At her worst, she equates the subtle with prudery. Her seeming freedom from men, her refusal to commit herself completely even in marriage, may be seen as fear of anything beyond the casual relationship and the one night stand. It is as if West, doubting her sexual capacity, were driven to exaggerate her prowess. Her need for a steady stream of men coming up to "see me sometime" makes her the equivalent of the Don Juan who, fearing impotence, must forever make new conquests. The Mae West who at 77 appears in *Myra Breckinridge* as a lascivious Hollywood agent collecting well-endowed young boys, like the West who appears at interviews with a collection of studs, is embarrassing when she does not offend. To qualify, each young man must possess not only the standard "six feet," but also a required "seven inches." "I don't care about your credits," she adds to an aspiring young actor, "as long as you're oversexed." The irony is gone. The heroic side of West is besmirched, suggesting that her interest all along has been in the exploitation of sex, at its best daring for its day, but no mark of emancipation. *Myra Breckinridge* shows us West as merely a distortion of the female, a travesty of self-parody which convinces us of the truth of its opposite, that compulsive sex is neither desirable nor pleasureable, that despite her bravura, West did women less a favor than a disservice.

In *Myra Breckinridge* and at the worst moments of all the films, West is the least liberated creature imaginable, retaining no portion of herself beyond the sexual. Her abundant self-confidence becomes no more than a concealment of the retrograde. It is this West which, making virtue of necessity (woman's enslavement) deploys style to conceal what it would have been far more liberating to expose. Those who applaud West's performances at the re-run houses on St. Marks Place do not

Mae West with her adoring servants—with Louise Beavers in *She Done Him Wrong* and Soo Yong in *Klondike Annie*. "There are aspects of her films that pander to the most corrupt values of the Hollywood of her day: the black maids named Beulah or Pearl, invariably fat and childish, the racist portrayals of sinister Chinese, such as the infamous Chan Lo of *Klondike Annie's* San Francisco Chinatown, the "savage" Indian horde which Flower Belle overwhelms and such salty, questionable ballads as 'I'm an Occidental Woman in an Oriental Mood for Love'" (MELLEN, pages 665–666).

differentiate the Mae West of *She Done Him Wrong* from the West of *Myra Breckinridge*. She is cheered there primarily by some men perhaps because she seems to them to represent the ultimate of sexual degradation in a woman. In her aggressiveness West imparts at times an aura of the transvestite, making a mockery of female sexuality by flaunting what are no more than ordinary female attributes.

Yet there is also the Mae West whose appeal as a new woman approaches the universality of Chaplin. "What would you do without me?" a producer asks Mae in *The Heat's On*. "Much better," is the reply and she goes on to prove it. West was the *auteur* of films redolent with wit in which the punchline always went to the woman. It should not be forgotten that she worked in a medium devoted to glorifying male prowess and female incapacity. And it took a courage heroic in its time (she was jailed for "indecency" as the author of one of her plays) to present Hollywood with a reversal of roles and a manifest contempt for the culture which had for so long demeaned the capacities of women.

1973

VII

Film: Psychology, Society, and Ideology

What are the nature and sources of film's psychological and political power? Is there something special about the film medium that confers this power? Is this power repressive or liberating? Can it be criticized and controlled? Questions of this sort have always been asked about cinema, but in recent years film studies have focused on them with unusual intensity. Many of these studies have relied on the Marxist notions of superstructure and ideology and on Freudian ideas about the development and constitution of the self. Writers in this tradition have been committed to exposing the ideological biases of classic narrative film and, in the writings of feminist authors, to revealing its sexist procedures and assumptions. In this section the reader will find some of the most arresting recent writing on the psychological and social bases of film, as well as essays by important precursors of present tendecies such as Walter Benjamin and Parker Tyler.

In his classic paper, the pre-war Marxist critic, Walter Benjamin, reflects on alterations in the artistic superstructure that the capitalist mode of production produces. In the past, art works have been unique objects, possessing "aura" and traditional "authority." They played a ritual role, contemplated by men who kept a "natural" distance from them. But the contemporary masses went to see things closer, spatially and humanly. They overcome the uniqueness of the work of art by accepting a mechanical reproduction of it as an equivalent.

These reproductions are no longer hallowed cult objects but consumer goods sold on the market; rather than absorbing their beholders they are absorbed by them. Reactions to these "works of art" are rarely personal and are almost completely determined by the mass audience to which the individual is subordinated. Indeed, films have now become one of the most powerful agents of mass political movements—in them the mass has for the first time come face to face with itself. In Benjamin's view, the film and the audience's relation to it are so different from all that has gone before that he is inclined to think that photography has transformed the very nature of art.

The editors of *Cahiers du cinéma* who, since the student uprisings of 1968 in Paris, have been central to the discussions represented in this section, assume that every film is part of the ideological superstructure which reflects a society's economic base. Inevitably, therefore, a Hollywood film will reflect the ideology of American capitaliam. This ideological undertaking will, among other things, require the repression of politics and of eroticism. Thus, *Young Mr. Lincoln* attempts to suppress the realities of politics by presenting Lincoln's career as one based on an idealist morality superior to mere politics. "The enterprise consisting of the concealment of politics (of social relations in America, of Lincoln's career) under the idealist mask of Morality has the effect of regilding the cause of Capital with the gold of myth, by manifesting the 'spirituality' in which American Capitalism believes it finds its origins and sees its eternal justification. The seeds of Lincoln's future were already sown in his youth—the future of America (its eternal values) is already written into Lincoln's moral virtues, which include the Republican Party and Capitalism." Although films inevitably reflect the ideology of the society that produces them, they do not necessarily give that ideology a full and unhampered passage. A "reading" of the film may turn up internal tensions, features of the film text that constitute an internal criticism of its ideology. This may be true even of a director like Ford, who is consciously sympathetic to that ideology. Indeed, the editors of *Cahiers* find that Ford's Lincoln is characterized by a violence which displays his truly repressive character and which, according to J.P. Oudart, shows the distance that Ford, or his "writing," keeps between himself and the idealist propositions that he uses.

In a more recent elaboration of the *Cahiers* point of view, Jean-Louis Comolli concentrates less on displaying the way in which society's ideology manifests itself in the works of a particular director, or film, and more on the way the entire apparatus of cinema is implicated in that ideology. In contrast to

the idealist conception of Bazin and Mitry, who view the evolution of cinematic language as a consequence of the internal
development of science and technology, Comolli proposes a
materialist conception: the development of film language implies the work of a social machine that anticipates and confirms the economic, ideological, and social profitability of cinematic products and techniques. "The machine is always social
before it is technical." The second half of the nineteenth century "lives in a sort of frenzy of the visible." The mechanical
reproduction of which Benjamin spoke makes things more visible, while the mechanical eye of the photographic machine
supplants the human eye and, as Brakhage noted, guarantees
the identity of the visible with "the norms of valid perception." But this ideological identification of the real with normal vision, which arises from the Western metaphysical and
representational tradition of perspectival viewing, falsely
identifies the cinema apparatus with the camera and ignores
or suppresses the ideological function of the non-photographic
elements of cinema such as the sound track and laboratory
techniques. Bazin believes that deep focus was adopted because it revealed the natural world in its full ambiguity and
unedited unity. But for Comolli, deep focus simply serves the
ideological purposes of miscognition, to offer its space as
" 'natural,' and hence to mask the play of differences," hiding
the work which the spectator always performs (what Scholes
termed "narrativity") when viewing a constructed image. "The
most analogical representation of the world is not, is never, its
reduplication." The spectator profoundly understands that the
spectacle which cinema presents and represents is not life.
Realist representations are successful because the spectator is
willing to "play along," willing to be fooled (a reformulation
of Coleridge's classic "willing suspension of disbelief"). It is
this potential disbelief and disillusion which allow cinema to
work against the reassuring, mystifying representations of
ideology.

In his essay "Technology and Ideology in the Cinema,"
American film scholar James Spellerberg describes the process
by which the views of the *Cahiers* critics, and particularly those
of Comolli, were refined in response to hostile criticism. He
distinguishes between the ideology of representation, which
is the main focus of Comolli's essay, and the ideology of specularization, which is examined in the work of Comolli's *Cahiers* colleague, Jean-Louis Baudry. For Baudry, the viewing
situation is analogous to the mirror stage of Lacan's Freudian
psychology and it presupposes the identification of the viewer
with the camera. For this identification to work, the cinematic

apparatus must be hidden or repressed so that the film image appears to be a characteristic of the natural world directly transmitted by the camera, and not an effect produced by the medium itself. In this way the ideology of specularization, like the ideology of representation, sustains the illusions of the metaphysic of seeing.

Both Spellerberg and Comolli reveal that theories about the cinematic apparatus inevitably imply theories about the psychological processes of the spectator. Not surprisingly, the cinema spectator has been compared with both the reader of a novel and the viewer of a play. Like the reader of a novel, the viewer of a film, sitting in a darkened hall, enjoys a degree of solitude. Like the viewer of a play, the movie-goer sits in a public place and reacts to humanly significant events in the company of other human beings. André Bazin, who distinguished between the "community" that views a play and the "mass" that watches a film, tries to hold both of these features in balance. But most theorists emphasize one or the other.

As we have seen, for Stanley Cavell, watching a film preserves the modern sense of privacy, offering the viewer both invisibility and an absence of responsibility. The experience is essentially voyeuristic and even pornographic. Parker Tyler's view of the film experience is even more explicitly sexual and psychological. For him, the "dark-enshrouded" passivity of the movie house encourages "the daylight dream." In this state, the movie screen transcends its role as a mirror of nature, and the viewer's unconscious mind can read the film's images symbolically. Tyler realizes that the Hollywood film (as opposed to the European film) cannot meet the standards of high art. But the resonant images of a Hollywood film mirror mythic cultural values and evoke primitive responses in the mass audience. Modern movie stars, "the gods and goddesses of Hollywood," are vestiges of the old Greek divinities and they gratify our deepest sexual fantasies. Comparative mythology and psychoanalysis have made us aware of the persistence of deep psychic needs, and the Hollywood film responds to these needs in a way that contemporary popular religions fail to do.

In his more recent work, Christian Metz also looks to psychoanalysis for an explanation of cinema's power. He applies ideas of Lacanian psychoanalysis to an examination of the ideology of specularization. For Metz, the uniqueness of the cinema lies in the duality of its signifier. Cinema is capable of an unprecedented range of perceptions (it is a machine of the visible), but these perceptions are stamped with unreality to an unusual degree (the cinematic apparatus does not succeed in identifying the visible with the real). What is perceived is not really the object, but its shades, its phantom, its double, its *replica* in a new kind of mirror. But this mirror differs from the primordial mirror of Lacanian analysis. In the Lacanian mirror, before which the mother holds the child, the child perceives its own image and its ego is formed by its identification with this likeness. In the cinema, the spectator identifies with himself as a pure act of perception. He identifies, that is, with the camera. But what makes the spectator's absence from the screen possible is the fact that the spectator has already experienced the primordial mirror.

For the spectator, film unfolds in that definitively inaccessible "elsewhere" in which the child sees the amorous play of the parental couple, who, like the actors in a film, are similarly ignorant of the voyeur or spectator and leave him alone. The filmic spectator is a privileged onlooker whose participation in the scene he witnesses is impossible. In this sense, the cinematic signifier is not only "psychoanalytic"; it is more precisely Oedipal. The cinema retains some of the prohibitions peculiar to the vision of the primal scene. But the institutionalization of the cinema legalized this practice, making it socially permissible. Going to the cinema is one lawful activity among others. Still, it constitutes a peephole opening on to something slightly more crazy, slightly less acceptable, than what one does the rest of the time.

For Laura Mulvey, the English critic and filmmaker, psychoanalysis helps to explain the pleasure and unpleasure offered by narrative film. In her essay "Visual Pleasure and Narrative Cinema," she argues that narrative film provides what Freud calls "scopophilic" pleasure, the pleasure of viewing another as an erotic object. In a narrative film, this activity characteristically takes the form of looking at women as erotic objects. But narrative film, echoing the experience of the child at Lacan's mirror, also provides the contrasting narcissistic pleasure of identification with the projected images, in particular with that of the male character, who makes things happen and controls them. Woman is, however, also a source of unpleasure since she represents the threat of castration and, in so being, motivates the voyeuristic and fetishistic mechanisms that attempts to circumvent her threat. (Mulvey studies their operation in the films of Sternberg and Hitchcock.)

None of these mechanisms is, however, intrinsic to film, and the pleasures of mainstream film can be challenged by breaking down the cinematic codes and the formative external structures that support them. Indeed, racial filmmakers have already begun to undermine the ideologically inspired illusion of three-dimensional space in which the spectator's surrogate performs and in which the look of the spectator is denied intrinsic force. This deconstruction is accomplished by freeing the look of the camera into its materiality in space and time and by transforming the scopophilic gaze of the audience into a detached and dialectical one. These changes destroy the pleasures and privilege of the "invisible guest" and highlight the ways film has depended on voyeuristic mechanisms. Women, whose images have continually been stolen and used for this purpose, cannot view the decline of traditional film with anything more than sentimental regret.

In her "Recent Developments in Feminist Criticism," Christine Gledhill of the British Film Institute rejects the anti-realist epistemology implicit in much neo-Marxist and neo-Freudian thought, along with the assumption that feminism must ally itself with an anti-realist cinema. Under the influence of Althusser, some feminists have thought that, since lived experience is the inevitable materialization of the dominant ideology, a realist cinema lacks the resources to escape that ideology. Under the influence of Lacan, many have also thought that the threat of castration is necessary to the production of the speaking subjects and for entrance into the paternalistically dominated symbolic order. But for the subject to speak, the possibility of castration must be overcome or concealed. For this reason female sexuality cannot be expressed. This mechanism of suppression is at play in the voyeurism and fetishism that govern the presentation of women in the narrative film, and it is this feature that leads Mulvey to endorse an alternative cinema. For Gledhill, however, it is a mistake to make language and the signifying process so exclusively central to social analysis. By concentrating exclusively on the semiotic production of meaning, theorists create a cultural condition in which the effectiveness of social, economic, and political practice threatens to disappear altogether. To say that language has a determining effect on society is a different matter from saying that society is nothing but its languages and signifying practices (as French theorists like Roland Barthes, Jacques Derrida, and Louis Althusser have tended to do). In the end, it is difficult for Gledhill to see how, if a radical ideology such as feminism is to be defined as a basis for practical political action, it is going to be possible to avoid some kind of realist epistemology.

WALTER BENJAMIN
THE WORK OF ART
IN THE AGE OF
MECHANICAL
REPRODUCTION

*"Our fine arts were developed, their types and uses were estab-
lished, in times very different from the present, by men whose
power of action upon things was insignificant in comparison with
ours. But the amazing growth of our techniques, the adaptability
and precision they have attained, the ideas and habits they are
creating, make it a certainty that profound changes are impending
in the ancient craft of the Beautiful. In all the arts there is a physical component which can no longer be considered or treated as it
used to be, which cannot remain unaffected by our modern knowledge and power. For the last twenty years neither matter nor space
nor time has been what it was from time immemorial. We must
expect great innovations to transform the entire technique of the
arts, thereby affecting artistic invention itself and perhaps even
bringing about an amazing change in our very notion of art."*
                    —Paul Valéry, PIÈCES SUR L'ART,
                    "La Conquête de l'ubiquité," Paris.

PREFACE

When Marx undertook his critique of the capitalistic mode of
production, this mode was in its infancy. Marx directed his efforts
in such a way as to give them prognostic value. He went back to
the basic conditions underlying capitalistic production and through
his presentation showed what could be expected of capitalism in

the future. The result was that one could expect it not only to exploit the proletariat with increasing intensity, but ultimately to create conditions which would make it possible to abolish capitalism itself.

The transformation of the superstructure, which takes place far more slowly than that of the substructure, has taken more than half a century to manifest in all areas of culture the change in the conditions of production. Only today can it be indicated what form this has taken. Certain prognostic requirements should be met by these statements. However, theses about the art of the proletariat after its assumption of power or about the art of a classless society would have less bearing on these demands than theses about the developmental tendencies of art under present conditions of production. Their dialectic is no less noticeable in the superstructure than in the economy. It would therefore be wrong to underestimate the value of such theses as a weapon. They brush aside a number of outmoded concepts, such as creativity and genius, eternal value and mystery—concepts whose uncontrolled (and at present almost uncontrollable) application would lead to a processing of data in the Fascist sense. The concepts which are introduced into the theory of art in what follows differ from the more familiar terms in that they are completely useless for the purposes of Fascism. They are, on the other hand, useful for the formulation of revolutionary demands in the politics of art.

I

In principle a work of art has always been reproducible. Manmade artifacts could always be imitated by men. Replicas were made by pupils in practice of their craft, by masters for diffusing their works, and, finally, by third parties in the pursuit of gain. Mechanical reproduction of a work of art, however, represents something new. Historically, it advanced intermittently and in leaps at long intervals, but with accelerated intensity. The Greeks knew only two procedures of technically reproducing works of art: founding and stamping. Bronzes, terra cottas, and coins were the only art works which they could produce in quantity. All others were unique and could not be mechanically reproduced. With the woodcut graphic art became mechanically reproducible for the first time, long before script became reproducible by print. The enormous changes which printing, the mechanical reproduction of writing, has brought about in literature are a familiar story. However, within the phenomenon which we are here examining from the perspective of world history, print is merely a special, though particularly important, case. During the Middle Ages engraving and etching were added to the woodcut; at the beginning of the nineteenth century lithography made its appearance.

With lithography the technique of reproduction reached an essentially new stage. This much more direct process was distinguished by the tracing of the design on a stone rather than its incision on a block of wood or its etching on a copperplate and permitted graphic art for the first time to put its products on the market, not only in large numbers as hitherto, but also in daily changing forms. Lithography enabled graphic art to illustrate everyday life, and it began to keep pace with printing. But only a few decades after its invention, lithography was surpassed by photography. For the first time in the process of pictorial reproduction, photography freed the hand of the most important artistic functions which henceforth devolved only upon the eye looking into a lens. Since the eye perceives more swiftly than the hand can draw, the process of pictorial reproduction was accelerated so enormously that it could keep pace with speech. A film operator shooting a scene in the studio captures the images at the speed of an actor's speech. Just as lithography virtually implied the illustrated newspaper, so did photography foreshadow the sound film. The technical reproduction of sound was tackled at the end of the last century. These convergent endeavors made predictable a situation which Paul Valéry pointed up in this sentence: "Just as water, gas, and electricity are brought into our houses from far off to satisfy our needs in response to a minimal effort, so we shall be supplied with visual or auditory images, which will appear and disappear at a simple movement of the hand, hardly more than a sign." Around 1900 technical reproduction had reached a standard that not only permitted it to reproduce all transmitted works of art and thus to cause the most profound change in their impact upon the public; it also had captured a place of its own among the artistic processes. For the study of this standard nothing is more revealing than the nature of the repercussions that these two different manifestations —the reproduction of works of art and the art of the film—have had on art in its traditional form.

II

Even the most perfect reproduction of a work of art is lacking in one element: its presence in time and space, its unique existence at the place where it happens to be. This unique existence of the work of art determined the history to which it was subject throughout the time of its existence. This includes the changes which it may have suffered in physical condition over the years as well as the various changes in its ownership. The traces of the first can be revealed only by chemical or physical analyses which it is impossible to perform on a reproduction; changes of ownership are subject to a tradition which must be traced from the situation of the original.

The presence of the original is the prerequisite to the concept of authenticity. Chemical analyses of the patina of a bronze can help to establish this, as does the proof that a given manuscript of the Middle Ages stems from an archive of the fifteenth century. The whole sphere of authenticity is outside technical—and, of course, not only technical—reproducibility. Confronted with its manual reproduction, which was usually branded as a forgery, the original preserved all its authority; not so *vis à vis* technical reproduction. The reason is twofold. First, process reproduction is more independent of the original than manual reproduction. For example, in photography, process reproduction can bring out those aspects of the original that are unattainable to the naked eye yet accessible to the lens, which is adjustable and chooses its angle at will. And photographic reproduction, with the aid of certain processes, such as enlargement or slow motion, can capture images which escape natural vision. Secondly, technical reproduction can put the copy of the original into situations which would be out of reach for the original itself. Above all, it enables the original to meet the beholder halfway, be it in the form of a photograph or a phonograph record. The cathedral leaves its locale to be received in the studio of a lover of art; the choral production, performed in an auditorium or in the open air, resounds in the drawing room.

The situations into which the product of mechanical reproduction can be brought may not touch the actual work of art, yet the quality of its presence is always depreciated. This holds not only for the art work but also, for instance, for a landscape which passes in review before the spectator in a movie. In the case of the art object, a most sensitive nucleus—namely, its authenticity—is interfered with whereas no natural object is vulnerable on that score. The authenticity of a thing is the essence of all that is transmissible from its beginning, ranging from its substantive duration to its testimony to the history which it has experienced. Since the historical testimony rests on the authenticity, the former, too, is jeopardized by reproduction when substantive duration ceases to matter. And what is really jeopardized when the historical testimony is affected is the authority of the object.

One might subsume the eliminated element in the term "aura" and go on to say: that which withers in the age of mechanical reproduction is the aura of the work of art. This is a symptomatic process whose significance points beyond the realm of art. One might generalize by saying: the technique of reproduction detaches the reproduced object from the domain of tradition. By making many reproductions it substitutes a plurality of copies for a unique existence. And in permitting the reproduction to meet the beholder or listener in his own particular situation, it reactivates the object reproduced. These two processes lead to a tremendous shattering of tradition which is the obverse of the contemporary crisis and renewal of mankind. Both processes are intimately connected with the contemporary mass movements. Their most powerful agent is the film. Its social significance, particularly in its most positive form, is inconceivable without its destructive, cathartic aspect, that is, the liquidation of the traditional value of the cultural heritage. This phenomenon is most palpable in the great historical films. It extends to ever new positions. In 1927 Abel Gance exclaimed enthusiastically: "Shakespeare, Rembrandt, Beethoven will make films . . . all legends, all mythologies and all myths, all founders of religion, and the very religions . . . await their exposed resurrection, and the heroes crowd each other at the gate." Presumably without intending it, he issued an invitation to a far-reaching liquidation.

III

During long periods of history, the mode of human sense perception changes with humanity's entire mode of existence. The manner in which human sense perception is organized, the medium in which it is accomplished, is determined not only by nature but by historical circumstances as well. The fifth century, with its great shifts of population, saw the birth of the late Roman art industry and the Vienna Genesis, and there developed not only an art different from that of antiquity but also a new kind of perception. The scholars of the Viennese school, Riegl and Wickhoff, who resisted the weight of classical tradition under which these later art forms had been buried, were the first to draw conclusions from them concerning the organization of perception at the time. However far-reaching their insight, these scholars limited themselves to showing the significant, formal hallmark which characterized perception in late Roman times. They did not attempt—and, perhaps, saw no way—to show the social transformations expressed by these changes of perception. The conditions for an analogous insight are more favorable in the present. And if changes in the medium of contemporary perception can be comprehended as decay of the aura, it is possible to show its social causes.

The concept of aura which was proposed above with reference to historical objects may usefully be illustrated with reference to the aura of natural ones. We define the aura of the latter as the unique phenomenon of a distance, however close it may be. If, while resting on a summer afternoon, you follow with your eyes a mountain range on the horizon or a branch which casts its shadow over you, you experience the aura of those mountains, of that branch. This image makes it easy to comprehend the social bases of the contemporary decay of the aura. It rests on two circumstances, both of which are related to the increasing significance of the masses in contemporary life. Namely, the desire of contemporary masses to bring things "closer" spatially and humanly, which is just as ardent as their bent toward overcoming the uniqueness of every reality by accepting its reproduction. Every day the urge grows stronger to get hold of an object at very close range by way of its likeness, its reproduction. Unmistakably, reproduction as offered by picture magazines and newsreels differs from the image seen by the unarmed eye. Uniqueness and permanence are as closely linked in the latter as are transitoriness and reproducibility in the former. To pry an object from its shell, to destroy its aura, is the mark of a perception whose "sense of the universal equality of things" has increased to such a degree that it extracts it even from a unique object by means of reproduction. Thus is manifested in the field of perception what in the theoretical sphere is noticeable in the increasing importance of statistics. The adjustment of reality to the masses and of the masses to reality is a process of unlimited scope, as much for thinking as for perception.

IV

The uniqueness of a work of art is inseparable from its being imbedded in the fabric of tradition. This tradition itself is thoroughly alive and extremely changeable. An ancient statue of Venus, for example, stood in a different traditional context with the Greeks, who made it an object of veneration, than with the clerics of the Middle Ages, who viewed it as an ominous idol. Both of them, however, were equally confronted with its uniqueness, that is, its aura. Originally the contextual integration of art in tradition found its expression in the cult. We know that the earliest art works originated in the service of a ritual—first the magical, then the religious kind. It is significant that the existence of the work of art with reference to its aura is never entirely separated from its ritual function. In other words, the unique value of the "authentic" work of art has its basis in ritual, the location of its original use value. This ritualistic basis, however remote, is still recognizable as secularized ritual even in the most profane forms of the cult of beauty. The secular cult of beauty, developed during the Renaissance and prevailing for three centuries, clearly showed that ritualistic basis in its decline and the first deep crisis which befell it. With the advent of the first truly revolutionary means of reproduction, photography, simultaneously with the rise of socialism, art sensed the approaching crisis which has become evident a century later. At the time, art reacted with the doctrine of *l'art pour l'art*, that is, with a theology of art. This gave rise to what might be called a negative theology in the form of the idea of "pure" art, which not only denied any social function of art but also any categorizing by subject matter. (In poetry, Mallarmé was the first to take this position.)

An analysis of art in the age of mechanical reproduction must do justice to these relationships, for they lead us to an all-important insight: for the first time in world history, mechanical reproduction emancipates the work of art from its parasitical dependence on ritual. To an ever greater degree the work of art reproduced becomes the work of art designed for reproducibility. From a photographic negative, for example, one can make any number of prints; to ask for the "authentic" print makes no sense. But the instant the criterion of authenticity ceases to be applicable to artistic production, the total function of art is reversed. Instead of being based on ritual, it begins to be based on another practice—politics.

V

Works of art are received and valued on different planes. Two polar types stand out: with one, the accent is on the cult value; with the other, on the exhibition value of the work. Artistic production begins with ceremonial objects destined to serve in a cult. One may assume that what mattered was their existence, not their being on view. The elk portrayed by the man of the Stone Age on the walls of his cave was an instrument of magic. He did expose it to his fellow men, but in the main it was meant for the spirits. Today the cult value would seem to demand that the work of art remain hidden. Certain statues of gods are accessible only to the priest in the cella; certain Madonnas remain covered nearly all year round; certain sculptures on medieval cathedrals are invisible to the spectator on ground level. With the emancipation of the various art practices from ritual go increasing opportunities for the exhibition of their products. It is easier to exhibit a portrait bust that can be sent here and there than to exhibit the statue of a divinity that has its fixed place in the interior of a temple. The same holds for the painting as against the mosaic or fresco that preceded it. And even though the public presentability of a mass originally may have been just as great as that of a symphony, the latter originated at the moment when its public presentability promised to surpass that of the mass.

With the different methods of technical reproduction of a work of art, its fitness for exhibition increased to such an extent that the quantitative shift between its two poles turned into a qualitative transformation of its nature. This is comparable to the situation of the work of art in prehistoric times when, by the absolute emphasis on its cult value, it was, first and foremost, an instrument of magic. Only later did it come to be recognized as a work of art. In the same way today, by the absolute emphasis on its exhibition value the work of art becomes a creation with entirely new functions, among which the one we are conscious of, the artistic function, later may be recognized as incidental. This much is certain: today photography and the film are the most serviceable exemplifications of this new function.

VI

In photography, exhibition value begins to displace cult value all along the line. But cult value does not give way without resistance. It retires into an ultimate retrenchment: the human countenance. It is no accident that the portrait was the focal point of early photography. The cult of remembrance of loved ones, absent or dead, offers a last refuge for the cult value of the picture. For the last time the aura emanates from the early photographs in the fleeting expression of a human face. This is what constitutes their melancholy, incomparable beauty. But as man withdraws from the photographic image, the exhibition value for the first time shows its superiority to the ritual value. To have pinpointed this new stage constitutes the incomparable significance of Atget, who, around 1900, took photographs of deserted Paris streets. It has quite justly been said of him that he photographed them like scenes of crime. The scene of a crime, too, is deserted; it is photographed for the purpose of establishing evidence. With Atget, photographs become standard evidence for historical occurrences, and acquire a hidden political significance. They demand a specific kind of approach; free-floating contemplation is not appropriate to them. They stir the viewer; he feels challenged by them in a new way. At the same time picture magazines begin to put up signposts for him, right ones or wrong ones, no matter. For the first time, captions have become obligatory. And it is clear that they have an altogether different character than the title of a painting. The directives which the captions give to those looking at pictures in illustrated magazines soon become even more explicit and more imperative in the film where the meaning of each single picture appears to be prescribed by the sequence of all preceding ones.

VII

The nineteenth-century dispute as to the artistic value of painting versus photography today seems devious and confused. This does not diminish its importance, however; if anything, it underlines it. The dispute was in fact the symptom of a historical transformation the universal impact of which was not realized by either of the rivals. When the age of mechanical reproduction separated art from its basis in cult, the semblance of its autonomy disappeared forever. The resulting change in the function of art transcended the perspective of the century; for a long time it even escaped that of the twentieth century, which experienced the development of the film.

Earlier much futile thought had been devoted to the question of whether photography is an art. The primary question—whether the very invention of photography had not transformed the entire nature of art—was not raised. Soon the film theoreticians asked the same ill-considered question with regard to the film. But the difficulties which photography caused traditional aesthetics were mere child's play as compared to those raised by the film. Whence the insensitive and forced character of early theories of the film. Abel Gance, for instance, compares the film with hieroglyphs: "Here, by a remarkable regression, we have come back to the level of expression of the Egyptians. . . . Pictorial language has not yet matured because our eyes have not yet adjusted to it. There is as yet insufficient respect for, insufficient cult of, what it expresses." Or, in the words of Séverin-Mars: "What art has been granted a dream more poetical and more real at the same time! Approached in this fashion the film might represent an incomparable means of expression. Only the most high-minded persons, in the most perfect and mysterious moments of their lives, should be allowed to enter its ambience." Alexandre Arnoux concludes his fantasy about the silent film with the question: "Do not all the bold descriptions we have given amount to the definition of prayer?" It is instructive to note how their desire to class the film among the "arts" forces these theoreticians to read ritual elements into it—with a striking lack of discretion. Yet when these speculations were published, films like L'Opinion publique and The Gold Rush had already appeared. This, however, did not keep Abel Gance from adducing hieroglyphs for purposes of comparison, nor Séverin-Mars from speaking of the film as one might speak of paintings by Fra Angelico. Characteristically, even today ultrareactionary authors give the film a similar contextual significance—if not an outright sacred one, then at least a supernatural one. Commenting on Max Reinhardt's film version of A Midsummer Night's Dream, Werfel states that undoubtedly it was the sterile copying of the exterior world with its streets, interiors, railroad stations, restaurants, motorcars, and beaches which until now had obstructed the elevation of the film to the realm of art. "The film has not yet realized its true meaning, its real possibilities . . . these consist in its unique faculty to express by natural means and with incomparable persuasiveness all that is fairylike, marvelous, supernatural."

VIII

The artistic performance of a stage actor is definitely presented to the public by the actor in person; that of the screen actor, however, is presented by a camera, with a twofold consequence. The camera that presents the performance of the film actor to the public need not respect the performance as an integral whole. Guided by the cameraman, the camera continually changes its position with respect to the performance. The sequence of positional views which the editor composes from the material supplied him constitutes the completed film. It comprises certain factors of movement which are in reality those of the camera, not to mention special camera angles, close-ups, etc. Hence, the performance of the actor is subjected to a series of optical tests. This is the first consequence of the fact that the actor's performance is presented by means of a camera. Also, the film actor lacks the opportunity of the stage actor to adjust to the audience during his performance, since he does not present his performance to the audience in person. This permits the audience to take the position of a critic, without experiencing any personal contact with the actor. The audience's identification with the actor is really an identification with the camera. Consequently the audience takes the position of the camera; its approach is that of testing. This is not the approach to which cult values may be exposed.

IX

For the film, what matters primarily is that the actor represents himself to the public before the camera, rather than representing someone else. One of the first to sense the actor's metamorphosis by this form of testing was Pirandello. Though his remarks on the subject in his novel *Si Gira* were limited to the negative aspects of the question and to the silent film only, this hardly impairs their validity. For in this respect, the sound film did not change anything essential. What matters is that the part is acted not for an audience but for a mechanical contrivance—in the case of the sound film, for two of them. "The film actor," wrote Pirandello, "feels as if in exile—exiled not only from the stage but also from himself. With a vague sense of discomfort he feels inexplicable emptiness: his body loses its corporeality, it evaporates, it is deprived of reality, life, voice, and the noises caused by his moving about, in order to be changed into a mute image, flickering an instant on the screen, then vanishing into silence. . . . The projector will play with his shadow before the public, and he himself must be content to play before the camera." This situation might also be characterized as follows: for the first time—and this is the effect of the film—man has to operate with his whole living person, yet forgoing its aura. For aura is tied to his presence; there can be no replica of it. The aura which, on the stage, emanates from Macbeth, cannot be separated for the spectators from that of the actor. However, the singularity of the shot in the studio is that the camera is substituted for the public. Consequently, the aura that envelops the actor vanishes, and with it the aura of the figure he portrays.

It is not surprising that it should be a dramatist such as Pirandello who, in characterizing the film, inadvertently touches on the very crisis in which we see the theater. Any thorough study proves that there is indeed no greater contrast than that of the stage play to a work of art that is completely subject to or, like the film, founded in, mechanical reproduction. Experts have long recognized that in the film "the greatest effects are almost always obtained by 'acting' as little as possible. . . ." In 1932 Rudolf Arnheim saw "the latest trend . . . in treating the actor as a stage prop chosen for its characteristics and . . . inserted at the proper place." With this idea something else is closely connected. The stage actor identifies himself with the character of his role. The film actor very often is denied this opportunity. His creation is by no means all of a piece; it is composed of many separate performances. Besides certain fortuitous considerations, such as cost of studio, availability of fellow players, décor, etc., there are elementary necessities of equipment that split the actor's work into a series of mountable episodes. In particular, lighting and its installation require the presentation of an event that, on the screen, unfolds as a rapid and unified scene, in a sequence of separate shootings which may take hours at the studio; not to mention more obvious montage. Thus a jump from the window can be shot in the studio as a jump from a scaffold, and the ensuing flight, if need be, can be shot weeks later when outdoor scenes are taken. Far more paradoxical cases can easily be construed. Let us assume that an actor is supposed to be startled by a knock at the door. If his reaction is not satisfactory, the director can resort to an expedient: when the actor happens to be at the studio again he has a shot fired behind him without his being forewarned of it. The frightened reaction can be shot now and be cut into the screen version. Nothing more strikingly shows that art has left the realm of the "beautiful semblance" which, so far, had been taken to be the only sphere where art could thrive.

X

The feeling of strangeness that overcomes the actor before the camera, as Pirandello describes it, is basically of the same kind as the estrangement felt before one's own image in the mirror. But now the reflected image has become separable, transportable. And where is it transported? Before the public. Never for a moment does the screen actor cease to be conscious of this fact. While facing the camera he knows that ultimately he will face the public, the consumers who constitute the market. This market, where he offers not only his labor but also his whole self, his heart and soul, is beyond his reach. During the shooting he has as little contact with it as any article made in a factory. This may contribute to that oppression, that new anxiety which, according to Pirandello, grips the actor before the camera. The film responds to the shriveling of the aura with an artificial build-up of the "personality" outside the studio. The cult of the movie star, fostered by the money of the film industry, preserves not the unique aura of the person but the "spell of the personality," the phony spell of a commodity. So long as the movie-makers' capital sets the fashion, as a rule no other revolutionary merit can be accredited to today's film than the promotion of a revolutionary criticism of traditional concepts of art. We do not deny that in some cases today's films can also promote revolutionary criticism of social conditions, even of the distribution of property. However, our present study is no more specifically concerned with this than is the film production of Western Europe.

It is inherent in the technique of the film as well as that of sports that everybody who witnesses its accomplishments is somewhat of an expert. This is obvious to anyone listening to a group of newspaper boys leaning on their bicycles and discussing the outcome of a bicycle race. It is not for nothing that newspaper publishers arrange races for their delivery boys. These arouse great interest among the participants, for the victor has an opportunity to rise from delivery boy to professional racer. Similarly, the newsreel offers everyone the opportunity to rise from passer-by to movie extra. In this way any man might even find himself part of a work of art, as witness Vertoff's *Three Songs About Lenin* or Ivens' *Borinage*. Any man today can lay claim to being filmed. This claim can best be elucidated by a comparative look at the historical situation of contemporary literature.

For centuries a small number of writers were confronted by many thousands of readers. This changed toward the end of the last century. With the increasing extension of the press, which kept placing new political, religious, scientific, professional, and local organs before the readers, an increasing number of readers became writers—at first, occasional ones. It began with the daily press opening to its readers space for "letters to the editor." And today there is hardly a gainfully employed European who could not, in principle, find an opportunity to publish somewhere or other comments on his work, grievances, documentary reports, or that sort of thing. Thus, the distinction between author and public is about to lose its basic character. The difference becomes merely functional; it may vary from case to case. At any moment the reader is ready to turn into a writer. As expert, which he had to become willy-nilly in an extremely specialized work process, even if only in some minor respect, the reader gains access to authorship. In the Soviet Union work itself is given a voice. To present it verbally is part of a man's ability to perform the work. Literary license is now founded on polytechnic rather than specialized training and thus becomes common property.

All this can easily be applied to the film, where transitions that in literature took centuries have come about in a decade. In cinematic practice, particularly in Russia, this change-over has partially become established reality. Some of the players whom we meet in Russian films are not actors in our sense but people who portray *themselves*—and primarily in their own work process. In Western Europe the capitalistic exploitation of the film denies consideration to modern man's legitimate claim to being reproduced. Under these circumstances the film industry is trying hard to spur the interest of the masses through illusion-promoting spectacles and dubious speculations.

XI

The shooting of a film, especially of a sound film, affords a spectacle unimaginable anywhere at any time before this. It presents a process in which it is impossible to assign to a spectator a viewpoint which would exclude from the actual scene such extraneous accessories as camera equipment, lighting machinery, staff assistants, etc.—unless his eye were on a line parallel with the lens. This circumstance, more than any other, renders superficial and insignificant any possible similarity between a scene in the studio and one on the stage. In the theater one is well aware of the place from which the play cannot immediately be detected as illusionary. There is no such place for the movie scene that is being shot. Its illusionary nature is that of the second degree, the result of cutting. That is to say, in the studio the mechanical equipment has penetrated so deeply into reality that its pure aspect freed from the foreign substance of equipment is the result of a special procedure, namely, the shooting by the specially adjusted camera and the mounting of the shot together with other similar ones. The equipment-free aspect of reality here has become the height of artifice; the sight of immediate reality has become an orchid in the land of technology.

Even more revealing is the comparison of these circumstances, which differ so much from those of the theater, with the situation in painting. Here the question is: How does the cameraman compare with the painter? To answer this we take recourse to an analogy with a surgical operation. The surgeon represents the polar opposite of the magician. The magician heals a sick person by the laying on of hands; the surgeon cuts into the patient's body. The magician maintains the natural distance between the patient and himself; though he reduces it very slightly by the laying on of hands, he greatly increases it by virtue of his authority. The surgeon does exactly the reverse; he greatly diminishes the distance between himself and the patient by penetrating into the patient's body, and increases it but little by the caution with which his hand moves among the organs. In short, in contrast to the magician—who is still hidden in the medical practitioner—the surgeon at the decisive moment abstains from facing the patient man to man; rather, it is through the operation that he penetrates into him.

Magician and surgeon compare to painter and cameraman. The painter maintains in his work a natural distance from reality, the cameraman penetrates deeply into its web. There is a tremendous difference between the pictures they obtain. That of the painter is a total one, that of the cameraman consists of multiple fragments which are assembled under a new law. Thus, for contemporary man the representation of reality by the film is incomparably more significant than that of the painter, since it offers, precisely because of the thoroughgoing permeation of reality with mechanical equipment, an aspect of reality which is free of all equipment. And that is what one is entitled to ask from a work of art.

XII

Mechanical reproduction of art changes the reaction of the masses toward art. The reactionary attitude toward a Picasso painting changes into the progressive reaction toward a Chaplin movie. The progressive reaction is characterized by the direct, intimate fusion of visual and emotional enjoyment with the orientation of the expert. Such fusion is of great social significance. The greater the decrease in the social significance of an art form, the sharper the distinction between criticism and enjoyment by the public. The conventional is uncritically enjoyed, and the truly new is criticized with aversion. With regard to the screen, the critical and the receptive attitudes of the public coincide. The decisive reason for this is that individual reactions are predetermined by the mass audience response they are about to produce, and this is nowhere more pronounced than in the film. The moment these responses become manifest they control each other. Again, the comparison with painting is fruitful. A painting has always had an excellent chance to be viewed by one person or by a few. The simultaneous contemplation of paintings by a large public, such as developed in the nineteenth century, is an early symptom of the crisis of painting, a crisis which was by no means occasioned exclusively by photography but rather in a relatively independent manner by the appeal of art works to the masses.

Painting simply is in no position to present an object for simultaneous collective experience, as it was possible for architecture at all times, for the epic poem in the past, and for the movie today. Although this circumstance in itself should not lead one to conclusions about the social role of painting, it does constitute a serious threat as soon as painting, under special conditions and, as it were, against its nature, is confronted directly by the masses. In the churches and monasteries of the Middle Ages and at the princely courts up to the end of the eighteenth century, a collective reception of paintings did not occur simultaneously, but by graduated and hierarchized mediation. The change that has come about is an expression of the particular conflict in which painting was implicated by the mechanical reproducibility of paintings. Although paintings began to be publicly exhibited in galleries and salons, there was no way for the masses to organize and control themselves in their reception. Thus the same public which responds in a progressive manner toward a grotesque film is bound to respond in a reactionary manner to surrealism.

XIII

The characteristics of the film lie not only in the manner in which man presents himself to mechanical equipment but also in the manner in which, by means of this apparatus, man can represent his environment. A glance at occupational psychology illustrates the testing capacity of the equipment. Psychoanalysis illustrates it in a different perspective. The film has enriched our field of perception with methods which can be illustrated by those of Freudian theory. Fifty years ago, a slip of the tongue passed more or less unnoticed. Only exceptionally may such a slip have revealed dimensions of depth in a conversation which had seemed to be taking its course on the surface. Since the *Psychopathology of Everyday Life* things have changed. This book isolated and made analyzable things which had heretofore floated along unnoticed in the broad stream of perception. For the entire spectrum of optical, and now also acoustical, perception the film has brought about a similar deepening of apperception. It is only an obverse of this fact that behavior items shown in a movie can be analyzed much more precisely and from more points of view than those presented on paintings or on the stage. As compared with painting, filmed behavior lends itself more readily to analysis because of its incomparably more precise statements of the situation. In comparison with the stage scene, the filmed behavior item lends itself more readily to analysis because it can be isolated more easily. This circumstance derives its chief importance from its tendency to promote the mutual penetration of art and science. Actually, of a screened behavior item which is neatly brought out in a certain situation, like a muscle of a body, it is difficult to say which is more fascinating, its artistic value or its value for science. To demonstrate the identity of the artistic and scientific uses of photography which heretofore usually were separated will be one of the revolutionary functions of the film.

By close-ups of the things around us, by focusing on hidden details of familiar objects, by exploring common place milieus under the ingenious guidance of the camera, the film, on the one hand, extends our comprehension of the necessities which rule our lives; on the other hand, it manages to assure us of an immense and unexpected field of action. Our taverns and our metropolitan streets, our offices and furnished rooms, our railroad stations and our factories appeared to have us locked up hopelessly. Then came the film and burst this prison-world asunder by the dynamite of the tenth of a second, so that now, in the midst of its far-flung ruins and debris, we calmly and adventurously go traveling. With the close-up, space expands; with slow motion, movement is extended. The enlargement of a snapshot does not simply render more precise what in any case was visible, though unclear: it reveals entirely new structural formations of the subject. So, too, slow motion not only presents familiar qualities of movement but reveals in them entirely unknown ones "which, far from looking like retarded rapid movements, give the effect of singularly gliding, floating, supernatural motions." Evidently a different nature opens itself to the camera than opens to the naked eye—if only because an unconsciously penetrated space is substituted for a space consciously explored by man. Even if one has a general knowledge of the way people walk, one knows nothing of a person's posture during the fractional second of a stride. The act of reaching for a lighter or a spoon is familiar routine, yet we hardly know what really goes on between hand and metal, not to mention how this fluctuates with our moods. Here the camera intervenes with the resources of its lowerings and liftings, its interruptions and isolations, its extensions and accelerations, its enlargements and reductions. The camera introduces us to unconscious optics as does psychoanalysis to unconscious impulses.

XIV

One of the foremost tasks of art has always been the creation of a demand which could be fully satisfied only later. The history of every art form shows critical epochs in which a certain art form aspires to effects which could be fully obtained only with a changed technical standard, that is to say, in a new art form. The extravagances and crudities of art which thus appear, particularly in the so-called decadent epochs, actually arise from the nucleus of its richest historical energies. In recent years, such barbarisms were abundant in Dadaism. It is only now that its impulse becomes discernible: Dadaism attempted to create by pictorial—and literary—means the effects which the public today seeks in the film.

Every fundamentally new, pioneering creation of demands will carry beyond its goal. Dadaism did so to the extent that it sacrificed the market values which are so characteristic of the film in favor of higher ambitions—though of course it was not conscious of such intentions as here described. The Dadaists attached much less importance to the sales value of their work than to its uselessness for contemplative immersion. The studied degradation of their material was not the least of their means to achieve this uselessness. Their poems are "word salad" containing obscenities and every imaginable waste product of language. The same is true of their paintings, on which they mounted buttons and tickets. What they intended and achieved was a relentless destruction of the aura of their creations, which they branded as reproductions with the very means of production. Before a painting of Arp's or a poem by August Stramm it is impossible to take time for contemplation and evaluation as one would before a canvas of Derain's or a poem by Rilke. In the decline of middle-class society, contemplation became a school for asocial behavior; it was countered by distraction as a variant of social conduct. Dadaistic activities actually assured a rather vehement distraction by making works of art the center of scandal. One requirement was foremost: to outrage the public.

From an alluring appearance or persuasive structure of sound the work of art of the Dadaists became an instrument of ballistics. It hit the spectator like a bullet, it happened to him, thus acquiring a tactile quality. It promoted a demand for the film, the distracting element of which is also primarily tactile, being based on changes of place and focus which periodically assail the spectator. Let us compare the screen on which a film unfolds with the canvas of a painting. The painting invites the spectator to contemplation; before it the spectator can abandon himself to his associations. Before the movie frame he cannot do so. No sooner has his eye grasped a scene than it is already changed. It cannot be arrested. Duhamel, who detests the film and knows nothing of its significance, though something of its structure, notes this circumstance as follows: "I can no longer think what I want to think. My thoughts have been replaced by moving images." The spectator's process of association in view of these images is indeed interrupted by their constant, sudden change. This constitutes the shock effect of the film, which, like all shocks, should be cushioned by heightened presence of mind. By means of its technical structure, the film has taken the physical shock effect out of the wrappers in which Dadaism had, as it were, kept it inside the moral shock effect.

XV

The mass is a matrix from which all traditional behavior toward works of art issues today in a new form. Quantity has been transmuted into quality. The greatly increased mass of participants has produced a change in the mode of participation. The fact that the new mode of participation first appeared in a disreputable form must not confuse the spectator. Yet some people have launched spirited attacks against precisely this superficial aspect. Among these, Duhamel has expressed himself in the most radical manner. What he objects to most is the kind of participation which the movie elicits from the masses. Duhamel calls the movie "a pastime for helots, a diversion for uneducated, wretched, worn-out creatures who are consumed by their worries . . . , a spectacle which requires no concentration and presupposes no intelligence . . . , which kindles no light in the heart and awakens no hope other than the ridiculous one of someday becoming a 'star' in Los Angeles." Clearly, this is at bottom the same ancient lament that the masses seek distraction whereas art demands concentration from the spectator. That is a commonplace. The question remains whether it provides a platform for the analysis of the film. A closer look is needed here. Distraction and concentration form polar opposites which may be stated as follows: A man who concentrates before a work of art is absorbed by it. He enters into this work of art the way legend tells of the Chinese painter when he viewed his finished painting. In contrast, the distracted mass absorbs the work of art. This is most obvious with regard to buildings. Architecture has always represented the prototype of a work of art the reception of which is consummated by a collectivity in a state of distraction. The laws of its reception are most instructive.

Buildings have been man's companions since primeval times. Many art forms have developed and perished. Tragedy begins with the Greeks, is extinguished with them, and after centuries its "rules" only are revived. The epic poem, which had its origin in the youth of nations, expires in Europe at the end of the Renaissance. Panel painting is a creation of the Middle Ages, and nothing guarantees its uninterrupted existence. But the human need for shelter is lasting. Architecture has never been idle. Its history is more ancient than that of any other art, and its claim to being a living force has significance in every attempt to comprehend the relationship of the masses to art. Buildings are appropriated in a twofold manner: by use and by perception—or rather, by touch and sight. Such appropriation cannot be understood in terms of the attentive concentration of a tourist before a famous building. On the tactile side there is no counterpart to contemplation on the optical side. Tactile appropriation is accomplished not so much by attention as by habit. As regards architecture, habit determines to a large extent even optical reception. The latter, too, occurs much less through rapt attention than by noticing the object in incidental fashion. This mode of appropriation, developed with reference to architecture, in certain circumstances acquires canonical value. For the tasks which face the human apparatus of perception at the turning points of history cannot be solved by optical means, that is, by contemplation, alone. They are mastered gradually by habit, under the guidance of tactile appropriation.

The distracted person, too, can form habits. More, the ability to master certain tasks in a state of distraction proves that their solution has become a matter of habit. Distraction as provided by art presents a covert control of the extent to which new tasks have become soluble by apperception. Since, moreover, individuals are tempted to avoid such tasks, art will tackle the most difficult and most important ones where it is able to mobilize the masses. Today it does so in the film. Reception in a state of distraction, which is increasing noticeably in all fields of art and is symptomatic of profound changes in apperception, finds in the film its true means of exercise. The film with its shock effect meets this mode of reception halfway. The film makes the cult value recede into the background not only by putting the public in the position of the critic, but also by the fact that at the movies this position requires no attention. The public is an examiner, but an absent-minded one.

EPILOGUE

The growing proletarianization of modern man and the increasing formation of masses are two aspects of the same process. Fascism attempts to organize the newly created proletarian masses without affecting the property structure which the masses strive to eliminate. Fascism sees its salvation in giving these masses not their right, but instead a chance to express themselves. The masses have a right to change property relations; Fascism seeks to give them an expression while preserving property. The logical result of Fascism is the introduction of aesthetics into political life. The violation of the masses, whom Fascism, with its *Führer* cult, forces to their knees, has its counterpart in the violation of an apparatus which is pressed into the production of ritual values.

All efforts to render politics aesthetic culminate in one thing: war. War and war only can set a goal for mass movements on the largest scale while respecting the traditional property system. This is the political formula for the situation. The technological formula may be stated as follows: Only war makes it possible to mobilize all of today's technical resources while maintaining the property system. It goes without saying that the Fascist apotheosis of war does not employ such arguments. Still, Marinetti says in his manifesto on the Ethiopian colonial war: "For twenty-seven years we Futurists have rebelled against the branding of war as antiaesthetic . . . . Accordingly we state: . . . War is beautiful because it establishes man's dominion over the subjugated machinery by means of gas masks, terrifying megaphones, flame throwers, and small tanks. War is beautiful because it initiates the dreamt-of metalization of the human body. War is beautiful because it enriches a flowering meadow with the fiery orchids of machine guns. War is beautiful because it combines the gunfire, the cannonades, the cease-fire, the scents, and the stench of putrefaction into a symphony. War is beautiful because it creates new architecture, like that of the big tanks, the geometrical formation flights, the smoke spirals from burning villages, and many others. . . . Poets and artists of Futurism! . . . remember these principles of an aesthetics of war so that your struggle for a new literature and a new graphic art . . . may be illumined by them!"

This manifesto has the virtue of clarity. Its formulations deserve to be accepted by dialecticians. To the latter, the aesthetics of today's war appears as follows: If the natural utilization of productive forces is impeded by the property system, the increase in technical devices, in speed, and in the sources of energy will press for an unnatural utilization, and this is found in war. The destructiveness of war furnishes proof that society has not been mature enough to incorporate technology as its organ, that technology has not been sufficiently developed to cope with the elemental forces of society. The horrible features of imperialistic warfare are attributable to the discrepancy between the tremendous means of production and their inadequate utilization in the process of production—in other words, to unemployment and the lack of markets. Imperialistic war is a rebellion of technology which collects, in the form of "human material," the claims to which society has denied its natural material. Instead of draining rivers, society directs a human stream into a bed of trenches; instead of dropping seeds from airplanes, it drops incendiary bombs over cities; and through gas warfare the aura is abolished in a new way.

"*Fiat ars—pereat mundus*," says Fascism, and, as Marinetti admits, expects war to supply the artistic gratification of a sense perception that has been changed by technology. This is evidently the consummation of "*l'art pour l'art.*" Mankind, which in Homer's time was an object of contemplation for the Olympian gods, now is one for itself. Its self-alienation has reached such a degree that it can experience its own destruction as an aesthetic pleasure of the first order. This is the situation of politics which Fascism is rendering aesthetic. Communism responds by politicizing art.

1935

A COLLECTIVE TEXT
BY THE EDITORS
OF *CAHIERS DU CINÉMA*
JOHN FORD'S
YOUNG MR. LINCOLN

Lincoln is not the product of popular revolution: the banal game of universal suffrage, ignorant of the great historical tasks that must be achieved, has raised him to the top, him, a plebeian, a self-made man who rose from being a stone breaker to being the Senator for Illinois, a man lacking intellectual brilliance, without any greatness of character, with no exceptional value, because he is an average, well meaning man. (Friedrich Engels and Karl Marx, Die Presse, 12-10-1862.)

At one point in our interview, Mr. Ford was talking about a cut sequence from Young Mr. Lincoln: *and he described Lincoln as a shabby figure, riding into town on a mule, stopping to gaze at a theatre poster. "This poor ape," he said, "wishing he had enough money to see Hamlet." Reading over the edited version of the interview it was one of the few things Ford asked me to change; he said he didn't much like "the idea of calling Mr. Lincoln a poor ape."* (Peter Bogdanovich, John Ford, Studio Vista, London, 1967.)

Young Mr. Lincoln: American film by John Ford. *Script:* Lamar Trotti. *Photography:* Bert Glennon. *Music:* Alfred Newman. *Art director:* Richard Day, Mark Lee Kirk. *Set decorations:* Thomas Little. *Editor:* Walter Thompson. *Costume:* Royer. *Sound assistant:* Robert Parrish. *Cast:* Henry Fonda (Abraham Lincoln), Alice Brady (Abigail Clay), Arleen Wheelan (Hannah Clay), Marjorie Weaver (Mary Todd), Eddie Collins (Efe Turner), Pauline Moore (Ann Rutledge), Ward Bond (J. Palmer Cass), Richard Cromwell (Matt Clay), Donald Meek (John Felder),

Judith Dickens (Carrie Sue), Eddie Quillan (Adam Clay), Spencer Charters (Judge Herbert A. Bell), Milburn Stone (Stephen A. Douglas), Cliff Clark (Sheriff Billings), Robert Lowery (juror), Charles Tannen (Ninian Edwards), Francis Ford (Sam Boone), Fred Kohler, Jr. (Scrub White), Kay Linaker (Mrs. Edwards), Russel Simpson (Woolridge), Charles Halton (Hawthorne), Clarence Wilson (Dr. Mason), Edwin Maxwell (John T. Stuart), Robert Homans (Mr. Clay), Jack Kelly (Matt Clay boy), Dickie Jones (Adam Clay boy), Harry Tyler (barber), Louis Mason (clerk), Jack Pennick (Big Buck), Steven Randall (juror), Paul Burns, Frank Orth, George Chandler, Dave Morris, Dorothy Vaughan, Virginia Brissac, Elizabeth Jones. *Producer:* Kenneth Macgowan. *Executive producer:* Darryl F. Zanuck. *Production:* Cosmopolitan/Twentieth Century Fox, 1939. *Distribution:* Associated Cinemas. Length: 101mn.

1

This text inaugurates a series of studies the need for which was indicated in the editorial of issue No. 218 [*Cahiers du Cinéma*]. We must now specify the objects and method of this work, and the origin of its necessity which has hitherto been merely affirmed.

1. Object: a certain number of "classic" films, which today are *readable* (and, therefore, anticipating our definition of method, we will designate this work as one of reading) insofar as we can distinguish the historicity of their inscription:* the relation of these films to the codes (social, cultural . . .) for which they are a site of intersection, and to other films, themselves held in an intertextual space; therefore, the relation of these films to the ideology which they convey, a particular "phase" which they represent, and to the events (present, past, historical, mythical, fictional) which they aimed to represent.

For convenience we will retain the term "classic" (though obviously in the course of these studies we will have to examine, and perhaps even challenge it, in order finally to construct its theory). The term is convenient in that it roughly desig-

---

*This usage of inscription (*l'inscription*) refers to work done by Jacques Derrida on the concept of *écriture* in *Theorie d'ensemble* (Collection Tel Quel, 1968) which will be taken up in a future issue of *Screen. Cahiers'* point here is that all individual texts are part of and inscribe themselves into one historically determined "text" (*l'histoire textuelle*) within which they are produced; a reading of the individual text therefore requires examining both its dynamic relationship with this general text and the relationship between the general text and specific historical events.—ED. *Screen.*

nates a cinema which has been described as based on analogical representation and linear narrative ("transparence" and
"presence") and is therefore apparently completely held
within the "system" which subtends and unifies these concepts. It has obviously been possible to consider the Hollywood cinema as a model of such "classicism" insofar as its
reception has been totally dictated by this system—and limited to a kind of non-reading of the films assured by their apparent non-writing, which was seen as the very essence of
their mastery.

2. Our work will therefore be a *reading* in the sense of a *re-
scanning* of these films. That is, to define it negatively first: (a)
it will not be a (yet another) commentary. The function of the
commentary is to distill an ideally constituted sense presented
as the object's ultimate meaning (which however remains elusive indefinitely, given the infinite possibilities of talking
about film): a wandering and prolific pseudo-reading which
misses the reality of the inscription, and substitutes for it a
discourse consisting of a simple ideological delineation of
what appear(s) to be the main statement(s) of the film at a
given moment.

(b) Nor will it be a new *interpretation*, i.e., the translation of
what is supposed to be already in the film into a critical system (meta-language) where the interpreter has the kind of absolute knowledge of the exegetist blind to the (historical) ideological determination of his practice and his object-pretext,
when he is not a hermeneute à la Viridiana slotting things into
a pre-ordained structure.

(c) Nor will this be a dissection of an object conceived of as
a closed structure, the cataloguing of progressively smaller and
more "discrete" units: in other words, an inventory of the elements which ignores their predestination for the filmmaker's
writing project and, having added a portion of intelligibility to
the initial object, claims to deconstruct, then reconstruct that
object, without taking any account of the dynamic of the inscription. Not, therefore, a mechanistic structural reading.

(d) Nor finally will it be a demystification in the sense
where it is enough to re-locate the film within its historical determinations, "reveal" its assumptions, declare its problematic
and its aesthetic prejudices and criticise its statement in the
name of a mechanically applied materialist knowledge, in
order to see it collapse and feel no more needs to be said. This
amounts to throwing the baby out with the bathwater without
getting wet. To be more precise, it would be disposing of the
film in a moralist way, with an argument which separates the
"good" from the "bad," and evading any effective reading of

it. (An effective reading can only be such by returning on its own deciphering operation and by integrating its functioning into the text it produces, which is something quite different from brandishing a method—even if it is Marxist-Leninist—and leaving it at that.)

It is worth recalling that the external and mechanistic application of possibly even rigorously constructed concepts has always tried to pass for the exercise of a theoretical practice: and—though this has long been established—that an artistic product cannot be linked to its socio-historical context according to a linear, expressive, direct causality (unless one falls into a reductionist historical determinism), but that it has a complex, mediated and *decentred* relationship with this context, which has to be rigorously specified (which is why it is simplistic to discard "classic" Hollywood cinema on the pretext that since it is part of the capitalist system it can only reflect it). Walter Benjamin has insisted strongly on the necessity to consider literary work (but similarly any art product) not as a reflection of the relations of production, but as having a place *within* these relations. (Obviously he was talking of progressive works, past, present, and to come: but a materialist reading of art products which appear to lack any intentional critical dimension concerning capitalist relations of production must do the same thing. We will return later at greater length to this basic notion of "the author as producer.") In this respect we must once again quote Macherey's theses on literary production (in particular those concerning the Leninist corrections to Trotsky and Plekhanov's simplistic positions on Tolstoy) and Badiou's concerning the autonomy of the aesthetic process and the complex relation historical truth/ideologies/author (as place and not as "internalisation")/work.

And that, given this, denouncing ideological assumptions and ideological production, and designating them as falsification and error, has never sufficed to ensure that those who operated the critique themselves produced truth. Nor what's more has it sufficed to bring out the truth about the very things they are opposing. It is therefore absurd to demand that a film account for what it doesn't say about the positions and the knowledge which form the basis from which it is being questioned; and it is too easy (but of what use?) to "deconstruct" it in the name of this same knowledge (in this case, the science of historical materialism which has to be practised as an active method and not used as a guarantee). Lest we be accused of dishonesty, let us make it clear that the points made in paragraph (d) refer to the most extreme positions within *Cinethique*.

3. At this point we seem to have come up against a contradiction: we are not content to demand that a film justify itself vis à vis its context, and at the same time we refuse to look for "depth," to go from the "literal meaning" to some "secret meaning"; we are not content with what it says (what it intends to say). This is only an apparent contradiction. What will be attempted here through a re-scansion of these films in a process of active reading, is to make them say what they have to say *within* what they leave unsaid, to reveal their constituent lacks; these are neither faults in the work (since these films, as Jean-Pierre Oudart has clearly demonstrated—see the preceding issue [No. 222]—are the work of extremely skilled filmmakers) nor a deception on the part of the author (for why should he practice deception?); they are *structuring absences,* always displaced—an overdetermination which is the only possible basis from which these discourses could be realised, the unsaid included in the said and necessary to its constitution. In short, to use Althusser's expression—"the internal shadows of exclusion."

The films we will be studying do not need filling out, they do not demand a teleological reading, nor do we require them to account for their *external* shadows (except purely and simply to dismiss them); all that is involved is traversing their statement to locate what sets it in place, to double their writing with an active reading to reveal what is already there, but silent, to make them say not only "what this says, but what it doesn't say because it doesn't want to say it" (J. A. Miller, and we would add: what, while intending to leave unsaid, it is nevertheless obliged to say).

4. What is the use of such a work? We would be obliged if the reader didn't envisage this as a "Hollywood revisited." Anyone so tempted is advised to give up the reading with the very next paragraph. To the rest we say: that the structuring absences mentioned above and the establishment of an ersatz which this dictates have some connection with the sexual *other scene*, and that "other scene" which is politics; that the double repression—politics and eroticism—which our reading will bring out (a repression which cannot be indicated once and for all and left at that but rather has to be written into the constantly renewed process of its repression) allows the answer to be deduced; and this is an answer whose very question would not have been possible without the two discourses of overdetermination, the Marxist and the Freudian. This is why we will not choose films for their value as "external masterpieces" but rather because the negatory force of their writing provides enough *scope* for a reading—because they can be re-written.

2. HOLLYWOOD IN 1938–39

One of the consequences of the 1929 economic crisis was that the major banking groups (Morgan, Rockefeller, DuPont, Hearst, General Motors, etc.) strengthened their grip on the Hollywood firms which were having problems (weakened by the talkies' "new patents war").

As early as 1935, the five Major Companies (Paramount, Warner, MGM, Fox, RKO) and the three Minor (Universal, Columbia, United Artists) were totally controlled by bankers and financiers, often directly linked to one company or another. Big Business's grip on Hollywood had already translated itself (aside from economic management and the ideological orientation of the American Cinema) into the regrouping of the eight companies in the MPPA (Motion Pictures Producers Association) and the creation of a central system of self-censorship (the Hays code—the American bank is known to be puritanical: the major shareholder of the Metropolitan in New York, Morgan, exercised a real censorship on its programmes).

It was precisely in 1935 that, under the aegis of the Chase National Bank, William Fox's Fox (founded in 1914) merged with Darryl F. Zanuck's 20th Century Productions, to form 20th Century Fox, where Zanuck became vice-president and took control.

During the same period, and mainly in 1937–38 the American cinemas suffered from a very serious drop in box-office receipts (this is first attributed to the consequences of the recession, then, with the situation getting worse, to lack of regeneration of Hollywood's stock of stars); the bank's boards, very worried, ordered a *maximum reduction in costs of production.* This national marketing crisis (in a field in which Hollywood films previously covered their entire costs, foreign sales being mainly a source of profits) was made even worse by the reduced income from foreign sales; this was due to the political situation in Europe, the gradual closure of the German and Italian markets to American films, and the currency blockade set up by these two countries.

3. THE USA IN 1938–39

In 1932, in the middle of the economic crisis, the Democrat Roosevelt became President, succeeding the Republican Hoover whose policies, both economic (favourable to the trusts, deflationist) and social (leaving local groups and charitable organisations to deal with unemployment: cf. *Mr. Deeds*

Goes to Town, Capra) had been incapable of avoiding the crisis and also of suppressing its effects. Roosevelt's policies were the opposite; federal intervention in the whole country's economic and social life, States as private powers (New Deal); establishment of federal intervention and public works agencies, impinging on the rights and areas previously reserved to State legislature and private companies (a controlled economy, social budget etc.): so many measures which encountered violent opposition from the Republicans and Big Business. In 1935 they succeeded: the Supreme Court declares Roosevelt's federal economic intervention agencies to be unconstitutional (because they interfere with the rights of the States). But Roosevelt's second victory in 1936 smashed these manoeuvres, and the Supreme Court, threatened with reform, ended up by recognising the New Deal's social policies and (among others) the right to unionise.

At the level of the structures of American society, the crisis and its remedies have caused the strengthening of the federal State and increased its control over the individual States and the Trust's policies: by its "conditional subsidies," its nationwide economic programmes, its social regulations, the federal government took control of vast areas which had previously depended only on the authority of the States and on the interests of free enterprise. In 1937, "the dualist" interpretation of the 10th amendment of the Constitution—which forbade any federal intervention in the economic and social policies of the States (their private domain)—was abrogated by the Supreme Court from its judgments. This strengthening of federal power at all levels had the effect of *increasing the President's power*.

But, as early as 1937, a new economic crisis emerged: economic activity dropped by 37% compared to 1929, the number of unemployed was again over 10 million in 1938, and despite the refloating of major public works, stayed at 9 million in 1939 (cf. *The Grapes of Wrath*). The war (arms industries becoming predominant in the economy) was to help end the new crisis by allowing full employment. . . .

Federal centralism, isolationism, economic reorganisation (including Hollywood), strengthening of the Democrat-Republican opposition, new threats of internal and international crisis, crisis and restrictions in Hollywood itself; such is the fairly gloomy context of the *Young Mr. Lincoln* (1939) undertaking.

It is no doubt difficult, but necessary to attempt to estimate the total and respective importance of these factors to the project and the ideological "message" of the film. In Hollywood, more than anywhere else the cinema is not "innocent." Creditor of the capitalist system, subject to its constraints, its crises, its contradictions, the American cinema, the main instrument of the ideological super-structure, is heavily determined at every level of its existence. As a product of the capitalist system and of its ideology, its role is in turn to reproduce the one and thereby to help the survival of the other. Each film, however, is inserted into this circuit according to its specificity, and there has been no analysis if one is content to say that each Hollywood film confirms and spreads the ideology of American capitalism: it is the precise articulations (rarely the same from one film to the next) of the film and of the ideology which must be studied (see 1).

4. FOX AND ZANUCK

20th Century Fox (which produced *Young Mr. Lincoln*), because of its links with Big Business, also supports the Republican Party. From its inception the Republican Party has been the party of the "Great Families." Associated with (and an instrument of) industrial development, it rapidly became the "party of Big Business" and follows its social and economic directives: protectionism to assist industry, anti-unionist struggle, moral reaction and racism (directed against immigrants and Blacks—whom the party had fleetingly championed in Lincoln's time: but it is common knowledge that this was due once again to economic reasons and to pressures from religious groups, groups which fifty years later, were to lead a campaign against everything that is "unamerican").

In power from 1928 to 1932 with Hoover as president, the Republican Party is financed by some of Hollywood's masters (Rockefeller, DuPont de Nemours, General Motors, etc.). At the elections in 1928, 87% of the people listed in *Who's Who in America* supported Hoover. He has put the underwriters of Capital at key posts in the administration: the Secretary to the Treasury is none other than Mellon, the richest man in the world (take an example of his policies: he brings down the income tax ceiling from 65% in 1919 to 50% in 1921, and 26% in 1929).

Forced by Roosevelt to make a number of concessions, American Big Business goes to war against the New Deal as soon as the immediate effects of the depression decrease (for example, the private electricity companies withdraw their advertising—which, in the USA, is equivalent to a death sentence—from the newspapers which support Roosevelt and his

Tennessee Valley Authority) and they do everything in their power to win the 1940 election.

All this allows us to assume that in 1938–39, Fox, managed by the (also) Republican Zanuck, participated in its own way in the Republican offensive by producing a film on the legendary character Lincoln. Of all the Republican Presidents, he is not only the most famous, but on the whole the only one capable of attracting mass support, because of his humble origins, his simplicity, his righteousness, his historical role, and the legendary aspects of his career and his death.

This choice is, no doubt, all the less fortuitous on the part of Fox (which—through Zanuck and the contracted producer Kenneth Macgowan—is as usual responsible for taking the initiative in the project, and not Ford) that during the preceding season, the Democrat Sherwood's play "Abe Lincoln in Illinois" had been a great success on Broadway. With very likely the simultaneous concern to anticipate the adaptations planned in Hollywood of Sherwood's play (John Cromwell's film with Raymond Massey came out the same year and, unlike Ford's, was very successful), and to reverse the impact of the play and of Lincoln's myth in favour of the Republicans, Zanuck immediately put *Young Mr. Lincoln* into production— it would, however, be wrong to exaggerate the film's political determinism which cannot, under any circumstances, be seen, in contrast, for example, to Zanuck's personal productions, *The Grapes of Wrath*, or *Wilson*, as promoting the company's line.

Producer Kenneth Macgowan's past is that of a famous theatre man. Along with Robert Edmund Jones and Eugene O'Neill, he has been manager of the Provincetown Playhouse; they had had a considerable influence on American theatre. A friend of Ford's, whom he met at RKO during the period of *The Informer*, he moved over to Fox in 1935 (there he produced *Four Men and a Prayer* among others) and became the man responsible for historical biographies which constitute the core of the company's productions.

Young Mr. Lincoln is far from being one of Fox's most important productions in 1939, but this film was shot in particularly favourable conditions; it is one of the few cases in which the original undertaking was least distorted, at least at the production stage: of thirty films produced by Macgowan in the eight years he spent at Fox (1935–43) this is one of the only two which were written by only one scriptwriter (Lamar Trotti) (the other being *The Return of Frank James*, written by S. M. Hellman). Another thing to remark on: these two scripts were written in close collaboration with the directors, who were, therefore, involved at a very early stage instead of being chosen at the last minute, as is the custom, even at Fox (the "directors studio"). Ford even says of the script: "We wrote it together" (with L. Trotti) a rare if not exceptional statement coming from him.

Lamar Trotti had already written two comedies on old America for Ford (of the species known as "Americana"), *Judge Priest* and *Steamboat Round the Bend*, before specialising in historical films with Fox (such as *Drums Along the Mohawk*, directed by Ford after *Young Mr. Lincoln*).

The background to a whole section of the script is the obsession with lynching and legality which is so strong in the thirties' cinema, because of the increase in expeditive justice (lynching), the consequences of gangsterism, the rebirth of terrorist organsations such as the KKK (cf. Lang's *Fury*, Mervyn LeRoy's *They Won't Forget*, Archie Mayo's *Black Legion*). Trotti, a southerner (he was born in Atlanta and had been a crime reporter before editing a local Hearst paper), combined one of Lincoln's most famous anecdotes with a memory from his youth. "When Trotti was a reporter in Georgia he had covered the trial of two young men accused of murder at which their mother, the only witness, would not tell which son had committed the crime. Both were hanged" (Robert G. Dickson, "Kenneth Macgowan" in *Films in Review*, October 1963). In Lincoln's story, a witness stated having seen, in the moonlight an acquaintance of Lincoln's (Duff Armstrong) participate in a murder. Using an almanac as evidence, Lincoln argued that the night was too dark for the witness to have seen anything and thus obtained Armstrong's acquittal with this plea.

5. FORD AND LINCOLN

Ford had already spent the greater part of his career with Fox: he made thirty-eight movies between 1920 and 1935! Since Zanuck's take over, he had made four movies in two years, the first, in 1936, *The Prisoner of Shark Island* ("I haven't killed Lincoln"). Thus it was to one of the company's older and more trustworthy directors that the project was entrusted. The same year, again with Zanuck, Ford shot *Drums Along the Mohawk* (whose ideological orientation is glaringly obvious: the struggle of the pioneers, side by side with Washington and the Whigs against the English in alliance with the Indians) and, in 1940, *The Grapes of Wrath*, which paints a very gloomy portrait of the America of 1938–39. Despite the fact that he calls himself a-political we know that Ford in any case greatly admires Lincoln as a historical figure and as a person: Ford, too, claims humble peasant origins—but this closeness with Lincoln as a man is, however, moderated by the fact that Ford is also, if not primarily, Irish and Catholic.

In 1924 already, in *The Iron Horse,* Lincoln appears as favouring the construction of the intercontinental railway (industry and unification); at the beginning of *The Prisoner of Shark Island,* we see Lincoln requesting "Dixie" from an orchestra after the Civil War (this is the tune which he "already" plays in *Young Mr. Lincoln*): symbolically, the emphasis is put on Lincoln's unifying, nonvindictive side and his deep southern sympathies by means of the hymn of the Confederation; in *Sergeant Rutledge* (1960) he is evoked by the Blacks as their Saviour; the anti-slavery aspect; in *How the West Was Won* (1962) the strategist is presented; finally in *Cheyenne Autumn* (1964), a cornered politician turns to a portrait of Lincoln, presented as the model for the resolution of any crisis.

Each of these films thus concentrates on a particular aspect either of Lincoln's synthetic personality or of his complex historical role; he thus appears to be a sort of universal referent which can be activated in all situations. As long as Lincoln appears in Ford's fiction as a myth, a figure of reference, a symbol of America, his intervention is natural, apparently in complete harmony with Ford's morality and ideology; the situation is different in a film like *Young Mr. Lincoln* where he becomes the protagonist of the fiction. We will see that he can only be inscribed as a Fordian character at the expense of a number of distortions and reciprocal assaults (by him on the course of fiction and by fiction on his historical truth).

6. IDEOLOGICAL UNDERTAKING

What is the subject of *Young Mr. Lincoln?* Ostensibly and textually it is "Lincoln's youth" (on the classic cultural model—"Apprenticeship and Travels"). In fact—through the expedient of a simple chronicle of events presented (through the presence and actualisation effect specific to classic cinema) as if they were taking place for the first time under our eyes, it is the *reformulation* of the historical figure of Lincoln on the level of the myth and the eternal.

This ideological project may appear to be clear and simple— of the edifying and apologetic type. Of course, if one considers its statements alone, extracting it as a *separable ideological statement* disconnected from the complex network of determinations through which it is realised and inscribed —through which it possibly even criticises itself—then it

706   FILM: PSYCHOLOGY, SOCIETY, AND IDEOLOGY

is easy to operate an illusory deconstruction of the film through a reading of the demystificatory type (see 1). Our work, on the contrary, will consist in activating this network in its complexity, where philosophical assumptions (idealism, theologism), political determinations (republicanism, capitalism) and the relatively autonomous aesthetic process (characters, cinematic *signifiers,* narrative mode) specific to Ford's writing, intervene simultaneously. If our work, which will necessarily be held to the linear sequentiality of the discourse, should isolate the orders of determination interlocking in the film, it will always be in the perspective of their relations: it therefore demands a recurrent reading, on all levels.

7. METHODOLOGY

Young Mr. Lincoln, like the vast majority of Hollywood films, follows linear and chronological narrative, in which events appear to follow each other according to a certain "natural" sequence and logic. Thus two options were open to us: either, in discussing each of the determining moments, to simultaneously refer to all the scenes involved; or to present each scene in its fictional chronological *order* and discuss the different determining moments, emphasising in each case what we believe to be the main determinant (the key signification), and indicating the secondary determinants, which may in turn become the main determinant in other scenes. That first method thus sets up the film as the object of a reading (a text) and then supposedly takes up the totality of its overdetermination networks simultaneously, *without taking account of the repressive operation* which, in each scene, determines the realisation of a key signification; while the second method *bases itself on the key signification of each scene,* in order to understand the scriptural operation (overdetermination and repression) which has set it up.

The first method has the drawback of turning the film into a text which is *readable a priori;* the second has the advantage of making the reading itself participate in the *film's process of becoming-a-text,* and of authorising such a reading only by what authorises it in each successive moment of the film. We have therefore chosen the latter method. The fact that the course of our reading will be modelled on the "cutting" of the film into sequences is absolutely intentional, but the work will involve breaking down the closures of the individual scenes by setting them in action with each other and *in* each other.

8. THE POEM

After the credits (and in the same graphic style: i.e., engraved in marble) there is a poem which consists of a number of questions which "if she were to come back on earth," Lincoln's mother would ask, concerning the destiny of her son.

(a) Let us simply observe for the moment that the figure of the mother is inscribed from the start, and that it is an absent Mother, already dead, a symbolic figure who will only later make her full impact.

(b) The enumeration of questions on the other hand programmes the development of the film by designating Lincoln's problematic as being that of a choice: the interrogative form of this poem, like a matrix, generates the binary system (the necessity to choose between two careers, two pies, two plaintiffs, two defendants, etc.) according to which the fiction is organised (see 14).

(c) In fact, the main function of the poem, which pretends that the questions posed therein haven't yet been answered (whereas they are only the simulation of questions since they presume the spectator's knowledge of Lincoln's *historical character*), is to set up the dualist nature of film and to initiate the process of a double reading. By inviting the spectator to ask himself "questions" to which he already has the answers, the poem induces him to look at history—something which, for him, has already happened—as if it were "still to happen." Similarly, by on the one hand playing on a fictional structure of the "chronicle" type ("natural" juxtaposition and succession of events, as if they were not dictated by any determinism or directed towards a necessary end), and on the other hand by contriving, in the scenes where a crucial choice must be made by the character, a margin of *feigned indecisiveness* (as if the game had not already been played, Lincoln had not entered history, and as if he was taking every one of his decisions on the spot, in the present), the film thus effects a *naturalisation* of the Lincolnian myth (which already exists as such in the mind of the spectator).

The retroactive action of the spectator's knowledge of the myth on the chronicle of events and the naturalist rewriting of the myth in the divisions of this chronicle thus impose a reading in the future perfect. "What is realised in my story is not the past definite of what once was since it is no more, nor the perfect of what has been in what I am, but the future perfect of what I will have been for what I am in the process of becoming" (Lacan).

A classic *ideological* operation manifests itself here, normally, through questions asked after the event whose answer, which has already been given, is the very condition for the existence of the question.

9. THE ELECTORAL SPEECH

First scene. A politician dressed in townclothes (John T. Stuart, later to become Lincoln's associate in Springfield) addresses a few farmers. He denounces the corrupt politicians, who are in power, and Andrew Jackson, President of the USA; he then introduces the local candidate whom he is sponsoring: young Lincoln. The first shot, in which we see Lincoln, shows him sitting on a barrel leaning backwards, in shirtsleeves, wearing heavy boots (one recognises the classic casualness of Ford's hero, who has returned and/or is above everything). In the next shot, addressing the audience of farmers, Lincoln in a friendly tone (but not without a hint of nervousness) declares: "My politics are short and sweet like your ladies' dances; I am in favour of a National Bank and for everybody's participation in wealth." His first words are "You all know who I am, plain Abraham Lincoln"—this is meant not only for the spectators in the film, who are anyway absent from the screen, but also to involve the spectator of the movie, brought into the cinematic space; thus this treatment in the future perfect is immediately confirmed (see 8).

This programme is that of the Whig party, at that time in opposition. It is in essence the programme of nascent American capitalism: protectionism to favour national industrial production, National Bank to favour the circulation of capital in all the states. The first point traditionally has a place in the programme of the Republican Party (it is thus easily recognisable to the spectator of 1939); the second calls to mind a point in history: while in power before 1830, the Whigs had created a National Bank (helping industrial development in the North) whose powers Jackson, who succeeded them, attempted to weaken: the defence of this bank was thus one of the demands of the Whigs, who later became Republicans.

(a) The specifically *political* notations which introduce the film, have the obvious function of presenting Lincoln as the candidate (that is, in the future perfect, the President, the champion) of the Republicans.

(b) But the scorn which is immediately shown towards the "corrupt politicians" and the strength in the contrast of Lincoln's programme which is simple as "a dance," have the effect of introducing him (and the Republicans in his wake) as

the opposition and the remedy to such "politics." Furthermore
we will see later that it is not only his opponents' politics
which are "corrupt," but all politics, condemned in the name
of morality (the figure of Lincoln will be contrasted, with that
of his opponent Douglas, with that of the prosecutor, as the
defender of Justice versus the politicians, the Uncompromising versus the manipulators).

This disparagement of politics carries and confirms the *idealist* project of the film (see 4 and 6): moral virtues are worth
more than political guile, the Spirit more than the Word (cf. 4,
6, 8). (Likewise, politics appears again, later, as the object of
discussion among drunks—quarrel between J. P. Cass and his
acolyte—or of socialite conversation: carriage scene between
Mary Todd and Douglas).

But what is most significant here is that the points of the
electoral programme are *the only indications* of a *positive relation*
between Lincoln and politics, all others being negative (separating Lincoln from the mass of "politicians").

(c) We may be surprised that a film on Lincoln's youth
could thus empty out the truly political dimension from the career of the future President. This massive omission is too useful to the film's ideological purpose to be fortuitous. By playing once again on the spectator's knowledge of Lincoln's
political and historical role, it is possible to establish the idea
that these were founded on and validated by a Morality superior to all politics (and could thus be neglected in favour of
their Cause) and that Lincoln always draws his prestige and
his strength from an intimate relationship with Law, from a
(natural and/or divine) knowledge of Good and Evil. Lincoln
starts with politics but soon rises to the moral level, divine
right, which for an idealist discourse—originates and valorises all politics. Indeed, the first scene of the film already
shows Lincoln as a political candidate without providing any
information either on what may have brought him to this
stage: *concealment of origins* (both his personal—family
origins and those of his political knowledge, however basic:
that is "his education") which establishes the mythical nature
of the character; or on the results of this electoral campaign
(we know that he was defeated, and that the Republicans' failure resulted in the shelving of the National Bank, among other
things): as if they were in fact of no importance in the light of
the already evident significance of fate and the myth. Lincoln's
character makes all politics appear trivial.

But this very *repression* of politics, on which the ideological
undertaking of the film is based, is itself a *direct result* of political assumptions (the eternal false idealist debate between

morality and politics: Descartes versus Machiavelli) and at the level of its reception by the spectator, this repression is not without consequences of an equally political nature. We know that the ideology of American Capitalism (and the Republican Party which traditionally represents it) is to assert its divine right, to conceptualise it in terms of permanence, naturalism and even biology (cf. Benjamin Franklin's famous formula: "Remember that money has genital potency and fecundity") and to extol it as a universal Good and Power. The enterprise consisting of the concealment of politics (of social relations in America, of Lincoln's career) under the idealist mask of Morality has the effect of regilding the cause of Capital with the gold of myth, by manifesting the "spirituality" in which American Capitalism believes it finds its origins and sees its eternal justification. The seeds of Lincoln's future were already sown in his youth—the future of America (its eternal values) is already written into Lincoln's moral virtues, which include the Republican Party and Capitalism.

(d) Finally, with the total suppression of Lincoln's political dimension, his main historico-political characteristic disappears from the scene of the film: i.e., his struggle against the Slave States. Indeed, neither in the initial political sequence, nor in the rest of the film is this dominant characteristic of his history, of his legend even, indicated, whereas it is mainly to it that Lincoln owes his being inscribed into American history more than any other President (Republican or otherwise).

Strangely enough, only one allusion is made to slavery (this exception has the value of a signal): Lincoln explains to the defendants' family that he had to leave his native state since "with all the slaves coming in, white folks just had a hard time making a living." The fact that this comment emphasises the economic aspects of the problem at the expense of its moral and humantarian aspects would appear to contradict the points outlined above (primacy of morality over politics) if Lincoln had not spoken these words in a scene (see 19) where he puts himself in the imaginary role of the son of the poor farmer family. He recalls his own origins as a poor white who, like everyone else, suffered from unemployment. The accent is thus put on the economic problem, i.e., the problem of the whites, not the blacks.

The *not-said* here, this exclusion from the scene of the film of Lincoln's most notable political dimension, can also not be fortuitous (the "omission" would be enormous!), it too must have *political significance*.

On the one hand, it was indeed necessary to present Lincoln as the unifier, the harmoniser, and not the divider of America (this is why he likes playing "Dixie": he is a Southerner). On the other hand, we know that the Republican Party, abolitionist by economic opportunism, after the Civil War rapidly reappeared as more or less racist and segregationist. (Already, Lincoln was in favour of a progressive emancipation of the blacks, which would only slowly give them equal rights with the whites). He never concealed the restrictions he asked for concerning the integration of blacks. Considering the political impact that the film could have in the context described above (see 3, 4) it would have been in bad taste on both these accounts to insist on Lincoln's liberating role.

This feature is thus silenced, excluded from the hero's youth, as if it had not appeared until later, when all the legendary figure's other features are given by the film as present from the outset and are given value by this predestination.

The shelving of this dimension (the Civil War) which is directly responsible for the Lincolnian Legend thus allows a political use of this legend and, at the same time, by castrating Lincoln of his historico-political dimension, reinforces the idealisation of the myth.

But the exclusion of this dominant sign from Lincoln's politics is also possible because *all the others* are rapidly pushed out (except for the brief positive and negative notations mentioned above which in any case are in play as *indicators* — of the general repression of politics — and of stamping of the Republican cause by the seal of the Myth) and because this fact places the film immediately on the purely ideological plane (Lincoln's a-historical dimension, his symbolic value).

Thus what *projects the political meaning* of a film is not a directly political discourse: it is *a moralising discourse.* History, almost totally reduced to the time scale of the myth with neither past nor future can thus, at best, only survive in the film in the form of a *specific repetition:* on the teleological model of history as a continuous and linear development of a pre-existing *seed,* of the future contained in the past (anticipation, predestination). Everything is there, all the features and characters of the historical scene are in their place (Mary Todd who will become Lincoln's wife, Douglas whom he will beat at the presidential elections, etc., right up to Lincoln's death: in a scene which Fox cut, before the film was first released, one could see Lincoln stop in front of a theatre presenting Hamlet and facing one of the (Booth family) troupe of actors—(his future murderer), the problematic of deciding (see 14) and of unifying is already posed. . . . The only missing thing is the main historical feature, this being the one on which the myth was first constructed.

But such repression is possible (acceptable by the spectator) only inasmuch as the film plays on what is *already known* about Lincoln, treating it as if it were a factor of *non-recognition* and at the limit, a not-known (at least, something that nobody wants to know any more, which for having been known is all the more easily forgotten): it is the already constituted force of the myth which allows not only its reproduction, but also its reorientation. It is the universal knowledge of Lincoln's fate which allows, while restating it, the omission of parts of it. For the problem here is not to build a myth, but to negotiate its realisation and even more to rid it of its historical roots in order to liberate its universal and eternal meaning. "Told," Lincoln's youth is in fact *rewritten* by what has to filter through the Lincolnian myth. The film establishes not only Lincoln's total predestination (teleological axis) but also that *only that to which he has been shown to be predestined* deserves immortality (theological axis). A double operation of addition and subtraction at the end of which the historical axis, having been abolished and mythified, returns cleansed of all impurities and thus recuperable to the service not just of Morality but of the morality re-asserted by capitalist ideology. Morality not only rejects politics and surpasses history, it also rewrites them.

10. THE BOOK

Lincoln's electoral speech seems to open up a fiction: electoral campaign, elections. . . . A problem is presented, which we have the right to expect to see solved, but which in fact will not be solved. To use the Barthesian formula, we have the elements of a hermeneutic chain: enigma (will he or won't he be elected?) and non-resolution. This chain is abandoned by the use of an abrupt fictional displacement: the arrival of the family of farmers. Lincoln is called away to help them. This family comprises the father, the mother and two twelve year old boys. They want to buy some material from Lincoln thus informing us of his occupation: he is a shopkeeper. But the family has no money: Lincoln offers them credit, and confronted by the mother's embarassment, argues that he himself has acquired his shop on credit. The situation is resolved by the use of barter: the family owns a barrel full of old books (left behind by the grandfather). Delighted at the mere mention of a book (legendary thirst for reading) Lincoln respectfully takes one out of the barrel: *as if by chance,* it is Blackstone's "Commentaries." He dusts the book, opens it, reads, realises that it is about Law (he says: "Law") and is delighted that the book is in good condition (the Law is indestructible).

Henry Fonda, in *Young Mr. Lincoln* (1939), "dusts the book, opens it, reads, realizes that it is about Law (he says: 'Law') and is delighted that the book is in good condition (the law is indestructible). . . . It's a *family* . . . of pioneers who are *passing through* that give Lincoln the opportunity of coming in contact with Law . . ." (EDITORS, page 712). Henry Fonda and Pauline Moore in *Young Mr. Lincoln.* "It is in nature that Lincoln communes with Law: It is at the moment of this communion that he meets Woman . . ." (EDITORS, page 715).

(a) It's a *family* (see 19) of pioneers who are *passing through* that give Lincoln the opportunity of coming in contact with Law: emphasis on the luck-predestination connection as well as on the fact that *even without knowing it* it is the humble who transmit Law (religiously kept by the family as a legacy from the ancestor). On the other hand we have here a classic Fordian fictional feature (apart from the family as a displaced centre): meeting and exchange between two groups whose paths need not have crossed (a new fictional sequence is born from this very meeting; it is first presented as a suspension and simple digressive delay of the main narrative axis, later it constitutes itself as being central, until another sequence arises, functioning in the same mode, Ford's total fiction existing finally only as an articulation of successive digressions).

(b) Lincoln makes a brief but precise speech in praise of credit: "I give you credit"—"I don't like credit" (says the farmer-woman incarnating the dignity of the poor)—"I myself bought my shop on credit": when one is aware of the role played by the extension of credit in the 1929 crisis, this kind of publicity slogan uttered by an American hero (who later, with ever increasing emphasis, will be the Righteous man) tends to appear as a form of exorcism: without credit, the development of capital is impossible; in a period of recession (1935–40), when unemployment is high, and wages have gone down, the maintenance of the level of consumption is the only thing which allows industry to carry on.

(c) The fact that Law is acquired by barter introduces a circuit of debt and repayments which is to run through the film (see 23).

d) The principle function of this sequence is to introduce a number of constituent elements of the symbolic scene from which the film is to proceed by *varying* and activating it (in this sense it is the true expository scene of the fiction, the first scene becoming pretextual and possibly even *extra-textual*): The Book and the Law, the Family and the Son, exchange and debt, predestination. . . . This *setting up* of the fictional matrix means *putting aside* the first sequence (political speech): a simple digression, first believed to be temporary, but then seen to be in fact the first step in the operation of the repression of politics by morality which will continue through the whole film (see 9).

11. NATURE, LAW, WOMAN

Third sequence: lying in the grass under a tree, near a river, Lincoln is reading Blackstone's "Commentaries." He sum-

marises its theories in a few sentences: "The right to acquire
and hold property . . . the right to life and reputation . . .
and wrongs are a violation of those rights . . . that's all there
is to it: right and wrong. . . ." A young woman appears and
expresses surprise that he should lie down while reading. He
gets up and answers: "When I'm lying down, my mind's
standing up, when I'm standing up, my mind lies down."
They walk along the river discussing Lincoln's ambitions and
culture (poets, Shakespeare, and now Law). They stop and
while she is talking he starts to stare at her and tells her that
he thinks she is beautiful. This declaration of love continues
for a few moments, centered on the question of those who do
and those who don't like redheads, then the young girl leaves
the scene (the frame, the shot). Alone, Lincoln approaches the
river and throws a stone into it. Close up of the ripples on the
water.

(a) The first anecdotic *signifié* of the scene refers to Lincoln's
legend: like any layman in law in the States at that time, Lincoln discovers Law in Blackstone. His "Commentaries" were
young America's legal Bible and they largely inspired the 1787
constitution. They are, in fact, no more than a summary and a
confused vulgarisation of 18th Century English Law. The second anecdotic *signifié* (again made explicit in the following
scene) is Lincoln's first acknowledged love affair, his relationship with Ann Rutledge—presented in the legend and the
film as the ideal wife (who shares similar tastes) whom he will
never meet again.

(b) Centred on Lincoln, the scene presents the relationship
Law-Woman-Nature which will be articulated according to a
system of complementarity and of substitution-replacement.

It is in nature that Lincoln communes with Law:

It is at the moment of this communion that he meets
Woman: the relationship Lincoln-Woman replaces the relationship Lincoln-Law since Woman simultaneously interrupts
Lincoln's reading of the book by her arrival and marks her appreciation of Lincoln's knowledge and encourages him in his
vocation as man of knowledge and Law.

The declaration of love is made according to the classic
(banal) cultural analogy Nature-Woman, in Nature (on the
bank of a river). But above all the promotion of the river to the
status of the woman corresponds to the Woman's (the wife's)
disappearance from the sequence (which in the fiction turns
out to be definitive); this promotion is signalled by the throwing of the stone (see 18).

Just as culturally determined and codified as the relationship
Nature-Woman, the equivalence Nature-Law is here un-

derlined precisely by the fact that the Law book is Blackstone, for whom all forms of Law (the laws of gravitation as well as those which regulate society) grow from a natural Law which is none other than God's law. In the final analysis, this supreme law separates Good from Evil, and is indeed called upon to legislate on the soundness of other human laws (the spirit against the word, see 6, 7, 9). Consequence: the acquisition and the defence of property are here presented as being based on the natural, indeed, on the divine (cf. the ideology of capitalism, 4, 9).

12. THE TOMB, THE BET

The ripples caused by the stone falling in the river dissolve into ice breaking up on the same river, as a transition between the scenes. A "dramatic" music underlines this passage. Lincoln arrives near a tomb covered in snow, near the river, at the spot where the preceding scene took place. Ann Rutledge's name can be read on the marble stone. Lincoln places a bunch of flowers on the tomb, while soliloquising on the return of spring ("the woods are already full of them too, the snow when it's drifting . . . ice breaking up . . . coming of the spring"). He says he is still hesitant on the path to follow: whether to stay in the village or to follow Ann's advice, go to town and choose a legal career. He picks up a twig of dead wood: if it falls towards Ann, he will choose law, if not, he will stay in the village. The twig falls on Ann's side. Lincoln, kneeling down, says: "Well Ann, you win, it's the Law" and after a moment of silence "I wonder if I could have tipped it your way just a little."

(a) The dissolve, which links the scene of the declaration of love (see 11) to that of the loved one's tomb, gives the impression that the transition from one to the other follows the same time-scale as the transition from summer to spring (the breaking ice) according to a symbolic (classic) opposition of the seasons: life/death (and resurrection). There is at the same time a smooth (continuous) succession from one season to the other, and a brutal contrast (Ann alive in one shot, dead in the next) between the two scenes. The effect of temporal continuity reinforces the violence of the contrast (the fictional shock) between life and death.

This process of temporal sequence and continuity (which is specific to great classical cinema) has in fact the function of absorbing referential time by juxtaposing and connecting two events (romance, death) separated by what will appear only later (at his arrival in Springfield) to be an interval of many years. This elimination has the effect of presenting Lincoln's first decisive choice (to become a lawyer) as if it had been neither thought out nor elaborated, nor rational: it *denies him the time of reflection*, it abolishes all *work*. Thus, once again, following the film's general strategy, it submits the hero to predestination, by reducing referential time to cinematic time: new *coup de force* by the film.

(b) Lincoln's definitive acceptance of Law is thus, once again, made under Woman's direct influence (we have seen in 11 the nature of her relationship with Law and Nature) and is in phase with the awakening of nature. But despite the fact that this decision is inevitable, both because of the logic of the symbolic axis Woman-Nature-Law, and because of the spectator's knowledge of Lincoln's fate, the film skilfully creates suspense, pretending that luck could change the course of events. As with Hitchcock with whom suspense, far from being weakened by our knowledge of the outcome, is increased at each viewing by this knowledge, the tension built up in the scene, far from being compromised by our knowledge of Lincoln's future (perfect), is increased by it. The film's supreme guile then consists in reintroducing—deceptively—at the very end of the scene the indication of intention, a voluntary choice on Lincoln's part ("I wonder if I could have tipped it your way just a little") which is, in fact, no more than a feigned delegation of power: as if Lincoln's already-accomplished destiny were referring to him to decide its path, following Spinoza's principle of "verum index sui," of truth as indicator of itself, *the self-determination of an already determined figure.*

13. THE PLAINTIFFS

Lincoln's arrival in Springfield. He sets himself up as a solicitor. Two Mormon farmers consult him, intending to take legal action. One owes the other money and the second has satisfied himself by violently beating up the first; therefore the first is claiming damages of an amount roughly equivalent to his debt. Having read the two plaintiffs' statements, Lincoln informs them of the quasi equivalence of their respective debts, the difference being equal to his bill; faced with their hesitation he threatens the use of force, if they don't accept his compromise. The farmers agree to pay him, and one of them tries to give him a fake coin. Lincoln first notices this by the sound it produces, then by biting the coin, and the scene ends on Lincoln's very insistent stare fixed on the forger.

(a) Lincoln's first legal act in the film is the solution of an extremely commonplace case. In fact, this anecdote which introduces the viewer to the violence of social relations in Lincoln's period, indicates his legal function which throughout the film is to repress violence even, as a final resort, by the use of a specifically legal violence (incarnated in Lincoln's physical strength but, most of the time, simply manifested by a verbal threat).

(b) The scene insists on Lincoln's supreme *cleverness*, in resolving any situation, the Law being able to decide either by taking one side against the other, or like here, by craftily restoring the balance between the two sides of the scales. This second solution is obviously preferred by the film because it emphasises Lincoln's legendary unifying role.

(c) Lincoln knows about money: he is not interested in its origin (credit, exchange, debt form, a circle) but it has a ring, a consistency, a value. It is precisely about a money-swindle that Lincoln's *castrating power* (see 16 and 22) is manifested for the first time, as an empty, icy, terrifying stare and his speed at hitting his opponents where it hurts, characteristics which will constitute the terrifying dimension of Lincoln's figure accentuated from scene to scene. Here for the first time the supreme process of Law eclipses the anecdotal character of Lincoln.

It will be observed that this terrifying dimension widely exceeds all the connotative *signifiés* (whether psychological—"I'm a farmer too, you can't fool me," or moral—reprobation, or situational, etc.) which could be applied to it. The irreducible character of Lincoln's castrating figure will persist throughout the film, transcending, altering the ideological discourse.

14. THE CELEBRATIONS

It is in order to take part in the Independence Day celebrations that Lincoln is in such a hurry to conclude the quarrel between the farmers. This celebration is made up of a number of episodes, announced in a programme, the order of which we will follow: (a) a parade (in which Lincoln meets Douglas, his opponent, and Mary Todd, his future wife); (b) a pie judging contest in which Lincoln is the judge (and during which the family from the first scene reappear); (c) a Tug of War (across a pond) in which Lincoln takes part (and in the course of which there is an incident between the family and two roughnecks); (d) a rail splitting contest (longitudinal section of a tree trunk) which Lincoln wins; (e) the burning of tar barrels.

(a) Lincoln is confronted by a historical evocation of

America: the local militias parade past him, followed by the
veterans of the war against Spain, and finally the survivors of
the War of Independence, whom Lincoln salutes by removing
his top hat. But Lincoln's slightly ridiculous solemnity is underlined on the one hand by the other spectators' joyful exuberance, and on the other by a succession of grotesque incidents, coupled with the veterans' shabby appearance, very
much in the Fordian tradition.

(b) The principle of Justice (whether or not to choose) is
here realised through a series of derivatives which exhaust all
its modalities: either Lincoln literally splits a rail in two, and
thus separates himself from, places himself above his opponents (adventitious meaning: affirmation of the physical
strength of literally his cutting edge): or he doesn't hesitate to
give *his* side, that is the right side, a helping hand, to help it
win (by tying the rope to a horse-drawn cart): Law represented by its ideal figure has every right: just as it doesn't hesitate to use force (see 13, 16) so it doesn't shrink before the use
of cunning and deception; a deception whose scandalous
aspect is masked by the triviality of the stake; and the "Fordian
gag" aspect of the action. Finally, more subtly, faced with the
undecidable character of a situation (the ethic, or gastronomic,
impossibility of preferring the product of one cook to that of
another) the fiction itself must, by abandoning the scene, censor the moment of choice and not show Lincoln making an impossible choice, both for the sake of the scene and for that of
the myth.

(c) The celebration sequence is made up of a series of fictionally autonomous *sketches* which are in fact determined by
the necessity of presenting a certain number of Lincoln's features. This mode of narration continues and stresses that of
the preceding scenes: namely a succession of sequences whose
length can vary but which are all subject to the *unity of action*.
Indeed each of them establishes a situation, presents, develops
and syntagmatically encloses an action (whether this latter is
resolved in terms of the diegesis or not: nothing said of the
consequences of the electoral speech, no decision about the
pies). (Insofar as it closes a scene only, the closure does not
preclude the later reinvestment of any one of the elements
which the scene has elevated to the status of a signifier: for example, the Law book or the Mother).

In fact it is at the moment of its greatest systematisation (a
series of headings) that this mode of narration is *infiltrated by
the first elements of a new narrative principle* (that of the detective story enigma and its solution: a hermeneutic chain which
articulates all the following sequences). Indeed, during the dif-

ferent episodes of the celebration, characters who will all play a more or less important role in the problem are present: Douglas and Mary Todd, the Clay family, the two bad boys, and a few extras who will reappear at the lynching and the trial. This new narrative device is reinforced (at the end of the celebration) by a scene (between Carrie Sue and her fiancé, Matt, the younger Clay son) which seems to reproduce Hollywood's most banal clichés (chatter of lovers, discussion of the future: how many children); in fact it is important insofar as it is the first scene from which Lincoln is physically absent. He is, however, constantly mentioned: first, indirectly, by Carrie Sue, who is very excited by the celebration and makes her fiancé promise to bring her back every year (what can be here taken as a simple whim, the manifestation of innocent joy and desire—the innocence briefly unmasked when she tells Matt she wishes "we was married right now. . ."—will be revealed and accentuated in all the scenes where Carrie Sue is present as the systematic denial of the violent erotic attraction provoked—not in her alone—by Lincoln of the direction indicated by the film in 19 where Lincoln identifies her with Ann Rutledge); then, directly, by the fiancé who says: "I wish it was going to be that fella's splitting them rails again," taking it on himself to formulate on her behalf *what she cannot say*.

15. THE MURDER

The new plot, which this scene develops and which is to dominate the rest of the film, started, as we noted, with the appearance of a number of elements which disturb the course of the celebration and its narrative presentation; the deputy sheriff (Scrub White) and his friend (J. Palmer Cass) somewhat worked up and high, pester Adam's (one of the Clay sons) wife. A fight breaks out, and is stopped by the mother's (Abigail Clay) intervention. This forgotten quarrel brutally reemerges during the final act of the celebration: the burning of the tar barrels. The two brothers and Scrub White start fighting again; this results in the death of the latter.

We have purposely not described the scene here; it is literally *indescribable*, insofar as it is the realisation—through the succession and length of the shots, abrupt changes of angle, play on distance, the reactions, and the behaviour of the participants, the successive arrival of witnesses—of an amazing system of *deception* which affects all the characters implicated in the event, and blinds them as well as the spectator. The radical difference between Ford's procedure here, and other films of the enigma, must at first give the spectator only scraps of knowledge and deprive him of a number of clues, the revelation of which, after the event, will provide the solution to the plot; whereas here, on the contrary, everything is given, present, but undecipherable, and it can only be deciphered at the second, *informed,* look.

The system of deception here set up is effective because *it develops as the scene progresses:* all the characters are caught up in it and duped, thus making it more powerful; and the spectator, witnessing these successive mystifications and called upon to agree with all, is thus the most deceived.

But we must also note that the effect of the deception continues and is *legitimised* by the substitution of a deceptive question: *which of the two brothers killed him?* for the real question: who killed him? The former question implies that the latter has already been answered, thus (successfully) suppressing the first: it will only be brought back by Lincoln (see 22).

All the different characters of the scene—*among them the spectator*—have either an active or a passive relationship to the deception—either way strengthening its influence. The spectator, who will be completely duped, is the initial witness of the fight: for him a perfectly plausible causal chain is constituted (except for one thing which we will specify): a cause of death: the shot; an effect: the wounded man's moans as he lies on the ground; reactions of the guilty: the two brothers, frightened, take refuge near their mother who has just arrived. There is only one element to contradict this causal chain: before hearing the shot, we see Scrub White's arm, which holds the weapon, turned away. But this element of confusion (Scrub White appearing to be seriously wounded by his own weapon when it was pointed elsewhere) far from invalidates this first setting up of the deception; on the contrary, it provokes distraction, thus permitting the intervention of a new factor (Cass's arrival) to pass almost unnoticed: the wounded man's death throes at this point can easily be accommodated by a classic typology: dying-in-one's-best-friend's-arms.

Cass, arriving during this break in attention, kneels down by his friend, placing himself *between him and the spectator* (long shot). He gets up in a *close up* shot, holding a bloody knife (a weapon which had not previously been seen): a shot which *independently of his drama* (as in Kuleshov's experiment) *is classically a shot of the guilty* (which is indeed what Cass is, since it is he who gave his friend this fatal knife wound but we will only learn this at the end of the movie, *even though all this has already been shown but rendered not-readable*).

The two sons Adam and Matt behave, even before Cass's arrival (ever since the shot was fired), like guilty men. Cass saying "He's dead" confirms them in this guilt; each one believes the other to be guilty but takes responsibility for the crime to protect his brother.

The mother intervenes when the shot is fired, and, seeing a man aground and her two sons alive but frightened, enters into the system of deception in her turn, believing them to be guilty. This feeling is strengthened when Cass gets up showing the knife, a knife which she recognises, believing then that she knows which of her two sons is guilty. But since they both accuse themselves, she plays the game and refuses to say which one she believes to be guilty (refusing to sacrifice one for the sake of the other). This refusal reinforces the deception because it accepts the displacement of the question: the mother thinks she keeps a secret, but it is the wrong one.

The spectator in his turn accepts this second causal chain: since the victim has been murdered with a knife by one of the two brothers, the gun shot from now on appears to him as a trivial episode, even a digression.

Thus what is happening here is precisely the cinematic questioning of direct vision, of perception insofar as it conceals the structure. The work that needs to be done to make the scene legible is not a search for hidden meanings, but the bringing to light of the *meaning which is already there:* which is why, paradoxically, it is our type of reading (see 1) of the film *in its entirety* which is called for and justified by this central scene.

This sequence and the preceding one (dialogue between the lovers) constitute, as we have already said, *a new fiction, from which Lincoln is absent.* He only comes into it when everything is decided (the crime committed, the accused taken away by the sheriff): neither actor, nor witness, *a priori* uninvolved in the problem, he *has no knowledge of it.* This is a necessary condition, in terms of Lincoln's mythical role, for the truth to emerge by magical rather than scientific means: to solve this crime story situation Lincoln will use means very different from those of an enquiry along ordinary thriller lines.

16. THE LYNCHING

(a) Introduced at the end of the celebration by the burning of the barrels (a commonplace episode in American celebrations, but here dramatically emphasised by the double fictional and historical context: KKK/fascist *auto-da-fés*), the cycle of violence (fight, crime) will culminate with the lynching. (The scene thereby acquires extra political significance because in the years 1925–35 a large number of lynchings took place in the USA—see films from that period, e.g., *Fury*.) This violence carries with it an acceleration of the narrative: between the moment when the defendants are taken away and the one when the lynching starts, there are only a few seconds, the time of a reframing; during this time Lincoln offers his legal services to the mother. She asks who he is, since she doesn't recognise him as the man who once gave her credit (this is not without importance, see the circulation of the debts 19) whereas he has just recognised her as the woman who gave him the Book. He answers, after a pause, "I'm your lawyer, ma'am."

(b) Inside the prison, under attack from the lynchers, there is a violent contrast between the understandable nervousness of the defendants and the sheriff and the unjustifiable panic of Cass (who has just been promoted deputy sheriff); for the second time—and here again in a non-readable way—the film exposes Cass as the culprit, i.e., as the man who is afraid of being lynched.

(c) Lincoln's action, insofar as he represents Law, can only be the, if necessary, violent, prohibition of any non-legal violence. Since the whole film is meant to manifest Lincoln's absolute superiority to all those who surround him, the scene of the lynching provides the opportunity for a masterly demonstration of it in a number of set scenes, each new stage of his victory increasing his castrating violence; this is inversely proportional to the expenditure of physical violence (since, in the ideological discourse, Law must have power insofar as it is legitimised by its own statement, not through physical strength, which is used as a last resort and often simply as a verbal threat). Here the escalation of legal repression is effected in many stages: 1. alone, Lincoln physically repels the lynchers' assault (courage and physical strength), 2. he incites one of the leaders to single combat, this the man evades (verbal threat based on knowledge of the opponent's weakness), 3. he defuses the crowd's anger by a cunning speech (so cunning, that the mother, not knowing *who he is*—i.e., in the fiction a good man, and in the myth President Lincoln—takes his speech literally and is very disturbed, before *believing* in him); he is also humorous (shifting to another level: complicity/familiarity with the crowd), 4. he throws back on the crowd the threat of its own violence by showing it that each one of them one way or the other, could be lynched (intimidation producing terror), 5. addressing one individual amongst the lynchers, whom he knows to be a religious man, he threatens him with retribution in the name of the Bible (ultimate recourse to divine writing as an instance of the Law). Lincoln's castrating triumph is sanctioned in the film itself not only by the subsiding of the crowd's anger, but very precisely by the lowering of the tree trunk, which on Lincoln's order is dropped by the lynchers—who are dispersing. (Note that it is with this same tree trunk that the lynchers attempted to break open the prison door, protected by Lincoln's body.)

17. THE DANCE

Invited by Mary Todd to a dance (the invitation card, congratulating him on his attitude in this "recent deplorable uprising" says, "My sister invites you . . .": here again, denial of desire), Lincoln abandoning his boots, vigorously shines his black high button shoes, and with the same unusual concern to be smart cuts his hair (see the anecdote told by Eisenstein about the new President moving to Washington: "he went as far as cleaning his own boots. Somebody said: *Gentlemen never clean their boots—And whose boots do real gentlemen clean?*"). The dance is in full swing, elegant and very genteel. Lincoln enters the lobby and is immediately surrounded by elderly gentlemen whom he entertains with funny stories (which we cannot hear). He is asked about his family ("Are you by any chance a member of the well-known Lincoln family from Massachusetts?"—"I'd say the evidence is against it if they own land"). Mary Todd responds absentmindedly to Douglas's advances, she is only interested in Lincoln. She goes to him and demands that he ask her to dance. He replies that he would very much like to dance with her, but warns her that he is a very poor dancer. He follows her to the middle of the dance floor, they start to dance a kind of waltz, then a polka, which Mary Todd suddenly interrupts and drags Lincoln to the balcony.

(a) The dance sequence is more or less compulsory in Ford's films. These dances almost always have the function first of setting up and ordering a ritual *miming ideal harmony*, which in fact is far from regulating the relations of the social group; then later, to disturb, unmask and destroy this simulation of harmony by the intervention of a foreign element. Here Lincoln's social heterogeneity gives place to the realisation of his symbolic otherness (figure of the Law): this involves him (socially and sexually) in a seduction relationship which simultaneously *integrates and excludes him;* this causes a confusion which is not resolved dramatically, unlike what takes place in other Ford films (cf. the dance in *Two Rode Together, Fort Apache* for example).

(b) The scandal of Lincoln's difference is even more noticeable to the spectators than to the characters of the scene. First it is apparent at the *physical* level, his shape, size, gait, rigidity, his undertaker look (Lincoln's mythical costume), then, while he is dancing, in the lack of co-ordination and rhythm in his movements. On the other hand, the social difference (made clear in the scene where Lincoln is dressing for the dance), emphasised by the question about his family, is immediately defused of any political significance and deflected into an amiable originality (it is out of the question according to the film's ideological system, that his class origins should play anything but a positive role).

(c) But it is at the symbolic level that the scandal is most apparent. In terms of the logic of castration, Lincoln's status, whereas it is realised in the lynching scene in its active form (castrating action), figures here in the passive form: that of *inversion* (the fact that these two dimensions—the action of castrating/being castrated—belong together will be made obvious in the balcony scene). Indeed, Mary Todd fully takes the initiative. First she expresses her resentment at Lincoln's coldness (in her conversation with Douglas); then she accuses Lincoln of not making the first move, and demands that he dance with her; finally she brings the dance to a sudden halt and drags him out to the balcony. Thus if the dance scene signifies the hero's social recognition (reward), the dance with Mary Todd puts him into a real castration, the retroactive effect of the lynching scene (which already implied it logically, writing it into the unconscious of Ford's text). There the castrating action was made on the basis of a castration which becomes effective in the dance scene and particularly in the balcony scene.

18. THE BALCONY

As soon as he is on the balcony, Lincoln is enchanted by the river. Mary Todd waits for a moment for Lincoln to speak or show some interest in her. Then she draws aside, leaving him alone in front of the river.

(a) Dance, balcony, river, moonlight, couple: all these elements create a romantic, intimate, sentimental atmosphere. The scene, however, mercilessly destroys this atmosphere (whose physical signifieds could be already read as more fantastic than romantic) to introduce the dimension of the Sacred.

(b) The transfer from one dimension to the other is effected by Lincoln's enchantment with the river: the commonplace accessory of the "romantic scene" is shifted to another scene and is at the same time the agent of this shift: another scene (from which Mary Todd, having no place, withdraws) in which a process of displacement-condensation takes place so that the river simultaneously evokes the first woman Lincoln loved (Ann Rutledge)—an evocation here emptied of any nostalgic or sentimental character—and (see 11) the relationship Nature-Woman-Law. The river is here the ratification of Lincoln's contract with Law. Lincoln, faced with his fate, accepts it; the classic moment of any mythological story. Here the hero sees his future written and accepts its revelation (the balcony, also a typical accessory of romantic love scenes, is here promoted, by Lincoln's gesture and the camera angle, to the anticipated role of the presidential balcony). Correlatively, Lincoln's renunciation of pleasure is written here: from now on Ann Rutledge's death must be read as the real origin both of his castration and of his identification with the Law; and the "inversion" of the dance scene as well as its relation to the lynching scene take on their true meaning: Lincoln does not have the phallus, he is the phallus (see Lacan, "La signification du phallus").

19. THE FAMILY

Immediately after the lynching Lincoln accompanies the mother (Mrs. Clay) and her two daughters-in-law back to their wagon. He tells her, "My mother would be just about your age if she were alive, you know she used to look a lot like you." After the scene of the balcony and before the opening of the trial, he goes to visit the family. On his way to the Clay farm, as he passes the river again, his companion tells him, "I've never known a fella look at a river like you do; fella would think it was a pretty girl the way you carry on" (see 11, 18).

(a) The scene in the farm yard acts as a reminder: Lincoln fantasises himself in the role of son of the family. First, by chopping wood (see 14), he evokes the time when this was his daily task—and compares himself to the son of the family. Then, one by one all the elements of the scene remind him of his house, his garden, his trees, the members of his family; he himself asserts the sequence of these equivalences: Mrs. Clay = his mother, Sarah = his dead sister, whose name was also Sarah, Carrie Sue = Ann Rutledge; and even the dish which is being cooked is his favourite dish: turnips. This insistent parallelism between the Lincoln family and the Clay family is carried through to the *absence* of the father: total exclusion in the case of Lincoln's father who is not even mentioned; the disappearance from the fiction of Mr. Clay (present in the first scene) is explained by an "accident." The rejection of the

Name of the Father logically corresponds to Lincoln's identification with the Law (his installation in the place of the great
Other) which can neither guarantee itself nor originate itself
through any other law than itself. We can here diagnose the
paranoia which governs the symbolics of the film.

This reliving of memories also has the function of stressing
Lincoln's social origins (see 9).

(b) This climate of nostalgic effusion—unique in the
film—is brutally interrupted by one of Lincoln's fixed stares
which can from now on be understood as the mark of his possession by Law. Giving up the role of son, he becomes inquis-
itor, interrupts the mother by asking her persistently which of
her two sons is guilty. Terrified she refuses to answer (as she
had done earlier in front of the sheriff, and will do later in
front of the prosecutor). Her consternation affects Lincoln and
makes him immediately cast off his attitude of investigator; he
gives up both trying to discover the mother's secret (but it is a
useless secret) and separate the two sons (for the problematic
of one or the other, he substitutes that of all or nothing) and
once again symbolically takes their place beside the mother.
Let us add that the film firmly avoids a possibility which could
have been exploited: namely that the question of the choice
between the two sons might upset Lincoln himself, make him
doubt or worry for a moment: Lincoln is totally ignorant of the
lamma sabbachtani.

(c) But this scene has the simultaneous function of continuing the circuit of debt and gift which links and will continue to
link Lincoln and the mother, and of providing it with an *origin:* fictionally introduced by the exchange—unequal in Lincoln's favour—of the material for the Book (see 10), it seems at
the symbolic level to go back to the time when the child "used
to stretch out while my mother read to me"; the situation is
here reversed since Mrs. Clay can't read and it is Lincoln—
still paying off this debt of which Mrs. Clay is unaware—who
reads her the letter from her sons (note the way in which he
pronounces the first words of this letter: "Dear Ma").

The origin of Lincoln's knowledge is here given for the second time (see 11) as being feminine-maternal; the same equivalence Woman-Nature-(Mother)-Law is once again posed, the
identification of Lincoln to the Law being related to the preliminary identification of the Law with Nature and Woman-
Wife-Mother; the debt contracted by Lincoln towards his
mother (she teaches him to read) as well as Mrs. Clay (she
gives the Book) and Ann Rutledge (she pushes him towards
knowledge) can only be "paid back" by his assumption of this
mission, and his incarnation of the Law. Let us not insist on

the assumptions behind this series (see 6), but notice that the circulation of the debt and its resolution are here enriched with an extra indicator: to answer, under the mother's dictation, the sons' letter, Lincoln asks Sarah for some paper; she gives him an almanac. Thus it is from the same family that Law and Truth originate: through the Book (the carrier of the Law) and the almanac: first used as a support for writing (letter from the mother to the imprisoned sons), it will reveal the truth when *exhibited by Lincoln* (see 22); it carries the solution to the enigma, it is the sign of Truth.

20. THE TRIAL

(a) The trial, a classic feature of Hollywood cinema, represents the staging of American legalist ideology and constitutes a microcosm of the social whole (sample of the different social strata represented by this or that type, this or that "silhouette"); confidence in the forms of legality is based precisely on this representativeness of the trial: it is America itself which constitutes the Jury, and who cannot be wrong, so that the Truth cannot fail to manifest itself by the end of the proceedings (carried out according to an almost ritualised alternation of comic and tragic moments). We have here a slight departure from this traditional trial, since the question is not to prove the culpability or the innocence of a defendant, but to *choose* (according to the principle of alternatives which has regulated the whole film) between two defendants. But here, as everywhere else, the constraints of the film's ideological strategy will compel Lincoln to *choose not to choose*, either (see 13) by deciding to re-establish the balance between the two parties, or (see 14) by indefinitely postponing the choice, or even, in the trial, by positively refusing to decide, thus trying to save both brothers, be it at the risk of losing both; all things which label and confirm Lincoln as a unifier and not a divider.

(b) During the different stages of the trial, Lincoln appears successively 1. As the weigher of souls: he quickly estimates the moral value of the members of the jury (and he does this according to norms which escape common understanding, even conventional morality: he accepts a man who drinks, lynches, loafs about, because by admitting to these faults, he manifests his deeper honesty). 2. As entertainer of the crowd (jokes, little stories, etc . . .) which put him in contrast with the prosecutor, a starchy man of mean appearance. 3. As manifesting his castrating power over Cass, whom he immediately attacks without apparent reasons: intimidation, vicious interrogation, and totally displaced onomastic play on words, thun-

dering looks: all these things imply a premonition of Cass's
guilt on Lincoln's part, which is not backed up by any knowledge but is nonetheless the Truth. For throughout the film
Lincoln relates not to knowledge, but to Truth (= Law). 4. As
the spirit opposed to the word, the natural and/or divine Law
to social Laws which are their more or less perfect transcription (he interrupts the prosecutor's cross-examination of the
mother by telling him, "I may not know so much of Law, Mr.
Prosecutor, but I know what's right and what's wrong"). 5. As
the righteous against the corridor filibusterer, morality against
politics (i.e., his political opponent Douglas's asides with the
prosecutor and with Cass).

(c) But this first day of the trial ends in a defeat for Lincoln,
brought about by a sensational development: Cass's second
testimony. From humanitarian concern, to save at least one of
the two defendants, he goes back on the first evidence he gave,
and claims to have been an eye-witness of the murder (thanks
to the moonlight) and points out the murderer: the elder of the
two brothers. In the hermeneutic chain ("which one has killed?") this reversal of the situation introduces a deceptive answer. A new question is thus posed: how will Lincoln sort this
one out, not only to win the trial, but also to remain faithful to
his refusal to choose?

21. THE NIGHT

(a) As before any "great crisis" in Hollywood cinema, there
is a pause: the scene of the family vigil in the prison—whose
function, in very classically codified form, is to instil a sense of
expectancy allowing a dramatic resurgence. Here the demands
of this code (tension-relaxation-tension) are precisely fulfilled:
no information is given which makes the drama progress (the
family's communion in song replacing/forbidding all explanatory dialogue); it is a "precarious situation lived through with
serenity." But the lack of any allusion on the part of the other
members of the family to the guilt of the elder brother is itself
sufficient to ratify Cass's accusations against him; the fact that
it is not questioned—as if it presented no problem—seems to
authenticate it.

In the duration of the scene, its adherence to the code seems
perfect and even excessive: the convention is accepted and
pushed to its extreme by the Fordian inscription (for everything which delineates the family group in Ford is grafted
here), even to bestowing its character of strangeness on the
scene (static frame, scenes shot from the front, strong light-

dark contrasts, position of the characters, choir). But this adherence on repeated reading is revealed to be a deception.
When we know that the real culprit is neither of the brothers,
the absence of any discussion between them or with their family has the effect of a real *coup de force* at the price of which the
miraculous dimension of Lincoln's revelation of the Truth is
made possible. The scene is thus regulated—with great skill—
by *the necessity of making the code* (the waiting period in which
the group communes in silence or song—when words are useless, even improper) *responsible for the censorship of any information* about the defendants' innocence. If the scene is silent,
it is because anything that might be intimated would inevitably have lifted the deception from the enigma and ruined the
magic of Lincoln's act.

(b) The second part of this night of vigil starts, concerning
Lincoln, on the same model: the hero's solitude and meditation before the decisive test. Lincoln is in his rocking chair by
his office window, playing the Jew's harp. This isolation signifying his defeat is strengthened by two events: 1. Douglas
and Mary Todd go past his window in a carriage; they both
look at him condescendingly; Mary Todd turns away and says
to Douglas: "You were discussing your political plans Mr.
Douglas, please go on." 2. The judge appears in Lincoln's office and, arguing from his long experience, suggests a double
compromise: to get help the next day from a more experienced
lawyer (he suggests Douglas) and to agree to plead guilty to
save the other brother. Lincoln categorically refuses: "I'm not
the sort of fella who can just swap horses in the middle of the
stream."

In 1. the change in size between the first long shot of the
carriage and the close up when Mary Todd speaks, a trick of
the direction which eliminates the "real" distance by changing
the axis (high angle shot) and the width of the shot so that
Lincoln appears to be right above the carriage, and Mary
Todd's words cannot then fail to reach him, thanks to this
unrealistic-proximity—compel the viewer to interpret them as
being addressed not to Douglas (Lincoln's eternal contrast) but
to Lincoln, and their political contents *standing* for an erotic
content. "You were discussing your political plans Mr. Douglas, please go on" can be read as, "I couldn't possibly do so
with you Lincoln, *nor make love*" at a time when everything in
Mary Todd's behaviour, look, and gestures points to her obvious spite, and to her speech as a denial of her desire. In the
film's other scenes the repression taking place alternately between the erotic and the political (Law as repressed desire and

as natural/divine morality) becomes here, in a single sentence, the repression of the erotic by the political.

In 2. Lincoln's paranoid features are confirmed: his refusal of all help, of any compromise, his hallucinatory faith in his own power, his certainty of being Chosen, his rigidity, the holding out to the bitter end.

22. VICTORY

Second day of the trial. Lincoln calls the main prosecution witness, Cass, back to the witness box, and by his questions makes him *repeat* his statement of the previous day point by point: it was in fact thanks to the full moon that he was able to witness the scene; it is to save one of the two brothers that he has gone back on his first statement. Mary Todd, like the rest of the public doesn't see the point of Lincoln's insistence to have things which are already known repeated. Lincoln pretends to let Cass go again, and just as he is about to leave the well of the Court, he suddenly asks him, "What d'you have against Scrub White, what did you kill him for?" Pulling the almanac out of his hat he thrusts it forward, saying: "Look at page 12: see what it says about the moon; it says it was in it's first quarter and set at 10.21 p.m., forty minutes before the murder" and, addressing Cass, "You lied about this point, you lied about the rest." From this point onwards Lincoln harasses Cass with questions until, collapsing, in a broken, shrill voice, he confesses: "I didn't mean to kill him. . . ." The confession obtained, Lincoln casually turns away from his victim and, addressing the prosecutor: "Your witness," while Cass's former supporters surround him threateningly.

(a) The almanac: a *signifier* first present in the scenes where the mother asks Lincoln to write to her imprisoned sons for her (see 19) as a simple support for writing, reappears on the first day of the trial (where it is on Lincoln's table, near his hat), then in the night scene where Lincoln is fingering it with apparent casualness. It is finally produced as *sign* of the Truth at the end of the second day of the trial, when Lincoln pulls it out of his hat like a conjuror.

We have here the typical example of a signifier running through the film without a signified, representing nothing, acquiring the status of a sign under Lincoln's revelation (the almanac representing proof of the truth for everyone) *but without ever having been an indicator*. Thus the thriller process of deduction is *completely eliminated* in favour of a scriptural logic which demands that such a signifier be produced as a veiled term whose very concealment and sudden final revelation would constitute a *mise en scene* inseparable from the meaning it induces, the mark of the unconscious determination of its writing into Ford's text. Veiled, 1, in the extent to which it realises the operation of repression of (erotic/criminal) violence in the fiction, whose return is effected according to a rhetoric of negation, and, 2, because its only *place* is that of a term whose sole function is to effect a mediation (between the criminal and the crime, between the mother and the sons), it is thereby doomed to disappearance as it is produced and to be included/excluded from the propositions in which it is actualised, by the very fact that it determines the production of their meaning; this is so to the extent to which the *signifier* of truth must remain veiled as long as truth is not stated, since at no moment is it presented as a clue (which would imply a work, the exercise of a knowledge, even a manipulation, which is not the case here). Lincoln's powers are thus not presented as the exercise of the art of detective deduction, but as a paranoid interpretation which short-circuits its process. Thus the proof of the crime seems to be materialised by the mere faculty which Lincoln has of producing the signifier as the concrete result of his omnipotent powers of Revelation.

But the manifestation of this omnipotence at the end of the film, made necessary by the ideological project (Lincoln, a mythical hero representing Law and guarantor of Truth), takes place at the end of the series of relations of co-presence between Lincoln and the almanac (three scenes where it is present without Lincoln knowing what to do with it in terms of the truth) and in such an unlikely and arbitrary (magical) way that it can be read in the following ways: 1, effectively as omnipotence, 2, as a pure fictional *coup de force* implying an imposition of Ford's writing on Lincoln's character (Lincoln's omnipotence is then *controlled and limited* by Ford's omnipotence, the latter not adopting the best possible viewpoint on his character, which would have been to show him as himself having the revelation of the Truth, and not merely as its agent) and 3, as Lincoln's *impotence* insofar as he appears subject to the power of the signifier (the almanac) and in a position of radical non-recognition regarding it, such that one can just as well say that the truth revolves around Lincoln (and not Lincoln around the truth) and that it is not Lincoln who uses the signifier to manifest the truth, but the signifier which uses Lincoln as mediator to accede to the status of the sign of truth. 2 and 3 (one specific to the film's writing, the other to its reading: but as we have stated in the introduction, we do not hesitate to force the text, even to rewrite it, insofar as the film only

constitutes itself as a text by integration of the reader's knowledge) *manifest a distortion of the ideological project by the writing
of the film.*

(b) Once the truth is revealed, Lincoln harasses Cass with
brutal questions until he obtains his confession. 1. Lincoln
must obtain from the culprit the confirmation of what he has
just stated to be truth; on the one hand to finalise the fiction
(save the two brothers, solve the mystery: but at the same
time, this solution is the admission that the enigma was, in
fact, a mere deception set up by the film); and on the other
hand to be confirmed in the eyes of the other characters as
possessor of the truth (if it is in fact enough for the spectator—
who knows who Lincoln is—to see him reveal the truth to
believe it, the characters of the fiction, his enemies, those who
have witnessed his failure of the previous day, etc . . . cannot
be so easily satisfied with his word). 2. Lincoln's insistence
and violence at this moment can be read, first, as the classic
harshness of rampant Justice, but mainly as the culmination of
Lincoln's castrating power (see 16), which is attested by the
fact that Cass, around whom the whole film has accumulated
the clichés of hypervirility, collapses in tears when he confesses, crying like a child. 3. This excessive violence of the
characterisation of Lincoln in the writing of the film, which is
motivated neither by the needs of Lincoln's cause (he could
triumph without terror) nor by those of the fiction (Cass could
confess without resisting) shows an imbalance with the idealised figure of Lincoln· even if this violence in the writing
implies no intentional criticism of the character Lincoln, it
makes visible—by its own scriptural excesses—the truly repressive dimension of the figure which this writing dictates,
and deroutes what could have been edifying or hagiographic
in the ideological project of the film.

23. "TOWARDS HIS DESTINY"

After his victory, Lincoln leaves the court alone. Four people
are waiting for him, among them Mary Todd and Douglas. She
congratulates him, looking at him seductively. Douglas then
comes to shake his hand: "I give you my sincere promise
never to make the mistake of underrating you again." Lincoln
replies, "Neither of us will underrate each other again." He is
about to go but is called back, "The town's waiting." He moves
towards the door, fully lit, and the crowd can be heard ap-
plauding off-set.

(a) Victorious, Lincoln is *recognised* by those who doubted

him: this type of scene (recognition of the hero) belongs to a
very classic register. But the way in which the scene is filmed,
the camera at a slightly low angle shot, disposition of the
groups, Lincoln's rather weary solemnity, the tone in which
he is called ("the town's waiting") and, chiefly, when he goes
to the threshold, his entry into a beam of violent light, the
frontal low angle shot when he faces the crowd whom he
greets by removing his hat, the very harsh lighting of the end
of this scene, all set this sequence in a very specifically theatrical dimension: congratulations backstage after the performance, recall to the stage of the primadonna. But the fact that,
by spatial displacement, this *encore* takes place not in the court
in front of the spectators of the trial, but on another stage (the
street, the town, the country) and in front of a crowd *which is
not shown* (which is no longer only the inhabitants of Springfield but of America) retroactively shows the performance of
the trial (definitely given as theatrical by the entrances, the
recalls, the repeats, the attitude of the spectators, the wings,
etc.) to be a simple rehearsal (provincial tour) and what is to
follow on the other stage (which the whole film has played on
as something having already happened which no one could be
ignorant of) will be the real performance (national tour); and
the *encore* is, in fact, the true entrance on the stage of the
legend. At the moment when he is *discovered* (intercepted) by
the others as Lincoln, and stripped of his character, he can
only act it out, play his own role. This interception is very precisely indicated in the film by the violent call of the brilliant
light: the reference to German expressionism (even to horror
films: *Nosferatu*)—much admired by Ford, as we well know—
is therefore compulsory at this point.

(b) Preceding the film's last shots which will only serve to
heighten this tragic dimension, we have the scene of farewell
to the Clays; like all other scenes with the family (as a function
of its status in relation to Lincoln) it is treated in an intimate,
familiar way, without solemnity. A scene in which the fiction
will terminate the double circuit of the symbolic debt linking
Lincoln to Mrs. Clay and of the desire which drives Carrie Sue
(as we have seen she is a substitute for Ann Rutledge) towards
a Lincoln who can no longer love her; first the mother insists
on paying Lincoln and gives him a few coins which he accepts, saying: "Thank you ma'am its mighty generous of you";
then Carrie Sue leaps to his neck and kisses him, saying: "I
reckon I'd just about die if I didn't kiss you Mr. Lincoln." This
confirms everything in Carrie Sue's attitude, which already ex-
ceeded the simple feeling of gratitude towards Lincoln, showing her to be driven by the desire, which, throughout the film,

makes her "play" around him, thus allowing her kiss to be read as a form of "acting out," a substitute for orgasm.

(c) Final scene: Lincoln takes leave of his companion (who is simultaneously a classic theatrical confidant and a sort of Sancho Panza, who is at his side in a number of scenes in the film) by telling him, "I think I might go on apiece . . . maybe to the top of that hill." The confidant goes out of frame. A storm threatens. Lincoln is slowly climbing the hill. A last shot shows him facing the camera, with a vacant look, while threatening clouds cross the background and the "Battle Hymn of the Republic" begins to be heard. Lincoln leaves the frame. Rain begins to fall violently and continues into the final shot of the film (his statue at the Capitol) while music intensifies.

Here again, it is the excesses of Ford's writing (accumulation of signs of the tragic, of ascent: hill—mythical reference—storm, lightning, rain, wind, thunder, etc.) which, by overlaying all the clichés, underlines the monstrous character of the figure of Lincoln: he leaves the frame and the film (like *Nosferatu*) as if it had become impossible for him to be filmed any longer; *he is an intolerable figure*, not because he has become too big for any film on account of the ideological project but rather because the constraints and violences of Ford's writing have exploited this figure for their own ends and manifested its excessive and monstrous dimensions, have no further use for it and so return it to the museum.

24. WORK OF THE FILM

With the fiction reaching saturation point here, what culminates in the final sequence is nothing other than the effects of meaning, re-scanned by our reading through the film as a whole, taken to their extreme. That is: the unexpected results (which are also contrary in relation to the ideological project) produced by the inscription—rather than flat illustration—of this project within a cinematic texture and its treatment by a writing which, in order to carry through the project successfully, maximising its value *and only that* (it's obvious that Ford takes practically no distance in relation to the figure and the ideology of Lincoln), is led to: such distortions (the setting up of a system of deception); such omissions (all those scenes, necessary in the logic of the crime thriller but whose presence could have lessened the miraculous dimension of Lincoln's omnipotence: the confrontation with the accused, the least one could expect of a lawyer); such accentuations (the dramatisation of the final scenes); such scriptural violence (be it for the

repression of violence—the lynching, the trial); such a sys-
temisation of determination and election (throughout a film
which, at the same time, wants to play on a certain suspense
and free choice without which the fiction could neither develop nor capture interest); in short to such a *work* that, today,
simply delimiting its operation and the series of means it puts
into action allows us to see the price at which such a film could
be made, the effort and detours demanded to carry the project
through.

And which Jean-Pierre Oudart in the following conclusion,
the point of departure of our study, cannot but repeat.

25. VIOLENCE AND LAW

I. A discourse on the Law produced in a society which can
only represent it as the statement and practice of a moralist
prohibition of all violence, Ford's film could only reassert all
the idealist representations which have been given it. Thus it
is not very difficult to extract from it an ideological statement
which seems to valorise in all innocence the ascetic rigour of
its agent, making it into the unalterable value which circulates
throughout the film from scene to scene; it is also easy to observe that this cliché, presented as such in the film and systematically accentuated, is not there merely to ensure the ac-
ceptability of the Fordian inscription. Without this cliché
which provides the fiction with a kind of metonymic continuity (the same constantly re-asserted figure)—whose necessity
is moreover overdetermined, its function being more than
simply setting up a character whose "idealism" can most conveniently be signified by the external signs of the very puritan
sense of election—the film would appear, in fact does appear
in spite of it, to be a text of disquieting unintelligibility;
through its constant disconnections, it places us in a forced
position for the reading and in fact its comprehension demands:
(1) That one first take no account of this at once insistent
and fixed statement;
(2) That one listens carefully to what is stated in the succession of so obviously "Fordian" scenes which support this
statement, and in the relations between the figures, all more or
less part of the Fordian fiction, which constitute these scenes;
(3) That one tries to determine how all these are involved;
i.e., to discover what the operation by which Ford inscribes
this character into his fiction consists of, insofar as, despite
appearances, it is not superimposed on Ford's "world," does

not traverse it like a foreign body, but finds through this inscription into his fiction a designated place as representative of his Law; for the filmmaker promotes the character to the role to which his (legendary) historical referent destines him only at the price of his subjection to the (Fordian) fictional logic. This determined his entry there in advance, insofar as his role was already written and his place already set out in Ford's fiction. The work of Ford's écriture only becomes apparent in this film through the problem involved in producing the character in this role, in that he took a place which was already occupied.

II. It is the character of the mother that incarnates the idealised figure of Ideal Law in Ford's fiction. Moreover, it is often, as in *Young Mr. Lincoln*, the widowed mother, guardian of the deceased father's law. It is for her that the men (the regiment) sacrifice the cause of their desire, and under her presidency that the Fordian celebration takes place; this in fact consists in a simulacrum of sexual relations from which all effective desire is banned. But it is in the constantly renewed relationship of this group with another (the Indians), in the dualism of Ford's universe that the inscription of the structural imperative of Law which dictates the deferment of desire and imposes exchange and alliance is realised, in violence, guided by the mediating action of the hero (often a bastard) who is placed at its intersection.

III. In *Young Mr. Lincoln* one of the results of using a single character for both roles is that he will have both their functions, which will inevitably create, by their interference and their incompatibility (insofar as one secures the taboo on the violence of desire, the other is agent of its inscription), disturbances, actions which oppose the order of Ford's world, and it is remarkable that each comical effect always shows them up (there is no film in which laughter is so precisely a sign of a constant disorder of the universe). The compression of their functions will in fact be used only on the one level of the castration of the character (signified at the ideological level by its puritan cliché, and at the same time written, in the unconscious of the text, as the effect of the fictional logic on the structural determination of the character) and of his castrating action, in a fiction ruled by Ideal Law alone since the dualism of Ford's world is abandoned in favour of the mass-individual opposition. (In fact the political conflict intervenes only as a secondary determination of the fiction and literally only acts backstage.) In fact, we see that:

(1). The character's calling originates in his renouncing the pleasures of love; it is strengthened because he resists its attraction: Lincoln becomes so well integrated in the fiction and so vigilant against the violences and plots which take place there only because he refuses to give in to the advances constantly made to him by women, affected by a charm which is due only to the prestige of his castration.

(2). This extreme postponement of the hero's desire soon becomes meaningful since it permits him to become the restorer of Ideal Law, whose order has been perturbed by a crime which the Mother has not been able to prevent but which she will attempt to stifle.

This shows that:

(1). The puritan cliché which Ford emphasises has the very precise function of promoting the character to his role as mediator, insofar as the pleasure which he rejects allows him to thwart any attempt at sexual and political corruption; it thus simultaneously guarantees the credibility of the figure of Lincoln and the position of the character as the figure of Ideal Law in Ford's fiction. At the obvious price of installing him within a castration, whose comical aspects Ford uses sufficiently to indicate how indifferent he is to producing an edifying figure, and how much more attentive he is to the disturbing results of its presence in the fiction: for example, in the dance scene in which his character perturbs the harmony, where the agent of Law behaves like a kill-joy, thus making visible what the harmony of the Fordian celebration would conceal.

(2). The fact that the character literally takes the place of the Mother, i.e., takes on simultaneously her ideal position and her function (since he assumes responsibility for her children, and promises to feed them well in the new home which the prison becomes), gives rise to a curious transformation of the figure, as this repetition of roles is effected under the sign of a secret which the Mother must (believes she does) keep to try to prevent any violence—even, inconceivably, that of the Ideal Law which she incarnates—against her children; and by thus incubating the crime she projects her role into a quasi erotic (almost Hitchcockian) dimension never presented as such by Ford, since usually the fiction protects her from any relationship with the crime (since it is part of her function to be ignorant of violence). This is comically reintroduced in the final scene of the trial, when the real proof (an almanac on a sheet of which should have been written the letter of love which Lincoln was planning to write for her, only to lull her attention and extract confessions from her) is pulled out of Lincoln's hat; it was necessary for the re-establishment of Law that by the end of the trial a signifier (the proof of the crime) be produced whose very occultation renders it erotic; and that it must necessarily be produced by the figure of Law to fit into the fictional logic since it is from this ideal Law that originated the cancellation of the criminal act in the fiction, the statement of the taboo on violence (on pleasure), the position of the Mother as the figure of forbidden violence (pleasure), the possession of the phallus by this figure (as a signifier of this pleasure) and the production of the proof of the crime as if it were a phallic signifier obviously proceeding from the same statement. In such fictions this usually means, either that the weapon, the trace of the crime, acts like a letter which Law must decipher, since its very proscription has written it, or that the confession be produced by the criminal as a return of the repressed in an erotic form. The two results are here compressed, Law producing the proof of the crime (the writing which reveals the murderer) as if it were a phallic object which Ford's comedy presents like the rabbit pulled out of the conjuror's hat; the improbable levity with which Ford brings the trial to its close really can only be read as a masking effect which conceals to the end the "human" context, thus allowing the logic of the inscription to produce this gag as its ultimate effect, a final consequence of Lincoln's re-enactment of the Mother's role, a fantastic return of the mask.

IV. The fact that the overdetermination of this inscription of the Lincoln figure, as agent of the Law, in Ford's fiction by all the idealised representations of Law and its effects produced by the bourgeoisie, far from having been erased by Ford, has been declared by his writing and emphasised by his comedy, shows what a strange ideological balancing act the filmmaker has insisted on performing, and what strange scriptural incongruities he has insisted on exploiting; to the extent that by the fictional constraints he gave himself, by giving up the usual bisection of his fiction and the sometimes truly epic inscription of Law thereby articulated (which recalls Eisenstein in *The General Line*) he could only produce the Law as a pure prohibition of violence, whose result is only a permanent indictment of the castrating effects of its discourse. Indeed to what is the action of his character reduced if not hitting his opponents at their weakest point—weaknesses which Ford always perversely presents as being capable of provoking a deadly laughter? So that the sole but extreme violence of the film consists of verbal repression of violence which, in certain scenes (the unsuccessful lynching) is indicated as really being a death sentence, a mortal interdict which has no equivalent except maybe in Lang, and which shows the distance Ford, or rather his writing, keeps between himself and the idealist propositions which he uses.

V. For, with a kind of absolute indifference to the reception
given to his stylistic effects, the filmmaker ends by practising
stubbornly a scriptural perversion, which is implied by the fact
that, paradoxically, in a film meant to be the Apology of the
Word, the last word is always given to the iconic signifier, entrusted by Ford with the production of the determining effects
of meaning. And as in this film what is to be signified is
always either the (erotic, social, ideological) separation of the
hero relative to his surroundings, or the immeasurable distance between him and his actions, or the absence of any common denominator between the results he obtains and the
means he uses, and those obtained by his opponents (insofar
as he holds the privilege of the castrating speech), Ford succeeds, by the economy of means which he uses to that effect—
his style forbidding him the use of effects of implicit valorisation of the character, which he could have drawn from an "in-
teriorised" writing—in simultaneously producing the same
signifier in completely different statements: (for example, in
the moonlight scene, where the moonlight on the river indicates, at the same time, the attempted seduction, the past
idyll, and the hero's "idealist" vocation); or even in renewing
the same effect of meaning in totally different contexts (the
same spatial disconnections of the character used in the dance
scene and the murder scene). So that the intention of always
making sense, of closing the door to any implicit effect of
meaning, of constantly re-asserting these same meanings, in
fact results—since to produce them the filmmaker always ac-
tualises the same signifiers, sets up the same stylistic effects—
in constantly undermining them, turning them into parodies
of themselves. (With Ford parody always proceeds from a de-
nunciation of the writing by its own effects.) The film's ideological project thus finds itself led astray by the worst means it
could have been given to realise itself (Ford's style, the inflexible logic of his fiction), mainly to the benefit of a properly
scriptural projection (obtained not by the valorisation after the
event of previously constituted effects of meaning, but proceeding directly from the inscription, produced anew and resolved in each scene, of the character in Ford's fiction), of the
effects of the repression of violence: a violence whose repression, written thus, turns into exorcism and gives to its signifiers, in the murder and the lynching scenes, a fantastic contrast which contributes considerably to the subversion of the
deceptively calm surface of the text.

1970

JEAN-LOUIS COMOLLI
MACHINES OF THE VISIBLE

INTRODUCTION

One of the hypotheses tried out in some of the fragments here gathered together would be on the one hand that the cinema—the historically constitutable cinematic statements—functions with and in the set of apparatuses of representation at work in a society. There are not only the representations produced by the representative apparatuses as such (painting, theatre, cinema, etc.), there are also, participating in the movement of the whole, the systems of the delegation of power (political representation), the ceaseless working-up of social imaginaries (historical, ideological representations) and a large part, even, of the modes of relational behaviour (balances of power, confrontations, manoeuvres of seduction, strategies of defense, marking of differences or affiliations). On the other hand, but at the same time, the hypothesis would be that a society is only such in that it is *driven by representation*. If the social machine manufactures representations, it also manufactures *itself* from representations—the latter operative at once as means, matter and condition of sociality.

Thus the historical variation of cinematic techniques, their appearance-disappearance, their phases of convergence, their periods of dominance and decline seem to me to depend not on a rational-linear order of technological perfectibility nor an autonomous instance of scientific "progress" but much rather on the offsettings, adjustments, arrangements carried out by a social configuration in order to represent itself, that is, at once to grasp itself, identify itself and itself produce itself in its representation.

What happened with the invention of cinema? It was not sufficient that it be technically feasible, it was not sufficient that a camera, a projector, a strip of images be technically ready.[1] Moreover, they were already there, more or less ready, more or less invented, a long time already before the formal invention of cinema, 50 years before Edison and the Lumière brothers. It was necessary that something else be constituted, that something else be formed: the *cinema machine*, which is not essentially the camera, the film, the projector, which is not merely a combination of instruments, apparatuses, techniques. Which is a machine: a *dispositif* articulating between one another different sets—technological certainly, but also economic and ideological. A *dispositif* was required which implicate its motivations, which be the arrangement of demands, desires, fantasies, speculations (in the two senses of commerce and the imaginary): an arrangement which give apparatus and techniques a social status and function.

The cinema is born immediately as a social machine, and thus not from the sole invention of its equipment but rather from the experimental supposition and verification, from the anticipation and confirmation of its *social profitability;* economic, ideological and symbolic. One could just as well propose that it is the spectators who invent cinema: the chain that knots together the waiting queues, the money paid and the spectators' looks filled with admiration. "Never," say Gilles Deleuze and Claire Parnet, "is an arrangement-combination technological, indeed it is always the contrary. The tools always presuppose a machine, and the machine is always social before it is technical. There is always a social machine which selects or assigns the technical elements used. A tool, an instrument, remains marginal or little used for as long as the social machine or the collective arrangement-combination capable of taking it in its *phylum* does not exist.[2] The hundreds of little machines in the nineteenth century destined for a more or less clumsy reproduction of the image and the movement of life are picked up in this "phylum" of the great representative

[1]See "Technique et idéologie," *Cahiers du cinéma*, no. 229 (May–June 1971), pp. 9–15; translation, "Technique and ideology: camera, perspective, depth of field," *Film Reader*, no. 2 (1977), pp. 132–38.
[2]Gilles Deleuze and Claire Parnet, *Dialogues* (Paris: Flammarion, 1977), pp. 126–27.

machine, in that zone of attraction, lineage, influences that is created by the displacement of the social co-ordinates of analogical representation.

The second half of the nineteenth century lives in a sort of frenzy of the visible. It is, of course, the effect of the social multiplication of images: ever wider distribution of illustrated papers, waves of prints, caricatures, etc. The effect also, however, of something of a geographical extension of the field of the visible and the representable: by journies, explorations, colonisations, the whole world becomes visible at the same time that it becomes appropriatable. Similarly, there is a visibility of the expansion of industrialism, of the transformations of the landscape, of the production of towns and metropolises. There is, again, the development of the mechanical manufacture of objects which determines by a faultless force of repetition their ever identical reproduction, thus standardising the idea of the (artisanal) copy into that of the (industrial) series. Thanks to the same principles of mechanical repetition, the movements of men and animals become in some sort more visible than they had been: movement becomes a visible mechanics. The mechanical opens out and multiplies the visible and between them is established a *complicity* all the stronger in that the codes of analogical figuration slip irresistibly from painting to photography and then from the latter to cinematography.

At the very same time that it is thus fascinated and gratified by the multiplicity of scopic instruments which lay a thousand views beneath its gaze, the human eye loses its immemorial privilege, the mechanical eye of the photographic machine now sees *in its place,* and in certain aspects with more sureness. The photograph stands as at once the triumph and the grave of the eye. There is a violent decentring of the place of mastery in which since the Renaissance the look had come to reign; to which testifies, in my opinin, the return, synchronous with the rise of photography, of everything that the legislation of the classic optics—that geometrical *ratio* which made of the eye the point of convergence and centring of the perspective rays of the visible—had long repressed and which hardly remained other than in the controlled form of anamorphoses: the massive return to the front of the stage of the optical aberrations, illusions, dissolutions. Light becomes less obvious, sets itself as problem and challenge to sight. A whole host of inventors, lecturers and image showmen experiment and exploit in every way the optical phenomena which appear irrational from the standpoint of the established science (refraction, mirages, spectrum, diffraction, interferences, retinal persistence, etc.). Precisely, a new conception of light is put together, in which the notion of wave replaces that of ray and puts an end to the schema of rectilinear propagation, in which optics thus overturned is now coupled with a chemistry of light.

Decentred, in panic, thrown into confusion by all this new magic of the visible, the human eye finds itself affected with a series of limits and doubts. The mechanical eye, the photographic lens, while it intrigues and fascinates, functions also as a *guarantor* of the identity of the visible with the normality of vision. If the photographic illusion, as later the cinematographic illusion, fully gratifies the spectator's taste for delusion, it also reassures him or her in that the delusion is in conformity with the norm of visual perception. The mechanical magic of the analogical representation of the visible is accomplished and articulated from a doubt as to the fidelity of human vision, and more widely as to the truth of sensory impressions.

I wonder if it is not from this, from this lack to be filled, that could have come the extreme eagerness of the first spectators to *recognise* in the images of the first films—devoid of colour, nuance, fluidity—the identical image, the double of life itself. If there is not, in the very principle of representation, a force of disavowal which gives free rein to an analogical illusion that is yet only weakly manifested by the iconic signifiers themselves? If it was not necessary at these first shows to forcefully deny the manifest difference between the filmic image and the retinal image in order to be assured of a new hold on the visible, subject in turn to the law of mechanical reproduction . . .

I. THE CAMERA SEEN

The camera, then.

For it is here indeed, on this *camera-site*, that a confrontation occurs between two discourses: one which locates cinematic technology in ideology, the other which locates it in science. Note that whether we are told that what is essential in the technical equipment which serves to produce a film has its founding origin in a network of scientific knowledges or whether we are told that that equipment is governed by the ideological representations and demands dominant at the time it was perfected, in both cases—discourse of technicians on the one hand, attempts to elaborate a materialist theory of the cinema on the other—the example given is *always* that which produces the cinematic *image,* and it *alone,* considered from the sole point of view of *optics.*[3]

Thus what is in question is a certain *image* of the camera: metonymically, it represents the whole of cinema technology, it is the part for the whole. It is brought forward as the *visible part* for the *whole of the technics.* This symptomatic displacement must be examined in the very manner of posing the articulation of the couple Technology/Ideology.

To elect the camera as "delegated" representative of the whole of cinematic equipment is not merely synecdochical (the part for the whole). It is above all an operation of reduction (of the whole to the part), to be questioned in that, *theoretically,* it reproduces and confirms the split which is ceaselessly marked in the technical practice of cinema (not only in the practice of film-makers and technicians and in the spontaneous ideology of that practice; but also in the "idea," the ideological representation that spectators have of work in cinema: concentration on shooting and studio, occultation of laboratory and editing) between the *visible* part of the technology of cinema (camera, shooting, crew, lighting, screen) and its *"invisible"* part (black between frames, chemical processing, baths and laboratory work, negative film, cuts and joins of editing, sound track, projector, etc.), the latter repressed by the former, generally relegated to the realm of the unthought, the "unconscious" of cinema. It is symptomatic, for example, that Lebel, so concerned to assert the scientific regulation of cinema, thinks to deduce it only from geometrical optics, mentioning only once retinal persistence which nevertheless is what brings into play the specific difference between cinema and photography, the synthesis of movement (and the scientific work which made it possible); at the same time that he quite simply forgets the other patron science of cinema and photography, photochemistry, without which the camera would be no more precisely than a *camera obscura.* As for Pleynet's remarks, they apply indiscriminately to the quattrocento *camera obscura,* the seventeenth century magic lantern, the various projection apparatus ancestors of the *cinématographe* and the photographic apparatus. Their interest is evidently to indicate the links that relate these diverse perspective mechanisms and the camera,

[3]With M. Pleynet—"Economique, idéologique, formel" (interview), *Cinéthique,* no. 3 (1969)—the focus of attention is voluntarily and *first of all* on *one* of the component elements of the camera, the *lens.* For J.-P. Lebel—*Cinéma et idéologie* (Paris: Editions sociales, 1971), chapter I—who cites the phenomenon of "persistence of vision," the reference-Science, constantly invoked, is *geometrical optics:* the laws of the propagation of light.

but in so doing they risk not seeing exactly what the camera hides (it does not hide its lens): the film and its feed systems, the emulsion, the frame lines, things which are essential (not just the lens) to cinema, without which there would be no cinema.

Hence it is not certain that what is habitually the case in practice should be reproduced in theory: the reduction of the hidden part of technics to its visible part brings with it the risk of renewing the domination of the visible, that *ideology of the visible* (and what it implies: masking, effacement of work) defined by Serge Daney:

> Cinema postulated that from the "real" to the visual and from the visual to its filmed reproduction a same truth was infinitely reflected, without distortion or loss. In a world where "I see" is readily used for "I understand," one conceives that such a dream had nothing fortuitous about it, the dominant ideology—that which equates the real with the visible—having every interest in encouraging it. . . . But why not, going further back still, call into question what both serves and precedes the camera: a truly blind confidence in the visible, the hegemony, gradually acquired, of the eye over the other senses, the taste and need a society has to put itself in spectacle, etc. . . . The cinema is thus bound up with the Western metaphysical tradition of seeing and vision whose photological vocation it realizes. What is photology, what could be the discourse of light? Assuredly a teleological discourse if it is true, as Derrida says, that teleology "consists in neutralizing duration and force in favour of the *illusion* of simultaneity and form."[4]

Undeniably, it was this "hegemony of the eye," this specularisation, this ideology of the visible linked to Western logocentrism that Pleynet was aiming at when stressing the pregnancy of the quattrocento perspective code in the basic apparatus: the image produced by the camera cannot do otherwise than confirm and reduplicate "the code of specular vision such as it is defined by the renaissant humanism," such that the human eye is at the centre of the system of representation, with that centrality at once excluding any other representative system, assuring the eye's domination over any other organ of the senses and putting the eye in a strictly divine place (Humanism's critique of Christianity).

Thus is constituted this situation of *theoretical paradox:* that it is by identifying the domination of the camera (of the visible) over the whole of the technology of cinema which it is

---

[4]Serge Daney, "Sur Salador," *Cahiers du cinéma,* no. 222 (July 1970), p. 39.

supposed to represent, inform and programme (its function as *model*) that the attempt is made to denounce the submission of that camera, in its conception and its construction, to the dominant ideology of the visible.

If the gesture privileging the camera in order to set out from it the ideological chain in which cinema is inscribed is theoretically grounded by everything that is implied in that apparatus, as in any case by the determining and principal role of the camera in the production of the film, it too will nevertheless remain caught in the same chain unless taken further. It is therefore necessary to change perspective, that is, to take into account what the gesture picking out the camera sets aside in its movement, in order to avoid that the stress on the camera—necessary and productive—is not reinscribed in the very ideology to which it points.

It seems to me that a materialist theory of the cinema must at once disengage the ideological "heritage" of the camera (just as much as its "scientific heritage," for the two, contrary to what seems to be stated by Lebel, are in no way exclusive of one another) and the ideological investments in that camera, since neither in the production of films nor in the history of the invention of cinema is the camera alone at issue: if it is the fact that what the camera brings into play of technology, of science and/or ideology is determining, this is so only in relation to other determining elements which may certainly be secondary relative to the camera but the *secondariness* of which must then be questioned: the status and the function of what is covered over by the camera.

To underline again the risk entailed in making cinema function theoretically entirely on the *reduced model* of the camera, it is enough to note the almost total lack of theoretical work on the sound track or on laboratory techniques (as if the sight of light—geometrical optics—had blocked its work: the chemistry of light), a lack which can only be explained by the dominance of the visible at the heart of both cinematic practice and reflection. Is it not time, for example, to bring out the ideological function of two techniques (instruments + processes + knowledges + practice — interdependent, together to realise an *aim*, an objective which henceforth constitutes that technique, founds and authorises it), both of which are on the side of the hidden, the cinematic unthought (except by very few film-makers: Godard, Rivette, Straub): *grading* and *mixing?*

II. COVERING OVER AND LOSS OF DEPTH OF FIELD

No more than in the case of the "close-up" is it possible to postulate a continuous chain (a filiation) of "depth-of-field shots" running through the "history of cinema." No more than in the case of the "close-up" (or of any other term of cinematic practice and technical metalanguage) is the history of this technical disposition possible without considering determinations that are *not exclusively technical* but economic and ideological: determinations which thus go beyond the simple realm of the cinematic, working it over with series of supplements, grasping it on other scenes, having other scenes inscribe themselves on that of cinema. Which shatter the fiction of an autonomous history of cinema (of its "styles and techniques"). Which effect the complex articulation of this field and this history with other fields, other histories. Which thus allow the taking into account, here for the particular technical procedure of depth of field, of the regulation of the functions it assumes—that is to say, of the *meanings* it assumes—filmic signifying production through codes that are not necessarily cinematic (in this instance: pictorial, theatrical, photographic), allow the taking into account of the (economic/ideological) forces which put pressure for or against the inscription of this regulation and these codes.

For historian—aestheticians like Mitry and theoreticians like Bazin to have let themselves fall for a determination of filmic writing and of the evolution of cinematic language by the advances of technology (development and improvement of means), to fall, that is, for the idea of a "treasure house" of techniques into which film-makers could "freely" dip according to the effects of writing sought, or, again, for an "availability" of technical processes which located them in some region outside of systems of meaning (histories, codes, ideologies) and "ready" to enter into the signifying production, it was necessary that the whole technical apparatus of cinema seem so "natural" to them, so "self-evident," that the question of its utility and its purpose (what is it used for) be totally obscured by that of its utilisation (how to use it).

It is indeed of "strength of conviction," "naturalness"—and, as a corollary, of the blindness on the part of the theoreticians—that we must talk. Mitry, for example, who notes the fact that deep focus, almost constantly used in the early years of cinema, disappears from the scene of filmic signifiers for some 20 years (with a few odd exceptions: certain films by

Renoir), offers strictly technical reasons as sole explanation for this abandonment, hence establishing technology as the last instance, constituting a closed and autonomous circuit within which technical fluctuations are taken as determined only by other technical fluctuations.

From the very first films, the cinematic image was "naturally" an image in deep focus; the majority of the films of Lumière and his cameramen bear witness to that depth which appears as constituent of these images. It is in fact most often in out-of-doors shooting that depth in the period finds its field. The reason is indisputably of a technical nature: the lenses used before 1915 were, Mitry stresses, "solely f35 and f50," "medium" focal lengths which had to be stopped down in order to produce an image in depth, thus necessitating a great deal of light, something to be found more easily and cheaply outside than in the studio.

One must then ask why, precisely, these "medium" focal lengths only were in use during the first 20 years of cinema. I can see no more pertinent reason than the fact that they restore the spatial proportions corresponding to "normal vision" and that they thereby play their role in the production of the impression of reality to which the *cinématographe* owed its success. These lenses themselves are thus dictated by the codes of analogy and realism (other codes corresponding to other social demands would have produced other types of lenses). The depth of field that they permit is thus also that which permits them, that which lays the ground for their utilisation and their existence. The deep focus in question is not a supplementary "effect" which might just as well have been done without; on the contrary, it is what had to be obtained and what it was necessary to strive to produce. Set up to put its money on, and putting its money wholeheartedly on, the identification—the desire to identify, to duplicate, to recognise specularly—of the cinematic image with "life itself" (consider the fantastic efforts expended over decades by hundreds of inventors in search of "total cinema," of complete illusion, the reproduction of life with sound and colour and relief included), the ideological apparatus cinema could not, in default of realising in practice the technical patent for relief, neglect the production of effects of relief, of effects of depth. Effects which are due on the one hand to the inscription within the image of a vanishing perspective and on the other to the movements of people or other mobile elements (the La Ciotat train) along vanishing lines (something which a photograph cannot provide, nor *a fortiori* a painting; which is why the most perfect *trompe-l'oeil* minutely constructed in conformity with the laws of perspective is powerless to trick the eye). The two are linked: in order that people can move about "perpendicularly" on the screen, the light must be able to go and take them there, it requires a depth, planes spaced out, in short the code of artificial perspective. Moreover in studio filming, where space was relatively tight and lightning not always adequate, the backgrounds were often precisely painted *trompe-l'oeil* canvases which, while unable to inscribe the movement in depth of the characters, at least inscribed its perspective.

We know what perspective brings with it and thus what deep focus brings into the cinematic image as its *constitutive codes:* the codes of classic Western representation, pictorial and theatrical. Méliès, specialist in "illusion" and interior shooting, said as early as 1897 of his Montreuil "studio": "in brief, it is the coming together of a gigantic photographic workshop and a theatrical stage." No more exact indication could be given of the double background on which the cinematic image is raised, and not fortuitously but explicitly, deliberately. Not only is deep focus in the early cinematic image the mark of its submission to these codes of representation and to the histories and ideologies which necessarily determine and operate them, but more generally it signals that the ideological apparatus cinema is itself produced by these codes and by these systems of representation, as at once their complement, their perfection and the surpassing of them. There is nothing accidental, therefore, or specifically technical in the cinematic image immediately claiming depth, since it is just this depth which governs and informs it; the various optical instruments are regulated according to the possibility of restoring depth. Contrary to what the technicians seem to believe, the restoration of movement and depth are not effects of the camera; it is the camera which is the effect, the solution to the problem of that restoration.

Deep focus was not "in fashion" in 1896, it was one of the factors of credibility in the cinematic image (like, even if not quite with the same grounds, the faithful reproduction of movement and figurative analogy). And it is by the transformation of the conditions of this credibility, by the displacement of the codes of cinematic verisimilitude from the plane of the impression of reality alone to the more complex planes of fictional logic (narrative codes), of psychological verisimilitude, of the impression of homogeneity and continuity (the coherent space-time of classical drama) that one can account for the effacement of depth. It will not then be a question merely of technical "delays": such "delays" are themselves caught up in and effects of the displacement, of this replacement of codes.

It seems surprising indeed (at least if one remains at the level of "technical causes") that a process which "naturally" dominated a large proportion of the films made between 1895 and 1925 could disappear or drop into oblivion for so long without — leaving aside a few exceptions, Renoir being one — film-makers showing the slightest concern (so it seems).

Everything, Mitry assures us, stems from "the generalisation of panchromatic stock round about 1925." Agreed. But to say that — offered with the weight of the obvious — and to pass on quickly to the unsuitability of the lighting systems to the spectrum of this emulsion is exactly *not to say* what necessity attaches to this "generalisation," what (new) function the new film comes to fulfil that the old was unable to serve. It is to avoid the question as to what demands the replacement of an emulsion in universal use and which (if we follow Mitry) did not seem so mediocre by another which (still according to Mitry) was far from its immediate equal. As far as we know, it is not exactly within the logic of technology, nor within that of the economics of the film industry (in the mid-twenties already highly structured and well-equipped) to adopt (or impose) a new product which in an initial moment poses more problems than the old and hence incurs the expense of adaptation (modification of lighting systems, lenses, etc.) *without somewhere finding something to its advantage and profit.*

In fact, it is a matter not simply of a gain in the sensitivity of the film but also of a gain in *faithfulness* "to natural colours," a *gain in realism*. The cinematic image becomes more refined, perfects its "rendering," competes once again with the quality of the photographic image which had long been using the panchromatic emulsion. The reason for this "technical progress" is not merely technical, it is ideological: it is not so much the greater sensitivity to light which counts as "being more true." The hard, contrasty image of the early cinema no longer satisfied the codes of photographic realism developed and sharpened by the spread of photography. In my view, depth (perspective) loses its importance in the production of "reality effects" in favour of shade, range, colour. But this is not all.

A further advantage, that is, that the film industry could find "round about 1925" in imposing on itself — despite the practical difficulties and the cost of the operation — the replacement of orthochromatic by panchromatic stock depends again on the greater sensitivity of the latter. Not only did the gain in sensitivity permit the realignment of the "realism" of the cinematic image with that of the photographic image,[5] it also compensated for the loss of light due to the change from a shutter speed of 16 or 18 frames per second to the speed of 24 frames per second necessitated by sound. This "better" technical explanation, however, can only serve here to re-mark the coincidence of the coming of the talkie and the setting aside of depth, not to provide the reason for it. Although certain of its effects are, that reason is not technical. More than one sound film before *Citizen Kane* works with depth; the generalisation of large aperture lenses even does not exclude its possibility: with the sensitivity of emulsions increasing and the quantity of light affordable, there was nothing to prevent—technically—the stopping down of these lenses (if indeed, as Renoir did, one could not find any others). So it is not as final "technical cause" that the talking picture must be brought into the argument; it is that in a precise location of production—distribution (Hollywood) it re-models not just the systems of filmic writing but, with them and directing this bringing up to date, the ideological function of the cinema and the economic facts of its functioning.

It is not unimportant that it be—in Hollywood—at the moment when the rendering of the cinematic image becomes subtle, opens up to the shades of greys (monochrome translation of the range of colours), thus drawing nearer to a more faithful imitation of the photographic images promoted (fetishised) as the very norms of realism, that Speech and the speaking Subject come onto the scene. As soon as they are produced, sound and speech are plebiscited as *the "truth" which was lacking* in the silent film—the truth which is all of a sudden noticed, not without alarm and resistance, as having been

---

[5]In the general readjustment of codes of cinematic "realism" produced in Hollywood (according, of course, to its ideological and economic norms and objectives: for its profit and for that of bourgeois ideology) by the coming of sound, the codes of the strictly photographic "realism" of the filmic image are redefined specifically (but not exclusively) in relation to the increasingly important place occupied by the photographic image in bourgeois societies in relation to mass consumption. This place has something to do with that of gold (of the fetish): the photo is the money of the "real" (of "life") assures its convenient circulation and appropriation. Thereby, the photo is unanimously consecrated as general equivalent for, standard of, all "realism": the cinematic image could not, without losing its "power" (the power of its "credibility"), not align itself with the photographic norms. The "strictly technical" level of the improvements of optical apparatus and emulsions is thus totally programmed by the ideology of the "realistic" reproduction of the world at work in the constitution of the photographic image as the "objective representation" *par excellence*. Ideology system of coding, which in its turn that image renews.

lacking in the silent film. And at once this truth renders no longer valid all films which do not possess it, which do not produce it. The decisive supplement, the "ballast of reality" (Bazin) constituted by sound and speech intervenes straightway, therefore, as *perfection and redefinition of the impression of reality.*

It is at the cost of a series of blindnesses (of disavowals) that the silent image was able to be taken for the reflection, the objective double of "life itself": disavowal of colour, relief, sound. Founded on these lacks (as any representation is founded on a lack which governs it, a lack which is the very principle of any simulacrum: the spectator is anyhow well aware of the artifice but he/she prefers all the same to believe in it), filmic representation could find its production only by working to diminish its effects, to mask its very reality. Otherwise, it would have been rejected as too visibly factitious: it was absolutely necessary that it facilitate the disavowal of the veritable sensory castrations which founded its specificity and that it not, by remarking them, prevent such disavowal. *Compromises* were necessary in order that the cinema could function as ideological apparatus, in order that its delusion could take place.

The work of suturing, of filling in, of patching up the lacks which ceaselessly recalled the radical difference of the cinematic image was not done at all at one go but piece by piece, by the *patient accumulation of technical processes.* Directly and totally programmed by the ideology of resemblance, of the "objective" duplication of a "real" itself conceived as specular reflection, cinema technology occupied itself in improving and refining the initial imperfect *dispositif, always* imperfect by virtue of the ideological delusion produced by the film as "impression of reality." The lack of relief had been immediately compensated for (this is the original impression of reality) by movement and the depth of the image, inscribing the perspective code which in Western cultures stands as principal emblem of spatial relief. The lack of colour had to make do with panchromatic stock, pending the commercialisation of three-colour processes (1935–40). Neither the pianos nor the orchestras of the silent film could really substitute for "realistic sound": synchronised speech and sound—in spite of their imperfections, in truth of little weight at a time when it is the whole of sound reproduction, records, radios, which is affected by background noise and interference—thus considerably *displace the site and the means (until then strictly iconic)* of the production of the impression of reality.

Because the *ideological* conditions of production—consumption of the initial impression of reality (figurative analogy + movement + perspective) were changing (if only in function of the very dissemination of photo and film), it was necessary to tinker with its technical modalities in order that the act of disavowal renewing the deception could continue to be accomplished "automatically," in a reflex manner, without any disturbance of the spectacle, above all without any work or effort on the part of the spectator. The succession of technical advances cannot be read, in the manner of Bazin, as the progress towards a "realism plus" other·than in that they accumulate realistic supplements which all aim at reproducing—in strengthening, diversifying, rendering more subtle—the impression of reality; which aim, that is, to reduce as much as possible, to minimise the gap which the "yes-I-know/but-all-the-same" has to fill.

What is at stake in deep focus, what is at stake in the historicity of the technique, are the codes and the modes of production of "realism," the transmission, renewal or transformation of the ideological systems of recognition, specularity, truth-to-lifeness.

III. "MORE REAL" OR MORE VISIBLE?

The reinforcement of "effects of the real" is the first and foremost reason for Bazin's interest in deep focus. In a number of famous texts (notably *The Evolution of Cinematic Language* and *William Wyler or the Jansenist of Mise en Scène*) and with reference essentially to the films of Orson Welles and William Wyler (a choice which is not without overdetermining Bazin's discourse), he makes deep focus the means and the symbol of the irreversible accomplishment of the "realist vocation of the cinema," of the "realist rejuvenation of narrative."

A series of principles are set up which follow from what is for Bazin a truly *first principle:* "the immanent ambiguity of reality," which montage and even classic Hollywood editing had reduced to a single meaning, to a single discourse (that of the film-maker), "subjectivising the event to an extreme, since every element is owing to the decision of the *metteur en scène*"; whereas filming with deep focus safeguards the ambiguity because it participates in "an aesthetic of reality" and offers the spectator "the possibility of carrying out at least the final stage of the editing him or herself."

Thus 1) the real is ambiguous; 2) to give a representation of it that is fragmented (because of montage or the work of the writing) is to reduce this ambiguity and replace it with a "subjectivity" (a meaning: a "view of the world," an ideology); 3) because deep focus brings the cinematic image closer to the "normal" retinal image, to "realist" vision, and shows literally *more* things, *more "real,"* it allows the reactivation of that "ambiguity" which leaves the spectator "free"; aims, that is, at abolishing the difference between film and reality, representation and real, at confirming the spectator in his or her "natural" relationship with the world, hence at reduplicating the conditions of his or her "spontaneous" vision and ideology. It is not for nothing that Bazin writes (not without humour) in the course of a discussion of *The Best Years of Our Lives:* "Deep focus in Wyler's film is meant to be liberal and democratic like the consciousness of the American spectator and the film's heroes."

On the one hand, duplication of the ideological effects of the impression of reality, of the "normality" of specular representation; on the other, *revelation* (in its exact Christian sense) of "the natural ambiguity and unity" of the world.

To this "revelation" according to Bazin of "the immanent ambiguity of reality" by deep focus, Mitry opposes "the fact that the real of film is a mediated real: between the real world and us, there is the film, the camera, the representation, in the extreme case where there is not in addition an author." He writes: "It is supremely naive to think (as Bazin does) that because the camera automatically records an element given in reality, it provides us with an objective and impartial image of that reality. . . . By the very fact that it is *given in an image,* the real captured by the camera lens is structured according to formalising values which create a series of new relations and therefore a new reality—at very least a new appearance. The *represented* is *seen* via *representation* which, necessarily, transforms it."

Secure in his insistence against Bazin on the distinction film/real, Mitry fails to see how, far from acknowledging the difference, film tends to reduce it by proposing itself as adequate to the norms of perception, by ceaselessly restoring the illusion of the homogeneous and the continuous, which is precisely the basis of Bazin's error—the postulation as the same value of the unifying functions of both perception and film representation. It was then inevitable that Mitry should end up sharing Bazin's view of deep focus. Against Bazin, he stresses the otherness of film to the real but fails to recognise the process of repression of which that otherness is the object and the place of the spectator in that process. The film is abstracted from its social inscription into an absolute realm where the "truth" of its nature ("fragmentation of the real into shots and sequences") takes precedence over that of its reading (reconstitution, suturation). Like Bazin—though not, of course, without shades of difference—he then comes to consider that, because it reduces such fragmentation, deep focus is indeed productive of an "increase in realism": it is seen as (ontological realism) capturing, as the classic shot does not, "the event globally, in its real space-time," restoring "to object and setting their density of existence, their weight of presence" (Bazin's formulations taken over by Mitry) and as (psychological realism) replacing "the spectator in the true conditions of perception"; that is to say, coherence, continuity and finally "ambiguity." On condition that deep focus does not become an omnivalent principle substitutive for every other formula of *mise en scène*, Mitry declares himself "perfectly in agreement with Bazin."

Nothing is less certain that that deep focus is in this way—particularly in the films of Welles and Wyler, the obligatory example since Bazin—responsible for an "increase in realism"; and this exactly in that it inscribes in the image, more successfully than any other filming process, the *representational code of linear perspective.*

We are thus faced with a contradiction: for Bazin the intervention of deep focus increases the realist coefficient of the cinematic image by completing the virtues (the virtualities) *already* inscribed in that image, by perfecting it, by giving literally *more field* to its "ontological realism." For Mitry this cannot be the case since by stressing the artificiality (the otherness) of the cinematic image, it is just such a "realism" that he refuses, merely conceding that deep focus—because it produces a "more global" and relatively less discontinuous space—comes closer to certain effects of ordinary perception; that is to say, it brings back and reinscribes in the image the (at least psychological) *conditions* of an increase in realism. For the first, this *more* is *added;* for the second, it tends to cancel out a *less,* to fill a lack. The contradiction between Bazin and Mitry is also a contradiction in Mitry, since the system of differences and specificities which constitutes the cinematic image as an other of the world, offered as its double, does not abolish the particular case of the deep focus image. In his illusion, Bazin is more coherent than Mitry, the person who denounces the illusion as such, for the stress on the constitutive differences and specific codings of the image must, as deep focus demonstrates, be accompanied by a simultaneous stress on the *work* of these codings (their *raison d'être* and their goal), which is to produce their own miscognition, to give themselves over as "natural" and hence to mask the play of differences.

It is from the basis of this *positive* contribution accorded deep

focus by both Bazin and Mitry that the *double game* of the coding of the cinematic image (its "transparency," since it is not
by being remarked as such that it functions) operates, insofar
as the "supplement of realism" that deep focus is held to produce cannot be produced without distorting and emphasising
the codes of "realism" already "naturally" at work in the image: a supplement that is *excessive* in relation to the system of
(perspective/cultural) norms which ground the impression of
reality and maintain the category of "realism.". . .

IV. NOTES ON REPRESENTATION

The most analogical representation of the world is still not,
is never, its reduplication. Analogical repetition is a false repetition, staggered, disphased, deferred and different; but it
produces *effects* of repetition and analogy which imply the disavowal (or the repression) of these differences and which thus
make of the *desire* for identity, identification, recognition, of
the desire for the *same*, one of the principal driving forces of
analogical figuration. In other words the spectator, the ideological and social subject, and not just the technical apparatus,
is the operator of the analogical mechanism.

There is a famous painting of the English school, *The Chol-
mondeley Sisters* (1600–10), which represents two sisters side by
side, each holding a baby in her arms. The two sisters look
very much alike, as do the babies, sisters and babies are
dressed almost identically, and so on. Confronted with this
canvas, one is disturbed by a repetition that is not a repetition, by a contradictory repetition. What is here painted is the
very subject of figurative painting: repetition, *with*, in this
repetition, all the play of the innumerable differences which at
once *destroy* it (from one figure to the other, nothing is identical) and *assert* it as violent *effect*. Panic and confusion of the
look doubled and split. The image is *in* the image, the double
is not the same, the repetition is a fiction: it makes us believe
that it repeats itself just because it does not repeat itself. It is
in the most "analogical" representation (never completely so),
the most "faithful," the most "realistic," that the *effects of representation* can be most easily read. One must be fooled by the
image in order to see it as such (and no longer as a projection
of the world).

Is it that cinema begins where *mise en scène* ends, when is
broken or left behind the machinery of performance, of the
actor and the scenario, when technical necessity takes off the
mask of art? That is roughly what Vertov believed and what is

repeated more or less by a whole avant-garde in his wake—
with categories such as "pure cinema," "live cinema," "cinéma vérité" —right up to certain experimental films of today. It
is not very difficult to see, however, that what is being celebrated in that tradition of "non-cinema" is a visible with no
original blemish that will stand forth in its "purity" as soon
as the cinema strips itself of the "literary" or "theatrical" artifices it inherited at its birth; a visible on the right side of
things, manifesting their living authenticity. There is, of course,
no visible not held in a look and, as it were, always already
framed. Moreover, it is naive to locate *mise en scène* solely on
the side of the camera: it is just as much, and even before the
camera intervenes, everywhere where the social regulations
order the place, the behaviour and almost the "form" of subjects in the various configurations in which they are caught
(and which do not demand the same type of performance: here
authority, here submission; standing out or standing aside;
etc.; from one system of social relation to another, the place of
the subject changes and so does the subject's capture in the
look of others). What Vertov films without *mise en scène* (as he
believes) are the effects of other *mises en scène*. In other words,
script, actors, *mise en scène* or not, all that is filmable is the
changing, historical, determined relationship of men and things
to the visible, are dispositions of representation.

However refined, analogy in the cinema is a deception, a lie,
a fiction that must be straddled—in disavowing, knowing but
not wanting to know—by the *will to believe* of the spectator,
the spectator who expects to be fooled and wants to be fooled,
thus becoming the first agent of his or her own fooling. The
spectacle, and cinema itself, despite all the *reality effects* it may
produce, always gives itself away *for what it is* to the spectators. There is no spectator other than one *aware* of the spectacle, even if (provisionally) allowing him or herself to be taken
in by the fictioning machine, deluded by the simulacrum: it is
precisely *for that* that he or she came. The certainty that we
always have, in our heart of hearts, that the spectacle is not
life, that the film is not reality, that the actor is not the character and that if we are present as spectators, it is because we
know we are dealing with a semblance, this certainty must be
capable of being doubted. It is only worth its risk; it interests
us only if it can be (provisionally) cancelled out. The "yes, I
know" calls irresistibly for the "but all the same," includes it
as its value, its intensity. We know, but we want something
else: to believe. We want to be fooled, while still knowing a
little that we are so being. We want the one and the other, to

be both fooled and not fooled, ot oscillate, to swing from knowledge to belief, from distance to adherence, from criticism to fascination.

Which is why realist representations are successful: they allow this movement to and fro which ceaselessly sets off the intensity of the disavowal, they sustain the spectator's pleasure in being prisoner in a situation of conflict (I believe/I don't believe). They allow it because they lay out a contradictory, representative space, a space in which there are both effects of the real and effects of fiction, of repetition and difference, automatic devices of identification and significant resistances, recognition and seizure. In this sense, analogical fiction in the cinema is bound up with narrative fiction, and all cinematic fictions are tightened, more or less forcefully, by this knot of disavowal which ceaselessly starts and starts again with the continual *petitio principii* of the "impression of reality." The capturing power of a fiction, whether the fiction of the analogical reproduction of the visible or the fictions of cinematic narrative, depends always on its self-designation as such, on the fact that its fictive character is known and recognised from the start, that it presents itself as an artificial arrangement, that it does not hide that it is above all an apparatus of deception and thus that it postulates a spectator who is not easily but *difficultly* deceivable, not a spectator who is blindly condemned to fascination but one who is complicit, willing to "go along."

Fictional deceits, contrary to many other systems of illusions, are interesting in that they can function only from the clear designation of their deceptive character. There is no uncertainty, no mistake, no misunderstanding or manipulation. There is ambivalence, play. The spectacle is always a game, requiring the spectators' participation not as "passive," "alienated" consumers, but as players, accomplices, masters of the game even if they are also what is at stake. It is necessary to suppose spectators to be total imbeciles, completely alienated social beings, in order to believe that they are thoroughly deceived and deluded by simulacra. Different in this to ideological and political representations, spectatorial representations declare their existence as simulacrum and, on that contractual basis, invite the spectator to *use* the simulacrum to fool him or herself. Never "passive," the spectator, works. But that work is not only a work of decipherment, reading, elaboration of signs. It is first of all and just as much, if not more, to play the game, to fool him or herself out of pleasure, and in spite of those knowledges which reinforce his or her position of non-fool; it is to maintain—if the spectacle, its play make it possible—the mechanism of disavowal at its highest level of intensity. The more one knows, the more difficult it is to believe, and the more it is worth it to manage to.

If there is an iconic analogy as operative in cinema the contradictory work of difference, non-similitude, false repetition which at once found and limit the deception, then it is the whole edifice of cinematic representation that finds itself affected with a fundamental lack: the negative index, the restriction the disavowal of which is the symptom and which it tries to fill while at the same time displaying it. More than the representative apparatuses that come before it (theatre, painting, photography, etc.), cinema—precisely because it effects a greater approximation to the analogical reproduction of the visisble, because it is carried along by that "realist vocation" so dear to Bazin—is no doubt more profoundly, more decisively undermined than those other apparatuses by everything that separates the real from the representable and even the visible from the represented. It is what resists cinematic representation, limiting it on all sides and from within, which constitutes equally its force; what makes it falter makes it go.

The cinematic image grasps only a small part of the visible; and it is a grasp which—provisional, contracted, fragmentary—bears in it its impossibility. At the same time, film images are only a small part in the multiplicity of the visible, even if they tend by their accumulation to cover it. Every image is thus doubly racked by disillusion: from within itself as machine for simulation, mechanical and deathly reproduction of the living; from without as single image only, and not all images, in that what fills it will never be but the present index of an absence, of the lack of another image. Yet it is also, of course, this structuring disillusion which offers the offensive strength of cinematic representation and allows it to work against the completing, reassuring, mystifying representations of ideology. It is that strength that is needed, and that work of disillusion, if cinematic representation is to do something other than pile visible on visible, if it is, in certain rare flashes, to produce in our sight the very blindness which is at the heart of this visible.

1980

JAMES SPELLERBERG
TECHNOLOGY AND IDEOLOGY IN THE CINEMA

Since its inception the cinema has rarely, if ever, been considered innocent of complicity in ideology. For the most part, ideological critiques of the cinema have centered on elements of narrative, objects, and events depicted by the image, or aspects of diffusion and exploitation (for example, the star system). In the past eight years in France, however, another critique has developed in conjunction with the more traditional one. It centers on the ideological effects of the formal elements of the cinema. This critique is not without precedent but, in one of its most striking aspects—its discussion of the relation of cinema technology to ideology—it can be seen as a decisive intervention in the way the cinema is thought of and practiced in western Europe. Lately, some of the more significant texts which constitute this critique have become available in English translation. *Film Quarterly* has published both an article from *Cinéthique*, Jean-Louis Baudry's "Ideological Effects of the Basic Cinematographic Apparatus,"[1] and an essay by Daniel Dayan, "The Tutor-Code of Classical Cinema,"[2] which summarizes some of Jean-Pierre Oudart's work in *Cahiers du Cinéma*. With the recent appearance in *Film Reader*[3] of the first part of Jean-Louis Comolli's series of articles from *Cahiers*, as

---

[1]*Film Quarterly* 27 (2): 39–47. Translated from *Cinéthique* No. 7/8, pp. 1–8.
[2]*Film Quarterly* 28 (1): 22–31.
[3]*Film Reader* 2, pp. 125–141.

well as *Screen's* continuing work in the general field of cinema and ideology, it is likely that the issue of technology and ideology in the cinema will increasingly be taken up in this country as well. With this in mind, I would like to review some of the basic arguments in the French literature.

To date, this ideological analysis of cinema technology has been largely concerned with the way the cinema has taken over and elaborated a major ideological function served by painting before the advent of the movies. This analysis has been made in greatest detail in the writings of Jean-Louis Comolli as part of an attempt to establish a materialist history of the cinema. The analysis of painting prior to the coming of photography and the cinema has been more fully treated in Jean-Pierre Oudart's essays; these, therefore, serve as a useful background to Comolli's work. And Jean-Louis Baudry's article serves to give a brief statement of the whole argument which has been both expanded and reshaped by the other writers. I will therefore begin with Baudry's overview and Oudart's background essays before looking at Comolli's massive undertaking.

According to Baudry, the "ideological effects of the basic cinematographic apparatus" are produced in two major ideologies: that of representation and that of specularization. With the arrival of western science and the end of the era of geocentrism, a new mode of representation, artificial perspective, was developed, This mode of representation set up the perceiving subject as the origin of meaning: space was centered about the eye; the eye seemed to organize the representation as continuous, homogenous space. Such a space was different from that found in the art of other cultures. For example, Greek art, Baudry says, had a discontinuous, heterogeneous space with pictorial construction based on multiple points of view.[4] The space of the new mode of representation was designed to be organized by something outside it; the subject was the ordering principle separate from the material world represented. It was, therefore, a transcendental subject.[5]

Such is Baudry's explanation of the ideological role of perspective in painting from the Italian Renaissance to the coming of photography: it implied the existence of the subject. For

---

[4]Most of the writers in *Cahiers* and *Cinéthique* rely on the work of Pierre Francastel for their art historical background. See *Peinture et société: naissance et destruction d'un espace plastique de la renaissance au cubisme* (Lyon: Audin Editeur, 1951); also, *la réalité figurative. Éléments structurels de sociologie de l'art* (Editions Gonthier, 1965).

[5]The "subject" is seen as an imaginary construct, both the means by which the biological individual is inserted into the relations of production, and the means by which his/her function in these relations remain masked. See the essays by Altman and Rosen in this issue.

an effect to be truly ideological, however, it must be hidden. Jean-Pierre Oudart, as we shall see, will take up this issue with regard to artificial perspective. Baudry traces the system of artificial perspective through painting to photography to cinema, showing that the camera and its lenses were designed to reproduce this system. Although different focal lengths may alter perspective, historically the dominant model is the system of the Italian Renaissance, and the use of other lenses are only deviations from this norm.

The cinema apparatus has a further contribution to the ideology of representation. One of the key means by which perspective implies the presence of the subject is by depicting a continuous space which is organized by a single factor: the look of the spectator. This continuity, Baudry argues (drawing on Husserl), is a major attribute of the subject, postulating its existence and circumscribing its place. Potentially, the cinema reintroduces discontinuity into its representation through the differences between the images in the series of photographs it registers. Projection, however, negates and conceals this difference, allowing the spectator-subject to reign once again over a continuous space to which he or she gives meaning. "Limited by the framing, lined up, put at the proper distance, the world offers up an object endowed with meaning, an intentional object, implied by and implying the action of the 'subject' which sights it."[6] Moreover, narrative structure provides a continuity for the different views of the same space or the different spaces presented by the film. This narrative continuity of space, however, requires violence against the instrumental base. Numerous codes (e.g., of editing and camera movement) were developed to preserve continuity at this level. The suppression of technological discontinuity through these narrative-related codes suggests the enormous ideological stake involved in preserving the synthetic unity of the subject, the place where meaning originates. Baudry does not question why discontinuity should spontaneously be present at the technical level of the linking of images, and his silence on this point is symptomatic of a weakness in the argument, one which will be made apparent in Comolli's work on the ideology of representation.

The viewing situation, for Baudry, is analogous to the mirror stage in Lacanian psychology. His analysis of the viewing situation leads him to what he calls the ideology of specularization. It is not necessary for this essay to reproduce this

[6] Baudry, "Ideological Effects of the Basic Cinematographic Apparatus," *Film Quarterly* 27 (2): 43.

analysis;[7] it suffices to say that this second ideology also results in the constitution of a unifying subject as source of all
meaning. This ideology of the viewing situation, based on the
identification of the viewer with the camera, complements the
ideology produced by the images viewed. "Ultimately, the
forms of narrative adopted, the 'contents' of the image are of
little importance so long as an identification remains possible."[8] What is necessary is that the cinematic apparatus be
hidden or repressed, so the constitution of the subject appears
to be a characteristic of the natural world directly transmitted
by the cinema, rather than an effect of production of the medium itself.

While the ideology of specularization is elaborated by Oudart in his series of articles on the "suture" in classical cinema,[9]
and by Christian Metz in his more recent work,[10] it is the ideology of representation which has played the primary role in
the current critique of cinema technology, and it is this which
I will pursue. In a series of articles in *Cahiers du Cinéma*,[11] Jean-
Pierre Oudart traces the history of western painting from the
Quattrocento with reference to its pictorial system. "L'effet de
réel" is the name Oudart gives to the effect of the production
in painting (and cinema) of the system of representation, which
includes the spectator as the determinant or metteur-en-scène
of its space while at the same time concealing this very production. The codes of figuration (producing "l'effet de réalité")
used in the late medieval period include codes such as those
of iconic similarity. They were carried over into the early Renaissance, but were included in a completely different arrangement of the total space of the image. This new arrangement was dictated by the codes of representation (producing
what Oudart calls "l'effet de réel"), which function to produce
a "subjective" space, one that implies a subject outside it. These
two sets of codes now make up a system which is hidden from
the spectator; it causes its own misrecognition ("méconnaiss-
ance").

This subjective structure of pictorial representation implies
a "judgment of existence" by the spectator-as-subject: the subject then serves as the index of the represented's existence.

[7]See Altman's article in this issue.
[8]Baudry, p. 46.
[9]See Dayan, "The Tutor-Code of Classical Cinema," *Film Quarterly* 28 (1):
22–31.
[10]See Metz, "The Imaginary Signifier," *Screen* 16 (2): 14–76.
[11]"L'effet de réel," *Cahiers du Cinéma* 228, pp. 19–26, "Notes pour une théo-
rie de la représentation," *Cahiers du Cinéma* 229, pp. 43–45; and 230, pp. 43–
45.

The symbolic religious figures depicted in the middle ages become in the Renaissance typical contemporary figures who make an existential claim. They are present to the look of a spectator, and become real to him or her (thus the surface of the painting appears to have depth, to be a real space). The scene is constituted as a spectacle viewed by a spectator excluded from the field—the subject. The subject is already, in a sense, part of the system of representation, since its presence is implied by the image; the image is made for a subject. The subject is already inscribed in the signifying chain, yet this inscription is concealed. Oudart uses rhetorical terminology: film deceptively presents itself as the predicate of a subject outside its field, and the viewer, in turn, hallucinates the traces of his or her own inscription as the subject of the discourse. This hallucination takes the form of misrecognizing these traces as real objects. The imaginary is taken for the real; the viewer sees through the surface of the painting to a space with depth, the markings of the figurative codes become a real space with real objects.

This "effet de réel" is achieved by "inscribing the subject as a lack." The figurative space of the painting or film implies the subject, yet rigourously excludes it. The subject is therefore an absence, a necessary, structuring absence, present in some "scene" or "stage" (to use the theatrical metaphor adopted by many of the writers with whom we are concerned) outside the scene viewed by the spectator. Oudart uses this concept of the "double stage" of the classical cinema when writing of the suture that characterizes the editing employed in that cinema.[12] The ultimate aim of his analysis is to make possible the recognition of this system of representation, to situate it historically.

> If "l'effet de réel" is the product of the re-inscription of the subject in the system of scenic representation of western painting, at first under the form of a re-marking of the position of the spectator in the representation from which develops a figurative tradition persisting in the cinema, it must be recognized today as a particular and transitory mode of the inscription of the subject in a figurative system historically determined.[13]

This analysis of the western system of representation is basic to the most sustained ideological critique of cinema technology, the series of articles on *Cahiers* by Jean-Louis Comolli

---

[12]See Dayan, *op. cit.*, pp. 27–31; also, William Rothman's response, *Film Quarterly* 16 (1): 45–50.

[13]*Cahiers du Cinéma* 228, p. 26.

which appeared under the general title, "Technique et Idéolo-gie."[14] Comolli's work is sufficiently important to stand as representative of one type of theoretical work done in France on the issue. It is best seen in clear opposition to another Marxist position also developed in France. Here again a single author's work presents itself as representative and, indeed, is taken as such by the writers of *Cahiers* and *Cinéthique*. The text is Jean-Patrick Lebel's *Cinéma et Idéologie*,[15] an expansion of a series of articles that were first published in *La Nouvelle Critique*. Lebel is considered the spokesman for the Marxism of the French Communist Party, which *Cahiers* and *Cinéthique* reject as tending toward liberalism. They accuse Lebel of presenting common sense as an antidote to their "extremist" theorizing.

There is no question that, in a large part, Lebel's *Cinéma et Idéologie* is ". . . a rare mixed bag of outdated subjective notions like creative responsibility and objective idealist innovations which largely drew on structuralism."[16] But, before he begins to theorize on his own, Lebel undertakes a critique of the ideology-technology issue as presented in *Cinéthique* and *Cahiers* which cannot be dismissed so lightly. Comolli's articles appeared after Lebel's, and Comolli makes reference to Lebel's work, but his own work is still not entirely exempt from Lebel's criticisms.

Lebel makes the argument that the camera and lens[17] are ideologically neutral because they are scientific in nature — based on the laws of the propagation of light, etc. Comolli persuasively argues that the cinematographic apparatus was developed as a response to an ideological (as well as economic) demand, and the fact that its operation involves scientific laws does not mean it is not marked by that demand. Comolli insists that there is no autonomous history of film technology, and he also opposes the formalist notion of a limbo of various techniques from which the filmmaker can draw as he or she chooses. He cites the endless chain of technical reasons given

---

[14]*Cahiers du Cinéma* 229 (pp. 4–21), 230 (pp. 51–57), 231 (pp. 42–49), 233 (pp. 39–45), 234–235 (pp. 94–100), and 241 (pp. 20–24). Translation of No. 229, pp. 4–15 available in *Film Reader 2*. I have used the mimeographed BFI translation of Nos. 229–233, but have made all references to the French text, since the translation is not readily available.

[15]Paris: Editions sociales, 1971.

[16]"Cinéthique on Language et Cinéma," *Screen* 14 (1–2): 212. Translated from *Cinéthique* No. 13–14.

[17]Nearly every writer concerned with this issue makes a disclaimer that he is discussing the whole technological base of the cinema, not just the camera and the lens, but the major arguments are centered on camera and lens nonetheless.

for the phenomenon of the eclipse of deep focus in the thirties, reasons which alone are obviously inadequate. Nontechnical determinants must be brought in, and for this the guidance of theory is required. This is the basis for a materialist film history.

Traditional theories of communication treat their object as a process of exchange: a meaning is passed essentially unaltered from a sender to a receiver via a transparent channel. But communication must be seen as exchange and work. A technical process in the cinema is a signifying practice. It both transmits and produces meanings, which are activated by the "other scene" of history, economy, and ideology. It is not a transparent medium of communication, though in the classical cinema it may appear that way. A technique, Comolli states, is "where instruments + processes + knowledge + practice which back each other up are combined to realise an *aim*—an objective which then constitutes, founds and sanctions the technique."[18] This aim is determined by economics and ideology in a roughly causal scheme: the socioeconomic inscription of the cinema constitutes an ideological demand which produces both technology and cinematic form together.[19]

This is the theoretical groundwork which both requires and permits an ". . . analysis of the connections between cinematic technique and its economic and ideological determinations."[20] Such an analysis deals with the historical inscription of the technique—the effects of the economic, ideological, and technical factors which produce its appearance—and the pattern of the presence and absence of the technique in the practice of the cinema. Comolli's major example is deep focus because, he says, it has historically been exempted from the "neutrality" usually ascribed to technical forms (the reference is to Bazin), and because it embodies the codes of perspective. It is this latter reason which provides the opportunity to draw on and develop the notion of the ideology of representation. Like Baudry and Oudart (and Bazin before them), Comolli largely equates cinema with photography, and assumes the purpose of both is to appear to reproduce visible reality. He adopts for his argument Serge Daney's formulation of the postulate of the ideological cinema: reality is equivalent to the visible, and the visible is equivalent to the image or representation—there is no loss or distortion of truth. This is a proposition that Lebel attacks. The "impression of reality" that so concerns the writers of *Cahiers* and *Cinéthique*, he argues, is

[18]*Cahiers du Cinéma* 229, p. 8.
[19]*Cahiers du Cinéma* 229, p. 18.
[20]*Cahiers du Cinéma* 231, p. 44.

part of an idealist problematic. These writers remain prisoner to the thought of Bazin by merely inverting him.

There can be no question of the tremendous influence of Bazin's thought on the ideological critique of the cinema. Those aspects of film technique which most concern the writers of *Cahiers* and *Cinéthique* are directly related to those aspects which most concerned Bazin: deep focus, montage (as opposed to the long take), the close-up (as opposed to the long shot), and the frame. Bazin's analysis of these is usually taken as a point of departure, but is then subjected to a radical critique that, at its most successful, supersedes it. The problems exist in a different problematic; they are conceptualized differently. From Bazin's spectator exercising free will to the imaginary subject of the ideological critics there is too great a leap to say, as Lebel does, that the latter is merely an outgrowth of the former. Lebel continues, however, with a more telling criticism: this "impression of reality" becomes, for Comolli, Oudart, and Baudry, an abstract ideology which, once assigned to the cinema, blocks the real work of the analysis of concrete instances of cinematic practice. Comolli is acutely aware of this criticism, and approvingly quotes Kristeva concerning the error of collapsing cinema into ideology. However, in his actual analyses, he does not always remain true to his own caveats, exhibiting most notably a tendency to speak of a *single* cinema. Thus, what at one moment applies to an instance of the cinema at the next applies to the cinema as a whole. Pascal Bonitzer, in reference to Baudry, shows how this is a theoretical error which leads to error in practice as well as we shall see.

Comolli accepts Oudart's and Baudry's analysis of artificial perspective and explains how perspective was transferred to the cinema. In the nineteenth century, scientific advancement jeopardized the previously unquestioned faith in the accuracy of the human eye, which had been the model and the empirical proof for the codes of perspective and its ideological effects (the ideology of representation). But at the same time photography was invented and a machine took the place of the suspect eye. A machine now produced the perspective views, and a machine was considered objective and scientific. The ideological importance of perspective escaped unharmed, even strengthened. Then, around 1896, certain entrepreneurs discovered that showing "life as it is" was profitable, and the cinema was born (Comolli does not elaborate on why this "discovery" was made at this time). The circuit from painting to photography to cinema is completed, but carries the risk of reducing all cinema to the visual, something Comolli himself

criticizes[21] but does not always escape. At points in his argument primitive deep focus *becomes* the cinema. For example,
deep focus is labelled

> a sign that the ideological instrument cinema is itself produced
> within these codes and by these systems of representation,
> completing, perfecting, and surpassing them. . . . Deep focus
> is thus one of the principal determining factors regulating the
> cinematic image (and the camera).[22]

Such a statement is subject to two serious criticisms, both of
which are made by Lebel. The first, referred to above, involves
the assignment of an abstract and monolithic ideology to the
cinema.[23] At points in his discussion, Comolli appears to assume that the cinema has an essential nature determined by
its origins—a Bazinian notion he is at pains to refute. The
cinema arises about 1896 partly as a response to an ideological
demand. This demand then becomes an *ideological* "first time."
A large part of Comolli's study is devoted to an attack on idealist film history, as characterized by the works of Bazin and
Jean Mitry. Comolli argues that these historians take a particular instance of cinematic practice (that which is contemporary
with them) and treat it as *the* cinema, reading it back into the
past and searching for its origin or "first time" in order to
justify its existence as the result of evolution. Although Comolli bases his statement of the ideological demand for the first
cinema on historical analysis and not merely on a reading of
the present into the past (as he accuses Bazin and Mitry of
doing), the result is similar: "the 'First' valorises, inscribes,
comprehends and carries all the rest."[24] An "abstract mould
whose nature, function and meaning do not change"[25] has been
created.

The second criticism is that Comolli, and much of the discourse on the ideological nature of film technology, confuses
(in Lebel's words) the camera and the cinema.[26] Comolli correctly labels such a distinction formalist,[27] but the criticism does
point to a weakness in parts of Comolli's analysis, that of the
uncertain relation of the apparatus to its use, or of technology

---

[21]*Cahiers du Cinéma* 229, pp. 7–8.
[22]*Cahiers du Cinéma* 233, p. 43.
[23]Lebel, *op. cit.*, p. 43.
[24]*Cahiers du Cinéma* 231, p. 46.
[25]*Cahiers du Cinéma* 231, p. 48.
[26]Lebel, p. 28.
[27]*Cahiers du Cinéma* 231, p. 49.

to technique. Comolli situates technology as an element of technique ("instruments + processes + knowledge + practice"), but, in order not to attribute neutrality to the instruments, seems to postulate that the "aim" which "constitutes, founds and sanctions the technique" does the same to the technology. This presents the danger of making a fetish of the materiality of the cinema, as Lebel points out.[28] In addition, the possibility of deconstruction, of creating films which call into question the ideological effects of the cinema, becomes remote. How can a film be made without using the guilty instruments? This difficulty may, like the other ones pointed out by Lebel, spring from a nondialectical notion of ideology. Dominant ideology is dominant, not total, and the technology, as well as the signifying practice, of the cinema is created in the field of ideology and is subject to the stresses and contradictions of that field. Baudry also assigned to the cinema instruments a single ideological effect. As we saw, this required him to refrain from questioning why discontinuity was present in the linking of shots, a discontinuity necessitating the "violence" of the codes of continuity. A weakness of Baudry's argument is thus found in Comolli's argument as well.

In his discussion of sound, written after that of deep focus, Comolli carefully avoids many of the problems that are present in the earlier text. The coming of sound, he writes, is the coming of speech, but we must ask what speech, from where, and for whom it originates.

> It is not cinematographic speech in general which is in its essence reactionary or progressive, because there is no cinematographic speech "in general," but ideological and economic inscriptions of the speaking cinema, of which one, the Hollywood cinema, ideologically and economically imposes itself as model.[29]

Similarly, he does not discuss editing in general, but the radical break between montage and decoupage (classical continuity editing). Decoupage was developed by the Hollywood cinema in the twenties and was suited for use with the speech of the Hollywood cinema, since both operated to create continuity, to unify. Montage is a signifying work which requires a reading, whereas decoupage effaces itself in presenting an "already-there." Decoupage appears to present the scene, while montage clearly produces it.

Comolli is aware of Lebel's criticism that such an interpretation valorizes montage. Lebel writes, "We find ourselves here

[28]Lebel, p. 21.
[29]*Cahiers du Cinéma* 241, pp. 22–23.

in the presence of a normative and idealist vision of things, which attributes to a process an absolute meaning, given once and for all."[30] Deconstruction, Lebel argues, cannot be applied to the cinema instruments but only to forms and style, and there are no privileged forms of deconstruction; no form has a univocal signification. Comolli replies that such an argument is itself idealist. Montage does not equal materialism, but it is incorrect to ignore the fact that Eisenstein and Vertov practiced and defended montage as materialist while the idealist Bazin attacked it. Historically, decoupage has been party to the metaphysical conception of the filmic scene as reproduction and revelation of an "already-there," as if it did not in fact produce this scene. In this, Comolli shows sensitivity to the need to speak of a specific practice of the cinema rather than the cinema as a whole. Apparently, this will also be the case with his discussion of deep focus, if he continues it, since he indicates that the later use of deep focus is significantly different from the earlier. For example, in a caption to a still from *The Lady from Shanghai* (the death of Rita Hayworth — Hayworth looming in the foreground; tiny Welles in the extreme background), he notes that "the emphasis of the code of perspective denaturalises the scene. The code is given to be read; it functions as reading, and no longer as (primitive) 'nature.' "[31] In a caption to a still from Eisenstein, he notes that deep focus and montage are not incompatible: "It is montage and depth that are at the same time repressed by the talking Hollywood narrative, to the extent that the inscription of a depth that was no longer 'primitive' implied a work of writing [écriture]."[32] Of course, no substantial change in the lens has occurred in the change from primitive deep focus to readable deep focus, so the ascription of a particular ideological effect to cinema technology must be relativized. It is this modification that Comolli seems to imply in the later sections of his work, and which serves as an answer to Lebel.

> It is not the spectator, but the technique that progresses; the "realism" activated at great cost has, above all, for its object not the cognitive appropriation of the real, but the reinforcement of the credibility of the spectacle which is given as representing and recovering the real. Such at least is the axis in Hollywood, principal place at the same time of the diffusion of the perfection of techniques and the domination of the spectacular conception of the cinema.[33]

[30] Lebel, p. 52.
[31] *Cahiers du Cinéma* 233, p. 41.
[32] *Cahiers du Cinéma* 234–235, p. 97.
[33] *Cahiers du Cinéma* 234–235, p. 99.

The concluding proviso is all-important, and seems to agree
with a statement of Lebel:

> As a precise stage in the history of cinematic forms, a particular
> form can momentarily crystallize in itself certain ideological sig-
> nifieds, which explain as reaction the rejection of these forms
> and the valorisation of other processes or forms which, "util-
> ised" or invested in their turn by ideological signifieds, will be
> rejected for new forms or for a return to forms previously re-
> jected and now "purified," ideologically speaking, by the flow
> of history.[34]

Between these positions lies a subtle but decisive difference.
Lebel seems to imagine a field of cinematic forms which exists
separate from but always called up within history—a limbo.
Comolli sees "film signifiers as 'formations of compromise' between the pressure of ideology and the pressure of the text."[35]
The difference becomes more apparent as Lebel develops his
own theory. As Bonitzer notes, he ends up putting ideology
inside people's heads.[36]

Pascal Bonitzer is more cautious than Comolli in constructing his discourse so that it will be proof to Lebel's criticisms.
In "Fetichisme de la technique: la notion de plan,"[37] Bonitzer
argues that technical apparatus and technical practice can only
be separated as idealist abstractions. He claims that the writers
of *Cahiers* always imply the practice in which an apparatus is
used when they speak of the apparatus—and all practices are
invested by ideologies. In "Réalité' de la denotation"[38] and its
continuation, "Le Gros Orteil,"[39] Bonitzer is careful to refer to
a *practice*. The cinema is both scientific and ideological, he
states. It is an extension of the figurative system developed in
painting in the Renaissance, yet it is more than just an extension of perspective space. It is necessary to have a reading
across the surface of the image, leading to the "other scene"
of economy and history, rather than a viewing in depth, within
the perspective cube. The closeup can contribute to this, but
in the classical cinema, it has been incorporated into the narrative continuity. The closeup interests Bonitzer not in itself,
but because it can mark the discontinuity of filmic space. It is
neither more nor less fragmentary than any other shot but,

[34]Lebel, p. 199.
[35]*Cahiers du Cinéma* 230, p. 53.
[36]See "Pratique artistique et lutte idéologique," *Cahiers du Cinéma* 248, pp.
60–64.
[37]*Cahiers du Cinéma* 233, pp. 4–10.
[38]*Cahiers du Cinéma* 229, pp. 39–41.
[39]*Cahiers du Cinéma* 232, pp. 14–23.

unlike the others, is nearly always read as a fragment, one that, in the classical cinema, must be incorporated into a whole. Jean Mitry's history of the closeup is really a history of this attempt at incorporation. The closeup is therefore a point where the weakness of idealist film history shows through; it is not some "privileged figure" in the cinema. The films of the Dziga Vertov group, for example, use all shots as they do the closeup—for the effect of a dynamic break.

Bonitzer's most extended discussion of cinema technology occurs within a study of the space outside the frame. "Horschamp (un espace en défaut)."[40] It is this essay which most carefully treats the criticisms of Lebel through a critique of the work of Jean-Louis Baudry. The impression of reality, Bonitzer writes, is the result of an absence. The screen hides as well as shows: "*the cinematographic image is haunted by what is not found in it.*"[41] This absence is marked diachronically (between shots) and synchronically (outside the frame). Noel Burch speaks of the space outside the frame,[42] but always with reference to the framed space. Burch's type of offscreen space is utilized by the classical cinema to support the space within the frame, to give it realism. Reframing and reverse angle cutting testify to the reality of a scene by means of what is absent from that scene. The classical filmic space is instituted by a double operation — the exclusion of the materiality of the filmic scene, of the cinema processes and technology and their multiple determinants, and the investment of this excluded space with a fictive reality continuing the space within the frame. In classical cinema, the continuity and homogeneity of space must be observed above all else.

Baudry, Bonitzer says, analyzes a machine outside of all its historical, economic, political, and concrete signifying inscriptions. This forecloses both history and contradiction, so that ideology becomes the equivalent of idealism, existing as an abstract generality. Bonitzer finds that Baudry speaks of *the* repressive system and *the* cinema. The cinema is embodied in its technology, and this "*technical* reduction of 'cinema' rejoins here, according to another mode, the repression of history worked by Lebel."[43] Lebel is relativistic — the filmmaker, enlightened as to the possible ideological effects of various techniques and technology, can do as he or she sees fit. Baudry is absolutist — the filmmaker must expose the mechanics of the cinema, thereby exposing the ideology it supports. The first

[40]*Cahiers du Cinéma* 234–235, pp. 15–26.
[41]*Cahiers du Cinéma* 234–235, p. 16. Italics in original.
[42]See Burch, *Theory of Film Practice*. New York: Praeger, 1973.
[43]*Cahiers du Cinéma* 234–235, p. 24.

purifies the technology of all ideological overdetermination by means of its enlightened usage; the second makes it the source of all ideology. Baudry hypostatizes an ideological effect, making ideology a closed system outside history.

> [Baudry] does not emphasize the fact that the apparatus of the classic cinematographic scene is sustained by another scene implying continuity (extension and diffusion of the "field" [within the frame] outside the frame). Two (field and what is outside it) fuse into one ("reality," "subject"), [resulting in] the forclusion of the signifier, that which is heterogeneous to the subject.[44]

The filmic signifier is hidden by the establishment of subjective space.

Deconstruction involves dividing the one ("reality") into two (practice/effect of sense): the inscription is hereogeneous to the reality-effect of the fiction. A materialist scene is divided; it is a productive, contradictory scene irreducible to "realism." The fragments of the materialist scenes are heterogeneous; such scenes are both constructed and destroyed in the articulation and dialectical interaction of these fragments. But the inscription of both the field of practice and the historical scene where it plays can only be conceived as a strategy. In Vertov and Godard, showing the technology of the cinema has a positive ideological effect, but this is not necessarily the case in a different historical moment or in the presence of a different combination of forces. In Rouch's cinema, for example, the technology shown on screen is reinvested in the field of "truth."

Bonitzer presents deconstruction in a manner that does not fall subject to Lebel's criticism. At the same time, he aims for a theoretical correctness that will sharply separate his work from the proliferating discourse on cinema and ideology that has burst forth in France. The theoretical difficulties in Baudry's and Comolli's presentations of the critique of cinema technology bear fruit in such eclectic work as Christian Zimmer's *Cinéma et Politique*.[45] Zimmer ends up valorizing the work of Robbe-Grillet, who practices a purely formal subversion of the cinema, uninformed by materialist analysis. *Cahiers* denounces Robbe-Grillet as "the last word in anarchic technocratism,"[46] yet his work can be read as evidence of the appear-

[44]*Ibid.*
[45]Cinema 2000/Seghers. Paris: Editions Seghers, 1974. A review in English is available: D. I. Grossvogel, "Reappropriating the Political Film," *Diacritics* 5 (2): 45–53.
[46]Jean Narboni, "Sur quelques contresens," *Cahiers du Cinéma* 226–227, p. 117.

ance in practice of some of the theoretical deficiencies found in *Cahiers* and *Cinéthique*.

The only defense against "popularization" of the ideological critique of the cinema, such as Zimmer's, is increased theoretical rigor. In the study of technique and technology, the writers of *Cahiers* refined their position in response to hostile criticism. This particular field of inquiry has been set aside by *Cahiers*, but the recent availability of several important texts to American readers may reopen it in a new setting.

PARKER TYLER
FROM MAGIC AND MYTH OF THE MOVIES

PREFACE

That the movies offer nothing but entertainment is a myth in a sense never used or implied in the following pages. I am not denying that millions of America's movie fans succeed in finding only entertainment in the nation's theaters. Aside from the newsreels and the documentaries given impetus by the war, entertainment remains all that is consciously demanded by those paying rising prices at movie box offices. . . . Patrons of all art media may get more than they demand as well as less, and since the surplus is not precisely expected, it may register vaguely, obliquely, unconsciously. Especially is this true of the movie audience, if only because as a large mass it is critically inarticulate. I hope that my efforts may succeed in giving it some voice on the positive side— movie reviewers take care of its voice on the negative side—and I hope also that for the benefit of students and those hitherto indifferent to the "folk" art of cinema I may further demonstrate that Hollywood is a vital, interesting phenomenon, at least as important to the spiritual climate as daily weather to the physical climate. A myth foisted specifically on the movies proper rather than on the reaction of audiences is furnished by devotees of both stage and novel who scorn movies as below the serious level—as standing in relation to true art somewhat as the circus does to the legitimate stage. But unfortunately these judges, unaware of the ritual importance of the screen, its baroque energy and protean symbolism, are unwarrantably summary, basically uneducated in the movie medium.

. . . The true field of the movies is not *art* but *myth*, between which—in the sense "myth" is invariably used here—there is a perhaps unsuspectedly wide difference. Assuredly a myth is a fiction, and this is its bare link with art, but a myth is specifically a free, unharnessed fiction, a basic, prototypic pattern capable of many variations and distortions, many betrayals and disguises, even though it remains *imaginative* truth. It has one degraded function connected with the idea of entertainment I discussed above, as when the word itself becomes adjectival and is deliberately attached to that pseudonymous Baltic kingdom having no existence saving in fifth-rate novels and in the movies. It is unsound to make a fact such as the existence of the very nation where a story occurs into a fiction, for it is like taking the props out from under a building and assuming it will still stand. No matter how fantastic an action, its background must be firm. It is the status of background that determines the strength of a myth, the status of its perspective in human history.

Essentially the *scene* of imaginative truth, or art, is the mind itself, but in some manner this truth must be objective, capable of projection onto the screen of the world. In a sense man *is* his past, the past of his race, and all the beliefs he ever held. Reality cannot be made up from the material facts of his existence, his immediate sensory reactions; nor can it be fundamentally a world that never was. Certainly man has ceased to believe much he used to believe. "Oh, that is a myth," we say, meaning that even if significant, it is an ideal or an illusion, a thing that has no substance. But psychology has taught us the strange reality of chimeras, their symbolic validity; and comparative mythology has revealed the great persistence of psychic patterns, with special reference to the supernatural, whose continuity in human belief is sometimes surprisingly self-evident. At one time men believed the earth was flat. Today this is a purely ornamental myth; it has died because imagining the earth is flat has no relation to our desires or employments. At one time the pagans believed in Diana as goddess of the moon and the hunt. Today this also might be considered a decorative myth, something in the fairy-tale class. Yet like so many legends it holds a mesmeric appeal for the mind; Diana represents, as a matter of fact, a certain sexual type—the vigorous virgin, the woman resistant to love; and yet according to the legend Endymion made her lose her heart; that is, the man lived who could break down her defenses merely through his physical image. Obviously this sexual pattern is repeated today. The modern belief that the earth is round corresponds to the conditions of our planetary existence insofar as, proceeding on this premise, our astronomical calculations work out. The belief is consistent with *all the facts*. Today the fact that Diana once had for the pagans a reality she does not have for us means merely that the myth lives in another form. It is an ideal archetype, a part of human experience that has its home in the imagination. And yet . . . that which was true once may become true again. What was symbolized by the Diana myth in actual human experience is a permanent legacy of the race. So the essence of myth also has the status of permanent possibility . . . in short, *desires* may have the same power over the mind and behavior, indeed a much greater power, than *facts.*

In the following pages I have occasion to refer specifically to the great researches made in ancient magic by Sir James Frazer. That there are anthropological assumptions contradictory to various of Frazer's own premises is of no importance to the point I am making. In order to explain a single phenomenon, the priest cult of the King of the Wood at Nemi, Frazer accumulated into one work a prodigious array of ancient primitive beliefs and customs suggesting the limitless lineage of the relatively recent cult at Nemi. At this moment, as when his book was written, nobody is a devotee of this cult; nobody believes in the magic of the golden bough that had to be plucked by the aspirant to Diana's priesthood before he was empowered to kill in single combat the incumbent priest. And yet those who do not profoundly know anthropology might be astonished to learn how much of our personal lives is influenced by all the ancient magical and religious beliefs connected with this one cult. The whole history of the decay and fall of gods, the extermination of divine hierarchies, could be told with just the Nemian cult as basis. In discussing in later pages the male comics of the screen who entertained troops all over the world during the war, I show how they may be considered modern medicine men or primitive priests, scapegoats who transferred to themselves the inner fears of the soldier striving to be brave and made cowardice and bravery alike into a kind of joke. Consequently in relation to my argument the myth is not, as a psychological or historical nucleus of fact, necessarily to be judged as true or false, illusory or real, according to its specific labels, its historic status, its literal beliefs. Essentially myths are not factual but symbolic. I assume that movies are essentially likewise.

. . . Briefly movies, similar to much else in life, are seldom what they seem. In this sense—being, to begin with, fiction—movies are dreamlike and fantastic, their fantasy and examples of this are the folk myths of the absent-minded professor, of the efficiency expert, and of the eccentricity of genius. . . .

Naturally when I ally myth with superstition I am taking not only Frazer's view of the profound interrelatedness of myths but also Freud's view that beneath the upper levels of the mind lies a vast human capacity to think in terms of frantic passions and above all in terms of symbols. Even ten years ago it would have been thought impossible by movie moguls that a surrealist artist, Salvador Dali, should be employed to devise images to portray movie dreams, which in turn are subjected to psychoanalysis, a clinical process that provides the solution of the plot. . . .

The fundamental eye trickery that is a genius of the camera—you see the object, yet it isn't there—came to the fore in the movies and ever since then has mocked with its dynamic plasticity the very form from which it developed, the still camera. Today the movie has all the flexibility of the novel as well as the vision and speech of the stage. In striving through imaginative works to create the illusion of reality the movie screen must constantly transcend its own mirror nature of literal reflection. Camera trickery is really camera magic, for illusion can be freely created by the movie camera with more mathematical accuracy and shock value than by sleight-of-hand magic or stage illusion. The very homogeneity of cinema illusion—the images of the actors themselves are illusive, their corporal bodies absent—creates a throwback in the mood of the spectator to the vestiges of those ancient beliefs that I discuss in detail later in the chapter on supernaturalism, such as beliefs in ghosts, secret forces, telepathy, etc.

Moreover, the movie-theater rite corresponds directly to the profoundly primitive responses of the audience; the auditorium is dark, the spectator is relaxed, the movie in front of him requires less sheer mental attention than would a novel or stage play—less attention because all movement seems to exist on the screen; even the background changes easily, quickly; the whole world moves around the spectator, who is a still point. From the capacity of the screen for trick illusion, plus the dark-enshrouded passivity of the spectator, issues a state of daydream, which I termed in my previous book "the daylight dream" because it occurs in the dark: the screen is the focus of light, while the spectator is conscious in a darkness of the bedroom. It is in daydreams that magic seems to operate, in daydreams that things begin to seem rather than to be. "The movie theater," to quote directly from my previous book, "is the psychoanalytic clinic of the average worker's daylight dream." It is likewise in the process of psychoanalysis, where the *part*, truly recognized as symbol, transforms the meaning of the whole. The movie process is a complex myth of sheer synecdoche. People go to the movies merely to see a favorite player, or for the locale or period, or for the genre, or because they are bored almost to death. How, under these conditions, can anyone hope to appreciate the *whole* movie, especially since, to begin with, the movie can hardly be considered a whole?

No longer does man believe in myth or magic. No! For magic has been sifted and reorganized into science and governs only his material world, not the realm of his spirit, while comparative mythology and anthropology merely comprise school subjects. The sects of Christian religion have organized Western man's spiritual beliefs under one heading: the myth of Christ. Yet Christ's myth too can be related to pagan myths. The very fact that for children the Bible itself is but another series of fairy tales, weighted but little by a sense of historical fact, alone demonstrates my point as to the basic importance of myth with regard to popular or folk art. Our imaginary lives as children survive in us as adults and enrich our subsequent natures. So the fairy-tale lives of primitive races, our ancient antecedents, survive in the religions we formally believe in today as well as among those tribes still unassimilated to modern civilization. I do not claim any absolute value for the myth and magic of Hollywood or for those modern vestiges of the old Greek divinities I have dubbed "the gods and goddesses of Hollywood." On the contrary the principle I mean is one of relativity and metamorphosis rather than absolutism and changelessness: just as a word has synonyms and antonyms—so has a myth. In psychoanalytical symbolism, the deepest symbolism of the mind, the identity of objects is established by a complex frame of reference in which an image may represent one of three objects or all three objects at once. If, then, I say that the actors of Hollywood are an enlarged personnel of the realistically anthropomorphic deities of ancient Greece, I do not indulge in a mere bit of verbal humor, satiric or otherwise; on the other hand neither am I proposing or assuming the existence of an unconscious cult of supernatural worship. I feel I am but calling attention to the fact that the glamour actors and actresses of the movie realm are fulfilling an ancient need, unsatisfied by popular religions of contemporary times. Those men and women who perform for us are human, as we are; they have homes, children, love affairs; they suffer and die. And yet a magic barrier cuts across the texture of our mutual humanity; somehow their wealth, fame, and beauty, their apparently unlimited field of worldy pleasure—these conditions tinge them with the supernatural, render them immune to the bitterness of ordinary frustrations. It does not matter if this thought is a mythological exaggeration. It is a *tendency* of the popular imagination. The secret of the power of Hollywood gods and goddesses is that they seem to do everything anyone else does except that when they die—in movies—they die over and over; when they love, they love over and over. Even as the gods do, they undergo continual metamorphoses, never losing their identities, being Rita Hayworth or Glenn Ford no matter what their movie aliases. And like Jupiter in the modern comedy, *Amphitryon 38*, they can condescend, even be ridiculous. All that the public demands is what it always gets—

the power to make and break stars—but gods have always led basically mortal lives.

Lastly, in this and my previous book, do I have *a method?* Not in the sense that I am selling ideas, nor above all, is mine a method by which one can test the high or low esthetic content of a given movie. . . . If my method is worthy of a label, it is "psychoanalytic-mythological," often socially angled. I have invented little or nothing. I have merely applied it to new material and formulated in accordance with the reapplication. That I speak metaphorically, in dream symbols, and . . . in terms of my own "hallucination," is a fact I wish not only to admit but to proclaim. Yes, I have made up a collective myth of my own, and I confess that in so doing I have plagiarized Hollywood exhaustively. If I have interpreted many things as dreams are interpreted, I cite as belated authorities recent movies of psychoanalytical themes and dream-symbol material. Indirectly, however, I have only been obeying Hollywood's own law of fluidity, of open and ingenious invention. If I have formulated an element of moviedom to be known as "the supernatural hush" and interpreted it as applicable at once to the hush of a cathedral, the hush of a psychiatrist's clinic, the hush of an isolated lovers' session on Riverside Drive, and the hush of the studio while Jennifer Jones does a scene in *The Song of Bernadette*, I feel that I am defining a quality of the movies as one would classify an acidic combination in the laboratory. And if in one of the magic-lantern metamorphoses internal movie meanings are discussed in terms of doubting the evidence of the senses, I am merely following the technique of psychoanalysis as well as paralleling legal criticism of circumstantial evidence of crimes: *things are not always what they seem.* I hope to have revealed a deeper sort of truth than that to be found on surfaces and at the same time to have assembled here a little mythology, a kind of concordance, showing the frequently unconscious magic employed by Hollywood—a magic of dream creation that far transcends its literal messages.

1947

CHRISTIAN METZ
FROM THE IMAGINARY SIGNIFIER

IDENTIFICATION, MIRROR

"What contribution can Freudian psychoanalysis make to the knowledge of the cinematic signifier?": that was the question-dream I posed (the scientific imaginary wishing to be symbolised), and it seems to me that I have now more or less *unwound* it; unwound but no more; I have not given it an answer. I have simply paid attention to what it was I wished to say (one never knows this until one has written it down), I have only questioned my question: this unanswered character is one that has to be deliberately accepted, it is constitutive of any epistemological procedure.

Since I have wished to mark the places (as empty boxes some of which are beginning to fill without waiting for me, and so much the better), the places of different directions of work, and particularly of the last, the psychoanalytic exploration of the signifier, which concerns me especially, I must now begin to inscribe something in this last box; must take further, and more plainly in the direction of the unconscious, the analysis of the investigator's desire that makes me write. And to start with, of course, this means asking a new question: among the specific features of the cinematic signifier that distinguish the cinema from literature, painting, etc. which ones by nature call most directly on the type of knowledge that psychoanalysis alone can provide?

Perception, Imaginary

The cinema's signifier is *perceptual* (visual and auditory). So
is that of literature, since the written chain has to be *read*, but
it involves a more restricted perceptual register: only gra-
phemes, writing. So too are those of painting, sculpture, architecture, photography, but still within limits, and different
ones: absence of auditory perception, absence in the visual itself of certain important dimensions such as time and movement (obviously there is the time of the look, but the object
looked at is not inscribed in a precise and ordered time sequence forced on the spectator from outside). Music's signifier
is perceptual as well, but, like the others, less "extensive" than
that of the cinema: here it is vision which is absent, and even
in the auditory, extended speech (except in song). What first
strikes one then is that the cinema is *more perceptual*, if the
phrase is allowable, than many other means of expression; it
mobilises a larger number of the axes of perception. (That is
why the cinema has sometimes been presented as a "synthesis
of all the arts"; which does not mean very much, but if we
restrict ourselves to the quantitative tally of the registers of
perception, it is true that the cinema contains within itself the
signifiers of other arts: it can present pictures to us, make us
hear music, it is made of photographs, etc.)

Nevertheless, this as it were numerical "superiority" disappears if the cinema is compared with the theatre, the opera
and other spectacles of the same type. The latter too involve
sight and hearing simultaneously, linguistic audition and non
linguistic audition, movement, real temporal progression. Their
difference from the cinema lies elsewhere: they do not consist
of *images*, the perceptions they offer to the eye and the ear are
inscribed in a true space (not a photographed one), the same
one as that occupied by the public during the performance;
everything the audience hear and see is actively produced in
their presence, by human beings or props which are themselves present. This is not the problem of fiction but that of
the definitional characteristics of the signifier: whether or no
the theatrical play mimes a fable, its *action*, if need be mimetic, is still managed by real persons evolving in real time
and space, *on the same stage or "scene" as the public*. The "other
scene," which is precisely not so called, is the cinematic screen
(closer to phantasy from the outset): what unfolds there may,
as before, be more or less fictional, but the unfolding itself is
fictive: the actor, the "décor," the words one hears are all absent, everything is *recorded* (as a memory trace which is immediately so, without having been something else before), and

this is still true if what is recorded is not a "story" and does not aim for the fictional illusion proper. For it is the signifier itself, and as a whole, that is recorded, that is absence: a little rolled up perforated strip which "contains" vast landscapes, fixed battles, the melting of the ice on the River Neva, and whole life-times, and yet can be enclosed in the familiar round metal tin, of modest dimensions, clear proof that it does not "really" contain all that.

At the theatre, Sarah Bernhardt may tell me she is Phèdre or, if the play were from another period and rejected the fig-urative regime, she might say, as in a type of modern theatre, that she is Sarah Bernhardt. But at any rate, I should see Sarah Bernhardt. At the cinema, she could make the same two kinds of speeches too, but it would be her shadow that would be offering them to me (or she would be offering them in her own absence). Every film is a fiction film.

What is at issue is not just the actor. Today there are a theatre and a cinema without actors, or in which they have at least ceased to take on the full and exclusive function which characterises them in classical spectacles. But what is true of Sarah Bernhardt is just as true of an object, a prop, a chair for example. On the theatre stage, this chair may, as in Chekhov, pretend to be the chair in which the melancholy Russian no-bleman sits every evening; on the contrary (in Ionesco), it can explain to me that it is a theatre chair. But when all is said and done it is a chair. In the cinema, it will similarly have to choose between two attitudes (and many other intermediate or more tricky ones), but it will not be there when the spectators see it, when they have to recognise the choice; it will have dele-gated its reflection to them.

What is characteristic of the cinema is not the imaginary that it may happen to represent, but the imaginary that it *is* from the start, the imaginary that constitutes it as a signifier (the two are not unrelated; it is so well able to represent it because it is it; however it is it even when it no longer represents it). The (possible) reduplication inaugurating the intention of fic-tion is preceded in the cinema by a first reduplication, always-already achieved, which inaugurates the signifier. The imag-inary, by definition, combines within it a certain presence and a certain absence. In the cinema it is not just the fictional sig-nified, if there is one, that is thus made present in the mode of absence, it is from the outset the signifier.

Thus the cinema, "more perceptual" than certain arts ac-cording to the list of its sensory registers, is also "less percep-tual" than others once the status of these perceptions is envisaged rather than their number or diversity; for its perceptions are all in a sense "false." Or rather, the activity of perception which it involves is real (the cinema is not a phantasy), but the perceived is not really the object, it is its shade, its phantom, its double, its *replica* in a new kind of mirror. It will be said that literature, after all, is itself only made of replicas (written words, presenting absent objects). But at least it does not present them to us with all the really perceived detail that the screen does (giving more and taking as much, i.e. taking more). The unique position of the cinema lies in this dual character of its signifier: unaccustomed perceptual wealth, but at the same time stamped with unreality to an unusual degree, and from the very outset. More than the other arts, or in a more unique way, the cinema involves us in the imaginary: it drums up all perception, but to switch it immediately over into its own absence, which is nonetheless the only signifier present.

The All-Perceiving Subject

Thus film is like the mirror. But it differs from the primordial mirror in one essential point: although, as in the latter, everything may come to be projected, there is one thing and one thing only that is never reflected in it: the spectator's own body. In a certain emplacement, the mirror suddenly becomes clear glass.

In the mirror the child perceives the familiar household objects, and also its object par excellence, its mother, who holds it up in her arms to the glass. But above all it perceives its own image. This is where primary identification (the formation of the ego) gets certain of its main characteristics: the child sees itself as an other, and beside an other. This other other is its guarantee that the first is really it: by her authority, her sanction, in the register of the symbolic, subsequently by the resemblance between her mirror image and the child's (both have a human form). Thus the child's ego is formed by identification with its like, and this in two senses simultaneously, metonymically and metaphorically: the other human being who is in the glass, the own reflection which is and is not the body, which is like it. The child identifies with itself as an object.

In the cinema, the object remains: fiction or no, there is always something on the screen. But the reflection of the own body has disappeared. The cinema spectator is not a child and the child really at the mirror stage (from around six to around eighteen months) would certainly be incapable of "following" the simplest of films. Thus, what *makes possible* the spectator's absence from the screen—or rather the intelligible unfolding of the film despite that absence—is the fact that the spectator has already known the experience of the mirror (of the true mirror), and is thus able to constitute a world of objects without having first to recognise himself within it. In this respect, the cinema is already on the side of the symbolic (which is only to be expected): the spectator knows that objects exist, that he himself exists as a subject, that he becomes an object for others: he knows himself and he knows his like: it is no longer necessary that this similarity be literally *depicted* for him on the screen, as it was in the mirror of his childhood. Like every other broadly "secondary" activity, the practice of the cinema presupposes that the primitive undifferentiation of the ego and the non-ego has been overcome.

But *with what,* then, does the spectator identify during the projection of the film? For he certainly has to identify: identification in its primoral form has ceased to be a current necessity for him, but he continues, in the cinema—if he did not the film would become incomprehensible, considerably more incomprehensible than the most incomprehensible films—to depend on that permanent play of identification without which there would be no social life (thus, the simplest conversation presupposes the alternation of the *I* and the *you,* hence the aptitude of the two interlocutors for a mutual and reversible identification). What form does this *continued* identification, whose essential role Lacan has demonstrated even in the most abstract reasoning and which constituted the "social sentiment" for Freud (= the sublimation of a homosexual libido, itself a reaction to the aggressive rivalry of the members of a single generation after the murder of the father), take in the special case of one social practice among others, cinematic projection?

Obviously the spectator has the opportunity to identify with the *character* of the fiction. But there still has to be one. This is thus only valid for the narrative-representational film, and not for the psychoanalytic constitution of the signifier of the cinema as such. The spectator can also identify with the actor, in more or less "a-fictional" films in which the latter is represented as an actor, not a character, but is still offered thereby as a human being (as a perceived human being) and thus allows identification. However this factor (even added to the previous one and thus covering a very large number of films) cannot suffice. It only designates secondary identification in certain of its forms (secondary in the cinematic process itself, since in any other sense all identification except that of the mirror can be regarded as secondary).

An insufficient explanation, and for two reasons, the first of which is only the intermittent, anecdotal and superficial consequence of the second (but for that reason more visible, and that is why I call it the first). The cinema deviates from the theatre on an important point that has often been emphasised: it often presents us with long sequences that can (literally) be called "inhuman"—the familiar theme of cinematic "cosmomorphism" developed by many film theorists—sequences in which only inanimate objects, landscapes, etc. appear and which for minutes at a time offer no human form for spectator identification: yet the latter must be supposed to remain intact in its deep structure, since at such moments the film *works* just as well as it does at others, and whole films (geographical documentaries, for example) unfold intelligibly in such conditions. The second, more radical reason is that identification with the human form appearing on the screen, even when it occurs, still tells us nothing about the *place of the spectator's ego* in the inauguration of the signifier. As I have just pointed out, this ego is already formed. But since it exists, the question arises precisely of *where it is* during the projection of the film (the true primary identification, that of the mirror, forms the ego, but all other identifications presuppose, on the contrary, that it has been formed and can be "exchanged" for the object or the fellow subject). Thus when I "recognise" my like on the screen, and even more when I do not recognise it, where am I? Where is that someone who is capable of self-recognition when need be?

It is not enough to answer that the cinema, like every social practice, demands that the psychical apparatus of its participants be fully constituted, and that the question is thus the concern of general psychoanalytic theory and not that of the cinema proper. For my *where is it?* does not claim to go so far, or more precisely tries to go slightly further: it is a question of the *point* occupied by this already constituted ego, occupied during the cinema showing and not in social life in general.

The spectator is absent from the screen: contrary to the child in the mirror, he cannot identify with himself as an object, but only with objects which are there without him. In this sense the screen is not a mirror. The perceived, this time, is entirely on the side of the object, and there is no longer any equivalent of the own image, of that unique mix of perceived and subject (of other and I) which was precisely the figure necessary to disengage the one from the other. At the cinema, it is always the other who is on the screen; as for me, I am there to look at him. I take no part in the perceived, on the contrary, I am *all-perceiving*. All-perceiving as one says all-powerful (this is the famous gift of "ubiquity" the film makes its spectator); all-perceiving, too, because I am entirely on the side of the perceiving instance: absent from the screen, but certainly present in the auditorium, a great eye and ear without which the perceived would have no one to perceive it, the instance, in other words, which *constitutes* the cinema signifier (it is I who make the film). If the most extravagant spectacles and sounds or the most unlikely combination of them, the combination furthest removed from any real experience, do not prevent the constitution of meaning (and to begin with do not *astonish* the spectator, do not really astonish him, not intellectually: he simply judges the film as strange), that is because he knows he is at the cinema.

In the cinema the *subject's knowledge* takes a very precise form without which no film would be possible. This knowledge is dual (but unique). I know I am perceiving something imaginary (and that is why its absurdities, even if they are extreme, do not seriously disturb me), and I know that it is I who am perceiving it. This second knowledge divides in turn: I know that I am really perceiving, that my sense organs are physically affected, that I am not phantasising, that the fourth wall of the auditorium (the screen) is really different from the other three, that there is a projector facing it (and thus it is not I who am projecting, or at least not all alone), and I also know that it is I who am perceiving all this, that this perceived-imaginary material is deposited in me as if on a second screen, that it is in me that it forms up into an organised sequence, that therefore I am myself the place where this really perceived imaginary accedes to the symbolic by its inauguration as the signifier of a certain type of institutionalised social activity called the "cinema."

In other words, the spectator *identifies with himself*, with himself as a pure act of perception (as wakefulness, alertness): as the condition of possibility of the perceived and hence as a kind of transcendental subject, which comes before every *there is*.

A strange mirror, then, very like that of childhood, and very different. Very like, as Jean-Louis Baudry has emphasized, because during the showing we are, like the child, in a sub-motor and hyper-perceptive state; because, like the child again, we are prey to the imaginary, the double, and are so paradoxically through a real perception. Very different, because this mirror returns us everything but ourselves, because we are wholly outside it, whereas the child is both in it and in front of it. As an *arrangement* (and in a very topographical sense of the word), the cinema is more involved on the flank of the symbolic, and hence of secondariness, than is the mirror of childhood. This is not surprising, since it comes long after it, but what is more important to me is the fact that it is inscribed in its wake with an incidence at once so direct and so oblique, which has no precise equivalent in other apparatuses of signification.

Identification With the Camera

The preceding analysis coincides in places with others which have already been proposed and which I shall not repeat: analyses of *quattrocento* painting or of the cinema itself which insist on the role of monocular perspective (hence of the *camera*) and the "vanishing point" that inscribes an empty emplacement for the spectator-subject, an all-powerful position which is that of God himself, or more broadly of some ultimate signified. And it is true that as he identifies with himself as look, the spectator can do no other than identify with the camera, too, which has looked before him at what he is now looking at and whose stationing (= framing) determines the vanishing point. During the projection this camera is absent, but it has a representative consisting of another apparatus, called precisely a "projector." An apparatus the spectator has behind him, *at the back of his head,* that is, precisely where phantasy locates the "focus" of all vision. All of us have experienced our own look, even outside the so-called *salles obscures* [= cinemas], as a kind of searchlight turning on the axis of our own necks (like a pan) and shifting when we shift (a tracking shot now): as a cone of light (without the microscopic dust scattered through it and streaking it in the cinema) whose vicariousness draws successive and variable slices of obscurity from nothingness wherever and whenever it comes to rest. (And in a sense that is what perception and consciousness are, a *light,* as Freud put it, in the double sense of an illumination and an opening, as in the arrangement of the cinema, which contains both, a limited and wandering light that only attains a small part of the real, but on the other hand possesses the gift of casting light on it.) Without this identification with the camera certain facts could not be understood, though they are constant ones: the fact, for example, that the spectator is not amazed when the image "rotates" (= a pan) and yet he knows he has not turned his head. The explanation is that he has no

need to turn it really, he has turned it in his all-seeing capacity, his identification with the movement of the camera being
that of a transcendental, not an empirical subject.

All vision consists of a double movement: projective (the
"sweeping" searchlight) and introjective: consciousness as a
sensitive recording surface (as a screen). I have the impression
at once that, to use a common expression, I am "casting" my
eyes on things, and that the latter, thus illuminated, come to
be deposited within me (we then declared that it is these things
that have been "projected," on to my retina, say). A sort of
stream called the look, and explaining all the myths of mag-
netism, must be sent out over the world, so that objects can
come back up this stream in the opposite direction (but using
it to find their way), arriving at last at our perception, which
is now soft wax and no longer an emitting source.

The technology of photography carefully conforms to this
(banal) phantasy accompanying perception. The camera is
"trained" on the object like a fire-arm (= projection) and the
object arrives to make an imprint, a trace, on the receptive
surface of the film-strip (= introjection). The spectator himself
does not escape these pincers, for he is part of the apparatus,
and also because pincers, on the imaginary plane (Melanie
Klein), mark our relation to the world as a whole and are rooted
in the primary figures of orality. During the performance the
spectator is the searchlight I have described, duplicating the
projector, which itself duplicates the camera, and he is also the
sensitive surface duplicating the screen, which itself duplicates the film-strip. There are two cones in the auditorium:
one ending on the screen and starting both in the projection
box and in the spectator's vision insofar as it is projective, and
one starting from the screen and "deposited" in the spectator's
perception insofar as it is introjective (on the retina, a second
screen). When I say that "I see" the film, I mean thereby a
unique mixture of two contrary currents: the film is what I
receive, and it is also what I release, since it does not pre-exist
my entering the auditorium and I only need close my eyes to
suppress it. Releasing it, I am the projector, receiving it, I am
the screen; in both these figures together, I am the camera,
which points and yet which records.

Thus the constitution of the signifier in the cinema depends
on a series of mirror-effects organised in a chain, and not on
a single reduplication. In this the cinema as a topography resembles that other "space," the technical equipment (camera,
projector, film-strip, screen, etc.), the objective precondition of
the whole institution: as we know, the apparatuses too contain

a series of mirrors, lenses, apertures and shutters, ground glasses, through which the cone of light passes: a further re-duplication in which the equipment becomes a metaphor (as well as the real source) for the mental process instituted. Further on we shall see that it is also its fetish.

in the cinema, as elsewhere, the constitution of the symbolic is only achieved through and above the play of the imaginary: projection-introjection, presence-absence, phantasies accompanying perception, etc. Even when acquired, the ego still depends in its underside on the fabulous figures thanks to which it has been acquired and which have marked it lastingly with the stamp of the lure. The secondary process does no more than "cover" (and not always hermetically) the primary process which is still constantly present and conditions the very possibility of what covers it.

Chain of many mirrors, the cinema is at once a weak and a robust mechanism: like the human body, like a precision tool, like a social institution. And the fact is that it is really all of these at the same time.

And I, at this moment, what am I doing if not to add to all these reduplications one more whereby theory is attempting to set itself up? Am I not looking at myself looking at the film? This *passion for seeing* (and also hearing), the foundation of the whole edifice, am I not turning it, too, on (against) that edifice? Am I not still the voyeur I was in front of the screen, now that it is this voyeur who is being seen, thus postulating a second voyeur, the one writing at present, myself again?

On the Idealist Theory of the Cinema

The place of the ego in the institution of the signifier, as transcendental yet radically deluded subject, since it is the institution (and even the equipment) that give it this place, surely provides us with an appreciable opportunity the better to understand and judge the precise epistemological import of the idealist theory of the cinema which culminates in the remarkable works of André Bazin. Before thinking directly about their validity, but simply reading texts of this kind, one cannot but be struck by the great precision, the acute and immediately sensitive intelligence that they often demonstrate; at the same time they give the diffuse impression of a permanent ill-foundedness (which affects nothing and yet affects everything), they suggest that somewhere they contain something like a weak point at which the whole might be overturned.

It is certainly no accident that the main form of idealism in cinematic theory has been phenomenology. Bazin and other

writers of the same period explicitly acknowledged their debt
to it, and more implicitly (but in a more generalised fashion)
all conceptions of the cinema as a mystical revelation, as "truth"
or "reality" unfolding by right, as the apparition of what is
[l'étant], as an epiphany, derive from it. We all know that the
cinema has the gift of sending some of its lovers into prophetic
trances. However, these cosmophanic conceptions (which are
not always expressed in an extreme form) register rather well
the "feeling" of the *deluded ego* of the spectator, they often give
us excellent descriptions of this feeling and to this extent there
is something scientific about them and they have advanced
our knowledge of the cinema. But the *lure of the ego* is their
blind spot. These theories are still of great interest, but they
have, so to speak, to be put the other way round, like the
optical image of the film.

For it is true that the topographical apparatus of the cinema
resembles the conceptual apparatus of phenomenology, with
the result that the latter can cast light on the former. (Besides,
in any domain, a phenomenology of the object to be understood, a "receptive" description of its appearances, must be
the starting-point; only afterwards can *criticism* begin; psy-
choanalysts, it should be remembered, have their own phenomenology.) The *"there is"* of phenomenology proper (philosophical phenomenology) as an ontic revelation referring to a
perceiving-subject (= "perceptual *cogito*"), to a subject for
which alone there can be anything, has close and precise affinities with the installation of the cinema signifier in the ego as
I have tried to define it, with the spectator withdrawing into
himself as a pure instance of perception, the whole of the perceived being "out there." To this extent the cinema really is
the "phenomenological art" it has often been called, by Merleau-Ponty himself, for example. But it can only be so because
its objective determinations make it so. The ego's position in
the cinema does not derive from a miraculous resemblance between the cinema and the natural characteristics of all perception; on the contrary, it is foreseen and marked in advance by
the institution (the equipment, the disposition of the auditorium, the mental system that internalises the two), and also by
more general characteristics of the psychical apparatus (such
as projection, the mirror structure, etc.), which although they
are less strictly dependent on a period of social history and a
technology, do not therefore express the sovereignty of a "human vocation," but inversely are themselves shaped by certain
specific features of man as an animal (as the only animal that
is not an animal): his primitive *Hilflosigkeit*, his dependence
on another's care (the lasting source of the imaginary, of object

relations, of the great oral figures of feeding), the motor pre-
maturity of the child which condemns it to an initial self-recognition by sight (hence outside itself) anticipating a muscular
unity it does not yet possess.

In other words, phenomenology can contribute to knowledge of the cinema (and it has done so) insofar as it happens
to be like it, and yet it is on the cinema *and* phenomenology
in their common illusion of *perceptual mastery* that light must
be cast by the real conditions of society and man.

On Some Sub-Codes of Identification

The play of identification defines the cinematic situation in
its generality, i.e. *the* code. But it also allows more specific and
less permanent configurations, "variations" on it, as it were;
they intervene in certain coded figures which occupy precise
segments of precise films.

What I have said about identification so far amounts to the
statement that the spectator is absent from the screen *as perceived,* but also (the two things inevitably go together) present
there and even "all-present" as *perceiver.* At every moment I
am in the film by my look's caress. This presence often remains diffuse, geographically undifferentiated, evenly distributed over the whole surface of the screen; or more precisely
hovering, like the psychoanalyst's listening, ready to catch on
preferentially to some motif in the film, according to the force
of that motif and according to my own phantasies as a spectator, without the cinematic code itself intervening to govern
this anchorage and impose it on the whole audience. But in
other cases, certain articles of the cinematic codes or sub-codes
(which I shall not try to survey completely here) are made responsible for suggesting to the spectator the vector along which
his permanent identification with his own look should be extended temporarily inside the film (the perceived) itself. Here
we meet various classic problems of cinematic theory, or at
least certain aspects of them: subjective images, out-of-frame
space, looks (looks and no longer the look, but the former are
articulated to the latter).

There are various sorts of subjective image and I have tried
elsewhere (following Jean Mitry) to distinguish between them.
Only one of them will detain me for the moment, the one which
"expresses the viewpoint of the film-maker" in the standard
formula (and not the viewpoint of a character, another traditional sub-case of the subjective image): unusual framings,
uncommon shot-angles, etc. as for example in one of the

sketches which make up Julien Duvivier's film *Carnet de bal* (the sketch with Pierre Blanchar, shot continuously in tilted framings). In the standard definitions one thing strikes me: I do not see why these uncommon angles should express the viewpoint of the film-maker any more than perfectly ordinary angles, closer to the horizontal. However, the definition is comprehensible even in its inaccuracy: precisely because it is uncommon, the uncommon angle makes us more aware of what we had merely forgotten to some extent in its absence: an identification with the camera (with "the author's view-point"). The ordinary framings are finally felt to be non-framings: I espouse the film-maker's look (without which no cinema would be possible), but my consciousness is not too aware of it. The uncommon angle reawakens me and (like the cure) teaches me what I already knew. And then, it obliges my look to stop wandering freely over the screen for the moment and to scan it along more precise lines of force which are imposed on me. Thus for a moment I became directly aware of the *emplacement* of my own presence-absence in the film simply because it has changed.

Now for looks. In a fiction film, the characters look at one another. It can happen (and this is already another "notch" in the chain of identifications) that a character looks at another who is momentarily out-of-frame, or else is looked at by him. If we have gone one notch further, this is because everything out-of-frame *brings us closer to the spectator*, since it is the peculiarity of the latter to be out-of-frame (the out-of-frame character thus has a point in common with him: he is looking at the screen). In certain cases the out-of-frame character's look is "reinforced" by recourse to another variant of the subjective image, generally christened the "character's point of view": the framing of the scene corresponds precisely to the angle from which the out-of-frame character looks at the screen. (The two figures are dissociable moreover: we often know that the scene is being looked at by someone other than ourselves, by a character, but it is the logic of the plot, or an element of the dialogue, or a previous image that tells us so, not the position of the camera, which may be far from the presumed emplacement of the out-of-frame onlooker.)

In all sequences of this kind, the identification that founds the signifier is *twice relayed*, doubly duplicated in a circuit that leads it to the heart of the film along a line which is no longer hovering, which follows the inclination of the looks and is therefore governed by the film itself: the spectator's look (= the basic identification), before dispersing all over the surface of the screen in a variety of intersecting lines (= looks of the characters in the frame = second duplication), must first "go through"—as one goes through a town on a journey, or a mountain pass—the look of the character out-of-frame (= first duplication), himself a spectator and hence the first delegate of the true spectator, but not to be confused with the latter since he is inside, if not the frame, then at least the fiction. This invisible character, supposed (like the spectator) to be seeing, will collide obliquely with the latter's look and play the part of an obligatory intermediary. By offering himself as a crossing for the spectator, he inflects the circuit followed by the sequence of identifications and it is only in this sense that he is himself seen: as we see through him, we see ourselves not seeing him.

Examples of this kind are much more numerous and each of them is much more complex than I have suggested here. At this point textual analysis of precise film sequences is an indispensable instrument of knowledge. I just wished to show that in the end there is no break in continuity between the child's game with the mirror and, at the other extreme, certain localised figures of the cinematic codes. The mirror is the site of primary identification. Identification with one's own look is secondary with respect to the mirror, i.e. for a general theory of adult activities, but it is the foundation of the cinema and hence primary when the latter is under discussion: it is *primary cinematic identification* proper ("primary identification" would be inaccurate from the psychoanalytic point of view; "secondary identification," more accurate in this respect, would be ambiguous for a cinematic psychoanalysis). As for identifications with characters, with their own different levels (out-of-frame character, etc.), they are secondary, tertiary cinematic identifications, etc.; taken as a whole in opposition to the identification of the spectator with his own look, they constitute secondary cinematic identification in the singular.

"Seeing a Film"

Freud noted, *vis-à-vis* the sexual act that the most ordinary practices depend on a large number of psychical functions which are distinct but work consecutively, so that all of them must be intact if what is regarded as a normal performance is to be possible (it is because neurosis and psychosis dissociate them and put some of them out of court that a kind of commutation is made possible whereby they can be listed retrospectively by the analyst). The apparently very simple act of

seeing a film is no exception to this rule. As soon as it is subjected to analysis it reveals to us a complex, multiply interconnected imbrication of the functions of the imaginary, the real
and the symbolic, which is also required in one form or another for every procedure of social life, but whose cinematic
manifestation is especially impressive since it is played out on
a small surface. (To this extent the theory of the cinema may
some day contribute something to psychoanalysis, even if,
through force of circumstances, this "reciprocation" remains
very limited at the moment, the two disciplines being very
unevenly developed.)

In order to understand the fiction film, I must both "take
myself" for the character (= an imaginary procedure) so that
he benefites, by analogical projection, from all the schemata of
intelligibility that I have within me, and not take myself for
him (= the return to the real) so that the fiction can be established as such (= as symbolic): this is *seeming-real*. Similarly,
in order to understand the film (at all), I must perceive the
photographed object as absent, its photograph as present, and
the presence of this absence as signifying. The imaginary of
the cinema presupposes the symbolic, for the spectator must
first of all have known the primordial mirror. But as the latter
instituted the ego very largely in the imaginary, the second
mirror of the screen, a symbolic apparatus, itself in turn depends on reflection and lack. However, it is not phantasy, a
"purely" symbolic-imaginary site, for the absence of the object
and the codes of that absence are really produced in it by the
physis of an equipment: the cinema is a body (a *corpus* for the
semiologist), a fetish that can be loved.

THE PASSION FOR PERCEIVING

The practice of the cinema is only possible through the perceptual passions: the desire to see (= scopic drive, scopophilia, voyeurism), which was alone engaged in the art of the silent film, the desire to hear which has been added to it in the
sound cinema (this is the *"pulsion invocante,"* the invocatory
drive, one of the four main sexual drives for Lacan; it is well
known that Freud isolated it less clearly and hardly deals with
it as such).

These two sexual drives are distinguished from the others in
that they are more dependent on a lack, or at least dependent
on it in a more precise, more unique manner, which marks
them from the outset, even more than the others, as being on
the side of the imaginary.

However, this characteristic is to a greater or lesser degree proper to all the sexual drives insofar as they differ from purely organic instincts or needs (Lacan), or in Freud from the self-preservation drives (the "ego drives" which he tended subsequently to annex to narcissism, a tendency he could never quite bring himself to pursue to its conclusion). The sexual drive does not have so stable and strong a relationship with its "object" as do for example hunger and thirst. Hunger can only be satisfied by food, but food is quite certain to satisfy it; thus instincts are simultaneously more and less difficult to satisfy than drives; they depend on a perfectly real object for which there is no substitute, but they depend on nothing else. Drives, on the contrary, can be satisfied up to a point outside their objects (this is sublimation, or else, in another way, masturbation) and are initially capable of doing without them without putting the organism into immediate danger (hence repression). The needs of self-preservation can neither be repressed nor sublimated; the sexual drives are more labile and more accommodating, as Freud insisted (more radically perverse, says Lacan). Inversely, they always remain more or less unsatisfied, even when their object has been attained; desire is very quickly reborn after the brief vertigo of its apparent extinction, it is largely sustained by itself as desire, it has its own rhythms, often quite independent of those of the pleasure obtained (which seemed nonetheless its specific aim); the lack is what it wishes to fill, and at the same time what it is always careful to leave gaping, in order to survive as desire. In the end it has no object, at any rate no real object; through real objects which are all substitutes (and all the more numerous and interchangeable for that), it pursues an imaginary object (a "lost object") which is its truest object, an object that has always been lost and is always desired as such.

How, then, can one say that the visual and auditory drives have a stronger or more special relationship with the absence of their object, with the infinite pursuit of the imaginary? Because, as opposed to other sexual drives, the "perceiving drive"—combining into one the scopic drive and the invocatory drive—*concretely represents the absence of its object* in the distance at which it maintains it and which is part of its very definition: distance of the look, distance of listening. Psychophysiology makes a classic distinction between the "senses at a distance" (sight and hearing) and the others all which involve immediate proximity and which it calls the "senses of contact" (Pradines): touch, taste, smell, coenaesthetic sense, etc. Freud notes that voyeurism, like sadism in this respect, always keeps apart the *object* (here the object looked at) and the *source* of the drive, i.e. the generating organ (the eye); the voyeur does not look at his eye. With orality and anality, on the contrary, the exercise of the drive inaugurates a certain degree of partial fusion, a coincidence (= contact, tendential abolition of distance) of source and aim, for the aim is to obtain pleasure at the level of the source organ (= "organ pleasure"): e.g. what is called "pleasure of the mouth."

It is no accident that the main socially acceptable arts are based on the senses at a distance, and that those which depend on the senses of contact are often regarded as "minor" arts (e.g. the culinary arts, the art of perfumes, etc.). Nor is it an accident that the visual or auditory imaginaries have played a much more important part in the histories of societies than the tactile or olfactory imaginaries.

The voyeur is very careful to maintain a gulf, an empty space, between the object and the eye, the object and his own body: his look fastens the object at the right distance, as with those cinema spectators who take care to avoid being too close to or too far from the screen. The voyeur represents in space the fracture which forever separates him from the object; he represents his very dissatisfaction (which is precisely what he needs as a voyeur), and thus also his "satisfaction" insofar as it is of a specifically voyeuristic type. To fill in this distance would threaten to overwhelm the subject, to lead him to consume the object (the object which is now too close so that he cannot see it any more), to bring him to orgasm and the pleasure of his own body, hence to the exercise of other drives, mobilising the senses of contact and putting an end to the scopic arrangement. *Retention* is fully part of perceptual pleasure, which is thereby often coloured with anality. Orgasm is the object rediscovered in a state of momentary illusion; it is the phantasy suppression of the gap between object and subject (hence the amorous myths of "fusion"). The looking drive, except when it is exceptionally well developed, is less directly related to orgasm than are the other component drives; it favours it by its excitatory action, but it is not generally sufficient to produce it by its figures alone, which thus belong to the realm of "preparatives." In it we do not find that illusion, however brief, of a lack filled, of a non-imaginary, of a full relation to the object, better established in other drives. If it is true of all desire that it depends on the infinite pursuit of its absent object, voyeuristic desire, along with certain forms of sadism, is the only desire whose principle of distance symbolically and spatially evokes this fundamental rent.

The same could be said, making the necessary modifications of course, about the invocatory (auditory) drive, less closely studied by psychoanalysis hitherto, with the exception of writers like Lacan and Guy Rosolato. I shall merely recall that of all hallucinations—and what reveals the dissociation of desire and real object better than the hallucination?—the main ones by far are visual and auditory hallucinations, those of the senses at a distance (this is also true of the dream, another form of hallucination).

The Scopic Regime of the Cinema

However, although this set of features seems to me to be important, it does not yet characterise the signifier of the cinema proper, but rather that of all means of expression based on sight or hearing, and hence, among other "languages," that of practically all the arts (painting, sculpture, architecture, music, opera, theatre, etc.). What distinguishes the cinema is an extra reduplication, a supplementary and specific turn of the screw bolting desire to the lack. First because the spectacles and sounds the cinema "offers" us (offers us at a distance, hence as much *steals* from us) are especially rich and varied: a mere difference of degree, but already one that counts: the screen presents to our apprehension, but absents from our grasp, more "things." (The mechanism of the perceiving drive is identical for the moment but its object is more endowed with matter; this is one of the reasons why the cinema is very suited to handling "erotic scenes" which depend on direct, non-sublimated voyeurism.) In the second place (and more decisively), the specific affinity between the cinematic signifier and the imaginary persists when film is compared with arts such as the theatre in which the audio-visual given is as rich as it is on the screen in the number of perceptual axes involved. Indeed, the theatre really does "give" this given, or at least slightly more really: it is physically present, in the same space as the spectator. The cinema only gives it in effigy, inaccessible from the outset, in a primordial *elsewhere*, infinitely desirable (= never possessible), on another scene which is that of absence and which nonetheless represents the absent in detail, thus making it very present, but by a different itinerary. Not only am I at a distance from the object, as in the theatre, but what remains in that distance is now no longer the object itself, it is a delegate it has sent me while itself withdrawing. A double withdrawal.

What defines the specifically cinematic *scopic regime* is not so much the distance kept, the "keeping" itself (first figure of the lack, common to all voyeurism), as the absence of the object seen. Here the cinema is profoundly different from the theatre as also from more intimate voyeuristic activities with a specifically erotic aim (there are intermediate genres, moreover: certain cabaret acts, strip-tease, etc.): cases where voyeurism remains linked to exhibitionism, where the two faces, active and passive, of the component drive are by no means so dissociated; where the object seen is present and hence presumably complicit; where the perverse activity—aided if need be by a certain dose of bad faith and happy illusion, varying from case to case, moreover, and sometimes reducible to very little, as in true perverse couples—is rehabilitated and reconciled with itself by being as it were undividedly taken in charge by two actors assuming its constitutive poles (the corresponding phantasies, in the absence of the actions, thus becoming interchangeable and shared by the play of reciprocal identification). In the theatre, as in domestic voyeurism, the passive actor (the one seen), simply because he is bodily present, because he does not go away, is presumed to consent, to cooperate deliberately. It may be that he really does, as exhibitionists in the clinical sense do, or as, in a sublimated fashion, does that oft noted triumphant exhibitionism characteristic of theatrical acting, counterposed even by Bazin to cinematic representation. It may also be that the object seen has only accepted this condition (thus becoming an "object" in the ordinary sense of the word, and no longer only in the Freudian sense) under the pressure of more or less powerful external contraints, economic ones for example with certain poor strippers. (However, they must have consented at some point; rarely is the degree of acceptance zero, except in the case of *victimisation*, e.g. when a fascist militia strips its prisoners: the specific characteristics of the scopic arrangement are then distorted by the overpowerful intervention of another element, sadism.) Voyeurism which is not too sadistic (there is none which is not so at all) rests on a kind of *fiction*, more or less justified in the order of the real, sometimes institutionalised as in the theatre or strip-tease, a fiction that stipulates that the object "agrees," that it is therefore exhibitionist. Or more precisely, what is necessary in this fiction for the establishment of potency and desire is presumed to be sufficiently guaranteed by the physical presence of the object: "Since it is there, it must like it," such, hypocritical or no, deluded or no, is the retrenchment needed by the voyeur so long as sadistic infiltrations are insufficient to make the object's refusal and constraint necessary to him. Thus, despite the distance instituted by the look—which transforms the object into a *picture* (a *"tableau vivant"*) and thus tips it over into the imaginary, even in its real presence—that presence, which persists, and the active consent which is its real or mythical correlate (but always real as myth) re-establish in the scopic space, momentarily at least, the illusion of a fullness of the object relation, of a state of desire which is not just imaginary.

It is this last recess that is attacked by the cinema signifier, it is in its precise emplacement (*in its place*, in both senses of the word) that it installs a new figure of the lack, the physical absence of the object seen. In the theatre, actors and spectators are present at the same time and in the same location, hence present one to another, as the two protagonists of an authentic perverse couple. But in the cinema, the actor was present when the spectator was not (= shooting), and the spectator is present when the actor is no longer (= projection): a failure to meet of the voyeur and the exhibitionist whose approaches no longer coincide (they have "missed" one another). The cinema's voyeurism must (of necessity) do without any very clear mark of consent on the part of the object. There is no equivalent here of the theatre actors' final "bow." And then the latter could see their voyeurs, the game was less unilateral, slightly better distributed. In the darkened hall, the voyeur is really left alone (or with other voyeurs, which is worse), deprived of his other half in the mythical hermaphrodite (a hermaphrodite not necessarily constituted by the distribution of the sexes but rather by that of the active and passive poles in the exercise of the drive). Yet still a voyeur, since there is something to see, called the film, but something in whose definition there is a great deal of "flight": not precisely something that hides, rather something that *lets* itself be seen without *presenting* itself to be seen, which has gone out of the room before leaving only its trace visible there. This is the origin in particular of that "recipe" of the classical cinema which said that the actor should never look directly at the audience (= the camera).

Thus deprived of rehabilitatory agreement, of a real or supposed consensus with the other (which was also the Other, for it had the status of a sanction on the plane of the symbolic), cinematic voyeurism, *unauthorised* scopophilia, is from the outset more strongly established than that of the theater in direct line from the primal scene. Certain precise features of the institution contribute to this affinity: the obscurity surrounding the onlooker, the aperture of the screen with its inevitable keyhole effect. But the affinity is more profound. It lies first in the spectator's solitude in the cinema: those attending a cinematic projection do not, as in the theatre, constitute a true "audience," a temporary collectivity; they are an accumulation of individuals who, despite appearances, more closely resemble the fragmented group of readers of a novel. It lies on the other hand in the fact that the filmic spectacle, the object seen, is more radically ignorant of its spectator, since he is not there, than the theatrical spectacle can ever be. A third factor, closely linked to the other two, also plays a part: the *segregation of spaces* that characterises a cinema performance and not a theatrical one. The "stage" and the auditorium are no longer two areas set up in opposition to each other within a single space; the space of the film, represented by the screen, is utterly heterogeneous, it no longer communicates with that of the auditorium: one is real, the other perspective: a stronger break than any line of footlights. For its spectator the film unfolds in that simultaneously very close and definitively inaccessible "elsewhere" in which the child *sees* the amorous play of the parental couple, who are similarly ignorant of it and leave it alone, a pure onlooker whose participation is inconceivable. In this respect the cinematic signifier is not only "psychoanalytic"; it is more precisely Oedipal in type. . . .

LAURA MULVEY
VISUAL PLEASURE AND NARRATIVE CINEMA

I. INTRODUCTION

A. A Political Use of Psychoanalysis

This paper intends to use psychoanalysis to discover where and how the fascination of film is reinforced by pre-existing patterns of fascination already at work within the individual subject and the social formations that have moulded him. It takes as starting point the way film reflects, reveals and even plays on the straight, socially established interpretation of sexual difference which controls images, erotic ways of looking and spectacle. It is helpful to understand what the cinema has been, how its magic has worked in the past, while attempting a theory and a practice which will challenge this cinema of the past. Psychoanalytic theory is thus appropriate here as a political weapon, demonstrating the way the unconscious of patriarchal society has structured film form.

The paradox of phallocentrism in all its manifestations is that it depends on the image of the castrated woman to give order and meaning to its world. An idea of woman stands as lynch pin to the system: it is her lack that produces the phallus as a symbolic presence, it is her desire to make good the lack that the phallus signifies. Recent writing in *Screen* about psychoanalysis and the cinema has not sufficiently brought out the importance of the representation of the female form in a symbolic order in which, in the last resort, it speaks castration and nothing else. To summarise briefly: the function of woman in forming the patriarchal unconscious is two-fold, she first symbolises the castration threat by her real absence of a penis and second thereby raises her child into the symbolic. Once this has been achieved, her meaning in the process is at an end, it does not last into the world of law and language except as a memory which oscillates between memory of maternal plenitude and memory of lack. Both are posited on nature (or on anatomy in Freud's famous phrase). Woman's desire is subjected to her image as bearer of the bleeding wound, she can exist only in relation to castration and cannot transcend it. She turns her child into the signifier of her own desire to possess a penis (the condition, she imagines, of entry into the symbolic). Either she must gracefully give way to the word, the Name of the Father and the Law, or else struggle to keep her child down with her in the half-light of the imaginary. Woman then stands in patriarchal culture as signifier for the male other, bound by a symbolic order in which man can live out his phantasies and obsessions through linguistic command by imposing them on the silent image of woman still tied to her place as bearer of meaning, not maker of meaning.

There is an obvious interest in this analysis for feminists, a beauty in its exact rendering of the frustration experienced under the phallocentric order. It gets us nearer to the roots of our oppression, it brings an articulation of the problem closer, it faces us with the ultimate challenge: how to fight the unconscious structured like a language (formed critically at the moment of arrival of language) while still caught within the language of the patriarchy. There is no way in which we can produce an alternative out of the blue, but we can begin to make a break by examining patriarchy with the tools it provides, of which psychoanalysis is not the only but an important one. We are still separated by a great gap from important issues for the female unconscious which are scarcely relevant to phallocentric theory: the sexing of the female infant and her relationship to the symbolic, the sexually mature woman as non-mother, maternity outside the signification of the phallus, the vagina. . . . But, at this point, psychoanalytic theory as it now stands can at least advance our understanding of the status quo, of the patriarchal order in which we are caught.

B. Destruction of Pleasure is a Radical Weapon

As an advanced representation system, the cinema poses questions of the ways the unconscious (formed by the dominant order) structures ways of seeing and pleasure in looking. Cinema has changed over the last few decades. It is no longer the monolithic system based on large capital investment exemplified at its best by Hollywood in the 1930's, 1940's and 1950's. Technological advances (16mm, etc) have changed the economic conditions of cinematic production, which can now be artisanal as well as capitalist. Thus it has been possible for an alternative cinema to develop. However self-conscious and ironic Hollywood managed to be, it always restricted itself to a formal mise-en-scène reflecting the dominant ideological concept of the cinema. The alternative cinema provides a space for a cinema to be born which is radical in both a political and an aesthetic sense and challenges the basic assumptions of the mainstream film. This is not to reject the latter moralistically, but to highlight the ways in which its formal preoccupations reflect the psychical obsessions of the society which produced it, and, further, to stress that the alternative cinema must start specifically by reacting against these obsessions and assumptions. A politically and aesthetically avant-garde cinema is now possible, but it can still only exist as a counterpoint.

The magic of the Hollywood style at its best (and of all the cinema which fell within its sphere of influence) arose, not exclusively, but in one important aspect, from its skilled and satisfying manipulation of visual pleasure. Unchallenged, mainstream film coded the erotic into the language of the dominant patriarchal order. In the highly developed Hollywood cinema it was only through these codes that the alienated subject, torn in his imaginary memory by a sense of loss, by the terror of potential lack in phantasy, came near to finding a glimpse of satisfaction: through its formal beauty and its play on his own formative obsessions. This article will discuss the interweaving of that erotic pleasure in film, its meaning, and in particular the central place of the image of woman. It is said that analysing pleasure, or beauty, destroys it. That is the intention of this article. The satisfaction and reinforcement of the ego that represent the high point of film history hitherto must be attacked. Not in favour of a reconstructed new pleasure, which cannot exist in the abstract, nor of intellectualised unpleasure, but to make way for a total negation of the ease and plenitude of the narrative fiction film. The alternative is the thrill that comes from leaving the past behind without rejecting it, transcending outworn or oppressive forms, or daring to break with normal pleasurable expectations in order to conceive a new language of desire.

II PLEASURE IN LOOKING/FASCINATION WITH THE HUMAN FORM

A.   The cinema offers a number of possible pleasures. One is scopophilia. There are circumstances in which looking itself is a source of pleasure, just as, in the reverse formation, there is pleasure in being looked at. Originally, in his *Three Essays on Sexuality*, Freud isolated scopophilia as one of the component instincts of sexuality which exist as drives quite independently of the erotogenic zones. At this point he associated scopophilia with taking other people as objects, subjecting them to a controlling and curious gaze. His particular examples centre around the voyeuristic activities of children, their desire to see and make sure of the private and the forbidden (curiosity about other people's genital and bodily functions, about the presence or absence of the penis and, retrospectively, about the primal scene). In this analysis scopophilia is essentially active. (Later, in *Instincts and their Vicissitudes*, Freud developed his theory of scopophilia further, attaching it initially to pre-genital auto-eroticism, after which the pleasure of the look is transferred to others by analogy. There is a close working here of the relationship between the active instinct and its further development in a narcissistic form.) Although the instinct is modified by other factors, in particular the constitution of the ego, it continues to exist as the erotic basis for pleasure in looking at another person as object. At the extreme, it can become fixated into a perversion, producing obsessive voyeurs and Peeping Toms, whose only sexual satisfaction can come from watching, in an active controlling sense, an objectified other.

At first glance, the cinema would seem to be remote from the undercover world of the surreptitious observation of an unknowing and unwilling victim. What is seen of the screen is so manifestly shown. But the mass of mainstream film, and the conventions within which it has consciously evolved, portray a hermetically sealed world which unwinds magically, indifferent to the presence of the audience, producing for them a sense of separation and playing on their voyeuristic phantasy. Moreover, the extreme contrast between the darkness in the auditorium (which also isolates the spectators from one another) and the brilliance of the shifting patterns of light and shade on the screen helps to promote the illusion of voyeuristic separation. Although the film is really being shown, is there to be seen, conditions of screening and narrative conventions give the spectator an illusion of looking in on a private world.

Among other things, the position of the spectators in the cinema is blatantly one of repression of their exhibitionism and projection of the repressed desire on to the performer.

B.   The cinema satisfies a primordial wish for pleasurable looking, but it also goes further, developing scopophilia in its narcissistic aspect. The conventions of mainstream film focus attention on the human form. Scale, space, stories are all anthropomorphic. Here, curiosity and the wish to look intermingle with a fascination with likeness and recognition: the human face, the human body, the relationship between the human form and its surroundings, the visible presence of the person in the world. Jacques Lacan has described how the moment when a child recognises its own image in the mirror is crucial for the constitution of the ego. Several aspects of this analysis are relevant here. The mirror phase occurs at a time when the child's physical ambitions outstrip his motor capacity, with the result that his recognition of himself is joyous in that he imagines his mirror image to be more complete, more perfect than he experiences his own body. Recognition is thus overlaid with mis-recognition: the image recognised is conceived as the reflected body of the self, but its misrecognition as superior projects this body outside itself as an ideal ego, the alienated subject, which, re-introjected as an ego ideal, gives rise to the future generation of identification with others. This mirror-moment predates language for the child.

Important for this article is the fact that it is an image that constitutes the matrix of the imaginary, of recognition/misrecognition and identification, and hence of the first articulation of the "I," of subjectivity. This is a moment when an older fascination with looking (at the mother's face, for an obvious example) collides with the initial inklings of self-awareness. Hence it is the birth of the long love affair/despair between image and self-image which has found such intensity of expression in film and such joyous recognition in the cinema audience. Quite apart from the extraneous similarities between screen and mirror (the framing of the human form in its surroundings, for instance), the cinema has structures of fascination strong enough to allow temporary loss of ego while simultaneously reinforcing the ego. The sense of forgetting the world as the ego has subsequently come to perceive it (I forgot who I am and where I was) is nostalgically reminiscent of that pre-subjective moment of image recognition. At the same time the cinema has distinguished itself in the production of ego ideals as expressed in particular in the star system, the stars centring both screen presence and screen story as they act out a complex process of likeness and difference (the glamorous impersonates the ordinary).

C.   Sections II. A and B have set out two contradictory aspects of the pleasurable structures of looking in the conventional cinematic situation. The first, scopophilic, arises from pleasure in using another person as an object of sexual stimulation through sight. The second, developed through narcissism and the constitution of the ego, comes from identification with the image seen. Thus, in film terms, one implies a separation of the erotic identity of the subject from the object on the screen (active scopophilia), the other demands identification of the ego with the object on the screen through the spectator's fascination with and recognition of his like. The first is a function of the sexual instincts, the second of ego libido. This dichotomy was crucial for Freud. Although he saw the two as interacting and overlaying each other, the tension between instinctual drives and self-preservation continues to be a dramatic polarisation in terms of pleasure. Both are formative structures, mechanisms not meaning. In themselves they have no signification, they have to be attached to an idealisation. Both pursue aims in indifference to perceptual reality, creating the imagised, eroticised concept of the world that forms the perception of the subject and makes a mockery of empirical objectivity.

During its history, the cinema seems to have evolved a particular illusion of reality in which this contradiction between libido and ego has found a beautifully complementary phantasy world. In *reality* the phantasy world of the screen is subject to the law which produces it. Sexual instincts and identification processes have a meaning within the symbolic order which articulates desire. Desire, born with language, allows the possibility of transcending the instinctual and the imaginary, but its point of reference continually returns to the traumatic moment of its birth: the castration complex. Hence the look, pleasurable in form, can be threatening in content, and it is woman as representation/image that crystallises this paradox.

III. Woman as Image, Man as Bearer of the Look

A.   In a world ordered by sexual imbalance, pleasure in looking has been split between active/male and passive/female. The determining male gaze projects its phantasy on to the female figure which is styled accordingly. In their traditional exhibitionist role women are simultaneously looked at and displayed, with their appearance coded for strong visual and erotic impact so that they can be said to connote *to-be-looked-at-ness*. Women displayed as sexual object is the leit-motiff of erotic spectacle: from pin-ups to strip-tease, from Ziegfeld to Busby Berkeley, she holds the look, plays to and signifies male desire. Mainstream film neatly combined spectacle and narrative. (Note, however, how in the musical song and dance numbers break the flow of the diegesis.) The presence of woman is an indispensible element of spectacle in normal narrative film, yet her visual presence tends to work against the development of a story line, to freeze the flow of action in moments of erotic contemplation. This alien presence then has to be integrated into cohesion with the narrative. As Budd Boetticher has put it:

> What counts is what the heroine provokes, or rather what she represents. She is the one, or rather the love or fear she inspires in the hero, or else the concern he feels for her, who makes him act the way he does. In herself the woman has not the slightest importance.

(A recent tendency in narrative film has been to dispense with this problem altogether; hence the development of what Molly Haskell has called the "buddy movie," in which the active homosexual eroticism of the central male figures can carry the story without distraction.) Traditionally, the woman displayed has functioned on two levels: as erotic object for the characters within the screen story, and as erotic object for the spectator within the auditorium, with a shifting tension between the looks on either side of the screen. For instance, the device of the show-girl allows the two looks to be unified technically without any apparent break in the diegesis. A woman performs within the narrative, the gaze of the spectator and that of the male characters in the film are neatly combined without breaking narrative verisimilitude. For a moment the sexual impact of the performing woman takes the film into a no-man's-land outside its own time and space. Thus Marilyn Monroe's first appearance in *The River of No Return* and Lauren Bacall's songs in *To Have or Have Not*. Similarly, conventional close-ups of legs (Dietrich, for instance) or a face (Garbo) integrate into the narrative a different mode of eroticism. One part of a fragmented body destroys the Renaissance space, the illusion of depth demanded by the narrative, it gives flatness, the quality of a cut-out or icon rather than verisimilitude to the screen.

B.   An active/passive heterosexual division of labour has similarly controlled narrative structure. According to the principles of the ruling ideology and the psychical structures that back it up, the male figure cannot bear the burden of sexual objectification. Man is reluctant to gaze at his exhibitionist like. Hence the split between spectacle and narrative supports the man's role as the active one of forwarding the story, making things happen. The man controls the film phantasy and also emerges as the representative of power in a further sense: as the bearer of the look of the spectator, transferring it behind the screen to neutralise the extra-diegetic tendencies represented by woman as spectacle. This is made possible through the processes set in motion by structuring the film around a main controlling figure with whom the spectator can identify. As the spectator identifies with the main male[1] protagonist, he projects his look on to that of his like, his screen surrogate, so that the power of the male protagonist as he controls events coincides with the active power of the erotic look, both giving a satisfying sense of omnipotence. A male movie star's glamorous characteristics are thus not those of the erotic object of the gaze, but those of the more perfect, more complete, more powerful ideal ego conceived in the original moment of recognition in front of the mirror. The character in the story can make things happen and control events better than the subject/spectator, just as the image in the mirror was more in control of motor coordination. In contrast to woman as icon, the active male figure (the ego ideal of the identification process) demands a three-dimensional space corresponding to that of the mirror-recognition in which the alienated subject internalised his own representation of this imaginary existence. He is a figure in a landscape. Here the function of film is to reproduce as accurately as possible the so-called natural conditions of human perception. Camera technology (as exemplified by deep focus in particular) and camera movements (determined by the action of the protagonist), combined with invisible editing (demanded by realism) all tend to blur the limits of screen space. The male protagonist is free to command the stage, a stage of spatial illusion in which he articulates the look and creates the action.

---

[1]There are films with a woman as main protagonist, of course. To analyse this phenomenon seriously here would take me too far afield. Pam Cook and Claire Johnston's study of *The Revolt of Mamie Stover* in Phil Hardy, ed.: *Raoul Walsh*, Edinburgh 1974, shows in a striking case how the strength of this female protagonist is more apparent than real.

C.1   Sections III. A and B have set out a tension between a mode of representation of woman in film and conventions surrounding the diegesis. Each is associated with a look: that of the spectator in direct scopophilic contact with the female form displayed for his enjoyment (connoting male phantasy) and that of the spectator fascinated with the image of his like set in an illusion of natural space, and through him gaining control and possession of the woman within the diegesis. (This tension and the shift from one pole to the other can structure a single text. Thus both in *Only Angels Have Wings* and in *To Have and Have Not*, the film opens with the woman as object of the combined gaze of spectator and all the male protagonists in the film. She is isolated, glamorous, on display, sexualised. But as the narrative progresses she falls in love with the main male protagonist and becomes his property, losing her outward glamorous characteristics, her generalised sexuality, her showgirl connotations; her eroticism is subjected to the male star alone. By means of identification with him, through participation in his power, the spectator can indirectly possess her too.)

But in psychoanalytic terms, the female figure poses a deeper problem. She also connotes something that the look continually circles around but disavows: her lack of penis, implying a threat of castration and hence unpleasure. Ultimately, the meaning of woman is sexual difference, the absence of the penis as visually ascertainable, the material evidence on which is based the castration complex essential for the organisation of entrance to the symbolic order and the law of the father. Thus the woman as icon, displayed for the gaze and enjoyment of men, the active controllers of the look, always threatens to evoke the anxiety it originally signified. The male unconscious has two avenues of escape from this castration anxiety: preoccupation with the re-enactment of the original trauma (investigating the woman, demystifying her mystery), counterbalanced by the devaluation, punishment or saving of the guilty object (an avenue typified by the concerns of the *film noir*); or else complete disavowal of castration by the substitution of a fetish object or turning the represented figure itself into a fetish so that it becomes reassuring rather than dangerous (hence over-valuation, the cult of the female star). This second avenue, fetishistic scopophilia, builds up the physical beauty of the object, transforming it into something satisfying in itself. The first avenue, voyeurism, on the contrary, has associations with sadism: pleasure lies in ascertaining guilt (immediately associated with castration), asserting control and subjecting the guilty person through punishment or forgiveness. This sadistic side fits in well with narrative. Sadism demands a story, depends on making something happen, forcing a change in another person, a battle of will and strength, victory/defeat, all occuring in a linear time with a beginning and an end. Fetishistic scopophilia, on the other hand, can exist outside linear time as the erotic instinct is focussed on the look alone. These contradictions and ambiguities can be illustrated more simply by using works by Hitchcock and Sternberg, both of whom take the look almost as the content or subject matter of many of their films. Hitchcock is the more complex, as he uses both mechanisms. Sternberg's work, on the other hand, provides many pure examples of fetishistic scopophilia.

C.2   It is well known that Sternberg once said he would welcome his films being projected upside down so that story and character involvement would not interfere with the spectator's undiluted appreciation of the screen image. This statement is revealing but ingenuous. Ingenuous in that his films do demand that the figure of the woman (Dietrich, in the cycle of films with her, as the ultimate example) should be identifiable. But revealing in that it emphasises the fact that for him the pictorial space enclosed by the frame is paramount rather than narrative or identification processes. While Hitchcock goes into the investigative side of voyeurism, Sternberg produces the ultimate fetish, taking it to the point where the powerful look of the male protagonist (characteristic of traditional narrative film) is broken in favour of the image in direct erotic rapport with the spectator. The beauty of the woman as object and the screen space coalesce; she is no longer the bearer of guilt but a perfect product, whose body, stylised and fragmented by close-ups, is the content of the film, and the direct recipient of the spectator's look. Sternberg plays down the illusion of screen depth; his screen tends to be one-dimensional, as light and shade, lace, steam, foliage, net, streamers, etc, reduce the visual field. There is little or no mediation of the look through the eyes of the main male protagonist. On the contrary, shadowy presences like La Bessière in *Morocco* act as surrogates for the director, detached as they are from audience identification. Despite Sternberg's insistence that his stories are irrelevant, it is significant that they are concerned with situation, not suspense, and cyclical rather than linear time, while plot complications revolve around misunderstanding rather than conflict. The most important absence is that of the controlling male gaze within the screen scene. The high point of emotional drama in the most typical Dietrich films, her supreme moments of erotic meaning, take place in the absence of the man she loves in the fiction. There are other witnesses, other spectators watching her on the screen, their gaze is one with, not standing in for, that of the audience. At the end of *Morocco*, Tom Brown has already disappeared into the desert when Amy Jolly kicks off her gold sandals and walks after him. At the end of *Dishonoured*, Kranau is indifferent to the fate of Magda. In both cases, the erotic impact, sanctified by death, is displayed as a spectacle for the audience. The male hero misunderstands and, above all, does not see.

In Hitchcock, by contrast, the male hero does see precisely what the audience sees. However, in the films I shall discuss here, he takes fascination with an image through scopophilic eroticism as the subject of the film. Moreover, in these cases the hero portrays the contradictions and tensions experienced by the spectator. In *Vertigo* in particular, but also in *Marnie* and *Rear Window*, the look is central to the plot, osciliating between voyeurism and fetishistic fascination. As a twist, a further manipulation of the normal viewing process which in some sense reveals it, Hitchcock uses the process of identification normally associated with ideological correctness and the recognition of established morality and shows up its perverted side. Hitchcock has never concealed his interest in voyeurism, cinematic and non-cinematic. His heroes are exemplary of the symbolic order and the law—a policeman (*Vertigo*), a dominant male possessing money and power (*Marnie*)—but their erotic drives lead them into compromised situations. The power to subject another person to the will sadistically or to the gaze voyeuristically is turned on to the woman as the object of both. Power is backed by a certainty of legal right and the established guilt of the woman (evoking castration, psychoanalytically speaking). True perversion is barely concealed under a shallow mask of ideological correctness—the man is on the right side of the law, the woman on the wrong. Hitchcock's skilful use of identification processes and liberal use of subjective camera from the point of view of the male protagonist draw the spectators deeply into his position, making them share his uneasy gaze. The audience is absorbed into a voyeuristic situation within the screen scene and diegesis which parodies his own in the cinema. In his analysis of *Rear Window*, Douchet takes the film as a metaphor for the cinema. Jeffries is the audience, the events in the apartment block opposite correspond to the screen. As he watches, an erotic dimension is added to his look, a central image to the drama. His girlfriend Lisa had been of little sexual interest to him, more or less a drag, so long as she remained on the spectator side. When she crosses the barrier between his room and the

814   FILM: PSYCHOLOGY, SOCIETY, AND IDEOLOGY

block opposite, their relationship is re-born erotically. He does not merely watch her through his lens, as a distant meaningful image, he also sees her as a guilty intruder exposed by a dangerous man threatening her with punishment, and thus finally saves her. Lisa's exhibitionism has already been established by her obsessive interest in dress and style, in being a passive image of visual perfection: Jeffries' voyeurism and activity have also been established through his work as a photo-journalist, a maker of stories and captor of images. However, his enforced inactivity, binding him to his seat as a spectator, puts him squarely in the phantasy position of the cinema audience.

In *Vertigo*, subjective camera predominates. Apart from one flash-back from Judy's point of view, the narrative is woven around what Scottie sees or fails to see. The audience follows the growth of his erotic obsession and subsequent despair precisely from his point of view. Scottie's voyeurism is blatant: he falls in love with a woman he follows and spies on without speaking to. Its sadistic side is equally blatant: he has chosen (and freely chosen, for he had been a successful lawyer) to be a policeman, with all the attendant possibilities of pursuit and investigation. As a result, he follows, watches and falls in love with a perfect image of female beauty and mystery. Once he actually confronts her, his erotic drive is to break her down and force her to tell by persistent cross-questioning. Then, in the second part of the film, he re-enacts his obsessive involvement with the image he loved to watch secretly. He reconstructs Judy as Madeleine, forces her to conform in every detail to the actual physical appearance of his fetish. Her exhibitionism, her masochism, make her an ideal passive counterpart to Scottie's active sadistic voyeurism. She knows her part is to perform, and only by playing it through and then replaying it can she keep Scottie's erotic interest. But in the repetition he does break her down and succeeds in exposing her guilt. His curiosity wins through and she is punished. In *Vertigo*, erotic involvement with the look is disorientating: the spectator's fascination is turned against him as the narrative carries him through and entwines him with the processes that he is himself exercising. The Hitchcock hero here is firmly placed within the symbolic order, in narrative terms. He has all the attributes of the patriachal super-ego. Hence the spectator, lulled into a false sense of security by the apparent legality of his surrogate, sees through his look and finds himself exposed as complicit, caught in the moral ambiguity of looking. Far from being simply an aside on the perversion of the police, *Vertigo* focuses on the implications of the active/looking, passive/looked-at split in terms of sexual difference and the power of the male symbolic encapsulated in the hero. Marnie, too, performs for Mark Rutland's gaze and masquerades as the perfect to-be-looked-at image. He, too, is on the side of the law until, drawn in by obsession with her guilt, her secret, he longs to see her in the act of committing a crime, make her confess and thus save her. So he, too, becomes complicit as he acts out the implications of his power. He controls money and words, he can have his cake and eat it.

IV. SUMMARY

The psychoanalytic background that has been discussed in this article is relevant to the pleasure and unpleasure offered by traditional narrative film. The scopophilic instinct (pleasure in looking at another person as an erotic object), and, in contradistinction, ego libido (forming identification processes) act as formations, mechanisms, which this cinema has played on. The image of woman as (passive) raw material for the (active) gaze of man takes the argument a step further into the structure of representation, adding a further layer demanded by the ideology of the patriarchal order as it is worked out in its favourite cinematic form—illusionistic narrative film. The argument turns again to the psychoanalytic background in that woman as representation signifies castration, inducing voyeuristic or fetishistic mechanisms to circumvent her threat. None of these interacting layers is intrinsic to film, but it is only in the film form that they can reach a perfect and beautiful contradiction, thanks to the possibility in the cinema of shifting the emphasis of the look. It is the place of the look that defines cinema, the possibility of varying it and exposing it. This is what makes cinema quite different in its voyeuristic potential from, say, strip-tease, theatre, shows, etc. Going far beyond highlighting a woman's to-be-looked-at-ness, cinema builds the way she is to be looked at into the spectacle itself. Playing on the tension between film as controlling the dimension of time (editing, narrative) and film as controlling the dimension of space (changes in distance, editing), cinematic codes create a gaze, a world, and an object, thereby producing an illusion cut to the measure of desire. It is these cinematic codes and their relationship to formative external structures that must be broken down before mainstream film and the pleasure it provides can be challenged.

To begin with (as an ending), the voyeuristic-scopophilic look that is a crucial part of traditional filmic pleasure can itself be broken down. There are three different looks associated with cinema: that of the camera as it records the pro-filmic event, that of the audience as it watches the final product, and that of the characters at each other within the screen illusion. The conventions of narrative film deny the first two and subordinate them to the third, the conscious aim being always to eliminate intrusive camera presence and prevent a distancing awareness in the audience. Without these two absences (the material existence of the recording process, the critical reading of the spectator), fictional drama cannot achieve reality, obviousness and truth. Nevertheless, as this article has argued, the structure of looking in narrative fiction film contains a contradiction in its own premises: the female image as a castration threat constantly endangers the unity of the diegesis and bursts through the world of illusion as an intrusive, static, one-dimensional fetish. Thus the two looks materially present in time and space are obsessively subordinated to the neurotic needs of the male ego. The camera becomes the mechanism for producing an illusion of Renaissance space, flowing movements compatible with the human eye, an ideology of representation that revolves around the perception of the subject; the camera's look is disavowed in order to create e nonvincing world in which the spectator's surrogate can perform with verisimilitude. Simultaneously, the look of the audience is denied an intrinsic force: as soon as fetishistic representation of the female image threatens to break the spell of illusion, and the erotic image on the screen appears directly (without mediation) to the spectator, the fact of fetishisation, concealing as it does castration fear, freezes the look, fixates the spectator and prevents him from achieving any distance from the image in front of him.

This complex interaction of looks is specific to film. The first blow against the monolithic accumulation of traditional film conventions (already undertaken by radical film-makers) is to free the look of the camera into its materiality in time and space and the look of the audience into dialectics, passionate detachment. There is no doubt that this destroys the satisfaction, pleasure and privilege of the 'invisible guest', and highlights how film has depended on voyeuristic active/passive mechanisms. Women, whose image has continually been stolen and used for this end, cannot view the decline of the traditional film form with anything much more than sentimental regret.[2]

1975

---

[2]This article is a reworked version of a paper given in the French Department of the University of Wisconsin, Madison, in the Spring of 1973.

CHRISTINE GLEDHILL
RECENT DEVELOPMENTS
IN FEMINIST CRITICISM

WOMEN AND REPRESENTATION

A crucial issue of Feminist film criticism is the examination of the fact that "women as women" are not represented in the cinema, that they do not have a voice, that the female point of view is not heard. Recognition of this fact unites all attempts at a Feminist critique of the cinema. Sharon Smith, in the first issue of *Women and Film*, writes:

> Women, in any fully human form, have almost completely been left out of film. . . . That is, from its very beginning they were present, but not in characterizations any self-respecting person could identify with. (p. 13)

The introductory "overview" locates the female image in terms of stereo-types:

> These roles—child/woman, whore, bitch, wife, mother, secretary or girl Friday, frigid career woman, vamp, etc.—were all portrayed falsely and one dimensionally.

Naome Gilbert in the second issue of *Women and Film* develops a notion of the female image as representing the male "other":

> The female is portrayed with an archetypal ambivalence. The "Eternal Feminine" has been aesthetically more a principle for

818   FILM: PSYCHOLOGY, SOCIETY, AND IDEOLOGY

realizing male objectives than a person in her own right. Thus
the dynamic of myth and reality when converging upon a female aesthetic has been quintessentially objectifying. . . . the
terms of the female aesthetic have been imposed on the basis
of man's fears and desires.

Claire Johnston in "Women's Cinema as Counter-Cinema" introduces the notion of fetishism into this argument:

> Within a sexist ideology and a male-dominated cinema, woman
> is presented as what she represents for man. . . . The fetishistic
> image portrayed relates only to male narcissism' woman repre-
> sents not herself, but by a process of displacement, the male
> phallus. It is probably true to say that despite the enormous
> emphasis placed on woman as spectacle in the cinema, woman
> as woman is largely absent. (p. 26)

And in "The Place of Women in the Cinema of Raoul Walsh,"
Pam Cook and Claire Johnston develop this analysis:

> In the tradition of classic cinema and 19th century realism,
> characters are presented as "autonomous individuals". . . . but
> the construction of the discourse contradicts this convention by
> reducing these "real" women to images and tokens functioning
> in a circuit of signs the values of which have been determined
> by and for men. (p. 93)

The crucial question (which would be answered in very different ways by these different writers) is *why "women as
women" are not represented in the media, and whether this is always and must be the case in cinematic representation.* Further if
this is the case, *how is it* (seeing that female roles and stars are
not absent, from films), *that images of concrete women end up
signifying a male discourse, and women are drawn to the cinema
to consume such images. What does it mean to pass from the "real"
experiences of concrete women to their representation in film?*
Recent Feminist work on film has sought to utilize a theoretical approach to such questions that breaks with the dominant assumptions of the literary tradition taught in schools and
of journalistic critical practice, which treat film as an expressive medium revealing in the story of a character's experiences
and development truths about the human condition that can
be judged according to their depth, maturity, etc. Thus against
traditional concern with characters and stereotypes, this critical "break" confronts Feminists with the semiotic/structuralist
notion of textual production. The *Camera Obscura* editorial
spells out the implications of this shift for Feminist analysis as
involving:

a process of investigation and theoretical reflection on the mechanisms by which meaning is produced in film. (p. 3)

In other words, we cannot understand or change sexist images of women for progressive ones without considering how the operations of narrative, genre, lighting, *mise en scène*, etc. work to construct such images and their meanings.

More complexly we have to consider the relationship between these formal mechanisms and ideology. The crucial shift from interpretation of meaning to an investigation of the means of its production locates the identification of ideology in aesthetic structures and film-making practices themselves, which as organizing principles produce their own ideological effect in the material they organize.

The value of this semiotic redefinition of film as text for Feminist analysis is that it enables us to escape the simple enumeration of sexist stereotypes (to which there is a limit) and the discussion of characters as to the degrees of liberation they represent, which often depends more on the critic's personal point of view than anything that can be determined by a reading of the film.[1] Elizabeth Cowie has summoned up the problems with the still prevalent tendency in Feminist film criticism to identify the absence of women in films in terms of their failure to reflect the social reality of women:

> Films are criticised for not showing "women as women", or "as fully human." It (sic) is criticised as inadequate, as partial and one-sided in relation to a possible definition of women else where, or else it is seen as a negation of that definition. Film is therefore precisely denied as a process of production when it comes to definitions of women, of woman as signifier and signified in the system of the film. ("Woman as Sign," in *M/F* No. 1, 1978, p. 50)

Nevertheless there is a danger that, once the object of Feminist criticism is defined solely in terms of the cinematic production of meaning, we lose the ability to deal with its relationship to women as defined in society altogether. Ann Kaplan has noted, for instance, how the concern in Claire Johnston's early "Women's Cinema as Counter-Cinema" to assert an economic

---

[1] Julia Lesage comments on *Women and Their Sexuality in the New Film* that Mellen rejects characters she finds "unpleasant." Thus Chloe in Rhomer's *Chole in the Afternoon* is "plain, with shaggy, unwashed hair falling in her eyes. Her complexion is sallow and unaided by makeup. Her sloppiness is intensified by a decrepit raincoat without style." "Whose Heroines?" *Jump Cut*, No. 1 (May–June 1974), pp. 22–24.

determination on films as products of a particular set of socioeconomic relations disappears in her later essays.[2] *Camera Obscura 1* makes a number of acknowledgments of the social context of film production:

> A theoretical examination. . . . locates analysis at the intersec-
> tion of the process of construction of the text and the social
> context which determines and is represented in that text. (p. 3)

However, this interaction is not pursued in any detail in this
issue of the journal.* What is also missing from this formulation, and from much recent Feminist film theory, is any sense
of the reading process performed by the audience and of how
this may both *be determined by* and *determine* the effectivity of
a film's ideological impact.

Although it is necessary to move away from concrete women
in society in order to grapple with the social and aesthetic
specificity of cinematic practices, the current concern with how
meaning is produced tends to stop at producing readings of
films that are illuminating to Feminist film theorists, or at a
film-making practice whose first aim is to produce knowledge
of its own production; the problem facing Feminist work on
the cinema now is what knowledge can be derived from film
theory that can make an intervention into both the production
and distribution of films and the way they are understood and
used by women at large. This problem appears to be felt in the
recent work of Feminist film-makers who have also been concerned to reflect on and change the dominant modes of representation—for instance Laura Mulvey and Peter Wollen's venture into a modified narrative mode in *Riddles of the Sphinx* or
the London Women's Film Group's use of intercut narrative
and documentary interviews in *Whose Choice?*, a film intended
to introduce the abortion issue to schoolgirls. What is at issue,
then, is the possibility of radical representation for women's
cinema. And this invokes the thorny theoretical issues of the
rejection of realism and the adoption of psychoanalysis in recent Feminist film theory.

REPRESENTATION, VERISIMILITUDE, REALISM, NATURALISM, ILLUSIONISM

Feminist film theory must inevitably encounter and do battle with the hybrid phenomenon of realism as a dominant ex-

*The new issue that has just appeared has not yet arrived in England so I
have been unable to follow how the collective is proceeding.
[2]Kaplan, "Aspects of British Feminist Film Theory." (See note 1 above.)

pectation of cultural production in the late 19th and 20th centuries, which embraces both hegemonic and radical aspirations. As the subtitle to this section indicates, realism is discussed through a wide range of terms and concepts with different shades of reference and indicating different relations to ideology. For instance in Claire Johnston's "Women's Cinema as Counter-Cinema," a variety of different concepts are used: Barthes's notion of myth as a process of naturalization (describing a mechanism specific to bourgeois ideology); representation (a cultural activity not necessarily tied to realism, e.g., medieval painting); the laws of verisimilitude (implying consonance with what is generally accepted by a particular society to be true as opposed to what a "progressive" realism might want to reveal); the camera developed "to safeguard the bourgeois notion of realism" (a construct belonging to an anti-realist position) and which grasps only "the natural world of the dominant ideology" (referring to the world of phenomenal forms it is the aim of naturalism, as distinct from realism, to reflect). To this array of terms *Camera Obscura* adds a view of mainstream cinema as "illusionist," thereby introducing a modernist inflection which rescues the materials and processes of art production from vulgar, bourgeois utilitarian ends; and by re-printing the piece by Jean-Louis Baudry on the cinematic apparatus, the collective shifts the meaning of realism from the deployment of a specific set of aesthetic techniques with more or less ideological effects to the capacity of a technological apparatus to reproduce in the subject the psychoanalytic structure now termed the "reality effect."

First I want to examine in what ways the current critique of realism shows that its dominance as a general cultural attitude constitute a problem for Feminist cinema. Realism in this general sense is the first recourse of any oppressed group wishing to combat the ideology promulgated by the media in the interests of hegemonic power. Once an oppressed group becomes aware of its cultural as well as political oppression, and identifies oppressive myths and stereotypes—and in the case of women, female images that simply express male fantasies—it becomes the concern of that group to expose the oppression of such images and replace their falsity, lies, deceptions and escapist illusions with reality and the truth.

The problems of a simplistic use of the notion of cinematic realism are threefold. The first has to do with defining the "reality" of women and the fact that it is not self-evidently given. There clearly will be contradictions between what the condition of women is, what their struggles for change aim to achieve, and how these realities are recognized and understood by Feminists on the one hand, and non-Feminists on the other. So while it is certainly possible to point to what is absent from media screens—women at work, home as a workplace, struggles to change legal and economic structures, the issues of sexual politics, expressions of women's sexuality and so on—there is no simple alternative reality to fill the gap and displace the stereotypes, which will be instantly recognized and accepted by women at large. On the one hand the reality of women can only be grasped through a Socialist-Feminist analysis, the terms of which are not immediately available in phenomenal appearances. On the other, as has already been suggested, the mass media produce their own definitions of women which also have a concrete existence and determining effect on social reality. Stereotypes do not vanish on the production of an image of real women, or of Feminist aspiration. They are materialized in the way society is structured and the way we live our lives; they are part of our reality. Clearly then, as Roman Jakobson pointed out long ago, the claim to realism can be invoked by forces seeking to preserve or to challenge the status quo.[3] This means Feminist cultural analysis needs to question the power and role of recognition. On the one hand a female audience will not necessarily make a Feminist reading of what they see. On the other hand, recognition of a powerfully evoked woman's dilemma, as for instance in *Klute* or *Alice Doesn't Live Here Any More*, may lead us to accept the recuperative ideology through which this dilemma is resolved. Diane Giddis, for instance, in an article on *Klute*, makes a convincing case for the authenticity with which Pakula has grasped the dilemma of the would-be independent woman faced with both the need to love and the threat of assimilation by the male.[4] But this account is then recuperated into a commonplace of traditional criticism that a divided self is a bad thing, which any mature person must seek to unify, rather than the product of the social and psychic contradictions women live under which are amenable to political not personal solutions. The psychologism of this approach leads Giddis to validate Pakula's profoundly un-Feminist, though no doubt "true" ending, that the woman must accept her vulnerability and expose herself to assimilation in the relationship with the man.

This said, it seems to me that these problems need not, as they do in the thinking of many anti-realist theorists, lead to

[3]Roman Jakobson, "On Artistic Realism," in *Readings in Russian Poetics,* eds. Ladislav Matejka and Krystyna Ponovska (MIT Press, 1971).

[4]Diane Giddis, "The Divided Woman: Bree Daniels in *Klute,*" *Women and Film,* 1, Nos. 3/4 (1973), 57–61. Anthologized in *Movies and Methods,* ed. Bill Nichols. (U. Cal. Press, 1976).

an equation between 1) concrete reality, 2) its ideological con-figuration, the status quo, and 3) realism as a political goal in cultural production. Nor does it mean that recognition and identification cannot under certain conditions be utilized (or indeed done without). As I shall argue, for women to take up a Feminist position requires precisely an act of identifica-tion—with women as a group and of our oppressed place in society.

The second problem with a naive recourse to reality as a counter to stereotyping is that it ignores the need to engage with the multiple function of the cinema as entertain-ment/ritual/art/fiction, which, although it must exist politically, does not exist alone, or even predominantly, for politics. Hans Magnus Enzensberger has suggested that mass consumerism invokes real needs and desires which capitalism orchestrates commercially in order to exploit.[5] And Claire Johnston argues the inherent puritanism of narrowly realist attitudes, suggest-ing the necessity of engaging the "collective fantasies of women" in a Feminist cinema.[6] Women are crucially located in this consumerist culture and its utopian elaboration in en-tertainment, both in terms of our social-economic role and in terms of our image, which is used to materialize its appeal. Realism narrowly defined in terms of actuality is not a pow-erful enough weapon to disengage women's fantasy from its imbrication in consumerist structures; the relation of propa-ganda and consciousness-raising films to the utopian, con-sumerist thrust of entertainment has yet to be worked through.

The third problem of a simple realist approach to the media is that it ignores the fact that "realism" as a mode of cinematic production involves a complex inter-play of techniques and devices— that it has to be produced and is not simply evoked by the intention to be real or true. The value of semiology for *Camera Obscura* is that it "attempts to deconstruct the assump-tion of the naturalness of the iconic image" (p. 6). The issue here is a naturalism which subsumes cinema and film within the operation of the camera lens under the ideological propo-sitions that reality equals what we can see, that perception equals cognition, and that the camera offers a window on the world and does not lie. What such propositions do is deny the existence of those material socioeconomic forces which, though not immediately perceptible in phenomenal appearances, are responsible for their production. Thus reality figures not as a

[5]"Constituents of a Theory of the Media," *New Left Review*, 64 (Nov.–Dec. 1970).

[6]Claire Johnston, "Nelly Kaplan, An Introduction," *Notes on Women's Cin-ema, Screen* Pamphlet No. 2, p. 15.

product of society, amenable to human control and change, but of nature, a notion much exploited by bourgeois ideology.[7] By constituting the whole of cinematic production in the visual image, naturalism not only ignores the film-making apparatus but also that the iconic sign is caught up in other signifying systems — linguistic, aesthetic, social, fictional etc. — which together structure the film.

The view generated by the media of their own practices reproduces this ideology in that it refuses acknowledgment of the mediating intervention of the film-making process. This is supported by a technology and aesthetic system developed and improved in the service of a naturalist practice, which works precisely to substantiate the claim of the media to reveal the world in an unmediated fashion — for example, lightweight cameras, synchronous sound, and all the devices of direct cinema. it is important to show that this is an ideology that the media strive to perpetuate. However, I think it highly questionable whether a theory of realism should equate all varieties of realist practice with the goal of naturalism and so with the operation of bourgeois ideology; or the socioeconomic conditions of the production of a technology with the ultimate aesthetic/ideological effect it produces in the audience who inhabit a different set of conditions.

That "realism" is dominant as an epistemology and aesthetic goal since the Renaissance seems to be an inevitable part of materialist history in so far as we are seeking to free ourselves from superstition, religion, idealism in order to gain control over our material, social, and psychological world. Thus in the days of the revolutionary bourgeoisie, visual and fictional techniques were developed, aimed at grasping the concrete world of human practice rather than the spiritual hierarchy of feudalism. Certain forms of the realist practice have in the 20th century been theorized in different ways (e.g., Lukacs, Brecht) as the means of reflecting on and analyzing the socially constructed world, in order to produce an understanding of its constitutive forces, and underlying contradictions. However, the problem of hegemonic bourgeois ideology is to try to disguise the fact of reality as a social and historical production and to return it to the world of nature. So the realist endeavor is frequently dehistoricized and reduced to the reflection of the surface appearances of phenomenal reality under the new ethic of naturalism, which becomes the ideology of the media.

[7]The account of bourgeois ideology which I draw on in this article is that given by Stuart Hall, "Culture, the Media, and the 'Ideological Effect,' "*Mass Communication and Society,* eds. James Curran et al. (Arnold, 1977).

It seems important to stress these distinctions because the current anti-realist position has produced a monolithic construct which collapses realism into naturalism and invalidates the fact that different media forms—say a classic Hollywood revival, a modern blockbusting spectacular, the "Play for Today," or a TV documentary—refer to and construct reality in very different ways. To take this argument further, however, requires looking in more detail at the different positions used against realism. These arguments turn about the epistemological status of reality itself, or representation of reality in aesthetic discourse, and of signification as the production of meaning.

BARTHES'S CONCEPT OF MYTH

In "Myth Today," Barthes describes how bourgeois ideology inserts itself into modern semiotic cultural phenomena.[8] His concern is with how the fabric of bourgeois cultural life divests reality of its material, historical specificity and returns it to an eternal, unchanging world of nature which reflects the world of bourgeois values but disguises its name. In "Rhetoric of the Image," he concentrates on how this happens specifically in the photographic image,[9] which has an existential relation to the person or object it represents in a way that the world does not. For a totally hypothetical and, in practice, unrealizable instant, he suggests the photographic image is purely denotative—it is what it means and what it is. Similarly the social world is full of objects which have a purely utilitarian function—clothes exist to be worn, food to be eaten, houses to protect us from the weather and so on. The issue for Barthes is what happens when these objects or photographic images are caught up in a semiotic system and enter the processes of signification.

At this point in bourgeois culture, the denotative image ceases to have as its referent the person, object, or function as these exist materially and historically. The denotative sign becomes a signifier in the second order of signification—connotation. Within bourgeois culture this process constitutes a kind of semiotic vampirism. The connotative signifier drains the original purely denotative sign of its historical and material reference—what Barthes rather suspectly calls its meaning—and turns it into a support for a new bourgeois signifier, the

[8]Roland Barthes, *Mythologies* (Jonathan Cape, 1972).
[9]Roland Barthes, "The Rhetoric of the Image," *Working Papers in Cultural Studies No. 1* (Spring 1971).

naturalized concept of eternal truths or the "human condition."

> I am at the barber's, and a copy of *Paris-Match* is offered to me.
> On the cover, a young Negro in a French uniform is saluting,
> with his eyes uplifted, probably fixed on a fold of the tricolour.
> All this is the *meaning* of the picture. But, whether naively or
> not, I see very well what it signifies to me: that France is a great
> Empire, that all her sons, without colour discrimination, faith-
> fully serve under her flag, and that there is no better answer to
> the detractors of an alleged colonialism than the zeal shown by
> this Negro in serving his so-called oppressors.
>   As meaning, the signifier already postulates a reading, I grasp
> it through my eyes, it has a sensory reality. . . . there is a
> richness in it. . . . it belongs to history, that of the . . . Negro:
> in the meaning, a signification is already built. . . . it postu-
> lates a kind of knowledge, a past, a memory, a comparative
> order of facts, ideas, decisions.
>   When it becomes form, the meaning leaves its contingency
> behind; it empties itself, it becomes impoverished, history
> evaporates, only the latter remains. ("Myth Today," pp. 116–
> 117)

For feminism this theoretical construct has a great attraction.
As I have noted, it has long been a common-place of Feminist
analysis that women are culturally located outside history—
the world that is made and remade by the activity of real material men—and placed in an idealist sphere of nature, eternal
values etc. It is also commonplace that women exist in cultural
production as "the other," or the "eternal feminine," the necessary complement to the male, the opposite against which men
struggle for self-definition and manhood.

For Pam Cook and Claire Johnston, Barthes's concept of the
naturalized connotation offers an analysis of how the photographic image of woman becomes a signifier in patriarchal
discourse without any sense of violence being done to it. In
their study of *The Revolt of Mamie Stover* the image of woman
is a sign emptied of its hypothetical denotation referring to the
concrete individual woman photographed, meaning "this is a
woman" of "woman so-and-so," to become the dehistoricized
signifier of the patriarchal connotation—"non-male."

For the moment I want to hold in abeyance the question as
to whether the iconic image of woman must always produce a
patriarchal connotation, to look at a slightly different appropriation of Barthes for feminism made by Eileen McGarry. In
an article on "Documentary, Realism and Women's Cinema"
(*Women and Film*, Vol. 2, No. 7, Summer 1975) she takes up
Barthes's analysis of cultural objects and practices—such as

clothing, eating, etc. — as having first a pure function and then a semiotic signification to elaborate the theory that reality itself is coded, and that within a patriarchal social structure everything to do with women is coded in a sexiest way. In a film these social codes are overlaid with the codes of appearance for the actress or film star. She makes a convincing critique of Wiseman's *High School* in terms of the way he photographs and organizes the image of an elderly schoolteacher according to the stereotype "crabby old spinster," just as if he were organizing an actress in a role. Following this line of reasoning, what the audience recognizes as real is not an unmediated reality but the product of socially formed codes. Accepting that the world is perceived through such codes, the issue is whether reality is so monolithically coded in terms of bourgeois and sexist ideology as McGarry suggests. The argument as she presents it does not exclude the codings of dress, appearance, and gesture that connote, for instance, women's liberation (*The Woman's Film*), the oppression of women (*Women of the Rhondda*), or the struggle of women (*Women Against the Bill*).[10] Yet her view of the coding of reality appears to leave no room for the contradictions in the social formation which make Marxist-Feminist analysis and struggle possible.

It is not only reality which is monolithically conceived in this argument but also the audience. Eileen McGarry does suggest that an audience's class position may modify the operation of the codes, but her argument seems to imply that this is at the level of selective perception. Stuart Hall is one of the few cultural analysts who has tried to give the decoding process an active rather than passive dimension in a model of different possible reading processes — hegemonic, negotiated, and oppositional.[11] And Elizabeth Cowie has convincingly argued that a Feminist reading of particular films or filmic processes in general is not an inevitable consequence of the film itself:

Sexism in an image cannot be designated materially as a content in the way that denotative elements such as colours or ob-

[10]*Woman's Film* by the Newsreel Group, USA 1971; *Women of the Rhondda* by the London Women's Film Group 1973; *Women Against the Bill* by Esther Ronay and members of the NottingHill Women's Liberation Group.

[11]Stuart Hall, "Encoding and Decoding in the TV Discourse," paper available from Centre for Contemporary Cultural Studies, University of Birmingham, England. The *hegemonic* decoding is one that takes the reading preferred by the dominant ideology; the *negotiated* decoding attempts to maintain the preferred reading in tandem with understandings drawn from a class position which is in contradiction (though disguised contradiction) to the dominant ideology; and the *oppositional* decoding transforms the readings offered by the dominant ideology into what they mean for an oppositional discourse.

jects in the image can be pointed to. Rather it is the development of new or different definitions and understandings of what
men and women are and their roles in society which produces
readings of images as sexist; the political perspective of feminism produces a further level of connotative reading. ("Women,
Representation and the Image," *Screen Education*, Summer 1977)

This argument suggests that the fact that we are able to see the
school teacher in Wiseman's *High School* as a sexist stereotype
at all is not because sexism resides inside the image itself, but
because the Women's Liberation Movement has produced a
Feminist perspective which enables us to read the connotation
of the teacher in other than naturalized patriarchal terms. In
this respect no artistic practice, realist or otherwise, can ensure
either a conservative or radical reading on the part of the audience.

There is a further problem in the contribution of semiotics
to cultural analysis, which compounds the question of realism
in film. As I have already suggested, Barthes tries to take account of the existential relation between photographic image
and person or object photographed by hypothesizing a purely
denotative moment when phenomenal meaning and existence
unite. So the fact that the iconic image can then be caught up
into other signifying systems constitutes a kind of cheat on the
premise of an original pure denotation. Eileen McGarry takes
up this aspect of Barthes's semiology:

When reality becomes a pro-filmic event it becomes the first
stage in a process of signification — i.e., the functional element
of human existence which makes it *more* than signification is
eliminated. People and objects are abstracted to the level of pure
sign. ("Documentary, Realism and Women's Cinema," p. 52)

Her earlier insistence, along with Barthes, that reality is not
transparently given but is itself a coded social construct and
that images similarly produce meaning according to a system
of semiotic codes is important as an intervention against naturalist ideologies. However, the route she takes from here into
the anti-realist position suggests that this acknowledgment involves one also in renouncing the goal of a realist representation aimed at probing that production in terms that can make
a connection with the experience people gain through their
social and political practices. In other words, if the iconic image is unable to deliver us images of women in our pure
"function" and "meaning," it does not seem to me the logical
next step to assert that our reality cannot be signified so as to
be better understood; if the functional elements of human ex-

istence are suppressed in the process of semiotic signification, may they not be spoken about in the organized message? This tendency to critique the realist endeavour for not rendering the "real" in its full immediacy does seem to stem in part from Barthes's nostalgia for the hypothesized and fleeting moment of pure denotation.[12]

ALTHUSSER AND IDEOLOGY

My appeal to experience and understanding at the end of the last section introduces a different strand in the anti-realist position, which turns on the problematic relation of individual consciousness and experience to a materialist understanding of reality and derives from a theory of ideology propounded by Louis Althusser. How far can the acts of recognition daily performed in the practical activity of women and men be informed by or produce an understanding of the nature of the social process in which they are caught up? To a large extent the possibility or otherwise of a cognitive artistic practice which can aim to produce understanding about the world stands or falls on the answer to this question.

Whereas many Marxist theorists — Lukacs and Brecht as two major and often opposed exponents of Marxist aesthetics — have sought to develop the terms of a realist practice capable of producing an understanding of the real world in its social practices and historical production, the Althusserian position claims that the attempt to represent the social formation can produce only "the natural world of the dominant ideology."[13] Behind this view lie two crucial concepts developed by Althusser, first, "ideology in general," and second, the ideological category of the subject. Althusser proposes a distinction between "ideology in general," which is necessary to the functioning of any society, and specific ideologies belonging to particular social formations at particular points in their history — bourgeois ideology, for instance. "Ideology in general" is theorized as a material force rather than merely a set of false ideas circulating in people's heads that should by now have been changed by Socialist teaching and example. It acts as a material support to specific ideologies, and is a structure providing the necessary mediation between (1) the forces and relations of production, (2) the social institutions they give rise to, and (3) the individuals who have to live through them. Ideology enables men and

[12]Terry Lovell has critiqued Barthes in these terms in "Cultural Studies," *Screen*, 14, No. 3 (Autumn 1973).

[13]Claire Johnston, "Women's Cinema as Counter-Cinema," *Notes on Women's Cinema*, Screen Pamphlet No. 2 (Sept. 1972), p. 28.

women to make sense of their world and feel in control of it. However, it is in their practical activity rather than in their ideas that ideology materializes itself; in fact it provides the terms of such activity.

> Ideology is indeed a system of representations, but in the majority of cases these representations have nothing to do with "consciousnes": they are usually images, and occasionally concepts, but it is above all as *structures* that they impose on the vast majority of men (sic), not via their "consciousness". They are perceived accepted-suffered cultural objects and they act functionally on men (sic) via a process that escapes them. Men (sic) "live" their ideologies . . . as their *"world"* itself. . . . the "lived" relation between men (sic) and the world, including History (in political action or inaction), passes through ideology, or better, is ideology itself. ("Marxism and Humanism," p. 233)

As such, ideology is a necessary component of human society; "it . . . is not an aberration or a contingent excrescence of History; it is a structure essential to the historical life of societies" (p. 232).

Ideology is able to materialize itself in the activities of women and men precisely because they operate under the illusion of being concrete individuals at the center of and to a measure initiating their lived experience, because they perform the daily acts of recognition which maintain and perpetuate the structures and institutions of the social formation. Althusser theorizes the ideological nature of identity and recognition through the psychoanalytic category of the subject developed by Lacan (which I will come to later):

> You and I are *always already* subjects, and as such constantly practice the rituals of ideological recognition, which guarantee for us that we are indeed concrete, individual, distinguishable and (naturally) irreplaceable subjects. (pp. 161–62)

> All ideology hails or interpellates concrete individuals as concrete subjects, by the functioning of the category of the subject. (p. 162)

This attack on the dominant discourse of Western philosophy since the Renaissance, aimed at irrevocably shifting humanist Man from the scene of history and women and men from the scene of their daily lives, also puts the "real" back a stage, not simply beyond the reach of phenomenal appearances, but making it inaccessible to the conscious social practice of men and women. Everyday life and its struggles can only be experienced in ideological terms; knowledge about the causes and nature of these struggles is produced only by theoretical practice:

> Ideology . . . is identical with the "lived" experience of human existence itself. This "lived" experience is not a given, given by a pure "reality," but the spontaneous "lived experience" of the ideology in its peculiar relationship to the real. (Althusser, "A Letter on Art," p. 205)

This position clearly has gave consequences for an artistic practice seeking to represent the real world. The problem is compounded by the fact that in capitalism it is bourgeois ideology that uses "ideology in general" for a material support. For the work of bourgeois ideology is understood to be aimed at dissolving class membership with its resulting contradictions into individuals, producing and maintaining them in the illusion of their non-contradictory discreteness, autonomy, freedom, and centrality. To do this it has to reorganize sociality into forms that obscure the fact of society as a historical social production and an interrelated totality grounded in contradiction. This requires the masking, displacing, or imaginary unifying of contradiction in terms of such myths as "nature" or the unchangeable "human condition." Thus in bourgeois ideology the members of the social formation find themselves isolated individuals who confront over and against them society as a preconstituted given appearing to derive from nature.[14]

In these terms the mechanisms of recognition and identification are complicit at the level both of "ideology in general" and bourgeois ideology. The former would appear to provide a sound support system for the latter in the inaccessibility to conscious experience of "the real" and in the formation of the subject. Thus in analyses of realist aesthetics, this distinction between "ideology in general" and "bourgeois ideology" often appears to get lost, so that bourgeois ideology becomes monolithic and inescapable to the point that the room for manoeuver available to social practices such as artistic production is very limited.

For Feminist cultural practice this position constitutes a serious problem. The Women's Liberation Movement, for instance, has set great store on the interrogation of personal experience and consciousness-raising as a form of work aimed at uncovering the political in the personal and creating new

[14]See note 8.

identifications for individual women where the recognition of a gender position in terms of the category *women*, as opposed to the patriarchal abstractions "woman," the "eternal feminine," etc., is precisely to leave behind an individual identification and begin to recast the self in terms of a group membership. The first issue of *Camera Obscura* can be seen as attempting to negotiate this contradiction between women's movement politics, their corresponding demands of Feminist film-making, and the anti-representational emphasis of recent film theory. Stating their allegiance to neo-Marxist structural theory developed in terms of feminism by Claire Johnston, Pam Cook, Laura Mulvey and others, the collective claims a break with the classic (Hollywood) text and the dominant "realist" mode of film production. Accounting for their interest in the avant-garde work of Yvonne Rainer, they state:

> We felt that the Feminist problematic—the complex and ambiguous permutations of male dominance/female submission—could not be presented as a political and therefore changeable, problem using the conventional modes of representation. (p. 59)

In consequence *Camera Obscura* rejects "identification" as a mechanism in the classic text or documentary for making a political intervention and this means taking a distance from much of the early film-making of the Women's Liberation Movement. The problem with *Janie's Janie*, for instance, is that "we can rather easily imagine *not* identifying with Janie, the subject." In Yvonne Rainer's films, on the other hand, their "formal construction . . . forces the audience to analyze the problems which the films demonstrate." (p. 59). . . .

If we have a certain freedom not to identify with Janie, it is unclear how Yvonne Rainer's films can "force" an audience into an appropriate analytical activity. This problem is the subject of an interesting debate between the collective and Rainer over the relation between the function of mainstream and avant-garde practices:

> CO: In *The Mother and the Whore* you *are* provided with situations that you can identify with, that you can see yourself in, but you've given no conceptual tools to analyze the situation. It has to do with questions of perception, with the way we see things. . . . these films provide you with a ready-made experience. Once you're inside that fictional world, you may see situations you can identify with, but when you come back out of that world, out of the theater, it's hard to transfer that filmed situation outside because it's so much tied to the characters and

the emotional situations inside the film. When you watch a film that you have to think about in order to determine its coherence or relevance, you are engaging in an active process which is exactly the same inside and outside the film. You don't have to rethink the milieu of the film in order to examine the situation it presents.

YR: I couldn't agree more. However, I think one of the problems in talking about what films do is, you start talking about some kind of Everyperson. . . . Perhaps it is a mistake to compare narrative films from the standpoint of those which use distancing devices and those which do not. How can we say which type of film will make "people" think, or make them active, and which will not? A friend of mine thought that *The Mother and the Whore* summed up the male-female predicament in a nutshell. I got bogged down in the talkiness, the actors, my difficulty with Leaud, a thousand and one details . . . As she talked about it I had to agree with her. What other film has so explicitly dealt with the child-man's expectations of women? She, my friend, came out of that movie critical and objective. I, poor soul, was adrift in that other tradition. It is very difficult to cross over to the other shore. (pp. 83–84)

The issue raised here is whether the audience is as automatically taken over by the identificatory mechanisms of mainstream cinema as the antirealist position suggests, or whether there is not a considerable degree of work required on the part of the audience in negotiating what a particular fictional world offers according to where they are placed in society. Similarly, although it is clear that the view of the media as "a window on the world" must be firmly resisted, it is not clear that the audience, even while accepting that view as a general proposition, automatically accept it on any and every occasion. It seems more likely that the audience will be as contradictory in its utilization of media products as any other aspect of society—though not necessarily consciously so. Disproving the epistemological claims of a particular medium or artistic practice is a different thing from analyzing its ideological effects in a particular concrete conjuncture. Thus, I would argue that *Camera Obscura's* rejection of early women's film-making is both right and wrong:

We feel that most of these filmmakers fell into the trap of trying to employ an essentially male-oriented bourgois notion of film — the notion of film as a window on the world, and have simply chosen to shoot out of other windows than did most filmmakers before the women's movement. (p. 60)

It is not clear that "shooting out of other windows" could not be a very illuminating and subversive activity. For instance, Ann Kaplan has suggested that although the movement films do not demystify the system of representation, they can "reorder the signs within the convention, giving us unfamiliar images of women; we make unfamiliar identifications, sympathies and alliances and are given new perceptions" ("Aspects of British Feminist Film Theory," p. 52).

There seems to be a danger in the current critique of realism of taking the claims for the media at their face values and so ignoring the fact that phenomenal appearances rendered in film have nevertheless to be read through a variety of signifying and social codes which are distributed differently among audiences. In the end what continually eludes attempts to confront the realist text is the question: at what level we are to understand its realism to be constituted and so available for interrogation. Are we dealing with an aesthetic form, an epistemological construct, a political practice, or an ideological claim surrounding media production?

More recently the technology of the cinema has been critiqued from the anti-realist perspective on psychoanalytic grounds. The ideological realism of the cinema is not now only a matter of the deployment of techniques of verisimilitude; rather the "reality effect" is ensured through the apparatus of cinematic projection, by the production of the individual spectator in the place of the subject—unified outside contradiction. Crucial to this production is the psychoanalytic representation of woman and her fetishized cinematic counterpart.[15]

PSYCHOANALYSIS AND FEMINIST FILM THEORY

In "The Place of Women in the Cinema of Raoul Walsh," Pam Cook and Claire Johnston move from Barthes's "myth" to Lacanian psychoanalysis. Thus reasons are found why the iconic image of woman must produce a patriarchal meaning, and why "women as women" are silent in our culture. At the same time the grounds for the rejection of a possible radical

[15]For accounts of the anti-realist polemic, see: Paul Willamen, "On Realism in the Cinema," *Screen*, 13, No. 1 (Spring 1972); Colin McCabe, "Realism in the Cinema: Notes on some Brechtian Theses," *Screen*, 15, No. 2; Peter Wollen, *"Vent d'Est:* Counter Cinema," *Afterimages* No. 4 (Autumn 1972). And for Feminist applications of these positions, see: Eileen McGarry, "Documentary, Realism and Women's Cinema," *Women and Film*, 2, No. 7 (Summer 1975); "Feminism and Film: Critical Approaches," editorial, *Camera Obscura 1* (Fall 1976).

realism are shifted to a concern with iconic representation which now subsumes all forms of realism. In these terms, representation has less the force of a purposive cultural activity than of a compulsive psychoanalytic mechanism centering on the female figure. Laura Mulvey gives an unequivocal statement of this in "Visual Pleasure and Narrative Cinema":

> The paradox of phallocentrism in all its manifestations is that it depends on the image of the castrated woman to give order and meaning to its world. (p. 6)

In Pam Cook and Claire Johnston's account, the cinematic image presents the body of woman as a spectacle for the erotic male gaze, at the same time rendering her as "non-male," so that her image may become the substitute phallus necessary to counter the castration threat to men posed by woman's lack of a penis. Thus the very act of representation ipso facto involves the objectification of women and the repression of female sexuality.

THE PLACE OF THE WOMAN IN THE LACANIAN CINEMA[16] PLENITUDE AND IDENTITY/BREAST AND "MIRROR PHASE"

The article in *Camera Obscura* by Jean-Louis Baudry and the most recent writings of Claire Johnston[17] cite the reality effect not in techniques of verisimilitude, but in the construction in the spectator of a certain position in relation to the film. This position produces a highly desired state of being termed "plenitude" or "unity." There are several aspects to this notion of unity: the desire to be united with reality, with the others who confer on one a sense of identity with one's own self, with one's words and their meanings. What is terrifying to us is the notion of separation, difference, and lack. An intimation of this desired state of being is first experienced by the baby at the breast, but this illusion of plenitude in unity with the mother is soon thrown into question by the experience of separation and loss when the mother leaves the baby to go about her own affairs. The pleasure of the cinema lies in

[16]The account of Lacanian psychoanalysis given here is largely drawn from: Steve Burniston and Chris Weedon, "Ideology, Subjectivity and the Artistic Text," *Working Papers in Cultural Studies* No. 10 (1977); Laura Mulvey, "Visual Pleasure and Narrative Cinema," *Screen*, 16, No. 3 (Autumn 1975); Colin MacCabe, "Principles of Realism and Pleasure," *Screen*, 17, No. 3.

[17]Claire Johnston, "Towards a Feminist Film Practice: Some Theses," in *Edinburgh '76 Magazine* No. 1, *Psychoanalysis/Cinema/Avant-Garde*.

its reconstruction in the spectator of an illusory sense of this imagined early experience of unity.

As the baby develops, however, it enters a second phase of illusory unity described as the "mirror phase," in which the baby's emerging subjectivity achieves an *imaginary* unity with its own idealized image reflected in a mirror—a fragmentation first indicated in the return look of the mother/"other" that confirms for the baby the identity between itself and its reflection. This forms the basis of the fragmentation through which the ego is formed to become conscious of self. In "Towards a Feminist Film Practice: Some Theses,"[18] Claire Johnston describes how the filmic text constructs a place for the spectator, which reproduces this illusory identification. This is achieved by an identification with the imaginary spectator implied in the presentation of a shot ("this scene is being looked at by someone)" which in the reverse shot is then transferred to a fictional character, so denying the return look of the image and the separateness of the concrete viewer in the auditorium and stitching her or him into the fiction (suture) and into the subject place where the filmic text constructs.

DIFFERENCE: CASTRATION AND LANGUAGE

If unity and identity are illusions, then the crucial reality is difference, the master concept of psychoanalysis. The splitting of self which takes place when the ego separates out from the imaginary unity of image and self-image during the mirror phase is coincident with the beginnings of language. With the ego and language begins the differentiation in the world of objects and others from each other and from the self, and at the same time the gradual establishment of an individual subject in the place marked out for it through a series of prohibitions and approbiations. The child gradually finds out who it is, who it has to become. Finally and most crucially for an analysis of patriarchy, the child acquires the sexed place indicated by the pronoun positions of "he" and "she" and everything that is predicated socially and culturally on them.

The crucial role of difference in this process arises from the structural linguistics of Ferdinand Saussure. He argued that there are no positive terms in language—single words united and full with their single meanings and their referents in the real world—but only a system of related differences or oppositions. For instance, the meaning of the word "sheep" in English is not the meaning of "mouton" in French because En-

18See note 18.

glish also has "mutton," which French does not. "Sheep" only has meaning in terms of its difference from "mutton" (and from a whole series of other interconnected differences, to pursue which would mean reading the dictionary of the English language). According to the logic of psychoanalysis, the starting place in this relay of differences is the first perception of sexual difference in the woman's lack of a penis.

DIFFERENCE, LACK, AND THE PHALLUS

In this instance the term difference becomes highly loaded. It is not a matter of functional oppositions as in the difference of "t" and "d" or "sheep" and "mutton." Sexual difference is said to be the key opposition in which presence (the phallus symbolized by the penis) is faced with absence (no penis).* Here for the emerging human subject a bitter paradox enters. Plenitude is only experienced in terms of the mother; for a short time, she "is the phallus" (symbol of plenitude) for the child—retrospectively, that is, for the mother offers that plenitude the possibility of which the phallus will later come to represent as a memory. But then the child is faced, not only with the fact of the mother's necessary absences, but also with her betrayal of her exclusive relation to the child in that she is possessed also by the father. Thus the maternal identification is broken by the entry of "the father"—the third term representing the look of "the other" suppressed during the mirror phase—whose prohibition against incest turns the perception of sexual difference into the threat of castration. The traumatic experience of this oppositional difference sets in motion the acquisition of the organized relay of linguistic differences which constitute language and so the human subject.

The drive which will impel the child onward from the realization of castration into culture and the resolution of the Oedipus complex will be haunted by the memory of his original illusory experience of plenitude when baby and world were at one. As this subject is constructed through language, so desire is constituted as the attempt to recapture these illusions, through language, which is its only means of knowing the world and so of gaining control over it. But the language user has to submit to the rules of a language he or she has not made; moreover there is an unbridgeable gap between the uttering ego, the moment of utterance, and reception of the ut-

---

*Penis and phallus should not be confused. While the penis refers to the anatomical organ, the phallus, which the penis is able to symbolize, represents the object of desire as it is structured under patriarchy.

terance by the other. The desire of the subject is doomed to failure. Hence the double importance of the iconic media which appear to promise an escape from the constraints of language and a return to the pleasure of an achieved unity between subject and reality.

MALE ENTRY INTO THE SYMBOLIC

At this point we can examine the differential entry of the male and female child into the patriarchal order, a difference that turns on the crucial role of the penis/no penis opposition in the institution of language. The mother originally represents the place of the phallus but then with the entry of the third term betrays the child by her lack. For the boy, the father's penis demonstrates a comforting and recuperative presence. Thus the penis stands in for the phallus, the key signifier, the importance of which is that it is a kind of end-stop to the otherwise endless chain of signifiers. It represents the possibility of arriving back where one wants to be, a kind of finality which makes the production of meaning possible from the play of difference. The patriarchal fact that the penis can be the signifier of the phallus is paralleled by the boy's reassuring expectation that one day he will himself wield such a penis, taking the place of his father, and once more gain symbolic possession of his mother in the person of his wife. The terror of castration and lack can be evaded at the same time as the fact of difference facilitates entry into the symbolic order of human culture. Thus through the correspondence between his anatomy and the possibility of wielding language the boy can escape from the illusory unity of the imaginary and enter the symbolic, the sphere of articulation, of signification, and the expression of desire.

WOMEN AND THE SYMBOLIC ORDER

If the boy enters into a position of command within the patriarchal symbolic order, what is the girl's position in patriarchy? For our purposes there are two questions: What is the relation of women to language as speaking subject? What is the role of the representation of women in cultural artifacts? Put simply: *Can women speak, and can images of women speak for women?* The answers seem negative. First, women anatomically play a key part in the production of the symbolic (language and culture), but by virtue of this role (castration) women can only have a negative relation to language; they cannot wield control over the symbolic; they do not carry in themselves the symbol of the signifier, the phallic authority for signification, only the absence which sets the signifier in place. Thus their entry into human discourse must be tentative, highly negotiated, and ambiguous. Second, though the threat of castration is necessary to the production of the speaking subject, in order for the subject to speak, the possibility of castration must not have taken place or has to be concealed. Thus female sexuality cannot be expressed; the symbolic activity of language and culture is set into motion in an attempt to liquidate the very lack that women represent. For women themselves to attain mastery within this system they would have to want to liquidate themselves. Hence the enigmatic silence of women.

So the answer to the first question (can women speak?) is no, or only in a highly negotiated fashion, because the subject position from which mastery of language is possible is a male construct—one which women help to form but which we cannot operate.

> Woman's desire is subjected to her image as bearer of the bleeding wound, she can exist only in relation to castration and cannot transcend it. She turns her child into the signifier of her own desire to possess a penis (the condition, she images, of entry into the symbolic). Either she must gracefully give way to the word, the Name of the Father and the Law, or else struggle to keep her child down with her in the half-light of the imaginary. Woman then stands in patriarchal culture as signifier for the male other, bound by a symbolic order in which men can live out his phantasies and obsessions through linguistic command by imposing them on the silent image of woman still tied to her place as bearer of meaning, not maker of meaning. (Laura Mulvey, "Visual Pleasure and Narrative Cinema." p. 7)

Not only can women not speak, but fully realized femininity is an unknown condition:

> Because under patriarchy we are condemned to live by our sexed identities, the ideological definitions of the "masculine" and the "feminine," Juliet Mitchell makes a strong case for seeing femininity in patriarchal culture as to some extent a repressed condition, which can only be acquired partially and in a distorted form. Perhaps it can only be fully understood in its symptoms, as in the case of hysteria ("a disorder with feminine characteristics"—Freud which embodies both the representation of desire and its prohibition. It would seen to me that within patriarchal culture there is a "definitely defined male sexuality" which can find expression (the fetishization of woman as spectacle is one example) while female sexuality is indeed repressed, its real nature only fully knowable with the overthrow

of patriarchal culture itself. (Claire Johnston,[19] "Femininity and
the Masquerade: *Anne of the Indies*," p. 43)

WOMEN AND REPRESENTATION

In these terms, then, the answer to the second question is
similarly negative: images of women cannot speak for women.
Because of the role played by the image of woman in the formation of the (masculine) subject, representations of women
in cultural artifacts are bound to return to and play on the re-
gressive desire to reestablish for the viewer the desired unity
with the real—thrown into question by the possibility of castration—difference. So "woman as woman" can be presented
in classic film representation, only as a fetishized image constituting a denial of female sexuality and desire. Claire Johnston describes how this fetishization is achieved cinematically
and at the same time reverses the claims usually made for Mae
West.

> Many women have read into her parody of the star system and
> her verbal aggression an attempt at the subversion of male
> domination in the cinema. If we look more closely there are
> many traces of phallic replacement in her persona which sug-
> gest quite the opposite. The voice itself is strongly masculine,
> suggesting the absence of the male, and establishes the
> male/non-male dichotomy. The characteristic phallic dress pos-
> sesses elements of the fetish. The female element which is in-
> troduced, the mother image, expresses male oedipal fantasy. In
> other words, at the unconscious level, the persona of Mae West
> is entirely consistent with sexist ideology; it in no way subverts
> existing myths, but reinforces them. ("Women's Cinema as
> Counter-Cinema," p. 26)

The connotation "non-male" or "substitute phallus" required by patriarchal ideology is imposed through a system of
iconic rather than fictional or narrative codes, so that women
are realized filmically as "to-be-looked-at" images rather than
in speech or action.

> Lighting, camera angles, the cutting between actors and use of
> close shot v. long shot—all the techniques of filming are used
> to differentiate radically the presentation of men and women on
> the screen . . . techniques normally used . . . for women in
> films . . . essentially produce a specularity in relation to the
> character in a way which places her role in the film as iconic

[19]*Jacques Tourneur,* eds. Claire Johnston and Paul Willamen (Edinburgh Film
Festival, 1975).

rather than diegetic; i.e., the classical sexual objectification of women in films. (Elizabeth Cowie, "Feminist Film Criticism: A Reply," *Screen*, Vol. 16, No. 1, p. 138)

Laura Mulvey in "Visual Pleasure and Narrative Cinema" uses the Lacanian interpretation of this visual objectification of women to argue that because the superabundant iconicity of the female image also threatens an eruption of extreme unpleasure—castration—classic Hollywood cinema has developed various devices and structures to give the male hero and, by proxy, the male spectator, control over her enchanting and threatening image. Given the crucial role of the female representation in patriarchal culture, these forms control the material of any film.

> Patriarchal ideology is an effect of the form of the film text itself, and may even in isolated cases be at variance with the beliefs of the author. . . . This domain of form imposes itself on the film-maker whether or not he or she likes it, defining the limits and meanings of the work of art itself. (Claire Johnston, "Feminist Politics and Film History," *Screen*, Vol. 16, no. 3, p. 122)

A Feminist film-maker, then, finds the root of patriarchy in the very tools she wishes to employ to speak about women. So what is required of her is the development of a counter-cinema that will deconstruct the language and techniques of "classic cinema" at the point where the patriarchal subject is formed and female desire repressed: *castration*.

In her article on *Anne of the Indies*, Claire Johnston sees the girl child's masquerade, her disguise as a pirate, as a destructive refusal of the feminine position within the symbolic order. In so doing she asserts sexual difference in the face of the male fear of castration. Johnston defines this in terms of the Barthesian notion developed in *The Pleasure of the Text* and *S/Z*, of "radical heterogeneity." In these terms, the means of attack on patriarchy consists in the assertion of castration and the fundamental difference it opens up. In "Towards a Feminist Film Practice: Some Theses" she argues that the union of signifier and signified in patriarchal and classic filmic discourse ipso facto represses the feminine because it constitutes a denial of difference. Thus Woman is "the unnameable, the unsaid." Feminist practice must work toward dislocating and restructuring the symbolic order in order to change the function, in the moment of perception of sexual difference, of the entry of the third term in the production of the symbolic signifier; thus a new subject will be created and a new order of language that will assert rather than repress sexual difference.

PSYCHOANALYSIS AND IDEOLOGY

It is important for Feminist analysis of patriarchal culture to understand how psychoanalysis affects our understanding of the nature of reality, for in changing this it changes our point of attack. In this respect the impact of Lacanian psychoanalysis has to be understood in its conjunction with Althusser's theory of ideology. The chief issue for feminism is the patriarchal construction of the subject (to which both women and men have to conform). This construct is both the origin and ssp-port of ideology in general, in the sense that the illusions of identity, personal experience, and language use that are necessary to social life offer, as it were, the soil in which specific ideologies can seed and naturalize themselves; and simultaneously constitute the point at which the "feminine" is repressed. The first question that arises is the problematic relation of the patriarchal symbolic order to the material existence of men and women and their social practices, which in orthodox Marxist terms constitute the reality, it is the struggle of human beings to transform. The problem with orthodox Marxism, it is claimed, is that socioeconomic determinants are seen as operating within already constituted and therefore potentially autonomous subjects.[20] Thus the recourse to Lacan seeks a "materialist" theory of the subject in the discovery of the so-called primary processes that construct the true subject. The problem here is that the theoretical juncture of Lacan and Althusser in the de-centering of individuals from their consciousness seems to remove them from much else as well, for although the Lacanian subject accounts for different sexual locations in the symbolic order, it says little about class; the constitutive force of language, primary in both a chronological and formative sense, appears to displace the effectivity of the forces and relations of production in the social formation. Sexual difference is made homologous to the Marxist concept of contradiction, the driving force of history. Desire, the motivation of human endeavor, is seen as the compulsive wish to overcome this contradiction—if such it is—in order to regain the original unity experienced in babyhood. It is difficult to see how the dialectical process of history and class struggle is to be articulated in relation to this. Moreover the construction of the subject construct *individuals;* it is unclear what effectivity class or racial location has on the production of individuals or in what sense individuals can be said to belong to *social groups.*

[20]For a discussion of this problem see the collective article by the editorial board of *Ideology and Consciousness* No. 1 (1977).

For women this has grave consequences. On the one hand we are faced with almost total repression of femininity within patriarchal culture; on the other with the intensification in the 20th century of struggles around the economic and political emancipation of women. The issue then, is the relation of the construction of the subject to the social structure; for Feminists this could be posed as a question about the relation of the penis to the phallus. For if the trauma of castration is relieved by the phallus, what needs explaining is why the penis is able to escape the linguistic rule of negativity and signify it. *Unless patriarchy is a product of chance, the role of the penis as support for the symbolic signifier seems to be predicated on patriarchal dominance as an already constituted fact.* This seems to be implicitly acknowledged in the account Steve Burniston and Chris Weedon give of the Lacanian system and of the moment of entry of the "third term" into the castration complex. Explaining that the Father in this system is symbolic of patriarchal law and not necessarily coincident with a real father, they say:

> In the situation with which the child is faced at the moment of the intervention of the Father in the pre-Oedipal relation, the paternal authority is inseparable from maleness. The penis, the distinguishing mark of maleness and thus the possibility of direct identification with the Father (if only *in prospect*), thus becomes the crux of the complex. ("Ideology, Subjectivity and the Artistic Text," in *Working Papers in Cultural Studies*, No. 10, p. 220)

The hiatus between women as constructed in language and women as produced by historical, social, and economic forces is more marked if we try to envisage the relation of patriarchy to capitalism and bourgeois ideology. In these terms patriarchy is coincident with ideology in general and would appear to precede, even be a condition of, any other form of oppression. This raises two general problems. First, a Feminist theory and cultural practice that seeks practical political effectivity must be able to take account of the intersection of gender with class and racial difference among others. In political terms it would seem essential to have recourse to some form of recognition through which women can make a first identification with themselves as women and as an oppressed group and at the same time relate this identification to their class experience. The second problem is the magnitude of the task facing Feminists if patriarchy can be shifted only by an assault on the structure of the subject and ideology in general. Our understanding of this task has been given us in terms of psycholinguistic representational structure to which fictional and cinematic forms of representation are understood as being homologous. But we are clearly in a very weak political position if rupturing the place of the subject in representation is our chief point of entry.

There clearly is a danger in posing the question in chicken-and-egg terms. But the problem remains if we are to locate an effective point of Feminist attack; how are the socioeconomic structures of power and subordination articulated with the repression of femininity in the psycholinguistic construction of the subject? and how can one level effect changes in the other? . . .

CONCLUSION

Recent developments in Feminist film theory rest on the meeting of three different strands in neo-Marxist analysis: 1) the Althusserian designation of lived experience, empirical reality, as the materialization of ideology; 2) the Lacanian theory of the primacy of language in the construction of the subject in which visual representation of woman plays a key role; and 3) the designation of cinema as an iconic medium ideologically complicit with an epistemology of vision based on the self-evident character of phenomenal appearances, and devoted to re-playing the process of the construction of the subject in order to reconfirm the ideological unity of the patriarchal subject outside contradiction.

The ultimate problem, it seems to me, lies in the attempt to make language and the signifying process so exclusively central to the production of the social formation. Under the insistence on the semiotic production of meaning, the effectivity of social, economic, and political practice threatens to disappear altogether. There is a danger of conflating the social structure of reality with its signification, by virtue of the fact that social processes and relations have to be mediated through language, and the evidence that the mediating power of language reflects back on the social process. But to say that language has a determining effect on society is a different matter from saying that society is nothing but its languages and signifying practices.

Once the social construction of reality and women is defined in terms of psychoanalytic signifying practice alone, the process of realist representation can only be ideologically complicit, for it is itself based on an imaginary unity between signifier and signified and the suppression of difference from which originates our illusory sense of the real world in the first place.

Thus in Barthes's *The Pleasure of the Text* and *S/Z*, part of his rejection of realism is that it demands that writers make a choice between meanings; for within the anti-realist epistemology, the only way to avoid ideology is to put off the signified—the moment of closure, of ideological fixity—for as long as possible, to stay within process, the infinite play of meanings. From the point of view of the Women's Liberation Movement, or any other political grouping, this demand has serious implications; there are some meanings associated with the image of women that have to be rejected forcibly. In the end it is difficult to see how if a radical ideology, such as feminism, is to be defined as a means of providing a framework for political action, one is not going to put one's finger on the scales, enter some kind of realist epistemology.

BIBLIOGRAPHY

Affron, Charles. *Star Acting*. New York: Dutton, 1977.

Agee, James. *Agee on Film: Reviews and Comments*. Boston: Beacon Press, n.d.

Agel, Henri. *Le Cinéma et la sacré.* Paris: Éditions du Cerf, 1961.

———. *Poetique du cinéma*. N.p.: Éditions du Signe, 1973.

Altman, Rick, ed. *Genre: The Musical*. London: Routledge and Kegan Paul, 1981.

Andrew, J. Dudley. *The Major Film Theories*. New York: Oxford University Press, 1976.

———. *André Bazin*. New York: Oxford University Press, 1978.

——— *Concepts in Film Theory*. New York: Oxford University Press, 1984.

Arnheim, Rudolf. *Art and Visual Perception*. Berkeley and Los Angeles: University of California Press, 1954.

———. *Film as Art*. Berkeley and Los Angeles: University of California Press, 1966.

——— *Visual Thinking*. Berkeley and Los Angeles: University of California Press, 1969.

Ayfre, Amédée. *Cinéma et mystère*. Paris: Éditions du Cerf, 1969.

———. *Le Cinéma et sa vérité*. Paris: Éditions du Cerf, 1964.

———. *Conversion aux images?* Paris: Éditions du Cerf, 1964.

Balázs, Béla. *Theory of the Film: Character and Growth of a New Art*. New York: Dover Publications, 1970.

Barnouw, Eric. *Documentary: A History of Non-Fiction Film*. New York: Oxford University Press, 1974.

Barr, Charles. "CinemaScope: Before and After." *Film Quarterly* XVI, No. 4, Summer 1963.

Barsam, Richard Meran. *Nonfiction Film: A Critical History*. New York: Dutton, 1972.

————. *Nonfiction Film: Theory and Criticism.* New York: Dutton, 1975.

Barthes, Roland. *Elements of Semiology.* Translated by Annette Laversy and Colin Smith. New York: Hill and Wang, 1967

————. *Mythologies.* Selected and edited by Annette Laversy. New York: Hill and Wang, 1972.

———— *Image-Music-Text.* Translated by Stephen Heath. New York: Hill and Wang, 1977.

Battcock, Gregory, ed. *The New American Cinema.* New York: Dutton, 1967.

Bazin, André. *What is Cinema?* Volume I. Berkeley and Los Angeles: University of California Press, 1971.

————. *What is Cinema?* Volume II. Berkeley and Los Angeles: University of California Press, 1971.

Benjamin, Walter. *Illuminations.* Edited and with an introduction by Hannah Arendt. New York: Harcourt Brace, 1968.

Bergman, Andrew. *We're in the Money.* New York: Harper Collophon, 1972.

Bergson, Henri. *Laughter,* in *Comedy.* Edited by Wylie Sypher. Garden City, New York: Doubleday Anchor, 1956.

Bluestone, George. *Novels into Film.* Berkeley and Los Angeles: University of California Press, 1966.

Bobker, Lee R. *Elements of Film.* New York: Harcourt Brace, 1969.

Bordwell, David, and Kristin Thomson. *Film Art: An Introduction.* Reading, Mass.: Addison and Wesley, 1979.

Brakhage, Stan. "Metaphors on Vision." *Film Culture,* No. 30, Fall 1963.

Braudy, Leo. *The World in a Frame.* Garden City, N.Y.: Anchor Press, 1976.

———— and Morris Dickstein, eds. *Great Film Directors: A Critical Anthology.* New York: Oxford University Press, 1978.

Burch, Noël. *Theory of Film Practice.* Translated by Helen R. Lane and with an Introduction by Annette Michelson. New York: Praeger, 1973.

Carroll, Noël. "Address to the Heathens." *October* 23 (1982), 89–163.

Caughie, John, ed. *Theories of Authorship.* (British Film Institute Series) London: Routledge and Kegan Paul, 1981.

Cavell, Stanley. *The World Viewed: Reflections on the Ontology of Film.* New York: Viking, 1971.

————. *Pursuits of Happiness: The Hollywood Comedy of Remarriage.* Cambridge: Harvard University Press, 1981.

Cawelti, John. *The Six-Gun Mystique.* Bowling Green, Ohio: Bowling Green Popular Press, n.d.

Clarens, Carlos. *An Illustrated History of the Horror Film.* New York: Capricorn Books, 1968.

Cocteau, Jean. *Cocteau on the Film.* Translated by Vera Triall. New York: Roy Publishers.

Cohen, Keith. *Film and Fiction/The Dynamics of Exchange.* New Haven: Yale University Press, 1979.

Cohen-Séat, Gilbert. *Essai sur les principes d'une philosophie du cinéma.* Paris: Presses Universitaires de France, 1958.

————. *Problemes du cinéma et de l'information visuelle*. Paris: Presses Universitaires de France, 1961.

Corliss, Richard. *Talking Pictures: Screenwriters in the American Cinema*. New York: The Overlook Press, 1974.

Cripps, Thomas. *Slow Fade to Black: The Negro in American Film 1900–42*. New York: Oxford University Press, 1977.

DeLaurentis, Teresa, and Stephen Heath, eds. *The Cinematic Apparatus*. New York: St. Martin's Press, 1980.

Derrida, Jacques. *Writing and Difference*. Chicago: University of Chicago Press, 1978.

Doesburg, Theo van. "Film as Pure Form." *Form* (Cambridge), No. 1, Summer 1966.

Durgnat, Raymond. *Films and Feelings*. Cambridge, Mass: The M.I.T. Press, 1967.

Dyer, Richard. *Stars*. (British Film Institute Series) New York: New York Zoetrope, 1978.

Earle, William. "Revolt Against Realism in the Films." *The Journal of Aesthetics and Art Criticism* XXVII, No. 2, Winter 1968.

Eco, Umberto. *A Theory of Semiotics*. Bloomington, Ind.: Indiana University Press, 1976.

Eisenstein, Sergei M. *Film Form*. Edited and translated by Jay Leyda. New York: Harcourt Brace, n.d.

————. *The Film Sense*. Edited and translated by Jay Leyda. New York: Harcourt Brace, n.d.

Farber, Manny. *Negative Space*. New York: Praeger Publishers, 1971.

Faure, Élie. *The Art of Cineplastics*. Boston: Four Seas Company, 1923.

Fenin, George N. and William K. Everson. *The Western*. New York: Grossman, 1973.

Ferguson, Otis. *The Film Criticism of Otis Ferguson*. Edited and with a preface by Robert Wilson. Foreword by Andrew Sarris. Philadelphia: Temple University Press, 1971.

Film Comment. "Hollywood Screenwriters" (Special Issue). VI, No. 4, Winter 1970–71.

Film Comment. "The Men with the Movie Cameras" (Special Issue). June 1972.

Fredericksen, Donald L. *The Aesthetic of Isolation in Film Theory: Hugo Munsterberg*. New York: Arno Press, 1977.

Geduld, Harry. *Film Makers on Film Making*. Bloomington: Indiana University Press, 1981.

Gessner, Robert. *The Moving Image: A Guide to Cinematic Literacy*. New York: Dutton, 1968.

Gouhier, Henri. *L'essence du théâtre*. Paris: Plon, 1948.

————. *Le théâtre et l'existence*. Paris: Auber, 1952.

Grierson, John. *Grierson on Documentary*. Edited by Forsyth Hardy. New York: Harcourt Brace, 1947.

Harrington, John. *The Rhetoric of Film*. New York: Holt, Rinehart, and Winston, 1973.

Harvey, Sylvia. *May Sixty-Eight and Film Culture*. (British Film Institute Series) New York: New York Zoetrope, 1980.

Haskell, Molly. *From Reverence to Rape: The Treatment of Women in the Movies*. New York: Holt, Rinehart, and Winston, 1974.

Hauser, Arnold. *The Social History of Art*. Four volumes. New York: Knopf, n.d.

Heath, Stephen. *Questions of Cinema*. Bloomington: Indiana University Press, 1981.

———. "Le Père Noël." *October* 26 (1983) 63–115.

Henderson, Brian. *A Critique of Film Theory*. New York: Dutton, 1980.

Hjelmslev, Louis. *Essais linguistiques*. Copenhague: Nordisk Sprog-og kulturforlag, 1959.

———. *Prolegomena to a Theory of Language*. Bloomington, Ind.: Indiana University Publications in Anthropology and Linguistics, 1953.

Houston, Beverle, and Marcia Kinder. *Self and Cinema*. Pleasantville, N.Y.: Redgrave Publishing Company, 1980.

Huss, Roy and Norman Silverstein. *The Film Experience: Elements of Motion Picture Art*. New York: Harper and Row, 1968.

Jacobs, Lewis. *The Rise of the American Film: A Critical History*. New York: Teacher's College Press, 1967.

Jarvie, I. C. *Movies and Society*. New York: Basic Books, 1970.

Jowett, Garth. *Film: The Democratic Art*. Boston: Little, Brown, 1976.

Kael, Pauline. *I Lost It at the Movies*. Boston: Little, Brown, 1965.

Kaplan, E. Ann, ed. *Women in Film Noir*. (British Film Institute Series) New York: New York Zoetrope, 1980.

Kauffmann, Stanley. "Notes on Theater-and-Film." *Performance* I, No. 4, October, 1972.

——— with B. Henstell. *American Film Criticism*. New York: Liveright, 1972.

Kawin, Bruce F. *Mindscreen: Bergman, Godard and First-Person Film*. Princeton: Princeton University Press, 1978.

Kelman, Ken. The Reality of New Cinema, in *The New American Cinema*, Edited by Batteock. New York: Dutton, 1967.

Kinder, Marcia, and Beverle Houston. *Close Up: A Critical Perspective on Film*. New York: Harcourt, Brace, Jovanovich, 1972.

Kitses, Jim. *Horizons West*. Bloomington, Ind. and London: Indiana University Press, 1970.

Kozarski, Richard. *Hollywood Directors, 1914–1940*. New York: Oxford University Press, 1976.

Kracauer, Siegfried. *From Caligari to Hitler*. New York: Noonday, 1959.

———. *Theory of Film: The Redemption of Physical Reality*. London, Oxford, New York: Oxford University Press, 1960.

Lacan, Jacques. *Ecrits: A Selection*. New York: W.W. Norton, 1977.

Langer, Susanne, K. *Feeling and Form*. New York: Scribner's, 1953.

Lawder, Standish D. *The Cubist Cinema*. New York: New York University Press, 1975.

Lawson, John Howard. *The Creative Process*. New York: Hill and Wang, 1964.

Lebovici, Serge. "Psychoanalyse et cinéma." *Revue internationale de filmologie* II, No. 5.

Lessing, Gotthold Ephraim. *Laocoon: An Essay Upon the Limits of Painting and Poetry*. New York: Noonday, n.d.

Lévi-Strauss, Claude. Structural Analysis in Linguistics and in Anthropology, in *Structural Anthropology*. New York: Basic Books, 1963.

Leyda, Jay. *Kino, A History of Russian and Soviet Film.* New York: Macmillan, 1960.

Liehm, Antonin J. *Closely Watched Films: The Czechoslavak Experience.* Armonk, N.Y.: N. E. Sharpe, 1974.

Lindgren, Ernest. *The Art of the Film.* Revised edition. London: Allen and Unwin, 1963.

Lindsay, Vachel. *The Art of the Moving Picture.* Revised edition. New York: Macmillan, 1922.

Lotman, Jurij. *Semiotics of the Cinema.* Translated by Mark E. Suino. Ann Arbor: University of Michigan Press, 1976.

Lovell, Terry. *Pictures of Reality: Aesthetics, Politics, Pleasure.* (British Film Institute Series) New York: New York Zoetrope, 1980.

Macbean, James Roy. *Film and Revolution.* Bloomington, Ind.: University of Indiana Press, 1975.

MacCann, Richard Dyer. *Film: A Montage of Theories.* New York: Dutton, 1966.

McConnell, Frank. *Storytelling and Mythmaking: Images from Film and Literature.* New York: Oxford University Press, 1979.

Manvell, Roger. *Film.* London: Penguin Books, 1946.

———. *Shakespeare and the Film.* New York: Praeger, 1971.

Marcel, Gabriel. "Possibilités et limites de l'art cinématographique." *Revue internationale de filmologie* V, Nos. 18–19.

Marinetti, Flippo T. *Selected Writings.* Translated by Arthur A. Coppotelli and R. W. Flint. New York: Noonday, 1972.

Martin, Marcel. *La langage cinématographique.* Paris: Éditions du Cerf, 1955.

Martinet, André. *Elements of General Linguistics.* Translated by Elisabeth Palmer. London: Faber and Faber, 1960.

Mast, Gerald. *The Comic Mind: Comedy and the Movies.* New York: Bobbs-Merrill, 1973.

———. *Film/Cinema/Movie: A Theory of Experience.* New York: Harper and Row, 1977.

Mellen, Joan. *Big Bad Wolves: Masculinity in American Films.* New York: Pantheon Books, 1978.

Merleau-Ponty, Maurice. *The Film and the New Psychology,* in *Sense and Non-sense.* Translated by Hubert L. and Patricia A. Dreyfus. Evanston, Ill.: Northwestern University Press, 1964.

Metz, Christian. *Film Language: A Semiotics of the Cinema.* Translated by Michael Taylor. New York: Oxford University Press, 1974.

———. *Language and Cinema.* Translated by Donna Jean Umiker-Seboek. The Hague: Mouton, 1974.

——— *The Imaginary Signifier: Psychoanalysis and the Cinema.* Translated by Celia Britton et al. Bloomington: Indiana University Press, 1982.

Meyerhold, Vsevolod. *Meyerhold on Theater.* Edited by Edward Braun. New York: Hill and Wang, 1969.

Mitry, Jean. *Esthétique et psychologie du cinéma.* Two Volumes. Paris: Éditions Universitaires, 1963–65.

Moholy-Nagy, László. *Vision in Motion.* Chicago: University of Chicago, 1947.

Monaco, James. *How to Read a Film.* New York: Oxford University Press, 1981.

Montagu, Ivor. *Film World*. Baltimore: Penguin, 1964.
Morin, Edgar. *Le Cinéma on l'homme imaginaire*. Paris: Éditions de Minuit, 1956.
———. *The Stars*. Translated by Richard Howard. New York. Grove Press, 1960.
Münsterberg, Hugo. *The Film: A Psychological Study*. New York: Dover, 1969.
Newcomb, Horace, ed. *Television: The Critical View*. 3rd edition. New York: Oxford University Press, 1982.
Nichols, Bill, ed. *Movies and Methods*. Berkeley and Los Angeles: University of California Press, 1976.
Nicoll, Allardyce. *Film and Theatre*. New York: Thomas Y. Crowell, 1937.
Olson, Elder. *The Theory of Comedy*. Bloomington, Ind., and London: Indiana University Press, 1968.
Orwell, George. Boys' Weeklies, in *Collection of Essays*. New York: Doubleday, 1954.
Panofsky, Erwin. "Style and Medium in the Motion Pictures." *Critique* I, No. 3, January–February 1947.
Perkins, V. F. *Film as Film: Understanding and Judging Movies*. Baltimore, Penguin, 1972.
Powdermaker, Hortense. *Hollywood, the Dream Factory*. Boston: Little Brown, 1960.
Pudovkin, Vsevolod I. *Film Technique and Film Acting*. Edited and translated by Ivor Montagu. New York: Grove Press, 1960.
Quarterly Review of Film Studies. "Interdisciplinary Approaches to Film Study" (Special Issue). I, No. 2, Summer 1976.
———. "Film and Semiotics" (Special issue). II, No. 1, Winter 1977.
Reisz, Karel. *The Technique of Film Editing*. New York: Hastings House, 1968.
Renan, Sheldon. *An Introduction to the American Underground Film*. New York: Dutton, 1967.
Richter, Hans. "The Film as an Original Art Form." *Film Cultura*, I, No. 1, January 1955.
Ritchie, Donald. *The Japanese Movie*. Rev. ed. Toyko: Kodansha International Ltd., 1982.
Rotha, Paul, Road Sinclair, and Richard Griffith. *Documentary Film*. London: Faber and Faber, 1966.
Russo, Vito. *The Celluloid Closet: Homosexuality in the Movies*. New York: Harper and Row, 1981.
Sadoul, Georges. *Histoire générale du cinéma*. Five Volumes. Paris: Éditions Denoël, 1946–54.
Sarris, Andrew. *The American Cinema: Directors and Directions 1929–1968*. New York: Dutton, 1969.
———. Notes on the *Auteur* Theory in 1962, in *Film Culture Reader*. Edited by Sitney. New York: Praeger, 1970.
———. "Notes on the *Auteur* Theory in 1970." *Film Comment* VI, No. 3, Fall 1970.
———. "Film Criticism in the Seventies." *Film Comment* XIV, No. 1, January 1978.
de Saussure, Ferdinand. *Course in General Linguistics*. Translated by Wade Baskin, New York: McGraw-Hill, 1966.

Schnitzer, Luda and Jean, and Marcel Martin, eds. *Cinema in Revolution: The Heroic Age of the Soviet Film.* New York: Hill and Wang, 1973.

Seldes, Gilbert. *The Great Audience.* New York: Viking, 1950.

———. *The Movies Come From America.* New York: Scribner's, 1937.

———. *The Public Arts.* New York: Simon and Schuster, 1956.

Sitney, P. Adams, ed. *Film Culture Reader.* New York: Praeger, 1970.

———. *Visionary Film: The American Avant-Garde.* New York: Oxford University Press, 1974.

——— ed. *The Essential Cinema: Essays on the Films in the Collection of Anthology Film Archives.* New York: Anthology Film Archives and New York University Press, 1975.

——— ed. *The Avant Garde Film, A Reader of Theory and Criticism.* New York: New York Univesity Press, 1978.

Sklar, Robert. *Movie-Made America.* New York: Random House, 1975.

Sontag, Susan. *Against Interpretation.* New York: Farrar, Straus & Giroux, 1966.

———. *Styles of Radical Will.* New York: Farrar, Straus & Giroux, 1966.

———. *On Photography.* New York: Farrar, Straus & Giroux, 1977.

Spottiswode, Raymond. *A Grammar of the Film.* Berkeley and Los Angeles: University of California Press, 1950.

Stephenson, Ralph, and J. R. Debrix. *The Cinema as Art.* Baltimore: Penguin, 1965.

Tudor, Andrew. *Theories of Film.* New York: Viking, 1973.

Tyler, Parker. *The Hollywood Hallucination.* New York: Simon and Schuster, 1970.

———. *Magic and Myth of the Movies.* New York: Simon and Schuster, 1970.

———. *Sex Psyche Etcetera in the Film.* Baltimore: Penguin, 1971.

Vorkapich, Slavko. "Toward True Cinema." *Film Culture,* No. 19, March 1959.

Warshow, Robert. *The Immediate Experience.* New York: Doubleday Anchor, 1964.

Williams, Christopher, ed. *Realism and the Cinema: A Reader.* London: Routledge and Kegan Paul, 1980.

Wolfenstein, Martha, and Nathan Leites. *Movies, a Psychological Study.* Glencoe: The Free Press, 1950.

Wollen, Peter. *Signs and Meaning in the Cinema.* New and enlarged. Bloomington, Ind., and London: Indiana University Press, 1972.

Wood, Michael. *America at the Movies.* New York: Basic Books, 1975.

Youngblood, Gene. *Expanded Cinema.* New York: Dutton, 1970.